The WILLIAM E. McLELLIN *Papers*, 1854-1880

William E. McClellin, ca. 1870

The WILLIAM E. McLELLIN *Papers*, 1854-1880

Stan Larson and

Samuel J. Passey, editors

George D. Smith, foreword

Signature Books • Salt Lake City • 2007

Signature Books is a registered trademark of Signature Books Publishing, LLC.

www.signaturebooks.com

Jacket design by Ron Stucki

The William E. McLellin Papers, 1854-1880 was printed on acid-free paper and was composed, printed, and bound in the United States of America.

2011 2010 2009 2008 2007 5 4 3 2 1

LIBRARY OF CONGRESS CATALOGING-IN-PUBLICATION DATA
McLellin, William E. (William Earl)
The William E. McLellin papers, 1854-1880 / edited by Stan Larson and Samuel J. Passey.
p. cm.
Includes bibliographical references and index.
ISBN-13: 978-1-56085-144-8 (alk. paper)
ISBN-10: 1-56085-144-9 (alk. paper)
1. Church of Jesus Christ of Latter-day Saints—History—19th century. 2. Mormon Church—History—19th century. McLellin, William E. (William Earl)—Correspondence. I. Larson, Stan. II. Passey, Samuel J., 1979- III. Title.

BX8611.M33 2007
289.3092—dc22
[B]

2007016184

In memory of

Steven F. Christensen

and Kathleen W. Sheets

CONTENTS

Appendixes

FOREWORD

George D. Smith

William Earl McLellin's writings document aspects of a community of believers that coalesced around Joseph Smith in nineteenth-century America, showing the church's place in its historical context. McLellin's notebooks and letters portray the Mormons from their inception in the 1830s up to the 1880s when they began to evolve from a mystical Christian offshoot into a modern world church. In the twenty-first century, his perspective provides a marker for comparing that bygone spiritualist movement with a church much less isolated from competing faith ideas and society's widespread skepticism.

McLellin's name became prominent in 1983-86 through the forger Mark W. Hofmann. When Hofmann invented a phantom "McLellin Collection" based on historical references, portions of the apostle's writings were found to reside in LDS archives. Some of these were published by the University of Illinois Press and *BYU Studies* thirteen years ago. Now other portions of the collection–including additional material at LDS archives and documents housed at the Marriott Library and Community of Christ archives–become available for the first time.

One of the original twelve apostles of the Church of the Latter Day Saints, as Mormons then presented themselves, McLellin advocated the genuine antiquity of the Book of Mormon. However, when questions emerged in 1837 Kirtland, Ohio, about founder Joseph Smith's connection to a live-in housekeeper, Fanny Alger, then issues of money and control of property, divided church leadership, McLellin criticized his once-beloved leader. Most pointedly, he questioned additions to an 1831 revelation regarding a second priesthood. A year after this dispute, McLellin was tried and excommunicated along with fellow stalwarts

---

George D. Smith is publisher and president of Signature Books, president of the Smith-Pettit Foundation which sponsors research into Mormon history, and a board member of the quarterly journal, *Kenyon Review*. Among his published works, he is the editor of *An Intimate Chronicle: The Journals of William Clayton* and the anthologies *Faithful History: Essays on Writing Mormon History* and *Religion, Feminism, and Freedom of Conscience: A Mormon/Humanist Dialogue*.

Oliver Cowdery, Apostles Luke and Lyman Johnson, David Whitmer, John Whitmer, and in 1839 William W. Phelps and Frederick G. Williams, all of whom had joined in the dissent against Joseph Smith.

Yet even after the prophet's death in 1844, McLellin remained close to the Smith family. It was McLellin whom the prophet's primary wife, Emma Smith, had told in Kirtland of seeing her husband, through a barn door, positioned on a hay mow with a young servant girl. McLellin recalls the struggle within the Smith family as Frederick Williams and others encouraged Joseph to offer a public apology. McLellin later related these incidents to the prophet's son, Joseph Smith III. An apostle at the time Joseph Jr. was offering new revelation to the church, McLellin was able to record early LDS events as an eyewitness, in their cultural context.

His treatises on many aspects of religion offer a fascinating glimpse into his struggle to fit his own religious dogma within the confines of any established religion of his day. Furthermore, his notebooks and letters highlight his own evolving theology. Throughout, he cites flaws he felt were apparent in the various branches of the faith. Because he had left Joseph at an early juncture, his commentaries described Mormonism as he remembered it—as it was taught in the pre-Nauvoo era. His writings therefore offer an important perspective into the thinking of one who was with the church early on as both a leader and critic.

EDITORS' PREFACE

JOHN TRAUGHBER WAS TWENTY YEARS OLD in 1874-75 when he first met former LDS apostle William E. McLellin, who was sixty-eight at the time.[1] Traughber had investigated and may have already joined the Reorganized Church of Jesus Christ of Latter Day Saints and was intensely drawn to Mormon history.[2] McLellin proved to be a trove of information about events that were fading into legend, providing the perspective of someone who, although a believer in early Mormonism, was not connected to any of the various Restoration groups.[3] In Traughber's eyes, the older man's unique perspective of history and theology was invaluable.

Traughber lived on his family's farm about fifty miles east of Independence, Missouri–close enough to pay an occasional visit to the McLellins, who lived at the Centerplace of Zion, but far enough away to make communication by mail more practical.[4] Thus, some of their surviving correspondence provides a glimpse into the content of their extended conversations. Traughber wrote of McLellin: "I valued him much. He and I were true friends, yet for the last two years of his life we were as far apart in religion as the poles of the earth."[5]

---

1. McLellin was born 18 January 1806 about fifty miles east of Nashville, Tennessee. For a short biography, see Richard P. Howard, "Mormonism's 'Stormy Petrel,'" in this volume. Traughber was born 23 November 1854 near Norborne, Missouri (John Logan Traughber Jr., "Records and Genealogies," on-line at *Carroll County Missouri Genealogy* (www.rootsweb.com/~mocarrol/pioneers/traughberfamily.htm). Their correspondence began in March 1875 (see Letter 14, p. 500). Readers should know that although McLellin spelled his name variously as McClellan, McClellin, McLelin, McLellin, M'Lelin, M'Lellin, and McLellan, for consistency sake we give it as McLellin; see Letter 24, p. 518n.

2. Richard E. Turley Jr., "The Provenance of William E. McLellin's Journals," in *The Journals of William E. McLellin, 1831-1836*, eds. Jan Shipps and John W. Welch (Urbana: University of Illinois Press, 1994), 257.

3. McLellin is presumed to have been excommunicated by a bishop's court on 11 May 1838. Curiously, the record does not specify what action was taken (Dean C. Jessee, ed., *The Papers of Joseph Smith* [Salt Lake City: Deseret Book, 1992], 2:240-41). Afterward, McLellin wandered from one Mormon sect to another, affiliating with Latter Day Saints who followed George M. Hinkle, William Law, Sidney Rigdon, James Strang, Martin Harris, David Whitmer, and Granville Hedrick before going his own way as an independent Mormon (Howard, "Stormy Petrel"; also Notebook 5, p. 323; Notebook 7, p. 379).

4. See Letter 4, p. 449; Letter 5, pp. 450-51; Letter 6, p. 455; Letter 24, p. 518n; Traughber, "Records and Genealogies," Notebook 7, p. 422n.

5. Notebook 1, p. 189n.

Possibly, McLellin was becoming more vocal in his criticism of the RLDS Church, even though his own wife, Emeline, would join the RLDS after William's death.[6] On the other hand, though Traughber may have defended the RLDS to McLellin, he had secretly become a skeptic, questioning not only the Reorganization and the Book of Mormon but also Christianity and the Bible.[7] Still, he realized the importance of McLellin's writing and memory. For a time, he considered editing a collection of McLellin's papers or writing a biography of his one-time mentor.

McLellin died in 1883.[8] The next year, Emeline moved to live with her son in Troy on the extreme eastern side of Missouri. In relocating, she began bequeathing her husband's papers to Traughber, who had been a good friend of the family. Traughber's inscription on the bottom of a page in a McLellin notebook reads: "I received this book from the Express Office at Norborne, Mo., Nov. 10, 1884. It was sent to me as a present by Mrs. Emeline McLellan now of Troy, Mo."[9]

Traughber may have temporarily moved to the southern part of the state when he married in 1888, perhaps to be near his wife's parents, as indicated by the fact that their first child was born in Taney County.[10] However, the couple was soon back in the Norborne area, where their next three children were born. In late 1897 or early 1898, they embarked on an entirely new adventure, heading west as homesteaders in Texas—taking the McLellin memorabilia with them—first to the Houston area and later to the upstate town of Doucette, about fifty miles west of Louisiana. Coincidentally, a few years later Emeline relocated to Denison,

---

6. See William D. Russell, "Portrait of a 'True Believer' in Original Mormonism," in this volume; also Turley, "Provenance," 257.

7. In a short journal Traughber kept in 1885, he mentions attending the local Protestant church, adding that he "almost wept" when the minister "spoke from a humanitarian standpoint of the brotherhood of man; but his God and his Christ I cared nothing about." Throughout the journal, Traughber invokes the angels' protection; places some confidence in premonitions and dreams; and mentions correspondence with various RLDS members (J. L. Traughber, Jr., "A Journal Commencing May 3rd, 1885," on-line at *Carroll County Missouri Genealogy* (www.rootsweb.com/~mocarrol/pioneers/traughberjournal. htm). See also "Dr. McLellan's Change of Views" (Notebook 1, p. 189n) and "On Inspired Books" (Notebook 4, pp. 320-22n), wherein Traughber confesses disbelief in both Christianity and Mormonism.

8. Larry C. Porter, "The Odyssey of William Earl McLellin: Man of Diversity, 1806-83," in Shipps and Welch, *Journals of McLellin,* 355-57.

9. Notebook 4, p. 320n.

10. Traughber married Mattie E. Felkins on 1 January 1888. Their first child was born in the same place on April 24, but no year is given; their next child was born in Carroll County in March 1891 (Traughber, "Records and Genealogies"). See also Traughber's inscription in Notebook 1, p. 189n, dated "Taney Co., Mo., Feb. 27 1889." Of course, the Traughbers may have been visiting on these occasions.

Texas, about sixty miles north of Doucette, where she lived with her daughter. It is not known if the two families remained in contact.[11]

Mattie Elmira Felkins Traughber, John Logan Traughber, and some of their children. *Courtesy J. Willard Marriott Library, University of Utah*

As time passed and Traughber lost enthusiasm for the documents he had safeguarded so long, he began looking for a buyer of the McLellin papers. He found an eager customer in LDS President Joseph F. Smith, who sent mission president Samuel O. Bennion to Texas in 1908 to meet with Traughber. Acting for the LDS Church, Bennion purchased McLellin's missionary diaries, four notebooks, and a bound copy of the 1833 Book of Commandments for fifty dollars.[12] When the items arrived in Salt Lake City, they were consigned to the First Presidency's vault and eventually forgotten.

They may have remained so, but for a series of dramatic events eighty years later involving greed, blackmail, forgery, and murder. In the early 1980s, Mark Hofmann—later revealed to be both a forger and murderer—rose to fame for discovering early Mormon documents. Then on the morning of 15 October 1985, Steve Christensen and Kathleen Sheets were killed by pipe bombs in two separate locations. That afternoon Hofmann talked with LDS Apostle Dallin H. Oaks in his office about a long-lost "McLellin collection" Hofmann said he had found and would sell to the church. Later that month church leaders stated in a press conference that they did not have a McLellin collection. In a surprising development, the *Salt Lake Tribune* announced on Thanksgiving Day 1985 that McLellin's papers had been found in Houston, Texas.

In March 1986, Dean C. Jessee, a member of the Joseph Fielding

11. Traughber, "Records and Genealogies"; compare Turley, "Provenance," 257; Porter, "Odyssey of McLellin," 358.

12. Samuel O. Bennion to Pres. Joseph F. Smith and Counselors, 12 Feb. 1908, in Central States Mission Historical Record, LR 1562/11, 1:224-29, Archives, Historical Department, Church of Jesus Christ of Latter-day Saints, Salt Lake City, Utah.

Smith Institute at Brigham Young University, remembered seeing McLellin's name in the church's Joseph F. Smith collection and reported this information to the LDS Church Archives. A search was made, and finally another McLellin collection was found in the First Presidency's vault. However, the LDS Church did not make this discovery known to police investigators. It was not until 1992 that the managing director of the LDS Historical Department, Richard Turley, announced that the church had discovered a collection of McLellin papers six years earlier.[13]

Lynn Packer, a member of the KSL television news team that covered the Hofmann story, pointed out some parallels between the 1908 and 1985 episodes:

> Twice Mormon officials arbitrated receiving the McLellin papers, first in 1908 and again in 1985. Twice the church attempted to get the collection ahead of supposed church enemies ... Twice a mission president would become involved in the deal. And twice fear of public censure and secrecy played a role in the outcome of the McLellin deals. Had the church, at any time between 1908 and 1985, made the McLellin collection available to even its own historians, Hofmann's McLellin fraud would have ended before it began.[14]

McLellin's early missionary diaries from 1831 to 1836 were published by Jan Shipps and John W. Welch in 1994.[15] The editors explained why they decided to publish the diaries but not McLellin's notebooks, also owned by the LDS Church: "His unfinished essays from the 1870s are held in the LDS Archives. We decided not to include these materials mainly because of their length, because of their late dates, and because some of them are derivative or not even original with McLellin."[16] Larry C. Porter's biographical essay mentioned the notebooks in a footnote, but their contents were not otherwise utilized.[17]

---

13. Richard E. Turley Jr., *Victims: The LDS Church and the Mark Hofmann Case* (Urbana: University of Illinois Press, 1992), 248-49. Three other books on Hofmann are Linda Sillitoe and Allen D. Roberts, *Salamander: The Story of the Mormon Forgery Murders* (Salt Lake City: Signature Books, 1988); Robert Lindsey, *A Gathering of Saints: A True Story of Money, Murder, and Deceit* (New York: Simon and Schuster, 1988); and Steven Naifeh and Gregory White Smith, *The Mormon Murders: A True Story of Greed, Forgery, Deceit, and Death* (New York: Weidenfeld and Nicolson, 1988).

14. Lynn Packer, "Lost and Found," *Utah Holiday*, Nov. 1992, 37.

15. Jan Shipps and John W. Welch, eds., *The Journals of William E. McLellin, 1831-1836* (Provo and Urbana: BYU Studies and University of Illinois Press, 1994).

16. Ibid., xviii, xx.

17. Porter, "Odyssey of McLellin," in Shipps and Welch, *Journals of McLellin,* 353, 376n324: "Although they are late-in-life reflections, the notes usually address topics that at-

In 1995 the University of Utah Marriott Library purchased from Traughber's son three other McLellin notebooks that had come to light ten years earlier. The library soon decided to publish all the extant notebooks, which cover the period from 1854 to 1880. In the process of preparing a typescript of the six known notebooks—three at the LDS Archives and three at the University of Utah—it was discovered that a seventh notebook fragment was housed in the archives of the Reorganized Church of Jesus Christ of Latter Day Saints (now the Community of Christ).

We also made a concerted effort to gather all of McLellin's letters covering the same period, 1854-80. However, as editors we would be remiss if we did not express suspicion that a number of letters from McLellin to Joseph F. Smith in the late 1870s and early 1880s may still reside in the First Presidency's vault. There are twelve letters of Smith to McLellin, 1878-83, extant in the LDS archives,[18] so presumably the correspondence in the other direction exists but is unavailable to the public. We see in this collection (Letters 2 and 12) how McLellin wrote to Joseph Smith's oldest son and namesake, speaking politely but forthrightly about a number of issues such as polygamy. Likewise, it seems probable that in his letters to Joseph F. Smith, a son of Hyrum Smith, McLellin would have written just as frankly about serious topics. What we do not know is whether Joseph F. Smith may have destroyed the McLellin letters. It seems most likely that in purchasing McLellin's diaries and notebooks in 1908, he would have filed the letters with the rest of the McLellin material in the vault.[19]

THE SEVEN MCLELLIN NOTEBOOKS

Notebook 1 consists of 140 pages and seven loose fragments. Four of these fragments were identified and attached to the appropriate pages before being encased in protective coverings. The remaining three fragments are together less than 1 cm^2. All are in an acid-free folder containing Notebook 1. The inscription on the cover reads: "Chester, Geauga Co. Ohio. April 15. 1854. W. E. McLellin." The date 1854 appears between the essays "On man, spiritual existences, influences and powers"

---

tracted McLellin's attention almost half a century earlier. These materials sometimes advance views that differ from or contradict his earlier positions, but McLellin never acknowledges those differences."

18. Ibid., 354.

19. On 24 September 2007, we asked Richard Turley for permission—not to see the contents of the First Presidency vault, but to consult an inventory of its contents. We have yet to receive a reply.

and "Of Dispensations," near the end of the notebook. The essay, "The call to the ministry," is dated 10-11 March 1857. The notebook contains nine other essays, among which "The work of the Holy Spirit among men" contains an update made in 1871. The original is located in the John L. Traughber Collection at the J. Willard Marriott Library (MS 666).

Only a small portion of Notebook 2 is available. The original fragment itself is not extant, so one has to rely on glass-plate negatives of the cover which reads "W. E. McLellan's Book Jan. 4th 1871" and two partial pages. These images were taken in the 1920s or 1930s by C. Edward Miller of the RLDS Church, evidently from the notebook then in the possession of William O. Robertson of Louisville, Kentucky. In 1929, Paul M. Hanson quoted from pages 166-67 of this particular notebook[20] and added that it consisted of 264 pages and bore the date of 15 January 1872. In the 1980s the photographs were transferred to safety film, and now paper copies are available at the Community of Christ Archives in Independence, Missouri (Miscellaneous Letters and Papers, P13, fd 2287). The Community of Christ has also donated copies to the Marriott Library (William E. McLellin Collection, Accession 1827).

The cover inscription to Notebook 3 reads: "W. E. McLellan, Jan 1877." Another indication of the date is McLellin's response to a sermon delivered in October 1876. There are four essays in this notebook. The original is in the Historical Department archives of the Church of Jesus Christ of Latter-day Saints (William Earl McLellin Collection, MS 13538).[21]

Notebook 4, with the cover inscription, "The Bible. Queries respecting it In 1877," is a 140-page document in two signatures, one 124 pages and the other 16 pages, consisting mainly of assorted verbatim quotations on various aspects of the Bible selected and transcribed by McLellin from sources available to him. The notebook is divided into two major parts. The first contains fourteen sections, often focusing on

---

20. Hanson, "Unwavering Testimony," *Saints' Herald*, 9 Jan. 1929, 34-35.

21. At the end of Notebook 3, McLellin inserted ten pages of his manuscript copies of four revelations of Joseph Smith (D&C 22, 45, 65, 66; RLDS 20, 45, 65, 66), as well as the printed Maudsley engraving of Joseph Smith with Smith's signature. The McLellin text of D&C 65 is printed in John W. Welch and Trevor Packer, "The Newly Found Manuscript of Doctrine and Covenants Section 65," *BYU Studies* 33/2 (1993): 331-36, and a discussion of all four revelations is in Shipps and Welch, *Journals of McLellin*, 233-54. The McLellin texts provide more specific and more correct information. For instance, Section 22 (RLDS 20) was given on 16 April 1830, not just April 1830; D&C 65 was given on 30 October 1831, not just October 1831, and explained a verse of the Lord's Prayer (Matt. 6:10); D&C 66 was given on 29 October 1831 in Hiram, Ohio, not 25 October 1831 at Orange, Ohio.

the Old Testament, and is titled "Who wrote the books of the Bible?" The second part contains seven sections having to do with the New Testament, similarly beginning with "Who were the writers of the books of the New Testament?" McLellin's sources included Adam Clarke's *Commentary and Critical Notes on the Holy Bible,* Ephraim Chambers's *Cyclopaedia,* and commentaries by Charles Buck, Johann Jahn, John Kitto, and other unnamed authors. Only those portions for which there is a high degree of probability that McLellin himself was the author are included in this volume. We added Traughber's comments and six-page essay as a concluding footnote. The original notebook is at LDS Archives (MS 13538).

Notebook 5, "Some of my thoughts in 1878. Why I am not an L. D. Saint of any click [clique] or party," as McLellin wrote on the cover, contains two sections. The first, "Some principles and practices of the Church of Christ," exists in two versions–one in this notebook and the other in the third part of Notebook 7. The original notebook is in LDS Archives (MS 13538).

McLellin's title for Notebook 6 is "Some of my history and also about peep-stones." Ironically, there is nothing in it of his personal history or about peep-stones, and we have therefore assigned it a title more indicative of the contents, "On Original Sin." The notebook is a forty-page document, one signature in length, consisting of eleven essays. One of the eleven essays is untitled and has been assigned the designation "If a Person Exercises Faith," drawn from the first line of the essay. Apparently "Faith," located at the back of the notebook on page 40 and covering about three-fourths of the page, was the first essay written into the notebook. On the back of that page (manuscript page 39), an essay, "Aaronic Priesthood," was begun and continued for only five lines before it was crossed out. Next, three sentences about faith based on Heb. 11:1 were written on manuscript page 11, then crossed out; about the same time a half-page essay, "If a Person Exercises Faith," was written on manuscript page 10. Then the entire notebook was turned upside down and McLellin transcribed seven essays, using pages 1-10 for the first essay and pages 12-27 for the remaining six. These are all related to the writings of the Methodist Albert Taylor Bledsoe, editor of *The Southern Review.* There are at least three instances in which McLellin specifically mentions Bledsoe: (1) in reference to the latter's essay on "Augustinism: Original Sin"; (2) in a note that reads "but A. T. Bledsoe writes" near the beginning of "Knowledge and free Agency"; and (3) in explaining near the end of "The Mind and Will" that "many extracts" of

Bledsoe's works were quoted. While sometimes McLellin quotes Bledsoe verbatim, other times he appears either to paraphrase or summarize or simply makes his own comments on the subject at hand. For this reason, all seven essays are included here. After these essays were written, McLellin added page numbers 1-27, for some reason omitting 19 and 25, then later in a new color of ink wrote an essay entitled "The Holy Ghost," using pages 28-38. Lastly he wrote "Of Faith," a revised version of the first essay "Faith," using pages 38-40. The only date in the notebook is 15 August 1878 for "The Holy Ghost." The original notebook is located in the Marriott Library (MS 666).

We have assigned the title, "Reasons Why I Am Not a 'Mormon,'" to Notebook 7 from the first line, "I will here give some of the reasons why I am not (what is called,) a Mormon, or a Latter Day Saint of any of its various parties." The notebook has three sections. The first, which McLellin left untitled, is devoted to the theme indicated, followed by two essays which McLellin did assign titles to: "Joseph Smith's errors and wrongs" and "Some principles and practices of the church of Christ"—the latter summarizing much of what preceded it. The approximate date of 1880 is confirmed by McLellin's reference to a September 1830 revelation to Oliver Cowdery: "Nearly fifty years have passed since that revelation was given." The original notebook is located in the Marriott Library (MS 666).[22]

THE TWENTY-SIX LETTERS

The first letter in this section, the only one from LDS Archives (MS 6237),[23] is McLellin's four-page epistle to LDS Apostle Orson Pratt, sent in April 1854. It is designated as Letter 1 due to the chronological arrangement of the present volume.

Of the twenty-six letters presented, eleven of which survive as holographs, nine reside in the Community of Christ Archives. Of these, Letter 2 from 1861, written to Joseph Smith III, was composed on a single sheet of paper, folded in two to make four pages (P13, f137). McLellin again wrote to Joseph III in 1872, herein Letter 12, begun in July but not dated until September.[24] Letter 4 contains no date but has been placed

22. There is an eighth McLellin notebook on the "Ruins of Central America and Yucatan," located in LDS Archives, but since it is comprised entirely of extracted quotations from John L. Stephens's book, *Incidents of Travel in Central America, Chiapas, and Yucatan,* it is not reproduced here. Traughber's comments on it are given in Appendix B.

23. For McLellin's published articles and letters from 1832 to 1849, see Appendix A.

24. In addition to the original at the Community of Christ Archives, a typescript is available in the Scott G. Kenney Collection, Ms 587, Bx 8, Fd 15, Marriott Library.

in the context of May 1869 according to internal evidence (f2287).

Several letters are addressed to "dear friends," including Letter 5, July 1869, composed on a single folded sheet (f185), and Letter 7, February 1870, written on a smaller sheet, unfolded, for which the original lacks the bottom portion where the autograph would have been (f191). Other mailings to "friends" include Letter 9 from October 1870 (f198) and Letter 11 from February 1872 (f198).

Letter 13 is to "Dear Mary, and all the friends," August 1872 (f215), and is unsigned but is in McLellin's handwriting. The letter was longer than the four existing pages; nevertheless, most of it was copied verbatim from the letter to Joseph III which McLellin was composing at the same time. In the top margin of the first page, someone added in pencil the words "McClellands letter to Aunt Mary."

Letter 10 survives only in portions. It was originally sent to RLDS writer Isaac Sheen, then recopied in October 1871 to Mark H. Forscutt, assistant editor of the Reorganized Church's *True Latter Day Saints' Herald.* The *Herald* published it in four parts, which makes it possible to reproduce the full text here.[25]

Some of the letters were addressed to Latter-day Saint publications, or to third parties who submitted them for publication on McLellin's behalf, and are available only in printed form. Letter 3, for instance, was published in *The Truth-Teller,* presumably addressed to its editor, Granville Hedrick, sometime in 1864.[26] Hedrick prefaced it: "With pleasure we publish the following letter from Br. W. E. McClellan, who came into the Church in 1831, and was ordained one of the quorum of the twelve, by Joseph Smith."

Similarly, Letter 6 to Davis H. Bays, November 1869, was published in the *True Latter Day Saints' Herald.*[27] The italics in the published version are assumed to have mirrored McLellin's underlinings. Letter 8, May 1870, again to Bays, also appeared in the *Herald*[28] and again has italics. Letter 20 to Thomas Fuller was written sometime in 1877. Fuller's brother-in-law, Charles W. Lamb, extracted a portion of it in a letter to David Whitmer's publication, *The Return.*[29]

No original exists for Letter 25, probably written sometime in 1878

---

25. *The True Latter Day Saints' Herald,* 1 Mar., 1 June, 15 July, 1 Aug. 1872, 153-55, 341-42, 435-37, 472-74.

26. *The Truth Teller* [Bloomington, Ill.], Oct. 1864, 57-58.

27. *True Saints' Herald,* 15 May 1870, 290-91.

28. Ibid., 15 Sept. 1870, 553-57.

29. *The Return,* Nov. 1890, 364.

or 1879. However, an extract was included in W. Wyl's 1886 book, *Mormon Portraits.*[30] Wyl published two other passages from McLellin's letters,[31] since located within the excerpts of letters McLellin sent to Traughber in December 1878 and January 1879. This allows us to make some tentative observations on the reliability of Wyl's transcriptions. By comparing the two copies, we can see that Wyl was careful but did change punctuation and spelling, added italics for emphasis, and omitted some phrases and sentences without ellipses.

Excerpts of Letters 14-19 and 21-24 to John Traughber, written from 1875 to 1879, reside in the Marriott Library (MS 666, Bx 2, Fd 40). Traughber made partial copies in his thirteen-page summary, prefaced: "The following extracts are taken from letters which I received from the late Dr. William E. McLellan. Between the years 1875 and 1882 I corresponded a great deal with the Doctor, and received from him a great deal of information on the early history of Mormonism and the acts and doings of Joseph Smith and some of his principal men."

Letter 26 was written to James T. Cobb in August 1880 and is found in the New York Public Library. Larry C. Porter previously printed the text in a historical journal and again in an LDS weekly newspaper insert.[32]

SIX INTERPRETATIONS OF MCLELLIN'S PAPERS

To better understand this collection, we solicited assistance from six scholars who have expertise in Mormon history and asked them to contribute interpretative essays. Together, the essays span the spectrum of opinion regarding McLellin's life and writings and the significance of the current compilation.

Introducing readers to the protagonist is Richard P. Howard, Church Historian Emeritus of the Community of Christ. Howard gives a well-researched summary of the one-time apostle's life. Borrowing a term used by another historian in describing McLellin, Howard titled his essay "Mormonism's 'Stormy Petrel.'" It is a slightly revised version of an essay Howard originally wrote in 1994.[33] In it, he gives particular

30. W. Wyl, *Mormon Portraits; or, The Truth about the Mormon Leaders from 1830 to 1886* (Salt Lake City: Tribune Printing and Publishing, 1886), 295. "W. Wyl" was a pseudonym for Wilhelm Ritter von Wymetal.

31. Ibid., 308-09.

32. Larry C. Porter, "William E. McLellan's Testimony of the Book of Mormon," *Brigham Young University Studies* 10 (Summer 1970): 485-87; "McLellin Expresses Feelings in Letter," *Church News* insert, *Deseret News,* 8 Dec. 1985, 6, 10.

33. "William E. McLellin: 'Mormonism's Stormy Petrel,'" in *Differing Visions: Dis-*

attention to how McLellin drifted in and out of almost every existing branch of Mormonism over the course of his life until he concluded that no church on earth represented the purity of the movement he had converted to in 1831.

Dawn House, a veteran reporter, editor, and columnist for *The Salt Lake Tribune,* gives a fascinating autobiographical account in "Discovery of the McLellin Papers" of how she tracked down the real McLellin collection in Texas. She tells how it ended up in private hands and how Hoffmann had come to learn of its existence but not its location. House has been known since her journalism start in Provo for her ability to dig deeply into sources in covering important stories.

Thomas G. Alexander is an award-winning Professor Emeritus of History at Brigham Young University. He chose to explore the tendency to romanticize the past, to remember one's youth with fondness and imagine great moments in history in idyllic settings. "The Past as Decline from a Golden Age: Early Mormonism's Restorationist Tendency" cautions readers about this human flaw, the effect on the mind of a nostalgic yearning for a mythologized past.

Continuing this theme, D. Michael Quinn, former Professor of History at Brigham Young University, explores McLellin's tendency to excise personal involvement in controversial historical events. Quinn suggests that to the degree McLellin's reporting was incomplete, it should not be considered the last word or the end of the story. For his title's essay, Quinn draws from McLellin's own words: "'My Eyes Were Holden in Those Days': A Study of Selective Memory."

John-Charles Duffy is a doctoral candidate at the University of North Carolina, Chapel Hill. He offers a fresh, contemporary perspective in his essay, "Reinventing McLellin: A Historiographical Review." Duffy demonstrates how Mormons have reframed McLellin's life and works over the years to portray him alternately as an apostate and traitor, fence-sitter, or a modern version of the Apostle Paul. Today, there are those who herald McLellin's disclosure of how the story of Mormonism was rewritten in the late 1830s, while others emphasize the fact that McLellin never recanted his belief in the Book of Mormon.

William D. Russell, a Professor Emeritus of Social Studies at Graceland University in Lamoni, Iowa, describes McLellin as a fundamentalist whose beliefs and practices did not change over time and who was incapable of accepting new doctrines, especially if they contradicted ear-

---

senters in Mormon History, ed. Roger D. Launius and Linda Thatcher (Urbana: University of Illinois Press, 1994), 76-101.

lier teachings. In "Portrait of a 'True Believer' in Original Mormonism," he empathizes with the apostle's search for meaning, if not with McLellin's obsession with perfection. Russell respects McLellin's honesty, intellectual curiosity, and spirituality. Whatever else, McLellin was not the brooding, taciturn critic some have assumed. From what one can detect from his correspondence and historical incidents, McLellin appears more likely to have been a socially comfortable, engaging individual, although one for whom truth was the ultimate prize and integrity the most important personal trait.

EDITORIAL PROCEDURES

We have retained the original spelling, capitalization, and apparent misspellings of proper names. Occasionally, minor punctuation problems have been silently corrected: "go to!." is changed to "go to!" It is not always possible to determine if a capital or lowercase letter was intended. To distinguish between "planed" and "planned," we present the latter as "plan[n]ed." In some cases, we have printed a bracketed correct letter for an incorrect one–"o[n]" where McLellin wrote "or." Other explanatory material is placed in square brackets, such as extrapolations of names and places identified by McLellin with initials and abbreviations.

We have inserted raised letters and interlinear words within the running line of text. In cases where it could be of interest to know which words were added at a later time, such information is given in the footnotes. Odd strokes that sometimes appear above or below certain letters are omitted.

Sometimes McLellin emphasized a word by writing it more vertically, with thicker ink strokes, represented in this volume by a **bold face type**. Elsewhere he emphasized words by underscoring them with a single, double, or triple line or by underscoring every other word, all of which we have standardized as single underlinings. We have also standardized long and short dashes to a constant length.

Crossed-out words are displayed with an overstrike; words written over erasures are given as: "~~they~~ their." If the underlying word is undecipherable, it is ignored.

We indicate page breaks in brackets as "[page 5:]" to indicate the break between pages 4 and 5. Absent a manuscript source, we have given the printed source's pagination. Indented paragraphs were sometimes added to make the text easier to read.

McLellin's penmanship included a descending ligature for words with a final *g* or *s*. He also sometimes added a curved line to indicate something approximating "and so on," for which we have substituted a tilde (~) as a rough approximation. When McLellin opened but failed to close with quote marks, or vice versa, we have added them within brackets if obvious and otherwise left the text as is with that internal ambiguity. For omissions within long quotations, McLellin used plus signs + + + to function like modern ellipsis dots (...).

We have added the source for scriptural quotations within square brackets. If McLellin provided the source but his quotation was different in some way from the standard text, "[cf.]" alerts the reader to this. Citations of Latter-day Saint scriptures are given with both LDS and RLDS references: "LDS D&C 21:5; RLDS D&C 19:2b."

Square brackets have been changed to parentheses to differentiate McLellin's and Traughber's punctuation from ours. A note explains this in each instance. If a word or words on a page cannot be deciphered, "[illegible]" appears. We have identified alterations and given our own editorial comments in numbered footnotes. We have used daggers for passages McLellin deleted or Traughber added, then placed the deleted or added copy at the bottom of the page with the footnotes, again designated by a dagger rather than an arabic number. Some of these annotations were written in a purple ink which bled through to the other side of the page, which is noted. Traughber's comments on "McLellin's 'Ruins of Central America and Yucatan'" are presented in Appendix B.

As with the letters, we numbered the notebooks according to their relative chronological dates. If an essay lacked a title, we gave it a bracketed derivative title. For instance, a section of Notebook 5 begins: "I will tell some of the reasons why I do not believe in the 'Reorganized Church of Jesus Christ of Latter day Saints.'" For this, we gave the title as "Reasons Why I Do Not Believe in the Reorganized Church" and placed it in brackets so the reader knows it was our addition.

MCLELLIN AND THE LDS CHURCH IN THE 1830s

Mormons generally remember McLellin as a fair-weather Saint—one who was loyal until faced with hardship.[34] The documents tell a different story of a stalwart who, on his many proselytizing missions, persevered through severe weather, sickness, and other obstacles in tattered clothes and worn boots needing repair.[35] He and his companions

34. For a discussion of this view of McLellin, see John-Charles Duffy, "Reinventing McLellin," in this volume.

35. Shipps and Welch, *Journals of McLellin,* 37, 44, 67, 112, 114, 123, 140-41, 145-46, 149, 178, 184-85, 190, 193-95, 216, 219, 224-25.

begged free food and lodging because they traveled without purse or scrip.[36] On one occasion he cut a hole in the ice to perform two baptisms, suffering a prolonged bout of diarrhea and lung congestion as a result.[37] The next week, "Brother Joseph [Smith] came to my bed side and laid his hands upon me and prayed for me and I was healed." Thereupon, McLellin arose, went out, and preached for an hour.[38]

He was called on his first mission in August 1831, a week after his baptism into the Church of Christ (later renamed the Church of the Latter Day Saints), only a month after hearing the Mormon missionaries.[39] At first he held back, watching and learning from his companion, but when given the opportunity he surprised himself by his ability to speak and quickly became known as one of the new church's most powerful orators.[40] In his preaching, he conveyed an urgency and single-minded commitment to finding the pure in heart to "prepare to meet the Lord at his second coming which was nigh at hand."[41] This was typical for the period—the same message was repeatedly rehearsed in other Mormon sources.[42] The Book of Mormon had been published the previous year. It was itself evidence of the approaching end of time,[43] as were such gifts of the spirit as miracle healings and speaking in tongues.[44]

---

36. Ibid., 63, 89-91, 98, 102, 122, 133, 183, 191-92.

37. Ibid., 66-67. McLellin adds that it was snowing during the baptism. Afterward, they repaired to a friendly non-member's house where McLellin preached for an hour on the gift of the Holy Ghost.

38. Ibid.

39. Ibid., 34; Porter, "Odyssey of McLellin," 295-97.

40. Shipps and Welch, *Journals of McLellin*, 36, 41.

41. Ibid., 39, 42, 111. McLellin advised people to "flee to Zion [Independence, Missouri] and save their souls" (94) and regretted when "none proposed or offered themselves as candidates for Zion" (113). One entry reads: "I ex[h]orted them to obedience and unfolded the glories of heaven and of Zion until the Lord poured out his spirit in my heart till I ceased to ex[h]ort and I just shouted and praised the Lord and offered my hand to all to go with me to Zion" (65).

42. Grant Underwood, *The Millenarian World of Early Mormonism* (Urbana: University of Illinois Press, 1993), 24-31.

43. Jan Shipps detects in McLellin's diaries "the importance of the coming forth of the Book of Mormon as a signal that the end was near": "LDS preachers seem to have pointed ... to [the Book of Mormon's] coming forth as the opening event in the dispensation that was serving as the 'winding-up scene' before the curtain rose on the *eschaton.* The Book of Mormon was therefore presented as the ultimate sign of the times, indicating the Saints' conviction that people in the United States in the 1830s were living at the end of time" (Shipps and Welch, *Journals of McLellin*, 3, 6).

44. McLellin recorded three episodes of speaking in tongues and several faith healings in a two-week period, 17-31 August 1834 (ibid., 134-38; see also 157, 176, 179, 191-92, 217, 219). For an 1877 reference, see Notebook 3, p. 272.

The world of Kirtland, Ohio, in the 1830s was far removed from anything Latter-day Saints today might find familiar. It would be another two decades before the core narratives of the church's founding, basic theological teachings, and behavioral admonitions would be completed. In Kirtland, the membership was taught that God is "a personage of spirit," not a deity with a physical body, as would become the doctrine in the 1840s.[45] According to all available documentary evidence, no one in Kirtland had heard of Joseph Smith's First Vision, and they would not know of it until it was publicly disclosed in 1840; in fact, the First Vision would not be incorporated into standard LDS teaching and discourse until the twentieth century.[46] Even late in life, McLellin seems unaware of this vision narrative.[47] For instance, he came to think it was wrong for Joseph Smith and Oliver Cowdery to have called themselves apostles because they were "witnesses of the true translation from the plates–the Book of Mormon; but not of Jesus Christ in any sense. ... They could not be apostles of Jesus unless they had seen him."[48] McLellin added that "the Apostles of Christ at Jerusalem, and all his Disciples in America saw, heard, and felt, hence they could bear a firm witness and testimony that they most positively knew what they declared.

45. Doctrine and Covenants, 1835, 52-54. When the Doctrine and Covenants was first published, it was organized with the doctrine first and the covenants second. The first part was a catechism of official teachings in seven lectures, popularly known as the "Lectures on Faith." The second part contained 102 revelations.

46. Of the ten known references to the First Vision in Joseph Smith's lifetime, the earliest is from an 1832 ledger book in which Joseph wrote that in his "sixteenth year" he prayed for mercy, upon which a pillar of light rested upon him and he saw a vision of Jesus: "the Lord opened the heavens upon me and I saw the Lord and he spake unto me saying Joseph my son thy sins are forgiven thee." This brief account, which was not published, lacked the theological import of seeing two personages in bodily form. In any case, the first public disclosure of the vision was in Orson Pratt's 1840 tract, *A[n] Interesting Account of Several Remarkable Visions* (Dean C. Jessee, "The Earliest Accounts of Joseph Smith's First Vision," and James B. Allen and John W. Welch, "The Appearance of the Father and the Son to Joseph Smith in 1820," in *Opening the Heavens: Accounts of Divine Manifestations, 1820-1844,* eds. John W. Welch, with Erick B. Carlson [Provo and Salt Lake City: BYU Press and Deseret Book, 2005], 1-75; compare R. Scott Lloyd, "A Genuine Vision: Scholars Have Rebutted Arguments from Naysayers, *Church News,* 26 May 2007, 7, 10). Summarizing the evidence, Jessee speculated that "should the foregoing historical sources pertaining to Joseph Smith's First Vision seem sparse in some respects, those gaps are primarily the result of inadequate record keeping of his many conversations and discourses on the subject or related topics" (26). For the incorporation of the First Vision into LDS consciousness in the twentieth century, see Kathleen Flake's chapter, "Re-Placing Memory," in *The Politics of American Religious Identity: The Seating of Senator Reed Smoot, Mormon Apostle* (Chapel Hill: University of North Carolina Press, 2004), 109-37, esp. 118.

47. However, McLellin does know of the new teaching that God has a physical body (Notebook 6, p. 367).

48. Notebook 7, p. 404.

Did Smith & Cowdery thus know? They did not. They never in the early days of the church so professed or declared."[49]

An interesting aspect of McLellin's writings through 1880 is how closely they reflected the common beliefs of the LDS Church in the 1830s. The church moved on in a theological sense while he remained stationary, as if stuck in time. He professed that he had always been Trinitarian.[50] He remained a believer in peep-stones and defended them as a biblically mandated means of revelation.[51] He believed he had a "ministering angel" that would "occasionally speak to my mind and to my heart."[52] He continued to believe in prophetic dreams, that the windows of heaven remained open for each individual to receive personal revelation, as taught by the Book of Mormon, and not that one person alone held sole authority to communicate God's will to His people.[53] In his earliest notebook, McLellin discussed Paul's letter to the Corinthians, writing: "We maintain that believers in the Lord can obey those precepts now, can obtain the gifts of the Spirit of God now, can rise as high in the knowledge of God now, as at any former period of time in this world's history." If people exercised these gifts, "then we would see more primitive order & saint-like holiness."[54]

Further observations by McLellin may leave some contemporary Latter-day Saints bewildered. For instance, McLellin wrote: "I heard Joseph tell his experience of his ordination and the organization of the church, probably, more than twenty times, to persons who, near the rise of the church, wished to know and hear about it. I never heard of Moroni, John [the Baptist], or Peter, James, and John."[55] In fact, accord-

49. Ibid., p. 424.

50. Notebook 6, pp. 369-73. His Trinitarianism was docetic rather than orthodox since he believed that Jesus became the Christ at his baptism (Notebook 1, pp. 179, 198). This could suggest a midpoint in the drift in LDS theology from the 1835 Lectures on Faith, which taught that "these three [Father, Son, and Holy Spirit] are one," to the 1843 "Items of instruction given by Joseph Smith the Prophet, at Ramus, Illinois": "The Father has a body of flesh and bones as tangible as man's; the Son also" (LDS D&C 130).

51. Notebook 4, pp. 299-303.

52. Shipps and Welch, *Journals of McLellin,* 364n95; compare 92, 101-02.

53. McLellin wrote that "man has an interior sight, and when this inmost being becomes quickened and the mind and eyes opened to see, natural objects being lost to view, the man is said to be in a trance, or to see a vision," adding that "almost all the prophets had visions from God" (Notebook 1, p. 208). "A vision is a supernatural rep[re]sentation of an object to a person when awake. It is seeing with the eyes of the mind. It is interior or spiritual sight. It is looking at things by the inner man" (Notebook 4, p. 299). These visions are nevertheless "as real ... as if seen with the natural eyes" (Notebook 1, ms. p. 209).

54. Notebook 1, p. 165.

55. Letter 8, p. 462.

ing to existing documentation, priesthood restoration by Jesus' mentor and apostles was not known until 1835. In Kirtland it was generally assumed that angels were a different species from humans and unrelated to anything earthly. No one imagined that a human being could return to earth as an angel. Not only had McLellin never heard of such a thing, he found it distressing, first because there was no biblical precedent, and second because spirits were assumed to be naked, presenting an unseemly scene to his mind.[56] It was an unnamed "holy angel" of glory that had directed Joseph Smith to the gold plates, McLellin maintained to his dying day, not a resurrected being.[57] McLellin accepted the restoration of priesthood but not the accounts involving John the Baptist and three biblical apostles.[58] It is interesting that in his early missionary diaries, Mclellin's choice of pronoun for an angel is "it," not "he."[59]

The goal of the present compilation is not to resolve questions surrounding the institutionalized founding narratives but to try to understand the Kirtland environment and the context in which McLellin wrote. Repeatedly, McLellin's theological statements point to potential areas for additional research into the Kirtland religious environment. The under-explored question is what it may have meant to be a Mormon in the 1830s without a knowledge of the First Vision, the Angel Moroni, or priesthood restoration by angelic messengers.[60]

For Latter-day Saints today, the most visible image of Kirtland remains the House of the Lord, or temple. Just knowing that the edifice served a different function than modern LDS temples reminds one of a

56. Notebook 5, p. 332; Notebook 7, pp. 386, 403-04, 413.

57. See Appendix D. It also seems significant that in Joseph Smith's 1832 account, the angel refers to Moroni in third person: "... and it came to pass when I was seventeen years of age I called again upon the Lord and he shewed unto me a heavenly vision for behold an angel of the Lord came and stood before me and ... he revealed unto me that in the Town of Manchester Ontario County N.Y. there was plates of gold upon which there was engravings which was engraven by Maroni & his fathers" (in Dean C. Jessee, ed., *The Papers of Joseph Smith* [Salt Lake City: Deseret Book, 1989], 8).

58. Shipps and Welch, *Journals of McLellin,* 29, 92; Letter 8, p. 462.

59. Shipps and Welch, *Journals of McLellin,* 79-80.

60. "The word priesthood is not found in the Book of Commandments, as far as printed in this city in 1833," McLellin wrote (Letter 8, p. 473). Brian Q. Cannon speculates that "details regarding the restoration of the Aaronic Priesthood, including John the Baptist's role in that event, however, were seldom if ever shared prior to 1832 'owing to a spirit of persecution,' as Joseph Smith indicated in 1838." Cannon's date of 1832 embraces Joseph Smith's 1832 reference to "reception of the holy Priesthood by the ministring of Aangels to adminster the letter of the Gospel" and Oliver Cowdery's 1834 account, which nevertheless fail to mention John the Baptist or the three biblical apostles, the Aaronic priesthood or Melchizedek priesthood ("Seventy Contemporaneous Priesthood Restoration Documents," in Welch and Carlson, eds., *Opening the Heavens,* 215-63).

past age, and with neither cross nor angel atop the spire, it shows that the church had not yet settled on a symbol to communicate a break with the past and the expectation of Christ's imminent return. To continue a metaphor, the LDS Church was like a train moving toward an undetermined destination; McLellin had disembarked, the train continued on, and McLellin found the progression disconcerting. He criticized the introduction of new material into the revelations that had been previously published, for instance.[61] For future generations, these revisions would alter what it would mean to be Mormon.[62] Just how far the LDS churches had moved from their origins over a half century is evident in McLellin's correspondence with former colleagues such as Orson Pratt, with whom he struggled to find common ground.[63]

McLellin's memories present an interesting challenge for researchers. He was ordained an apostle in 1835 and must have accepted that Joseph Smith and Oliver Cowdery had authority to give him such a commission. Where did he believe that authority came from? On what basis did McLellin accept this, given his later criticism of the church's priest-

---

61. Perhaps the most controversial change was the addition of more than 400 words in the middle of a sentence in Section 28 of the Book of Commandments. The original 1833 version read: "... for the hour cometh that I will drink of the fruit of the vine with you, on the earth, and with all those whom my Father hath given me out of the world." The 1835 version (LDS D&C 27, RLDS D&C 26) read: "... for the hour cometh that I will drink of the fruit of the vine with you, on the earth, and with Moroni, whom I have sent unto you to reveal the Book of Mormon, ... and also with Elias, ... and also John the son of Zacharias, ... which John I have sent unto you, my servants, Joseph Smith, jr. and Oliver Cowdery, to ordain you unto this first priesthood which you have received, ... and also Elijah, ... and also, with Joseph, and Jacob, and Isaac, and Abraham your fathers; ... And also with Peter, and James, and John, whom I have sent unto you, by whom I have ordained you and confirmed you to be apostles and especial witnesses of my name, ... and also with all those whom my Father hath given me out of the world" (H. Michael Marquardt, *The Joseph Smith Revelations: Text and Commentary* [Salt Lake City: Signature Books, 1999], 72-73). The information about Peter, James, and John ordaining Smith and Cowdery to be apostles was new; a connection to the Melchizedek priesthood was still not explicit and would not be until Joseph Smith wrote in 1838-39 that John the Baptist had "acted under the direction of Peter, James, and John who held the keyes of the Priesthood of Melchizedek, which Priesthood he said would in due time be conferred on us," published in the *Times and Seasons,* Aug. 1842, 866.

62. McLellin wrote about the church publication committee assigned to revise the revelations, saying they "changed them so much that a man would scarcely know them to meet them in a brush-heap!" (Letter 22, pp. 510-11).

63. McLellin struggles in his response to Pratt, who had sent him a call to repentance. "Yours, bearing the Baltimore post-mark, of the 21st inst., lies before me," McLellin wrote, "and I feel gratified at the earnest spirit, and warm manner in which your letter was written. It called to my mind afresh reminisances both pleasing and painful." McLellin sends his love to Pratt's first wife, Sarah, adding: "I well remember the night you immersed her in lake Ontario" (Letter 1, pp. 433, 439). McLellin retains a polite tone of mannered civility, which is characteristic of all his letters.

hood? He did not believe that John the Baptist and Peter, James, and John had conveyed authority to Smith and Cowdery, and he rejected the notion of two different priesthoods on the earth at the same time.[64] Having denounced Smith's and Cowdery's self-designation as apostles, would this not imply a repudiation of McLellin's previous ordination? He does not say. There is much he is silent on.

This does not materially change the reliability of McLellin's central claims, which were that the church had revised its doctrines and history, making the current orthodoxy the result of theological development and the "traditional story" a revised version. These issues ought to be carefully scrutinized by future researchers to determine more precisely the nature of the Mormon experience of the 1830s. McLellin points the way to topics that might add much to our understanding of how Mormon history and theology seemed to evolve together.

Was McLellin a fanatic or simple seeker? The writers in this volume differ in answering this, most assuming that McLellin fell somewhere between sainthood and villainy. In spite of the variation, all agree that Mc Lellin's recollections are of historical value. Where McLellin does not give as much information as we would like, his omissions, particularly to avoid self-incrimination, seem to be due to pride rather than an intent to distort or exaggerate. His focus is on principles, as he understood them, not personalities. We encourage readers to make his writings a starting point in examining and comparing other eyewitness accounts of events in LDS history. Interpretation is always a matter of judgment. However, in terms of the evidence upon which our interpretations are based, McLellin's contribution is an important part of the mix.

ACKNOWLEDGMENTS

We extend our appreciation to George Smith for his encouragement throughout the course of this project and for his foreword, in which he deftly alerts readers to the significance of the McLellin collection and its miraculous discovery. Our appreciation also to Dick Howard, Dawn House, Tom Alexander, Mike Quinn, John-Charles Duffy, and

64. Writing for his own Mormon separatist publication, *Ensign of Liberty,* in 1847, McLellin referred approvingly to Joseph Smith's ordination by "the angel John, the Baptist," and by "Peter and James and John" (quoted in Brian Q. Cannon, "Seventy Contemporaneous Priesthood Restoration Documents," in Welch and Carlson, *Opening the Heavens,* 255-56; see also Shipps and Welch, *Journals of McLellin,* 141, 181, 299, 335, 343). Perhaps this was the kind of imprecision McLellin had in mind when he admitted in 1875: "I wrote several letters that were published in the *Herald* ... I admitted more then than I could conscientiously do now, after my own mature deliberations and investigations" (Letter 15, p. 501).

Bill Russell for the background and context for understanding McLellin. Dorothy Mortensen proofread the notebooks, and her sharp eyes many times transformed a notation of "[illegible]" into McLellin's intended word. H. Michael Marquardt shared his research on McLellin and donated photocopies of the *Gospel Herald, New Hampshire Gazette, Voree Herald,* and *Zion's Reveille* to the McLellin Collection (Accn 1827) in the Marriott Library.

The New York Public Library gave permission to print McLellin's 1880 letter to James T. Cobb. Ronald E. Romig of the Community of Christ Archives generously provided access to letters and a fragmentary notebook. Randall Dixon of the LDS Archives allowed us to examine the three original McLellin notebooks and the original of McLellin's 1854 letter to Orson Pratt. Russell Taylor of the Harold B. Lee Library at Brigham Young University provided a copy of Alvin Knisley's *Biographical Dictionary of the Latter Day Saints Ministry*. Gregory C. Thompson, associate director of Special Collections at the Marriott Library, provided constant support, and Susan Brusik of the Marriott Library's Interlibrary Loan Department acquired numerous books not available in Utah. James Tharp of the Mid-Continent Public Library of Independence, Missouri, provided us with biographical information on several historical figures, and Kirk Watson helped us compile the Biographical Notes. Larry W. Conrad supplied early sources on the RLDS belief in the plurality of Gods. Ed Voorhees gathered information on Elijah Banta. Steve Walters shared information on William Kinkade. Our greatest debt is to the direct descendants of William McLellin who kindly gave permission to publish his notebooks and letters—Kenneth L. Clark Jr. of Longview, Texas, and Betty Clark Heller of Memphis, Tennessee. And lastly Patty Larson and Samantha Passey for their longsuffering patience throughout this project.

Essays

1.

MORMONISM'S "STORMY PETREL"

RICHARD P. HOWARD

Dale L. Morgan, preparing his bibliographies of the churches of the Mormon dispersion, dubbed William E. McLellin (1806-1883) Mormonism's "stormy petrel."[1] Morgan's image of McLellin suggests the use of such modifiers as emotional, impulsive, opinionated, irritable, and controlling, at least in describing McLellin's nature. Considerable evidence supports this description, making McLellin a lively study in dissent. During a long life, he flitted from one Mormon faction to another, searching for what he perceived as the absolute truth of the gospel. His was a desperate and seemingly frustrating search for God.

Born on 18 January 1806 in Smith County, Tennessee, McLellin's search shows up in one of his earliest known letters. Writing on 4 August 1832 about his conversion to the Latter Day Saints, he described how two separate teams of Mormon elders visited him in his home at Paris, Illinois, in July 1831. Both groups were en route to Jackson County, Missouri, in preparation for the establishment of a zionic community there. The preaching of David Whitmer, one of the three witnesses to the divinity of the Book of Mormon and a member of the second team to visit Paris, so deeply impressed on McLellin the gospel message that he im-

---

RICHARD P. HOWARD is Church Historian Emeritus of the Community of Christ, where he served nearly three decades beginning in 1966, also as Director of Archives. He is the author of *The Church through the Years* (two volumes); *Restoration Scriptures: A Study of Their Textual Development*; and with his wife, Barbara, *Tell the Sacred Story*; as well as editor of *The Memoirs of President Joseph Smith III*. He is a past president of both the John Whitmer Historical Association and the Mormon History Association.

1. Dale L. Morgan, "A Bibliography of the Churches of the Dispersion," *Western Humanities Review* 7 (Summer 1953): 264. In mid-nineteenth century parlance, a "storm petrel" was "a person who delights in conflict, or whose appearance on the scene heralds trouble" (*Shorter Oxford English Dictionary*, 5th ed., 2002, s.v.). The comparison is particularly apt because *petrel* is thought to have been derived from *Peter*, and sea petrels are so named because they appear to walk on water as they feed.

mediately left his settled life to follow Mormonism:[2] "My curiosity was roused up and my anxiety also to know the truth. –And though I had between 30 & 40 students and the people generally satisfied with me as Teacher–yet I closed my school on the 29th July and on the 30th I mounted Tom and left for Indepen[dence]."[3]

McLellin arrived in Independence on 18 August 1831 only to find that Joseph Smith Jr., the Mormon prophet, and many of the elders who had come to Missouri had already left to return to Ohio. However, he acquainted himself with the saints there and was baptized two days later. On 24 August he was ordained an elder, and the next day he headed eastward with Hyrum Smith. On this trip he preached his first missionary sermon, one and a half hours in length, on 28 August 1831 and perceived his hearers were touched by God's spirit. Encouraged by this, McLellin later preached to a packed court house at Jacksonville, Illinois, writing that "the house though large was full of Judges, Lawyers, Doctors, Priests and People I think about 500. I spoke 3 hours and when done I cannot describe the joy of some, the consternation of others, and the anger of others."[4]

On their way to Kirtland, Ohio, the Mormon stronghold, William and Hyrum veered to Paris, where William finished some personal business, bought Hyrum a horse, and preached to some friends and relatives. They eventually arrived in Kirtland on 18 October 1831. A week later, at a church conference at nearby Orange, William first met Joseph Smith. William's account of this meeting demonstrated something of his fundamental commitment to Joseph and the Latter Day Saints: "On the 25th Oct I attended a conference.... General peace and harmony pervaded the conference and much instruction to me. From thence I went home with Jos[eph] and lived with him about three weeks; and from my acquaintance then and until now I can truely say I believe him to be a man of God. A Prophet, a Seer and Revelator to the church of christ."[5] At this meeting McLellin asked Smith to inquire of God's will for his life, and Smith responded through revelation in rather minute detail.[6]

---

2. McLellin was at that time a school teacher in Paris; a wife, Cynthia Anne, whom he had married on 30 July 1829, had recently died (Lyndon W. Cook, *The Revelations of the Prophet Joseph Smith: A Historical and Biographical Commentary of the Doctrine and Covenants* [Salt Lake City: Deseret Book, 1985], 106-07).

3. William E. and Emiline McLelin to Beloved Relatives [Samuel McLellin], 4 Aug. 1832, Community of Christ Archives, Independence, Missouri. This is a rare instance in which McLellin spells his last name as "McLelin."

4. McLelin and McLelin to Beloved Relatives.

5. Ibid.

McLellin was ordained at the conference to the office of high priest.[7]

McLellin's faculty for misjudging his social environment, which he demonstrated repeatedly in following years, came out during a church conference at Hiram, Ohio, in early November 1831. Church leaders were considering publication of revelatory documents by Joseph Smith. McLellin saw himself as superior in literary attainment and ability to most of those around him, including Smith, and apparently boasted that he could write a revelation surpassing the ones available to the church through its prophet. Smith gave him a chance to try his hand. Predictably, McLellin's effort not only failed of its immediate objective, but the elders also rallied around Smith and bore witness to his revelatory prowess. Years later, after McLellin was out of the church, Smith wrote of the event:

> William E. McLellin, as the wisest man, in his own estimation, having more learning than sense, endeavored to write a commandment like unto one of the least of the Lord's, but failed, it was an awful responsibility to write in the name of the Lord. The elders and all present, that witnessed this vain attempt of a man to imitate the language of Jesus Christ, renewed their faith in the fulness of the gospel, and in the truth of the commandments and revelations which the Lord had given to the church through my instrumentality; and the elders signified a willingness to bear testimony of their truth to all the world.[8]

Thereafter Smith sent McLellin on a mission, perhaps in part to get him out of Kirtland.[9] McLellin left for the eastern states, but within a few weeks his complaints about being sent away had reached Smith, who admonished him through revelation at the January 1832 conference at Amherst, Ohio, and sent him with Luke Johnson on another mission, this time to the southern states.[10] Although McLellin continued to do

---

6. Doctrine and Covenants 66 commended McLellin for his repentance and specifically urged him to resist the temptation to commit adultery. He was also sent eastward on a missionary tour in the company of Samuel H. Smith, brother of Joseph. McLellin's reward was the promise of "a crown of eternal life at the right hand of my Father, who is full of grace and truth" (RLDS D&C 66:5g; LDS D&C 66:12).

7. Donald Q. Cannon and Lyndon W. Cook, eds., *Far West Record: Minutes of the Church of Jesus Christ of Latter-day Saints, 1830-1844* (Salt Lake City: Deseret Book Co., 1983), 14.

8. "History of Joseph Smith," *Times and Seasons*, 15 April 1844, 496. Present at this special conference, according to the minutes in Cannon and Cook, *Far West Record*, 15, were "Joseph Smith, Jun., Oliver Cowdery, David Whitmer, John Whitmer, Peter Whitmer, Jun., Sidney Rigdon, William E. M'Lellin, Orson Hyde, Luke Johnson, Lyman E. Johnson."

9. RLDS D&C 68:1; LDS D&C 68:1-12.

10. RLDS D&C 75:2; LDS D&C 75:6-11.

missionary work, he remained in Middlebury, Ohio, then suddenly returned to Kirtland and married Emeline Miller on 26 April 1832.[11] His record of unwillingness to carry out the wishes of Joseph Smith probably accounted for McLellin's 3 December 1832 excommunication, although he was apparently reinstated soon thereafter.[12] Perhaps fittingly, the last time McLellin's name appeared in Smith's revelatory instructions it was a rebuke. A document of 8 March 1833 read: "I [God] am not well pleased with my servant William E. M'Lellin." The document admonished the backslider, who had by that time settled in Independence, to repent of his many failings.[13] In sum, the initial interactions between McLellin and Joseph Smith revealed a distance portending McLellin's eventual separation from the church.

McLellin stayed in Independence until late 1833 when mob action forced him, with some 1,200 other church members, to flee to Clay County. There he remained for nearly a year. On 3 July 1834, he became a member of the Missouri High Council under the presidency of David Whitmer, further cementing the close relationship these two men had enjoyed since McLellin first learned of Mormonism. On 9 July McLellin started for Kirtland with Joseph Smith and several other men, although he became ill and had to stay behind until he recovered. He nevertheless settled in Kirtland in the fall of 1834.

Perhaps another instance of McLellin's relationship with Whitmer is evident from 14 February 1835 when McLellin began his brief tenure as a member of the Quorum of Twelve Apostles. The members of this quorum were chosen by the three witnesses to the Book of Mormon, one of whom was Whitmer. The prayer of blessing given McLellin at the time may have influenced the convert's self-perception:

---

11. Emeline Miller was born 4 September 1819 in Vermont. She and William were married for many years and had six known children: Charles William, Sarah Emeline, James Martin, Helen Rebecca, Albert Eugene, and Marcus Nelson. Of this event, Joseph Smith wrote to his wife, Emma Smith, on 6 June 1832: "I am not pleased to hear that William Mclelin has come back and disobayed the voice of him who is altogether Lovely for a woman[.] I am astonished at Sister Emaline yet I cannot belive she is not a worthy sister[.] I hope She will find him true and kind to her but have no reason to expect it[.] his Conduct merits the disapprobation of every true follower of Christ." Mormon Collection, Chicago Historical Society; LaMar C. Berrett, "An Impressive Letter from the Pen of Joseph Smith," *BYU Studies* 11 (Summer 1971): 517-23.

12. Joseph Smith Jr., "History, 1832," entry for 3 Dec., in Dean C. Jessee, ed., *Personal Writings of Joseph Smith,* rev. ed. (Salt Lake City and Provo: Deseret Book and Brigham Young University Press, 2002), 22.

13. RLDS D&C 87:8c; LDS D&C 90:35. McLellin had settled in Independence on 16 June 1832.

> Wisdom and intelligence shall be poured out upon him, to enable him to perform the great work that is incumbent upon him; that he may be spared until the Saints are gathered; that he may stand before kings and rulers to bear testimony, and be upheld by holy angels; and the nations of the earth shall acknowledge that God has sent him; he shall have power to overcome his enemies; and his life shall be spared in the midst of pestilence and destruction, and in the midst of his enemies. He shall be a prince and savior to God's people. The tempter shall not overcome him, nor his enemies prevail against him; the heavens shall be opened unto him, as unto men in days of old. He shall be mighty in the hands of God, and shall convince thousands that God has sent him; and his days may be prolonged until the coming of the Son of Man. He shall be wafted as on eagles' wings, from country to country, and from people to people; and be able to do wonders in the midst of this generation. Even so. Amen.[14]

Almost at the same time that he was called to be an apostle, McLellin's almost constant troubles with the church leadership became public. In the summer of 1835 he was disfellowshipped, but then restored on 25 September 1835 without a clear reconciliation. From this point on he seems to have lost confidence in some leaders in the church, although the attraction of Mormonism still held sway. He could not leave the church, although he definitely considered doing so. That push-pull relationship with the church would become a part of McLellin's life ever after.[15]

Public disputes between McLellin and the hierarchy arose with the Kirtland church's disintegration and the flight of its leaders to Far West, Missouri, in the winter of 1837-38. Progress toward church stability did not materialize as he had hoped, and the failures of the organization to meet serious challenges of an economic and political, as well as spiritual, nature created a serious crisis of conscience for McLellin. It seems from the scant records available for this period that he lost faith in the leadership and had second thoughts about continuing as a Latter Day Saint. This was a not an uncommon development at the time. The most serious dissent of the church up to that point took place during this period, and it prompted the withdrawal or excommunication of numerous church members. Among them were several high officials, one of whom was McLellin's mentor, David Whitmer.[16]

---

14. B. H. Roberts, ed., *History of the Church of Jesus Christ of Latter-day Saints. Period I: History of Joseph Smith, the Prophet,* 2d ed. rev. (Salt Lake City: Church of Jesus Christ of Latter-day Saints, 1978), 2:190-91.

15. Cook, *Revelations,* 107.

16. On this important topic, see Marvin S. Hill, "Cultural Crisis in the Mormon King-

As church leaders relocated to Far West, McLellin became increasingly disenchanted. His dissent was known to the senior leadership. Apostle David W. Patten took the opportunity at the 7 April 1838 conference to speak against him and four other apostles.[17] Finally on 11 May, a bishop's court tried McLellin for transgression. Joseph Smith was in attendance but related nothing of the outcome, only that he spoke at the trial. In editing Smith's account for publication years later, B. H. Roberts inserted a footnote on this subject. He commented:

> The text is silent in relation to what action was taken respecting William E. McLellin, and the Far West Record is silent upon the subject also. In fact the minutes of the trial before the Bishop are not written in that record at all. It is known, however, from other sources that William E. McLellin was finally excommunicated from the church at Far West. Thence forward he took an active part in the persecution of the Saints in Missouri, and at one time expressed the desire to do violence to the person of Joseph Smith, while the latter was confined in Liberty prison.[18]

In the period that followed, McLellin became a diligent opponent of the Mormon leadership but not necessarily of the Saints. He charged that Smith, with his lieutenants, had lost the vision of the early church and had been seduced by power and affluence. There is some evidence that while Joseph Smith and other leaders were in jail in November 1838, McLellin led a search party through Smith's home "to confiscate books and papers that might prove damaging to the Mormons. The Danite constitution was reportedly found in a trunk filled with the Prophet's personal papers."[19] Smith wrote in an epistle from Liberty jail in Clay County, Missouri, in December that turncoats William "McLellin, John Whitmer, David Whitmer, Oliver Cowdery, Martin Harris, are too mean to mention; and we had liked to have forgotten them."[20]

From 1838 through 1843, McLellin essentially retreated from the Mormon scene. When the church was forced out of Missouri at the end of 1838, he moved to Hampton, Illinois, near Rock Island, began prac-

---

dom: A Reconsideration of the Causes of Kirtland Dissent," *Church History* 49 (September 1980): 286-97.

17. Cannon and Cook, *Far West Record,* 160. All these apostles except William Smith, the prophet's brother, were later cut off from the church.

18. Roberts, *History of Church,* 3:31-32n.

19. *Missouri Republican,* 10 Nov. 1838, quoted in Stephen C. LeSueur, *The 1838 Mormon War in Missouri* (Columbia: University of Missouri Press, 1987), 180.

20. Joseph Smith Jr. to the Church in Caldwell County, 16 Dec. 1838, in Roberts, *History of Church,* 3:232. The names of these and others were dropped out of the version of Smith's letter published in *Times and Seasons* 1 (April 1840): 85.

tice as a physician, and remained aloof from Mormonism until the autumn of 1843. He then began several intensive years of affiliation with a quick succession of dissenting factions. These affiliations culminated in his forming a group of his own at Kirtland from 1847 to 1849. Nearly twenty years after that group fell apart, McLellin spent several months affiliated with the faction led by Granville Hedrick at Independence.

The first of the factions to attract McLellin was George M. Hinkle's church at Buffalo, Iowa Territory, across the Mississippi from McLellin's home. Hinkle, another Mormon dissident from the 1838 period, had gathered a group in 1840 of about a hundred members, which struggled for existence for several years. McLellin appeared at a conference of Hinkle's group on 16 September 1843 and accepted ordination to "be united with elder Hinkle in bearing the glad tidings of salvation to the world." McLellin apparently "straightway preached this to be the true, the only true church of God now on the earth."[21]

By mid-1844, both Hinkle and McLellin were active as apostles, jointly launching a church periodical, the *Ensign,* with McLellin as editor. This gave him a forum for presenting his views about Mormonism. For instance, he had an intense disgust for the activities of Brigham Young and the Twelve in control of the institutional machinery. When the editor of the nearby *Davenport Gazette* mistakenly suggested that Hinkle's group was "Mormon," McLellin offered the first of many published attacks on what he would later refer to as "Twelveitism": "One thing we have to say, and we want it distinctly understood—we have no bond of union or fellowship existing between us and the Mormons (so called.) Yet we do not feel disposed to persecute or injure them, or needlessly make any thrusts at them. We are for the Latter Day Saints to have and enjoy their rights as other churches; and when they trample upon the laws, and disregard other men's rights, then we are for their punishment."[22] In this mild put-down of Mormons, McLellin followed Hinkle's lead, who was careful to convey the wickedness of Nauvoo Mormonism while appearing if not conciliatory then at least indifferent, with a live-and-let-live attitude.[23]

McLellin did not remain a part of Hinkle's group long. By October 1844 he was gone, and had he not voluntarily departed Hinkle would have forced him out on charges of apostasy. Hinkle strongly criticized McLellin for reneging on the church and gospel:

21. "Conference Minutes," *The Ensign* [Buffalo, Iowa], Oct. 1844, 62.

22. "Our Politics," *The Ensign,* Aug. 1844, 30.

23. Ibid., 31-32.

> It is awful to reflect upon the many thrilling discourses, positive declarations, and pointed testimonies borne from the public stand by this individual ... since last April.... [N]o man of this age has made a louder pretence to the miraculous gifts of the gospel than Dr. McLellin.... He was, Paul-like, in his zeal against [those] ... who apostatized or departed from the Church.... [H]e [had] remarked, that when any one left this Church they were bound to lie; for, said he, the Devil will lead them to it.... He then determined to leave the church; and from thence forward sought to do all the mischief in his power.

Hinkle was convinced McLellin had fallen into the same trap the apostle had detected in the course of other apostates. "I am now convinced that he intends to destroy the faith of all those who he can have influence over," Hinkle added. "I deem it my duty to thus put you on your guard."[24]

From there, for a brief season in late 1844 and early 1845, McLellin affiliated with William Law's dissident group situated in the Hampton, Illinois, area. Law had been a member of the First Presidency, but bolted from the church with his family and a few friends in the spring of 1844 over doctrinal differences with Joseph Smith. McLellin cast his lot with people whom he called the "faithful" members of the First Presidency. He tried to bring Sidney Rigdon into this group of reformers on 23 December 1844, suggesting that the scattered Saints could unite under Rigdon and Law—the only surviving members of the First Presidency—as the proper successors to the slain Joseph Smith: "The Lord has shown to me that by a union of President Law and yourself, together with each [of] your friends, that all the honest in heart among the Latter Day Saints and throughout the world will UNITE also, and form that company who will follow the saviour robed in white linen 'clean and white.'"

Even as he was making this proposal, McLellin also raised the possibility of his visiting Pittsburgh and joining Rigdon's movement. He wrote to Rigdon:

> You used to tell me that "I was a man after your own heart." One thing I know that on my first visit to Ohio, from no man did I receive so much intelligence concerning the divine volume as from yourself. But you could seldom act yourself in consequence of the abominable jealousy of him [Joseph Smith] with whom you were connected. And I am told by the brethren here that for the last five years you have been rather a spectator than an active adviser in those measures at Nauvoo, which have brought death upon the prophet and lasting disgrace upon the church. This gives me more confi-

---

24. George Hinkle, *The Ensign*, Oct. 1844, 57-59.

dence in you, and I am determined from this time forward to "be a man after God's own heart."[25]

In a postscript McLellin referred to thrice-weekly meetings he was attending at William Law's home, in which they enjoyed the spirit of God in prophecy. He seemed clearly a part of Law's tiny following at that point, but he was leaning plaintively toward Rigdon by the start of 1845.

An especially attractive feature for McLellin was Rigdon's penchant for blistering the Nauvoo Quorum of the Twelve. Leaving Law's group, by March 1845 McLellin was in Pittsburgh and had his anti-Twelve views published in Rigdon's periodical. He considered the Twelve to be men who had fallen so far, they were beyond redemption. He affirmed the church's proper leaders were comprised of a presidency of three, headed by Rigdon. His praise of Rigdon was nothing short of a eulogy. In urging the primacy of the presidency over the authority of the Twelve, he closed by hinting that he himself should like to stand with Rigdon in that inspired leadership: "I feel my interest identified with his, and I feel also to stand by him in all righteousness before God, while he stands as a man of God to plead with the world."[26]

Predictably, McLellin played an active role in Rigdon's April 1845 Conference of the Church of Christ.[27] Rigdon proposed a committee of Samuel Bennett, Jeremiah Hatch Jr., McLellin, Joseph M. Cole, and George W. Robinson to draft a preamble and resolutions on the Mormon Nauvoo problem. The goal was twofold: to take a definite stand against the perceived Nauvoo apostasy and to inform the world of the chasm between those in Nauvoo and the "true faith" of the Church of Christ. The committee met and delivered to the conference a document entitled "Preamble and Resolutions of the Church of Christ." The preamble noted the necessity of differentiating themselves from the larger Nauvoo population. It lamented how Nauvoo Mormons had perverted the gospel and defied the laws of God and the nation. The committee then framed these resolutions:

Resolved, That we hold no fellowship with the people calling them-

25. McLellin to President S. Rigdon, 23 Dec. 1844, in *Latter Day Saint's Messenger and Advocate,* 15 Jan. 1845, 92.

26. McLellin to Brother [Samuel] Bennett, 15 Mar. 1845, in *Latter Day Saint's Messenger and Advocate,* 15 Mar. 1845, 151.

27. By this time McLellin favored the name "Church of Christ" as the only acceptable title for followers of Christ. As he moved into Rigdonism, his influence on this matter seems apparent. Rigdon's periodical henceforth became the *Messenger and Advocate of the Church of Christ.*

selves the church of Jesus Christ of Latter Day Saints, and can have no communion with them, unless they repent and obey the principles of righteousness and truth.

Resolved, That we maintain the truth and the truth only, at all hazards; renouncing at once, and for ever, the unsanctifying dogma, that it is sometimes lawful to lie.

Resolved, That our subjection to the law of God impels us to yield implicit obedience to the law of the land.

Resolved, That we maintain and do earnestly contend for the faith which was once, and is again, delivered to the saints, contained in the Bible, Book of Mormon and Book of Covenants.

Resolved, That we feel it a solemn and imperative obligation, we owe to God and our fellow men, to disseminate to the extent of our ability, correct information regarding certain pernicious doctrines and practices which are secretly taught by the leaders and many of the members, of the society called the church of Jesus Christ of Latter Day Saints; verily believing them demoralizing and destructive, combining all the worst features of barbarism, and containing all the elements of the wildest anarchy, and would if unchecked by the power of truth, ultimately extinguish the species.[28]

McLellin's signature to these resolutions showed that at this stage he was focusing his dissent on Mormonism as it then existed at Nauvoo.

Other indications of McLellin's swift rise in Rigdon's group included his selection as a member of the Quorum of Seventy-three, along with his old comrade George M. Hinkle, and his designation as a member of the Quorum of Twelve.[29] A clerk of the conference, McLellin also played a central role in the discussion of important issues, speaking several times at key points in the conference. Early in the week, just after Rigdon had been unanimously sustained as prophet, seer, revelator, and translator to the Church of Christ, McLellin stood, took Rigdon's hand, and pledged "to stand by him and his family in all righteousness before God until the time of the end."[30] Two days later on 9 April, he confirmed a vision and revelation proclaimed by Rigdon.[31] Later in the conference

---

28. "Minutes," *Messenger and Advocate of the Church of Christ,* 15 Apr. 1845, 176.

29. Hinkle, writing in April 1845, told his followers in Buffalo, Iowa, of essentially a merger between his group and Rigdon's Church of Christ. He said all differences that had arisen between himself and McLellin no longer existed and that full confidence between them had been restored. *The Ensign,* Apr. 1845, 156-57.

30. "Minutes," 7 Apr. 1845, in *Messenger and Advocate of the Church of Christ,* 15 Apr. 1845, 169. Rigdon followed this demonstration by immediately nominating Samuel James and Ebenezer Robinson as his counselors in the First Presidency. The conference accepted both unanimously. Had McLellin intended his effusive vow of fealty to Rigdon to make him part of Rigdon's presidency, he must have been disappointed at the result.

31. *Messenger and Advocate of the Church of Christ,* 1 May 1845, 185-86.

he reported his own revelation and covenant. In it he had been commissioned to be a steward over the bones of Joseph M. Cole, a fellow apostle and member of the Quorum of Seventy-three who was also present at the conference but who, according to McLellin's revelation, would be slain before Christ's Second Coming.[32]

On the last day the conference unanimously endorsed the 1835 Doctrine and Covenants as the revelation of God and law of the church. Later McLellin would reject it, but at this point in the development of his antipathy for Brigham Young's Twelve, his endorsement was tantamount to rejecting the Nauvoo editions of 1844 and1845. His full break from all the major features of Latter Day Saintism except the Book of Mormon would await the formation of his own schismatic group in 1847.

Reports of the Rigdon conference of April 1845 soon reached Nauvoo. One elder, David Pettegrew, back in Nauvoo from a mission to the eastern states, had contact with some of the Rigdon branches since January 1845. He read the Rigdon conference minutes and reacted strongly:

> I left Nauvoo the 28th of last January, in company with Elder Willard Snow, for the southeast part of Indiana. When we arrived we found great trouble in the branches which we had built up three years before. There were men among them of another spirit—the doctrine of Rigdon, and it was marvelous to witness the "wicked spirit" of those who had turned away from the faith. I never realized before the abomination and wickedness of dissenters. They drew after them a multitude of the baser sort, who stood and delighted to hear them ridicule and slander the prophet and people of God; by which "*the way of truth was evil spoken of.*"

Warming to a denunciation of McLellin, Pettigrew recalled an event corroborated in no other source thus far:

> It brings to mind what I witnessed in Jackson county, in 1833, a few months before we were driven from that place. The power of God was manifest on that land in our meetings, held by the elders. I remember in one of those meetings it was made known by prophecy and revelation, through T. B. Marsh, as the spirit gave utterance, "that McLellin would carry the things the Lord was revealing to his people, to the world, and would use his influence against the church to destroy it."
>
> McLellin wondered why T. B. Marsh uttered words against him: —Then another arose and bore testimony to what Marsh had foretold, by

32. "Minutes," *Messenger and Advocate of the Church of Christ,* 15 Apr., 1 May 1845, 168, 189.

> the same spirit; and a third arose and testified also, and we marveled! we sorrowed! we wondered! I shall never forget that scene. It was true, and when I read the Pittsburgh papers, and saw McLellin in with Rigdon, it brought the prophetic language of 1833, to my mind, and confirmed it. *McLellin goes against the church to destroy it!*[33]

Such characterizations did not bother McLellin, even if he knew about them. On 28 May 1845, he sent a letter to "Presidents Rigdon and Robinson" that reflected great optimism in the eventual triumph of their cause against the Nauvoo Twelve. He told of a revelation to go to Tennessee to visit his father, whom he was told he would baptize, and who in turn would give him a father's blessing. All of this had come to pass, he wrote. Even more, he had prophesied the future in response to a question from his congregation, "Are you a prophet of God?" He commented: "The future was opened up before me and I rolled it off with a voice that started some of them from their seats. And I must say that I even felt some astonished myself at what *I saw and declared.* The meeting closed, the people dispersed." While receiving his father's blessing McLellin's soul caught fire and the future world opened to him, revealing "important events and scenes through which you and I will have to pass shoulder to shoulder, hand to hand, and heart to heart, before we shall see this world redeemed, sin destroyed, satan bound, and the saints rise, and all the righteous enter into the rest of God, and dwell on the face of this earth in perfect peace."[34]

From late May through August 1845, McLellin traveled and preached widely for Rigdon's Church of Christ. From Hampton, Illinois, to Philadelphia he labored tirelessly, preaching, baptizing, and helping local people resolve their conflicts. J. H. Newton, a member in Philadelphia, wrote feelingly of McLellin's "olive branch" qualities of ministry and paid tribute to the way in which McLellin had quickened the believers there in their faith and commitment.[35]

From the sketchy evidence extant, by early 1846 McLellin had become convinced the faithful of the church ought to gather at Kirtland. It also appears that by that time McLellin was no longer firmly a part of Rigdon's organization. In trying to influence others to this position,

---

33. David Pettegrew to *Times and Seasons,* 1 May 1845, 893.

34. McLellin to Sidney Rigdon and Ebenezer Robinson, in *Messenger and Advocate of the Church of Christ,* 1 July 1845, 253.

35. Two McLellin letters telling of his labors that summer appear in the *Messenger and Advocate of the Church of Christ,* 15 July, 15 Aug. 1845, 267-68, 302-03; see 315-16 for Newton's letter.

McLellin wrote to Leonard Soby in Philadelphia about the gathering and direction of the Rigdonites. Soby promptly alerted Rigdon of this dissent on 2 February, questioning McLellin's course: "Why does he write to me to destroy my confidence in those I love? Oh I see the spirit of the Devil in this."[36] Rigdon explained that McLellin and some others had "apostatized from the church and kingdom of the living God, and are lifting their puny arms against the work of the Almighty." He printed extracts of two McLellin letters in the *Messenger and Advocate* and noted that McLellin had left the fold altogether. His heart was at Kirtland—stronghold for the kingdom of God, in which place he soon would try to find the "rest of God."[37]

In April 1846 McLellin moved to Shalersville, Ohio, to practice medicine until moving to Kirtland the following October. During that time he apparently flirted for a few months with the movement of James J. Strang. In a letter to David Whitmer on 2 December 1846, he stated that Strang had made overtures to him and even listed him as a member of his Quorum of Twelve. McLellin, however, disavowed any official affiliation with Strang, later attacking the leadership in his *Ensign of Liberty*. In May 1848 he accused Strang of instituting strange oaths, covenants, bizarre ceremonies, and blood rituals and labeled him a "third-rate infidel," a "false prophet, and a base hearted man, whose great aim is to destroy others in order to build himself up."[38]

Seven months earlier, however, McLellin had passed through Voree, Wisconsin, the site of Strang's headquarters, to visit him and his followers. In October 1847 he engaged in a debate with Strang. The two men had a heated exchange on the issue of McLellin's affiliation and whether he had ever been on friendly terms with one of Strang's colleagues, John C. Bennett. McLellin hotly denied both points, and Strang responded by reading three letters from McLellin, two to Bennett and the other to Strang himself, into the record of the debate. He challenged McLellin to deny that he had written the letters. McLellin remained silent in the face of the challenge. The three letters, together with Strang's comments about them, ended the discussion quickly, and McLellin never mentioned the matter again, even in his own publications. Summarized, the letters established the following

36. *Messenger and Advocate of the Church of Christ,* Mar. 1846, 463.

37. Ibid., 463-64.

38. "J. J. Strang's L. D. Saintism," *The Ensign of Liberty, of the Church of Christ* [Kirtland, Ohio], May 1848, 91.

points about McLellin's membership in Strang's group and his previous friendship with John C. Bennett:

1. His friendship with Bennett dated from 1831, and they had lived and practiced medicine in the same town in 1844, presumably in Hampton, Illinois. On the basis of that friendship, McLellin had asked Bennett to write him a recommendation as a physician and a gentleman. McLellin proposed entering into a medical partnership with Bennett, indicating a willingness to spend the winter in Voree trying to work it out.

2. He encountered Strang in Kirtland and had several long conversations with him. He found Strang intelligent and gentlemanly and respected his claims as president of the Latter Day Saints.[39]

3. He longed to be "with his Brethren" in Voree for the 6 October 1846 conference but his workload was too heavy. He expected to visit Voree in "only a few months" but was pleased with the close friendship he had with Bennett.

4. To Bennett, McLellin praised Strang and enclosed a separate message to be delivered to Strang with the statement: "The nearer the relation and the more the intimacy between J. J. S. and myself the better for the cause."

5. He pressed Bennett to be his advocate for a responsible station in Strang's organization: "You may promise in my name all that you may think I am (by indefatigable perseverance) capable of performing.... Some things in this [letter] you will show to none save my friend Pres. J. J. Strang. In him I have all confidence."[40]

6. To Strang, McLellin affirmed his gratitude for their lengthy August 1846 visit with each other at Kirtland. McLellin pledged his active participation in church work, describing his determination in this regard to be "almost unbounded." His "soul pants to dwell among the BRETHREN." He urged Strang to postpone the next conference until 6 June 1847 and to defer "appointment of all important presiding officers" until then so McLellin would be able to attend.[41]

7. He stated his unchanging position regarding his "taking the oversight and management of some important business on my arrival" at Voree and hoped Strang had not changed in his support. McLellin was

---

39. McLellin to My Old and much Respected Friend [John C. Bennett], 14-18 Aug. 1846, in *Gospel Herald* [Voree, Wisc.], 2 Dec. 1847, 164.

40. McLellin to Dear Doctor [John C. Bennett], 30 Sept. 1846, in *Gospel Herald,* 2 Dec. 1847, 165.

41. McLellin to Pres. J. J. Strang, 27 Sept. 1846, in *Gospel Herald,* 2 Dec. 1847, 165.

willing to help with the printing press for the church next spring but awaited Strang's advice.[42]

In their debate Strang exploited the sentiments McLellin had expressed in his letters to show how much at variance they were with his verbal and other published statements. In all probability McLellin was disillusioned by Strang's decision to pass him over for a top leadership role and thereafter began distancing himself from the group. Near the end of October 1846, McLellin, no doubt wounded by Strang's neglect, moved his family to Kirtland and began preparing for the launching of his own "Church of Christ." On 2 December he sat down to write a long and critically important epistle to his old friend David Whitmer in Richmond, Missouri.

His object in writing was to urge Whitmer to accept a calling as prophet, seer, and revelator to the church. That calling, McLellin argued, had been imposed on Whitmer on 8 July 1834 in Clay County, Missouri, by Joseph Smith. After the Zion's Camp debacle, just before returning to Kirtland, Smith had organized the Missouri High Council and set apart other leaders, including Whitmer as president of the church in Missouri. Writing in retrospect, McLellin reinterpreted this ordination in a wholly different light. What had not occurred to McLellin before, he now wrote in the most definite and persuasive language he could summon:

> You will remember, he [Joseph Smith] appointed a special conference at L. Wight's, on the 8th of July, 1834. Benj. Winchester and Leonard Rich have both told me that he laid his hands on you, in that conference, and appointed and ordained you to be the Lord's Seer, "in his stead," provided anything should befal himself, so as to remove him from time. I was at that conference part of the day, and well remember that I saw you ordained. Should Joseph transgress, he should not have power except to appoint another. Now all acquainted with his history, from that day to the day of his death, know perfectly well that he never had power with God to accomplish any one great or good object that he ever commenced. Every thing seemed to be marred in his hands, until finally he died "as a fool dieth," at the hands of his enemies.
>
> Now brother David, ... inasmuch as the Lord has appointed you, you cannot shrink from your duty, and then have any hope of eternal life. You must obey, or sink in utter darkness forever.... But my dear brother, the church is bleeding at every pore, for the want of faithful Shepherds to take the oversight of the flock.

42. Ibid., 166.

> ... The church now calls upon you to come and take your place, and make the seat of the FIRST LEADERS in the church here in Kirtland. For this was the first Stake of Zion ever pointed out, in this generation. We have the promise that in this place, we shall have an endowment from on high. Then the Elders, thus prepared, shall go to Gentile and then to the Jew, in all the world, in power.[43]

What is striking about the letter is how it denounces Joseph Smith and claims Whitmer's ordination to the Missouri presidency was directly consequent to Smith's transgression. This assertion rested on McLellin's interpretation of Doctrine and Covenants, section 43:2 (LDS 43:4-6). By this theory, Smith had no further prophetic authority from then on; he was a fallen prophet during the last decade of his life. McLellin then directed his anger at the Nauvoo Twelve, as well as other factional groups: "The apostate Twelve have fled to the wilderness, with a large body of followers, to endure the severity of the judgments of God, in their destruction, which is certain. Rigdon lives near Chambersburg, Pa., surrounded by only a *few* followers; but few as they are, their hearts are full of desires for blood and war. –Strang pitched his head quarters in Voree, Wisconsin, and has made the *notorious* Dr. J. C. Bennett his chief counsellor and *Pontiff. Big title truly*."[44]

McLellin then pled at length that Whitmer make this a matter of prayer and come and take his place. For whatever reasons, Whitmer chose not to respond to McLellin's letter. When McLellin published it in the *Ensign of Liberty* in April 1847, he noted that Whitmer had given him no answer.

McLellin's patience at Whitmer's long silence had already worn thin by mid-January 1847. He, Martin Harris, and several other elders met on 23 January in Kirtland to name their organization officially "The Church of Christ." Two weeks later the first conference of the new group convened there, and one of their first actions was to hear and approve a committee report–written by McLellin, Leonard Rich, Jacob Bump, and three others–on the reasons for the emergence of the Church of Christ. Now in much more detail than McLellin had written to Whitmer, the "fallen prophet" theory began to take on a life of its own. They faulted Joseph Smith and other top leaders for a broad range of offenses:

1. Renaming the church in May 1834 as the "Church of the Latter Day Saints" when the original name had been designated by revelation.

---

43. McLellin to My old, well tried, and beloved friend, David Whitmer, 2 Dec. 1846, *Ensign of Liberty*, Apr. 1847, 18-19.

44. Ibid., 19, emphasis in original.

2. Leading the militaristic Zion's Camp against the peace enjoined by the gospel. That the camp had ended in disaster was evidence of the Lord's displeasure.

3. Presuming to lead the church after he had appointed his successor, David Whitmer, in 1834.

4. Making Sylvester Smith a scapegoat for his own sins committed during the military expedition of Zion's Camp.

5. Engineering the "endowment" at the Kirtland Temple in March and April 1836, which failed to meet expectation because the Lord would not endow His spirit in those who had drifted so far from divine purpose.

6. Establishing a mercantile at Kirtland stocked with goods bought on credit when the Lord had commanded "to owe no man."

7. Founding a bank without a charter from the state legislature in clear violation of Ohio law.

8. Engaging in land speculation with the city plat at Kirtland.

This set of indictments was similar to those offered by other dissenters from the 1837-38 period, aiming mostly at the church's involvement in secular affairs. This was not the end of the assessment, however. The committee went on to denounce excesses in Nauvoo, seeing them as the logical outcome of the earlier transgressions. "Finally," because of these sins,

> the protecting, or rather the preventing power of God is withdrawn. "The wolves are on the scent," the Prophet and Patriarch of the Latter Day Saints are again taken prisoners, and soon the massive doors of the Carthage prison grate upon their hinges, as they are closed for the *last time* upon these strange, singular, and unfortunate men. Soon a lawless banditti of mobocrats rush forward and surround the walls of their prison. Infuriate madness, with the blackness of darkness of the infernal regions, sits on their brows. Wilful murder is in their hearts. Another moment, and the–Hark! What do we hear? O! 'Tis the death groans of Joseph and Hyrum Smith. Ah!! see them fall!!! The fatal lead has pierced their vital parts. Their life's blood has crimsoned the jail of Hancock County. O! ye unfortunate men, we feel to bewail the manner of your end. O! that you had kept the strict commandments of your God, and then lived in righteousness, and led the people of the Church of Christ onward to that "rest which remaineth to the people of God."[45]

Having dispensed with Joseph Smith's prophetic authority in this

---

45. McLellin, report of his committee to a conference of the Church of Christ at Kirtland, Ohio, 6 Feb. 1847, in *Ensign of Liberty,* Mar. 1847, 11, emphasis in original.

report, McLellin proceeded to demolish the factional leaders. For example, the *Ensign of Liberty* for April 1847 featured a long, stinging rebuke of James Strang's claims.[46] Meanwhile, McLellin undertook lengthy missionary tours both east and west to capture followers of Rigdon, Strang, and Young. He met with Strangites in Pittsburgh, where they were led by J. M. Greig, who reported to Strang:

> I thought it important that you should know that "Scrutator's" angel [McLellin] has recently favored this region of country with a visit, professedly to confirm the appointment of one David Whitmer to the successorship of Joseph Smith in the Seer's office; but really to *boost* himself into notoriety, and get subscribers to the *Ensign of Liberty*. I will give you some specimens of his statements here and in Brighton, that you may judge of his *work* and its probable influence upon the minds of the saints here—premising that in Brighton as well as in this place he had the privilege of saying all that he would to the saints. We gave up our meeting to him in both places, that he might deliver his message. I have not room to give but a few of the many queer and contradictory statements of ... [McLellin:] "I cannot be mistaken (said he) about the history of the church, for I have a *good memory*." But when asked how he came to join G. M. Hinkle, and afterwards, by special revelation, go 500 miles to join S. Rigdon, if he witnessed the appointment and ordination of David Whitmer to the Seer's office? his answer was—I *forgot* it....
>
> "Joseph Smith had no power or authority to lead the church after 1834."
>
> "No man can understand the Book of Doctrine and Covenants unless familiar with all the circumstances under which it was written."
>
> The above are fair samples of his teaching. The effect of such teaching with the brethren of this place has been only to strengthen and confirm them in the truth. There is an old saying that, "Give the *Devil* rope enough and he will hang himself." We gave McLellin all the rope he asked for, and he has *snarled* himself up so badly that Oliver's revelations about Voree will never be able to straighten him up. I would advise the saints, whenever Mc. or any of the "immortal trio" at Kirtland [Martin Harris, William McLellin, Leonard Rich] visit them, to *keep them talking*. Only encourage them to *talk* and they will talk the "truth all to pieces."[47]

Greig's letter was probably indicative of a general response to McLellin's traveling ministry, given the early demise of McLellin's Church of Christ in late 1849.

---

46. *Ensign of Liberty*, Apr. 1847, 29-32. The attack discredited the "letter of appointment" by Joseph Smith of 18 June 1844, Strang's angelic ordination, and his claims to having produced translations of ancient sacred writings.

47. "Extracts of Letters," *Gospel Herald*, 7 Oct. 1847, 118-19.

On a western tour McLellin spent nearly a week with the Whitmers in Richmond, probably to press David Whitmer into action as church prophet. However, in publishing his record of the visit, McLellin told nothing of his main purpose in going there. At most, he was able to say of the visit: "Union of feeling, and harmony of action, governed our every movement. Brethren and friends, let me say to you, 'All is right, all is well,' with those witnesses."[48]

James J. Strang lost no time in chiding McLellin for being so evasive about his critical contacts with the Whitmers. He caustically honed in on McLellin's vexing leadership problem, saying the former apostle had struck out on

> a journey of four months to visit Whitmer and converse face to face, and returns without one scrap from him, and not even the assurance that he will accept the station of prophet. We have for a long time suspected that Whitmer and Cowdery[49] did not lend themselves to Mc.'s humbug, and now we are more assured of it than ever. If all was union and harmony, *what* was done so harmoniously? ... *If* WM. E. MCLELLIN COULD HAVE GOT **ONE SINGLE WORD** *from* DAVID WHITMER OR OLIVER COWDERY, *wherewith to prop up his cause, he would have made speed to give it the* GREATEST POSSIBLE PUBLICITY.[50]

Allowing for Strang's antipathy toward McLellin, one must still wonder just what transpired in September 1847 between McLellin and his Missouri hosts. Not until August 1849—the last issue of the *Ensign of Liberty*—did McLellin report anything of substance regarding his encounter with the Whitmers. And what he wrote confirms why he had said so little about the events before; his Missouri venture had failed, according to the details he now divulged:

1. McLellin, Hiram Page, and David, Jacob, and John Whitmer met and four of them administered to David Whitmer for "strength to do his duty."

2. They approved the revelation to McLellin of 10 February 1847 at Kirtland, providing for rebaptisms, reconfirmations, and reordinations to all who wished to unite with the Church of Christ.

---

48. McLellin, "Our Apology—And Our Tours," *Ensign of Liberty,* Dec. 1847, 34.

49. McLellin had seen Oliver Cowdery at the latter's home near Voree the previous July, not in Richmond in September.

50. "David Whitmer, Ensign of Liberty, and McLellinism," *Gospel Herald,* 13 Jan. 1848, 197. Strang challenged Whitmer to stop playing this waiting game, to publicize his position openly. "If he thinks he is a prophet let him say it, and we will publish it.... If ye be honest men speak."

3. David received four revelations, mostly directing McLellin to continue his work in Kirtland and to expose the errors of apostasy in the various schismatic groups. The Whitmers and Page were enjoined to stay in Missouri against the day when they should reclaim their inheritances in Zion.

4. David saw a vision in which McLellin was to possess a beautiful chest filled with precious things: wisdom and knowledge from God. This confirmed to McLellin a similar vision he had in April 1844 concerning these gifts to himself.

5. Acting on the pattern they had endorsed for others, they rebaptized, reconfirmed, and reordained each other, including David Whitmer "to all the gifts and callings to which he had been appointed through Joseph Smith, in the general assembly of the inhabitants of Zion in July 1834" but *not* to be a prophet and president of McLellin's Church of Christ.[51]

From this event the irrepressible McLellin could see the grave implications of that September meeting for his future. No wonder he had not cared to publish this record before. The closer he studied what had happened, the longer it took him to deal with the reality of his ultimate rebuff. The Whitmers had treated him with civility, even hospitality. But there was no mistaking their intent. They would not yield to McLellin's ingratiating presence and pressure among them. If it took four revelations and a vision to send McLellin away reasonably happy, then so be it. Back to Kirtland he had gone in 1847, hoping to keep alive his tiny, struggling band of dissenters.

McLellin's flagging hope for David Whitmer's seership vanished as he read, published in the August issue of the *Olive Branch*—the periodical of the James C. Brewster-Hazen Aldrich Church of Christ also at Kirtland—Hiram Page's letter of 24 June 1849. Page, speaking for himself and his Whitmer relatives in Richmond, renounced what was of value to McLellin from the proceedings of the "conference" of September 1847. Page acknowledged McLellin's honorable motives in trying to affirm the Whitmers as good and honest people. The Whitmers, however, took exception to McLellin's claim of direction by the Holy Spirit in coming there and insisting that they organize in some church capacity. Page saw through to the center of McLellin's thinking that the church "must come through him, which would give a sanction to all that he had done, which would give a more speedy rise to the cause than any thing else could; and by our ho[l]ding [sustaining] him up, he could

51. McLellin, "Our Tour West in 1847," *Ensign of Liberty,* Aug. 1849, 99-105.

build up the church according to its true order, which would be a source of consolation to us. But we had not as yet come to an understanding, but consented to the organization after *three days successive entreaties*. Now we acknowledge that the organization *was not in accordance* with the order of the Gospel Church."[52]

McLellin's Missouri heroes had resolutely distanced themselves from him to the point that his claims to credibility were severely impaired. He could not make a career out of condemning Latter Day Saint apostates, so his wisest course would be to shift the focus of his life. In 1849 he retreated from the scene of debate and apology, moved to Linden, Michigan, and pursued his medical profession.

Mormonism was at the center of McLellin's being, however, and seemed to signal him now and then to reenter the fray whenever events caught his attention. Such an event was the coming of Joseph Smith III to the prophetic office of the Reorganized Church of Jesus Christ of Latter Day Saints in April 1860. In his inaugural address on 6 April, young Smith had affirmed some things about his father and about early Mormon history that differed radically from what McLellin remembered and had written about so vehemently back in the 1840s.

McLellin read the address, as well as other writings of the Reorganization leaders. He thought about what to do and finally, on 10 January 1861, wrote to Smith with the aim of educating the young prophet. The long letter's primary teaching points were as follows:

1. The church should never have had two priesthoods, as the Levitical priesthood was strictly Old Testament.

2. Christ was the last and great high priest; there was no need for any later high priests at any time. High priests in the Restoration were added later, not meant to be a part of the original church structure.

3. Joseph Smith Jr. taught and practiced polygamy. All young Smith needed to do on this point was ask his mother, who had told McLellin during his trip to Nauvoo in 1847 that this was so.

4. Joseph Smith Jr. was not as good a man as his son had proclaimed him to be in his 1860 inaugural address.

52. Hiram Page to Alfred Bonny, Isaac N. Aldrich, and M. C. Ishem, 24 June 1849, in *Olive Branch, or Herald of Peace and Truth to All Saints*, Aug. 1849, 27-29, with editor's commentary on P. 30. In more specific terms, Page rejected, among other things, (1) the office of high priest, (2) the office of seer, stating that the endowment of the Holy Spirit was free to all who join the Church of Christ, and (3) the idea of the gathering to a single center. The editor noted that Page had thoroughly discredited McLellin, whom he described as "our most violent opposer" since the Brewster-Aldrich Church of Christ began in Kirtland in June 1848.

5. Joseph Smith Jr. died owing $200,000 because of his ruinous financial speculations.

6. The church under Joseph Smith Jr. had strayed from the original pure teachings. The Twelve in Utah represented what was taught during the uninspired last years of his life.

7. The Doctrine and Covenants was an inferior work to the Book of Commandments.

8. Proper church leadership should be clothed with apostolic power. Joseph Smith III had no credentials along that line.

9. So many factions had risen and fallen, the Reorganization would no doubt meet the same fate. What, McLellin asked, was different about the Reorganization that would equip it to survive?[53]

There is no evidence that Joseph Smith III answered McLellin's letter. How seriously he took McLellin's instruction can be guessed from the fact that by his own admission, Joseph III never spoke to his mother about the polygamy question until February 1879. This was in spite of a second letter from McLellin in 1872 that urged him, among other things, to ask Emma about the matter.

Another evidence of McLellin's continuing interest in Mormonism was his letter to the editor of the *Truth Teller,* a periodical of Granville Hedrick's group in Independence. Writing in 1864 from his Michigan home, McLellin advanced the idea that the singular hallmark of ordained ministry in every age was the process of direct revelation between God and the minister.[54] McLellin did not argue with anything said in the periodical; he simply shared his insights. The editor printed his letter without comment.

The next evidence of McLellin's reviving interest in Mormonism was his announcement that he had united with Hedrick in Independence. Writing from Brownsville, Missouri, on 12 July 1869, McLellin told some friends why he had become a "Hedrickite":

> In the first place he delivered a number of prophecies which have already come to pass. So his friends who heard him declare. I could tell you what they were—but no matter now.... They go back [to] the original principles as taught at first in 1830 and up to 1834 when they declare that Joseph fell. Dont You know that I published in the "Ensign" in 1847 that Jos. fell in

53. McLellin to Joseph Smith [III], 10 Jan. 1861, Community of Christ Archives; see Letter 2, p. 440.

54. He now spelled his name "McLellan" and did so consistently the rest of his life. Much earlier he had occasionally spelled it "McLelin." Some early church records show his name as "M'Lellin."

> 1834.... We set aside all extras as doctrine or principle which cannot be sustained by the New Testament, and that inestimable inspired book of Mormon. I went up to Independence to attend their conference which was to have been the 28 of May, but was put off until the 4th of June. They had meetings every day between the 28th and the 4th. So I had a good opportunity to investigate. And I set and said nothing during the meeting & conference, but on the 5th I stated to them precisely my position, that I was willing to believe Hedrick was a Prophet, and the church had chosen him to preside over the whole church, and I was willing to take him to preside. I hea[r]d, after he got there on the 1st, a great deal of his teaching, and of his decisions, I was willing to admit I could see wisdom in them. Hence I united with them.[55]

McLellin also preached his first sermon in nearly twenty years at Hedrick's conference on 6 June 1869. Hedrick was more than pleased. While at the conference McLellin decided to move to Independence. Although he referred to his wife as "not very pious, or spiritual minded," she "is willing to go with me to Zion." He bought a frame home near the Independence square for $1,500 and moved into it a few weeks later.[56]

McLellin's union with Hedrick's group lasted only a few months. He left them on 3 November. Near the same time, his wife joined the Reorganized Church. In February 1870 he wrote about his feelings for those he had left: "There are some fifteen or twenty of us here who cannot go with the Hedrick party. They are in reality nothing but Latter Day Saints. True they dont hold to polygamy, but they hold to many wild notions of that *infamous ism*." He seemed to lean once again toward David Whitmer's presidency, having recently written and read to Whitmer his considered view on that matter. McLellin wanted to publish strong claims for Whitmer's prophethood, but Whitmer was not sanguine. He told him to do it only if McLellin "would publish it under [his] own signature."[57] An echo of the summer of 1847, to be sure.

McLellin's dissent in his final years was primarily in the form of written letters, both private and public, against the claims of the Reorganized Church. An apparent anomaly was when he sided with Reorganization missionaries in jousting with Utah Mormons. Common ground? No. McLellin fought the Mormons because he believed their doctrines, stemming mostly from Joseph Smith's later years, were false. Reorga-

---

55. McLellan to Our Very Dear Friends, 12 July 1869, Community of Christ Archives; see Letter 5, p. 450.

56. Ibid.

57. McLellan to My dear Friends, Feb. 1870, Miscellaneous Letters and Papers, Community of Christ Archives; see Letter 7, p. 456.

nized missionaries contended with Mormons because they denied their doctrines were ever taught or practiced by Joseph Smith. So McLellin also read Reorganized Church periodicals and tracts and went into his warring mode against the RLDS because Joseph Smith III and his followers did not know their history. Or even worse, if they did, they lied about it.

McLellin's approach would be to use his old ideas from the *Ensign of Liberty* magazines and rewrite them to meet the new challenges. The basic points of argument did not change greatly. He proceeded from a clear and deeply felt bias, expressed succinctly in a letter he wrote in October 1870:

> I have been reading and writing most of the summer and fall[;] so far I have quite a book of manuscript, I expect to publish it some day but shall not until I get spiritual minded brethren around me to read and scan each treatise. I want it to contain pure truth and nothing else. I have five foolscap pages, reviewing [the teachings of Davis] Bays and [Isaac] Sheen. And I have not spared! I perfectly dispise their **miserable** misrepresentations. I cant believe them honest, or that they want to know the **truth**. I tell You I know Josephisim is built on a flimsy, sandy foundation, and God's truth will wash all the sand from under it! All Latter Day-ism is nothing on earth but sectarianism!![58]

McLellin also expressed a growing closeness to David Whitmer, spending time with the little Whitmer fellowship where he felt the word of God to his soul. He rejoiced in not having contention with any sect or party, seeing himself as simply basking in the presence of God. In this sense McLellin did not view his running letters of debate with the Reorganization as contention. Rather, he was simply enlightening those who walked in darkness. It was not his mission to convert and baptize "Josephites." He was only intent on setting the record straight and, having done that, waiting for more questions to explore from differing perspectives.

In this context, McLellin wrote letters to various inquirers, or to writers whose published views were offensive to the truth as McLellin saw it. Upward of a dozen such letters are either on file in the Community of Christ Archives or were published in the *Saints' Herald* during the 1870s. Most deal with the same issues, hobbies McLellin had been riding for much of his adult life. By the 1870s his dissenting voice, although

58. McLellan to My dear old friends, 21, 25 Oct. 1870, Community of Christ Archives; see Letter 9, p. 464.

strident and at times boorishly repetitious, had lost whatever appeal it might have had to open-minded investigators. He had become a crank. When he died at his Independence home on 24 April 1883, few mourned his passing. McLellin was indeed Mormonism's stormy petrel: moody, blustery, self-absorbed beyond words to tell, yet an indefatigable crusader for the relative truths he knew as absolute truth.

2.

DISCOVERY OF THE MCLELLIN PAPERS

DAWN HOUSE

On Tuesday morning, 15 October 1985, rare documents dealer Mark Hofmann was to hand over a collection of nineteenth-century books, journals, and letters believed to be worth tens of thousands of dollars to businessman Steven Christensen. Hofmann claimed he had "two apple crates worth of material" written by early Mormon apostate William McLellin that would shake the foundations of the Church of Jesus Christ of Latter-day Saints. Hofmann intimated that the so-called "McLellin Collection" had embarrassing information on church founder Joseph Smith's secret polygamous relationships and first-person accounts by early Mormons that contradicted official versions of the church's divine origins in the 1820s.

Hours before the scheduled meeting, Christensen died when he stooped to pick up a booby-trapped package propped up against his office door at the Judge Building in downtown Salt Lake City. The brown paper package, addressed to Christensen, contained a mercury-switch pipe bomb packed with black powder, steel piping, and cement nails. The device exploded when Christensen grabbed it, peppering his chest with shrapnel. The force of the explosion was so intense that it tore Christensen's office door from its hinges and blew the steel nails through walls, wounding an office worker across the hall. The worker

---

DAWN HOUSE has been with *The Salt Lake Tribune* since 1983—nine years as a reporter, then editor of the Justice and Safety Desk, and now a columnist for the business section. She also teaches a class in journalism at Utah State University. In 1998 she and a team of reporters were finalists for a national IRE Freedom of Information Award. When she came to the Mark Hofmann story, it was because another reporter covering the document discoveries had asked to be reassigned due to pressure from his Mormon family. "For months before the bombings, I repeatedly asked Hofmann if he had the collection," House said. "He was always evasive and repeatedly refused a face-to-face meeting. It was frustrating because his telephone numbers constantly changed." She decided to confront him at his home, but was diverted, on the day Steve Christensen died.

told police she first had heard a deafening boom and then what sounded like a whimpering child. The cry had come from thirty-one-year-old Christensen as he lay dying on the hallway floor. His wife was expecting their fourth child, who would be born on his father's birthday several weeks after Steve's death.

About three hours after the first blast, a second bomb exploded at the home of Gary Sheets, Christensen's business partner. Sheets's wife, fifty-year-old Kathleen, was killed when she picked up a package addressed to her husband from the driveway of their suburban Salt Lake County home. Police speculated that she may have taken a step or two before she tilted the package, setting off the deadly explosion. Kathleen left four children behind, including eighteen-year-old Gretchen who would become a police officer for the department that had investigated her mother's murder.

At first, investigators vacillated between two theories of the murders. Because Christensen was a well-known collector of historical documents, many having to do with the Mormon Church, his death might have involved a fanatic enraged by those acquisitions. Or the killings may have been linked to Christensen's and Sheets's CFS (Coordinated Financial Services) investment company, which had folded months before, losing millions of dollars for thousands of investors. The next day, Hofmann was critically injured when a bomb went off in his car a few blocks away from where Christensen had been killed. Parts of Hofmann's fingers were blown off and his kneecap was horribly mangled, but he survived.

The three bombings left Salt Lake City—Utah's capital and headquarters of the LDS Church—in a panic. The topic of the day was eerily similar at lunch tables and offices throughout the normally peaceful Salt Lake Valley: Where would a bomb explode next? Before the third blast, police had received hundreds of phone calls from jittery intellectuals, church critics, business people, document collectors, and just about anyone who received an unanticipated package. Everyone was nervous, investigators would later note, except Hofmann. Police focused on him the day Christensen was killed after tipsters mentioned to reporters, who relayed the information to investigators, that Hofmann often wore the same type of green and white Olympus High School letterman's jacket seen by two witnesses the morning of the first murder. A father and son told police they had gotten on the elevator at the Judge Building shortly before the bombing with a man who had been wearing such a jacket, carrying a package addressed to Christensen.

When Hofmann's name surfaced as a suspect, friends rallied to his defense. Aside from having no criminal record, Hofmann was a nationally known document dealer with dozens of spectacular finds to his credit. Among his dazzling discoveries were the so-called 1828 Anthon transcript, purportedly containing characters copied by Joseph Smith from gold plates, promissory notes bearing the signature X of mountain man Jim Bridger, a purported Charles Dickens's manuscript, and the Oath of a Freeman—the first printed document in America, valued at more than $1.5 million. The Library of Congress had considered buying the latter during the summer of 1985.

Hofmann had become a celebrity of sorts in the Mormon community because of several historical documents he had come across that were particularly embarrassing to the church, such as an 1825 letter in which Joseph Smith purportedly wrote about digging for magical buried treasure. Whether Hofmann was friend or foe was a matter of confusion, but church officials seemed both to embrace and fear him. They purchased his discoveries or encouraged trusted members to secure documents rather than allow them to fall into the hands of what one church leader described as "our enemies."

Hofmann's most infamous find was the so-called "Salamander Letter," dated 1830 and said to have been written by early Mormon Martin Harris. The letter described how a white salamander, rather than the Angel Moroni, guarded the golden plates. Christensen bought the letter for $40,000 and hired researchers with ties to the Mormon Church to place the controversial correspondence into a nineteenth-century setting when folk magic such as water-witching was common. But while Hofmann had a solid reputation in the documents world, police investigating the bombing deaths were highly skeptical that any one person could find so many historically significant and valuable documents. "Where does he get them?" asked Salt Lake County Sheriff Pete Hayward several days after the bombings. "All of a sudden there's this one guy who keeps coming up with these things, worth all that money. These kinds of documents don't just lie around for years and years. I know for a fact that fifty of us couldn't find these papers in fifty years if we were looking for them. But he keeps coming up with them."

That assessment was not shared by world-renowned document dealer Kenneth Rendell, who in the 1970s exposed the infamous Hitler diaries as a forgery, or Charles Hamilton, author of *Great Fakes and Famous Forgers*. Rendell, who authenticated Hofmann's Salamander Letter, and Hamilton, who pronounced the 1825 Joseph Smith letter genuine, were critical of police accusations. After all, investigators had no evidence that any of the documents Hofmann had sold were bogus. Eventually Utah forensics expert George Throckmorton and his partner, William J. "Bill" Flynn, revealed the deceptively simple forgery scheme after scrutinizing dozens of Hofmann's documents under a microscope. They discovered that many of them had a single razor-sharp edge and that the paper's ink had tiny cracks. Throckmorton and Flynn concluded that Hofmann had cut blank pages from old books so that when a bogus document was tested, the paper content would be consistent with the historical period Hofmann claimed. Working from his basement, always off-limits to his children and wife Doralee, Mark carefully forged signatures and even entire letters, then chemically aged the ink to make the writing look old. "As far back as I can remember, I have liked to impress people through my deceptions," Hofmann would later confess. "In fact, some of my earliest memories are of doing magic and card tricks. Fooling people gave me a sense of power and superiority. I believe that is what led to my forging activities."

Even though police had no motive, they knew they had their killer the day they questioned him at LDS Hospital in Salt Lake City. He was evasive but insistent the bomb had gone off as he was getting into his car. An expert from the ATF (Alcohol, Tobacco, and Firearms) agency who had picked through Hofmann's bombed-out blue Toyota MR2 said he was lying. Hofmann had been inside his car prior to the blast, probably leaning over the console, when he dropped the device while trying to arm it.

To prove Hofmann's guilt would require tedious gumshoe work in what detectives would call the most complicated and convoluted investigation ever conducted in Utah. It would be four long months before prosecutors were confident enough to file charges in a case that was entirely circumstantial. Investigators painstakingly traced to Hofmann receipts from a Radio Shack for materials to make bombs, chemicals bought in a toy store to age ink, and orders for printing plates to forge such items as the Jim Bridger notes and the Oath of a Freeman. Tellingly, Hofmann had no provenance for any of the documents he had marketed, insisting that every seller had demanded complete secrecy. It turned out that collectors had purchased a variety of phony Americana documents from Hofmann, such as a Betsy Ross letter (none are known to exist) and a purported Charles Dickens manuscript, "The Haunted Man." He seemed to specialize, however, in documents related to Mormonism. In fact, no one individual or group acquired more documents from Hofmann than the LDS Church or its leaders, paying a total of

$57,100 for seven documents and trading valuable historical materials for forty-one items. All of Hofmann's papers eventually were proved forgeries.

Detectives learned that Christensen died because he had given Hofmann an ultimatum: Deliver the so-called McLellin Collection that Tuesday morning or be exposed as a dirty dealer. Hofmann had lied so many times about when he would have the documents that Christensen believed Hofmann was either selling off the collection piecemeal or marketing the entire package to more than one investor. Hofmann, in fact, had been double-dealing. He was peddling the collection or parts of it, sight unseen, to six different buyers. Weeks before the bombings, Hofmann had told Christensen he was short on cash and needed $185,000 to buy the collection from a family living somewhere in Texas. Acting as a middleman to get the sensitive documents into friendly hands, Christensen contacted a high Mormon official, Hugh Pinnock, who quickly arranged for a bank signature loan for that amount. David Sorensen, a wealthy mission president and businessman, agreed in turn to buy the collection for $185,000 and donate it to the church as long as the materials were authenticated. Christensen was the one the churchmen were relying on to examine the documents. Meanwhile, the signature loan became due and Hofmann had not produced the collection. Frantic and unable to locate Hofmann, Christensen called a mutual friend and asked him to warn Hofmann that he would be sued and possibly sent to jail if he did not repay the $185,000 loan.

Hofmann later confessed to killing Christensen "to take the pressure off," while his second bomb at the Sheets's home was "a pure diversion" to confuse police. Hofmann showed a psychopathic indifference to life at his 1988 parole hearing when he acknowledged that anyone could have been killed when he placed the bomb on the Sheets's driveway under cover of darkness, "Mrs. Sheets, a child, a dog, whoever." He added, "In any case, the hoped-for diversion would be effective." He conceded it was unfortunate Christensen and Sheets had to be killed but thought "they might have died in a car accident anyway," he told parole board members. "I try not to think about it, as far as thinking about various victims or whatever."

The McLellin Collection was to have been Hofmann's largest and most ambitious con. The idea struck him when he learned of an authentic 1901 letter stored in the Theodore Schroeder Collection in the New York Public Library that for decades had gone unnoticed. In the early 1970s historian D. Michael Quinn, then a Yale University graduate student, had come across the letter and immediately realized its significance. It was from John L. Traughber, a Texas homesteader, aspiring author, and devotee of William E. McLellin. The latter was a charter member of the 1835 Quorum of Twelve Apostles, one of the major governing bodies of the Mormon Church, and a bitter and eloquent critic of Joseph Smith. For a book Traughber had hoped to write, he had spent years gathering journals, letters, and documents from McLellin. By the turn of the twentieth century, however, Traughber's book was just a loose pile of yellowed pages, sometimes written on the back of broadsides. He had failed to eke out a living on his farm in Mobile, a hardscrabble Texas town that no longer exists. Traughber was forty-five years old, supporting a wife, six children, and a fifty-five-year-old brother. "I want to get away from this flooded burnt up land and go to some place where there is irrigation," Traughber wrote. "I am essentially an agriculturalist but I have been lessened by floods and droughts till I am in straitened circumstances." He had corresponded regularly with Theodore Schroeder, a Salt Lake City lawyer and amateur historian, hoping to sell the documents he had acquired from McLellin for a sum that would be "materially good."

"I have some little manuscript books written by Dr. W. E. McLellin," Traughber wrote in a letter dated 21 August 1901. "I also have his journal for parts of the years 1831-2-3-4-5-6. I have over thirty letters compactly written by Dr. McLellin containing much on the subject of Mormonism. Yes, I could be induced to part with what I have on the subject of Mormonism provided I could get enough for it to do me some good. If I dispose of any of it, I want to make a clean sweep and wipe my hands from all that pertains to the matter." Traughber also had one of McLellin's notebooks, miscellaneous theological and philosophical writings, holographic copies of correspondence, extracts from published works, affidavits, notes, and reminiscences mostly pertaining to Mormonism.

In a letter dated 11 July 1901, Traughber offered to sell an 1833 Book of Commandments, an early version of the Mormons' sacred collection of revelations called the Doctrine and Covenants. The Book of Commandments was never officially released. Most of the sheets of the printed but unbound book were destroyed by a Missouri mob. Collectors say Books of Commandments are rare: fewer than two dozen are known to have survived. Traughber wrote that McLellin had given him a copy, "one page gone. Dr. McLellin ... told me that he had a printer boy to gather up the sheets out of the streets after the mob had torn down the printing office in Independence," Traughber wrote. "He had two copies–one he had bound in Cincinnati, the other the one I have. The fact that it was picked out of the street after the mobbing gives it a little extra historical value." Schroeder did not buy the collection but saved Traughber's letters and donated them with other correspondence to the New York Public Library.

Some seventy years later when Quinn spotted Traughber's letter, he reasoned that a descendant of Traughber might have some of the McLellin material stored in an attic or garage. It might not be too difficult to track the family, Quinn thought, because the name had an unusual spelling. He mailed letters to every household in Texas with the surname of Traughber, inquiring about historical documents.

No one replied. Traughber's elderly son, Otis, received Quinn's letter but threw it away–and he, indeed, owned the McLellin documents. Discouraged, Quinn turned to Hofmann, who by then was a well-respected documents dealer. "From 1970 to 1977, I tried to track down the diaries and I had come to a dead end," said Quinn. "I sent Hofmann a copy of my notes from the Traughber letter and said, 'Good luck.'"

As a reporter for the *Salt Lake Tribune,* I had often tried to contact Hofmann for an interview about the McLellin Collection. He had been hinting for months, through friends and acquaintances, that he had found the documents. But he was evasive and secretive, often changing telephone numbers, never showing up or calling when he said he would, and answering questions with a single word or two. In July 1985, three months before the murders, he confirmed to me that he had located the collection and incredibly added that it included Facsimile 2. This was a reference to the Egyptian papyri Joseph Smith had used in producing the Book of Abraham. Traughber had never mentioned in his letters that he had Facsimile 2, indicating in retrospect how greedy and entangled Hofmann had become in his own forgery scheme. I unwittingly wrote a newspaper story about Hofmann's claims, an article he would later use as part of his con.

Not long after Christensen's death, the McLellin Collection came to the attention of detectives. They found in Hofmann's bombed-out car a $100,000-plus cashier's check written to Hofmann and signed by Christensen. It seemed the money was for the McLellin material and some pieces of papyri they heard about. Later they would discover Hofmann had bought a papyrus from a New York dealer and cut it up, thinking he could pass them off as fragments of Facsimile 2. The investigators also learned that Hofmann had met with Mormon apostle Dallin H. Oaks the day Christensen was killed to discuss the status of the collection. Oaks asked Hofmann if he planned to go ahead with a meeting the next day to close the deal despite Christensen's death. Hofmann said yes and Oaks thanked him for agreeing to sell the collection to someone friendly to the church. Hofmann was injured before the rescheduled meeting could take place, which left the specter of the McLellin papers hovering over the crime: If Hofmann had the documents, it might show his innocence. If he did not, he would have had a motive to kill.

Like many historians and researchers, I knew about Traughber's letter, which meant the documents had existed in Tyler County, Texas, at least in 1901. The next logical step would be to track down Traughber's descendents who might know where the materials would be. And if Hofmann had purchased the collection, he would have had to contact Traughber's descendents at some point in his search. If I could find Traughber's descendents, they could tell me if Hofmann had ever gotten in touch with them. In short, I would do Traughber's genealogy.

I walked across town to the LDS genealogy library. As I searched through U.S. census records, probate court documents, marriage indexes, and cemetery listings from the church's vast archives, I thought it bizarre that the information I was seeking might figure into a modern-day murder investigation. I learned that Traughber was born in 1854 in Missouri, where he likely met McLellin (1806-1883), a schoolteacher who was ordained a Mormon apostle in 1835 and excommunicated three years later. McLellin was one of the most educated of the founding apostles and served as secretary to the original Quorum of Twelve. The much younger Traughber knew McLellin in his later, more rebellious years when McLellin was a country doctor and by this time railing against the Mormon Church. By 1900, Traughber was forty-five years old, living in Texas, and supporting his wife, Mattie, their four sons and two daughters, ages one to eleven, and Traughber's older brother Harmon. Traughber would die eight years later. By 1910, Mattie, now forty-two, was struggling to support their seven children and her nineteen-year-old daughter, son-in-law, and infant granddaughter. Mattie sold the farm and moved to Polk County, where she buried a second husband, W. W. Armitage, and two children, one of them an eight-year-old boy who died in a sawmill accident while helping support the family.

Oma Armitage, a daughter from Mattie's second marriage, was the first relation I called. I asked about Mattie, who seemed to have struggled with poverty much of her life. Armitage said her mother married an "old gentleman" she herself remembered fondly and died "in peace and

From his home in Houston, Texas, Otis Traughber displayed pages from McLellin's last notebook, written in about 1880. Photograph by Lynn Johnson. Courtesy *The Salt Lake Tribune.*

Otis Traughber (center) conveys the McLellin papers to the University of Utah in 1995. Otis's father, John L. Traughber Jr. was a one-time Mormon and confidant of McLellin in Missouri, prior to the Traughbers' move to Texas. Also in the photograph are Gregory C. Thompson (left), Associate Director for Special Collections and Services, J. Willard Marriott Library; George D. Smith (right), publisher and president, Signature Books Publishing. Photograph by Lynn Johnson. Courtesy *The Salt Lake Tribune*

A sample display of three notebooks from the McLellin collection at the Marriott Library. The cover image on Notebook 7 (foreground) is the manufacturer s decorative flourish rather than something from McLellin himself. To the left, Notebook 6 lies open to pages 28-29. On bottom is Notebook 1. Photograph by Lynn Johnson. Courtesy *The Salt Lake Tribune*

happiness." Armitage vividly recalled how Mattie had safeguarded books on Mormons which her mother's first husband had collected more than two generations earlier. She referred me to Otis, living in Houston, an elderly half-brother.

It was clear that although family members knew little about Mormonism, they valued the collection because it was all they had of Traughber's life work. Even John Ernest Traughber, eighty-two, who was living in California and had not kept in touch with the family, recalled that his father, a schoolteacher and book salesman, had some kind of collection. "We moved to Doucette and Livingston and because of our movings, I don't know what happened to his collection," John said. "My father was interested in lots of things. When he would read a book and see a discrepancy, he wrote between the lines. It was an interesting habit." As John talked, his mind wandered. "I left home twenty-three years ago," he said. "It was nice I did it, but it was shameful. I lost myself in the shuffle of society.... I retired in 1962 with thirty years of service. I was a chief petty officer. It's a strange thing, history, and stories. It seems as though I've been weaned away from the whole bit."

When I telephoned Otis Traughber, he was gracious but unwilling to discuss exactly what documents he had until the murder investigation was completed in Salt Lake City. He said that when he read about the bombings in the newspaper, he realized with a shock that it had something to do with a McLellin Collection–like the documents he too had. He gathered up his father's collection, he told me, and stored it in a bank deposit box. Although Otis was only three when his father died, he knew about much of what his father had gathered and his father's intention of writing a book. "My father knew McLellin and his widow," said Otis. "I have three books, letters–McLellin letters–I'm reasonably sure, papers and other documents. I've looked at these things for a long time, even when I was a little boy. It's all I had of my father's." He had never heard of Mark Hofmann.

This was the first time since two people had been killed some five weeks before that I had serious doubts about Hofmann's innocence. When I pressed Otis Traughber to see the collection, however, he again refused. But what if I flew down, I asked, examined the documents and wrote a story about them without revealing his name? "Perhaps," he answered. "But I'll have to discuss this with the family." My first break. I had already talked with several of Otis's siblings. They knew me. I had spent time answering their questions. I hoped they trusted me. On Thanksgiving morning, I again called Otis Traughber, and he agreed that I could come to Houston. I asked if I could bring along a historian who would provide some expertise. He said no. He did not want anyone else involved. I booked a ticket for a flight that same day before Otis Traughber could change his mind. I quickly popped a turkey in the oven for my family and made a quick call to Dean C. Jessee, a historian at Brigham Young University. I wanted to know how I would go about examining a collection of historical documents. "Make a list of each document and something about what each of them contains," he said. "Try to get a fence around the collection. See what's in it and how it is related to some kind of whole."

In less than an hour, *Salt Lake Tribune* photographer Lynn Johnson and I made the eight-hour flight, with layover, to Houston. The next morning we drove to a well kept, single-level rambler in a middle-class Houston suburb. Otis, eighty, met us in the driveway while his wife, Neola, stood in the doorway. Both were smiling. They were Southern gentlefolk welcoming their guests. After introductions and talk about the weather, we sat around the kitchen table, stacked with nineteenth-century books and yellowed documents. Otis Traughber proudly showed me his father's distinctively written manuscript of loose pages, which seemed to be the bulk of the collection. What caught my attention, though, was a notebook written by McLellin listing fifty-five reasons why he was no longer a Mormon. "I dont believe, In a Prophet being placed at the Head of the church as Leader and sole Dictator," McLellin wrote. "I dont believe, in holding general conference to make rules and laws for the government of the church of Christ." "I dont believe, in only one man to receive and give off revelations for the whole church. Its unch[r]istian." Reading McLellin's words in his own bold script seemed to underscore his defiant spirit.

Otis was watching me. "These things have been in the family for more than 100 years," he said. "My father had no desire to tear down anything. He only had an interest in history." Among the piles of papers was a journal John L. Traughber himself had compiled. He wrote that the only traditional Mormon belief McLellin retained was a faith in the divine origin of the Book of Mormon. "I believe that if Dr. McLellin could have been freed from the idea that the book of Mormon was a divine revelation, he would have made it hot for the Mormons," Traughber had written, "more so than he ever did." Still, as I leafed through the pages, I wondered if this was actually the collection that John Traughber had written about to Schroeder. There seemed to be papers missing such as a McLellin journal for the years 1831-36. Could there be more papers somewhere else? John Traughber himself may have answered part of my question in another journal entry. He wrote that he had traveled to Missouri shortly after McLellin's death to ask his widow if she had any more documents he might acquire. She told him she burned some of them and gave others away, "as they were of no use to her."

After several hours of politely watching me read through the documents, Otis excused himself and strolled out to the garage to smoke a cigar. He had converted a small section to a smoking area where he had set up a folding metal chair and a portable television. "I tell him he can smoke inside the house and he always says it would bother me," Neola said in a labored voice. Recently she had suffered a stroke. "I always say it never bothers me, but he does it anyway." The next day Otis unknowingly gave me some bad news. Before I left Utah for Houston, word had somehow leaked that I had found the collection. My editors instructed me to write a story before I left town to protect my scoop, though without using Traughber's name. I had no idea how the leak occurred. Reporters, staffers, and receptionists talk, I guessed. Reporter Marnie Funk at the rival *Deseret News* started calling every Traughber in Texas. When she got to Otis, he refused to speak with her.

"I told her I would not talk about the documents," Otis said. "But that only confirmed to Marnie that you do have documents," I said. "I'm afraid the *Deseret News* is going to publish your name." "I knew it would be a risk when I said you could come," he replied. "It's not your fault. Whatever happens, happens."

Before I returned to Utah, I treated Otis to lunch at a neighborhood cafeteria, which he allowed only after I assured him it would be a *Tribune* business expense. Later I asked a favor. Would he be willing to wait until I published my stories on the collection before talking to other reporters? He chuckled and said he'd be happy to comply. The day after my first article on the collection appeared, reporters and camera people from Utah and Texas swarmed the Traughbers' home to get an interview. Faithful to his promise, Otis shut the front door on anyone who knocked. A *Deseret News* columnist, Milt Holstein, referred to the Traughbers' front door as the most photographed ever. But Otis refused to budge on his commitment even after my articles were published. I told him over the phone that the reporters would go away if he spoke to them, even briefly, but he decided that "too many cooks spoil the broth." The first reporter Otis slammed the door on was Marnie Funk, who returned to Salt Lake City empty handed. Her story said the Traughbers refused to speak to anyone other than the *Tribune* because I had paid them, calling the imagined bargain "a classic case of checkbook journalism."

This false accusation hinted at the rivalry between the two newspapers, which can be traced to a more than century old tension between the *Tribune,* founded by excommunicated Mormons and purchased by a Catholic mining magnate, and the *Deseret News,* the official town crier for the LDS Church. The competition between the two papers weaves a tapestry of dueling philosophies, jealousies, and contempt. The story of the McLellin Collection heightened the ill feelings because it tugged at the consciousness of Mormons and non-Mormons whose uneasy coexistence in Utah was mirrored by the mutual dislike staffers of the two newspapers had for each other. I remembered how honest and good the Traughbers were. Otis Traughber never blamed me when reporters surrounded his home, saying it was his decision alone. I also remembered how kind he was to his wife and how he blessed the meals and invited us to hold hands during the prayer as was their custom. And now the *Deseret News* was accusing the Traughbers of having been bought off.

Otis, who died in 1997, never did speak to another reporter. He said his only interest was in selling the collection to a university where his father's work could be studied. He hoped there would be enough money from the sale to establish a trust fund for his nieces and nephews. Otis was eighty years old when I met him, but it would take ten years of correspondence with the people at the University of Utah before he finally agreed to part with his father's papers.

"I want my father's work to be recognized," he often told me. "He deserved credit for his intense interest in history." As it turned out, the Traughbers drew additional attention after my series on the family's collection was published, this time from prosecutors at the Salt Lake County Attorney's Office. Within days of the story's publication, Otis received a subpoena to appear before a grand jury in Utah. Otis was distraught. He said he wanted to cooperate but did not want to leave his wife. No one had taken care of her but him since her stroke, and no matter how he tried to reassure her, she was convinced that if he traveled to Utah, whoever killed those other people with bombs would kill him too.

I called prosecutor Bob Stott, asking if Otis could testify in Houston; Otis was frail and terribly worried about his wife. Stott said he could not discuss grand jury proceedings. Angry, I went to my editor, Will Fehr. Within an hour, *Tribune* attorney Miles Holman was preparing a motion asking that Otis be allowed to testify in Houston. It was obvious the prosecutors had only one or two simple questions for him to answer.

Did he have a McLellin collection? Had Mark Hofmann ever contacted him about purchasing that collection? Otis's testimony would show that Hofmann was perpetrating a fraud, selling a collection he did not own.

By the end of the day, all Holman needed was Otis's approval so a motion could be filed in Third District Court to quash the subpoena. Over the phone, however, Otis was so upset he had difficulty speaking. In the background, I could hear his wife crying. "I don't know what to do," he stammered, relating his wife's increased anxiety. Still, he wanted to wait before taking any court action so prosecutors would have a chance to change their minds. I called the police investigators, who seemed much more sympathetic to the Traughbers. I said flatly that the *Tribune* was prepared to intervene on the couple's behalf. Next morning, Otis happily reported that the prosecutors had agreed to allow him to appear before a grand jury in Houston. "I knew they would," he added, completely confident in the American judicial system.

Two months later, on 3 February 1986, Hofmann was charged with two murder counts among a total of thirty counts of theft by deception and communications fraud involving dozens of forgeries. By spring, Hofmann was bound over for trial after a preliminary hearing. Absent from these proceedings was acting Mormon president Gordon B. Hinckley, who had personally purchased from Hofmann for $15,000 the letter linking the church founder to folk magic. The judge, Paul Grant, said President Hinckley was excused from testifying because of his busy schedule and health concerns.

It was evident the prosecutors were treating Hofmann somewhat generously as well. His attorneys assumed no one would want to see church officials, who had purchased the bulk of the forgeries, appear in court. In a church-dominated state where some 70 percent of the population is Mormon, matters involving the ecclesiastical hierarchy are considered sensitive. With this threat in their pocket, the defense attorneys were able to see to it there would be no trial. Instead, they advised Hofmann to plead guilty to greatly reduced charges of two counts of second-degree murder and two counts of communication fraud, which he did on 23 January 1987. The latter two counts had to do with the Salamander Letter and McLellin Collection. All other counts were dismissed. Former Salt Lake County prosecutor Gerry D'Elia, who quit before negotiations began, had qualms about the plea agreement: "I always thought it was a slam-dunk case," he said. "Once you deal with a case behind closed doors, there will always be speculation. It would have been better to put on the evidence and let a jury decide." As part of the plea agreement, Hofmann promised to divulge the details of his bombing and forgery scheme. At a press conference, prosecutor Stott defended the plea bargain, saying it would put Hofmann behind bars and "all the questions about the documents could be answered."

From the back of the room, however, Salt Lake County Sheriff Hayward grumbled that the case had been botched. The burly lawman edged startled journalists out of his way and fired a question of his own: Why had prosecutors struck a plea bargain with Hofmann before he complied with his part of the agreement? "That's not standard procedure," he complained. To this day, Hofmann still has not lived up to the plea deal that spared him the death penalty. When prosecutors came calling at the Utah State Prison where Hofmann is serving a life sentence, he abruptly ended the tenth interview, which turned out to be the final time he would meet with interrogators. In the 537 pages of interview transcripts, only four pages dealt with the murders.

Said Sheriff Hayward of the so-called debriefing: "Hofmann has told us nothing we didn't know before the plea bargain." Hofmann's own attorney, Brad Rich, conceded that his client's confession "was less interesting than it might have been. But you've got to remember this type of debriefing doesn't usually happen," he added. "Still, it's fair to say a lot of mysteries are left hanging."

One mystery was what happened to the papers John L. Traughber had described that his descendants did not have, such as McLellin's 1830s journals. Otis Traughber assumed his family had lost them in the ensuing decades because they were not as prized as their father's papers. "The only thing that was important to us was my father's writings," said Otis. "The McLellin papers we had probably were only those that got intermingled with my father's papers." Since the Traughbers did not have portions of the collection described in the 1901 letter, perhaps the McLellin family might know where they were. But after contacting several direct descendants in January 1986, I knew they had no such information. The response of family historian John McLellin of Council Bluffs, Iowa, was typical: "I knew McLellin was a medical doctor and he died in Independence, Mo., but I didn't know he was Mormon." Edythe Clarke Vails of Denison, Texas, knew her great-grandfather "was some sort of founding Mormon minister" but "never knew anything about documents, and I'm one of the last ones from my generation who is left." Said Richard Hollingsworth of Midland, Texas: "Talking to us is a dead end. There was a house fire in the early 1900s so whatever [McLellin's widow] Emeline might have had was destroyed."

What had been long forgotten by historians was that John Traughber himself had offered to sell his collection to the LDS Church, including his rare Book of Commandments. Although investigators had repeatedly asked Mormon leaders if the church had some sort of McLellin Collection, the official answer was no. Long after the investigation, however, the church acknowledged it did have McLellin documents that might have been relevant to the Hofmann murder case. In the early 1900s, LDS President Joseph F. Smith had recorded that he bought some of McLellin's papers from John Traughber "for no other reason than to prevent the writings of this unfortunate and erratic man ... from falling into unfriendly hands." That portion of the McLellin collection had languished in the vault of the First Presidency in the church's administration building until March of 1986 when, at the suggestion of historian Dean Jessee, Richard E. Turley, managing director of the LDS Historical Department, initiated an intensive search.

Turley located Traughber's letter and sent word to Hinckley, who authorized access to the First Presidency's vault, an area separate from normal church archives. "Hinckley and the other church officials then learned, to their astonishment, that the church had owned McLellin's journals and manuscripts all along," Turley wrote in his book *Victims: The LDS Church and the Mark Hofmann Case,* published in 1992. It became clear that "the McLellin items found in church possession were not the McLellin collection touted by Hofmann," which was simply further evidence that "Hofmann was a fraud," Turley wrote. Those who had known about the McLellin journals and papers in the First Presidency vault had remained silent because the items "did not fall within any of the subpoenas issued to the church, and thus officials were not legally obligated to mention them to anyone," Turley concluded, adding that it was assumed the collection would "be revealed" during the trial and was not, only because the case was settled by the plea bargain.

Prosecutor D'Elia said the information withheld from him did not alter the course of the investigation even though it would have been helpful to know. "Our biggest problem was the motive," he said. "That goes to the heart of the case." The documents the church purchased in 1908 to keep them from the church's enemies turned out, to everyone's surprise, to be mostly sympathetic to the faith. In 1994 *Brigham Young Studies* co-published the missionary journals, a letter, and manuscript copies of four revelations in *The Journals of William E. McLellin, 1831-1836.* The editors chose not to include three of McLellin's notebooks that proved to be critical of the church.

"It is a great irony that there was an assumption McLellin's diaries would be negative in regards to Joseph Smith when they were quite the opposite," wrote historian Jan Shipps, who co-edited the publication. "His later papers [notebooks kept out of public view by the LDS Church and other material that had remained in the Traughber family until sold to the University of Utah] also are important. They give a picture of someone who continued to search all his life for what he thought he had found in the beginning."

Hinckley became church president in 1995. Prior to the bombing investigation, he had been much more accessible and candid with reporters. Several months before the murders, I wrote a story for the *Tribune* saying the LDS Church had purchased Joseph Smith's 1825 money digging contract from Hofmann. When Hinckley read the article, which included a statement from church spokesman Jerry Cahill denying the church had the document, Hinckley instructed Cahill to issue a public statement confirming that he had bought the letter from Hofmann. Hinckley's forthrightness stood in contrast to Turley's reasoning that the church was not obligated to volunteer information to investigators trying to catch a killer.

On 6 May 1986 Ron Yengich, Hofmann's attorney, interviewed Hinckley and asked about the McLellin collection, but Hinckley neglected to mention that it had been found two months earlier. That same month both the prosecution and defense attorney entered a statement that Hinckley "has never seen nor possessed nor has any knowledge of the whereabouts of a document or a group of documents known as the McLellin collection," and Hinckley did not make any effort to correct this misstatement.

It is an ironic twist that a modern-day bombing investigation would bring public attention to McLellin, an apostle little known to most Mormons. Before the discovery of Traughber's collection, few materials from McLellin were known to exist. "I was not aware of any McLellin Collection anywhere in the country until police started talking about it," said Dean Jessee. The Reorganized Church of Jesus Christ of Latter Day Saints had a few McLellin letters, Jessee said in 1986, and the LDS Church even less.

John L. Traughber failed in his quest to write a book about McLellin and left his young family in poverty. However, his unfinished work was redeemed in 1995 when the University of Utah purchased the remaining portions of Traughber's collection of McLellin writings covering the period from 1854 to 1880. Interestingly, John Traughber had remained a McLellin devotee all his life: "I valued him much. He and I were true friends, yet for the last two years of his life we were as far apart in religion as the poles of the earth. Peace to his memory. Repose to his spirit." Although John Traughber is to be credited with having secured for future generations the thoughts and philosophies of McLellin, it is to his widow and children that the decades-long task fell to ensure that John's own efforts would not be overlooked, lovingly preserving his deepest musings along with those of McLellin.

A single entry in Traughber's journal tells how his life's work began. In 1884 he recorded that he rode to an express station, paid fifty cents in shipping charges, and took home a boxful of McLellin's journals, essays, letters, and one of the rare handwritten copies of a revelation dictated by Smith. In that same journal, Traughber ironically seemed to allude to the 1985 bombing investigation that would be conducted nearly eight decades after his death: "I hope that the long and industrious life of Dr. McLellin has not been in vain, and the record he has made concerning Mormonism will prove to be as much worth to mankind as he had desired it should," then Traughber added, "but it may be in a different way than he had expected."

3.

THE PAST AS DECLINE FROM A GOLDEN AGE

Early Mormonism's Restorationist Tendency

THOMAS G. ALEXANDER

What strikes me about William McLellin's personal writings, now available to us through the work of the current editors, is the human tendency to interpret the past selectively. Many of us try to imagine what it must have been like to have lived through certain great moments in history. In doing so, our imagination often edits events to emphasize the heroic and extraordinary, perhaps in contrast with the tedium of daily life. I would argue that the urge to similar historical nostalgia and reconstruction is even more pronounced in dissenters. After all, they have withdrawn from fellowship with friends and societies with which they once associated. In many cases they have a tendency to become increasingly critical in their perceptions of the differences between the organization they first knew and the organization they now see. They become, if anything, less satisfied, more irritable, and more restless, even than when they first parted ways. McLellin's life, at least, is evidence for this pattern.

As a twenty-five-year old, McLellin thought he had found a perfect organization in the fledgling Church of Christ, the name then borne by the organization later called the Church of Jesus Christ of Latter-day

---

THOMAS G. ALEXANDER is Lemuel Hardison Redd Professor of Western American History Emeritus at Brigham Young University. His many works include *Mormonism in Transition: A History of the Latter-day Saints*; *Things in Heaven and Earth: The Life and Times of Wilford Woodruff, a Mormon Prophet* (Best Book Award, Mormon History Association; Evans Biography Award, Mountain West Center); and as co-editor, *Great Basin Kingdom Revisited: Contemporary Perspectives*; *Manchester Mormons: The Journals of William Clayton, 1840-1842*; and volume five of *The Papers of Ulysses S. Grant*. He is past president of the Association of Utah Historians, Mormon History Association, and Utah State Historical Society and currently national president of Phi Alpha Theta and on the governing council of the Western History Association.

Saints. It may have been the purity of the church's call to biblical precedent that attracted McLellin. In any case, on 20 August 1831 he offered himself for baptism.[1] He then devoted himself to service in the church for five years, principally by teaching and by proselytizing as a missionary in the upper South and Midwest.

McLellin was born on 18 January 1806 in Tennessee and grew up in the north central Cumberland River counties of Smith and Jackson. Little is known of his family, educational, political, or religious background, but he seems to have been raised a Protestant and was probably also a seeker. Trained as a farmer, he gave up agriculture to work as a school teacher and a store clerk. In later life he practiced botanic medicine and edited a newspaper.

In July 1831, shortly after the death of his first wife, Cynthia Ann, while teaching school in Paris, Illinois, McLellin met missionaries Reynolds Cahoon and Samuel H. Smith, Joseph Smith's brother. Impressed by their teachings, he immediately closed his school and traveled to Independence, Missouri, to meet Joseph Smith. Joseph had left for Kirtland, Ohio, so David Whitmer, Harvey Whitlock, Martin Harris, and Hyrum Smith taught McLellin about the church. Hyrum baptized him and seems to have played the major role in his conversion. After Hyrum Smith and Edward Partridge ordained him an elder, William and Hyrum left with others for Kirtland.

McLellin married Emeline Miller and settled his family in 1832 in the major church centers of first Kirtland, Ohio, and then Independence, Missouri. Residing in Independence at the time of the expulsion of the Mormon settlers from Jackson County in 1833, he negotiated with the local anti-Mormon leaders over the disposition of the Latter-day Saints' property. Returning with Joseph Smith to Kirtland in July 1834, he labored as a troubleshooter and teacher for the church. Seven months later, on 14 February 1835, he was called to be a founding member of the Quorum of Twelve Apostles. In this position, McLellin ministered principally as a missionary and teacher until separating from the Latter-day Saint community in August 1836.

After leaving the body of the Saints, he resided variously in Illinois, Iowa, Pennsylvania, Ohio, Michigan, and Missouri. In 1845 he joined

---

1. Richard P. Howard's essay in this volume offers extensive evidence for the same tendency I explore here. Other details of McLellin's life are drawn from Larry C. Porter, "The Odyssey of William Earl McLellin: Man of Diversity, 1806-83," in *The Journals of William E. McLellin, 1831-1836,* eds. Jan Shipps and John W. Welch (Provo and Urbana: *BYU Studies* and University of Illinois Press, 1994), 291-378.

briefly with Sidney Rigdon, William Law, Martin Harris, and others in organizing the Church of Christ under Rigdon's leadership, using the original name of the Church of Jesus Christ of Latter-day Saints. He remained in the organization for only a few months before differences with Rigdon led to his withdrawal. Like William Smith, McLellin flirted briefly with James J. Strang's organization, though unlike Smith he apparently did not join. Residing for a time in and around Kirtland, he tried to promote the organization of a church with David Whitmer as its prophet. After that effort failed, he eventually returned to Missouri where, convinced by Granville Hedrick's revelations, he offered himself for baptism in 1869 in the Church of Christ (Temple Lot). His conversion to the Hedrickites lasted from June through November, about the same length of time as his membership in Rigdon's Church of Christ. McLellin corresponded at various times with Joseph Smith III and other leaders in the Reorganized Church of Jesus Christ of Latter Day Saints (now the Community of Christ). He also communicated with some of his old colleagues and met with members of the Church of Jesus Christ of Latter-day Saints.

When David Whitmer organized a Church of Christ in 1875, in spite of McLellin's long friendship with and admiration for Whitmer and his belief that Whitmer was Joseph Smith's chosen successor, he did not join. He decided Whitmer's church represented an unbiblical type of spiritualism. After searching for manna in a wilderness of faith for most of his life, in August 1880, about two and a half years before his death, McLellin summed up the feelings that had germinated over more than four and a half decades. "I have no faith in any party or faction of L.D.S.ism any where in the world," he wrote. "I live alone outside all churches. I most firmly believe that the Lord will establish the Church of Christ shortly, and then (if they will accept of me) I'll unite with them!!!" By contrast, he wrote, "I have more confidence in the Book of Mormon than any book of this wide earth!" Anyone who fights against the book, he wrote, "fights against truth–against purity–against light–against ... one of the truest, purist books on earth"[2]

Although these confessions of faith may seem contradictory, they parallelled in many ways the beliefs of David Whitmer, Oliver Cowdery, and Martin Harris–the three principle witnesses to the Book of Mormon. All three continued to bear strong testimonies of the Book of Mormon, although each left the LDS Church for various periods. Cowdery

2. McLellin to James T. Cobb, 14 August 1880; Letter 26, p. 521.

and Harris both rejoined the Utah church prior to their deaths; Whitmer and McLellin did not.[3]

Significantly, the seven notebooks and the letters published here offer a fascinating glimpse into the way the human mind reconstructs and reinterprets the past; at the same time they help us probe the views of a man we might call an independent restorationist.[4] As William Cronon reminds us, human beings remember and reconstruct the same events from the past in different ways. In doing so, they see divergent meanings in and extract diverse interpretations from those events.[5]

Thus, dissenters and conformists alike reconstruct the past with a view to making sense of their respective positions. As mentioned, dissenters detect a story of decline from a better time—from a Golden Age. It matters little whether the dissent appears in political, social, economic, or religious matters, partisans of various views select those facts and interpretations that help to explain their positions, to themselves if not to others. The American Revolution was either an illegal mistake or a war to defend liberty, depending on whether you were a British or American partisan. Americans fought each other in either the Civil War or the War between the States, depending upon whether you supported the North or South. The Second World War was spawned by American insensitivity or Japanese aggression, depending upon your perspective.

Just as in political matters, religious traditions spawn divergent readings of the past. The Jewish, Muslim, and Christian faiths each provide examples. In Christianity, the Protestants rejected the Catholic story as the former organized churches around the teachings of such leaders as Martin Luther, John Calvin, John Knox, and John Wesley. Divergent understandings—often stories of decline—led to the organization of the Baptists, Mennonites, Quakers, and Christian Scientists. The Pentecostals read the past differently from the Methodists, from which many came, and partisans of the New Thought movement saw a past unlike that of their former colleagues in Christian Science.[6]

---

3. On the three witnesses, see Richard Lloyd Anderson, *Investigating the Book of Mormon Witnesses* (Salt Lake City: Deseret Book, 1981), and numerous articles by Anderson on Whitmer, Cowdery, and Harris.

4. For the seeker impulse in Mormonism, see Dan Vogel, *Religious Seekers and the Advent of Mormonism* (Salt Lake City: Signature Books, 1994).

5. William Cronon, "A Place for Stories: Nature, History, and Narrative," *Journal of American History* 78 (Mar. 1992): 1347-76.

6. For general histories of religion in America, see Sidney E. Ahlstrom, *A Religious History of the American People,* 2 vols. (New York: Doubleday, 1975); Martin E. Marty, *Pilgrims in Their Own Land: Five Hundred Years of Religion in America* (Boston: Little, Brown, 1984).

During Joseph Smith's lifetime, competing revelations and interpretations within Mormonism itself led to divisions. Hiram Page, one of the eight witnesses to the Book of Mormon, proposed new revelations, and David Whitmer, one of the three witnesses, rejected a number of the changes in organization and doctrine.[7] McLellin came to believe that God would reveal his will through personal revelation for the governance of the church to those whom he called as prophets, independent of church office. Significantly, he read God's dealings with past generations as evidence for rejecting the view that the calling of prophet could be a church office. As an independent restorationist, he believed God would call seers and prophets directly rather than through the agency of other humans.

In a revelation announced in September 1830, Joseph Smith rejected Page's, and by implication Whitmer's and McLellin's, interpretation of prophetic calls. Shortly before, Page had received revelations through a seer stone. Smith's 1830 revelation, now published as Section 28 of the LDS Doctrine and Covenants (RLDS 27), resolved the controversy for those who continued to accept his leadership by designating him as the only prophet authorized to receive revelation for the entire church. Thereafter, others might receive revelations on matters under their stewardship, but only one person could receive it for the body of the saints.

Dissatisfied with Smith's views, like the antinomian Anne Hutchinson of the seventeenth-century Massachusetts Bay Colony, McLellin chose to resist dictation by any of the church leadership. Like Hutchinson, McLellin believed in governance by immediate personal revelation rather than by established church leaders.[8]

Within Mormonism, divergent readings of the past did not end with Joseph Smith's death. McLellin constructed a different story of the

---

7. On the controversy over Hiram Page, see B. H. Roberts, ed., *History of the Church of Jesus Christ of Latter-day Saints, Period I: History of Joseph Smith, the Prophet by Himself,* 2d ed. rev. (Salt Lake City: Church of Jesus Christ of Latter-day Saints, 1978), 1:109-111, 115; D&C 28, RLDS 27. On Whitmer's views, see David Whitmer, *An Address to All Believers in Christ by a Witness to the Divine Authenticity of The Book of Mormon* (Richmond, Mo.: by the author, 1887).

8. On Hutchinson and anti-clericism in New England, see David D. Hall, ed., *The Antinomian Controversy, 1636-1638: A Documentary History,* rev. ed. (Durham, N.C.: Duke University Press, 1990); Amy Schranger Lang, *Prophetic Woman: Anne Hutchinson and the Problem of Dissent in the Literature of New England* (Berkeley: University of California Press, 1987); Selma R. Williams, *Divine Rebel: The Life of Anne Marbury Hutchinson* (New York: Holt, Reinhart, and Winston, 1981). By contrast, McLellin's belief in free will and rejection of predestination differed with antinomian doctrines of Hutchinson and those who agreed with her.

Latter-day Saint experience than did Brigham Young, and each in turn differed from those scripted by Joseph Smith III, Sidney Rigdon, James J. Strang, and Granville Hedrick. After the Mormon exodus to Utah, Joseph Morris proposed new revelations for the church and the Godbeites offered spiritualistic seances. In the twentieth century, various new prophets have announced revelations to fundamentalists who reject the church's abandonment of polygamy. In Mexico, the Third Convention divided for a time, in part on the issue of Hispanic versus Nordic leadership.

The documents reproduced here help us to understand McLellin's reconstruction of the Latter-day Saint past. As he considered the changes in doctrine, organization, and disposition that took place between 1831 and 1836, he came to believe that God had withdrawn Joseph Smith's prophetic calling and that the church had experienced a decline beginning immediately after the translation of the Book of Mormon.

The notebooks and letters detail McLellin's objections. He cited changes in church organization and practice as evidence of Joseph's fall from grace. He rejected the division of the priesthood into two units, Aaronic and Melchizedek. He thought that God had called Christ as the only High Priest. He criticized the Prophet's changes in the revelations made in preparation for publication of the Book of Commandments and the Doctrine and Covenants. He denounced the march of Zion's Camp to assist the Saints in Missouri as the introduction of an unauthorized spirit of war into the community. He rejected doctrines such as plurality of gods, baptism for the dead, God's eternal progression, and plural marriage. He also repudiated practices such as the construction of a temple, the spirit of ostentation and speculation in Kirtland, the opening of the Kirtland Safety Society without a charter, and the organization of Danites in Missouri.

In addition to shining a light on the independent restorationist tendency in early Mormonism, the documents published here can be compared with the six diaries McLellin kept during the years of his activity between 1831 and 1836 to unpeel the layers of thought that time deposited over McLellin's understanding.[9] During the five-year period covered by the diaries, McLellin cultivated an intimate relationship with Joseph Smith and other church leaders. As reflections of his thoughts from 1831 through 1836, the diaries reveal a devoted disciple, mission-

9. See Shipps and Welch, *Journals of McLellin*.

ary, and apostle who moved rapidly into the upper echelon of the movement. By contrast, the letters and notebooks disclose McLellin's explanations of his later views. These include his reasons for believing the Book of Mormon, his reasons for leaving the LDS Church, and his reasons for declining to remain with any of the churches organized by Joseph Smith's followers after his death in 1844.

Significantly, the strong views, specific events, and vigorous objections expressed in the letters seem virtually absent from the diaries. This is extremely important since the views McLellin expressed in the later documents apparently served as a rationale for his rejection of the various churches that took their teachings from Joseph Smith.

Such changes in perceptions over time are not unusual. As Cronon pointed out, historians have long understood that human beings have an intense need to understand the end of a story. As a result, their present condition leads to a rethinking of past events.[10] We have learned that through the process of reflection, humans seek to make sense of their lives and experiences by rationalizing and reshaping their memory of events in ways that help them to understand both their previous actions and current situations. Some shape these events in a progressive or triumphalist mode, others see in the events decline from a golden age that existed in the past.

Though they differ from McLellin's experiences in large part because his view of the LDS story is of decline, the orthodox view is of progress, for which several examples from the Latter-day Saint past offer instances of this process.

We have, for example, no contemporary accounts of the transfiguration of Brigham Young into the image and voice of Joseph Smith at the meeting in Nauvoo, Illinois, on 8 August 1844. Clearly, the majority of those present at the time experienced some kind of group religious experience that confirmed Young's leadership. We know from the diaries of Wilford Woodruff and others, written at the time, that Young and the Twelve contended with Sidney Rigdon of the First Presidency for leadership of the church. We know that when the leadership called for a vote, the congregation supported the Twelve.[11] Only from retrospective accounts, however, do we learn of the transfiguration of Young into the appearance of Smith. Many Latter-day Saints had begun referring to "the

10. Cronon, "Place for Stories," 1354.

11. Scott G. Kenney, ed., *Wilford Woodruff's Journal, 1833-1898.* (Midvale, Utah: Signature Books, 1983-85), 2:434-40.

mantle of the prophet" descending on Young much like Elijah's mantle fell on Elisha when the former ascended to heaven in a chariot of fire.[12]

We find a second example in the famous "This is the place" statement allegedly made by Brigham Young at the mouth of Emigration Canyon on 24 July 1847. Incapacitated at the time with "mountain fever," which some medical scholars have identified as Colorado tick fever, Young recuperated in the back of Woodruff's carriage as the team pulled it to the mouth of the canyon. Woodruff's journal entries exult in praise over the valley, but they mention nothing about Young's famous "This is the place" declaration.[13]

As early as 1873, some in the church began to refer to the "This is the place" phrase. In a sermon that year, Erastus Snow, who had not been present at the time, said Young had uttered the words. In later sermons in 1892-93 and 1897, Woodruff, who was present, elaborated. In 1892 he said, "I brought President Young in my carriage into the valley of Salt Lake. He was sick, and he asked me to turn my carriage so that he could get sight of the valley. I did so. He cast his eyes over the valley and looked for some little time. When he got through he said, 'Brother Woodruff, drive on. Here is our home. This is the place God has pointed out for us to plant our feet. I have seen this place before.'"[14]

The re-envisioning of the Nauvoo meeting and the Emigration Canyon incident seems to have resulted from the efforts of participants to understand the deeper, even cosmic, meaning of these events. How had the Lord confirmed Brigham Young's call as Joseph Smith's successor? How had the Saints known that the Lord approved of their settlement in Salt Lake Valley? Such questions brought perceptions to mind—perhaps previously inchoate—that helped make sense of these events.

By contrast, instead of explaining a collective experience such as those in Nauvoo and Emigration Canyon, McLellin sought to understand his personal experience. For him, it had been a retrograde rather than a progressive experience. Once he had served as a leader in the nascent movement. He had stood with Brigham Young, Heber C. Kimball,

---

12. Lynne Watkins Jorgensen, "The Mantle of the Prophet Joseph Passes to Brother Brigham: A Collective Spiritual Witness," *BYU Studies* 36/4 (1996-97): 125-204. Cf. Richard S. Van Wagoner, "The Making of a Mormon Myth: The 1844 Transfiguration of Brigham Young," *Dialogue: A Journal of Mormon Thought* 28 (Winter 1995): 1-24.

13. Kenney, *Wilford Woodruff's Journal,* 3:233-35.

14. Erastus Snow, "Ancient Prophecy, Relating to the Time of the Restitution of All Things, To Be Fulfilled," *Journal of Discourses* 16 (1874): 207; Brian H. Stuy, ed., *Collected Discourses Delivered by President Wilford Woodruff, His Two Counselors, The Twelve Apostles, and Others* (Burbank, Calif.: BHS Publishing, 1989), 3:82-83, 424.

and Orson Hyde in the Quorum of the Twelve Apostles. Later in life he felt the need to tell his story—to explain to himself and others why he had left the LDS Church in 1836, why he had never rejoined the body of the Saints, and why he had never remained with any of the other churches. The explanations he gave during a later period clearly establish his disillusionment and his independent restorationism, something not evident in the diary entries.

Just as none of his diary entries formulate the reason for the break in the way McLellin later thought of it, a letter he wrote on 24 January 1837 reveals a much different point of view from the later documents. In this letter, responding to an invitation from the Council of the Twelve to rejoin them, McLellin does not assert his independence but asks for forgiveness and for the reinstatement of his ministerial license.[15]

The contemplated reconciliation did not take place, and as McLellin reflected on his perceptions and beliefs he came to understand that he had left the church because he disagreed with changes that had taken place. By 1870, further reflection led him to believe that as early as 1831 the church itself had fallen into apostasy. In a letter of 24 May to Davis H. Bayes, McLellin argued that the "Church of Christ," which was the name of the church when he joined it in 1831, "had ceased to exist."[16] He placed great stock in the belief that the change to Church of the Latter Day Saints on 3 May 1834 and subsequent changes which finally ended in the name Church of Jesus Christ of Latter-day Saints had resulted from such fundamental alterations in the nature of the church as to void its legitimate existence. He came to believe that with these and other revisions the church had forsaken its authority and Joseph Smith had lost the prophetic mantle.

After leaving the body of the Saints, while revisioning his own perceptions of the relationship between the church and God, McLellin continued to reflect and write on various other religious matters. He read widely and meditated on the meaning of passages in the Bible and Book of Mormon, the writings of the early Christian fathers, and the works of theologians and religious philosophers. He also thought about his experiences in the church. The notebooks offer a glimpse into his reflections on these topics. Significantly, much of the doctrine he continued to believe would seem quite familiar to Latter-day Saints. He believed in the great apostasy of the early Christian church from the teach-

15. McLellin to "My dear old Friends," 24 Jan. 1837, in Shipps and Welch, *Journals of McLellin*, 229-30.

16. See Letter 8, p. 458.

ings and authority of Christ. He wrote in support of continuous revelation and latter-day miracles. He spoke of repentance as forsaking sin and making restitution for wrongs committed. He considered baptism by immersion and the gift of the Holy Ghost as absolutely necessary for salvation. He believed in the restoration of the "ancient order of things," including the reestablishment of such offices as the First Presidency, Quorum of the Twelve, and Seventy. He said that Satan is a real spiritual person. He accepted the doctrine of gospel dispensations, though he arranged them somewhat differently from the way most Mormons would today. As a millennialist he believed in Christ's imminent return to the earth. He believed that the Bible contained mistakes and that other books should have been included in the scriptures. He rejected infant baptism. He believed in free agency, a view that he buttressed with the belief that God's omniscient knowledge does not nullify the human freedom to choose. He asserted that God lives in eternity where all things are present, rather than in time, as human beings do, where events take place in linear order.

Some of his views would seem strange to Mormons. Not all would agree with his view of time. He believed in a sort of numerology that determined the ordering of offices in the church. He argued that only Christ could hold the office of High Priest. In his view, God had a body of spirit, not of flesh and bones as well. He believed in direct revelation but rejected the view that such communications can come from God through seer stones.

Therefore, the documents that follow offer significant insight into early Mormonism. They reveal something of the range of views of those who believed in the Book of Mormon and in the teachings of Joseph Smith.[17] They offer a glimpse into the operation of the human mind in re-envisioning and reconstructing the past. They explore the thought of an independent restorationist, whose perception of decline in the Mormon past helps us understand why some people decided to leave the body of the Saints. They also reveal the continuing reflections of a man who had played a significant role in the early history of the Church of Jesus Christ of Latter-day Saints.[18]

---

17. At least since publication of Gordon S. Wood's "Evangelical America and Early Mormonism," *New York History* 41 (Oct. 1980): 359-86, we have understood something of the divergent views that existed within Mormonism. For a treatment of the range of contradictory symbols often held by early Mormons, see Jon M. Duncan, "Multiple Discourses in Early Mormon Religion," M.A. thesis, Brigham Young University, 1998.

18. I appreciate the suggestions of Ferenc M. Szasz, Ignacio M. Garcia, John W. Welch, and Jan Shipps for revisions of this article.

4.

"MY EYES WERE HOLDEN IN THOSE DAYS"

A Study of Selective Memory

D. MICHAEL QUINN

The title's quote is from William E. McLellin's December 1878 letter to John L. Traughber Jr.,[1] who preserved the former LDS apostle's diaries, unpublished religious treatises, and some of his letters. McLellin's diaries for 1831-36 have been published,[2] and he hoped to eventually publish his religious musings, which sometimes contained references to "dear reader." In addition, some of his letters were clearly written for publication. Of all this collection's documents from 1854 onward, the 1878 letter to John Traughber deserves the most attention as one of the more personally revealing and historically accurate writings. Composed less than five years before his death in 1883, it and another letter to Traughber in January 1879[3] stand almost alone in acknowledging McLellin's former faith in the religious teachings and activities of Joseph Smith Jr., the founding prophet of Mormonism.

And there lies the crux of the matter because McLellin, as an original member of the Quorum of the Twelve Apostles, cannot be dismissed as someone who did not know what he was talking about. Even if readers

D. MICHAEL QUINN was Professor of History, Brigham Young University, 1976-88, and Beinecke Senior Fellow and Associate, Department of History, Yale University, 2002-03. He is the author of *Early Mormonism and the Magic World View* (Best Book Award, Mormon History Association), *Elder Statesman: A Biography of J. Reuben Clark*, the two-volume *Mormon Hierarchy* series (*Origins of Power* and *Extensions of Power*), and *Same-Sex Dynamics among Nineteenth-Century Americans: A Mormon Example* (American Historical Association Award); he is editor of *The New Mormon History: Revisionist Essays on the Past.*

1. See Letter 22, p. 510; restated in Letter 23, p. 516.

2. Jan Shipps and John W. Welch, eds., *The Journals of William E. McLellin, 1831-1836* (Provo and Urbana: *BYU Studies* and University of Illinois Press, 1994).

3. See Letter 23, p. 516.

recoil at his criticisms, he was nonetheless present at many of the crucial events in early LDS history.

My analysis has this perspective on McLellin's perspective: he conveniently edited himself out of scenes he later came to despise. This is not to say there is not some truth in what he chose to report, at least from his later perspective, only that the passage of time and a healthy ego tended to accentuate his own virtue and cast others as definite villains. As with any source we consider, McLellin's selective memory must be checked against other eyewitness reports.

Unfortunately, McLellin's criticisms were not written at the time the events occurred. The evidence indicates that he was more or less content in the church during the period when the issues arose he would later criticize. I do not mean to suggest that it is wrong to reassess how one feels about matters that one approved in the past. Such reassessments are completely legitimate, but often the person will marshal evidence on one side or the other, whether or not by intent. Despite the passage of time and the bias of disillusionment, there is corroboration here and there of McLellin's critiques.

It is worth noting as a final caution that, like the disaffected witnesses of the Book of Mormon, McLellin clung to core doctrines of the Restoration. He retained faith in the Book of Mormon, in *some* angelic visitations, and in dispensations, millennialism, and living an upright life. He argued that the church had veered from its origins, not that he had. In fact, both moved significantly beyond their former points of concurrence.

He was not a participant in Mormonism when Joseph Smith organized the "Church of Christ" in 1830. He was an adherent in 1834 when it became the "Church of Latter Day Saints." Then Smith announced an 1838 revelation to name the organization "The Church of Jesus Christ of Latter Day Saints." Aside from criticizing the changes of name,[4]

---

4. See Notebook 7, pp. 388-89, 419; Letter 8, pp. 459-60; Letter 22, p. 511. For the early name changes, see *A Book of Commandments, For the Government of the Church of Christ, Organized According To Law, On the 6th of April, 1830* (Zion [Independence, Mo.]: W. W. Phelps and Co., 1833); "Minutes of a conference, of the authorities of the church of Latter Day Saints assembled in the house of the Lord in Kirtland, Sept. 17th, 1837," *Elders' Journal of the Church of Latter Day Saints*, Nov. 1837, [17]; "An Extract of Revelation," *Elders' Journal*, Aug. 1838, 52; Richard L. Anderson, "What Changes Have Been Made in the Name of the Church?" *Ensign*, Jan. 1979, 13-14; Bruce Douglas Porter, "Church of Jesus Christ of Latter-day Saints," and Susan Easton Black, "Name of the Church," in Daniel H. Ludlow, ed., *Encyclopedia of Mormonism: The History, Scripture, Doctrine, and Procedure of the Church of Jesus Christ of Latter-day Saints* (New York: Macmillan Publishing Co., 1992), 1:276-77, 3:979. During Joseph Smith's lifetime, the common spellings in church documents were "Latter

McLellin presented those years as milestones in his litany of disbeliefs. His full statement in 1878 is revealing: "But my eyes were holden in those days, because I had confidence in J. Smith."

Likewise, McLellin acknowledged in the same letter that even while he was becoming disenchanted with Mormonism in 1836, he hesitated to leave a proselytizing mission because "I was sent here by a prophet of the Lord (as I supposed)." Concerning his resignation from the Quorum of Twelve Apostles in 1836, he told Traughber some four decades later: "They almost perfectly knew me, and I now think they loved me." Even in a caustic letter to Apostle Orson Pratt, McLellin wrote of "Joseph Smith and his brethren, (for I once loved them)," and later repeated in the same letter: "Once I loved them and their society so dearly."[5]

Moreover, he affirmed that the founding Mormon prophet saw angels, despite McLellin's later expressions of disbelief in some of the claimed appearances to Joseph Smith. In an 1870 letter he wrote: "I do not say but [that] angels conversed with him, and gave him much instruction how to proceed. But that they ever ordained him I deny."[6] Ten years later he wrote for publication: "I have no doubt an angel ministered to Joseph, but it was not Moroni."[7]

McLellin's combination of faith and disbelief may puzzle modern believers and secular rationalists, but it was his perspective on Mormonism. The above quotes provide a useful context in which to consider some of the documents in this collection which question Mormon claims, teachings, and practices. For the day-to-day expression of McLellin's devotion, readers should consult his diaries for 1831-36.

During his most prominent service in those early years, McLellin was simultaneously an insider and outsider. When Smith organized the Quorum of Twelve Apostles in February 1835, he was among its members, and was related by marriage to three of the other apostles. His wife, Emeline, was first cousin to Luke S. Johnson, Lyman E. Johnson, and Orson Hyde's wife, Marinda Nancy Johnson. However, McLellin was the only apostle not born in New England or New York, and in the elite group of Yankee Mormons, he was the Southern outsider.[8]

Day," "Latter day," "Latterday," "Latter-Day," and "Latter-day." Since his death in 1844, different churches have adopted one of the above spellings as official. For McLellin's complaint about the church's name, see Richard P. Howard, "Mormonism's 'Stormy Petrel,'" in this volume.

5. See Letter 1, pp. 436-38.

6. See Letter 8, p. 462.

7. See Notebook 7, p. 392.

8. See my *Mormon Hierarchy: Origins of Power* (Salt Lake City: Signature Books and

Even his diaries reflected an outsider's point of view. Although he was the quorum's secretary and recorded its minutes for 1835-36,[9] he devoted his diary to daily activities in the "branches" and "missionfield" rather than reporting on events at LDS headquarters in Kirtland, Ohio.[10]

Moreover, while many knew of his Tennessee birth, apparently none of his LDS associates were aware that his mother was a Cherokee Indian.[11] Although the Book of Mormon advances the view that the "Lamanites" (Native Americans) are a "chosen people," McLellin's lifelong silence about this ancestry indicates that he was ashamed of his "half-breed" status.[12] Apparently unaware of the divided ethnicity, Larry C. Porter noted: "William makes no mention of his mother in any known source. She appears to have been either dead or out of the home during a substantial part of his life."[13]

McLellin's criticisms of Mormonism extended back to the period of 1829-30, before he was converted. Clearly he needed to draw on the views of actual witnesses for this material and interpret what he heard from them. A faithful member of the church from 1831-36, he might have had occasion to learn about earlier events from the founder himself, from other members of the Smith family, or from such ever-faithful Mormons as Alvah Beaman, Emer Harris, Joseph Knight, Newel Knight, or Orrin Porter Rockwell. In fact, there were more than seventy individuals in the church whose experiences dated back to its founding, with whom he could have spoken while still participating in the Quorum of the Twelve.[14] Several accounts by these early faithful members were avail-

---

Smith Research Associates, 1994), 466, 540, 552, 554-56, 563-64, 568-69, 571, 594, 606; Larry C. Porter, "The Odyssey of William Earl McLellin: Man of Diversity, 1806-83," in Shipps and Welch, *Journals of McLellin,* 302-03.

9. B. H. Roberts, ed., *History of the Church of Jesus Christ of Latter-day Saints. Period I: History of Joseph Smith, the Prophet,* 2d ed. rev. (1902-32; Salt Lake City: Deseret Book, 1978), 2:209-10, 219, 222, 238, 395; Quorum of the Twelve Apostles minutes, 1835-1836, manuscript, Archives, Historical Department, Church of Jesus Christ of Latter-day Saints, Salt Lake City, with detailed transcriptions in my research papers at the Beinecke Rare Book and Manuscript Library, Yale University, New Haven, Connecticut.

10. Shipps and Welch, *Journals of McLellin.*

11. Quinn, *Origins of Power,* 563; Bob L. Andrews, "McClellan Family Sketch," *Smith County Historical and Genealogical Society Newsletter* 1/2, 39.

12. This insulting term was in universal usage among Anglo-Americans during the early 1800s. See "Half Breed" in Bruce Grant, *Concise Encyclopedia of the American Indian,* rev. ed. (New York: Wings Books, 1989), 145.

13. Porter, "Odyssey of McLellin," 292.

14. Larry C. Porter identified by name seventy-three people present at the organizational meeting of 6 April 1830. See his "Organizational Origins of the Church of Jesus

able in print before McLellin's 1880 treatise in the present collection,[15] while others were published later[16] or remain in manuscript form.[17]

After McLellin's departure from Mormonism, his main sources about the pre-1831 period were fellow dissidents Oliver Cowdery, Martin Harris, Hiram Page, and the Whitmer family, primarily David and John Whitmer. These five were among the eleven men Joseph Smith chose as special witnesses of the Book of Mormon.[18] Of the dissident sources, McLellin's longest and apparently closest association was with David Whitmer, who published two pamphlets emphasizing the same criticisms McLellin expressed about Joseph Smith's 1829-30 activities.[19]

It was from these dissidents that McLellin learned what the docu-

---

Christ, 6 April 1830," in *Regional Studies in Latter-day Saint Church History: New York,* ed. Porter, Milton V. Backman, Jr., and Susan Easton Black (Provo: Department of Church History and Doctrine, Brigham Young University, 1992), 154-55.

15. Oliver Cowdery, Letters I-VIII, in *Latter Day Saints Messenger and Advocate*, Oct., Nov., Dec. 1834, 13-16, 27-32, 41-43; Feb., Mar., Apr. July, Oct. 1835, 77-80, 95-96, 108-12, 155-59, 195-202; "The History of Joseph Smith," published in installments from 1842 onward; Oliver Cowdery statement, 17 Oct. 1848, quoted by Reuben Miller in *Latter-Day Saints' Millennial Star,* 20 Aug. 1859, 544; Lucy Mack Smith, *Biographical Sketches of Joseph Smith the Prophet and His Progenitors for Many Generations,* ed. Orson Pratt (Liverpool, Eng.: S. W. Richards, 1853); Orrin Porter Rockwell's account in *Journal of Discourses* (London and Liverpool: Latter Day Saints' Book Depot, 1878), 19:37-38.

16. Oliver Cowdery, signed statement, 13 Jan. 1849, in Roberts, *History of the Church,* 1:42n; William Smith, *William Smith on Mormonism* (Lamoni, Iowa: Herald Steam Book and Job Office, 1883); "Newel Knight's Journal," in *Scraps of Biography: Tenth Book of the Faith-Promoting Series* (Salt Lake City: Juvenile Instructor Office, 1883), 46-104; Dean C. Jessee, ed., "Joseph Knight's Recollection of Early Mormon History," *Brigham Young University Studies* 17 (Autumn 1976): 29-39; remarks of Alvah Beaman and Orrin Porter Rockwell in Norman R. Bowen, ed., *A Gentile Account of Life in Utah's Dixie, 1872-73: Elizabeth Kane's St. George Journal* (Salt Lake City: Tanner Trust Fund, University of Utah Library, 1995), 70, 71-74; also various selections in Hyrum L. Andrus and Helen Mae Andrus, comps., *They Knew the Prophet* (1974; Salt Lake City: Deseret Book Co., 1999); Milton V. Backman Jr., *Eyewitness Accounts of the Restoration* (Salt Lake City: Deseret Book Co., 1986).

17. Emer Harris statement, Utah Stake General Minutes, 6 Apr. 1856, Local Record 9629, ser. 11, vol. 10, 268-78, LDS Archives.

18. Richard Lloyd Anderson, *Investigating the Book of Mormon Witnesses* (Salt Lake City: Deseret Book, 1981); Bruce G. Stewart, "Hiram Page: An Historical and Sociological Analysis of an Early Mormon Prototype," M.A. thesis, Brigham Young University, 1987; Phillip R. Legg, *Oliver Cowdery: The Elusive Second Elder of the Restoration* (Independence, Mo: Herald Publishing House, 1989); Lyndon W. Cook, ed., *David Whitmer Interviews: A Restoration Witness* (Orem, Utah: Grandin Book Co., 1991); Richard Lloyd Anderson, "Oliver Cowdery," Rhett Stephens James, "Martin Harris," and Keith W. Perkins, "David Whitmer," in Ludlow, *Encyclopedia of Mormonism,* 1:335, 2:574-76, 4:1564-66; Ronald E. Romig, "David Whitmer: Faithful Dissenter, Witness Apart," in *Differing Visions: Dissenters in Mormon History,* ed. Roger D. Launius and Linda Thatcher (Urbana: University of Illinois Press, 1994), 23-44; Bruce N. Westergren, ed., *From Historian to Dissident: The Book of John Whitmer* (Salt Lake City: Signature Books, 1995).

19. David Whitmer, *An Address to All Believers in Christ by a Witness to the Divine*

ments of this collection say concerning "Joseph's Canada revelation."[20] Hiram Page wrote a letter to McLellin explaining this failed effort to obtain a Canadian copyright for the Book of Mormon.[21] Martin Harris showed an original copy of the revelation to McLellin, who wrote: "J. Smith's revelation for Cowdery to go to Canada was never printed. M. Harris had the copy that I read, in manuscript."[22] David Whitmer also must have been a source for his information about this incident. Nonetheless, McLellin did not refer to Whitmer's account of Smith's second revelation, also by means of his seer stone, explaining why his prophecy regarding the Canadian mission proved false. Whitmer published the second revelation in 1887, admittedly after McLellin's death, but probably something that McLellin was aware of. In any case, the text read: "Some revelations are of God: some revelations are of man: and some revelations are of the devil."[23] Despite that statement's sensationalism, the official history of the LDS Church in 1930 quoted it and accepted the basic accuracy of Whitmer's narrative about this matter. On the other hand, outsiders regard the statement as evasive and flippant. In that respect, it seems odd that McLellin did not mention the second revelation.[24]

More valuable than the information he learned from others are McLellin's reports of what he himself witnessed during the time he was at church headquarters from 1831-38. Of course, his reminiscent statements must still be compared and contrasted with other eyewitnesses wherever possible.

For example, after the passage of forty years, McLellin questioned whether Joseph Smith was still using a seer stone in 1831: "When he finished the translation of the Book [of Mormon in 1829,] thereafter he did not see–that is he did not use his stone. So say all those who were in-

---

Authenticity of The Book of Mormon (Richmond, Mo: by the author, 1887) and *An Address to Believers in the Book of Mormon* (Richmond, Mo: by the author, 1887).

20. See Notebook 7, p. 404; Letter 12, p. 484; Letters 16, p. 503; Letter 17, p. 504.

21. Hiram Page to William [E. McLellin], 2 Feb. 1848, typescripts in Community of Christ Archives and LDS Archives of holographic letter subsequently stolen from Community of Christ Archives.

22. See Letter 17, p. 504.

23. Whitmer, *Address to All Believers in Christ,* 31.

24. B. H. Roberts, *A Comprehensive History of The Church of Jesus Christ of Latter-day Saints, Century I* (Salt Lake City: "by the Church," 1930), 1:163, 165-66: "Then there must be taken into account the probable purpose of God in permitting the Toronto misadventure, the lesson he would teach through it. How important for the Prophet's disciples to know that not every voice heard by the spirit of man is the voice of God; that not every impression made upon the mind is an impression from a divine source."

timate with him at the time. In Oct. 1831 I wrote a revelation as he delivered it. And I know he used no stone to see then."[25] Nonetheless, other eyewitnesses told a different story, mentioning Smith's use of a seer stone for years thereafter. Smith may have neglected to use it in McLellin's presence, but the latter's memory might have been simply faulty on this point.[26]

Occasionally McLellin clearly misstated the details of incidents he had personally witnessed. For example, he was emphatic about what was *not said* in the ordination of Joseph Smith during a meeting of January 1832 at Amherst, Ohio. "I myself attended the Amherst Conference, and know positively that he was only ordained President of the church. Priesthood was not mentioned in his ordination at that time and place."[27] However, the contemporary diary of Reynolds Cahoon stated: "Wednesday the Elders asembld for Conference[—]the first business[:] ordained the President of the high Preas[t]hood and others."[28] McLellin appealed to his eyewitness status to undermine a traditional claim,[29] but his recollection was mistaken.

---

25. See Letter 12, p. 484. Writing for publication about 1880, he became even more emphatic: "A Seer must have the Urim and Thummim, the Interpreters or Directors, or a Seer-stone of some kind in which to see, or he is not an inspired Seer of the Lord. After Joseph Smith finished the book of Mormon he never used a Seer-stone in which to see: hence was not a Seer" (Notebook 7, p. 405).

26. In a reminiscent account, Orson Pratt described the revelation Smith dictated to him in November 1830: "Joseph produced a small stone called a seer stone, and putting it into a Hat soon commenced speaking" (James R. B. Vancleave, grandson-in-law of David Whitmer, to Joseph Smith III, 29 Sept. 1878, Miscellaneous Letters and Papers, P13, fd 255, Community of Christ Archives, reprinted in Cook, *David Whitmer Interviews,* 239-40). Moreover, in a manuscript written at Kirtland on 7 October 1835, Newel K. Whitney wrote that Smith gave him and his wife a blessing "through the Urim and Thummim" (Joseph Smith Jr., blessing, 7 Oct. 1835, Newel K. Whitney Family Papers, box 6, fd 19, L. Tom Perry Special Collections, Harold B. Lee Library, Brigham Young University, Provo, Utah). McLellin was living in Kirtland at the time. In December 1841, Joseph showed the apostles what Brigham Young called a seer stone and Wilford Woodruff called the Urim & Thummim ("History of Brigham Young," *Latter-Day Saints' Millennial Star,* 20 Feb. 1864, 118-19; Elden Jay Watson, ed., *Manuscript History of Brigham Young, 1801-1844* [Salt Lake City: Smith Secretarial Service, 1968], 112a; Scott G. Kenney, ed., *Wilford Woodruff's Journal, 1833-1898,* [Midvale, Utah: Signature Books, 1983], 2:144, for 27 Dec. 1841, cf. 2:155; Susan Staker, ed., *Waiting for World's End: The Diaries of Wilford Woodruff* [Salt Lake City: Signature Books, 1993], 50). See also Parley P. Pratt, "Editorial Remarks," *Latter-Day Saints' Millennial Star,* July 1842, 47; George D. Smith, ed., *An Intimate Chronicle: The Journals of William Clayton* (Salt Lake City: Signature Books and Smith Research Associates, 1995), 133-34.

27. Letter 10, pp. 477-78; also quoted and discussed in Quinn, *Origins of Power,* 296-97.

28. Reynolds Cahoon, Diary, January 1832, LDS Archives; quoted and discussed in Quinn, *Origins of Power,* 40.

29. Roberts, *History of the Church,* 1:243n.

The year 1832 is the reference point for McLellin's criticism of Joseph Smith's marital arrangements. He wrote to Joseph Smith III in 1872 concerning his father: "Was he an <u>Adulterer</u> so long ago, and still a 'good man'[?]" McLellin said the church founder was seeing other women as far back as Joseph III's birth, which was in 1832.[30] This was based on McLellin's 1847 conversation with Smith's widow, he wrote. McLellin had already raised the issue with "young Joseph" eleven years earlier and recommended that he ask his mother for confirmation: "Joseph, if You will only go to your own dear <u>mother</u>, she can tell you that he believed in Polygamy and practiced it long before his violent death!"[31] Midway between these two letters, it must have unnerved Joseph III when his mother gave McLellin a favorable endorsement.[32]

However, that *ad hominem* argument definitely could backfire on McLellin. An 1831 revelation stated that "you have turned away from your iniquities" and spoke of "adultery–a temptation with which thou hast been troubled." He kept a manuscript copy of this revelation.[33] According to Hazen Aldrich, senior president of the Seventy from 1835 to 1837, McLellin abandoned a proselytizing mission with Luke Johnson in order to live with "a certain harlot."[34] This referred to the mission they

---

30. See Letter 12, p. 489 (also cited in Roger D. Launius, *Joseph Smith III: Pragmatic Prophet* [Urbana: University of Illinois Press, 1988], 199n27, 207n52, but without comment).

31. See Letter 2, p. 441.

32. Emma Smith Bidamon to Joseph Smith III, 2 Feb. 1866, quoted in Linda King Newell and Valeen Tippetts Avery, *Mormon Enigma: Emma Hale Smith,* 2d ed. (Urbana: University of Illinois Press, 1994), 291, with references to McLellin's letters on 274, 291.

33. LDS D&C 66:1, 10; RLDS D&C 66:1, 5; "The McLellin Manuscripts of Doctrine and Covenants Sections 22 (RLDS 20), 45, 65, and 66," in Shipps and Welch, *Journals of McLellin,* 246-51.

34. My quote corrects the spelling of "harlot." For Aldrich, see Quinn, *Origins of Power,* 466, 535.

John Greenhow, "To the Church of Jesus Christ," *Zion's Reveille,* 4 Feb. 1847, 16, stated that "McLellin, at a certain time, went out to preach the gospel, in company with Luke Johnson, and when he came to the house of a certain harlet[,] he concluded to tarry many days ... and left Mr. Johnson to wend his way alone. So says Hazen Aldrich." The truthfulness of this allegation was supported by an untitled statement in *Zion's Reveille,* 18 Feb. 1847, 23, which observed: "In Vol. 2, No. 4, p. 16, of Zion's Reveille, we made a statement in relation to Dr. Wm. E. McLellin's immoral conduct upon the authority of Hazen Aldrich; which, though TRUE, Brother Aldrich much regrets, from the fact that he does not wish his name to appear in connection with the controversy; more especially as he says Dr. McLellin has always treated him with kindness and [with] becoming respect. Brother Aldrich made the statement in a private conversation respecting Dr. McLellin's repeated defections, and gave no authority for its publication. This apology is due Brother Aldrich, though we had no idea until now that he regarded the matter as confidential."

Ten months later McLellin published an editorial which referred to Aldrich as one of "four noble hearted brethren" who had joined his fledgling effort to form a church with

began on 2 February 1832, which McLellin claimed he ended three weeks later because of doubts "in my mind whether man or the fountain of all wisdom had called me to preach."[35] Subsequent knowledge of the real reason was undoubtedly what led church headquarters to excommunicate McLellin on 3 December 1832.[36] Typical of Joseph Smith's willingness to quickly reinstate Mormons who expressed regret after receiving church discipline for sexual transgressions,[37] McLellin was baptized again before starting his next mission on 28 January 1833.[38] He became a member of the Quorum of the Twelve Apostles in 1835 despite the previous condemnations. McLellin's selective memory shielded more than his former position of faith.

"I think the Twelvites are, as nearly as they can, carrying out Joseph's measures,"[39] McLellin had written in his 1861 letter to Joseph III, "And I think that they are the wickedest people now on this wide earth." This added insult to injury because Joseph Smith III presided over a church that repudiated everything connected with Utah Mormons.[40]

David Whitmer at its head. See "Our Apology—and Our Tours," *The Ensign of Liberty,* Dec. 1847, 30; also Mar. 1847, 2, for McLellin as its editor.

35. McLellin diary, 2 Feb. (departure), 25 Feb 1832 (quote), in Shipps and Welch, *Journals of McLellin,* 70, 73, also 78n34 (for explanation he gave his family in August 1832 for having ended this missionary assignment the previous February).

36. Scott H. Faulring, *An American Prophet's Record: The Diaries and Journals of Joseph Smith* (Salt Lake City: Signature Books and Smith Research Associates, 1987), 10.

Apparently unaware of the *Zion's Reveille* account of McLellin's sexual transgression, Porter, "Odyssey of McLellin," 305, stated: "Meanwhile, in Kirtland a council met on December 3, 1832. Not satisfied with certain unspecified activities of McLellin, they examined his case and excommunicated him.... As no minutes of the actual charges in the case appear to have been preserved, it is difficult to identify the causes associated with this action. However, his previous failure to complete his assigned mission to the 'south countries' and unauthorized travel to Missouri may well have been key factors."

37. Nauvoo high council minutes, 6 Feb. 1841, LDS Archives, with copy in box 76, H. Michael Marquardt Papers, Manuscripts Division, J. Willard Marriott Library, University of Utah, Salt Lake City; Quinn, *Origins of Power,* 632 (Smith's 1841 forgiveness of Theodore Turley for "sleeping with two females"); D. Michael Quinn, *Same-Sex Dynamics among Nineteenth-Century Americans: A Mormon Example* (Urbana: University of Illinois Press, 1996), 267 (Smith's forgiveness of John C. Bennett's "adulterous connections" in 1841), 268 (Smith's forgiveness of Francis M. Higbee's "revolting, corrupt, and disgusting" sexual behavior in 1842), 410.

38. McLellin diary, 28 Jan. 1833, and Porter, "Odyssey of McLellin," 90, 305.

39. See Letter 2, p. 443. This echoed an 1845 essay in the official publication of the church founded by dissident leader Sidney Rigdon, with whom McLellin briefly affiliated. In "Carry Out the Measures of Joseph Smith," *Latter Day Saint's Messenger and Advocate* [Pittsburgh, Pa.], 1 Jan. 1845, 75, the editor argued that "those man worshippers who contend for the measures of Joseph Smith, irrespective of the law of God, are in love with the 'spiritual wife system.'"

40. Richard P. Howard, "The Emerging RLDS Identity," *Restoration Studies* 3 (1986):

Not that McLellin was the only dissenter who tied Brigham Young's teachings to his predecessor's initiatives. In an equally backhanded compliment to Young, the excommunicated Sidney Rigdon had earlier written: "In 1840 it [the LDS Church] culminated and its history tended in a different direction and found its level in the order of things which now exist in Utah."[41]

Various sources support the accuracy of McLellin's claims about what was not said, or at least what he *did not hear,* in any public meeting or private statement during the first years of his affiliation with the church. He wrote: "In 1831 I heard Joseph tell his experience ~~some twenty times probably~~, many times about angels visits, and about finding the plates, and their contents coming to light, but I never heard one word of John the baptist, or of Peter, James, and John's visit and ordination. Till It was told some ~~year~~ years ~~or two~~ afterward in Ohio."[42] McLellin told the founding prophet's son: "I never heard of it in the church for years, altho I carefully noticed things that were said."[43] In support of these statements, there is a letter from McLellin to his family in August 1832 where he explained and defended Mormonism at length. Aside from references to the angel that revealed the gold plates, the letter showed no knowledge of other angelic ministrations.[44] Likewise, Lucy Mack Smith made no reference to angelic restoration of authority in an 1831 letter she wrote to her brother about the new church.[45] Nor did Joseph Knight's 1833 manuscript history of Mormonism refer to angelic restorations of authority, despite his eagerness to discuss angelic ministrations.[46] Book of Mormon witness David Whitmer later stated that "neither did I ever hear of such a thing as an angel ordaining them until I got into Ohio about the year 1834—or later."[47] From 1834 onward, official publications and faithful Mormons referred to Joseph Smith and Oliver Cowdery receiving authority from John the Baptist in 1829

44-53; Roger D. Launius, "At the Barricades of the Gospel: The Conspiracy Theme in RLDS History," *John Whitmer Historical Journal* 13 (1993): 3-17; Howard, *The Church through the Years* (Independence, Mo.: Herald Publishing House, 1993), 2:84-90, 125-27.

41. Sidney Rigdon to William H. Payne, 9 July 1858, Rigdon Papers, LDS Archives.

42. See Notebook 7, p. 392; cf. Letter 8, p. 462; Letter 20, p. 508.

43. See Letter 12, p. 491.

44. McLellin to "Samuel McLelin" and "Beloved Relatives," 4 Aug. 1832, in Shipps and Welch, *Journals of McLellin,* 79-85.

45. Lucy Mack Smith to Solomon Mack Jr., 6 Jan. 1831, in Ben E. Rich, ed., *Scrap Book of Mormon Literature* (Chicago: Henry C. Etten and Co., [1911]), 1:543-45.

46. Jessee, "Joseph Knight's Recollection," 29-39.

47. David Whitmer, interviewed by Zenas H. Gurley, 14 Jan. 1885, in Cook, *David Whitmer Interviews,* 154.

and from Peter, James, and John in 1829 or 1830 (based on additions Joseph Smith made to the official record).[48]

The related issue was McLellin's concern about the publication of Joseph Smith's revelations in the 1835 Doctrine and Covenants. Comparing these to the texts of the same revelations published in 1832-33 at Independence, Missouri, McLellin wrote in one letter: "I think there is scarcely a revelation printed in that book but that is altered and changed. I have counted more than twenty material alterations in one revelation, by comparing it as printed here [in Independence] and [later] in Kirtland."[49] He elaborated: "They altered words, sentences and paragraphs. They took out passages and added others so as to entirely change the sentiment, and thus made them read very different."[50] Among the additions to pre-1833 revelations, he noted, were "whole paragraphs also, relative to priesthood & Presidency."[51]

---

48. *Latter Day Saints Messenger and Advocate*, Oct. 1834, 15-16; *Doctrine and Covenants of the Church of the Latter Day Saints* (Kirtland, Ohio: F. G. Williams and Co., 1835), 180, "Section L," vv. 2-3 (LDS D&C 27:8, 12; RLDS D&C 26:2-3); Oliver Cowdery statement, 28 Sept. 1835, in Joseph Smith Sr., Patriarchal Blessing Book, 1:9, 12, LDS Archives, with complete transcription (though dated 18 Dec. 1833), in Gregory A. Prince Collection, Marriott Library, University of Utah; *Times and Seasons,* 1 Aug. 1842, 865-66; Oliver Cowdery to Phineas Young, 23 Mar. 1846, quoted in Stanley R. Gunn, *Oliver Cowdery: Second Elder and Scribe* (Salt Lake City: Bookcraft, 1962), 250-51; Oliver Cowdery statement, 17 Oct. 1848, quoted by Reuben Miller in *Latter Day Saints' Millennial Star,* 20 Aug. 1859, 544; Roberts, *History of the Church,* 1:39, 41n, 42n, 43n, 43-44; Dean C. Jessee, ed., *The Papers of Joseph Smith* (Salt Lake City: Deseret Book, 1989), 31; Brian Q. Cannon et al., "Priesthood Restoration Documents," *Brigham Young University Studies* 35 (1995-96): 163-207.

For statements that the angelic visitation of Peter, James, and John occurred in 1830 some time after the church's founding, rather than 1829 as traditionally claimed, see Brigham Young in the *Journal of Discourses,* 10 (1864): 303; William W. Phelps, *Deseret Almanac: For the Year of Our Lord, 1852* (Salt Lake City: W. Richards, [1851]), 38; Richard L. Bushman, *Joseph Smith and the Beginnings of Mormonism* (Urbana: University of Illinois Press, 1984), 162-63, 241n55; Jay A. Parry and Larry E. Morris, *The Mormon Book of Lists* (Salt Lake City: Bookcraft, 1987), 7; Quinn, *Origins of Power,* 22-26.

On the other hand, Orson Pratt, *An Interesting Account of Several Remarkable Visions, and of the Late Discovery of Ancient American Records,* 2d Amer. ed. (New York: Joseph W. Harrison, 1841), 24-5, referred only to the restoration of authority by a single angel, John the Baptist; cf. Joseph Smith III and Heman C. Smith, *History of the Church of Jesus Christ of Latter Day Saints* (Lamoni, Iowa: RLDS Church, 1897), 1:64-65: "There is no historical evidence of such an event. Nor is there any evidence that Peter, James, and John were present, either when the instruction was given to ordain or when the ordination actually took place. The only historical account of their appearance is in the epistle quoted from above.... It is not safe then to write historically that Joseph Smith and Oliver Cowdery were ever ordained literally under the hands of Peter, James, and John. He who does so[,] writes recklessly and without sufficient evidence upon which to base his conclusion."

49. See Letter 10, p. 474.

50. See Notebook 7, p. 413.

51. See Letter 10, p. 479, including his further observation that "no such statement is

Actually, these observations, which can be characterized as *descriptive* statements, are consistent with the findings of LDS and RLDS (now Community of Christ) scholars who have compared the 1833 Book of Commandments with the Doctrine and Covenants published from 1835 onward.[52] Among the additions to original texts were references to the appearance of Peter, James, and John and their restoration of priesthood to Joseph Smith and Oliver Cowdery.[53] It is McLellin's *interpretation* of these changes where devout readers may have a problem.

Even more disconcerting, from my point of view, is that in his various presentations he concealed his own complicity in this process. In 1880 he wrote: "But they seemed to think themselves authorized to alter and change what they claimed to be the revelations of the Lord, to an alarming extent." He added: "I think to change the Lord's word is a great crime!"[54] However, this and most of his other accounts in later life only hint at the fact that he had first-hand knowledge of the revisions and did not object to them at the time. In his 1878 letter to Traughber, he specifically acknowledged his role, but without specifying its implications:

> The first of November, 1831, a council was called in Joseph's translating room. I presided, and of course would notice and know all that passed in that council. The object of the council was to determine relative to printing Joseph's revelations. Hours were spent in talking the matter over, and it was finally decided to have them printed. Joseph [Smith], Oliver [Cowdery] and Sidney [Rigdon] were appointed a committee to read them over and prepare them for the press.

He explained further: "In the revelations it was often said, 'Keep these things from the world.' These expressions were taken out, and many

---

in the book of Commandments as that John was ordained by an Angel when eight days old, as you stated. I know the paragraph relative to 'Traveling Bishops, high Priests etc.,' never was printed until 1835, in the book of Covenants. Harp on it as you please."

52. Robert J. Woodford, "A Survey of Textual Changes in the Doctrine and Covenants," in *The Seventh Annual Sidney B. Sperry Symposium: The Doctrine and Covenants* (Provo: Religious Instruction, Brigham Young University, 1979), 27-36; Karl F. Best, "Changes in the Revelations, 1833 to 1835," *Dialogue: A Journal of Mormon Thought* 25 (Spring 1992): 87-112; Richard P. Howard, *Restoration Scriptures: A Study of Their Textual Development,* 2d ed., rev. and enl. (Independence, MO: Herald Publishing House, 1995), 139-66; H. Michael Marquardt, *The Joseph Smith Revelations: Text & Commentary* (Salt Lake City: Signature Books, 1999).

53. Robert J. Woodford, "The Historical Development of the Doctrine and Covenants, Ph.D. diss., Brigham Young University, 1974, 1:392-403; Quinn, *Origins of Power,* 16; Gregory A. Prince, *Power from on High: The Development of Mormon Priesthood* (Salt Lake City: Signature Books, 1995), 10, 29-30.

54. See Notebook 7, pp. 413-14.

other alterations—material alterations—[were] made in their reading. I stood by hours and saw them do this work"[55] In this 1878 letter he specifically acknowledged for the first time that he himself had been there during the entire process of changing the revelations.

Yet this was only the first stage, and McLellin explained what was to come.

> But in April [1832], Joseph and Sidney came to Mo., and held another council, and appointed [William W.] Phelps, [Oliver] Cowdery and [John] Whitmer a committee to read over the revelations and alter them again, when they thought they could better the language. Thus, they were twice altered before they were printed [in 1832-33].[56]

After a mob of Missourians in 1833 destroyed the printing press and nearly all its press run of the Book of Commandments,[57] LDS leaders prepared to publish the thoroughly revised revelations, re-titled Doctrine and Covenants. McLellin was directly involved in the massive 1834-35 revisions of Smith's revelations, and wrote: "Another committee [Sept. 1834] is formed by adding Dr. [Frederick G.] Williams to the former one. This committee revised all the revelations [a third time], and changed them so much that a man would scarcely know them to meet them in a brush-heap!"[58]

What was his attitude while he stood by and watched his colleagues alter the texts of the divine revelations? The answer is contained in the 1878 letter: "But my eyes were holden in those days, because I had confidence in J. Smith." In other words, from 1831 to 1835 McLellin accepted that Joseph and Oliver were divinely "authorized to alter and change what they claimed to be the revelations of the Lord." In his state of mind at the time, this would have been his own faithful perspective. Even his leaving Mormonism in 1836 had nothing to do with changes in the revelations. What upset him was "to see speculation, pride and folly, drinking to excess by the leaders, &c, &c. I made up my mind to leave."[59] Decades later, when he no longer had that faith and his eyes no longer

55. See Letter 22, p. 510.

56. Ibid.

57. For more on this incident, see Ronald E. Romig and John H. Seibert, "First Impressions: The Independence, Missouri, Printing Operation, 1832-33," *John Whitmer Historical Journal* 10 (1990): 51-66; James B. Allen and Glen M. Leonard, *The Story of the Latter-day Saints* (Salt Lake City: Deseret Book, 1992), 94-95; Robert J. Woodford, "Book of Commandments," in Ludlow, *Encyclopedia of Mormonism,* 1:138.

58. See Letter 22, pp. 510-11.

59. See Letter 8, p. 459; also in Letter 1, pp. 435-36.

"were holden," he condemned the textual alterations as fraudulent.[60] In 1880 he concluded: "If any man had the original as first given and there read the alterations, he could not help being surprised at their changes. And why sane men should act so I cant conceive"[61] In fact, one must assume he knew very well why sane men acted in such a way because he had been one of them.

Another example of McLellin's failure to acknowledge his own participation in events that he later condemned concerns Joseph's and Oliver's visions in the Kirtland Temple. McLellin wrote: "All the Apostles of Christ at Jerusalem, and all his Disciples in America saw, heard, and felt, hence they could bear a firm witness and testimony that they most positively knew what they declared. Did Smith & Cowdery thus know? They did not. They never in the early days of the church so professed or declared."[62] Joseph Smith's manuscript diary of 3 April 1836 reads to the contrary:

> They saw the Lord standing upon the breast work of the pulpit before them, and under his feet was a paved work of pure gold, in color like amber: his eyes were as a flame of fire; the hair of his head was like the pure snow, his countenance shone above the brightness of the sun, and his voice was as the sound of the rushing of great waters, even the Voice of Jehovah, saying, I am the first and the last, I am he who liveth, I am he who was slain.

After the record of this theophany, Joseph Smith's diary described the appearance of angels who proclaimed themselves to be Moses, Elijah, and Elias. This was in the handwriting of Warren A. Cowdery,[63] who rejected Smith's leadership within two years. The Utah church published the above passage twenty-eight years before McLellin wrote his objection to Smith's claims, and the text was added to the 1876 Doctrine and Covenants.[64]

---

60. As observed by Best, "Changes in the Revelations," 98, 107, such changes could be interpreted as "either a clarification or a fraud."

61. See Notebook 7, p. 414.

62. Ibid., p. 424.

63. Jessee, *Papers of Joseph Smith,* 2:208n2, 209, 538; Lyndon W. Cook, *The Revelations of the Prophet Joseph Smith: A Historical and Biographical Commentary of the Doctrine and Covenants* (Salt Lake City: Deseret Book Co., 1985), 215, 220.

64. Cook, *Revelations of Joseph Smith,* 220. Unfortunately, an entry in Ludlow, *Encyclopedia of Mormonism,* 1:419, has misled all readers who have consulted it about D&C 110. In his article, "Doctrine and Covenants: Sections 109-110," S. Michael Wilcox claimed this vision-revelation was "first published one week after the events it described in the *Messenger and Advocate.*" As the only bibliographic source for his article, Wilcox listed "Sperry, Sidney B. *Doctrine and Covenants Compendium.* Salt Lake City, 1960." Contrary to Wilcox, no allu-

Nevertheless, correspondence with an eyewitness substantiates McLellin's sensational testimony about another event in the Kirtland temple during the spring of 1836. To Orson Pratt, then a member of the Quorum of the Twelve in Utah, McLellin wrote: "Orson, you cannot have forgotten the scenes of drunkenness during the pretended enduement in Kirtland in 1836. I shall never forget them...."[65] As McLellin later elaborated, drunkenness was the unintended consequence of the assembled elders drinking too much sacramental wine on empty stomachs after fasting.[66] Devout believers will want to dismiss McLellin's account as false, especially his description of the inebriated nausea of Samuel H. Smith, brother of the founding prophet and witness of the Book of Mormon.[67] However, the letter to Apostle Pratt indicates a shared knowledge of this embarrassing event.

Yet again, his letter of January 1879 admitted that McLellin was also partly responsible for this drunkenness in the Kirtland temple. To Traughber, he wrote: "The Twelve were required to take large servers, and set glasses of wine and lumps of bread, and go through the house and serve the brethren. I did my part of the serving."[68] In other words, he was among those responsible for having served too much wine to the fasting men, something which undoubtedly embarrassed him in retrospect.

In the last dated letter in this collection, McLellin admonished Mormon antagonist James T. Cobb as follows: "I know a man can sit down and find crookedness in almost any thing by prying closely into it."[69] It was wise advice and unusually temperate. That said, his treatment of the drunkenness in the temple would fall into the same category of hyper-criticism.

Of course, he wanted to emphasize the more substantive issue of truthfulness or falsehood in later claims about heavenly manifestations in the temple. On this score, it is interesting that he conflated several solemn assemblies and successive days of temple dedication into one incident, leaving the reader to wonder whether he was implying that the

---

sion to Section 110, nor quote from it, appeared in the *Messenger and Advocate* issues of April-May 1836, nor was this claimed by Sperry, at least not in the 1960 second edition, pp. 596-606, which I consulted.

65. See Letter 1, p. 436.

66. See Notebook 7, pp. 421-22; Letter 12, p. 494.

67. See Letter 12, p. 494.

68. See Letter 23, p. 516.

69. See Letter 26, postscript, pp. 522-23.

drunkenness was representative or anomalous. From Joseph Smith, we read, in addition to the previously quoted account of the April 1836 service, that at an earlier temple gathering on 21 January he saw "the Father and the Son," and "I saw father Adam, and Abraham and Michael." In fact, "many" others in attendance are said to have seen "glorious visions also,—angels ministered unto them, as well as my self," and "some of them saw the face of the Saviour...."[70]

These reports were not limited to Mormonism's elite. For example, a convert of six months, Stephen Post recorded in January 1836 that "some saw visions and angels[—]many Angels were in the room which were seen by some who had strong faith." After the temple dedication on the morning of 27 March, Post wrote: "President F. G. Williams arose & testified that in the A.M. an angel of God came into the window (at the back of the pulpit) while Pr. Rigdon was at prayer & took his seat between him and Father Joseph Smith sen[ior] & remained there during the prayer." This visionary claim was even in Kirtland's newspaper of March 1836. Post recorded that during the evening, "Angels of God came into the room, [and] cloven tongues rested upon some of the Servants of the Lord, like unto fire...."[71] For nearly five months, there continued to be reports of metaphysical manifestations in the Kirtland temple.[72]

One may legitimately disbelieve these testimonials or dismiss them as delusional, but McLellin denied that such claims even existed: "When that noble structure the Temple in Kirtland was dedicated, after only being partly finished, it was done without any power being sent forth, or manifested in any degree to the large congregation assembled in it. I was present and know what I say."[73] Since even the rank-and-file made contemporary notations about spiritual events in the temple at this time, it is difficult to believe that Apostle McLellin was unaware of these reports from January through the spring of 1836. It would have been more accu-

---

70. See Faulring, *American Prophet's Record*, 118-19, 120; Jessee, *Papers of Joseph Smith*, 2:156-57, 158. The words "and Michael" have been deleted from LDS D&C 137:5.

71. Stephen Post, Diary, summary for 28-31 Jan., 27 Mar., 29 Mar. 1836, LDS Archives; also microfilm copy, Marriott Library; *Latter Day Saints Messenger and Advocate*, Mar. 1836, 281 ("President F. G. Williams bore record that a Holy Angel of God came and set between him and J. Smith sen.").

72. Roger D. Launius, *The Kirtland Temple: A Historical Narrative* (Independence, Mo: Herald Publishing House, 1986), 62-71; Karl Ricks Anderson, *Joseph Smith's Kirtland: Eyewitness Accounts* (Salt Lake City: Deseret Book, 1989), 111-13, 169-77, 182-85, including a one-page summary of experiences reported in the temple to 1 May 1837; Charles C. Rich, diary, 16 May 1836, Lee Library.

73. See Letter 12, p. 493.

rate (and charitable) for McLellin to say that he saw no otherworldly manifestations himself, even though others made such claims.

Five months after the temple dedication, McLellin abandoned the church to which he had devoted almost exactly five years of his life. In the last document of this collection, he explained: "I left the church in Aug. 1836, not because I disbelieved the Book [of Mormon] or the (then) doctrines preached or held by the Church, but because the Leading men to a great extent left their religion and run into and after speculation, pride, and popularity!"[74] At this time he gave his ministerial license to Joseph Smith as a sign of his formal withdrawal from Mormonism, but received it back later.

The return of his LDS ministerial license is another example of McLellin's selective memory. "I wrote a letter to J. Smith, and sent him my license; but they returned it to me two years afterward, and I have it yet." He added: "I never united with Joseph after I then quit him, although they sent me back my license; but this was through the influence of the Twelve. They could not bear the idea of having one leave their number and company."[75] He accurately stated that the Twelve wanted him to return to activity and initiated contact with him for that purpose. The fact that their request occurred within months of his departure, rather than years, is relatively unimportant to the accuracy of his reminiscence. However, the wording of his response to the apostles in January 1837 is crucial: "Suffice it to say,–I am sorry for the course that I have pursued.–Can You, Will you forgive me? Will Brother Joseph forgive me? And will the Church forgive me? If so write to me immediately and let me know it. And please to obtain from President Smith my licence and send it to me, so that I may again feel that I have authority to lift up my voice in the midst of this generation."[76] Rather than receiving back his apostolic license as an unsolicited gesture, he was the one who requested that the Twelve return it to him. Rather than remaining aloof from the leadership after August 1836, McLellin asked Joseph Smith's forgiveness in 1837.

---

74. See Letter 26, postscript, pp. 522-23. The extensively revised revelations in the 1835 Doctrine and Covenants were obviously among "the (then) doctrines preached or held by the Church" in 1836, and by this statement he did not disbelieve those revised revelations at the time he left Mormonism.

75. See Letter 22, p. 513; also Donald Q. Cannon, "Licensing in the Early Church," *Brigham Young University Studies* 22 (Winter 1982): 96-105. The nineteenth-century spelling was often "licence."

76. McLellin to "My dear old Friends" [Quorum of Twelve], 24 Jan. 1837, in Shipps and Welch, *Journals of McLellin,* 230.

Later that same year, Kirtland's economy crashed, after which the church experienced massive disaffections among the leaders and members. With one exception, McLellin's statements in this collection add little to our understanding of the community's land speculation, commercialism, and disastrous experiment in banking. Aside from his tone, which is hostile, he is consistent with other eyewitnesses and with modern scholarship.[77] However, he does add one anecdote that conveys in graphic details the materialism that gripped LDS headquarters in the mid-1830s:

> Soon fine dressing and fine parties were the go; and soon a fine ride was determined upon. Some fifteen couples hired fine carriages, [with] fine harness and fine horses and when all was in readiness, they sat out for Cleveland, some 19 miles distant. They drove round and round through the streets. People gazed and inquired: "Who's all this?" "O, it's Joe Smith, the Mormon prophet, and his company." They put up at a first class tavern; called for a room, refreshments, and something to drink. Some of them became intoxicated and they broke up about $200 worth of dishes and furniture. Next morning they paid their bill, and sat out for home. They stopped at Euclid—half-way—and took dinner, and again drank freely; and after they sat out for home, they commenced running [i.e., racing the] horses and turned over a buggy and broke it up so they had to haul it home on a wagon. But all went swimmingly. We are great merchantmen, money plenty! But no confessions were ever required or made in the church for this wild goose chase.[78]

Assuming the account is true—which is to say that McLellin's sources accurately recounted what happened—it may offer some insight into the attitudes of the Mormon elite before Kirtland's economy crashed. What personal knowledge did McLellin have of this event? He told Traughber: "My lady was not in condition, so I did not go on this ride; but two of the men who did go told me about it"[79] He had direct knowledge of the ex-

---

77. Parley P. Pratt to Joseph Smith, 23 May 1837, in Richard Livesey, *An Exposure of the Mormons ...* (Preston, Eng.: J. Livesey 1838), 9; Mary Fielding Smith letters to Mercy R. Fielding Thompson, July-Oct. 1837, in Kenneth W. Godfrey, Audrey M. Godfrey, and Jill Mulvay Derr, eds., *Women's Voices: An Untold History of the Latter-day Saints, 1830-1900* (Salt Lake City: Deseret Book, 1982), 60-68; Marvin S. Hill, C. Keith Rooker, and Larry T. Wimmer, "The Kirtland Economy Revisited: A Market Critique of Sectarian Economics," *Brigham Young University Studies* 17 (Summer 1977): 391-475; Anderson, *Joseph Smith's Kirtland,* 193-223; Wimmer, "Kirtland Economy," in Ludlow, *Encyclopedia of Mormonism,* 2:792-93; Allen and Leonard, *Story of the Latter-day Saints,* 117-25.

78. See Letter 22, pp. 512-13; also Letter 12, p. 490.

79. See Letter 22, p. 513.

cursion because he was invited, but we must depend on two unnamed participants to judge the accuracy of the telling.

On the other hand, numerous sources verify what McLellin tells about the plight of dissenters, including witnesses to the Book of Mormon, who were forced to flee with their wives from Far West, Missouri, in June 1838.[80] Sidney Rigdon of the First Presidency warned the dissenters in a sermon,[81] after which First Presidency counselor Hyrum Smith and Assistant Counselor John Smith joined with eighty other Mormons in signing a written ultimatum to the dissenters: "depart, or a more fatal calamity shall befall you." This document became part of the court record in Missouri.[82] Ebenezer Robinson later wrote an autobiography in which he discussed signing this document.[83] Speaking of this, Joseph Smith's "Scriptory Book" noted: "These men took warning, and soon they were seen bounding over the prairie like the scape Goat to carry of[f] their own sins."[84] Understandably, John Whitmer and David Whitmer were less jocular in describing their panicky departure.[85] McLellin told Traughber, "Next morning they reached my house, and I entertained them for about a week, until they got their wives away from Far West."[86]

---

80. Ibid., p. 514.

81. Anson Call, statement to B. H. Roberts (First Council of Seventy) and John M. Whitaker (Council secretary), 30 Dec. 1885, typescript, 1, Whitaker file, Utah State Historical Society; John Corrill, *A Brief History of the Church of Christ of Latter Day Saints, (Commonly Called Mormons;) including an Account of Their Doctrine and Discipline; with the Reasons of the Author for Leaving the Church* (St. Louis, Mo.: by the author, 1839), 30; Orson Hyde, letter of 21 Oct. 1844, in *Nauvoo Neighbor,* 4 Dec. 1844, 1; John E. Thompson, "The Far West Dissenters and the Gamblers at Vicksburg: An Examination of the Documentary Evidence and Historical Context of Sidney Rigdon's Salt Sermon," *Restoration Studies* 5 (Jan. 1986): 21-27; William G. Hartley, *My Best for the Kingdom: History and Autobiography of John Lowe Butler, a Mormon Frontiersman* (Salt Lake City: Aspen Books, 1993), 46; Richard S. Van Wagoner, *Sidney Rigdon: A Portrait of Religious Excess* (Salt Lake City: Signature Books, 1994), 220-22.

82. *Document Containing the Correspondence, Orders &c In Relation to the Disturbances With the Mormons* ...(Fayette, Mo.: Boon's Lick Democrat, 1841), 103-07; Quinn, *Origins of Power,* 334n59, 335n60; D. Michael Quinn, "National Culture, Personality, and Theocracy in the Early Mormon Culture of Violence," *JWHA Nauvoo Conference Special Edition* (Independence, Mo.: John Whitmer Historical Association, 2002), 159-86.

83. Ebenezer Robinson, "Items of Personal History of the Editor," *The Return,* Oct. 1889, Feb. 1890, 145-47, 218-19.

84. Faulring, *American Prophet's Record,* 187; Jessee, *Papers of Joseph Smith,* 2:249, 249n1.

85. F. Mark McKiernan and Roger D. Launius, eds., *An Early Latter Day Saint History: The Book of John Whitmer, Kept by Commandment* (Independence, Mo.: Herald Publishing House, 1980), 165; David Whitmer to "Dear Brethren," ca. 9 Dec. 1886, in *Saints' Herald,* 5 Feb. 1887, 91; Westergren, *From Historian to Dissident,* 183-84.

86. See Letter 22, p. 514.

Furthermore, numerous sources verify McLellin's claim that faithful Mormons robbed and pillaged non-Mormon farms and settlements in 1838.[87] For example, lifelong Mormons like James Bracken, John L. Butler, Moses Clawson, Dimick B. Huntington, Oliver B. Huntington, Benjamin F. Johnson, and Justus Morse wrote manuscript accounts of their own participation in these Mormon raids against the farms and villages of non-LDS Missourians.[88] McLellin examined some of this booty that had been stockpiled by Mormons at Far West, "as many as ten wagon loads of goods." At the site of this stolen property he met "an old man who said he came about 60 miles for his goods." However, this dissenting apostle provided the context: "But in justice I must say it was a state of warfare, and the old setlers—the Missourians[—]robbed the L.D.S., and burned down their houses, and destroyed their thousands [of dollars worth of property]. It was a scene of murder and bloodshed all around."[89] In his letter to Apostle Pratt, he added the following comment: "But their bad conduct did not, nor could not justify the church in their course."[90]

Nevertheless, as another example of McLellin's demonstrable pattern of omitting his own role in activities he condemned, he had also aided the anti-Mormon Missourians. A contemporary newspaper reported that he led an October 1838 search of Joseph Smith's Far West home "to confiscate books and papers that might prove damaging to the Mormons."[91] Beginning in 1864, traditional Mormon histories claimed McLellin "took an active part with the mob in Missouri, in robbing and driving the Saints,"[92] and even "expressed the desire to do violence to the person of Joseph Smith while the latter was confined in

87. Ibid.; Notebook 7, p. 393.

88. James B. Bracken Sr., statement in Andrus and Andrus, *They Knew the Prophet,* 79; Moses Clawson, "Reminiscences," Lee Library; Dimick B. Huntington, "Journal from 1808 to Salt Lake City," Lee Library; Oliver B. Huntington manuscript autobiography, book 1, 37-38, Lee Library; Benjamin F. Johnson, *My Life's Review* (Independence, Mo.: Zion's Printing and Publishing, 1947), 39; Justus Morse affidavit, 23 Mar. 1887, LDS Archives, and complete transcription in Marquardt Collection, fd 3, box 22, Marriott Library; Stephen C. LeSueur, *The 1838 Mormon War in Missouri* (Columbia, Mo.: University of Missouri Press, 1987), 119, 134-36; Hartley, *My Best for the Kingdom,* 42, 69; E. Dale LeBaron, *Benjamin Franklin Johnson: Friend to the Prophets* (Provo: Grandin Book, 1997), 21.

89. See Notebook 7, p. 393; Letter 22, p. 515.

90. See Letter 1, p. 437.

91. *Missouri Republican,* 20 Nov. 1838, quoted in LeSueur, *The 1838 Mormon War,* 180; Howard, "Mormonism's 'Stormy Petrel'"; Van Wagoner, *Sidney Rigdon,* 225n32.

92. "History of William E. McLellin," *Latter Day Saints' Millennial Star,* 17 Dec. 1864, 809, quoted in Andrew Jenson, *Latter-day Saint Biographical Encyclopedia* (Salt Lake City: Andrew Jenson History Co., 1901), 1:83.

Liberty prison." According to Mormon sources, the non-Mormon sheriff prevented this "flogging."[93] On the other hand, McLellin denied such allegations and told Traughber he refused to obey a Missouri officer's instructions to "knock him down!" while Joseph Smith was a prisoner.[94]

There are contradictory statements from McLellin within the current collection itself, among which McLellin's most emphatic statements about priesthood office changed dramatically over time. A change of view is legitimate, but McLellin did not acknowledge that he altered his position on such fundamental matters. For example, his 1854-57 notebook, which was intended for publication, stated: "The kingdom of heaven cannot fully exist among men without three men at its head, called of God by the voice of revelation, and acknowledged in their office by the voice of the kingdom–to stand as a council of first presidency."[95] By contrast, in 1880 McLellin wrote: "I dont believe, in setting up three men as first Presidents of the church, instead of twelve Apostles at the Head."[96]

During these last decades of his life, his views likewise changed concerning modern apostles. In 1854-57 he wrote: "And now again in this age when all the councils of the 'church of Christ' stand in their proper places, there will be a twelve, to bear the same relation in his kingdom which the same council of men did in ancient times. They will be apostles, yes, special witnesses of the work of the preparation for the second coming of Christ."[97] About 1864 he enthused: "The Apostolship was the highest legal ministerial authority ever exercised in the 'Church of Christ,' at its commencement, and in the great work of the last days, the Apostles will be looked up to as the 'mouth-piece of God' to all true believers."[98] In contrast to this affirmation of "ministerial authority," he wrote eight years later that "an Apostle is not an administrative offi-

93. "History of McLellin," 809. The narrative reads: "While Joseph was in prison at Richmond, Mo., McLellin, who was a large and active man, went to the sheriff and asked for the privilege of flogging the Prophet. Permission was granted on condition that Joseph would fight. The sheriff made known to Joseph McLellin's earnest request, to which Joseph consented, if his irons were taken off. McLellin then refused to fight unless he could have a club, to which Joseph Smith was perfectly willing; but the sheriff would not allow them to fight on such unequal terms." This was Roberts's source in writing of this episode in *History of the Church,* 3:32n; *Comprehensive History of the Church,* 2:443.

94. See Letter 15, p. 502.

95. See Notebook 1, p. 175.

96. See Notebook 7, p. 381.

97. See Notebook 1, p. 176.

98. See Letter 3, p. 447.

cer."[99] In 1880 he concluded: "I do not believe, that he [Joseph Smith] or any man ever had authority to appoint and ordain Apostles of Christ."[100]

Equally interesting in his 1854-57 summary of faith-promoting events which would occur before the Millennium, he listed "the coming forth of ancient sacred records" and "the re-organization of the church of Christ," as well as "the endowment of the Lord's ministerial authorities with power from on high ..."[101] His list so closely paralleled LDS sacred history, it has to be seen as favorable commentary on the early days of Mormonism. By 1870-71, when he no longer saw the possibility for reformation or revitalization of Mormonism according to his preferences, he was able to write: "As to the endowment in Kirtland, I state positively, it was no endowment from God."[102] In fact, McLellin reversed his views about this spiritual "endowment" within weeks or months of having positively referenced it in his earliest notebook. To Orson Pratt on 29 April 1854, he wrote that "in 1836 they sought an endowment from on high. But I have no fears to say, they made a perfect failure."[103]

McLellin's most extraordinary reversal involved Book of Mormon witness David Whitmer's right to succeed the founding prophet. In 1869 McLellin wrote: "I believe David Whitmer was legally and properly appointed and ordained on the 8th day of July, 1834, by Joseph Smith ... and that he holds that authority sacred to-day"[104] Incredibly, by 1878 McLellin could write that "Smith's ordination of David Whitmer [as] Prophet & Seer on the 8th day of July 1834 were all without authority from God, all wrong, null & void."[105] In an 1879 letter to Traughber, he repeated his new belief that Whitmer's 1834 ordination had been "illegal and void" and was "outside of the revelations of God to man."[106] However, from 1847 to the early 1870s, McLellin had reported that he himself received revelations affirming Whitmer's ordination.[107] A letter in this collection gives the exact text of McLellin's 1870 revelation on this matter: "Did I not say to you through my servant David that I re-

---

99. See Letter 12, p. 492.

100. See Notebook 7, p. 380.

101. See Notebook 1, pp. 146-47.

102. See Letter 10, p. 476.

103. See Letter 1, p. 435. This letter's interpretative change allows more precise dating of Notebook 1 to the first months of 1854.

104. See Letter 6, p. 455.

105. See Notebook 5, p. 324.

106. See Letter 24, p. 518.

107. For McLellin's revelation of 10 Feb. 1847, see *Ensign of Liberty,* Jan. 1848, 56; Aug. 1849, 100-01, 104; Smith and Smith, *History of the Church,* 3:85.

quired you to fulfil all the **ministry** to which I the Lord had caused you to be ordained in in my church; and also to fulfil all the special revelations which I had ever given you[?]"[108] Since 1846, it was William E. McLellin who prodded the reluctant Whitmer to form a church based on the 1834 ordination.[109] However, when Whitmer did so in 1876, it was without involving McLellin, and his former advocate lost no time in repudiating the ordination on which Whitmer's new organization was based.[110] It seems clear that wounded pride was the source of this reversal.

In fact, by 1879 McLellin had repudiated so many former beliefs that only his faith in the Bible and Book of Mormon remained. Traughber wrote:

> The poor old man, after having run about after pretended prophets for years, finally laid them all aside who pretended that God had commissioned them to rule men. The Book of Mormon, was, when he died, March, 1883, the only part of all Mormonism that he gave unqualified assent to; and I believe that if he had had a few years more of healthy life, he would have freed himself of the last vestige of the folly of all Mormon pretensions ...[111]

It is impossible to know whether Traughber was right about McLellin's trajectory–whether the former apostle would have eventually rejected everything Mormon. Although speculation on Traughber's part, this conclusion was based on observing the path McLellin was following.

A reporter of events and witness of decisive moments in early Mormonism, McLellin nevertheless remained behind while the bulk of the LDS hierarchy moved to Illinois and then to Utah. In Missouri and elsewhere, he remained in close contact with and sometimes even in neighborly proximity to such important figures as David and John Whitmer, whose observations extended to Mormonism's beginnings. McLellin

---

108. See Letter 9, p. 466.

109. McLellin to David Whitmer, 2 Dec. 1846, in *Ensign of Liberty,* Apr. 1847, 17-20; McLellin statement, *Ensign of Liberty*, Mar. 1848, 78; Hiram Page to William [E. McLellin], 6 June, 8 Oct. 1848; Hiram Page to Alfred Bonny, Isaac N. Aldrich, and M. C. Ishem, 24 June 1849, in *Olive Branch,* Aug. 1849, 28; Quinn, *Origins of Power,* 188-89; Romig, "David Whitmer," and Howard, "William E. McLellin," in Launius and Thatcher, *Differing Visions,* 38, 88-89, 92-94, 96.

110. Ebbie L. V. Richardson, "David Whitmer: A Witness to the Divine Authenticity of the Book of Mormon," M.A. thesis, Brigham Young University, 1952, 130, 132-34, with a list of elders and priests but not McLellin; Quinn, *Origins of Power,* 189; also differing interpretations in Romig, "David Whitmer," and Howard, "William E. McLellin," in Launius and Thatcher, *Differing Visions,* 38-39, 42n62, 96-97, 101n58.

111. See Traughber's annotation, "Dr. McLellan's Change of Views," Notebook 1, p. 189.

could confidently report what they told him about the processes by which Joseph Smith dictated his translation of the Book of Mormon years before McLellin's own 1831 conversion. When the new church had two gathering places in the early 1830s, one in Kirtland and one in Independence, McLellin was frequently in both. When Joseph Smith dictated "Thus saith the Lord" revelations from 1831 to 1835, McLellin was in the room, at least when he was in town and not on a preaching assignment from the prophet. When Smith wanted those revelations prepared for publication, McLellin was on the committee that oversaw their preparation and "revision." When the new Quorum of the Twelve Apostles needed a secretary to record the minutes of its meetings in 1835, they chose him. When the first Mormon temple was dedicated in 1836, he participated in every meeting. When some of the highest LDS leaders became disaffected in Kirtland in 1837 and in Far West in 1838, he was also at their side. He joined the "old settlers" of Missouri in the religious civil war that resulted in the near-execution of Smith and forced exile of all non-dissenting Mormons from the state.

As a chronicler of early Mormonism, McLellin had crucial access and participation. If his decades-later reporting needs cross-referencing to check for completeness and bias, that is also true for every other account by a participant remembering back into the past. It would please McLellin to know that he remains a controversial, aggravating, and essential source for early Mormonism.

5

REINVENTING MCLELLIN

A Historiographical Review

JOHN-CHARLES DUFFY

Historical literature on Mormon apostle William E. McLellin has been sparse, and much of what exists has been written only recently. The monumental bibliography *Studies in Mormon History* lists twenty relevant sources–a relatively small number–and the online update to the bibliography adds only two more entries after 1997. A little over half of this material was published after 1993; indeed half a dozen of the entries come from the 1994 volume in which *BYU Studies* and University of Illinois Press co-published McLellin's missionary journals. Of the ten entries predating 1993, only a handful are centrally about McLellin; in the others, he plays a minor role.[1]

In short: Mormon historians have had little to say about William McLellin until recently. In the early 1990s, there was a minor surge of interest, a hefty portion of it connected with his missionary journals. The present volume, containing the apostle's notebooks and letters, rides the same wave. Why this sudden interest in a formerly obscure figure from Mormonism's early history? The answer: a confluence of developments affecting the LDS Church during the 1980s and 1990s that unexpectedly made McLellin's life and writings useful for supporting

---

JOHN-CHARLES DUFFY is a William N. Reynolds Fellow pursuing doctoral work at the University of North Carolina at Chapel Hill, where he is currently helping coordinate the American Religions Timeline Project. He has published on Mormon topics in the *American Transcendental Quarterly*, *John Whitmer Historical Journal*, *Sunstone*, and elsewhere and received honors from the Mormon History Association (Lester E. Bush Award for Best Thesis) and Dialogue Foundation (New Voices Award for New Writers). In addition, he has presented and critiqued papers related to Mormon history at meetings of the American Academy of Religion and American Society of Church History.

1. James B. Allen, Ronald W. Walker, and David J. Whittaker, *Studies in Mormon History, 1830-1997: An Indexed Bibliography* (Urbana and Provo: University of Illinois Press and BYU Smith Institute for LDS History, 2000); *Studies in Mormon History*, on-line at http://mormonhistory.byu.edu.

various agendas of LDS officials, scholars, and intellectuals. Those developments include the Hofmann forgery/murder scandal of the mid-1980s during which Hofmann claimed to have found McLellin's long-lost journals; the serendipitous discovery of the real McLellin journals in the First Presidency vault the following year; the rise of a new form of LDS religiosity centered on Jesus Christ and the Book of Mormon as a witness of Christ; concern on the part of Latter-day Saints to clarify that theirs is a Christian religion; the appearance of revisionist histories that placed occult practices at the center of Mormon origins; and much-publicized conflicts between some LDS scholars or "intellectuals" and the leadership of their church.

What relevance does this have to what we know about William McLellin? In fact, as Latter-day Saints promoted a more self-consciously Christian message, wrote critical reviews of histories of the occult in early Mormonism, and debated the place of intellectualism and dissent in the church, they found McLellin's writings to be a convenient source for evidence of precedent for their positions. In the process, McLellin was reinvented—again and again. Before the 1990s, he had been a bit player in Mormon historiography, usually typecast in the role of an arrogant, vicious apostate. The surge of writing about him during the 1990s produced different versions of his life. For the publication of his missionary journals in 1994, he was reclaimed as an apostle whose ministry revealed the Christ-centered nature of Mormonism. Controversies over intellectualism and dissent in the church produced at least three more biographical versions, all corresponding to idealized or stereotypical portraits of intellectuals circulating through LDS discourse in the early 1990s: McLellin as an unfairly maligned intellectual who had used his scholastic gifts in the service of the church; as a brave dissenter who was committed to truth and opposed unjust ecclesiastical power; and as a tragically willful individual who embraced ambiguity to rationalize his unwillingness to obey God's commandments. It remains to be seen whether future studies will break out of these three molds—McLellin as apostate, McLellin as Christian witness, and McLellin as intellectual—to pursue new directions in Mormon history.

"To Act the Part of Judas": McLellin as Apostate

McLellin was a minor but vilified character in the historiography of early Mormonism until recent years. Although he was among the original Quorum of the Twelve, ordained in 1835, he was excommunicated three years later during the Missouri-Mormon war, one of the casualties in the purge of high-ranking, disaffected leaders that included Oliver Cowdery and David Whitmer. Because McLellin never returned to the church, he passed out of the sacred history as far as the Utah-based Saints were concerned. Following Joseph Smith's death, McLellin briefly associated with movements led by Sidney Rigdon and David Whitmer, and he spent his final years in Independence, Missouri, suggesting that he retained some sense of connection to a Mormon community; but he died unaffiliated with any Mormon body.[2]

Two events dominated the standard narrative of McLellin's life in early LDS literature. First, he played a role in events surrounding the revelation canonized as section 67 of the Doctrine and Covenants. In that revelation, received in response to a discussion of the language used in the revelations about to be published as the Book of Commandments, the Lord challenged church elders to write a revelation equal to Joseph Smith's. McLellin, a schoolteacher by profession, accepted the challenge and failed. For a century and a half, this was the most oft-repeated story involving McLellin; it may still be today. McLellin's second most-cited role in the foundational narrative, prior to the historiographical developments of the 1990s, was his participation in mob violence against the Saints during the Missouri-Mormon war. LDS histories reported that McLellin gloated over Joseph Smith and other leaders who had been arrested by Missouri troops and that McLellin requested the privilege of flogging Smith, then allegedly looted Smith's home while the latter was incarcerated.

These representations of McLellin became enshrined in Mormon historiography during the latter half of the nineteenth century thanks to biographical sketches written by Wilford Woodruff, George Q. Cannon, and Andrew Jenson.[3] Repeated in church manuals and other publi-

2. The most substantial McLellin biography to date is Larry C. Porter, "The Odyssey of William Earl McLellin: Man of Diversity, 1806-83," in *The Journals of William E. McLellin, 1831-1836,* eds. Jan Shipps and John W. Welch (Provo and Urbana: BYU Studies and University of Illinois Press, 1994), 291-378.

3. Wilford Woodruff, "History of William McLellin," *Deseret News,* May 12, 1858; George Q. Cannon, *Life of Joseph Smith the Prophet* (1888; Salt Lake City: Deseret Book, 1986), 127, 265, 271; Andrew Jenson, *Historical Record* 5 (Mar. 1886), 38-39. As Professor Grandstaff points out in his review of the revelation episode, Jenson's sketch in the *Historical Record* largely copied Woodruff's account, who in turn took his information from the manuscript copy of the yet unpublished *History of the Church* (Mark R. Grandstaff, "Having More Learning than Sense: William E. McLellin and the Book of Commandments Revisited," *Dialogue: A Journal of Mormon Thought* 26 [Winter 1993], 25-28). It may be apropos that Woodruff was called to the Twelve to fill a vacancy left by the excommunication of the group that included McLellin.

cations over the years, this way of narrating McLellin's life has been replicated as recently as 2001 in the brief biography that appeared in a BYU Religious Studies Center publication, *Prophets and Apostles of the Last Dispensation.*[4] These biographies cast McLellin as an apostate, a stock role in Mormon imagination since Joseph Smith's day. The apostate is characterized by arrogance, violence, and vice (often sexual)–the same qualities assigned to Mormons in nineteenth-century anti-Mormon polemics. In the Mormon imagination, apostasy is always a consequence of personal failing. Andrew Jenson, echoing Wilford Woodruff, explained McLellin's excommunication in 1838 as a result of his having "quit praying and keeping the commandments of the Lord, and indulged himself in his sinful lusts."[5] George Q. Cannon attributed the apostasy of McLellin, Thomas B. Marsh, and others to their being "unable to bear the pressure and to face the terrors of the time," which is to say the horrors of the Missouri war.[6] Useful for slighting McLellin's character was a passage in the Doctrine of Covenants instructing him to "commit not adultery–a temptation with which thou hast been troubled" (66:10). Also useful was an episode in which McLellin reportedly asked permission to fight Joseph Smith on condition that Smith be shackled or that McLellin be allowed to wield a club. Retellings of this incident served to depict McLellin as unscrupulous and cowardly.[7]

When McLellin is made to play the apostate, as in Cannon's *Life of Joseph Smith the Prophet,* his motivations in the episode involving the manufacture of a revelation are assumed to be "vanity and self-conceit." Elder Cannon understood that section 67 was received because McLellin had presumed to "criticize" the language of the prophet's revelations.[8] (As we will see, this understanding was challenged by Professor Mark Grandstaff at the end of the twentieth century.) Understood in these terms, the imitation of divine revelation became a drama not unlike biblical confrontations between Moses and the priests of Pharaoh (Exod. 7-8) or Elijah and the priests of Baal (1 Kings 18). In those stories, God's true prophets were challenged by competitors who tried unsuc-

---

4. Lawrence R. Flake, *Prophets and Apostles of the Last Dispensation* (Provo: BYU Religious Studies Center, 2001), 355-57. Lawrence cites two sources for his information: the edition of McLellin's journals edited by Shipps and Welch and an *LDS Church News* story published shortly after the Hofmann bombings headlined "McLellin Became Enemy of Church."

5. Jenson, *Historical Record,* 39.

6. Cannon, *Life of Joseph Smith,* 265.

7. Jenson, *Historical Record,* 39.

8. Cannon, *Life of Joseph Smith,* 127.

cessfully to work identical wonders. Likewise, McLellin "sacrilegiously essayed to write a commandment in rivalry of those [revelations] bestowed direct from God upon the church. But [McLellin] failed miserably in his audacious effort."[9] The revelation episode showed McLellin was "an apostate 'from the beginning,'" arrogant in his learning, and a man "who allowed flaws in his personality and not in the church or its leaders to eventually lead him astray."[10] A *Church News* article asserted in 1992 that McLellin had exhibited "a proud and rebellious nature."[11]

Narratives of McLellin-as-apostate contain echoes of additional scriptural stories. Grandstaff proposes that "the story of McLellin is typical of a genre which correlates dissent with biblical figures such as Satan, Cain, or Judas or with Book of Mormon characters such as Nehor and Korihor."[12] Elder Cannon, in fact, explicitly described McLellin as having conspired "to act the part of Judas against the prophet." According to Cannon's account, after Smith and other leaders had been arrested, McLellin "taunted them with their impending fate, declaring that there was no hope for them." Possibly there is an echo here of the chief priests and soldiers who taunted Jesus before and during his crucifixion.[13]

A gentler variation on McLellin-as-apostate appeared in 1970 when Larry C. Porter wrote a short piece about the former apostle for the *BYU Studies* feature, "The Historian's Corner." Porter reproduced a letter McLellin had written in 1880 to James Cobb, a detractor who hoped McLellin would help him debunk the Book of Mormon. In this Cobb was disappointed: while McLellin had lost faith in Joseph Smith and all existing churches, he remained passionate in his conviction the Book of Mormon was divine.[14] Porter thus invoked McLellin as a witness who retained his testimony of the Book of Mormon despite having parted ways over other issues. Latter-day Saints were already accustomed to citing to similar effect the testimonies of the Three Witnesses—Oliver Cowdery, Martin Harris, and David Whitmer—all of whom had been excommunicated. McLellin's apostasy was central to Porter's representation of him. However, rather than condemn him, Porter used McLellin's apostate status to lend greater force to the renegade's unflagging testimony of

9. Ibid.

10. Grandstaff, "More Learning than Sense," 24, 26.

11. "Writings Shed Light on Church History," *LDS Church News,* Oct. 24, 1992.

12. Grandstaff, "More Learning than Sense," 45.

13. Cannon, *Life of Joseph Smith,* 265, 271.

14. McLellin's letter to Cobb appears in this volume as Letter 26.

the Book of Mormon.[15] This partial rehabilitation of McLellin foreshadowed a more enthusiastic reclaiming of the lapsed apostle by LDS scholars in the early 1990s.

Judas Becomes Paul: McLellin as Christian Witness

In 1985, McLellin's name was propelled from obscurity into the center of tragedy and scandal when Mark Hofmann claimed to have located boxes of materials McLellin had collected before his death.[16] Among the items in the collection, the document dealer said, were the papyrus fragment containing Facsimile 2 from the Book of Abraham, an Emma Smith affidavit attesting that Joseph Smith's First Vision had occurred in the context of discovering the Book of Mormon rather than in the sacred grove, and the only known copy of an unpublished revelation instructing Smith he could make a substantial amount of money by selling the copyright of the Book of Mormon in Canada, an expectation that proved untrue.

Like other fraudulent finds by Hofmann, the McLellin collection was reputed to contain documents that undermined canonical versions of LDS tradition. Several years before Hofmann's supposed discovery of the McLellin material, Egyptologist Edward Ashment had theorized that Facsimile 2 was a typical funerary text imaginatively doctored by Smith; the alleged discovery of the original papyrus threatened to confirm Ashment's theory.[17] The Emma Smith affidavit promised to lend further credence to an argument already current among detractors and historical revisionists: that the canonical account of Joseph Smith's First Vision was a self-serving elaboration of what had actually been a commonplace conversion experience. And the discovery of the Canadian copyright revelation was bound to throw the spotlight on an embarrassing failure in church history, inviting skepticism about whether Smith was actually directed by God. In addition, Hofmann reported that the collection contained journals written by McLellin during the early years of the church. Coming hard on the heels of Hofmann's discovery of the so-called "salamander letter" and other documents tying the origins of

---

15. Larry C. Porter, "William E. McLellin's Testimony of the Book of Mormon," *BYU Studies* 10 (Summer 1970), 485-87; see also Porter, "Odyssey of McLellin," 292.

16. My summary of these events is synthesized from Linda Sillitoe and Allen Roberts, *Salamander: The Story of the Mormon Forgery Murders,* 2nd ed. (Salt Lake City: Signature Books, 1989), esp. ch. 14; Richard E. Turley, Jr., *Victims: The LDS Church and the Mark Hofmann Case* (Urbana: University of Illinois Press, 1992), esp. ch. 6.

17. Edward H. Ashment, "The Facsimiles of the Book of Abraham: A Reappraisal," *Sunstone,* Dec. 1979, 33-48.

Mormonism to Smith's magical treasure-hunting practices, the discovery of the journals raised the specter of further uncomfortable revelations about early church history.

Steve Christensen, the businessman who had purchased the salamander letter from Hofmann, recognized the "potential damage which this material [the McLellin collection] would cause the Church," according to his journal.[18] Lacking funds to purchase the new material, Christensen brokered a meeting between Hofmann and LDS general authority Hugh Pinnock. Elder Pinnock in turn, after unsuccessfully petitioning Dallin H. Oaks for church funds to purchase the collection,[19] facilitated a nearly $200,000 loan from Zions First National Bank. With the loan, Hofmann could purchase the collection and donate it to the church, just as Christensen had done with the salamander letter. According to the plan Pinnock helped put together, Hofmann would pay the bank loan with funds obtained from the sale of a rare piece of Americana to the Library of Congress. The plan unraveled when the Library of Congress realized the document Hofmann was pitching to them was a forgery. In a desperate bid to evade financial ruin or detection, Hofmann planted the pipe bombs that killed Christensen and Kathleen Sheets, wife of one of Christensen's business associates. Hofmann himself was wounded by a third pipe bomb, a turn of events that led eventually to his exposure as a forger. Hofmann's McLellin collection apparently never existed, not even as a forgery.

After the bombings brought McLellin into the news, but before Hofmann was known to be a forger, the church tried to limit the potential for damage. An *LDS Church News* headline within two weeks of the bombings informed readers bluntly that "McLellin Became Enemy of Church." By implication, McLellin was such an unreliable witness–one with an axe to grind–that whatever challenges to church history his collection might raise should be viewed skeptically.[20]

Within a few years, however, Mormon scholars promoted an about-face regarding McLellin's reliability as a historical witness. This reversal was the result of a dramatic and *bona fide* new documents discovery. In March 1986, employees of the church's historical department, in the course of seeking information about McLellin in response to the Hofmann scandal, discovered that McLellin's real journals were already

18. Sillitoe and Roberts, *Salamander,* 326.

19. On Pinnock asking Oaks for church funds to purchase the collection and Oaks's negative response, see Turley, *Victims,* 192.

20. "McLellin Became Enemy of Church," *LDS Church News,* Oct. 27, 1985.

in the First Presidency's vault. Joseph F. Smith had authorized their purchase in 1908 from a former RLDS member who had obtained them from McLellin's widow. President Smith's desire was to keep the journals out of "unfriendly hands"—the same concern Hofmann exploited eighty years later. Once in hand, the journals were locked away in the First Presidency vault and forgotten for three-quarters of a century until researchers happened onto correspondence regarding the purchase.[21]

Although the journals were plainly relevant to the Hofmann prosecution, the church chose not to announce their existence for six years. In 1991 a course of action was agreed upon whereby the documents were released to LDS historian Richard Bushman at Columbia University and to friendly non-LDS historian Jan Shipps at Indiana University–Purdue University Indianapolis. Shipps later explained that this was done to funnel media inquiries "to historians not connected with the LDS Church Historical Department."[22] Finally in October 1992, the *Church News* broke the story of the journals' discovery.[23] By then, Bushman and Shipps had confirmed the journals contained nothing startling. Moreover, Shipps had received permission from church leaders to publish a scholarly edition, which appeared in 1994, co-edited by Shipps and John Welch, founder of the Foundation for Ancient Research and Mormon Studies (FARMS) and recently appointed editor of *BYU Studies*. The journals were jointly published by *BYU Studies* and the University of Illinois Press, the church retaining copyright.

The circumstances invite one to interpret publication of the journals as an attempt to save face after the Hofmann scandals—to show the church had nothing to hide and nothing to fear from its history. Shipps's editorial introduction acknowledged frankly that when Hofmann claimed to have discovered McLellin's journals, "many ... expected—and some feared—that any contemporaneous documents in a collection of McLellin's papers would ... add to a perception of early Mormonism as a hotbed of occultism and hermetic hocus-pocus."[24]

The real journals, felicitously, presented nothing of the kind. On the contrary, McLellin's journals depicted Mormonism in a way Latter-day Saints at the end of the twentieth century would be inclined to find especially congenial. Shipps explained:

21. Richard E. Turley, Jr., "The Provenance of William E. McLellin's Journals," in Shipps and Welch, eds., *Journals of McLellin,* 257-61; Turley, *Victims,* 248-50.

22. Jan Shipps, "Another Side of Early Mormonism," in Shipps and Welch, eds., *Journals of McLellin,* xiii.

23. "Writings Shed Light on Church History," *LDS Church News,* Oct. 24, 1992.

24. Shipps, "Another Side," 3.

> Instead, what these narratives from the 1830s depict is a struggling missionary band preaching not only a millennialist message that, to be sure, reflected the importance of the coming forth of the Book of Mormon as a signal that the end was near, but also a message whose true anchor was nonetheless the Christian scriptures.... [The journals] are not significant because they either extend knowledge about or challenge early Mormonism's radical and esoteric aspect; they do not speak to this side of the story at all. They are important because they point to an often overlooked (or summarily dismissed) part of the story of early Mormonism, i.e., the movement's rootedness in Christianity and the extent to which its representatives preached the Mormon gospel within that familiar framework.[25]

In a word, the McLellin journals attested that Mormons were Christian. Contrary to widespread perceptions in the present, Mormonism fell within the "familiar" American Christian framework, its "true anchor" the Christian Bible. The Mormon religion was not, in its essence, "radical" or "esoteric." To use an expression of Gordon B. Hinckley made famous by *Newsweek*, Mormons were not "weird."[26] John Welch made the point more directly than Shipps in his introductory essay: "These documents confirm that the early Mormon experience was not eccentric or aberrational, but was deeply rooted in the Bible, in the gospel of Jesus Christ ..."[27]

The McLellin journals' portrayal of early Mormonism as Christian was welcomed by twentieth-century Latter-day Saints because it coincided with their self-conscious emphasis on Christ-centeredness since the late 1970s. This emphasis was partly in reaction to an increase in anti-Mormon polemics by Protestant evangelicals and fundamentalists who were alarmed by Mormonism's increasing public profile outside the Intermountain West and concerned to clarify the boundaries between themselves and a people whose political and cultural values resembled their own but whose religious beliefs they deemed heretical. The film *The God Makers* was the premier example of this anti-Mormon revival.[28]

The rise in Christ-centered Mormon discourse after the 1970s was also connected to the popularity of a new form of LDS piety during the presidency of Ezra Taft Benson, a piety centered on the Book of Mormon as a witness of Jesus Christ and an invitation to experience his

25. Ibid., 3-4.

26. Kenneth L. Woodward, "A Mormon Moment," *Newsweek*, Sept. 10, 2001, 48.

27. John W. Welch, "The Acts of the Apostle William E. McLellin," in Shipps and Welch, eds., *Journals of McLellin*, 14.

28. Jan Shipps, *Sojourner in the Promised Land* (Urbana: University of Illinois Press, 2000), 350-51.

grace. Landmarks in the promotion of this piety included the addition of the subtitle "Another Witness of Jesus Christ" to the Book of Mormon; the summation of the church's threefold mission as inviting all to come to Christ; Benson's call to flood the earth with the Book of Mormon; the release of a new set of missionary discussions that emphasized Christian themes before teaching the LDS view of a general Christian apostasy; and the rehabilitation of the concept of grace for LDS audiences by BYU religious professor Stephen Robinson in his popular book, *Believing Christ*.[29] When Shipps announced that the McLellin journals revealed Mormonism, though built on faith in the Book of Mormon, was "nonetheless" Christian, she was in effect providing the Saints with historical precedent for the Christ-centered, Book of Mormon-focused piety that had emerged in the 1980s. She confirmed that this piety was a return to the movement's roots rather than an innovation.

As a witness for the Christian essence of Mormonism, the McLellin journals were therefore useful to late twentieth-century LDS scholars who aimed to rebut histories that "exoticized" Mormonism by tracing its origins to occult traditions: magic, alchemy, hermeticism.[30] During the 1980s the need to make sense of the salamander letter and related Hofmann forgeries had forced Mormon historians to investigate seriously for the first time Joseph Smith's involvement in folk magic and treasure-digging. Even after Hofmann's discoveries proved forgeries, historians had accumulated enough independent evidence of Smith's magical activities, such as seeking treasure with a peep stone, that some accommodation had to be made for these non-canonical aspects of Smith's early life.[31] Still, Smith's involvement with occult traditions re-

---

29. See Boyd K. Packer, "Scriptures," *Ensign*, Nov. 1982; "June Videoconference: 'Accomplishing the Mission of the Church,'" *Ensign*, Sept. 1987; Ezra Taft Benson, "Flooding the Earth with the Book of Mormon," *Ensign*, Nov. 1988; Stephen E. Robinson, *Believing Christ: The Parable of the Bicycle and Other Good News* (Salt Lake City: Deseret Book, 1992). All *Ensign* articles were accessed on-line at www.lds.org. See John-Charles Duffy, "The New Missionary Discussions and the Future of Correlation," *Sunstone*, Sept. 2005, 32-34.

30. John-Charles Duffy, "Clyde Forsberg's Equal Rites and the Exoticizing of Mormonism," *Dialogue: A Journal of Mormon Thought* 39 (Spring 2006): 4-34. My use of "occult" is consistent with Howard Kerr and Charles L. Crow, eds., *The Occult in America: New Historical Perspectives* (Urbana: University of Illinois Press, 1983). Though eluding precise definition, "occult" encompasses hermetic traditions, magic, astrology, mesmerism, spiritism, and in the twentieth century parapsychology and UFOs. Not unexpectedly, LDS historians have preferred to use less negatively freighted terms such as "folk magic." I use "occult" precisely to drive home the discomfort this subject causes many Latter-day Saints.

31. For examples of different ways LDS scholars try to absorb evidence of Smith's occult activities with minimum disruption to the canonical narrative, see Richard Lloyd Anderson, "The Mature Joseph Smith and Treasure Searching," and Ronald W. Walker,

mained uncomfortable for many Latter-day Saints. LDS scholars severely criticized two books published following the Hofmann scandal that emphasized the occult in early Mormonism to the point of making it central to the story: D. Michael Quinn's *Early Mormonism and the Magic World View* and John L. Brooke's *The Refiner's Fire*.[32] Brooke's book was especially obnoxious to LDS critics because it bore the imprint of Cambridge University Press and won the prestigious Bancroft Prize for history. Reflecting on the controversy later, Shipps observed that "many LDS scholars seem to think the positive responses to Brooke's work are latter-day expressions of prejudice against Mormonism, the academic equivalent of the accusation that Mormonism is a cult."[33] Quinn's book appeared before the McLellin journals, but LDS reviewers of *The Refiner's Fire*, including Richard Bushman and Philip Barlow, were able to cite the journals to argue that the faith of early Mormons was a variation on common primitivist or millenarian themes, not hermetic ones. These LDS scholars held up McLellin's eyewitness account of Mormonism to show that Brooke's reconstruction was a distortion.[34]

If McLellin's journals were to be used to demonstrate the Christian, not esoteric, essence of Mormonism, then McLellin himself had to be rehabilitated. Remember that in 1985, to preempt the potentially embarrassing claims of Hofmann's McLellin collection, the *LDS Church News* had cast doubt on McLellin's reliability as a historical witness. Publication of the journals required LDS scholars to reverse that strategy: McLellin had to be reliable, at least during the period covered by the diaries (1831-36). Furthermore, McLellin's preaching had to be taken as representative. This meant he had to be presented as a consummate insider to the faith community, not "an apostate 'from the beginning,'" as the historiography up to this point had tended to cast

---

"Joseph Smith: The Palmyra Seer," *BYU Studies* 24 (Fall 1984, publication delayed until 1986): 489-560; 461-72; Richard L. Bushman, *Joseph Smith and the Beginnings of Mormonism* (Urbana: University of Illinois Press, 1984), 69-76.

32. D. Michael Quinn, *Early Mormonism and the Magic World View* (Salt Lake City: Signature Books, 1987); John L. Brooke, *The Refiner's Fire: The Making of Mormon Cosmology, 1644-1844* (New York: Cambridge University Press, 1994). For harsh comments from LDS critics, see Stephen E. Robinson in *BYU Studies* 27 (Fall 1987): 88-95; William A. Wilson in ibid., 96-104; William J. Hamblin, Daniel C. Peterson, and George L. Mitton in *BYU Studies* 34 (Winter 1994): 167-81; Davis Bitton in ibid., 182-92; Hamblin, Peterson, and Mitton, "Mormon in the Fiery Furnace: Or Loftes Tryk Goes to Cambridge," *FARMS Review of Books* 6/2 (1994): 3-58.

33. Shipps, *Sojourner in Promised Land*, 205-06.

34. Richard Bushman, "The Mysteries of Mormonism," *Journal of the Early Republic* 15 (1995): 501-08; Philip L. Barlow, "Decoding Mormonism," *Christian Century*, 17 Jan. 1996, 52-55.

him.[35] McLellin's status as apostate had to be downplayed in favor of his ministry as apostle.

John Welch undertook the task of reinventing McLellin in his introductory essay. The re-invention was dramatic: where Elder Cannon had compared McLellin to Judas, Welch hinted at a comparison to the apostle Paul. By titling his essay "The Acts of the Apostle William E. McLellin," Welch linked the journals to the account of Paul's missionary journeys in the New Testament. He drew enthusiastic parallels between the book of Acts and the Mormon communities and missionary activities described in McLellin's writings. "Whatever implications or conclusions one may choose to draw from these points," Welch wrote, "the parallels between the experiences reported in Acts and in the McLellin journals are extensive, pervasive, and illuminating."[36] The parallels he cited included a focus on faith, repentance, baptism, and the laying on of hands for the gift of the Holy Ghost; the expectation of Christ's imminent return; missionaries' use of scriptural quotations to support their message; dramatic spiritual outpourings such as tongues, visions, and prophecy; and recurring experiences of persecution and adversity. Welch also underscored McLellin's insistence that the Book of Mormon was an indispensable source text for preaching. Although Welch acknowledged that McLellin may have been unusual among Mormon missionaries in that regard, the apostle's reliance on the Book of Mormon was noteworthy because it offered precedent for the centrality of the book during the Benson presidency.[37]

Jan Shipps, in her introductory essay, and Laurel Thatcher Ulrich in her guest foreword, described the journals as important because they offered a window into the religious environment of early nineteenth-century America.[38] But this would not be the principal use LDS scholars would make of the journals. For most, McLellin's journals were used to support efforts in the late twentieth century to assert that the Latter-day Saint movement was Christian. Impressed as Welch and others were by McLellin's mission journeys, the more intriguing journey may be the historiographical one that had brought McLellin, by way of the Hofmann scandal, from perfidious apostate to a model for Mormonism's Christian witness.

---

35. Grandstaff, "More Learning than Sense," 24.

36. Welch, "Acts of McLellin," 18.

37. Ibid., 19-22.

38. Shipps, "Another Side," 4-5; Laurel Thatcher Ulrich, foreword to Shipps and Welch, eds., *Journals of McLellin,* x-xi.

"Alternative Voices" and "Differing Visions": McLellin as Intellectual

Around the same time Welch and other scholars were rehabilitating McLellin for the sake of attesting to the Christian essence of Mormonism, other authors were attempting to refurbish the former apostle's reputation as an arrogant, dissenting intellectual. In a *Dialogue* article published in late 1993, Mark Grandstaff, a professor of history at BYU, argued that McLellin's role in the revelation episode had been consistently misunderstood by LDS writers beginning with Wilford Woodruff in 1858. According to the telling made standard by Woodruff, Cannon, and Jenson, McLellin and other elders had criticized the language of the early revelations, leading the Lord to challenge them to do better. McLellin vainly accepted the challenge, the story went, but exposed his folly by his humiliating failure. Grandstaff argued that the historical evidence for this version of events was weak. Returning to the sources, he reconstructed the events surrounding section 67 of the Doctrine and Covenants and found the challenge to write a better revelation had not been prompted by criticism of Joseph Smith. Rather, it had been a response to uncertainty about what testimony could be affixed to the published revelations given that some of the elders, although not all, had received a specific spiritual witness that the revelations were divine. The challenge to produce an imitation came directly from the Lord as an offer of another form of witness: an empirical confirmation the revelations were produced by superhuman means. McLellin was presumed to be the most intellectually equipped of those present and was "duly appointed" to undertake the challenge–then duly failed, as the test required him to do.[39]

Grandstaff cited a number of general conference addresses and church teaching materials that over the years had used the revelation imitation as a cautionary tale against intellectualism and criticism of church leaders. A 1954 manual, *Teachings of the Doctrine and Covenants,* drew the moral that "the intellectual who discovers ... mistakes in grammar must beware lest the finding leads him to undermine the sure word of God and result in a loss of his own faith." A 1978 lesson incorporated the revelation episode under the subheading "The Critic's Failure." In the same year Grandstaff published his article, the adult Sunday school (Gospel Doctrine) class manual "cited D&C 67 and McLellin's chal-

39. Grandstaff, "More Learning than Sense," 23-48. The apt expression "duly appointed" comes from Professor Porter's paraphrase of Grandstaff's revisionist account, which Porter seems to find plausible. Porter, "Odyssey of McLellin," 299-300.

lenge of the revelations as proof" of Joseph Smith's 1839 statement that "those who found fault with church leaders were on the 'high road to apostasy.' Moreover," Grandstaff reported, "the text inferred that those 'who question' like McLellin could lose their 'crown of eternal life.'"[40]

Grandstaff objected that this misrepresented McLellin's actual role. McLellin was not a puffed up critic deflated by the Lord, as church literature depicted him. Rather, McLellin had used his intellectual gifts by church request to provide what was supposed to be empirical evidence of the authenticity of Smith's revelations. "Those who desired to make McLellin into an example of criticism, irreverence, and apostasy may have done their history a great disservice," Grandstaff complained. But there was more at stake here than historical accuracy. Painting McLellin as a dissident intellectual had deleterious consequences for intellectuals in the present-day church. "The McLellin story establishes a paradigm from which an intellectual's dissatisfaction with the church or church leadership can be understood and rationalized by Mormon membership"—the paradigm being that the "one who questions ... is a potential candidate for apostasy." Grandstaff voiced protest over this stigmatizing of intellectuals: "It is time to stop fearing intellectual inquiry ... Ultimately, only truth will set us free."[41]

The BYU professor's revision of the revelation episode appeared at a time of public conflict between general authorities, aligned with orthodox LDS scholars such as those associated with FARMS, and Mormon "intellectuals," as they were typically called, who questioned received LDS doctrines and history or challenged church leadership on matters such as women and the priesthood, devotion to Mother in Heaven, homosexuality, ecclesiastical authority, and academic freedom at BYU. Specific points of contest included:

- Addresses by Elder Oaks during the late 1980s warning against "alternative voices" and forbidding criticism of church leaders, even if the criticism was true.[42]

- A public feud between Signature Books and writers associated with FARMS who accused Signature of producing apostate or anti-Mormon literature.[43]

---

40. Grandstaff, "More Learning than Sense," 30-31.

41. Ibid., 45.

42. Dallin H. Oaks, "Criticism," *Ensign,* Feb. 1987; Oaks, "Alternate Voices," *Ensign,* May 1989.

43. Eugene England, "Healing and Making Peace in the World and the Church," *Sun-*

• The questioning or disciplining of members who commented to the media on changes to the temple ceremonies in 1990.[44]

• A 1991 First Presidency statement urging members not to participate in symposia that injured the church; the Sunstone Symposium appeared to be the statement's chief target.[45]

• The disfellowshipment or excommunication of six controversial LDS writers in the month of September 1993: Lavina Fielding Anderson, Avraham Gileadi, Maxine Hanks, D. Michael Quinn, Paul Toscano, and Lynne Knavel Whitesides.[46]

• The firing of two BYU professors, Cecilia Konchar Farr and David Knowlton, whose writings or public statements on sensitive topics such as abortion, feminism, and the assassination of LDS missionaries in Latin America had angered some church leaders.[47]

This context lends urgency to Grandstaff's plea that Latter-day Saints "stop fearing intellectual inquiry." By challenging the long history of criticism of McLellin's alleged dissent and intellectualism, Grandstaff was indirectly responding to attacks on Mormon intellectuals of the early 1990s. His article appeared in print, in fact, within months of the September 1993 excommunications.

Another work from the same period that aimed to redeem McLellin from the label "dissenter"—or at least to infuse that label with positive value—was the anthology *Differing Visions,* edited by Roger Launius and Linda Thatcher in 1994, a collection of essays on prominent Mormons who had reputations for dissent. The roll call of dissenters ran the whole span of Mormon history, from David Whitmer to Sonia Johnson.[48] RLDS historian Richard P. Howard provided the anthology's essay on McLellin (reprinted in this volume). In certain respects, Howard's representation of McLellin followed patterns that Grandstaff had chal-

stone, Dec. 1991, 38; Daniel C. Peterson, "Editor's Introduction: Questions to Legal Answers," *Review of Books on the Book of Mormon* 4 (1992): vii-lxxvi.

44. "Comments on Temple Changes Elicit Church Discipline," *Sunstone,* June 1990, 59-61.

45. "Church Issues Statement on 'Symposia,'" *Sunstone,* Oct. 1991, 58-59.

46. "Six Intellectuals Disciplined for Apostasy," *Sunstone,* Nov. 1993, 65-73.

47. Bryan Waterman and Brian Kagel, *The Lord's University: Freedom and Authority at BYU* (Salt Lake City: Signature Books, 1998), chap. 6.

48. Roger D. Launius and Linda Thatcher, eds., *Differing Visions: Dissenters in Mormon History* (Urbana: University of Illinois Press, 1994).

lenged.[49] Like Mormon historians before him, Howard treated the revelation incident as a sign of McLellin's arrogance and portrayed the apostle as someone whose character flaws had sown the seeds of his apostasy from the beginning of his encounter with Mormonism. McLellin was "impulsive, opinionated, irritable, and controlling," as well as "moody, blustery, self-absorbed beyond words to tell." His first meetings with Joseph Smith "revealed a distance portending McLellin's eventual separation from the church." By the end of his life, McLellin's "dissenting voice, although strident and at times boringly repetitious, had lost whatever appeal it might have had to open-minded investigators. He had become a crank."[50]

Where Howard was not shy about portraying McLellin in a less flattering light, the editors of *Differing Visions* leaned toward hagiography in their views of dissenters. In their introduction, Launius and Thatcher cast dissent as a noble profession in the tradition of Anne Hutchinson. Indeed, Mormonism itself, they wrote, originated as a radical form of religious dissent. Mormons were therefore wrong to portray dissidents as "apostates, charlatans, or even psychopaths." Many of the dissidents had been "honest seekers for religious truth" as well as "pluralists" who "decried what they perceived as an omnipresent pressure to conform." They had protested "tyranny" and called on leaders "to function more democratically."[51] Launius and Thatcher named McLellin specifically as one of those whom historians had "characterized as misbegotten, woeful malcontents" with arguments that were "without foundation." Vague aspersions cast on the character of the dissenters, according to the editors, avoided questions about the competency of "the church or its leadership."[52] The historiography on McLellin-as-apostate indeed matched this characterization, as we have seen. To a surprising extent, so did Howard's essay for *Differing Visions*. Granted it was not as harsh as earlier polemical histories, but still it followed the pattern the editors identified: interpreting apostasy as a consequence of McLellin's character rather than as a just protest against unjust authority. Launius and Thatcher seemed to favor the latter interpretation.

A paper read at a 2001 symposium of the Joseph Fielding Smith In-

---

49. In part, this may be due to Howard's essay having been prepared before Grandstaff's work was published: Howard's notes cited neither Grandstaff's 1993 *Dialogue* article nor the newly published McLellin journals.

50. Richard P. Howard, "William E. McLellin: 'Mormonism's Stormy Petrel,'" in Launius and Thatcher, eds., *Differing Visions,* 76, 78, 97.

51. Launius and Thatcher, eds., *Differing Visions,* 3, 7, 9-10.

52. Ibid., 13.

stitute for Latter-day Saint History indicated that at least one observer recognized–and objected to–Launius and Thatcher's attempt to celebrate McLellin as an intellectual. In his paper, Steven Harper, an editorial assistant for *BYU Studies* who helped prepare the McLellin journals for publication, recounted how, while working on the journals, he became preoccupied with understanding why McLellin was briefly excommunicated at the end of 1832, six years before his final break with the church. The quandary, Harper explained, was that McLellin's behavior did not differ substantially from that of "many other Latter-day Saints for whom Joseph voiced no contempt and whose membership in the church was not questioned. What was going on?" The answer came to Harper in what he described as a sudden flash of insight as he was lying awake one night in 1993-94.[53]

Explaining his insight, Harper presented McLellin as someone who had relied on reason to an extent unusual among his co-religionists. Reliance on reason is not necessarily a fault: Harper noted the Lord himself had instructed McLellin to use reasoned evidence in his missionary preaching (D&C 66:7). But McLellin was also prone to "willfulness," and that trait combined with his intellectualism proved a spiritual danger.[54] When his mission became difficult, McLellin "rationalized" disobedience–abandoning his mission, taking a wife, moving to Independence on his own initiative and buying property there. McLellin "construct[ed] a rational case" for these actions despite having been specifically prohibited from doing so and despite his spiritual and empirical witness that Joseph Smith was a prophet.[55] To resolve the "cognitive dissonance," caused by having an undeniable testimony yet being unwilling to follow the prophet's instructions, McLellin embraced "an ambiguous conviction" which let him "construct a conception of Joseph Smith 'as a true prophet ...' yet allow for liberty to disregard such parts of the revelations as McLellin found unduly intrusive."[56] To support this, McLellin gathered evidence of Smith's fallibility, such as the Canadian copyright revelation, and made counter-accusations of wrongdoing. It was these rationalizations, Harper concluded, for which McLellin merited excommunication.

53. Steven C. Harper, "Drawing Lessons from a Life: William E. McLellin, 1831-1832," *Lives of the Saints: Writing Mormon Biography and Autobiography*, ed. Jill Mulvay Derr (Provo: BYU Smith Institute for Latter-day Saint History, 2002), 77.

54. Ibid., 78-79.

55. Ibid., 81.

56. Ibid., 82.

Harper's portrayal of McLellin reproduced stock images of intellectuals deployed by church leaders during the final decades of the twentieth century. During the general conference immediately following the high-profile excommunications of September 1993, Elder James E. Faust decried the "arrogance in thinking that any of us may be more spiritually intelligent, more learned, or more righteous than the Councils called to preside over us."[57] A few years earlier, in a much-discussed 1989 address, Elder Oaks had warned the Saints against "alternate voices" who rely on reason to criticize the church.[58] In the same general confession in which Oaks delivered his "alternate voices" address, Glenn L. Pace warned against "inappropriate intellectualism" that "leads one to testify that he knows the gospel is true but believes the Brethren are just a little out of touch" to justify "selective obedience."[59] Two decades before that, Elder Boyd K. Packer had opined in his famous sermon, "The Mantle Is Far, Far Greater than the Intellect," that a scholar who drew attention to the foibles of church leaders did so to "justify his own weaknesses."[60] The notion that critics of the church are in reality rationalizing their own faults has been a recurring theme in LDS discourse.[61] Harper assigned to McLellin the same attributes or motives church leaders imputed to intellectuals and other critics: arrogance, a need to rationalize disobedience, and a selective testimony that professes to accept some teachings of church leaders while rejecting others.

The image of McLellin as dissenting intellectual was a variation on the image of McLellin as apostate; but in Harper's hands, McLellin was treated less harshly than in the classic apostasy narratives of Woodruff, Cannon, and Jenson. Harper's McLellin was more tragic than treasonous. Nor did Harper betray any hint of satisfaction at seeing a haughty intellectual brought low—there are no accusations of perfidy or seething about sacrilege. Harper aimed for a more balanced approach: McLellin, he wrote, "was both an apostle and an apostate and deserving at times of both descriptions."[62]

---

57. James E. Faust, "Keeping Covenants and Honoring the Priesthood," *Ensign,* Nov. 1993.

58. Oaks, "Alternate Voices."

59. Glenn L. Pace, "Follow the Prophet," *Ensign,* May 1989.

60. Boyd K. Packer, "The Mantle Is Far, Far Greater Than the Intellect," *BYU Studies* 21 (Summer 1981): 264-66.

61. For examples that bookend the period from the 1970s to the 2000s, see N. Eldon Tanner, "Judge Not, That Ye Be Not Judged," *Ensign,* July 1972; Neal A. Maxwell, "Remember How Merciful the Lord Hath Been," *Ensign,* May 2004.

62. Harper, "Drawing Lessons," 77.

Still, his account remained a cautionary tale against the dangers of intellectualism, written to counter Launius's and Thatcher's depiction of dissent as noble.[63] Harper did not respond to Launius and Thatcher directly, but twice in the essay he took up the key phrase from their anthology—"differing visions"—in a way that subverted Launius's and Thatcher's positive valorization of the term. In Harper's usage, "differing vision" became a synonym for rationalization, as when he wrote of McLellin: "His 'differing vision' had to justify chosen behaviors ... while accommodating an ironclad conviction that the Book of Mormon was an authentic ancient scripture ... No matter what the revelation said, McLellin was going to Zion, thinking of property, and choosing to marry."[64] At the level of subtext, Harper's essay warned intellectuals along the same lines general authorities had during the period Harper was working on the McLellin journals. If Professor Welch turned McLellin from Judas into Paul, we could say Harper made McLellin over in the image of Paul Toscano. Or rather, Harper made McLellin over into a sympathetic but disapproving stereotype of Paul Toscano and other dissenters of the 1990s: the image of the wayward intellectual, a tragic figure brought down by pride and disobedience.

Conclusion: New Directions for McLellin Scholarship?

Until the 1980s-90s, Mormon histories relied on the stock image of the apostate in representations of William McLellin. He was presented as a Judas-like figure who had joined the Missouri mobs to wage war against the Saints. He had reveled in the prospect of Joseph Smith's death at the hands of the Missouri militia, had pillaged Smith's home, and was so base he sought permission to assault the prophet in an unfair fight. McLellin had also vaunted his intellectual capacities over Smith's prophetic calling, leading him to criticize the language of the prophet's revelations and imagine he could do better. As rendered in this historiographical strain, the revelation episode made McLellin an archetype of all presumptuous critics who exalt their education over the authority of church leaders and who, as surely as McLellin, would reap the shame they deserve.

During the 1990s, two new historiographical strains emerged, offering different renderings of McLellin for the Saints' consideration. The discovery of the real McLellin journals in the aftermath of the

63. The didactic purpose of Harper's essay is evident from the title: "Drawing Lessons from a Life."

64. Ibid., 82.

Hofmann scandal prompted scholars to extend a posthumous hand of fellowship to McLellin, reclaiming him as an apostle, not just an apostate—as someone whose views, at least from 1831-36, represented the mainstream of Mormon religiosity. Latter-day Saints became interested in reclaiming the apostle once it became clear his journals could be employed to demonstrate (a) the church had nothing to fear from its history and (b) the occult elements of early Mormonism, which had received so much press following the Hofmann forgeries, were marginal to what was, in its essence, a Christian religion along familiar lines. The need to use McLellin for these purposes produced a spate of friendly portrayals, representing a marked departure from the polemics that had characterized previous LDS treatments of McLellin-as-apostate.

At the same time, those troubled by the church's stigmatizing of intellectuals tried to rehabilitate McLellin's reputation as an honest critic, especially in connection with the revelation episode. This reclaiming was part of a larger project in which Grandstaff, Launius, and Thatcher, among others, positively re-valorized intellectualism or dissent. An orthodox rejoinder by Steven Harper, published by BYU's Smith Institute, interpreted McLellin's character and motives in a way that reinforced official church rhetoric, reminding readers that intellectuals are people who rationalize their own disobedience. Harper's McLellin was a softer variation on the image of McLellin as apostate.

Both strains of the new McLellin historiography of the 1990s—McLellin as witness to the Christian content of Mormonism and McLellin as an intellectual critic—were fused to questions about how to interpret Mormonism today. The journals were published to exorcize the sensationalism attached to the Mormon founding as a result of the Hofmann scandal. McLellin's account of early Mormonism mattered to LDS scholars not only, or even primarily, for the light it cast on the past but for the support it lent in the present to the Saints' protests against being tarred as non-Christian cultists. Meanwhile, competing representations of McLellin-as-intellectual reflected late twentieth-century conflicts over intellectualism in the church. In short, McLellin's life and writings have served the Saints not so much as a window on the past but as a mirror for present-day concerns. To shift metaphors: the historiography has been a fertile field where LDS writers can work out present-day issues and advance current agendas in the community of faith.

What alternative directions might there be for McLellin scholarship, especially now that a corpus of McLellin's writings beyond his 1831-36 missionary journals is available in published form? McLellin studies of the 1990s focused on three questions, all familiar from other contexts: "Are Mormons Christian?" "Is there a place for critical questioning in the church?" and "What are the spiritual pitfalls of intellectualism?" There are other questions that can be posed, other historical projects to pursue. William G. Hartley, in an essay written to accompany the published journals, offered a catalogue of insights into early Mormon organization and practice he had gleaned from those documents.[65] Shipps recognized the journals as a resource for studying LDS communities removed from the centers at Kirtland and Missouri where most historians have fixed their attention.[66] I have already mentioned Shipps's and Ulrich's promotion of the journals as illustrating the religious marketplace of the early Republic. Students of American religious history often use the autobiography of Methodist circuit rider Peter Cartwright as a window onto the nineteenth-century religious landscape.[67] In not so many words, Shipps and Ulrich proposed McLellin's journals for the same purpose. Yet McLellin's journals have not been used for that purpose, and the avenues for further historical inquiry signaled by Hartley, Shipps, and Ulrich have remained unexplored. The problem is that scholars of Mormonism—most of whom are still Mormons themselves—seem more interested in McLellin's life and writings for addressing contemporary controversies affecting the LDS Church than in expanding knowledge of the Mormon or general American religious past.

Publication of McLellin's letters and notebooks invites the sobering question: How will Mormon scholars and intellectuals use these new resources? If discussions continue to revolve around the themes that have dominated the historiography since the 1990s—intellectualism, dissent, Mormonism's Christian content—then opportunities to open new channels for scholarship will be lost. So too if these documents do not advance beyond supporting what have become familiar, if still controversial, challenges to canonical LDS church history: for instance, regarding whether or not Joseph Smith invented the priesthood-restoration narratives to bolster his own authority during the Kirtland period.[68]

The current publication offers an opportunity to ask new questions that place the McLellin documents into larger contexts. McLellin's per-

65. William G. Hartley, "The McLellin Journals and Early Mormon History," in Shipps and Welch, eds., *Journals of McLellin,* 263-289.

66. Shipps, "Another Side," 7-9.

67. W. P. Strickland, ed., *Autobiography of Peter Cartwright, the Backwoods Preacher* (New York: Carlton & Porter, 1857).

68. See Grant H. Palmer, *An Insider's View of Mormon Origins* (Salt Lake City: Signature Books, 2002), 224-25, for McLellin's journals and correspondence cited to this end.

sistent commitment, after separating from the church, to certain Book of Mormon teachings such as the necessity of spiritual gifts or the absurdity of infant damnation, makes his writings a useful source for thinking about: What doctrinal concepts most appealed to the first Mormon converts? How did Mormon teachings on those topics compare to teachings of other religious movements—that is, to what extent did these doctrines set Mormonism apart from its competitors in the religious marketplace? If we were to read McLellin's doctrinal writings alongside treatises by writers in the various Mormon churches (LDS, RLDS, and so on), could we identify themes or concepts that constitute a Mormon tradition defined more broadly than by membership in a particular institution, just as certain themes or emphases constitute Wesleyan, Baptist, or Adventist traditions, each encompassing more than a single denomination?

As noted above, Jan Shipps proposed McLellin's journals be used to develop a history of Mormonism beyond the gatherings at Kirtland and Independence to include communities on the periphery. Analogously, McLellin's interactions with individuals in a number of different churches after Smith's death, or with seekers waiting for a sign that the church ought to be re-instituted, invite us to construct a history that is more expansive than the history of one church. This would be an account of continuous interaction between different organizations descended from Joseph Smith, organizations whose histories are usually recounted separately, as well as interaction among Mormon-sympathetic seekers outside the rival churches. Such a history would accord with a turn among American religious historians away from institutional histories in favor of charting religious practices or "lived religion." It would accord with contemporary historians' interests in themes of contact, exchange, and boundary crossing. These recent trends have been slow to gain ground in the field of Mormon history.

Implicit in such historical projects would be yet another re-invention: McLellin as representing a kind of Mormon identity separate from institutional affiliation. Reinventing McLellin in this way would mean reinventing the way we do Mormon history, which itself would be a timely project at the beginning of the twenty-first century as Mormon studies has begun to find a home outside Mormon organizations. The publication of McLellin's notebooks and letters can therefore be an occasion to imagine a new kind of Mormon historiography, one guided more by the research agendas of American religious historians than by controversies within and around the present-day LDS Church.

6.

PORTRAIT OF A "TRUE BELIEVER" IN ORIGINAL MORMONISM

WILLIAM D. RUSSELL

As I read the documents in this collection, I developed an appreciation for Dr. William E. McLellin. I empathize with his struggle—his search to find a manifestation of the religion he loved and the book he treasured, while he simultaneously became disenchanted with the church he had enthusiastically joined and the prophet who had brought forth the Nephite record. The essentials of his faith are found in the 1830 Book of Mormon, in the belief that human beings are capable of direct encounter with God. He well stated this core principle of Mormonism in a letter published in 1864 in Granville Hedrick's *The Truth Teller.* McLellin wrote that there is "one universal, immutable law existing and governing the whole in all ages of man ... the Lord's right to speak, and men's right to hear and his duty to obey."[1] Sadly, none of the church organizations claiming allegiance to the Book of Mormon could claim McLellin for long. He was a "true believer" in original Mormonism. He could be called a prophetic figure, summoning the Saints to be true to the original genius of the movement.

WILLIAM D. RUSSELL recently retired from Graceland University, where he taught for forty years as a Professor of Political Science, History, and Religion, and later as chair of Social Sciences. He is a past president of the Mormon History Association; past editor of *Courage: A Journal of History, Thought, and Action;* and former assistant editor of the *Saints' Herald.* Among his many books and professional articles are *Treasure in Earthen Vessels: An Introduction to the New Testament* and *The Word became Flesh: Sermons on New Testament Texts;* he is a contributor to *Differing Visions: Dissenters in Mormon History* and *The Word of God: Essays on Mormon Scripture.* He is an active elder in the Community of Christ and serves as a member of the Human Rights Committee for the World Church, as well as Peace and Justice Coordinator for his mission center.

1. Larry Porter, "The Odyssey of William Earl McLellin: Man of Diversity," in Jan Shipps and John W. Welch, eds., *The Journals of William E. McLellin, 1831-1836* (Provo and Urbana: BYU Studies and University of Illinois Press, 1994), 348.

McLellin has not received the respect he deserves in Mormon studies because he chose not to remain with any of the churches he associated with. The LDS and RLDS[2] churches have both published extensively and often with a tendency to ascribe unworthy motives to people who departed from them. Emma Smith is a good example. Because she did not make the trek to Utah, she has rarely been treated well by LDS authors. Three of her sons became members of the RLDS First Presidency.[3] As seen by those who believe theirs is the "one true church," defectors like McLellin are portrayed as people who knew the truth and rejected it. Some think this amounts to an "unpardonable sin."[4] Someone like McLellin, who tried first one group and then another, is portrayed as a frustrated power-seeker, moving from one faction to another in search of high office.[5] This character assassination is unworthy of "Saints." Conversely, people who moved from one group to another before landing in the "right" church are seen by adherents as humble servants of God who did not seek power or high office and were not troubled by pride. They were sincere, devout disciples who struggled to find the truth and finally obtained it.

From this collection of McLellin's writings, it is clear to me that he was a sincere disciple who wanted to live in such a way that salvation would be his in the next life. On 29 April 1854 he wrote to Orson Pratt, "For I desire salvation more tha[n] all other things within the gift of God to man."[6] There was a sense of urgency because, like so many at the time including the Mormons, McLellin expected the millennium to come in

2. The Reorganized Church of Jesus Christ of Latter Day Saints (RLDS) changed its name to "Community of Christ" on 6 April 2001, but since virtually all of this article deals with things that occurred before 2001, I will use "RLDS" throughout.

3. A noteworthy exception is the award-winning biography of Emma Smith by Linda King Newell and Valeen Tippetts Avery, *Mormon Enigma: Emma Hale Smith, Prophet's Wife, "Elect Lady," Polygamy's Foe* (Garden City, New York: Doubleday, 1984). Emma's oldest son, Joseph III, was president of the RLDS Church for almost 55 years, 1860-1914. Emma's sons David Hyrum and Alexander Hale were also in the First Presidency but not at the same time.

4. See, for instance, Joseph Fielding McConkie and Craig J. Ostler, *Revelations of the Restoration: A Commentary on the Doctrine and Covenants and Other Modern Revelations* (Salt Lake City: Deseret Book, 2000), who mention McLellin under the heading, "They Shall Not Have Right to the Priesthood and Shall Be Damned," p. 949.

5. See Richard P. Howard, "Mormonism's Stormy Petrel," in *Differing Visions: Dissenters in Mormon History*, ed. Roger D. Launius and Linda Thatcher (Urbana: University of Illinois Press, 1994), 76-101.

6. Letter 1, p. 434. Seven years later he wrote to Joseph Smith III and said, "The Lord knows that I want to know and do the truth in all matters pertaining to my salvation" (Letter 2, p. 443).

the nineteenth century.[7] I do not think McLellin's primary motives were power and prestige, although I doubt anyone is totally selfless. I think Reinhold Niebuhr was right to assert that even the most noble action is tainted with self-interest and pride.[8] Albert Schweitzer, who had admirable motives for his medical mission to Africa, was probably not free from knowing how noble his actions would appear to others. Niebuhr's assertion applies both to the person who stays in the church and gains power and to those who, like McLellin, try one group after another but are never satisfied. Neither lacks pride. Human beings are too complex for "either/or" labels of "good" or "bad," unlike the Hebrew Bible's simplistic description of the kings of Israel and the generally one-dimensional characters described in the Book of Mormon.

As an example of how character assassination begins when someone defects from the church, Mormons have often assumed on very slim evidence that McLellin committed adultery. True, he was warned in a revelatory blessing on 25 October 1831: "Forsake all unrighteousness. Commit not adultery a temptation with which thou hast been troubled."[9] Perhaps we wonder how people like McLellin responded when the prophet chastised them in a revelation that became public. McLellin responded positively to this 1831 blessing, coming soon after he had joined the church. At the time, he believed it answered the questions he had about the church and his role in it. He believed it clearly gave him a reason to become involved in proselyting and would help him resist temptation in his travels–resolving whether he should remarry after his wife's recent death or postpone having a family until later.[10] It was not long–a little more than a year later–before McLellin was again chastised in a revelation: "I am not well pleased with many things; and I am not well pleased with my servant William E. McLellin, neither with my servant Sidney Gilbert."[11] Other unnamed individuals appeared to be out of pleasure with the Lord, according to this revelation. One might wonder if there was a difference between the Lord's attitude and Joseph Smith's.

7. The millennial theme was very prominent in his earlier diaries (Shipps and Welch, eds., *Journals of McLellin,* 3, 6-7, 39, 42-44, 63, 65, 83, 90-92, 94, 111, 113), and sometimes Mormons of that period sounded like millennialist William Miller. But the millennial theme is not nearly so strong in the later writings in this collection.

8. Reinhold Niebuhr's classic statement of his view regarding man's sinfulness is found in his two-volume work, *The Nature and Destiny of Man* (New York: C. Scribner's Sons, 1941-43).

9. RLDS D&C 66:5; LDS D&C 66:10.

10. Shipps and Welch, eds., *Journals of McLellin,* 249-250.

11. See introduction to RLDS D&C 53; LDS D&C 90:35.

For instance, I wonder if the reference to adultery in the 1831 revelation could have been a case of projection on Joseph Smith's part. Some might say he himself was tempted with the sin of lust, and we know there were times the Mormon prophet yielded to temptation. So perhaps he was projecting onto McLellin—a man whose wife had died and who was probably lonely—something he hated in himself. Where McLellin thanked the prophet for his blessing, presumably accepting the caution against sexual temptation,[12] should we therefore convict McLellin of adultery or should we rather praise his humility and willingness to be counseled? How different is this than drawing unsupportable conclusions about Jesus associating with prostitutes or Jimmy Carter, a devout Christian, admitting to lust prior to the 1976 U.S. presidential election?

There is an inherent tension in Mormonism—not only in the dominant LDS version but also in the RLDS and other related groups. On one hand, Joseph Smith sought to restore the "ancient order of things"[13] This assumes that God established true Christianity in the days of Adam, four thousand years before Christ, and in America six centuries before Christ. The true faith was lost in both civilizations but was restored by Jesus. Then it was lost and restored again by Joseph Smith. This implies a static gospel which should not be changed. All the truth that is needed in religion existed from the beginning and again at the time of Jesus. On the other hand, a core belief of the Restoration was that God reveals new truths to humankind,[14] implying that new truths might go beyond what was previously known and may be inconsistent with or even conflict with past "truths." Conservatives are especially attracted to the restoration of a sacred past, whereas liberals tend to be attracted to the idea of continuing revelation. As a true-blue conservative Mormon, McLellin was not particularly open to theological innovation.

Early Mormons can be divided into three broad categories. First, those who did not have serious problems with the unique new doctrines and practices Joseph Smith introduced, with the prophet's fertile

---

12. In Shipps and Welch, eds., *Journals of McLellin,* 250, hypothetical words are put in McLellin's mouth: "How can I escape the temptation of adultery and other sins which have burdened me, especially since the recent death of my wife?" This is proposed as a question McLellin may have had in mind when he asked Joseph Smith for a blessing.

13. See chapter 6, "The Restoration of All Things," in Richard L. Bushman, *Joseph Smith and the Beginnings of Mormonism* (Urbana: University of Illinois Press, 1984):179-88.

14. McLellin and his contemporaries would use the word "mankind," but we will use the more inclusive term "humankind," although it is doubtful that McLellin or other Mormons expect God to reveal his will to the females of the flock.

mind and imagination, and followed Brigham Young to Utah beginning in 1846. Second, those who had difficulties with these changes, especially the doctrinal alterations from the Nauvoo period, and ended up in the RLDS Church if they remained Mormons. Third, some early Saints, especially those associated with the Whitmers, who believed that Joseph Smith became a fallen prophet early in his career. McLellin fits this third category of early converts.

Ultimately the RLDS Church would reject all of the major innovations of Nauvoo,[15] including the plurality of gods, plurality of wives, temple rituals, and eradication of the line separating church and state, which had become a hallmark of the new American democracy. The lion's share of Saints who had initially followed such men as Alpheus Cutler, Sidney Rigdon, William Smith, James J. Strang, Charles Thompson, and Lyman Wight ended up in the Reorganized Church, which was led by Joseph Smith's oldest son, Joseph III, beginning in April 1860. Those among the RLDS fold who studied their church history seriously—which was not many—tended to conclude that the founder had strayed and was no longer a true prophet during the Nauvoo years. Those who did not study church history seriously fooled themselves into believing Brigham Young had introduced what were to them "abominable doctrines."

So the RLDS Church can be said to have rejected the Nauvoo theology in favor of the Kirtland theology—ideas that had developed by the end of the Kirtland period in 1838. Living in the Midwest among neighbors who were mostly Protestant, RLDS people were certainly more comfortable defending the Book of Mormon and contemporary revelation without having to defend polygamy, baptism for the dead, and what was probably the greatest Mormon "heresy," the concept of the plurality of gods, and with it eternal progression to godhood.[16] Meanwhile the Saints in Utah had the luxury of not having to face numerous critical neighbors of other faiths. They were freer to develop their unique be-

---

15. My Graceland College colleague Alma Blair started me thinking along these lines with his essay on the origins of the RLDS Church in F. Mark McKiernan, Alma R. Blair, and Paul M. Edwards, eds., *The Restoration Movement: Essays in Mormon History* (Lawrence, Kans.: Coronado Press, 1973), and I continued thinking about the topic in "The LDS Church and Community of Christ: Clearer Differences, Closer Friends," *Dialogue: A Journal of Mormon Thought* (Winter 2003): 177-90.

16. LDS President Gordon B. Hinckley, whose background is in public relations, seems to be distancing the church from the doctrine of the plurality of gods, suggesting it is an old idea the church doesn't really pay attention to anymore. See Hinckley's statements in Don Lattin, "Musings of the Main Mormon," *San Francisco Chronicle*, 13 Apr. 1997; David Van Biema, "Kingdom Come," *Time* magazine, 4 Aug. 1997.

liefs with little negative interaction from Doubting Thomases in the neighborhood or workplace. Most of those who were critical of the Nauvoo developments either left the church or declined to move to Utah and finally affiliated with the RLDS.[17]

McLellin fits a third type of early Mormon—one who had experienced difficulty already in Kirtland over the evolving theology and had left the church *before* it became established in Nauvoo. David Whitmer is the model for this position. The Whitmers and Hiram Page[18] were the Saints McLellin most respected because they remained true to the earliest teachings of the church and rejected later innovations in doctrine. Today the Church of Christ (Temple Lot), headquartered in Independence, is the best example of a church that still reflects this general view. Whitmer's *An Address to All Believers in Christ by a Witness to the Divine Authenticity of the Book of Mormon* (1887), published months before his death, is the best expression of this position, along with *An Address to All Believers in the Book of Mormon,* published the same year.[19]

William McLellin is in this camp, and his collected writings may in time come to equal or surpass Whitmer's as the classic statement of this third view.[20] Most of these people, including Whitmer and McLellin, had become disaffected in Ohio or Missouri, and it was the prophet's actions that brought about what is so incorrectly called "apostasy." In Christianity apostasy refers to a departure from faith in Jesus Christ, not a lack of faith in the humans who lead the institution. Over and over again in this collection, McLellin says he ceased activity in the church in 1836. However, for most of the rest of his life—including his final years—he sought and earnestly hoped for the establishment of a true "church of Christ" which could lift high the banner of primitive Christianity until the millennium, which he expected would arrive before the

17. What became the RLDS Church had its beginnings with an organizational meeting in 1852. It was eight years later that Joseph Smith III accepted the church leadership and a name was decided upon.

18. An interesting sidelight from the RLDS experience came in the late 1980s when a descendant of Hiram Page had two revelations leading to creation of an RLDS offshoot called the Restoration Church of Jesus Christ of Latter Day Saints. Norman Page had been a Seventy in the RLDS Church but had become disaffected. When he presented his first revelation, he candidly reminded his associates of his pedigree so they might want to be cautious about his claim.

19. David Whitmer, *An Address to All Believers in Christ* (Richmond, Mo.: By the author, 1887); David Whitmer, *An Address to All Believers in the Book of Mormon* (Richmond, Mo.: By the author, 1887).

20. For this reason, I am glad the Traughber family had the foresight to preserve the records published in this volume.

end of the century. Not surprisingly, McLellin briefly associated with various factions but left each because they collectively failed to meet his expectation of what constituted the "true church of Christ." He had high hopes for David Whitmer stepping forward to lead. As late as 1872, McLellin wrote to Joseph Smith III telling him that David Whitmer had been ordained in 1834 as Joseph Smith's successor, as Prophet, Seer, Revelator, and Translator.[21]

Like so many of the early Saints, William E. McLellin was converted first to the Book of Mormon.[22] The rest of his life, he maintained his belief in its truthfulness. In the last letter of the current collection, written to James T. Cobb in 1880, McLellin had this to say:

> But when a man goes at the Book of M. he touches the apple of my eye. He fights against truth—against purity—against light—against the purist, or one of the truest, purist books on earth. I have more confidence in the Book of Mormon than any book of this wide earth![23]

Joseph Smith dictated the Book of Mormon to scribes and it was thereafter printed by E. B. Grandin in March 1830 at Palmyra, New York. Through the remaining fourteen years and three months of his life, Joseph Smith paid relatively little attention to the Book of Mormon as he moved far beyond its theology and the religious practices set forth in it. The Book of Mormon presented a conservative Protestant version of Christianity that fit well within the religious environment of the United States in 1830. It especially appealed to those who resented the American elites who dominated religion, politics, law, and publishing.[24] Often the new doctrines that emerged from Joseph Smith during his later religiously fertile periods were not to be found in the Book of Mormon and were not a part of conservative Protestantism. It did not seem to bother Joseph Smith that his new theologies and practices sometimes conflicted with the Book of Mormon or even his own earlier revelations, if he even noticed.

Although McLellin was considered very learned for his day, he had a literalistic approach to interpreting the Bible. In his "Views on the Bible" (1877), he accepted as history the first eleven chapters of Genesis[25]— the

21. Letter 12, p. 487.

22. Letter 26, p. 521.

23. Ibid.

24. See Nathan Hatch, *The Democratization of American Christianity* (New Haven: Yale University Press, 1989).

25. Notebook 4, pp. 302, 309, 311, 315.

myths of Adam and Eve, Noah, and the Tower of Babel—which precede the saga of the Hebrew patriarchs Abraham, Isaac, and Jacob. He believed in a pure Adamic language.[26] He felt that any idea in conflict with previously revealed truth was wrong because God knew how to speak clearly and meant what he said.[27] This fundamentalist view applied to scriptural passages McLellin thought had not been corrupted by men. In an early writing in this collection, "A Treatise on Faith," his view was that when God spoke to man it was by an "infallible testimony to the mind."[28] Therefore, when Joseph Smith claimed new revelations which conflicted with the Book of Mormon or other past revelations, it was because Joseph had become confused in his mind about his source of inspiration and was not truly a prophet in those instances.

McLellin was not only well read but was possibly the most educated and brightest of all the members of the church of his day, as demonstrated in his letters and journals in this collection. He was systematic in his thinking, often spelling out his logic in a very orderly way, item by item, numbering each point.

McLellin was also legalistic, as seen in his 1871 letter to Isaac Sheen.[29] This way of thinking is unattractive to academics in areas of religion and history. For "New Mormon Historians" from the late 1960s, educated in well-regarded universities, McLellin appears to be extreme. He was well-versed for his time and reasonable within the assumption of scripture as truth, but he seems radical today, which might add to the difficulty of contemporary professional historians to evaluate him sympathetically.

It is not surprising that McLellin was considered by some to be the smartest man in the church. From his 1831-36 missionary journals,[30] we learn that soon after hearing the Mormon message, he bought a copy of "Brown's Bible Concordance."[31] Thereafter, on various missions, we learn that he purchased "Whelpley's Compend[ium] of History,"[32] "Mahomets' Alcoran,"[33] "Fox['s Book of] Martyrs,"[34] and something

26. Ibid., p. 302.
27. Ibid.
28. Notebook 1, p. 143.
29. Letter 10, pp. 471-72.
30. See Shipps and Welch, eds., *Journals of McLellin.*
31. Ibid., 33.
32. Ibid., 139.
33. Ibid., 186.
34. Ibid., 197.

called "All Religions and Ceremonies."[35] He has a list of books he wants to buy: "Jones' Church History, Goodrich's Ecclesiastical History," a "Dictionary of History," "Moshiem's Church History," "Creeds and Desciplines, Celcus History (Infidel)," and "American Antiquities."[36] When it is said that God wanted the elders to choose "the most wise among you" to demonstrate the impossibility of writing a revelation better than Joseph could,[37] the elders chose McLellin as the one who fit the bill.[38] McLellin gave it a try and wrote a revelation, later interpreted as a sign of arrogance on his part. Of course, the Saints witnessing this "contest" supported the prophet against McLellin in this strange "duel of revelations." BYU historians James Allen and Glen Leonard suggest McLellin was "humbled" when he discovered he could not equal the prophet's writings,[39] but this demonstration of prophetic superiority would have fooled no one. Nick the Greek would not have taken bets if he had been on the scene. To the contrary, I have not seen evidence that McLellin shared the verdict that Allen and Leonard report or that he even conceded defeat. In fact, McLellin says that two months later he went to Joseph Smith for a blessing, as he had done before, and Joseph suggested that this time McLellin should speak and Joseph write. Afterward, Joseph pronounced McLellin's blessing as much a revelation as Smith had ever produced.[40]

It appears McLellin continued to read and think about religious matters throughout his life. During his years in the church, 1831-38, modern biblical criticism was virtually unknown in the United States. Beginning in Germany in the late eighteenth century, it only gradually became known in the nineteenth century, first in England and later in

---

35. Ibid.; probably Thomas Robbins, comp., *All Religions and Religious Ceremonies* (Hartford: O. D. Cooke & Sons, 1823).

36. Ibid., 196-97. McLellin probably means William Jones, *The History of the Christian Church from the Birth of Christ to the Eighteenth Century, including the Very Interesting Account of the Waldenses and Albigenses* (New York: S. H. Cone, 1824); Charles A. Goodrich, *Outlines of Ecclesiastical History* (N.p.: 1829); Johann Lorenz Mosheim, *Institutes of Ecclesiastical History, Ancient and Modern* (New Haven: A. H. Maltby, 1832); Origen's *Contra Celsus*; and Josiah Priest, *American Antiquities and Discoveries in the West* (Albany: Hoffman & White, 1833); among others.

37. RLDS D&C 67:2; LDS D&C 67:5-8.

38. Porter, "Odyssey of McLellin," 299-300.

39. James B. Allen and Glen M. Leonard, *The Story of the Latter-day Saints* (Salt Lake City: Deseret Book, 1992), 78-79.

40. Shipps and Welch, eds., *Journals of McLellin,* 301. "Brother William," Joseph is quoted as having said, "that is the mind and will of God, and as much a revelation as I ever received in my life. You have written it by the true spirit of inspiration."

the United States.[41] In later years, judged by his own writings in this collection, McLellin became knowledgeable about Christian history and presented a good historical analysis in his 1877 journal section entitled "Views on the Bible."[42] He is well informed on the process of canonization. He was also fascinated with the "lost books" of the Bible, typical of Mormons of the various branches owing to Joseph Smith's belief that wicked men had distorted the sacred text and deleted material they did not like.[43] McLellin wrote that the Bible referred to nearly forty books which had become lost.[44] He believed other ancient writings, "received by holy men of old," also had been lost or destroyed.[45]

He seems to have thought some or many of these compositions would have qualified as scripture if they had survived. However, one might posit a counter view that these writings did not survive because early Christians did not consider them all that valuable. Therefore, the manuscripts were never thought worth the painstaking effort of copying them out by hand. Printing presses would not appear until the fifteenth century. A significant factor in canonization was the mere fact that the faith community had regarded certain writings as significant enough to be re-copied, and therefore survived.

Nevertheless, McLellin is familiar with the fact that seven books of the New Testament were not accepted as scripture in the first two centuries, unlike the other twenty of the "first list." These seven "books of the second list"[46] took much longer to find acceptance in the informal process of determining the canon.[47] McLellin's belief was that there should have been at least thirty-seven books in the New Testament.[48] Finally, I was impressed that our subject did not fall for the predictive prophecy assumption of some biblical fundamentalists since the nineteenth century who presume that the biblical authors predicted events that would soon transpire in our contemporary, modern world. Thus

41. My article, "The RLDS Church and Biblical Criticism: The Early Response," *John Whitmer Journal* 7 (1987), 62-68, showed the overall initial negative response to biblical scholarship.

42. Notebook 4, pp. 303-04.

43. Ibid., pp. 317-18.

44. Ibid., pp. 308-09.

45. Notebook 1, p. 167.

46. The seven New Testament books of the "second list" were Hebrews, James, 2 Peter, 2 John, 3 John, Jude, and Revelation.

47. Notebook 4, pp. 312-13.

48. Ibid., p. 315.

biblical writers predicted the two world wars, the rise of Hitler and Stalin and others.[49]

McLellin has great confidence in the holy men who wrote the Bible but regrets that we don't have the original documents so we can correct the transmission errors.[50] His thought was probably influenced by a wish that some of the biblical texts, especially the earlier ones, contained more information. He probably wished the Old Testament writers had told us how the true Adamic religion had gone astray.[51] His assumption was that what we have are abridged accounts,[52] leaving us deprived of much of God's revelation. I wonder, however, if we had the originals we would have more confidence in the Bible. It may be their absence that allows us to assume the best and put the best possible face on any interpretive problems that arise.[53]

McLellin holds to a high theology of scripture. For him, outside of direct intercourse with the Creator, everything else is conjecture, uncertainty.[54] Yet, he seems to accept the Bible and Book of Mormon at face value even though much of the Bible was corrupted in transmission.[55] Late in life McLellin wrote in "Reasons Why I Am Not a 'Mormon'" (ca. 1880): "God's voice is the highest evidence that can be presented to man's mind; but the word of fallible man is to a great degree uncertain, and consequently must be received with some doubts, until his revealments are proved by comparing with revelations going before."[56] This puts him in the position of valuing the older revelations, as uncertain as their texts might be, over seeking new light and truth, which he knew could result in instability in the church and raise conflicts. The strange scene of the dueling prophets—Smith versus McLellin—might have continued as a recurring theme if McLellin had continued in the church. Consider, for instance, the RLDS revelation of 1984 calling for the ordi-

49. Ibid., pp. 304-05.

50. Ibid., p. 313.

51. But since this idea, that Christ's religion existed four thousand years prior to Jesus of Nazareth at the time of Adam, is found in no other religious tradition than Mormonism, such support is not bound to surface. Possibly Joseph Smith got the idea from the Gospel of John, "In the beginning was the Word and the Word was with God and the Word was God" (1:1), and ran with it.

52. Notebook 4, pp. 309-311.

53. The idea of Biblical inerrancy or infallibility is a modern creation of the nineteenth century. To hold that any writing produced by human hands is infallible is a species of idolatry and therefore heresy.

54. Notebook 1, pp. 213-14.

55. See, for instance, ibid., p. 162.

56. Notebook 7, p. 423.

nation of women. Its conflict with past scriptures caused conservatives to break with the church. They did not consider the fact that the existing scriptures, ancient and latter-day, were produced in patriarchal societies where the idea of ordaining women would not have occurred. They often complained about the First Presidency editorial, "The Nature of New Revelation," published in the official church organ two months before the revelation was presented to the conference and in which it was asserted that new revelation need not always be consistent with past revelations.[57] McLellin probably would have joined with the conservatives in challenging "disjunctive revelation."

McLellin went beyond the conservative status quo and argued that if any current tenet was not supported by previous scripture, it was not true. He did not believe in the visitations of John the Baptist and of Peter, James, and John, partly because he had never heard these stories since the time he had converted to Mormonism and party because he could not find "in any of the inspired books where an angel ever performed an ordination."[58] If Joseph Smith had presented a revelation endorsing angelic ordination, McLellin probably would have rejected it because angelic ordination was not found in the scriptures he accepted, which were the Bible and the Book of Mormon. He viewed the Doctrine and Covenants as, at best, a mix of inspiration and the words of men. Therefore, it appears that since he, no doubt, regarded the Book of Mormon as an ancient text, his personal canon of scriptures was entirely ancient.[59]

Paradoxically, McLellin also wanted the canon to expand harmoniously at both ends. He hoped for the recovery of lost ancient texts and he wanted to be open to new revelation from God. "All the popular religionists of the nineteenth century deny to man the high moral or legal right to now hold direct intelligent intercourse with the Heavens," he wrote, and questioned that "'the Old and New Testaments <u>alone</u> are a sufficient rule of faith and practice for all Christians.' I was taught this

---

57. "The Nature of New Revelation," First Presidency editorial, *Saints' Herald*, Feb. 1984, 51-52. Many people assumed President Wallace B. Smith wrote the editorial, but it was written by his second counselor, Alan D. Tyree, as both Smith and Tyree have since confirmed to me. When President Smith approved the editorial, he did not know a revelation on women would be presented to the World Conference in April. The 1984 revelation is Section 156 in the RLDS Doctrine and Covenants.

58. Notebook 7, p. 403.

59. Non-Mormon readers of the Book of Mormon regard it as the work of Joseph Smith. Among RLDS and LDS members, there has been a move in recent years toward this view, but most of the rank-and-file probably still regard it as history.

from youth to manhood, but do not now believe it, nor can I ever again."[60]

McLellin's God was the accessible God of Mormonism, ready to respond to man's entreaties. This fit well within the Romantic worldview of prominent American intellectuals of the antebellum period.[61] This original Mormon assertion of God's accessibility was almost immediately limited by Joseph Smith's declaration that he alone would speak for God to the church; since his death, there has been very little of substance added to the Doctrine and Covenants. The LDS Church has only added two more sections dated later than 1844, plus the Official Declarations of 1890 and 1978.[62]

In much of his theology, McLellin appears to be a good Mormon as seen in his lengthy 1878 treatise "On Original Sin." He is opposed to infant baptism.[63] Sin is not sin unless it is voluntary.[64] Satan exists and was the first sinner, Eve second, Adam third.[65] He sees himself as a Trinitarian, consistent with the Book of Mormon but in conflict with the radically new concept of divinity fashioned by Joseph Smith during the Nauvoo years.

Although McLellin was a firm believer in the 1830 Book of Mormon and the idea of the availability of divine-human encounter, and although he shared the Mormon dream of a "true church of Christ" and the millennial return of the Savior, and even though he maintained for some time that Joseph and the church had fallen from grace in 1834, ultimately he concluded that there had been problems with Joseph Smith's leadership from the start. He did not doubt that Joseph had possessed the gift of translation, given McLellin's love for the Book of Mormon; and while it is not clear when McLellin came to doubt Smith had

60. Notebook 1, p. 215; see also p. 219.

61. See Stow Persons, *American Minds: A History of Ideas* (New York: Henry Holt, 1958), part 3: "The Mind of the American Democracy: 1800-1860."

62. Although twenty-six other sections and a eulogy to Joseph Smith were subsequently added, all date from 1844 or earlier. The RLDS Church has added fifty revelations since Joseph III became president. However, many of them deal with little more than calling individuals to high office in the church. A few are substantive, such as Section 116 calling for the ordination of African American men (1865) and Section 156 prescribing the ordination of women (1984). In the LDS Church, the revelation giving African-American men the priesthood was issued in 1978, a full 113 years after the similar RLDS revelation. An LDS friend tells me this gives him hope that in 2097 women will receive the priesthood in the Utah church.

63. Notebook 6, p. 338.

64. Ibid., p. 339.

65. Ibid., p. 342.

been a Prophet, Seer, and Revelator, he ultimately came to that conclusion. In 1878 he wrote a provocative treatise, "Why I am Not a Latter Day Saint," outlining five great and incorrect principles established at the beginning of the church.[66]

The first mistake had been ordaining Joseph Smith as Prophet, Seer, Revelator, and Translator on 6 April 1830. Smith had previously been recognized as having a gift of translation, but not the other three gifts: "As to the ordination of a Prophet or Seer, I know of no place in the word of God where a Seer, or inspired Prophet was ever ordained by man. It is not a ministerial office, but it is a direct gift from God. It is neither conferred or confirmed by ordination." To ordain a man to such an office was to respond to the desires of one's own heart "or from the promptings of Satan."[67] For a long time McLellin affirmed the validity of David Whitmer's July 1834 ordination as Joseph Smith's successor to be Prophet and Seer, but by 1878 had come to believe it was "without authority from God, all wrong, null & void."[68]

The second great mistake of the founding church was the assertion made by Joseph Smith that when the prophet spoke, his words were as if from the mouth of God. McLellin thought this "simply preposterous."[69]

Third was the claim, also made on 6 April 1830, that Joseph Smith and Oliver Cowdery were apostles of the Lord Jesus Christ. McLellin insisted that the apostles in Jerusalem and the disciples in the New World all "saw, heard and felt" Jesus Christ. No such assertion had been made by Joseph Smith while McLellin was in the church, and therefore Joseph Smith "should not have made so false a claim [to the apostleship] for himself and Cowdery."[70] McLellin probably did not hold this view when he himself was called to be an apostle in 1835, but by 1878 he had rejected the apostolic ordinations in the church, since these men had not seen, heard, or felt Jesus Christ. There is no evidence McLellin ever said he himself had seen Christ face-to-face. By his own admission much later, his "appointment and ordination was a perfect nullity!"[71]

---

66. Notebook 5, pp. 323-26.

67. Ibid., p. 323.

68. Ibid.

69. Ibid., p. 324.

70. Ibid., p. 325.

71. Ibid., p. 332. Jeffrey Lundgren, the ex-RLDS priest who became a cult leader and murdered a family of five, for which he was executed in Ohio in 2006, was consumed with a passion to see and feel Jesus Christ like the brother of Jared. Lundgren's theology was deeply rooted in the Book of Mormon. He thought of himself as a seer and was convinced he needed to "destroy" the Avery family because they were unrepentant.

Fourth was this instruction to Oliver Cowdery: "Thou shalt not command him who is at thy head and at the Head of the Church," meaning Joseph Smith.[72] McLellin felt "the Lord Jesus is Head of his Church, as much so as a man is head of the woman."[73]

Fifth was that Joseph Smith set himself up as the only one who could receive revelations for the church.[74] This was contrary to the genius of Mormonism—that everyone should have equal access to God. Joseph Smith's exclusive right to revelation was "one of the most unchristian and ruinous principles that Smith or any man ever did or could lay down," McLellin wrote.[75] He cited Moses, "Would God that all the Lord's people were prophets";[76] Joel and Acts, that God will "pour out of my Spirit upon all flesh";[77] Paul's first letter to the Corinthians, "For ye may all prophesy one by one, that all may learn, and all may be comforted";[78] and the Book of Revelation, "For the testimony of Jesus is the spirit of prophecy."[79] McLellin deeply believed in the core principle of Mormonism—that revelation is possible for everyone and not restricted to an elite group. Nathan Hatch has shown that the Book of Mormon expressed a populist belief current in several other movements of the day, including African-American Methodists, American Baptists, Campbellites, and white Methodists, in their rejection of cultural elites in such areas as the law, politics, religion, and publishing.[80] In the Book of Mormon the same principle was affirmed, that people need not rely on intermediaries to interpret God's will for them. In light of Joseph Smith's move away from that core principle, it is not surprising McLellin preferred the Book of Mormon perspective rather than Joseph's revelation limiting power to himself.

Given that McLellin came to see five mistakes made by Joseph Smith at the very beginning of the church's history, one can see why he believed that, as a result of these foundational errors, "many other wrongs would enter into it [Church of Christ] and so destroy its useful-

72. RLDS D&C 27:2; LDS D&C 28:6.

73. Notebook 5, p. 325. I found nothing in the McLellin writings which would suggest that he did not share the patriarchal worldview of his age, seeing women as subservient to men.

74. Book of Commandments 30:2; RLDS D&C 27:2; LDS D&C 28:2.

75. Notebook 5, p. 325.

76. Num. 11:29.

77. Joel 2:28; Acts 2:17.

78. I Cor. 14:31.

79. Rev. 19:10.

80. Hatch, "Democratization of American Christianity."

ness in the world."[81] Among these was an indictment of Joseph Smith's behavior during the Kirtland years, 1831-38, which coincided with McLellin's 1831 baptism and 1838 excommunication.

With regard to Joseph Smith's revelations, we should remember that it was not clear at first that these revelations would be made public, much less published, or finally that they should achieve canonical status.[82] This was a problem for McLellin and others in his day and has continued in the minds of some of the independent-minded members of the various Mormon churches. First of all, McLellin noted that in the early revelations it was often said, "Keep these things from the world,"[83] clearly implying it was not expected that they would be added to the cannon of scripture. But these expressions were taken out, along with other changes to the revelations prior to their publication. "I stood for hours and saw them do this work," McLellin recalled.[84] He complained that some of the revelations were altered two or three times between their first utterance and their appearance in the first edition of the Doctrine and Covenants in 1835. Nor did the decision to publish the prophet's revelations by itself prove they were to be regarded as scripture.

Changing the revelations was onerous for McLellin, given his view that God spoke clearly to man by "infallible testimony to the mind."[85] Man was not free to alter these communications, and doing so brought a curse rather than a blessing.[86] Therefore, "if J. Smith's revelations were sacred I pity the poor man who altered them."[87] McLellin is astonished that a sane man would do this.[88] The edited Doctrine and Covenants was useful "only as a relic of folly,"[89] wherein McLellin perceived "some truth" in the revelations, "mixed with much error and falsehood."[90]

We might recall Joseph Smith's and the early Saints' condemnation of the Roman Catholic Church for allegedly tampering with the sacred

---

81. Notebook 5, p. 326.

82. It would be interesting to determine how early Mormons moved from seeing the prophet's revelations as too private to be openly discussed to the idea that they should be published, then finally to the idea that the published revelations were scripture—as much as the Bible or Book of Mormon.

83. Letter 22, p. 510.

84. Ibid.

85. Notebook 1, p. 143.

86. Ibid., p. 217.

87. Notebook 7, p. 414.

88. Ibid., pp. 413-14.

89. Letter 22, p. 510.

90. Notebook 7, p. 413.

texts of the Old and New Testaments.[91] Similarly, the changes in LDS revelations were not a matter of improved clarity but reflected Joseph Smith's changing theology during his first five years as the prophet.

A serious problem exists for the various churches of Mormondom because Joseph's solutions to day-to-day problems became canonized and more or less binding on the membership to thereafter follow historically conditioned decisions. It appears McLellin saw these "revelations" for what they were, as administrative acts rather than eternal truths. Joseph Smith "delivered a revelation in 1830 positively contradicting a declaration in the book of Mormon, saying, "Teachers have not authority to baptize."[92] "I prefer the book of M[ormon]," McLellin continued, "hence his [Joseph Smith's] 'word' cannot be relied on as being positively certain." McLellin said he could cite many more examples, and he no doubt could have.[93] The supposed errors were so egregious, McLellin believed this was why God inspired a mob in Independence, Missouri, to destroy the Book of Commandments.[94] Changing revelations was not going to go unpunished.

Not only did Joseph Smith change the revelations when they were being prepared for publication, an examination of the content showed that some of them contradicted each other, the newer pronouncements standing in opposition to older ones, as well as in contradiction to ancient scripture. On 26 April 1832, the Order of Enoch was established with nine members, and Joseph said in his revelation that "this order I have appointed unto you to be an <u>everlasting order</u>, and unto your successors."[95] But as McLellin noted, "another revelation is given" in March 1833, "setting aside their brethren in Zion, and setting up another band of men."[96] McLellin quoted the new revelation: "You shall no longer be bound as a united order to your brethren in Zion, but you shall be called the united order of the stake of Zion, in the city of Shinehah (Kirtland).

91. McLellin was extremely unhappy with RLDS D&C 34:5 (LDS D&C 35:20), where Sidney Rigdon was directed to write as Joseph dictated a "new translation" of the Bible. McLellin was "intimately acquainted with the manner of this (said to be) translation." Joseph would read through his Bible and "<u>correct</u> whatever he thought was amiss. Hence it was not a translation." He pointed out that Joseph had no knowledge of the language involved. His changes were "sometimes for the worse." "It was no translation in any sense of the word" (Notebook 7, p. 408).

92. RLDS D&C 17:11; LDS D&C 20:58.

93. Notebook 5, p. 324.

94. Notebook 7, pp. 381, 396.

95. RLDS D&C 81:5; LDS D&C 82:20. The wording in the Doctrine and Covenants has very slight variations from McLellin's wording.

96. Notebook 7, p. 415.

... You are dissolved as a united order with your brethren."[97] McLellin observed that the "everlasting order only lasted two years!"[98] It actually lasted less than a year. As he wrote in 1878, the Doctrine and Covenants also sometimes contradicted the Book of Mormon.

In 1872 McLellin wrote to RLDS President Joseph Smith III to inform him that one of his father's revelations had proven to be false—the revelation for Oliver Cowdery and associates to travel to Canada for a Book of Mormon copyright.[99] McLellin told 39-year-old Joseph III, "Now if he delivered a word by pretended revelation which was positively false, then I ask how we can depend upon any of his future predictions?"[100] The revelation to convert the Indians also proved fallible: "You shall go unto the Lamanites and preach my gospel unto them, and cause my church to be established among them."[101] The revelation was "utterly false," McLellin explained.[102]

His two greatest problems over inconsistencies in the revelations were with (1) a proclamation of peace, followed almost immediately by a revelation calling the Saints to war; and (2) a revelation that changed the name of the church. According to McLellin's recollection, "at first was taught and practiced the principle of non-resistance for some years. Would not return evil for evil or railing for railing."[103] This was confirmed in August 1833 when "Smith professed to receive this word from the Lord, 'Renounce War, and proclaim peace.'"[104] In less than two months, the leaders reversed themselves and "renounced peace and proclaimed war."[105] This "was contrary to all revelation and to the best interests of the church, and was the prime cause of the entire church being driven from the county, over the Missouri river into Clay Co."[106] Possibly a major difference in perspective was that McLellin had focused on Jesus and the New Testament, while Joseph Smith may have been

---

97. RLDS D&C 101:9; LDS D&C 104:47-48, 53. Again, there are slight variants in McLellin's wording and that of the Doctrine and Covenants.

98. Notebook 7, p. 415.

99. Not surprisingly, this revelation was not included in the 1835 Doctrine and Covenants or in any later editions.

100. Letter 12, p. 492.

101. Book of Commandments 30:7.

102. Letter 12, p. 483.

103. Notebook 5, p. 326.

104. RLDS D&C 95:3; LDS D&C 98:16.

105. Notebook 5, p. 326.

106. Ibid.

preoccupied with Old Testament passages in which God had directed his people to wage war.[107]

Zion's Camp was "the great reason," according to McLellin, "why the church was driven from this [Jackson] county and never allowed to return again."[108] What we in the Community of Christ like to call "Christ's peaceable kingdom" did not last more than a year.[109] McLellin detailed how the men of Zion's Camp died young or in horrible circumstances as evidence of God's displeasure, in McLellin's view. Sixty or seventy men got cholera,[110] and of those, fourteen died[111] in this fruitless expedition. Key leaders of the expedition, as McLellin points out, died early, some ignominiously, to borrow a Book of Mormon term.[112] McLellin opined, "All this was contrary to the peaceable and glorious doctrines of the Lord Jesus Christ, to cease to do evil, and cease to resist evil."[113]

During the military expedition to Missouri, Joseph Smith got into a quarrel with Sylvester Smith over a camp dog and would have come to blows if the brethren had not separated them. Back in Kirtland, Joseph charged Sylvester with insubordination, to which Sylvester countered with his own charge of unsolicited abuse. The high council took two days and two nights to come to a decision in this case. Sylvester held the moral high ground, according to McLellin, but because a verdict against Joseph would have embarrassed the church, the judgment went against Sylvester.[114] Sylvester initially refused to sign the confession—until his brother took him outside and persuaded him to submit. McLellin says: "I do know there was never a more wicked official business performed

107. Could there by a contrast starker than the God of the book of Joshua compared to the teachings of Jesus we see in the Sermon on the Mount in Matthew and Luke?

108. Letter 22, p. 511.

109. A peace emphasis has emerged in the RLDS Church since 1984 when acceptance of Section 156 of the Doctrine and Covenants not only called for ordination of women but also for the soon-to-be-built temple in Independence to be "dedicated to the pursuit of peace, reconciliation, and healing of the spirit." President Wallace B. Smith presented the revelation. His successors, W. Grant McMurray and Stephen Veazey, have continued that emphasis. A favorite phrase of President Veazey is "Christ's peaceable kingdom."

110. Early in Notebook 7, McLellin says sixty men came down with cholera (p. 389). Later in the same notebook, he puts the number of casualties at "about sixty or 70" (p. 418), then settles on seventy (p. 428). It is one of the rare inconsistencies.

111. Letter 22, p. 512.

112. Notebook 7, pp. 389, 414-15, 418, 420, 428.

113. Notebook 5, p. 327.

114. It seems to me that in our churches, as well as in government, we blame the lowest official possible to protect the higher-ups. Here, as in so many cases, the highest official deserves plenty of blame.

on this wide earth." Once again, McLellin saw God's punishment at work because all those who served on the council allegedly "died an untimely, miserable death or did not live out half their days."[115]

Considering the many examples of time-sensitive revelations in the early history of the church, where one revelation replaced a former one, the RLDS First Presidency was right when in the mid-1980s they spoke of "disjunctive revelation" and endorsed the concept that new revelation is not always consistent with past revelation.[116] If conservative RLDS members who defected over the ordination of women and related issues had known their history, they would have acknowledged that Joseph Smith himself was the author of "disjunctive revelation." Often RLDS defectors have said they were restoring the church as it existed in 1830, but that is quite wrong because much of orthodox RLDS thought harks back to the Kirtland period, 1831-38, not 1830.

McLellin accepted the church as it existed when he was baptized in 1831. Eventually he concluded that "the Church of Christ fell in 1834, and J. Smith also fell, and was thereafter only president of that new church of Latter Day-ites."[117] McLellin relates this to the 1834 military campaign and the church's name change. In his view, they "suffered Satan to give them an entire 'false name.'"[118] The name was changed on 3 May 1834 from "Church of Christ" to "Church of Latter Day Saints."[119] In McLellin's later writings, he frequently chastised Joseph Smith for this affront, consistent with his belief in Mormonism in its original expression, reflected in the Book of Mormon. Since the Book of Mormon was the truest book, and "seven times in the book of Mormon the name is clearly stated to be the church of Christ, or the true church of Christ,"[120] these were the only two possible names for the church.

According to McLellin, when "the cholera afflict[ed] about sixty of the number of Joseph's 'braves' and some fourteen died ... Joseph Smith transgressed so as to be rejected." Thereafter the only power left to the prophet was to appoint his successor. McLellin believed David Whitmer's ordination satisfied that demand.[121]

---

115. Letter 12, p. 486.

116. First Presidency, "Nature of New Revelation."

117. Letter 10, p. 476.

118. Letter 8, p. 460.

119. Letter 22, p. 511; *Evening and the Morning Star*, May 1834.

120. Notebook 7, pp. 388-89.

121. Letter 8, p. 460. See D. Michael Quinn, "The Mormon Succession Crisis of 1844," *BYU Studies* 16 (Winter 1976): 187-233; Quinn, "Joseph Smith III's Blessing and the Mormons of Utah," *John Whitmer Historical Journal* 1 (1981): 12-27.

McLellin subscribed to a "dispensationalist theology" that was popular in the nineteenth century in and out of Mormonism. Community of Christ historian Mark Scherer has noted the Kirtland dispensationalism.[122] The central element was a distinction between the *law* dispensation and *gospel* dispensation. The law dispensation covered the period from Moses to Christ, its rules set forth in the Hebrew Bible as the legal standard against which people were judged. With Christ came a new dispensation wherein his gospel provided new guidelines for religious thought and action. These guidelines were to be in place until the millennium when presumably a new set of principles would be ushered in.[123] McLellin believed the priesthood during the law dispensation was the order of Aaron and the priesthood of the gospel dispensation was the Melchizedek priesthood. He could not understand why Joseph Smith would confuse the two and thereby create a false system. The order of Aaron, from the law dispensation, was no longer in effect during the gospel dispensation, as McLellin saw it.[124] This was his central critique of LDS priesthoods, that Joseph Smith combined authority and offices from two or more different dispensations.[125]

Shortly after Joseph Smith III became president of the RLDS Church, McLellin wrote to explain to him that the two conflicting priesthoods "never, no never should have been instituted" in the church.[126] He informed Joseph III that the Book of Commandments makes no mention of high priests or lesser priests but that this was changed when they published the 1835 Doctrine and Covenants.[127] Eleven years later in 1872, he told Joseph III that "there is not a word said in both the books [of] the New Testament and the book of M[ormon] about Aaronic, or Levitical, or Lesser priests as existing in the Gospel age."[128] Nine years later he told Davis H. Bays that "a Levitical priest never lived or ministered among the Nephites."[129] In a letter to RLDS

122. Mark A. Scherer, "'Called by a New Name': Mission, Identity, and the Reorganized Church," *Journal of Mormon History* 27 (Fall 2001).

123. Growing up in Michigan in the 1950s, I would occasionally hear speakers talk about various dispensations, sometimes asserting that specific things would be fulfilled "in this dispensation of time."

124. Notebook 1, pp. 198-99, 239-40.

125. Notebook 7, p. 389.

126. Letter 2, p. 440.

127. Ibid., p. 441.

128. Letter 12, p. 489.

129. Letter 8, p. 463.

editor Isaac Sheen, he said neither the Book of Mormon nor the New Testament know anything of "Aaronic priests."[130]

McLellin's view was that God revealed a particular form of church government to Adam, Enoch, Noah, and on to Abraham, but that the Bible was too succinct and "does not give us the particular form of church government."[131] He tried to harmonize the New Testament and Book of Mormon on this point.[132] In his letter to Sheen, he wrote:

> The word lesser priest, Aaronic priest, or Levitical priest, is not found in the Book of Mormon. The word High Priest or Priesthood is not found in the Book of Mormon, after Jesus personally ministered on this continent. The word priesthood is not found in the Book of Commandments, as far as printed in this city in 1833. Then all the support you have for two priesthoods in the church in the gospel age you have to take from that altered, mutilated, changed, mixed up, and bungled Book of Doctrine and Covenants. And the documents in it were twice, if not three times *altered* and changed before they came to light in that book. No man can be a High Priest or Aaronic or lesser priest either, in the gospel church in this age.[133]

As stated earlier, McLellin eventually accepted the New Testament understanding that the twelve apostles had seen the Christ but that the Mormon apostles had not and held no authority.[134] He rejected the office of patriarch, saying that Joseph Smith's "appointment and ordination of a Patriarch to bless the church has no precedent in God's word, hence null and voice. It was trying to combine the Patriarchal age with the Gospel era."[135]

Early in his post-LDS life, McLellin had in fact accepted the office of high priest. In 1845 he traveled to Tennessee and converted his father to the Sidney Rigdon/William Law church, baptized his father, and ordained him to that office.[136] David Whitmer later rejected the concept,[137] and McLellin followed suit. McLellin also criticized the ordination of bishops to oversee temporal affairs such as church property. Appointing Edward Partridge to administer church property had "no warrant in the word of God, nor in church history either," he told

130. Letter 10, p. 471.
131. Notebook 1, p. 174.
132. Letter 2, pp. 440-41.
133. Letter 10, p. 472.
134. Notebook 5, pp. 324-25.
135. Letter 12, p. 486.
136. Shipps and Welch, eds., *Journals of McLellin,* 343.
137. Ibid., 345.

young Joseph.[138] In Christian history, the bishop was the spiritual head of a large jurisdiction, sometimes a diocese. The bishop was not the pastor of a congregation or ward like the LDS bishop, and he or she was not a financial officer for a jurisdiction, as in the RLDS Church. McLellin thought it was "miserable" that Joseph Smith should have all men in the church ordained, further diluting the significance of priesthood structure.[139]

LDS and RLDS people have long revered the stories of the mountaintop spiritual experiences accompanying the "endowment" in the dedication services held in the Kirtland Temple in 1836. McLellin was there and reported that he was disappointed that the great spiritual endowment he had expected at these meetings had failed to materialize. In fact, the leaders drank wine on empty stomachs, he asserted, and drunkenness accounted for some of the strange behavior that went on. He recalls how Samuel Smith got so drunk he threw up, then had a prophecy while in that state.[140]

McLellin frequently says he peacefully withdrew in 1836 "and never held any connection with Joseph Smith until the day of his death."[141] He says he wrote a letter to Joseph Smith, enclosing his ministerial license and saying: "Suffice it to say, when any one asks me why I left you, I say to them, It was because I lost confidence in the Heads of the church."[142] It is difficult to tell if McLellin was involved in the church at all from August 1836 to his excommunication in 1838. Larry Porter reports that McLellin wrote a letter of withdrawal to the leadership in August 1836—probably the letter McLellin himself refers to above. Porter then says that, after the Twelve wrote to McLellin in December and urged him to come back, McLellin must have re-affiliated because a list of licensed LDS ministers in 1837 included him. In addition, at a September 1837 conference in Kirtland, McLellin was sustained as a member of the Twelve, again at a Far West conference in November. He was finally excommunicated in May 1838. Porter suggests McLellin was active in the church until then apparently because he was sustained with the Twelve, but I do not think we can infer that.[143]

---

138. Letter 12, p. 483.

139. Ibid.

140. Letter 22, p. 511; Letter 23, p. 516; also Letter 12, p. 492; Letter 13, p. 498; Shipps and Welch, eds., *Journals of McLellin,* 320.

141. Letter 14, p. 500.

142. Letter 23, p. 517; see also Letter 26, postscript, on why he left. He dates his departure as August 1836.

143. Porter, "Odyssey of McLellin," 322-23, in which McLellin's letter to "My dear old

Mormon historians have charged McLellin with mob action against the Saints during the conflict in Missouri. In the best history of that period, *The 1838 Mormon War in Missouri,* Steven LeSueur gives an even-handed account which is unlike most versions by Mormon writers who have placed virtually all the blame for this terrible series of events on the Missourians. BYU historian Larry Porter mentions only hostile actions by ex-Mormons and Missourians—thefts and violent actions like the Haun's Mill Massacre—against the Saints. Readers of the current collection will have trouble believing, for example, the statement Porter cites by Timothy B. Foote that McLellin said the Bible, Book of Mormon, and all religion are "matters of speculation and priestcraft from beginning to end, and 'Joe' is the biggest speculator of them all." Porter recounts tales of McLellin's hostility toward Joseph Smith and the Mormons, alleging that McLellin looted Smith's home. While it is probably not possible to know whether these accounts are accurate—or rather to what degree they were embellished—clearly the Saints' actions at the time against the Three Witnesses, who were mobbed by their fellow Mormons, indicate that what we have usually heard was only one side of this conflict. It was an especially dark period in the church and neither side should be pointing fingers at the other. In any case, McLellin's 6 December 1875 letter to John L. Traughber refutes the accusation that he had harassed Joseph while the latter was in the custody of law enforcement. Three years later in another letter to Traughber, McLellin relates the persecution of the Book of Mormon witnesses by the Saints.[144]

Among the more curious disclosures by McLellin is that he had not heard the Mormon tradition about the identity of the angel that visited Joseph Smith and told him about the Nephite record. That is not surprising because the identification of "Moroni" came much later, well after publication of the Book of Mormon in 1830. All but one of 202 narratives reprinted in John W. Welch's *Opening the Heavens: Accounts of Divine Manifestations, 1820-1844* state simply that an "Angel" gave Joseph Smith the plates.[145] There are some variants, but these are minor. In 1831 Lucy

Friends," 24 Jan. 1837 (Shipps and Welch, eds., *Journals of McLellin,* 229-30), also contributes to Porter's reasoning.

144. Letter 22, pp. 514-15.

145. John W. Welch, "The Miraculous Translation of the Book of Mormon," in John W. Welch, with Erik B. Carlson, eds., *Opening the Heavens: Accounts of Divine Manifestations, 1820-1844* (Provo and Salt Lake City: Brigham Young University Press and Deseret Book, 2005), 77-213, esp. "Documenting the Translation Chronology," pp. 118ff. The only mention of "Moroni" is a century later in a 1939 speech by William Pilkington (p. 140), based on his notes of an interview with Martin Harris, who died in 1875.

Smith used the term "Angel of the Lord." In 1835 Orson Pratt referred to an "angel from heaven." In 1848 Joseph Knight used the word "personage." In the 1880s John H. Gilbert said the "lord gave Joseph" the plates. David Whitmer, one of the witnesses to the Book of Mormon, called it a "messenger from God" and "Celestial Visitant," apparently never using even the term "angel."[146]

Since the orthodox Mormon story identifies the angel as Moroni, we just assume its identity must have been known from the beginning even though the sources do not so identify it. In the edition of McLellin's early missionary journals prepared by Jan Shipps and John W. Welch, the index lists "Angel Moroni" four times. Even so, "Moroni" is nowhere to be found except in a scholarly comment introducing a statement by David Whitmer, who is alleged to have said he was shown the gold plates by the Angel Moroni. The quotation from Whitmer does not mention Moroni.[147]

Writing to Davis H. Bays in 1870, McLellin recalled: "I never heard of Moroni, John, or Peter, James, and John. It was after [Joseph Smith] *fell* from God [in 1834] that these [two priesthoods] were put it. ... His history was gotten up after he fell from God."[148] It is not that McLellin doubted the existence of angels. To the contrary, his belief was constant throughout his life, reporting that his own ministering angel "would occasionally speak to my mind and to my heart, and its voice was as calm as a zephyr of a summer's morning, saying 'Be still, and trust in me, and I the Lord will be your deliverer.'"[149]

John W. Welch, on the other hand, believes he can read the traditional story in the gaps in McLellin's early writings. For instance, Welch wonders, when McLellin says he preached on "'the rise and progress of the Church,' how many of the visions of Joseph Smith were recounted? When he spoke about the two priesthoods or about Peter and the divine

146. Ibid., 161, 192, 167, 149, 154. Welch does not include Oliver Cowdery to W. W. Phelps, Letter VI, from the *Messenger and Advocate*, April 1835 (in Dan Vogel, comp. and ed., *Early Mormon Documents* [Salt Lake City: Signature Books, 1998], 2:437-44), which states, seemingly as an afterthought at the end of a long and rambling letter, that it was "the angel Moroni, whose words I have been rehearsing," or the reference in 1834 from an earlier interview with Joseph Smith by Leman Copley to "MORONI" and the "MONKEY," in E. D. Howe, *Mormonism Unvailed* (Painsville, Ohio: By the author, 1834), 276-77, emphasis in original. McLellin himself, in his early journals, referred to the angel of Palmyra as "it" rather than "he" (Shipps and Welch, eds., *Journals of McLellin*, 79).

147. Shipps and Welch, *Journals of McLellin*, 29, 79, 80, 264.

148. Letter 8, p. 461.

149. McLellin, in *Ensign of Liberty*, Jan. 1848, 62, in Shipps and Welch, eds., *Journals of McLellin*, 364n95.

authenticity given by God to the Church, did he comment on the restoration of the Aaronic and Melchesidec Priesthoods at the hands of heavenly messengers? McLellin's failure to record any of these details cannot be taken as evidence that he did not mention such points."[150] However, since nobody else mentioned these things in the early 1830s, why should we presume McLellin did?

Welch's overriding concern seems to be that early Mormons appear normal. That is quite a stretch. Mormonism was a radical sect that stood apart from American society in many ways. By the end of the twentieth century, the LDS Church and its people had become more mainstream, most of them voting for conservative political candidates and aligning themselves with social conservatism. They have actively opposed gay marriage, for example, forgetting that their own form of nineteenth-century marriage was considered abnormal by American society.[151] Mormons have embraced the nineteenth-century critique of their own marriage practices and gone on to point a finger of scorn at others.

Although McLellin was excommunicated prior to the Nauvoo period, he kept up with developments in Utah and within the other Mormon factions throughout his life. He was consistently critical of the doctrines and practices Joseph Smith had introduced in Nauvoo, which were continued in Utah, although he expressed nostalgia for his former acquaintances. He wrote to Orson Pratt in 1854: "I feel sorry to the bottom of my heart that Joseph Smith and his brethren (for I once loved them,) had not lived the pure principles of the doctrine of Christ. Then he [Joseph] would have been alive today." In such a scenario, McLellin still would have been in standing with Joseph and the Twelve.[152] He regretted that "the doctrine of Christ as it was first taught and practiced in the church organization [in] 1830, is scarcely now known among you, or if known is not esteemed or heeded."[153]

When Joseph Smith III accepted the RLDS presidency in 1860, he declared his conviction that his father had not been a polygamist. McLellin suggested that he ask his mother about it.[154] McLellin said Emma

150. Shipps and Welch, *Journals of McLellin,* 23.

151. See D. Michael Quinn, "Prelude to the National 'Defense of Marriage' Campaign: Civil Discrimination against Feared or Despised Minorities," *Dialogue: A Journal of Mormon Thought* 33 (Fall 2000), 1-52.

152. Letter 1, p. 436.

153. Letter 1, p. 434.

154. Letter 2, p. 441.

Smith had told him in 1847 that her husband had practiced both polygamy and adultery. To John Traughber, he explained:

> I visited Mrs. Emma Smith in Nauvoo, in 1847. She told me plainly and frankly that her husband did receive and deliver the Polygamic revelation himself, and she knew he practiced its provisions. And she said she knew he had committed adultery with girls previous to that.[155]

Young Joseph never asked his mother these embarrassing questions until the last year of her life in 1879, and his interview, in which he asks his mother carefully crafted questions and she responds with carefully crafted answers, was not published in the *Saints' Herald* until after Emma's death. This looked suspicious to the LDS, just as the RLDS suspected the validity of the King Follett sermon, having been first published, as it was, after Joseph Smith's death.[156] Not to make too much of the coincidence of Emma's death, one can still not help but wonder if Joseph III may have taken more liberty in editing the interview once his mother had died.

McLellin recognized that polygamy was sanctioned by the Bible in the accounts of the various patriarchal figures in the Old Testament. On the other hand, McLellin also believed the Old Testament had been corrupted by the centuries-long transmission process, so he could criticize its contents and polygamy in particular as, in fact, "a blot on the Bible."[157]

The greatest "heresy" of Mormonism, compared to classic Christian orthodoxy, was the doctrine of the plurality of gods and eternal progression to godhood. McLellin called it "the most ruinous of pure religion, of any that could be introduced."[158] To think "that man can ever be exalted or in any way become a God," he fumed, "is monstrous–an absurdity of the deepest die. Man become a God and reign over a glorified world with his numerous progeny by many wives and concubines. Plurality of Gods is connected with plurality of women. They cannot be separated."[159] McLellin quotes the classic text on monotheism from Isaiah: "Beside me there is no God; ... I know not any" (44:6, 8). He may have known that ancient Israel's God, Yahweh, was once seen as having

155. See Letter 15, p. 501.

156. Emma died in April. See Joseph Smith III, "The Last Testimony of Sister Emma," *Saints' Herald*, 1 Oct. 1879, 289-90; also Linda King Newell and Valeen Tippetts Avery, *Mormon Enigma: Emma Hale Smith, Prophet's Wife, "Elect Lady," Polygamy's Foe, 1804-1879* (Garden City, NY: Doubleday, 1984), 304.

157. Notebook 7, p. 394.

158. Ibid., p. 393.

159. Ibid.

equal standing with the gods of other nations. When the sixth-century "prophet of the Exile," Second Isaiah, first asserted the notion of "radical monotheism," it turned the former belief on its head.[160] However, Joseph Smith envisioned something much different than tolerance of the gods of other nations. His pantheon included everyday people, deified alongside their polygamous families.

It is no surprise that McLellin thought baptism for the dead was "nonsense and worse! Proxy never saved a soul since the world began, nor never will."[161] The RLDS were ambiguous about this principle for nearly a century until President Israel A. Smith was so against the practice that he sought unsuccessfully in the 1950s to have the three relevant revelations removed from the RLDS Doctrine and Covenants. He was unsuccessful not because the members believed in baptism for the dead but rather because they were reluctant to delete any sections from the canon of scripture that would suggest some weakness in the founding prophet. Twelve years after his death, the church moved the three documents to the back of the Doctrine and Covenants and then, twenty years later, dropped them entirely.[162]

McLellin criticized the combination of temporal and spiritual power in one person at the head of the church.[163] This was one of the complaints he included in his 1872 letter to Joseph Smith III—"this combining temporal and spiritual power together, like the Popes of Rome."[164] McLellin concluded by telling young Joseph his father was not a good man and that his death should not be hailed as martyrdom.

McLellin never affiliated with the RLDS Church, but his wife, Emeline, was baptized on 1 July 1888, five years after her husband's death. She was born in 1809 and lived until 1907.[165] William's main criticism of

---

160. Ibid. Biblical scholarship has established the multiple authorship of Isaiah. Certain parts, such as the radical monotheism statement in chapter 44 and the mention of Persian emperor Cyrus clearly by name were written later than the eighth century when Isaiah prophesied. The historical context, the literary style, and the theology of chapters 40ff. in Isaiah clearly demonstrate a later date than the eighth century. This, of course, raises a problem for the historicity of the Book of Mormon because it borrows from portions of Isaiah that were written after Lehi's departure in 600 BCE.

161. Notebook 5, p. 331; compare Notebook 3, p. 268; Notebook 7, p. 394; Letter 2, p. 443.

162. See Roger Launius, "An Ambivalent Rejection: Baptism for the Dead and the Reorganized Church Experience," *Dialogue* 23 (Summer 1990): 61-84.

163. Notebook 7, pp. 387-88, 390, 408, 415, 418, 422-23, 426.

164. Letter 12, p. 496.

165. Susan Easton Black, comp., *Early Members of the Reorganized Church of Jesus Christ of Latter Day Saints*, (Provo: BYU Religious Studies Center, 1993), 4:371-72.

the RLDS Church was that it denied that Joseph Smith had been a polygamist. That was reason enough for McLellin to dislike the Josephites—ironically touching on the same topic of dispute with the Brighamites—even though the RLDS themselves abhorred polygamy as much as McLellin did. But to contribute to the coverup was something the former apostle could not forgive.[166]

His second most important criticism was the conferral of lineal right to the office of president. McLellin said Joseph Smith had improperly incorporated the structure of the *law* dispensation, including lineage, into the structure of the *gospel* dispensation. This was too much for McLellin, who could find "not a word about hereditary rights in the gospel system—not a word!!"[167] Anti-polygamy and lineal succession within the office of church president had been the two central issues in creation of the RLDS Church. The idea of lineage was also applied to other offices. It was thought by many RLDS for many years that a man's priesthood office would naturally transfer to his son, although the son would have to be worthy.[168]

In 1878, McLellin's notebook, "Why I am Not a Latter Day Saint," mentioned additional reasons for antagonism toward the RLDS Church. For instance, he stated that in the gospel system it is not right for one man to be "President and Head of the Church" because Christ set on both continents apostles first, then prophets to work under the direction of the apostles—not vice versa.[169]

Two other objections were not necessarily true because the RLDS Church had not formally affirmed either the plurality of gods or baptism for the dead. McLellin was partly right on the plurality of gods. RLDS leaders in the 1860s debated whether it was an acceptable doctrine or not. McLellin probably knew that some in the church believed the doctrine and that it had not been repudiated. The RLDS rejection of baptism for the dead was similarly gradual and ambiguous.[170]

A closely related complaint by McLellin regarded the confusion over priesthoods since the RLDS Church accepted the two priesthoods established by Joseph Smith.

---

166. Letter 6, p. 454; Letter 2, p. 441.

167. Notebook 7, p. 393.

168. In 1957 when I was nineteen, my district president, Almer Sheehy, prophesied to me in a prayer meeting that "the lineal priesthood is within you." I was called to be a priest very shortly thereafter and many years later an elder, both offices my father held. However, I am unlikely to attain the office of high priest, which my father eventually held.

169. Notebook 7, p. 393.

170. Notebook 5, p. 329; Launius, "Ambivalent Rejection."

Another objection was tithing. McLellin correctly noted that tithing is not affirmed in the New Testament. However, he was incorrect regarding the Book of Mormon's stance on this.

He thought the RLDS Church was based on self-appointed authority: "I do not believe that John the Baptist came and ordained J. Smith and O. Cowdery."[171]

To an unidentified "Dear Mary," McLellin mentioned that he was sending advice to Joseph III, which he suspected would go unheeded: "Wo[e] betide his cause, for it will sink, and never be heard of in celestial glory."[172] To Joseph III himself, McLellin did not mince words: "I feel sorry that you took the position you did. Had you come out squarely on <u>original</u> principles then you would have been right. But my hopes are now very slim."[173] Despite such unequivocal rejection of the RLDS for the reasons stated, what is equally significant is how much McLellin shared in common with the Reorganization. He held pretty much the same beliefs and reservations as the dissenters in all the various splinter groups which did not go West, including the RLDS.

Another striking characteristic of McLellin is that even when presenting his views with some forcefulness, he seems to have been ever the gentleman. His letter to young Joseph is just one example that could be given, wherein he wrote: "I feel no e[n]mity to any man for differing with me in views, on religious matters," then ended with: "Prosperity to You in all righteous endertakings. W.E.M."[174]

Conclusion

As we Mormons write our histories of the early church, we tend to discount the views of those who separated themselves from the flock—those like William E. McLellin who trusted their own counsel over that of the institution. How much better to try to find out why such people separated from the church. Sometimes the fault resided with the leaders. Looking back over McLellin's life and the history of Mormonism, there is an even greater question: Why has Mormonism fractured so? Perhaps because Mormons are so sure they are right, coupled with the goal of restoring the purity of a gospel which allegedly existed at the time of Adam. That can imply that any change is heresy, while simultaneously those who hold too fervently to the past are in equal danger of

171. Notebook 5, pp. 331-32.
172. Letter 13, p. 496.
173. Letter 12, p. 489.
174. Ibid., p. 492.

apostasy. Human institutions inevitably change over time, so there will always be conservative dissenters challenging changes in churches that claim to be restoring lost truths. The contemporary Mormon polygamists, called fundamentalists, are a good example of this.[175]

McLellin's adult life is a sad story of a sincere, devout believer in the Book of Mormon who continually studied and prayed and engaged in extensive correspondence advocating the truth as he saw it. The true church of Christ, he concluded, had never appeared during his lifetime. If he were still alive today, at over 200 years old, he might still be waiting and still frustrated.

Critics of McLellin often suggest that he turned from what he had once believed and for no good reason. It seems that John W. Welch, in his annotations of McLellin's diaries, wants to make it appear that McLellin's later views contradicted his earlier ones. While McLellin did alter his beliefs in some minor respects as the years went by, it would be much more accurate to say that the LDS Church changed and McLellin's beliefs remained relatively stable–belief in the Book of Mormon and the importance of heavenly communication with human beings. Later developments by Joseph Smith brought seismic shifts in the church's theology and practice, and this is what McLellin objected to. As he saw it, the church had departed from the truth; he was trying to cling to the truth. It should not be difficult to understand this because it is so similar to that of LDS and RLDS fundamentalists, for whom the changes initiated by the leadership of their churches constitute a bridge too far.

I see William E. McLellin as an essentially likeable person–not a crank, not a power-hungry fanatic or an immoral person. He was a true conservative who quite logically became distressed with the innovations he observed. Joseph Smith was God's instrument for translating our most reliable scripture, then Joseph wandered into darkness, leading the church into uncharted paths. The founder made serious mistakes beginning the day he organized the church, and equally in succeeding years. Therefore, his death at an early age was no surprise for McLellin. After all, the prophets had said to repent or be destroyed.[176] The way McLellin saw it, this was unintentionally prophetic.

McLellin's writings from his later years reflect a "mature" view of

175. For a good account of twentieth-century Mormon polygamy from an orthodox Mormon perspective, see Brian C. Hales, *Modern Polygamy and Mormon Fundamentalism: The Generations after the Manifesto* (Salt Lake City: Greg Kofford Books, 2005).

176. Mosiah 7:55 (LDS 12:8); Alma 6:21; 7:14, 38; 8:34; 13:7; 21:18 (LDS 8:16; 9:12, 24; 10:23; 21:6; 45:16); Hel. 3:127 (LDS 10:14).

one who continued to study religion seriously and related what he learned to the Mormon experience. We should not ignore him or assume that what he said was untrue simply because he became more critical of Joseph Smith as he and Mormonism changed.

Notebooks

1

A TREATISE ON FAITH, 1854-1857

Chester, Geauga Co. Ohio.
April 15. 1854. W. E. McLellin

A treatise on Faith

All things are possible to him that believeth Mar[k] 9:23.
"According to your faith be it unto you" [Matt. 9:29] –Jesus.

1. Among the principles of the gospel of Christ, we think ~~the first~~ one of the[1] most important links[2] in the grand chain, is faith.–Paul by inspiration said in Heb. 11:6, "He that cometh to God must believe that he is, and that he is a rewarder of them that diligently seek him." And "without faith it is impossible to please him."

2. Probably more has been written on that word in Theology, called faith, than any other in the English language; or rather upon the principle or idea contained in the word, or communicated to the mind by it.

3. The definition given in holy writ, has not satisfied the curious, nor quieted the contentious; and theologians have ransacked their brains and the great and small libraries of the world, to find a better or different definition than that simply given by the apostle Paul in Heb 11:1, "Faith is the substance (i.e., the ground or confidence,) of things hoped for, the evidence of things not seen." This definition suits us very well. But Buck[3] in his theological dictionary, says "Faith is the assent which we give to a proposition advanced by another, the truth of which we do not immediately perceive from our own reason and experience,

---

The first essay in this notebook, "A Treatise on Faith," should be compared with McLellin's two-part article, "On Faith," which appeared in *The Ensign*, 15 July, Sept. 1844, 8-11, 38-40. Absent a title for this notebook, outside of "Chester, Geauga Co. Ohio. April 15. 1854. W. E. McLellin," which McLellin wrote on the cover, we have applied the title of the first essay to the entire notebook as a general designation of the contents.

1. McLellin added "of the."
2. McLellin added the "s" to make "links."
3. For a summary of Charles Buck's life, see the Biographical Notes.

or it is a judgement or assent of the mind, the motive whereof is not any intrinsic evidence, but the authority or testimony of some other who reveals or relates it. The Greek noun translated faith, comes from a verb which signifies to persuade,[4] the nature of faith being a persuasion and assent of the mind, arising from testimony or evidence." Brown,[5] in his Dictionary of the Bible says: "Faith properly signifies, a persuasion and assent to truth upon the authority [page 2:] of another, and is opposed to doubting."

4. Webster,[6] in his Dictionary of the English language, says: 1. "Faith is the assent of the mind to the truth of what is declared by another, resting on his authority and veracity, without other evidence. 2. The assent of the mind to the truth of a proposition advanced by another; belief, on probable evidence. 3. In theology the assent of the mind or understanding to the truth of what God has revealed,"&c. "Belief of the revealed truths of religion." –Hooker.[7] Swift[8] says, "Faith is trust in God."

5. We might multiply authors on the subject–this all-absorbing subject; but we think the above will answer as to the definition of learned men; Therefore we proceed to another part of the subject. Mr Buck, in his Theological dictionary, has given us an explanation of seven different kinds of faith, viz: divine, human, historical, the faith of miracles, a temporary faith, faith in respect to futurity, and faith in Christ. And Mr. Brown adds, "Saving faith," which would make eight. We have been some astonished that men with gifted minds, with the revelations of God in their hands, as contained in the scriptures, with good common sense, and with all the light of the sciences as now developed shining upon their minds, should be so speculative and wild in their notions about faith. For we never could learn from the sources of truth that there was or is but "one faith" [Eph. 4:5]. And that faith according to the apostle James is either a "living or dead faith" [cf. James 2:26]. If it produces action then we would call it living faith; but if no action is pro-

---

4. The beginning of this sentence illustrates how McLellin, not knowing Greek, made some adjustments to Buck's wording. Charles Buck, *A Theological Dictionary containing Definitions of All Religious Terms; A Comprehensive View of Every Article in the System of Divinity; An Impartial Account of All the Principal Denominations Which Have Subsisted in the Religious World from the Birth of Christ to the Present Day: Together with an Accurate Statement of the Most Remarkable Transactions and Events Recorded in Ecclesiastical History* (Philadelphia: J. J. Woodward, 1832), 180, gives this part of the sentence as "The Greek word, Πιστις, translated faith, comes from the verb Πειθω, to persuade."

5. For a summary of John Brown's life, see the Biographical Notes.

6. For a summary of Noah Webster's life, see the Biographical Notes.

7. For a summary of Richard Hooker's life, see the Biographical Notes.

8. For a summary of Jonathan Swift's life, see the Biographical Notes.

duced, of course it would be dead—dead because it would be motionless. [page 3:]

6. Now if philosophy too as well as scripture will bear us out in this point, then we hope all honest inquirers after <u>truth</u>, for the sake of truth will be profited, and all the "traditions of men," and "doctrines of devils" on this subject, may be found out and seen to be what they really are, that is, chaff, and nothing but chaff:—only words without knowledge, subverting the souls of men, and leading them farther, and farther astray from God and truth: Yea, mere vanity.

7. No rational or intelligent being has more than one mind, though that **mind** has various properties, or faculties which compose it. With the powers of the **mind** we examine every thing presented to us in which we are interested. Some individuals examine with one degree of scrutiny and some with another, owing to the peculiar construction of their minds; or rather to the degrees of intelligence which the individuals have acquired. Now if the faculties of the mind are the same in all, although in some weaker and others stronger, how is it that we can find different kinds of faiths? With the same powers of mind we believe every thing to which we assent; and with the same mind we reject every thing which does not come to us, as we think, sufficiently authenticated. Thence we come to the inevitable conclusion with the apostle that there is but "one faith." Although that may be exercised on different objects, and consequently produce varied results, yet there is but <u>**one** faith</u>.

8. We will here divide the faculties of the mind into the understanding, the the[9] heart, and the will. The understanding is that which perceives ideas, compares them one with another, and judges of their agreement or disagreement. It is the seeing or thinking faculty. Its operations are termed perceptions. The heart is that which loves, hates, and desires, is pleased or displeased. It is the seat of all those exercises which are pleasing or painful, and virtuous or [page 4:] vicious. It is the feeling faculty. Its operations are termed affections. The will is the determining faculty—that which determines or chooses to act. Its operations are termed volitions.

9. Imagination or fancy is that faculty or power of the mind which forms ideal pictures or images without evidence—without being perceived by the senses. Opinion is the persuasion of the mind. It is an idea formed from our reason without certain evidence or foundation; or it is an imaginative **idea** settled into a conviction merely from reasoning. Be-

9. McLellin wrote the word "the" twice, the first at the end of one line and the second at the beginning of the next.

lief is the settled conviction of the mind upon testimony. It is the credit given to evidence. It is the full assent of the mind to the truth of a proposition. And Faith is the concentration of all the foregoing into one point. It is belief carried to freedom from doubt. It is the confidence of things hoped for. It is the assurance of the existance of things not seen. It is actual trust in God. In man it is always the moving principle of spiritual power. By faith he draws all he ever obtains from the Eternal fountain. And without faith it is impossible to please God. Knowledge is the end of belief and faith. It is faith carried to possession and to positive and real[10] certainty. It is an actual acquaintance with persons, objects, principles, and things as they are, were & will be. It is the possession of facts and realities. It is our experience of things. It is the enjoyment of that in which we had believed. Knowledge is said to be power. And it is partly true. Knowledge is based on the immutable revelations of God. Faith is swallowed up in knowledge. We cant believe what we know. Knowledge is the focal point of faith, the result of faith, & the end of faith: It is that which we possess within ourselves. [page 5:]

10. Living faith is that principle which actuates us in all our right dealings both with or before God and man. Dead faith is that which does not produce action—does not show itself in active works. Faith is an act or exercise of the mind, placing confidence in that which is made known. And the effect produced upon the individual is always owing to the object about whom, or concerning which the evidence is given. If the testimony adduced is concerning the divine Being, and the mind or understanding assents to the truth of that which is proposed, then the effect produced upon the heart is what Mr. Buck would call "a divine faith." But it is not in reality a different kind of faith from any other living faith; but it is the powers of the mind called up to contemplate the Creator, and if we give credence or assent, then the effect produced is confidence in, reliance on, or assurance of the existance of God. It is not divine faith, but faith exercised in a divine personage. And if we suffer that assurance to work in us to will, then the effect or result ~~in us~~ is living faith. And if carried out it will produce right action towards him in whom that faith is centered. But if the evidence presented is concerning some natural or temporal object, and we assent to it, then only a natural or common result is produced in the mind; and if there is any motive produced by the testimony or in the object, to beget in us a will, then our action should always correspond with our interests, and it always will provided we are correctly taught and act rationally.

10. McLellin added "positive and real."

11. There are different kinds of evidence by which we assent to the truth of propositions, and of these but two are infallible. First: when the principles upon which the evidence is founded, are intuitive. [page 6:] Such is the evidence of Mathematical truths. Secondly: when God speaks from heaven to man by his own voice, by an angel, by an open vision, or by his Son; then that which is spoken is infallible testimony to the mind. The next highest evidence to the mind is experience. Such is the evidence on which natural and experimental philosophy stands. This is received immediately by the senses. But there is a possibility of being deceived by any one of our senses singly, since to a man having the jaundice badly things sometimes appear yellow. The organs of the ear may be diseased and we may think, ~~that we~~ and even affirm that we hear sounds, when we do not. The next and last class of evidence which we shall now notice is wherein we give our assent to the truth of a proposition on the veracity of others. Now, reviewing the above, we are intuitively certain that a whole is greater than a part. When our three senses of seeing, hearing, and feeling are brought into requisition by the vocal voice of the Lord, by the presence of his Son, or of an angel of light, the evidence will not admit of doubt; therefore it is infallible. Next we are experimentally certain that fire will burn. And lastly, we are by testimony convinced that Jesus of Nazareth was the Christ, the Son of God.

12. Jesus is said to be "the author and finisher of faith" [cf. Heb. 12:2]. And we read in the scriptures of the "proportion, measure, or degrees of faith." That is, of strong or weak faith, of great or little faith. We also read of the "common–mutual–unfeigned–precious–holy faith." Also [page 7:] "The law of faith, the spirit of–the righteousness–joy–mystery–word–work–obedience–the prayr–and the assurance of faith." "The trial–the breastplate–the shield–and the fight of faith. The unity, and the end of faith." And we also read that "faith is both a gift, and a fruit of the Holy Spirit."

13. The way that Jesus is the "author,["] i.e. beginner of faith is explained by the following quotation from the Apostle, "For there is no difference between the Jew and the Greek: for the same Lord over all is rich ~~is rich~~ unto all that call upon him. + + + How then shall they call on him in whom they have not believed? and how shall they believe in him of whom they have not heard? and how shall they hear without a preacher? and how shall they preach except they be sent? + + + So then faith cometh by hearing the word of God" [cf. Rom. 10:12, 14-15, 17]. Ah! is the ear the organ, hearing the sense or medium, preaching the word of God, and bearing testimony to truth the cause, and belief or

faith the effect produced. Is this sound reasoning? Let us turn it over and look at it again. Then in order to first produce the faith of Gospel, the Lord must first call a man or men by revelation—by direct revelation from heaven, set them apart i.e ordain them, or cause them to be ordained,[11] to his ministry, and ~~then~~ send them out to preach his gospel by the power of the "Holy Ghost sent down from heaven" [1 Pet. 1:12]. Thus, the Author of faith is "pleased by the foolishness of preaching to save them that believe" [cf. 1 Cor. 1:21]. ~~Belief or~~ faith then is a saving principle, connected with obedience. And thus "faith comes by hearing the word of God" [cf. Rom. 10:17]. And Jesus sending "the word" to us becomes the "Author of faith & of our eternal salvation" [cf. Heb. 5:9; 12:2]. [page 8:]

14. But again there is a faith spoken of in the New Testament, which no wicked man ever did or ever will receive. It is contrary to the nature of the Lord's dealing. He cannot enjoy it, cannot exercise it, cannot have it. The apostle Paul in speaking of the "spiritual gifts" which the Lord gave to his children, said, "To another faith by the same spirit" [1 Cor. 12:9]. The "birth of the spirit," succeeds the birth of the water. When men on the day of Penticost were cut to the heart by the force of truth, and inquired what they must do to be saved; inspiration said to them "Repent and be baptized every one of you, in the name of Jesus Christ, for the remission of sins; and (then and not till then,) ye shall receive the gift of the Holy Ghost" [Acts 2:38]. There is not a promise in "God's word" to any man or men of the gift of the Holy Spirit, until after faith, repentance, and baptism. There is not an example given in the New Testament where a wicked man ever received the gift of the Spirit before baptism. Without a birth of water and spirit no man ever yet entered into the kingdom of Christ. In thus "being born again" the external man is born of water and the internal man is born of the Holy Spirit, and thus man is "a new creature." He is translated from the kingdom of darkness into the kingdom of light. Thus ~~man~~ man receives the spirit of **the King** and by it he may obtain the "gift of faith," but without that spirit he cannot receive the "gift" or be exercised by it. The Lord's spirit does not dwell in unholy temples. An unbelieving wicked man is unholy; [page 9:] and in order to obtain and enjoy the Holy Spirit, he must "arise and be baptized and wash away his sins, calling upon the name of the Lord" [cf. Acts 22:16]. Then he is washed—then the temple is prepared for the reception of the Spirit; by which he can truly pray "Our Father who art in heaven" [Matt.

11. McLellin added "or cause them to be ordained."

6:9]. Then, and not till then, he can receive this "gift of faith." Then he can understand the force of Judas' enquiry "Lord how is it that thou wilt manifest thyself unto us and ~~dost~~ not unto the world?" [John 14:22]. This exercising the "gift of faith," with the other gifts of the Spirit, once was, ought to be now, and will be at the coming of the Savior, the distinguishing characteristic of the true believers.

15. It was this gift of faith by which the ancients did wonders. "Through faith they subdued kingdoms, wrought righteousness, obtained promises, + + + women received their dead raised to life again" [Heb. 11:33, 35]. &c. &c. It was by or through this "gift of faith"—by the immediate operation of the spirit of God, that every miracle which has ever been performed since the days of Adam to the present time, was and has been done—except those which have been performed by the power of Belzebub. For the servants of Satan have wrought miracles as well as the servants of God. No doubt both performed their wonders by faith; but their faith was centered in opposite objects—one in God, the other in the Devil.

16. To illucidate more clearly this "gift of faith," we will introduce an example. When Moses and the children of Israel had started from [page 10:] Egypt to Canaan, they halted on the banks of the Red Sea, enclosed by mountains and the Egyptian army. Nothing could save them but the interposition of Heaven. "By faith they passed th[r]ough the Red Sea as by dry land" [Heb. 11:29]. They believed in God from their forefathers, yet they could see no way of escape now. Here Moses was exercised by two of the "gifts of the spirit," viz: revelation and faith. Yet he had no faith now which directed him what to do, only to trust in God, until the Lord said to him, "Lift up thy rod, and stretch out thy hand over the sea, and divide it" [Ex. 14:16]. That moment the "gift of faith" was lit up in his soul. He lifted up his rod in faith. His friends were delivered. His enemies sunk. His soul magnified the Lord, and his stock of knowledge was increased. Thus the gift of faith is an immediate operation, act, or gift of the Spirit of God on the minds of all those who ever receive it. And yet it comes by "hearing the word of God" spoken at the time needed—at the time exercised. The difference between "the common faith," and "the gift of faith" is, one is a gradual, and the other is an immediate operation of the mind.

17. But dear reader, stop for a moment and think, if there is no church in christendom who is now contending for and enjoying the "spiritual gifts," or miraculous gifts by the spirit, and the gift of faith is one of these gifts; then can any church claim "the gift of faith"? We an-

swer no! distinctly no!! The ancients enjoyed the spiritual gifts[12] by faith in God. The same cause will produce the same effects, now as then.

18. But let us take another view of this subject. The Ap[os]tle Jude wrote to his brethren thus: "It was needful for me to write unto you, and [page 11:] exhort you that you should earnestly contend for the faith which was once delivered to the saints" [Jude 1:3]. To what saints did he refer? "Once delivered," in this place means previously delivered. Then we ask what this earnest contention should be for? Should it be about creeds, or forms, or doctrines, or notions of men? No. It should be ~~about~~ "for the faith." The gift of faith–living faith. Faith exercised in a living object producing action–yes, marvelous results. Then it would be the faith which was once delivered to the saints. It would not only be like their faith, but it would be the very same faith. But again, did the ancients believe that it was their privilege to receive immediate aid[13] [and] power from God? Yes: by them "the mouths of lions were stopped" [cf. Heb. 11:33]. Did they believe in receiving direct revelations from heaven for themselves? Yes. Paul says, "They obtained promises" [Heb. 11:33]. Do christians (as they are called,) of our day believe in receiving miraculous power from God–revelations from heaven now? No. Do they then have faith–the same faith that actuated the bosoms of the ancients? Do they have faith in the same objects, in the same things? If so, does it produce the same effects, the same results? No! O, no!! But where are those enjoyments? Where is that "like precious faith" [2 Pet. 1:1], by which all the ancient worthies lived and walked and held sweet[14] communion with heaven, with angels, with Jesus, and with his Father? O! where! where shall we find it in christendom at the present day? Have all those precious privileges fled from earth no more to return, until the Lord comes in his glory? He said while here, "Nevertheless when the Son of man cometh, shall he find Faith on the earth?" [Luke 18:8]. O, my Lord! if thou shouldst come now, as many [page 12:] believe thou wilt soon, then, O, then! where wouldst thou find that faith which actuated thy saints and martyrs? Or wouldst thou come and "smite the earth with a curse" [Mal. 4:6]? Nay, but there will be a people on earth before the burning day, who will serve the Lord aright; who will have faith, who will be prepared to meet and abide that consuming time–the glorious appearing of our Lord and his mighty angels, with all the heavenly throng. For Jesus said while on earth, in reference to this very point–"But as the days

12. McLellin added "gifts."

13. McLellin added "aid."

14. McLellin added "sweet."

of Noah were, so shall also the coming of the Son of man be" [Matt. 24:37]. In the days of Noah, among the wicked they knew not "until the flood came and took them all away" [Matt. 24:39]. But how was it with the righteous family of Noah, who obeyed the voice of revelation given to them in order to their safety? Did that day overtake them as a thief in the night? No. Noah "being moved with fear prepared an ark to the saving of his house" [Heb. 11:7]. If it will be before the second coming of Messiah, as it was in the days of Noah, then the Lord will call upon some man or men by direct revelations from heaven. They will hearken to his voice.—Will have faith in his word. Will prepare a plan of temporal safety. Will gather into it, and the Lord will then preserve them while "the day cometh that shall burn as an oven,["] (as he preserved Noah and Lot,) till his overflowing judgement consumes "all the proud and all that do wickedly" [Mal 4:1]. By faith the saints will stand that trying day. By "<u>the gift of faith</u>," th[e]y will outstrip the winds, and flee from the wrath to come. By faith they will be caught up to meet the Lord in the air, and so shall they ever be with the Lord. Amen. ~ [page 13:]

<u>Repentance</u>.

1. Repentance means an afterthought, or the soul recollecting its own actings, which produces uneasiness, anxiety, and sorrow in the review of what has been done amiss, and a desire of amendment. It consists in conviction of sin, sorrow for it, confession of it, hatred to it, renunciation of it or reformation from it,[15]—and so far as it is in the power of the sinner, restitution or restoration for the evil or injury done.

2. Repentance towards God is in immidiate connection with faith in our Lord Jesus Christ. A man or men sent of the Lord declare their message or preach the gospel "in demonstration of the spirit and of power, with the Holy Ghost sent down from heaven" [cf. 1 Cor. 2:4; 1 Pet. 1:12]. Those who hear and believe the truth of the principles declared, that belief or faith works in them a "repentance unto salvation" [2 Cor. 7:10].

3. On the day of Pentecost the Apostles and Elders received that "other Comforter" as a seal to their ministry, i.e. an enduement from their King, to qualify them to "go into all the world," and speak in all the languages and tongues of the earth in order "to preach the gospel to every creature which is under heaven" [cf. Mark 16:15].

4. Now, when the descent of the Holy Spirit and its effects upon the believers "was noised abroad, the multitude came together" [Acts 2:6] and heard the ministers of this heavenly kingdom speak understand-

15. McLellin added "or reformation from it."

ingly in sixteen different tongues "the wonderful works of God." The minds of the hearers were open to investigation, for "there were devout men dwelling at Jerusalem, from every nation under heaven" [cf. Acts 2:5]. Being devout or honest, they wished to know the truth. Peter stood up with the eleven, and uttered a solemn testimony, and taught them from the sacred scriptures, in which they professed faith, that Jesus was the Christ, and that "this Jesus had God raised up," and "he hath shed forth this [page 14:] which you now see and hear" [Acts 2:32-33]. When they heard this they were cut to the heart—that is, they heard the word of the Lord, and they saw the effect of the Holy Spirit: consequently, after believing the evidences, sorrow filled their hearts, which belief ~~in them~~ and sorrow produced in them a desire to reform and to be saved, hence they enquired "What shall we do?"

5. The answer by the spirit and power of the Lord Jesus, through the apostles, (Peter being mouth or having the keys,) was ready. What was the answer? Was it to believe in the Lord Jesus? No. Was it to be heartily sorry for their sins? No. Both these they had done, and it would be useless for divine wisdom to command men—intelligent men, to do things which they had just performed. But the query of the convicted, broken and contrite in heart, still reverberates, what, O! what shall we do? What shall be the next act of our lives after we have received faith "by hearing the word of God." We have heard, we do believe and we are sorry. Now, O! ye men of Israel, and brethren according to the covenant of God with Abraham, can we be saved or delivered from sin? If so, what should be our next act according to the principles of adoption, by which we can enter into the kingdom of Christ?

6. Repent: yes, repent is the divine command. But here we pause and query again, what is repentance? And we answer conviction, sorrow, reformation, and restitution. Reformation is a forsaking or turning away from sin; or as Daniel said to the king "Break off thy sins by righteousness, and thine iniquities by showing mercy to the poor" [Dan. 4:27]. Restoration is the act of returning, or making good to a person some right or thing of which he has been unjustly deprived. In repentance is included restitution for wrongs previously done to our fellow men, as far as it is [page 15:] possibly in our power. Then according to the above, belief produces conviction; conviction produces sorrow, and sorrow ought to produce reformation and restitution. As to the principle and practice of restitution belonging to gospel repentance, we have examined and reflected on the subject much, and have come to the settled conclusion that no man can amass wealth, or even obtain a penny by

fraud or false accusation, and then profess religion–the religion of heaven–and obtain the true spirit of holiness, and then live in the enjoyment of the smiles of the Lord, until he is not only convicted and sorry for, but also reforms from all his wicked deeds, and then restores to the injured. He must be like Zaccheus, "he stood and said unto the Lord, if I have taken any thing from any man by false accusation, I restore him four-fold" [Luke 19:8]. If the principle of restoration was not correct, or did not belong to repentance, why did Jesus, who knew every principle that belonged to his kingdom, say to him–"This day is salvation come to thy house" [cf. Luke 19:9]. But alas! how few of the professors of christianity of our day, or the churches to which they attach themselves, pay any regard to this divine rule? No, no! that would touch that which is dearer to them than their religion–that is, their property–their persestrings, and their honors. For confession & restitution would bring some strange things to light in our world. But they had better be brought to light here than at the day of judgement. And if they are not brought to light here, they must and will be there. For all secret things must be revealed, in order that a righteous judgement can take place–and take place it will for God has said it.

7. By repentance and forgiveness here, we secure a right to a position on the right hand of the Judge, and will hear him say to us,[16] "come ye blessed of my Father" [Matt. 25:34]. [page 16:]

Baptism

1. When the ordinance of baptism was first introduced into the world among men, is a matter of uncertanity–no record with which we are acquainted being explicit on the subject. That the Jews, as a people, were familiar with the ordinance, before "John came preaching in the wilderness of Judea," is plain, from the fact that so many among that people yielded to the "divine rite," whose pr[e]judices were so strong, and who were so much affraid of encroachments upon the law of Moses.–They yielded too, without raising the objection that it wa[s] a new, unwarranted, or unheard of ordinance, introduced contrary to the Mosaic law, in which they professed faith, and according to which they wished to have people think they lived and worshiped. Paul, in speaking of the congregation which left Egypt for Canaan under Moses, their Prophet, their[17] Leader and their[18] Lawgiver, says, "That all our

16. McLellin added "to us."

17. McLellin added "Prophet, their."

18. McLellin added "their."

fathers were under the cloud, and all passed through the sea; and were all baptized unto Moses in the cloud and in the sea" [1 Cor. 10:1-2]. The manner in which this baptism was performed, is not written in "the volume of Book." But we suppose they were baptized unto Moses in the sea, in the same manner as the Jews were baptized unto John's baptism in Jordan.

2. In writing upon this principle of the doctrine of Christ, or ordinance of his gospel, about which there has been so much contention in the world, we realize that we ought to properly understand the subject ourself, (and we think we do,) before we strike pen to paper [page 17:] in order to enlighten others. There are questions which naturally occur to the mind in the examination of this subject; such as the following: 1st How many baptisms are there? 2nd Who is a proper subject? 3rd Is baptism a saving ordinance? 4th Or what was its design? 5th And what is the proper mode of administration? 1st There are two baptisms of which we shall treat, one with water, and one with the Holy Ghost. "For John truly baptized with water; but ye shall be baptized with the Holy Ghost not many days hence" [Acts 1:5]. Paul in summing up the principles of the doctrine of Christ says, "Of the doctrine of baptisms"—isms, in the plural agreeing with the above—"with water and with the Holy Ghost." We shall, however, at this time treat of water baptism, and refer the reader to the latter part of this[19] ~~a~~ treatise ~~following this~~ for the baptism of the Holy Spirit. ~~and its effects~~.

3. 2nd The proper subject for baptism, is a believer in the Lord Jesus Christ. None who are incapable[20] of exercising faith and re~~pe~~pentence, should be baptized. A person who hears the word of truth, the gospel of salvation, preached or taught by a minister who has legal authority from the king, and who believes the ~~the~~ gospel with all the heart, and comes humbly forward with this faith in Christ, and in his ordinances, with conviction, sorrow, and reformation, and demands baptism of said minister, as the Eunuch did of Philip, such penitent believers must be admitted unto baptism into the "church of Christ." Faith in Christ, and repentance for sin always precedes the baptism of a sinner. This accords with what John said to the Jews, when he saw a multitude come to his baptism. "O, generation of vipers! who hath warned you to flee from the wrath to come? Bring forth, therefore, fruits meet for repentance" [Matt. 3:7-8]. It seems that John, who was full of the Holy Spirit [page 18:] from his

19. McLellin added "the latter part of this."

20. McLellin added "in" to make "incapable."

birth, thought that a person must be first warned of danger or wrath to come, believe the warning and bring forth fruits of reformation, before admission unto baptism. The Savior said, in commissioning his apostles for their ministry, "Go ye into all the world and preach the gospel to every creature: he that believeth and is baptized, shall be saved" [Mark 16:15-16]. Or as Matthew has it, "Go ye, therefore, and teach all nations, baptizing them in the name of the Father, and of the Son, and of the Holy Ghost" [Matt. 28:19]. Go teach or preach to all the world—to every creature, the good news of salvation, that men may hear,—may believe: or in other words, go ye and preach, that "faith may come by hearing the word of God" [cf. Rom. 10:17]. And then he that believeth and is baptized shall be saved.

4. The practice of all inspired men, whether Apostles, prophets, evangelists, pastors, or teachers, in building up the kingdom of heaven, in every instance where they established a church, accords with their command, to first teach or preach, and then to baptize the believers. Here we will introduce a few passages, taken from their history "Then they that gladly received his word were baptized: and the same day there were added about three thousand souls" [Acts 2:41].[21] But when they believed Philip preaching the things concerning the kingdom of God, and the name of Jesus Christ, they were baptized both men and women. Philip preaches to the Eunuch [about] Jesus. He hears and believes. The chariot stands still, and they both go down into the water, and he baptizes him. Lydia heard the ministers of Jesus preach the word—The Lord opened her heart that she attended unto the things which were spoken of by Paul, and then she was baptized. The affrighted jailor cried out to Paul and Silas, Sirs, what must I do to be saved? Believe on the Lord Jesus Christ, was the divine command. [page 19:] ["]And they spake to him and to all that were in his house, the word of the Lord; and he and all his were baptized straightway. And many of the Corinthians hearing, believed, and were baptized" [cf. Acts 16:30-33; 18:8]. What could be plainer? Preaching the word of the Lord produces faith, and faith produces conviction and sorrow, and sorrow works repentance, and then after truly repenting, the penitent is immersed in water, for the remission of his sins, and then he is precisely in a state for the baptism of the Holy Spirit.

5. But is baptism in water a saving ordinance? We answer, Yes. We

21. McLellin quoted this passage from the King James Version, but the word "gladly" is not found in the earliest and best Greek manuscripts and seems to have been added from the parallel passage at Acts 21:17.

know of but one plan of salvation, but one gospel, but one law of adoption, but one set of principles and ordinances, that all who come to Christ must obey. But cannot a person be saved by obeying a part of the ordinances of the gospel? And indeed cannot a sinner be saved by faith without obeying any ordinances at all? We have no right to promise eternal life to any, or claim it ourselves upon any principle or plan, except entire obedience to the **plan** of Jesus Christ revealed in the gospel. And we know of no way by which a man can exercise faith in Christ, and not have confidence in his ordinances. Any thing else than the whole plan of adoption, would not be <u>the</u> gospel, but <u>a</u> gospel; another gospel, or rather a perversion of the true gospel of the Savior: and consequently, according to Paul would bring a **curse** instead of a blessing. Jesus said to Nichodemus, "Except a man be born of water and of the Spirit, he cannot enter into the kingdom of God" [John 3:5]. Peter said, "The like figure whereunto, even baptism doth also now save us, by the resurrection of Jesus Christ" [1 Pet. 3:21]. Reader, would you say after reading the above, that any man—after the kingdom of Jesus was set up on the day of Pentacost, ever could be <u>saved</u> without baptism. If so, as all things must be governed by law, by what law, or rule, or principle is he sanctified and saved? If not by the gospel, then he would have to be by some other plan—one which God has not revealed in his word. Where could we find it? We know that men have sought out many inventions, [page 20:] in order to climb up—or to endeavor to get in some other way into "the kingdom of God," than the Lord's plan "of water and of spirit."

6. But what is the proper mode of administering baptism? This is a question of great importance, and it has been the subject of much—very much discussion among the learned as well as the illiterate. Many have been the sermons, the debates, the treatises, the pamphlets, & the books which have agitated the minds of men concerning this one ordinance of the great gospel plan. Hundreds, yea, thousands have read, and closely examined the arguments on both sides—yes, all sides of this question, which the ingenuity of the learned have proposed and discussed. And after this, the minds of men are as much agitated, as much unsettled, as to the **mode** of administration, as they ever have been since the days when John, the baptist, first "came preaching in the wilderness of Judea" [Matt. 3:1].

7. Shall we then assume to ourselves the vanity, that any thing we can write relative to this important ordinance, this mooted question, would settle it in the minds of the contending parties? Nay, if a revelation from heaven, or an angel from God, should be dispatched to earth, and

unfold all the mind of the Lord on this subject, it would not settle the question—only in the minds of a few. The great mass of professors would say, "the day of revelations from God to man has ceased to be, and angel's visits are not now expected on earth; therefore, we do not receive the testimony from the skies:—we believe it is all a delusion. This is a deplorable condition into which the world have placed themselves. They admit that they cannot settle the dispute from "the book," and they are not willing to let the Almighty settle it for them—consequently we see no other alternative only for them to remain in contention, in ignorance, in strife, in confusion, and in darkness, until the Lord comes—And when he comes he will find them caviling. [page 21:]

8. We shall state as to the mode that baptism by immersion in water is the only proper one. And as we have said, it is to be administered to believers only. And that too in order to be valid, must be attended to by a minister who has authority from Jesus so to do. John was a minister thus sent; and when the Jews round about Jordan in Judea came to him "he immersed them in Jordan. And Jesus when he was immersed went up straight-way out of the water" [cf. Matt. 3:13, 16]. He could not have gone up out of the water, had he not been in it. "And John also was baptizing in Enon near Salem because there was much water there" [John 3:23]. We cannot see the propriety of the expression <u>much water</u>, if a few drops only were required in baptism. Philip & the Eunuch "went down into the water—and came up out of the water" [cf. Acts 8:38-39], &c. This is to[o] plain to need comment. Interested priestcraft, notwithstanding, can find many difficulties in the way of immersion. However plain the word of God may speak they can reason it away, and hunt up some far-fetched logic to sustain their frail bark. They are willing to say Lord, Lord; but they do not the things which he says. They all admit that immersion in water is baptism—but contend that sprinkling with water is also. But once more, "The Lord opened Lydia's heart by a river side" [cf. Acts 16:13-14]. Here she and hers were baptized, as we would very naturally suppose, <u>in the river</u>; as the Savior was <u>in the Jordan</u>.

9. Baptism is spoken of under the figure of a birth—"Born of water." A birth is always a seclusion and a bringing forth. Immersion is the only mode of baptism that resembles a birth. That is, a covering up, and then coming up out of the water again. Again baptism is represented under the figure of a burial. "Therefore, we are buried with him by baptism into death" [Rom. 6:4]. Baptism then means an internment in water, as a burial means a covering up in the earth. And rising again from the water, resembles a resurrection of the body from the grave. The two

are similar, at least [page 22:] as nearly as figures generally represent. But again, Noah and his family were saved from the flood, by being enclosed in the ark. "The like figure whereunto even baptism doth also now save us" [1 Pet. 3:21]—We must be enclosed or enveloped. No other mode but immersion will do this. Then immersion, and that only, is gospel baptism.

10. Baptism has two kinds of subjects, and hence two objects to be accomplished in its administration. The first subject is a righteous man, and the second is a sinner. The one is immersed to "fulfill a righteous law." And the other for that, and for the remission of sins also. Jesus & Cornelius' baptisms in water, were not for the forgiveness of their sins, but to keep the righteous law of God—to be born of water as well as **Spirit**, in order to inherit God's kingdom. For it is a fixed law of God, that man organized of body and spirit must receive two baptisms in order to be born again—to be a new creature, that the kingdom of heaven might dwell within him. Jesus could not enter upon his great ministry on earth until his external man was immersed in water, and his internal man overwhelmed in the Spirit. Thus the Savior of the world was "born again—made new," that in him "all fullness might dwell" [Col. 1:19]. And man, sinful man must be immersed in water and in the Holy Spirit in order to rise to his high privilege, "that he too might be filled with all the fulness of God."

11. Man in his fallen state needs "to be cleansed from all the filthiness of the flesh and spirit" [cf. 2 Cor. 7:1]. And the gospel baptisms of water and spirit are peculiarly adapted to that end. They are the means the Lord has given for that object. Water for flesh, and spirit for spirit. Thus the whole man is "born again." And so important was the baptism of the Holy Spirit, its gift to man—its reception by man, that Jesus said to his deciples, when sorrow had filled their hearts, "It is expedient for you that I go away; for if I go not away, the Comforter will not come, but if I depart I will send him unto you" [John 16:7]. [page 23:]

12. The ordinance of the "laying of hands," was practiced by the inspired Apostles of Christ, in order that those who had been immersed in water, might be baptized with the Holy Spirit also, and thus enter the kingdom of God by the legal door into the sheepfold. When Samaria had believed the gospel under the preaching of Philip, Peter and John traveled about forty miles from Jerusalem to Samaria, in order that they might administer the ordinance of laying on of hands, that those believers might also be baptized with **the Spirit**. "Then laid they their hands upon them, and they received the Holy Spirit" [Acts 8:17]. In the begin-

ning of the gospel dispensation, the Apostles were very careful to know when they found disciples whether they had been "born of the Spirit." Pail's [Paul's] first question to the believers at Ephesus was, "Have you received the Holy Spirit since you believed?" And when they had been properly instructed and baptized in water, then Paul laid his hands upon them, and the Holy Spirit ["]came on them, and they spake with tongues and prophesied" [Acts 19:6]. They were then born anew, they were legally adopted into the "church of Christ" on earth. They were fellow citizens with the saints, and of the household of God. Thus the "new birth," is to be born of the water and of the Spirit both. And hence none can be legal heirs of the kingdom, only those ~~those~~ who have thus put on Christ. And thus to hear the word of God by the preaching of the gospel, to believe in Christ, to repent of sin, to be immersed in ~~in~~ water "for the remission of **sins**," to receive the laying on of hands, for the gift of the Holy Spirit, and to live in that Spirit bearing its fruits, and enjoying its gifts unto the end, is the only true gospel plan of salvation. And no other scheme can ever possibly secure to any individual a seat, at the right of the Majesty in the heavens. [page 24:]

The work of the Holy Spirit among men.

"That which is born of the Spirit, is spirit" [John 3:6]. Jesus.
"The manifestation of the Spirit is given to every man to profit withal" [1 Cor. 12:7]. Paul.

1. Upon this subject much has been written, and many, very many elaborate discourses delivered, by some of the most able reasoners in the different ages of the world. Within this century, and even during the last twenty five years, there has been much discussion and disputation upon the nature of the gift, and the work of the Holy Spirit. It is a subject that we have had under consideration ever since our first thoughts on Christianity: but more especially so for the last ~~twenty five~~ forty years.[22] During that time we have held several public discussions, (debates,) with men of superior powers of mind; consequently we think we understand some of the strong points on both sides of this all important subject. And after thus maturing the matter, we firmly believe that men may **now** exercise as much faith, and enjoy as much of the Holy Spirit, bear as

22. The explicit dates within this notebook are 1854 and 1857. Since McLellin joined the church in 1831, adding twenty-five years gives the year 1856, which fits in nicely within the known dates. Consequently, the change from "twenty-five" to "forty" in this instance probably indicates that McLellin is making the update sometime around 1871.

much of its fruit, and receive as many of its gifts, as men or societies ever did[23] in any former age of the world. ~~ever did.~~

2. We shall not in this treatise enter into all the speculations of gifted minds upon this subject, but content ourselves with stating plainly and frankly, our views, as we have done and shall do upon all subjects upon which we write. The nature of the influences, manifestations, operations, and gifts of the Holy Spirit, to true believers in Christ, ought to especially interest all and every person who desires eternal life.

3. The inspired apostle says, "If any man,—yes, any man, have not the spirit of Christ he is none of his" [Rom. 8:9]. Again, "as many as are led by the spirit of [page 25:] God, they are the sons of God" [Rom. 8:14]. Adam was "a **Son** of **God**" [Luke 3:38] by creation; and he communed familiarly with his Father, as a man talks with his friend, face to face—seemingly without a dimming[24] veil between them. He rested in the love, light, and glory of his Creator; until the Law under which he was plac[e]d was broken, and the fatal fruit swallowed—in consequence of which he was cast out, became an alien, subject to death, and a curse rested upon all the earth for his sake, or on account of his transgression. Therefore it became necessary that the plan of salvation should be revealed to man through Christ, by the power of the Holy Spirit working among men, in order that they might be redeemed from death.

4. The Spirit of Christ is that which the soul receives when, "the strong man armed," is cast out. It is that which makes the children, when adopted into the kingdom, cry "My Father, my Father"; that which makes their worship acceptable to the spiritual Head. It is alone the witness of that spirit with theirs by which they can know their acceptance with God. It is the wisdom and work of the Holy Spirit by which any man can know the things of God from those of the Devil. It is that in which they live and walk, and by which they will be sanctified and sealed unto the day of redemption. It is the earnest of their inheritance, until the redemption of their bodies: and finally, it is the Holy Spirit, which each saint enjoys, by which their mortal bodies will be quickened, and brought forth in the first resurrection—when all the righteous who have ever lived since Adam (except those translated, and those who rose immediately after Jesus rose,) will rise among the just, and put on glory, honor, immortality, and eternal life. It will be that by which their minds will then perceive, search, learn, expand, and comprehend the things of

23. McLellin added "men or societies ever did."

24. McLellin added "dimming."

God in eternity; "for the Spirit searches all things, yea, the deep things of God" [1 Cor. 2:10]. Now if in the redemption of fallen man, so much [page 26:] depends upon the agency or work of the Holy Spirit, we should certainly examine the subject closely, and see to it that we are not deceived in so important a matter.

5. We will now divide our subject into parts or heads, in order to illucidate it the more easily and clearly. First. What the Savior promised the Holy Spirit should do when shed forth. Secondly. What the fruits of the Spirit are in true believers. Thirdly. What the spiritual gifts are and were in the true Church. Fourthly. For what purpose those gifts were given by the Lord, and enjoyed by the members of the Church.[25] Fifthly. When did miraculous gifts cease in the church, and what were the causes of their not continuing? And finally, Will those "spiritual gifts" ever be restored, or be enjoyed by Christians before the last day?

6. First, then, is the Savior's promises. "Behold I send the promise of my Father upon you: but tarry ye in the city of Jerusalem until ye be endued with power from on high" [Luke 24:49]. When the believers in Christ received the ~~the~~ fulfilment of that promise, Peter stood up and rehearsed this prophecy of Joel, "And it shall come to pass in the last days, (saith God,) I will pour out of my Spirit upon all flesh: and your sons and your daughters shall prophesy, and your young men shall see visions, and your old men shall dream dreams: and on my servants and on my handmaidens, I will pour out, in those days, of my Spirit; and they shall prophecy" [Acts 2:17-18; cf. Joel 2:28-29]. "This Jesus hath God raised up, whereof we all are witnesses. And being by the right hand of God exalted, and having received of the Father the promise of the Holy Ghost, he hath shed forth this which you now see and hear" [Acts 2:32-33]. Reader, examine the following texts at your leisure, and then we will proceed again, viz: John xiv:16, 17, and 26. xv:26. xvi:7-13. From the foregoing we will condense or extract a few short sentences showing what Jesus promised that the Holy Spirit should do when received. "He shall teach you all things–shall bring all [page 27:] things to your remembrance–shall testify of me–will guide you into all truth–and he will show you things to come." Here five distinct points, or manifestations of the Holy Spirit are brought to view, to be realized when the disciples received that "unction from the Holy One" [1 John 2:20], by which they should know all things. It was to teach, to brighten the memory, to testify of Christ, to guide into all truth, and to show futurity. But says one, this promise was

25. McLellin added "of the Church."

to the apostles only, and not "to all them who believe on him through their word" [cf. John 17:20]. But he who held the keys of the kingdom of heaven, when he received his enduement on the day of Pentecost, while he was yet full of the Holy Spirit, extended the promise, "To all the Jews, and to their children, and to all that are afar off; even as many as the Lord our God shall call" [cf. Acts 2:39]. And on that day when the Apostles received their enduement, there were about one hundred and twenty who received it also, at the same time, both men and women. At Samaria, at the house of Cornelius, and at Ephesus the believers received the Holy Ghost, when they had obeyed the Gospel. And at Cornelius and at Ephesus they "spake with tongues and prophecied" [Acts 19:6], when the Holy Spirit was poured out upon them. And the Lord "put no difference between Jew and Gentile" [cf. Acts 15:9], in this important matter. But as to this gift belonging to all believers who obey the gospel, we will quote again, "And we (apostles,) are witnesses of these things and so is also the Holy Ghost, whom God hath given to them that obey him" [Acts 5:32]. This passage settles the whole matter that all—yes, male and female, Jew and Gentile, bond and free, received not a gift only, but received the Spirit itself.

7. Then, according to the above, every one born into the kingdom of Christ must receive the spirit of that kingdom. Jesus said so, "Except a man be born of water and of the Spirit, he cannot enter into the kingdom of God" [John 3:5]. [page 28:] And every inspired prophet since the world began believed the same great truth. Hence we see what Jesus promised, and also see the effects which were to follow—that the object of the gift of the Holy Spirit was to inspire, to justify, to sanctify, and then to glorify all who received it, and retained it unto the end.

8. Secondly. What the fruits of the Holy Spirit are in true believers. The fruit of the Spirit, growing out of its reception, or flowing from its effects upon the heart, is that without which no being can be a Christian. Because the fruit is a natural production, when the gospel truths are planted in the heart by the preaching of the word, and the reception of the Spirit. Paul said, "But the fruit of the Spirit is love, joy, peace, long-suffering, gentleness, goodness, faith, meekness, temperance, +++ righteousness and truth, against which there is no law" [cf. Gal. 5:22-23]. The above fruit of the Spirit as naturally flows from its reception as water runs down hill. And the very first thrill that rolls through the soul, when it receives that "other Comforter" is the holy fruit of the Spirit. And the last ecstatic thrill that such soul (if faithful,) will ever feel in time will be "Glory to God in the highest, on earth peace, and good will toward men"

[cf. Luke 2:14]. When a band or congregation of those who bring forth the fruit of the Spirit, fruit which accompanies salvation—the fruit which works by love and purifies the heart, in reality and not in name only, when such are united in a church capacity, and have inspired ministers, (God acknowledges none others,) then they may and it is their duty "to covet earnestly the best gifts" [1 Cor. 12:31], and thus grow into "an holy temple of the Lord" [cf. Eph. 2:21]. All "following after charity and desiring spiritual gifts also" [cf. 1 Cor. 14:1], and thus grow up into Christ their living Head in all things.

9. Thirdly, What the spiritual gift[s] were and are in the true Church. Now, reader, if you have prejudices they will do you no good, lay them all aside [page 29:] and travel with us into this weighty subject. Joel said "Your sons and your daughters shall prophesy, and your young men shall see visions, and your old men shall dream dreams" [Acts 2:17; cf. Joel 2:28]. Peter said, "As I began to speak the Holy Spirit fell on them (Cornelius' household,) as on us at the beginning. Foras much then as God gave them the like gift as he did unto us—what was I, that I could withstand God?" [Acts 11:15, 17]. Jesus said, "These signs shall follow them that believe: In my name shall they cast out Devils; they shall speak with new tongues, they shall take up serpants; and if they drink any deadly thing, it shall not hurt them; they shall lay hands on the sick, and they shall recover" [Mark 16:17-18]. Now if Joel, Peter, and Jesus' words were true—were fulfilled the **true believers** anciently were blessed with great[26] spiritual powers. Paul says, "Now there are diversities of gifts, but the same spirit—for to one is given by the spirit the word of wisdom; to another the word of knowledge; to another faith; to another gifts of healing; to another the working of miracles; to another prophecy; to another discerning of spirits; to another divers kinds of tongues; and to another the interpretation of tongues" [1 Cor. 12:4, 8-10]; "And again to another, the beholding of angels and ministering spirits" [Moro. 10:14]. All the above gifts and powers come by the spirit of Christ, and they were enjoyed in the beginning of the gospel dispensation, and that too by the brethren as well as by the Apostles.

10. Was it common in the first ages or centuries of the Christian era, for the believers who obeyed the gospel—the law of adoption—the law of liberty, to enjoy miraculous gifts by the Spirit of Christ? We unhesitatingly answer, Yes. On the day of Pentecost "the hundred and twenty ~~received the Spirit. "And they~~ were all filled with the Holy Spirit, and be-

26. McLellin added "great."

gan to speak with other tongues as ~~the Spirit~~ it gave them utterence" [cf. Acts 1:15; 2:4]. This caused the devout Jews to say, ~~How hear we every man in our own tongue wherein we were born?~~ "We do hear them speak in our tongues the wonderful works of God" [Acts 2:8, 11][27] At the house of Cornelius also, "While Peter yet spake these words, the Holy Spirit fell on all them who heard the word, +++ for they heard them speak with tongues and magnify God" [Acts 10:44, 46]. When the Ephesians received the word, "Paul laid his hands upon them, and the Holy Spirit came on them; and [page 30:] they spake with tongues and prophesied" [cf. Acts 19:6]. The above are thus indubitable evidences to establish this query in the affirmative. But these are not all. Paul to the Romans says, "Having then gifts differing according to the grace that is given to us, whether prophecy, let us prophesy according to the proportion of faith" [Rom. 12:6]. To the Corinthians, "To them that are sanctified in Christ Jesus; with all that in every place call upon the name of Christ, +++ in every thing ye are enriched by him, in all utterance and in all knowledge, even as the testimony of Christ was confirmed in you: so that ye come behind in no gift" [1 Cor. 1:2, 5-7]. To the Ephesians, who had "spoken with tongues and prophesied," he says, "When he (Jesus,) ascended up on high he led captivity captive, and gave gifts unto men" [Eph. 4:8]. Remember it was gifts. And among these gifts of inspired saints[28] were prophets–etc, signifying more than one. A man to be a prophet, must be so endued with the spirit of God, as to look into futurity, and tell of unborn events, that will roll upon the earth at some future day. To the Thessalonians, "Quench not the Spirit; dispise not prophesyings" [1 Thes. 5:19-20]. Not prophecies, for then he might have referred to the sayings of the old Hebrew Seers. Let us now take one quotation from Revelations "For (said the Angel,) the testimony of Jesus is the spirit of prophecy" [Rev. 19:10]. The Spirit of Christ, (which every son of God receives,) is that by which all the prophets of the Lord always spoke ever since the world began. "Holy men of God spake as they were moved by the Holy Ghost" [2 Pet. 1:21].[29] The foregoing accords with what Peter said at the setting up of the kingdom on Pentecost, "And you shall receive the gift of the Holy Ghost,[30] For the promise is to you, and to your

27. McLellin added "We do hear them speak in our tongues the wonderful works of God."

28. McLellin added "of inspired saints."

29. McLellin quoted from the King James Version. The earlier and better Greek texts have the translation: "but men moved by the Holy Ghost spoke from God." See explanation in this chapter, note 170.

30. McLellin added "And you shall receive the gift of the Holy Ghost."

children, and to all that are afar off, even as many as the Lord our God shall call" [Acts 2:38-39]. Jesus said, "If ye then, being evil, know how to give good gifts unto your children, how much more shall your heavenly Father give the Holy Spirit to them that ask him" [Luke 11:13]. Now reader, we want you to take up your New Testament and read, and carefully examine the 12th, 13th, and 14th chapters of 1st Cor., and we think You will answer this question as we [page 31:] have done in the affirmative, and say, Why, yes, the "spiritual gifts" were and are as necessary to the Christians, as the "fruit of the Spirit" in order for them "to grow in the knowledge of our Lord and Savior Jesus Christ" [2 Pet. 3:18].

11. Fourthly. What was the design of the spiritual gifts?

We think that the design was certainly accomplished under the immidiate eye and teaching of the Apostles—those men who held the spiritual destiny of the world in their hands: or, "who had the word of reconciliation committed unto them." Their teachings, of course was by the true spirit of wisdom, and we must have the same guide, for all truth is harmonious. Every one who understands plain English must admit the signs were to follow the believers in the gospel preached by the apostolic ministry, and not to follow the Apostles only—nor to go before, to produce faith in unbelievers. The design then was to benefit individuals, and the whole "flock of God."

12. But says an objecter, the only great design was to establish the truth of the gospel dispensation. Let us see. We want truth upon this subject and truth only. "And they (the ministers,) went forth and preached every where, the Lord working with them and confirming the word with signs following, amen" [Mark 16:20]. Now if the Lord's object in giving those signs was to produce faith in the word, instead of to confirm the believers, then the signs should precede faith and not follow ~~after~~ it should go before and not come after. But Jesus said, "These signs shall follow," which shows conclusively that they were given for the mutual benefit of all, both ministers and ~~layity~~ laity. But we want the true object of signs and gifts. Paul said, "But he that prophesyeth, speaketh unto men to edification, and exhortation and comfort" [1 Cor. 14:3]. "Now brethren, if I come to you speaking with tongues, what shall I profit you, unless I speak to you either by revelation or by knowledge, or by prophesying, or by doctrine! Even so ye, for as much as ye are zealous of spiritual gifts, seek that ye may [page 32:] excel to the edifying of the church. How is it then brethren? when ye come together every one of you hath a Psalm, hath a doctrine, hath a tongue, hath a revelation, hath an interpretation. Let all things be done unto edifying" [cf. 1 Cor. 14:6,

12, 26]. Paul tells the Ephesians for what the gifts were given, "For the perfecting of the saints, for the work of the ministry, and for the edifying of the body of Christ" [Eph. 4:12]. Language could not be more plain. Now if those gifts were given to the Apostles only, and only designed to aid them in their ministry, why then the language addressed to the church by the Apostle, "Seek that ye may excel, for the edification of the body of Christ" [cf. 1 Cor. 14:12].–Not the Head or ministry alone, but to edify the body–the whole "church of Christ." According to the above the object or design of spiritual gifts is clear and plain. That is, as a blessing to believers, but not to convert sinners.

13. And notwithstanding all creation seemed to be opposed to the ancient Christians, yet God was not[31] ashamed to be called their God–by giving them signs, gifts, and revelations according to their faith, and to the measure of the gift of Christ. And they were not ashamed to be called his people, by coveting and earnestly desiring those gifts, and exercising themselves in them in order to comfort and edify one another. They in that age brought forth the fruits of the spirit, and some churches[32] enjoyed all its gifts.

14. In reflecting upon those apostolic times, we have often been led to exclaim, O, glorious day! O, happy hour!! O, blessed people!!! Who thus walked with their God, and enjoyed his smiles!!!! "Of whom the world was not worthy" [Heb. 11:38]. They ascended the heights of the knowledge of God by bearing fruit, having gifts, working signs, having visions, and receiving direct revelations from heaven. Yes, says inspiration speaking to a church of them, who had become dead to the world but alive to their best interests–who had suffered all manner of persecutions; yea, the loss of all things, and counted them as naught, that they might win Christ–win heaven [page 33:]–win eternal life–win celestial glory in the mansion where God and Christ dwell. O, reader! Let us listen to the voice of the Spirit speaking to them thus: "Ye are come to mount Zion, and unto the city of the living God, the heavenly Jerusalem, and to an innumerable company of angels; to the general assembly and church of the first born, which are written or enrolled in heaven, and to God the judge of all, and to the spirits of just men made perfect, and to Jesus the mediator of the new Covenant" [cf. Heb. 12:22-24]. These people had united in a perpetual covenant to serve the Lord, and had kept their promise. They lived in the Spirit, and walked in the Spirit until they could say in truth, <u>the spirit teaches us all things</u>. Yes, all things in

31. McLellin added "not."

32. McLellin added "churches."

heaven, as well as on earth. For some or all of them were caught away by the power of the Spirit unto "the third heaven," and stood in the immediate presence of God and the Lamb. Yes, they associated with angels and spirits of just men made perfect. O, field of thought! Our mind expands while writing upon this exalted, glorious theme, and we can say with the Psalmist, "The Lord will give grace and glory; and no good thing will he withhold from them that walk uprightly. O Lord of hosts, blessed is the man that trusteth in thee, Amen" [cf. Ps. 84:11-12].

15. Fifthly. When did miraculous gifts cease to be enjoyed in the church?

It may be considered that this question is difficult of solution—hard to answer. But with the Bible in our hands, and the light of history before us, we will enter upon the important subject or task.[33] That those supernatural gifts by the spirit of God, were enjoyed by all classes in the "church of Christ," in the first ages of Christianity, we can see no room to dispute. The different branches of the church of Christ[34] at Rome, Corinth, Ephesus, Thessalonica, Jerusalem &c. enjoyed them and practiced upon them ~~in order~~ to their comfort, their edification, and their sanctification.

16. That those gifts continued to be manifest during the lifetime of the apostles, we do not know that any professed Christians dispute. But upon investigation we do [page 34:] not find that the churches of the present day are adorned with, nor edified by any spiritual gif[t]s. No! No!! Nor ever even hear them "earnestly contending for them," but often have we heard their preachers & members contend against them.

17. We then are led to inquire when did they cease? Did they die in the first century with the twelve apostles? Or did they cease when the last of those brethren, who received the Holy Spirit by the imposition of the apostles' hands, took their ascent to the Paradise of God? And did the Lord thus design that healings, tongues, prophecy, visions, dreams, revelations, &c. &c. should die with the apostolic age, or the first hundred years of the christian era? If so, we would say of our faith in this matter, as Paul said of the resurrection in his day, "Then our faith is vain. Our teaching is vain also. And we are yet in our sins" [cf. 1 Cor. 15:14, 17]. Because we firmly believe and teach, that we are commanded, if there is a mandate in God's word to be obeyed by any in this generation, "To follow after charity and desire spiritual gifts" [1 Cor. 14:1]. Divine wisdom we think would not thus command us if it were not our privilege

33. McLellin added "or task."

34. McLellin added "of the church of Christ."

to obtain—merely to mock us. We are aware of the consequences of this doctrine, for once establish it, and that proves an apostate or false state of all religious societies who have not the "spiritual gifts." And that people who first obtain the gifts, and authority from God to use them in wisdom must raise the Ensign, to all nations; must lift up their voice and cry, "Come out of her my people, that ye be not partakers of her sins, and that ye receive not of her plagues" [Rev. 18:4]. This cry or voice John said he heard from heaven. Now if no church can be found among all the present denominations of christendom who communes with heaven by or through the medium of the spiritual gifts, then no people on earth can raise that voice. No, nor even receive the warning when [page 35:] it comes. For men could not hear the voice and obey its entreaty "to come out of her," without a direct revelation from the Lord. And a revelation would be the exercise of one of the most precious of the "spiritual gifts."

18. The popular opinion is that gifts were given, or rather were exercised to produce faith in unbelievers—to establish the gospel dispensation. If this is true then we are entirely wrong on this point, for we believe and teach, that spiritual gifts and manifestations were given to confirm believers in the word of truth, and to comfort and edify the church—[and] were to follow believers, and not to go before to create or make faith: that faith comes by hearing the word of God, and not by seeing miracles. That spiritual gifts were given "for the edifying of the body of Christ" [Eph. 4:12], and not to convert sinners. But[35] That miracles will arrest the attention of the ungodly we would admit, and sometimes set them to listen to and examine the truth, but they never did nor never will produce faith.

19. Those gifts are spiritual things. "They are spiritually discerned. They are foolishness to a natural man—a wicked man. He cannot know them" [cf. 1 Cor. 2:14]. If they are thus, (and the apostle declares that they are,) to all carnal minded men; would it be rational to suppose that the Savior of the world would lay it down as a fundamental principle of his kingdom, that all wicked unbelieving people must be damned for unbelief, when the evidences to them were positive foolishness? We say no. The divine order when it embraced Gentile as well as Jew, was, "Go and preach," that men may hear the word of God, may believe, may repent, may be immersed, and may receive the Holy Spirit. Then by that Spirit they can discern the things of the spirit; can compare spiritual things with spiritual. Then the promise is that signs and gifts will follow, that

35. McLellin added in pencil the word "But" though it does not help the sentence.

the believers thus exercised might grow up together a spiritual house, to offer up spiritual sacrifices, acceptable to God by Jesus Christ.

20. We draw an argument for the enjoyment of spiritual gifts, from the express com[page 36:]mandments of inspiration to believers. Paul to the Corinthians says, "to all that in every place call upon the name of Jesus Christ," to "covet earnestly the best gifts" [1 Cor. 12:31]. What more express commandment could be given? Could stronger language be usesed? Covet, and do it earnestly. Paul said in the beginning of the twelfth chapter, "Now concerning spiritual gifts brethren, I would not have you ignorant" [1 Cor. 12:1]. Then, after giving us the names of nine of these gifts, and comparing them to the members of the natural body of a man, and showing thereby their indispensible use in the body of Christ, he uses the above emphatic language, to encourage and bind it upon all believers every where to seek after them with all their hearts. In chapter thirteen, he shows the "more excellent way" [1 Cor. 12:31] or the beauties, benefits, and excellencies of charity; without the enjoyment of which, all mysteries, faith, knowledge, and even "spiritual gifts," would be nothing.

21. Then the 14th chapter opens with another mandate from the skies to "follow after charity, and desire spiritual gifts; but rather that ye may prophesy" [1 Cor. 14:1]. And after contrasting the gift of prophecy with the gift of tongues, and showing that to prophesy was more profitable to the church, in the 39th verse he says: "Wherefore, brethren, covet to prophesy, and forbid not to speak with tongues" [1 Cor. 14:39]. Now here we would ask one important question,–["]Can professors of the present day obey these commandments in the New Testament,[36] or can they not?" If they can, then our position is settled at once; but if they cannot then we ask, what precept of the New Testament or of any of the word of God can they obey? We maintain that believers in the Lord can obey those precepts now, can obtain the gifts of the Spirit of God now, can rise as high in the knowledge of God now, as at any former period of this world's history. And if there was less contention in the world about forms, modes, doctrines, and creeds of men, and more earnest contending for "the faith once delivered to the saints" [Jude 1:3], for the power of godliness, and for the gifts of the Spirit, then we should see more primitive order & saint-like holiness. [page 37:]

22. But we will touch one more commandment (taken from ~~the~~ James,) before we dismiss this part of the subject. "Is any sick among you? Let him call for the Elders of the church, and let them pray over

36. McLellin added in pencil the words "in the New Testament."

him, anointing him with oil in the name of the Lord: and the prayr of faith shall save the sick" [James 5:14-15]. This was practiced by the ancient Christians, but how is it now among the professors of our day? O, when they are sick they run for a Doctor with his nauseous drugs, and even the most devoted among them trust their lives to his skill; and the Elder is not generally called until the case is considered hopeless, and even then not to "anoint them," but only to pray that they may be reconciled to death. O! what solemn mockery to pretend to be Christians, and to leave undone, and unobeyed some of the most important commandments of God. Truly men have "hewn to themselves cisterns, broken cisterns that will hold no water" [cf. Jer. 2:13], that is, no power from God.

23. But on the question, how long were those gifts to continue? We wish to say a few words. Paul, in speaking of the gifts which Christ gave unto men when he ascended up on high, says they were given, "For the perfecting of the saints, for the work of the ministry, and for the edifying of the body of Christ" [Eph. 4:12]. But when speaking in reference to the time that the gifts were to continue, he says, "Till we all come into the unity of the faith, and of the knowledge of the Son of God" [Eph. 4:13]. If no other scripture spoke plainly on the subject of the continuance of the gifts, and of the time they were to cease, this one would be sufficient. We have only to ask, have Christians ever enjoyed more of a oneness of faith and practice than in the Apostolic times? Have they ever had a more perfect knowledge of the Son of God than then? All, yes all, would say no. This admitted and our point is gained. For Paul said of his times, in contrast with a day that is yet to come, "For we know in part, and we prophesy in part"—we now see through a glass darkly, but then face to face" [1 Cor. 13:9, 12]. We might say, and we firmly believe, that those gifts & powers were given to remain, provided the church remained holy enough [page 38:] to retain them, "untill[37] the times of the restitution of all things" [Acts 3:21]. Then that which is in part shall be done away! And that too, by divine appointment—not as they have been done away, for the want of faith and obedience in the church.

24. But how long did those gifts continue to be enjoyed ~~by~~ in the church?

We answer—the last writer of the New Testament, between the years ninety and one hundred, enjoyed them to a very full extent. "I was in the Spirit on the Lord's day, and heard behind me, a great voice as of a trumpet" [Rev. 1:10]. But John's writings end the volume in the "Sacred Canon" as it now stands. And of course the remainder of our testimony

37. McLellin adds an "un" to his original "till" to produce the spelling "untill."

must be drawn from history. And if by that we prove that the "Spiritual gifts," continued for centuries afterward, then we upset a popular notion of this day both root and branch, viz: that those gifts were only given to remain during the lifetime of the Apostles.

25. Eusebius[38] is considered the father of ecclesiastic history,[39] and is refered to by almost all succeeding church historians. On page 86, he records that after the death of James,~~ the less~~, who presided over the church in Jerusalem, the other apostles were driven from the land of Judea; and while awful vengeance was hanging over that devoted city, "The whole body of the church at Jerusalem, having been commanded by a divine revelation given to men of approved piety before the war, removed from the city, and dwelt at a certain town beyond the Jordan, called Pella." That revelation for some cause or other, was not embodied in the "Sacred Canon." We would be glad to see it, for it was "The word of the Lord." It would be profitable "for doctrine, for reproof, for correction, and for instruction in righteousness" [2 Tim. 3:16]. But it is gone. And many other precious revelations, received by holy men of old are gone–have been destroyed, [page 39:] and in consequence thereof schisms and divisions prevail throughout the world. And men now instead of seeking and receiving knowledge from the same source, and in the same way that those "men of approved piety["] did, are "heaping to themselves teachers having itching ears, who turn away their ears from the truth unto fables" [cf. 2 Tim. 4:3-4]. The above proves that revelations at this period were received direct from heaven. These things were done about the year 70.

26. The seven churches of Asia received through John, the apostle, some very important revelations by the gifts of the Spirit, between the years 90 & 100.[40] In the sixth year of the reign of Adrian,[41] the Roman emperor, who succeeded Trajan[42] in the year 117, he came to Athens.

---

38. For a summary of Eusebius's life, see the Biographical Notes. For a modern account of the early Christian centuries, see Norbert Brox, *A Concise History of the Early Church* (New York: Continuum, 1995).

39. Since McLellin specifically mentions pages 86, 123, 186, 227, and 275, the particular edition of Eusebius's *Ecclesiastical History* can be identified. It is one of the mid-nineteenth-century New York editions of 480 pages, not the London editions of 431 pages. The translator was Christian Frederick Crusé. The ninth edition was published by Stanford and Swords in 1850 and the tenth by Thomas N. Stanford in 1856, both in New York.

40. For items 26-28, cf. McLellin's "The Work of the Holy Spirit among Men, *The Ensign,* Sept. 1844, 41-45.

41. Adrian was a common nineteenth-century spelling of Hadrian. For a summary of Hadrian's life, see the Biographical Notes.

42. For a summary of Trajan's life, see the Biographical Notes.

Quadratus[43] was then Pastor of the church in that city, having succeeded Publius.[44] He[45] drew up an apology for the christian religion, which he addressed and delivered to the Emperor. Eusebius has these remarkable sentences on page 123. "Of those that flourished in those times, Quadratus is said to have been distinguished for his prophetical gifts. There were many others also noted,[46] for, leaving their country, they performed the office of Evangelists to those who had not heard the faith.[47] The Holy Spirit also wrought many wonders as yet through them." During the second century lived and wrote those who are now styled the Fathers, because they lived and wrote so near the days of the Apostles. During the first part of the second century, miracles and miraculous ~~and miraculous~~ gifts were not uncommon, as the writings of these Fathers testify–but toward the close of that century, after the first race[48] from the apostles had all passed away, did those gifts then still continue? If we mak[e] this point plain, then we are safe.

27. Eusebius, page 186, quoting from Irenius,[49] writes thus "For even among [page 40:] the brethren frequently in a case of necessity, when a whole church united in much fasting and prayr, the spirit has returned to the ex-animated body and the man was granted to the prayrs of the saints.[50] Wherefore, also, those that were truly the disci-

---

43. For a summary of the life of Quadratus of Athens, who died in the 170s, see the Biographical Notes.

44. For a summary of Publius's life, see the Biographical Notes.

45. McLellin has incorrectly combined Eusebius's various references to two separate men named Quadratus. For a summary of the life of Quadratus, who was a prophet and Christian apologist, see the Biographical Notes.

46. At this point McLellin omits the following from Eusebius's account: "in these times, who held the first rank in the apostolic succession. These, as the holy disciples of such men, also built up the churches where foundations had been previously laid in every place by the apostles. They augmented the means of promulgating the gospel more and more, and spread the seeds of salvation and of the heavenly kingdom throughout the world far and wide. For the most of the disciples at that time, animated with a more ardent love of the divine word, had first fulfilled the Saviour's precept by distributing their substance to the needy."

47. McLellin omits the following from Eusebius: "whilst with a noble ambition to proclaim Christ, they also delivered to them the books of the holy gospels. After laying the foundation of the faith in foreign parts as the particular object of their mission, and after appointing others as shepherds of the flocks, and committing to these the care of those that had been recently introduced, they went again to other regions and nations, with the grace and co-operation of God."

48. Though obsolete, the word "race" was used in the nineteenth century to mean "generation."

49. For a summary of Irenaeus's life, see the Biographical Notes.

50. McLellin omits the following from Eusebius's account: "And again, he says, after other observations: 'But if they say that our Lord also did these things only in appearance,

ples of the Son of God, receiving grace from him, in his name performed those things for the benefit of the rest of man, and every one received the free gift from him. Some, indeed, most certainty and truly, cast out demons.[51] Others have knowledge of things to come, as also visions and prophetic communications. Others heal the sick by the imposition of hands, and restored them to health. And more, as we said above, even the dead have been raised and continued with us many years. And why should we say more? It is impossible to tell the number of gifts which the church throughout the world received from God, and the deeds performed in the name of Jesus Christ, who was crucified under Pontius Pilate, and this too every day for the benefit of the heathen, without deceiving any, or exacting their money. For as she had [']freely received from God, she also freely ministers[']" [cf. Matt. 10:8]. In another place the same author writes: "As we hear of many brethren in the church who have prophetic gifts, and who speak in all tongues through the spirit, and who also bring to light the secret things of men for their benefit, and who expound the mysteries of God. These gifts of different kinds also continued with those that were worthy until the times mentioned."

28. Irenius suffered martyrdom at Lyons in Gaul, (France,) during the fifth general persecution under Septimus Severus,[52] about the year 202. Hence he must have written the above near the close of the second century, after the death of all those who had received "the faith" immediately [page 41:] from the Apostles—after all had passed away who had received the Holy Spirit by the imposition of their hands. If so, and Irenius wrote the truth, then the point is settled: forever settled, that miraculous gifts outlived the apostolic age, and also the age of their immediate followers. Narcissus[53] was the thirteenth[54] in regular succession from the Apostles who presided over the church in Jerusalem, consequently he must have lived in the third century. Of him Eusebius says, page 227: "Many miracles are attributed to Narcissus by his countrymen, as they received the tradition handed down from the brethren." On page 275,

---

we shall refer them back to the prophetic declarations, and shall show from them that all those things were strictly foretold, and were done by him, and that he alone is the Son of God.'"

51. McLellin omits the following: "so that frequently those persons themselves that were cleansed from wicked spirits believed and were received into the church."

52. For a summary of Septimius Severus's life, see the Biographical Notes.

53. For a summary of Narcissus's life, see the Biographical Notes.

54. McLellin miscopied Eusebius, who says that Narcissus was the "thirtieth" in succession.

he mentions a vision and revelation of Dyonisius,[55] the pastor of the church at Alexandria, and even gives us the words of the pastor himself: "I was confirmed in my purpose by a vision sent me from heaven, when a voice came to me and commanded me in words," &c. He was the pupil of Origin,[56] and was co[n]temporary with Dyonisius of Rome,[57] who presided there in the year 280.[58] He presided over the church in Alexandria 17 years.

We will at this time present only one more quotation from Eusebius. Book of Martyrs,[59] chapter 11. Speaking of those who were associated with Pamphilus[60] in martyrdom, who was an associate of his own, and a thrice dear friend to him; he says: "These were twelve, who were distinguished by a prophetic and apostolic grace as well as number."[61] They lived and suffered in the commencement of the fourth century, during the last of the ten general persecutions.

29. We will now give one testimony from the pen of John Wesley.[62] We look upon it as being a strong one. We fear it is a little to[o] strong a pill for the Methodists of the present day: but the founder of Methodism compounded the dose, and being a Physician we will venture to administer it. 2d vol. Sermons, page 266.[63] Text,

> "But covet earnestly the best gifts; and yet show I unto you a more excellent way" [1 Cor. 12:31].

He says[64]

> In the preceding verses Paul has been speaking of the extraordinary gifts of the Holy Ghost: such as healing the sick, prophesying, in the proper sense of the word; that is, foretelling things to come, speaking with strange tongues [page 42:] such as the speaker had never learned; and the miracu-

---

55. For Dionysius the Great, see the Biographical Notes.

56. For Origen, see the Biographical Notes.

57. For St. Dionysius, see the Biographical Notes.

58. McLellin has the wrong year and perhaps meant to write 260 because Dionysius became bishop of Rome in 259, convened a synod in 260, and died in 268.

59. Eusebius's *Ecclesiastical History* contains ten books. Between books eight and nine is a work called "The Book of Martyrs" consisting of thirteen chapters.

60. For a summary of Pamphilus's life, see the Biographical Notes.

61. These twelve martyrs are Pamphilus of Caesarea, Valens of Aelia, Paul of Jamna, Porphyry, Seleucus of Cappodocia, Theodulus, Julianus of Cappodocia, and five unnamed individuals.

62. For a summary of John Wesley's life, see the Biographical Notes.

63. John Wesley, *Sermons on Several Occasions,* 2 vols. (New York: Nelson & Phillips, 1825).

64. McLellin adds in pencil "He says."

> lous interpretation of tongues. And these gifts the apostle allows to be desirable: yea, he exhorts the Corinthians, + + + to covet them earnestly, that thereby they might be qualified to be more useful to either christians or heathens. It does not appear that those extraordinary gifts of the Holy Ghost were common in the church for more than two or three centuries. We seldom hear of them after that fatal period, when the emperor Constantine[65] called himself a Christian; and from a vain imagination of promoting the Christian cause thereby, heaped riches, and power, and honor, upon the Christians in general; but in particular upon the christian clergy. From this time they almost totally ceased: very few instances[66] of the kind were found. The cause of this was not, (as has been vulgarly supposed,) because there was no more occasion for them, because all the world was become Christians. ~~The real cause was, the love of many~~ This is a miserable mistake: not the twentieth part of it was then nominally christians. The real cause was, the love of many, almost all christians, so called, waxed cold. The christians had no more of the Spirit of Christ than the other heathens. The Son of man when he came to examine his church, could hardly find "faith on earth." This was the real cause why the gifts of the Holy Ghost were no longer to be found in the christian church, because the christians were turned heathens again, and had only a dead form left.

The above sentiments of that distinguished historian and reformer, John Wesley, is plain and pointed, ~~and answers our last proposition~~ as language can make it.[67]

30. But we will give a few extracts from the pen of Wm. Kinkade,[68] a minister of the old christian church, who wrote his "ancient order of things," in the year of 1829. He is plain and pointed, and I ea[r]nestly urge a careful perusal. He say[s], "when I speak of the ancient order, I mean the order of the New Testament; one inch short of that will not satisfy me. In that book the church is called the body of Christ.["] "And gave him to be head over all things to the church, which is his body.["] Eph 1: 22-23 ~ [page 43:] "Now ye are the body of Christ, and members in particular." 1 Cor. 12:27. Of this body Christ is the head; and the members in particular, are the various members of the church, possessing different spiritual gifts; its principle of life is the Holy Spirit, by which the whole body was brought into existance, is agitated and kept in action. Hence Paul says, "For to one is given by the spirit, the word of wisdom; to another, the word of knowledge by the same spirit; to another, faith by

65. For a summary of Constantine's life, see the Biographical Notes.

66. McLellin adds "instances" to make the text agree with what Wesley said.

67. McLellin adds "as language can make it."

68. For a summary of William Kinkade's life, see the Biographical Notes.

the same spirit; To another the gifts of healing by the same Spirit; to another, the working of miracles, to another prophecy; to another the discerning of Spirits; to another, divers kinds of tongues; to another, the interpretation of tongues. But all these worketh that one and self same Spirit, dividing to every man severally as he will. For as the body is one; and hath many members, and all the members of that one body being many are one body, so also is Christ." 1 Cor. 12:8, 9, 10, 11, 12. Paul considers these different spiritual gifts[69] as being each in its place, as necessary and useful to the church, as the different members of the human body are to the man. Hence he says, "If the whole body were an eye, where were the hearing? If the whole were hearing where were the smelling? And if they were all one member, where were the body?" Verse 17.19 [1 Cor. 12:17, 19]. The government or discipline of the church, was among the primitive Christians, administered by divinely inspired men, whom God placed in the church, each one in his proper ~~place~~ order. Hence Paul says, "And he hath set some in the church; first Apostles; secondarily, prophets; thirdly, teachers; after that, miracles; then gifts of healing, helps, governments, diversities of tongues." Verse 28 [cf. 1 Cor. 12:28].

31. This is the ancient order of things; every one opposed to this, is opposed of primitive Christianity. To say God caused these gifts to cease, is the same as to say, God has abolished the order of the New Testament church. To say it is not the privilege of Christians in the present day to belong to such a church, is the same as to say it is not our privilege to be members of Christs spiritual body, because the church here discribed, "is the body of Christ." To divest the church of all these spiritual [page 44:] gifts, would be to take from the body of Christ the senses of hearing, smelling, seeing. &c. To say these miraculous gifts are not necessary nor useful to the church in the present day, would be as absurd as to say, eyes, ears, hands, &c. are not useful to a man. To say we only need one of these gifts, viz. faith, would be to reduce all the members to one. Then, "If all were one member, where were the body?"

32. In Eph. 4th Paul describes the church thus, "And he gave some apostles; and some prophets; and some evangelists; and some pastors and teachers, for the perfecting of the saints, for the work of the ministry, for the edifying of the body of Christ; till we all come in the unity of the faith, and of the knowledge of the son of God" [Eph. 4:11-13]. From this passage we learn two things relative to the primitive church; first,

69. McLellin adds "gifts."

that their ministers were the special gifts of God: and second, that those ministers were parts of Christ's body, were given to unite the saints in faith and love, guard them against wavering, and enable them to edify themselves in love. If infinite wisdom saw these gifts were necessary to make the church perfect that day, who has authority to say the church can be perfect without them in the present day? Surely the church has as great need of being united, built up and established in the present day, as it then had. These gifts constitute the ancient order of things; and if the church is perfect without them, she must have been very imperfect with them, because they were members of Christ's spiritual body; and if that body is perfect without them, they must have been redundant; and superflous members always render the body imperfect. If a child should be born with two heads and four legs we would call it an imperfect child. We have not such a church as the primitive Christians had; they had to[o] many spiritual gifts, or else we have not enough.

33. Some say these gifts were temporary; were only given to introduce Christianity before revelation was comple[te], and that God designed [unfinished].† [page 45:]

The kingdom of heaven

"Wherefore we receiving a kingdom which cannot be moved, let us have grace whereby we may serve God acceptably, with reverence and godly fear." Heb.12:28.

1. The finger of inspiration in other places calls this, "The kingdom of heaven, The kingdom of God's dear Son, The kingdom of Christ, The kingdom of God," &c. There are certain things without which no kingdom either earthly or heavenly, can exist. In order to establish and carry on a kingdom there must be a King, laws, subjects or citizens, and orders of ministry to publish and execute the laws, rules, and mandates of the kingdom. These things are inherent in the very nature and existance of a kingdom—and if it is temporal there must be territory also.

2. Jesus Christ is the King, and the great Head of his church and kingdom on earth. He it is from whom proceeds by direct revelation, all laws and rules of action for the regulation and government of all the children of God, both ministers and members. And in his character and administration, all those who live under his government, whether as ministers or as people, may expect such precepts, laws, and regulations

†The text continues on with the two leaves (four unnumbered pages) that were inserted into the notebook at this point but which we have placed at the end of the notebook, following the bound pages, as supplemental pages 137-40.

as will be best calculated to develop the human mind and energies so as to give to all, all that liberty, all that intelligence, and all that happiness which man is capable of receiving and enjoying in this world.

3. None are natural born citizens of the kingdom of heaven. All have to be born into it—have to be legally adopted in order to enjoy communion and fellowship with the King, with his ministry, with each other, and with all "the the[70] church of the first born whose names are written in heaven" [cf. Heb. 12:23]. But as none can obey the Gospel of adoption into the kingdom of Christ, without officers or ministers legally appointed to wait upon them, we shall next speak of the calling to the ministry, of their orders and stations in the kingdom; and of their responsibilities in carrying on the operations of church government for the salvation of men. [page 46:]

4. Without a direct revelation from heaven no man ever was called to be a minister of Christ since the world began or ever will be.[71] Thus men were called in the days of Enoch and Noah, of Moses and Peter and Paul;[72] and thus it was and will be in all days while the world shall stand, and while God shall acknowledge a people upon it. Enoch before he was translated received this testimony from heaven, "That he pleased God" [Heb. 11:5]. "Noah was a just man, and perfect in his generations, and Noah walked with God—and was warned of God of things not seen as yet" [Gen. 6:9; Heb. 11:7]. "And the Lord spake unto Moses face to face, as a man speaketh unto his friend" [Ex. 33:11]. The Savior said to Peter "Flesh and blood hath not revealed it unto thee, but my Father who is in heaven" [Matt. 16:17]. "Now there were in the church that was at Antioch, certain prophets and teachers. As they ministered to the Lord and fasted, the Holy Ghost said, seperate me Barnabas and Saul for the work whereunto ~~I have~~ called them. And when they had fasted and prayed, and laid their hands on them, they sent them away" [Acts 13:1-3]. Paul said to Timothy "Neglect not the gift that is in thee, which was given thee by prophecy, with the laying on of the hands of the presbytery" [1 Tim. 4:14]. It is then the spirit of prophecy which points out men to the ministry, and without that spirit we have no rule in the word of God by which a man ever was, or ever will be pointed out to be set apart as an officer or minister of Christ.

5. There are three special dispensations or periods of the Lord's dealings with men, which I shall notice in this treatise, viz. The leading

70. McLellin wrote "the" twice but marked neither for deletion.

71. McLellin adds "or ever will be."

72. McLellin adds "and Paul."

Israel from Goshen to Canaan, The ministry of Christ and his Apostles in "Preaching the gospel to all the world," And the period just before us of "The times of the restitution of all things, which God hath spoken by the mouth of all his holy prophets since the world began" [Acts 3:21].

6. The Bible in its succinct account does not give us the particular form of church government which God revealed unto Adam, to Enoch, to Noah, or to Abraham. It is not until the days of Moses that we have the order of heaven set forth among men in specific numbers, classes, ranks, grades, orders or councils of ministry:—the relation [page 47:] that these councils stand to each other, to the kingdom of Christ on earth, and to heavenly things themselves.

7. There are in the scriptures what may be called hallowed or special numbers. Three, seven, twelve, seventy. &c. are some of those numbers. They are special because the Lord has been pleased in the organization of his church or kingdom on earth, in the various ages of the world, to call and set apart his servants into classes or councils of ministers of three, seven, twelve seventy &c., in order to carry on the operations of his government among men. In those three periods above named we must find those peculiar numbers set in order, each one in its place, all operating and working together under Jesus, the King, or otherwise we find not the full development of that "kingdom which cannot be moved."

8. The kingdom of heaven cannot fully exist among men without three men at its head, called of God by the voice of revelation, and acknowledged in their office by the voice of the kingdom—to stand as a council of first presidency, to hold "the keys" of revelation and government for the whole church. There must be twelve men, called apostles disciples,[73] or special witnesses of the great object of the period in which they live. They must act ~~under the direction of~~ in unison ~~with~~ and the three be a part of the Twelve.[74] There must also be a council or Sanhedrim of seventy to assist the Twelve[75] "in bearing the burden of the kingdom." Then to have the whole government complete and to operate without schism there should be a council of seven to attend to the temporal affairs of the church to take charge of church property and[76] to over-

73. McLellin adds "disciples."

74. McLellin initially adds "in unison with" and deletes "under the direction of." He then appears to have crossed out "with" and replaced it with "and" and finished the statement by adding the words "be a part of the Twelve."

75. McLellin adds "the Twelve."

76. McLellin adds "to take charge of church property and."

see the interests of the poor, until all should become of one heart and one mind. "Perfectly joined together in the same mind, and in the same judgement" [1 Cor. 1:10].

9. In the days when God led Israel from Egypt to Canaan he called and qualified Moses, Aaron, and Hur to stand before him in the first presidency. And they acted in that station until Israel rebelled and "the law was added because [page 48:] of transgression" [cf. Gal. 3:19]. In the days of Christ's incarnation he called Peter, James, and John, and delivered to them "the keys of the kingdom of heaven" [Matt. 16:19], and thus left in their hands the presiding authority when he left the world. And his church when organized in "the fulness of times" [Eph. 1:10], in order to prepare a people for his second coming, in order to bring in that great millennial rest of one thousand years, must be organized according to the pattern of heavenly things, to hold "the keys" or men may be assured that God's hand will not be in the work.

10. The great object of Israel in the days of Moses was to obtain possession of the land of Canaan–"the lot of their inheritance" [cf. Num. 36:3]. The prime object of the Apostles of Christ was to get both Jew and Gentile to believe that Jesus was the Christ–the Messiah–the Son of God; and to publish his gospel to all nations; and to build up his church among all people. And when his kingdom is organized again on earth, the important object will be to restore ~~both~~ first the[77] Gentile and then the Jew to the knowledge of the true God–to the knowledge of his true and divine government, in the orders and powers of his chosen and faithful ministry; and thus bring in the "thousand years of rest" and peace to the whole earth.

11. In Israel the Lord chose twelve men as Apostles or special witnesses to them concerning the land of Canaan; and he sent them to search it out, that they might bear witness of it. Num. 13. Jesus, who came to restore the gospel to the world with all its grace and truth, chose twelve men to be his witnesses–his Apostles, to bear testimony of his name, his character, his doctrine, and his resurrection, "In Jerusalem, in all Judea, in Samaria, and unto the uttermost part of the earth" [Acts 1:8]. And now again in this age when all the councils of the "church of Christ" stand in their proper places, there will be a twelve, to bear the same relation in his kingdom which the same council of men did in ancient times. They will be apostles, yes, special witnesses of the work of the preparation for the second [page 49:] coming of Christ.

---

77. McLellin adds "first the."

(Presidency of Three.—See page 63.)†

12. In the days of Israel the Lord through Moses chose a Seventy, "Elders of the people, rulers among them," to stand with the **three** and, "to bear the burden of the people" [cf. Num. 11:16-17], so that Israel thus organized might prosper. In the meridian of time when Jesus went about doing good, "The Lord appointed other Seventy also, and sent them two and two before his face, as lambs among wolves" [Luke 10:1, 3]. Telling them to say to all people when they ministered that, "The kingdom of God is come nigh unto you" [Luke 10:9].[78] The church of Christ in order to fill the pattern given to Moses, and established by Jesus Christ must have a Seventy—one seventy and no more, to stand with the Three and the Twelve to minster righteousness, peace and joy in the Holy Spirit to all the world.

13. Thus we find in the days of Moses three, twelve, and seventy. In the period of Christ there were three, twelve, and seventy. And again in the "dispensation of the fulness of times" [Eph. 1:10], there must be councils established of three, twelve, and seventy. Thus the three dispensations ought to and must correspond with each other in their numbers in their councils in order to be "the kingdom of God—which cannot be moved" [cf. Dan. 2:44]. In the government of heaven, in the councils thus organized among men, the Lord anciently met with his servants, revealed his will to them, talked with them face to face, and led them (when they hearkened to his teachings,) by the right hand of his power. And so will he lead and protect his servants in the work of the last days, (and more too,) just as soon as these councils become properly organized, and then live in the spirit and practice of their calling.

14. When the Lord began to exercise his government over the children of Israel in order to lead them from Egypt to Canaan he organized among them a council or presidency of three men. And those men he called up on a mountain apart from the rest of the world, to act before him in a relation to each other, to the heavens, and to the camp of Israel, in a capacity different from all other men on earth: and that too on one of the most extraordinary occasions ever recorded in any history. Ex. 17. There that trio stood pleading with heaven, Moses in the [page 50:] center with uplifted hands, being braced by Aaron and Hur on either side; while Joshua leading the hosts of Israel struggled in the valley be-

†This heading, in the handwriting of John L. Traughber, refers to where Traughber wrote his conclusions on "Dr. McLellan's Change of Views."

78. The Greek verb means "has come."

neath not only for liberty, but even for their very existence as a nation or people on earth.

15. When Jesus came to earth to ~~re~~organize[79] his kingdom with a ministry in their proper relations to each other, to the kingdom, and to the heavens, he singled out Peter, James, and John—three men to stand as "pillars" [Gal. 2:9]: to the center one of whom be gave "the keys of his kingdom." And in order to qualify them to act in that important relation, he invited them to go with him into a high mountain apart, and then he unveiled to them his glory—and the beauty of the heavens. Mat. 17. He showed to them there the pattern of heavenly things. There Peter, James, & John gazed upon the three, Jesus, Moses, and Elias, who stood before them in their glorified attire. There they could see a perfect pattern of the God-head in heaven. There they could learn the benefit of "the keys" which Jesus had given them to use in spreading the gospel to all the world. There they received knowledge and qualifications above any others then living upon the face of the whole earth. Information which really qualified them to be **pillars**—pedestals to brace and stay the whole fabric of the apostolic church. Jesus had other apostles, but he made Peter, James, and John his ~~presiding~~, prime ministers on earth. To them was given power to unlock the kingdom to Jew and to Gentile. Peter was to that age what Moses was to the age in which he lived. And ~~again~~, when the Lord "sets his hand again the second time, to recover a remnant of his people" [cf. Isa. 11:11]—When the "dispensation of the fulness of times" [Eph. 1:10] has fully arrived—When "the hour of God's judgement is come" [cf. Rev. 14:7]—And the voice from heaven must be sounded to all the honest hearted in old Babylon "to come out of her my people, that ye be not partakers of her sins, and that ye receive not of her plagues" [Rev. 18:4]: When the Lord's set time "to favour Zion" arrives—Then we should confidently look for him to organize that last "kingdom which shall never be thrown down, or given to another people" [cf. Dan. 2:44]. To set it up with a first [page 51:] presidency or council of three at its head in its ranks[80]—to hold the "Keys" of the age—the period—the dispensation so that it might roll forth "to fill the whole earth with his glory" [cf. Dan. 2:35]. Such is its organization[81] or it will ~~never~~[82] prosper so as to bring in "that rest which remains to the people of God" [cf. Heb. 4:9].

79. The McLellin original has deleted the "re" in "reorganize," resulting in "organize."

80. McLellin adds "in its ranks."

81. McLellin originally wrote "Such must be its organization." Later he added above the line the words "is its," but the earlier wording of "must be its" was not deleted.

16. This council of three holds the highest authority which God ever gave to man on the earth. That man, who in any age or dispensation, occupies the center of the first ~~presidency~~ council[83] of the people of the Lord, as Moses and Peter did bears the same relation to the church, which the eternal Father does to all the heavenly hosts. He is in reality as Jethro said to Moses, "Be thou for the people to God-ward" [Ex. 18:19] that is, as the mouth of God. He is the Lord's Seer, the people's Prophet—He is to receive the law of the Lord from his mouth or messenger, and then to declare it to the people. He holds the keys of revelation, of translation, of government, and of power from [and] with[84] God. But inasmuch as the Son and the Holy Spirit are one with the Father in bearing record in heaven, so two counsellors are one with the Seer in bearing witness on earth—and also in the discharge of all his official duties. The pattern is complete. The first presidency of three in the kingdom of God on earth is a similitude of the three in the heavens, where God sits in the center, and in the midst of all his glories beholding their order and their harmony

17. From my youth up I have heard much speculation and reasoning about the doctrine of the trinity—the unity, &c., of the God-head. I have thought and read much on the subject, and have heard many comparisons drawn, (by the professedly learned,) in order to explain—to elucidate that deep, that all important doctrine. But I am free to confess that I never saw any thing that God had organized or made among men, until I saw this council or first presidency of three, wherein "the invisible things of him from the creation of the world are clearly seen, being understood by the things that are made, even his eternal power and God-head; so that they are left without excuse." [cf.] Rom. 1.20. In the organization of "the kingdom which cannot be moved," we can clearly see how this first council of three on earth, organized as a pattern of the three in [page 52:] heaven, shadows forth "his eternal power and God-head, so that men are left without excuse. And in order that Jesus might more fully show to his three prime ministers on earth how "The fulness of the God-head dwelt in him bodily" [cf. Col. 2:9], he took them up into an high mountain apart where they saw "his glory and the two men that stood with him" [Luke 9:32]. Here in this vision three glorified personages, (Jesus in the center,) appeared standing in the presence of the three apostles. In this glorious vision the pattern of the God-head was clearly seen on earth.

---

83. McLellin added "council."

84. McLellin added "with" but his original "from" is not deleted.

18. There are three who bear record in heaven, and they are one God—one council one court one tribunal.[85] There are three as a pattern of them to bear witness on earth, and they, (in all their official acts,) agree in one. The Father is the center of the three in heaven, from whom all light and intelligence springs to all heaven and earth; and the Seer on earth is the center, and with his two counsellors is the medium through whom must be revealed all laws for the instruction, regulation, and government of his kingdom, in order that all things may be done after the council of God's will, both in heaven and on earth.

19. A church or people claiming under the gospel dispensation to be the Lord's chosen ones, who have not a council of three, (and no more, nor no less,) at their head in their ranks,[86] in their organization, are in the dark and their works are in the dark—that is God does not reveal to them for their salvation; but they have to grope their way by the uncertain councils of uninspired men, who teach for doctrine the commandments and traditions of men—who teach fables. They may have cried Lord! Lord!! but they did not organize on the platform according to the pattern which Heaven had revealed to man in his sacred word as clearly as the noon-day sun beam. Therefore the Lord cannot own them as his. They have by their folly forced him to say "I know you not" [Matt. 25:12]—I never revealed myself to you, I never organized among you that order of things called "the kingdom of heaven"; and You therefore know me not, and you must stand aside. O my soul! think thou of the various church organizations in the world, which have no similarity to things in the heavens. Who have no council of three among them.

20. If we search through all the denominations of christendom, Catholic, Greek [page 53:] church, and all Protestanism, shall we find any or either of them with their ministry organized into councils of three, seven, twelve and seventy? If it were necessary to have that peculiar church organization in the times of Christ and his Apostles[87] olden times, "for the perfecting of the saints, for the work of the ministry, and for the edifying of the body of Christ" [Eph. 4:12], we would ask can any people now in this nineteenth century place themselves under a different form of church government and yet grow into perfection? Can they have that "Faith once delivered unto the saints" [Jude 1:3], and yet not have that order of ministry—not have those councils in the Priesthood

85. McLellin added "one court one tribunal."

86. McLellin added "in their ranks" but his original "at their head" is not deleted.

87. McLellin added "the times of Christ and his Apostles" but the words "olden times" are not deleted.

which the Lord thus distinctly placed in his kingdom through whom he could "preach the gospel with the Holy Ghost sent down from heaven" [cf. 1 Pet. 1:12]; and by whom he could administer "the Law of liberty" [James 1:25] for the government of his church? Nay, verily, nay. And here we can see one great reason why the different professedly religious denominations keep multiplying, or breaking to pieces and getting ~~and~~ still further and further[88] apart. It is because the Lord's form of church government has been rejected, and men—poor weak men have sought out many inventions, have formed up various canons of scripture. Creeds, Articles, disciplines, and confessions of faith to aid them in governing what they call the church of God. The Lord has left them to themselves because they desired it, and they are running to and fro, but still splits and divisions and denominations are increasing among them. Forms of church government are as abundant as the sects are, all differing the one from the other, each ~~one~~ party claiming theirs[89] to be the best—or nearest right; to have been drawn up by the most profound wisdom of men: all based upon or having been drawn (say they,) from the divine oracles of God. But remember dear reader it is only the wisdom of men drawn out in form or forms. It would spoil their religions in a moment, if they were to acknowledge that God had directly revealed to **them** one item in their various creeds.

21. The Catholics declare that the Pope is the head of their organization; he holds the keys of St Peter. Yet he has not two counsellors as Moses and Peter had. Here we can see a "falling away" from [page 54:] three to one, in the first council in the church. And in their orders of ministry following the Catholics seem still wider from the pattern given of the Lord. The Head of the Greek church is the Patriarch of Constantinople. One man, not three. The government of the church of England is Episcopal. The King or Queen is the supreme head. The Methodist church is governed by Bishops, and their numbers are increased at pleasure by their general conference, as there is a demand for their labours. But here we will stop following the sects and parties who claim to be christians, for the further we go down among them, the darker the picture grows relative to church government. And it matters not to us which of their creeds is best or worst, so that we cannot find the Lord's system among them. The express injunction of Heaven to Moses was, "See that thou make all things according to the pattern showed to thee in the mount" [cf. Ex. 27:8; Num. 8:4]. The Lord has given a pattern of minis-

88. McLellin added "and further."

89. McLellin added "theirs."

try in his word, and that people who establishes a "Kingdom which cannot be moved" [cf. Dan. 2:44], must do it precisely according to that pattern, or otherwise it will be shaken, moved, and blown to the four winds, when the "Lord of Hosts shall reign in Mount Zion, and in Jerusalem, and before his ancients gloriously" [Isa. 24:23].

22. But that people who gain the precise organization, patterned after heavenly things, governed by correct, holy, just, and good principles, and then are led by the true spirit of revelation; God will be their Father, Jesus their brother and friend, and Angels their messengers and ministers, and Prophets their associates and companions. Such a people will triumph—gloriously triumph over all the powers of darkness; and will finally bring in "the rest of God," and universal peace to the whole earth.

23. In the organization of the kingdom among men anciently they did not, (while they remained upright,) even once think of ~~ever~~ being governed by any other principle than by direct revelations from God through their Apostles or Disciples and[90] Prophets and Seers. They never assembled in general councils nor conferences in order to make creeds by their own wisdom to govern the church of God, "over which the Holy Spirit had made them overseers" [cf. Acts 20:28]. Nay, for that would have been a denial of their religion— [page 55:] of the fundamental principle which governed them. The principle of communing with God was the dearest one that ever animated the bosom of an ancient saint. Take that privilege away and such a being as a saint could not exist. Neither does the "Kingdom of God" exist on the earth except that principle and privilege exists in it; except the spirit of revelation has been given to organize it, to govern it, and then to carry it on to future triumph. It is that principle and privilege, and that only, which the ministers & members in that Kingdom possess of obtaining direct intelligence from heaven, by the voice of the Lord, by the visits of Angels, by open visions, by the gifts and powers of the Holy Spirit, and by and through inspired Prophets, that distinguishes it as "the kingdom which cannot be moved." Without the spirit of revelation and of direct intelligence being understood and possessed on earth among men, the Lord could not teach, lead, guide or direct his people. He could not[91] show them whether he loved them, or was displeased with them. Whether they were right, or whether they were wrong.

24. God is the fountain of all intelligence. And it is the spirit of revelation only that opens up to man the medium to that fountain. Let aside

---

90. McLellin added "Apostles or Disciples and."

91. McLellin added "not."

or deny that Spirit and principle and man is in the dark. He then is forced to grope his way through the world. He flies to inventing, but his wisdom is folly. His inventions of creeds to govern the church are subject to mutation, to alteration, to improvement, or to decay and death. After generations will set his forms, rules, and modes of worship aside, saying that he lived in a darker age—and then form new ones for themselves; and then divide and tear asunder those formerly bound together under the old established forms. Confusion and schisms arise—envy, jealousy, and every evil work follows. Thus the professedly religious world are going on, and have been for centuries past, and will be for ages to come, unless the Lord will be kind enough to raise up and to establish the "true church of Christ," and in it to place all the councils of three, seven, twelve, and seventy. And then to endow them with all the gifts and blessings "spoken of by all the holy Prophets since the world began" [cf. Acts 3:21]. To close, we say, that such a Kingdom would be the **home** of the faithful, and the "Joy and the Deliverer of the world." Amen. ~ [page 56:]

A Seer of the Lord.

"Before time in Israel when a man went to inquire of God, thus he spake: Come let us go to the Seer: for he that is now called a Prophet, was beforetime called a Seer." 1 Sam. 9.9.

1. A holy man, who possessed the Urim and Thummim, ~~viz.~~ or the[92] Directors and Interpreters, and the gift from God to use them for holy purposes; was in ancient times called a Seer. This instrument was prepared in olden time to strengthen men's faith in God, to interpret languages, & to aid them to see the past, the present, and the future. It was for the purpose of inquiring and receiving wisdom and knowledge direct from God. Hence it was the great, the sure, the certain, and the infallible medium of communication between God & his Seers.

2. The learned say the word Urim signifies Lights, and the word Thummim Perfections. If so, then when an answer was received through or by that medium there was no possibility of deception, because God was its light, and his answers were perfect. Whosoever had these things would be called a Seer, after the manner of old times. He would be a Revelator & a Prophet also. No mortal man could possess a greater gift from God.

3. The first mention we have of that sacred instrument in the Bible

92. McLellin added "or the."

was in the days of Moses. "And thou shalt put in the breastplate of judgement the Urim and the Thummin; and they shall be upon Aaron's heart when he goeth in before the Lord: and Aaron shall bear the judgement of the children of Israel upon his heart before the Lord continually." Ex. 28[:30]. "And he (Joshua) shall stand before Eleazar the Priest, who shall ask council for him, after the judgement of Urim before the Lord." Num. 27[:21]. In Moses last blessing on the tribes of Israel, when speaking of Levi he said, "Let thy Thummin and thy Urim be with thy holy one, whom thou didst prove at Massah." Deut. 33[:8]. "And when Saul inquired of the Lord, the Lord answered him not, neither by dreams, nor by Urim, nor by prophets.["] 1st. Sam. 28[:6]. Again when the captives returned from Babylon, some claimed [page 57:] to be of the priesthood, who could not trace their genealogy in the register: "Therefore they were as polluted put from the priesthood. And the Governor said to them, that they should not eat of the most holy things, till there stood up a priest with Urim and with Thummim." Ez[ra] 2[:62-63].

4. Many have been the speculations of the learned about what this instrument was, the time when it was first introduced, who prepared it, and what was its design. One thing however is certain, the man who held that sacred instrument in olden times, held it to inquire of God, in order to see—therefore he was called a Seer. But whether all those in ancient times called Seers held those peculiar eyes, is questionable—I am inclined to think they did not. The ~~office~~ gift of Seer is the most responsible, or the highest in the gift of God to man in this state of existance. That man who is the Lord's Seer holds the right to enjoy all the gifts of God which he ever bestows upon mortal man: and also authority to set apart men in all the offices in the church or kingdom of God. Even the Kings of the earth in olden times held their crowns because they were appointed and anointed by the Lord's Seers.[93]

5. It appears that but one Seer lived in the world at the same time, or at least in the same realm or dominion at the same date. The calling and appointment of a Seer is alone in the hands of the great God himself. And that one who is privileged to hold and act in that office in the Priesthood stands in the same relation to the church of Christ on earth, that Jehovah does to all the heavenly worlds, that is, he is Head on earth, as God is Head in heaven—only that God holds his power independently, and a Seer derives his directly from him, as did Adam in Eden, Abraham in Mesopotamia, and Samuel in the house of the Lord with Eli, or by the

93. McLellin originally wrote "Seer." (period included), then deleted the period and replaced it with both an "s" and another period to make the plural "Seers."

voice of an Angel sent on that errand direct from God: as did the Seers Moses and, Peter, and Joseph, ~~and also Joseph~~ Smith.[94]

6. The duty of a Seer is, as was said to Moses by Jethro his father-in-law, "Be thou for the people to God-ward." Ex. 18[:19]. That is, thy calling is to receive "a thus saith the Lord," direct from his mouth, and then declare it to the people. Also to denounce the judgements of God against individuals, communities or nations [page 58:] and to warn them of their danger: and to lead the people of the Lord aright in principle, in doctrine, in practice, and in government, so that their faith, and knowledge, and power with God might increase unto perfection.

7. Moses had the Urim and Tummin, (but when, where, or how he received it, or how it was prepared, the Bible does not inform us,) and being a Seer, that is, holding the highest ~~office~~ privilege in the gift of God to man, he could act in any other ~~office~~ station in all the congregation of Israel: and he could, by the direction of the Lord, set apart men to act in any or all the various offices necessary for the ministry and government of all the tribes of Jacob. Through the ministry and ~~priesthood~~ authority which he held and confered upon the first born[95] the gospel of Jesus (Heb. 4:2.) was preached in plainness to all the congregation of Israel, in order to make them "a kingdom of Priests" [Ex. 19:6], and to sanctify them and thus prepare them to enter "the rest of God." But they refused to be sanctified by the mild, the holy principles & practices of the "perfect law of liberty" [James 1:25]. They rebelled, and consequently "the law of carnal ~~commandments~~ rites and ordinances was added" [cf. Heb. 7:16; Gal. 3:19], and Israel was placed under a schoolmaster until Christ should come. And in consequence thereof the presiding authority was taken out of the hands of the Melchesidek order of priesthood and placed upon the Aaronic or Levitical order. Hence at Moses' Aaron's[96] demise the Urim was given to Eleazor his first born.[97]

8. Moses' appointment of a man to lead Israel across Jordan into Canaan did not, after the change of presidency in priesthood, entitle him to the Seer's office, that is, to hold the Urim. But when the law which was "a shadow of good things to come" [Heb. 10:1], was given, and authority given to the Aronic order of priests to administer it, those sacred Seer's stones were taken and placed in the breastplate, and that was fastened

94. For a summary of Joseph Smith's life, see the Biographical Notes.

95. McLellin added "and confered upon the first born."

96. McLellin added "Aaron's" but his original "Moses'" is not deleted. The former would be correct since Eleazar was the third son of Aaron by Elisheba.

97. McLellin added "his first born."

into a garment [page 59:] called the Ephod, worn by the high priest of the Aronic order. Consequently Moses could not confer it upon Joshua, but it legally and rightly belonged to Eleazor; and thus was Eleazor placed over Joshua—that is, he must by the use of the Urim inquire of God and then declare his will to the Leader of Israel's host. Hence the Lord said to Moses concerning Joshua, "thou shalt put some of thine honor upon him." God divided some of Moses' honor between Eleazor and Joshua. But both of them in the nature of things could not receive the authority vested in Moses. The right of presidency in the Melchesidec priesthood being taken away ~~with Moses~~ when the law was added,[98] well might it be recorded in the holy book that "There arose not a Prophet since in Israel, like unto Moses, whom the Lord knew face to face." Deut. 34[:10].

9. Moses was Prophet, Seer, Revelator, Law-giver, Judge, & Leader in Israel. And all that authority was united in his person, because ~~his priesthood~~ he was a type of Jesus,[99] was after the order of the Son of God. But after Israel's rebellion, and they had lost the rights of the gospel, and it was necessary there should be a change in the priesthood—or rather in the presidency of it, then Eleazor became Seer and Joshua Leader. Hence, it was a saying among them during the reign of the law, that "No man can see the face of God and live" [cf. John 1:18]. Without the Melchesidec priesthood it would be impossible. Consequently came the above expression about Moses. And hence came also a settled and fixed feeling among all the tribes of Jacob, who were under the authority of the ~~lesser~~ Aaronic priesthood, as expressed by Manoah to his wife, "We shall surely die, because we have seen God." Judges 13[:22].

10. One peculiarity we will mention here, when the Lord designed to accomplish a great work in the world among men, he called and qualified a Seer, he gave to him the "keys" of knowledge, and he also gave him two men to stand with him in his presidency as helps & counsellors. But when he only designed to warn a people who had forsaken him after the order had been established ~~the order~~,[100] and run into transgression after the establishment of a dispensation, then he only sent to them his Prophet or Seer, and one with him as assistant or scribe. [page 60:]

11. When Moses led Israel he had Aaron and Hur as assistants and counsellors with him in the first presidency. They then had power with God, the Seer in the center, and his helps on either side. "And Moses, Aaron and Hur, went up to the top of the hill, and it came to pass, when

---

98. McLellin added "when the law was added."

99. McLellin added "he was a type of Jesus."

100. McLellin added "after the order had been established the order."

Moses held up his hands that Israel prevailed; and when he let down his hands, Amalek prevailed. But Moses' hands were heavy; and they took a stone, and put it under him, and he sat thereon: and Aaron and Hur staid his hands, the one on the one side, and the other on the other side; and his hands were steady until the going down of the sun, + + + and Joshua discomfitted Amalek" [cf.] Ex.17[:10-13]. "And the Lord said unto Moses, come up to me unto the mount, and be thou there; and I will give thee tables of stone and a law, and commandments which I have written; that thou mayest teach them. And Moses rose up, and his minister Joshua; and Moses went up into the mount of God. And he said unto the Elders, tarry ye here for us, until we come again unto you: and, behold, Aaron and Hur are with you; if any man have any matters to do, let him come unto them." [cf.] Ex. 24[:12-14]. Why did it require them to be on the hill, while Joshua fought in the valley below in self defense? And why did Moses say to the 70 Elders, I leave Aaron and Hur with you; if difficulties arise, bring the matters before them? I answer, because they two with him formed the highest tribunal on earth. And Moses here laid down the principle that his counsellors had a right, by virtue of their office, to preside and give decisions in his absence.

12. But after Israel was planted in Canaan, the order of things being changed, then when the Lord warned them he usually sent a prophet alone, or only sent a servant or scribe with him. Instance Elijah, Elisha, and Jeremiah. 1st Kings 18. 2 Kings 4. Jer. 36.

13. Thus matters remained, with the Aaronic high priest holding the keys of authority until the Messiah "sprang out of Juda" [cf. Mic. 5:2], in order to again reestablish a higher order of Priesthood [page 61:] so as to bring in everlasting righteousness. His ministry or Priesthood was after the same order in which Adam, Abel, Enoch, Noah, Melchesidec, Abraham, Jethro, and Moses, ministered; the presidency of which, was taken away from the Hebrews when the ceremonial law was <u>introduced</u> or rather established.[101] But Jesus came, fulfilled the law, and took it out of the way; and when it was abolished there was no more need to retain the power in the hands of Levi to administer it. Christ held a superior priesthood. He held the keys of power, and had a right to confer them upon Peter, thus making him his Seer; and also gave him James & John to be his counsellors, in the great work of publishing the gospel of salvation to all the world.

14. The moment the priesthood was changed, or the keys with the

101. McLellin added "or rather established."

presid[e]ncy, were taken from the order of Aaron, and given to the higher order of Melchesidec, the responsibilities became as much greater as the gospel system was greater than the law. Hence the union of three in the first presidency. James and John were associated with Peter in holding the keys; so that the pattern of the eternal power and Godhead might be clearly seen on earth, as was said by Paul, Rom. 1:20. But the subsequent falling away from the true order of heaven, and all religious denominations taking to themselves power—that is, "heaping to themselves teachers, having itching ears + + + and were turned unto fables" [cf. 2 Tim. 4:3-4]. They built up systems of their own, "having <u>a</u> form of godliness, but denying the power thereof" [2 Tim. 3:5]. Each system, whether Catholic, Greek or Protestant, as it sprung up, stood in contradistinction to the other, but all of them living and acting without the aid of "a Seer of the Lord," through whom they might inquire concerning their isms and schisms, their tenets and notions—thus denying the Lord, and setting aside his peculiar form of church[102] government for the gospel age, and bringing in all the confusion, the jargon, and the distrust now experienced in the world.

15. Men now run to and fro, and hold conferences, councils, assemblies, and even a "World's convention," in order to inquire of each other, instead of doing as they [page 62:] did in olden time, to go and say, "Come, let us go to the Seer," that he may inquire of God, and receive light and truth—by new revelation—direct from the Fountain of all intelligence & wisdom. But if the Lord should raise up and qualify a Seer, and reveal his will through him, according to the order as stated above, all the world as it is now organized, among all denominations, would rise up and say, we have bible enough; we have the word of God enough, we have no need at the present day for a Seer to live among us. And yet they are all divided and subdivided into parties; each one claiming to be the nearest right, both in the doctrine and government of their isms. None knowing, yet all guessing, "I am more holy than thou, stand thou there." In the days of Aaron, the Urim and Thummim was placed in a breast-plate, and then that was placed into the bosom of the high priest's garment called the Ep~~h~~od. Whoever then among the priests held that garment, had also that curious instrument of power with God. Hence, when David, the anointed king of Israel, was brought into a strait in Keilah, he said unto Abiath[a]r, the priest—"Bring hither the Ephod" [1 Sam. 23:9]. And when it was brought he learned the mind of

102. McLellin added "church."

God. Again, when the Amalekites had smitten Ziklag, David's adopted city, and burned it with fire; David again applied to Abiath[a]r, saying, "I pray thee, bring me hither the Ephod" [1 Sam. 30:7]. And David inquired of the Lord saying, "Shall I persue this troop? Shall I overtake them? And he answered him, Persue: for thou shalt surely overtake them, and without fail recover all." 1 Sam. 30[:8]. Whoever was a holy man, and had the Urim, could always approach the Lord and obtain an answer; and it was in some way by the use of Seeing; hence the one who looked was called Seer. [page 63:]† [page 64:]

On Priesthood.

1. Priesthood is the office and character of a priest. It is an order of men, or of ministers set apart for sacred and holy offices; embracing quality, character, and condition. It sometimes signifies a confraternity of individuals as in brotherhood. Holy priests were always called of God by immediate or direct revelation, and then set apart, ordained, or consecrated unto him for the purposes of declaring or administering his

---

†The whole of p. 63 is in the handwriting of John L. Traughber, as follows:

Dr. McLellan's Change of Views

On pages 49 and 50 of this book the Doctor treats elaborately of the presidency of Three at the head of the church. While the arguments and illustrations there used are of the most positive character, it is but just to state that the Doctor's mind underwent a very radical change years after he had written what is contained in this book.

From the time when I first began correspondence with the Doctor, in 1875, he utterly repudiated the doctrine of a presidency of three, which he was at such pains to try to uphold when writing this book.

I write this, here, to clear the memory of the Doctor's last years from the blot of believing in this much adored doctrine of the Mormons. The poor old man, after having run about after pretended prophets for years, finally laid them all aside who pretended that God had commissioned them to rule men. The Book of Mormon, was, when he died, March, 1883, the only part of all Mormonism that he gave unqualified assent to; and I believe that if he had had a few years more of healthy life, he would have freed himself of the last vestige of the folly of all Mormon pretensions, from the claim of Smith to have had his first vision to the last gibberish spoken by some deluded fanatic who has faith in Smith.

Having cast his whole soul into Mormonism in 1831, Dr. McLellan had to be "whipped" out by the unanswerable logic of stern facts to which he could not shut his eyes; hence it took him more that half a lifetime to unlearn even as much of the damnable fraud as he did get free from.

I valued him much. He and I were true friends, yet for the last two years of his life we were as far apart in religion as the poles of the earth. Peace to his memory. Repose to his spirit.

J. L. Traughber.

Forsyth, Taney Co., Mo., Feb. 27, 1889.

laws among men. There are but two true priesthoods spoken of in the word of God, viz. The Melchesidec and the Aaronic or[103] Levitical. And in each of these there are different classes, orders, courses or degrees of office. By and through the authority of the Melchesidec order the Lord ministered among men from Adam until Moses. And the Levitical priesthood ministered among the tribes of Israel from Aaroon until John. But from the days of Christ until now, so far as the gospel has been preached by divine authority, "it has been by ~~priests~~ ministers of the Melchisedec order.

2. = The Melchisedec is the high priesthood—it is the holy order of the son of God. It is unchangeable, its power is endless, and its authority is universal. And as there have been but two priesthoods, so there have been but two codes of law given by inspiration from God to man. The gospel was the first and the last. The law of Moses to Israel was given intermediate. But the gospel is the unchangeable, the endless, and the universal "Law of Liberty" [James 1:25], declared from heaven for the salvation of fallen man. This high and holy order of priesthood is that sacred[104] authority in which the scheme of eternal redemption was first fixed before the foundation of this world was laid. It was the first authority which man ever received from his Creator by which to minister among men in holy things. And the gospel always was & always will be the law of that priesthood. [page 65:]

By its authority all the sacrifices ever acceptable to God were offered up, and all the spiritual powers exercised among men for their good—except those only which were attended to by the ~~Levitical~~ Aaronic order of priests during the reign of the Law. Truly this priesthood is emphatically called, "the holy order of God."

3. By a minister in this priesthood the gospel was preached to Abraham in ~~in~~ his day. Gal. 3:8. It was also thus preached to the whole camp of Israel to sanctify them that they might enter into rest. Heb 4:2. Yes, if Israel had obeyed the Lord's voice indeed, and kept his covenant, then they as a nation would have been unto God "a kingdom of priests." Ex. 19:6. If Israel as a nation had obeyed the Lord without rebellion, then the gospel with all its ordinances, its rights, and its blessing—together with its priesthood, would have remained among them; and they then as God's messengers and holy priests would have ministered it to all other nations of men. Then the law of Moses would not have been "added be-

---

103. McLellin added "Aaronic or."

104. McLellin added "sacred."

cause of transgression" [cf. Gal. 3:19], consequently the Aaronic or Levitical priesthood would never have been instituted or known in Israel, or in the world. Israel would thus have been made "the head and not the tail," of this lower creation. But they rebelled and the law ~~as~~ was given, and "it made men priests after the law of a carnal commandment" [cf. Heb. 7:16]. That is, a priesthood was given them which was not received because of faith and righteousness, but descended from father to son by lineal or[105] hereditary right. It came by lineage. All this was bound upon Israel as a yoke or schoolmaster "till the seed should come, to whom the promise was made" [Gal. 3:19]. The calling, and ordinance, and high priesthood is without beginning of days or end of years; being prepared from eternity to all eternity. Exceeding faith, repentance, and good works were always prerequisites to this priesthood; and hence priests of this holy order never could look upon sin with allowance or[106] save it were with abhorence. [page 66:]

4. There are in the Melchesidec priesthood different classes, or degrees of office, such as ~~Seer or Prophet~~, apostle, elder, ~~priest~~,[107] deacon &c. The qualifications of most of these officers may be gathered from the examples in past history, but to mark their specific duties any where in the written word of God so far as we now have it,[108] cannot be done–at least of all of them. But we find each of the above classes of officers or overseers distinctly mentioned as belonging to the gospel age, hence we claim that they belong to this holy order of the Son of God. But we have said that the authority of this priesthood was universal. By this we mean that it never was confined to any one man, or tribe, or nation of men. But that in every nation he who feared God, and worked righteousness and exercised exceeding great faith could and did receive office and authority in this high and holy priesthood. Its gifts and callings are from God directly; and are bestowed wherever men diligently, consistently, conscientiously, and honestly persue the highest degree of light which shines upon their minds. Melchesidec acted upon this principle, ~~conseq~~ and became[109] distinguished; consequently his name stands enrolled at the head of the order. The motto of all the priests in this order is,–that man who has the most spiritual intelligence, the highest degree of light,

105. McLellin added "lineal or."

106. McLellin added "with allowance or."

107. The word "priest" is faintly crossed out with four diagonal lines, which contrasts sharply with the bold horizontal lines deleting "Seer" and "Prophet."

108. McLellin added in faint handwriting "so far as we now have it."

109. McLellin added "and became."

and the greatest power with God has a divine right to stand at the head &[110] to direct and lead the people of God.

The Levitical Priesthood.

5. The law of Moses and the ~~Levitical~~ Aronic P.hood[111] ~~was~~ were introduced among the tribes of Israel, and for them especially for the particular purpose of administering the rights of that singular, that fiery law which was given to them.[112] It was confined to the tribe of Levi, and its highest office to Aaron, and to his oldest son succeeding. When no faultless male member of that tribe family[113] could be found, no Levitical Aaronic[114] priest could possibly officiate, or even exist. But where a legal priest of this order did live and minister, his duties were so particularly defined in and by that law that they must be performed according to it in order to be valid. Hence we [page 67:] can see that the Levitical Aaronic[115] priesthood was a circumscribed partial one, intended only for one nation, and given to and confined to but one tribe in that nation.

6. All the priests of this order from Aaron until John received their authority by lineage[116] pedigree, descent, or birthright. Therefore they were said to be made after the law of a carnal, i.e. fleshly commandment. Hence it was called a changeable priesthood, because it descended in a regular line from father to son. And because no priest of this order ever gained eternal life by translation. This whole institution of law and priesthood was by the order or disposition of Angels, instead of by the holy order of the Son of God. The apostle called it "the ministration of condemnation–and of death" [cf. 2 Cor. 3:7, 9]. But when the law defining its call, its consecration, its rights, its ceremonies, and its duties; and for the ministration of which it was instituted, was abolished, then the priesthood itself of course could no longer exist–It was abrogated also.

7. In this priesthood there were orders or distinct offices such as High Priest, chief priests, and Levites. And in king David's reign the priests were divided into twenty four classes or courses, each class min-

---

110. McLellin added in faint handwriting "to stand at the head &."

111. McLellin added "and the Levitical P.hood"; later he deleted the word "Levitical" and wrote "Aronic" on top of it.

112. McLellin added "which was given to them."

113. McLellin added "family" but his original "tribe" is not deleted.

114. McLellin added "Aaronic" but his original "Levitical" is not deleted.

115. McLellin again added "Aaronic" without deleting his original "Levitical."

116. McLellin added "lineage."

istering at the altar alternately a specified time. And this division seems to have existed until the days of Zacharias, the father of John the Baptist—who "was of the course of Abia" [Luke 1:5]. John ~~the~~ was a legal, lineal descendant of his fathers. He was the last legal priest of that order who ministered among men—He introduced the Messiah who brought in a priesthood with objects as much higher than the Levitical Aaronic[117] as heaven was higher than the earth.

Remarks.

8. Wherever a priest of ~~this~~ the order of Melchisedec lived and ministered, he would as assuredly preach the gospel of Christ as a Levitical priest would [page 68:] administer the ritual law of Moses. The Melchisedec order is and always was entirely independent of the Levitical Aaronic[118] order. But ~~the whole order of~~ Aaron ~~or Levi~~ and his sons[119] ~~was~~ were ~~instituted or~~ consecrated by ~~one or more of the order of Melchisedec~~ Moses the Prophet and Seer of God, and then Aaron consecrated the Levites,[120] and also all the rules of law regulating their the number, ~~their~~ the orders, and ~~their~~ the worship ~~was~~ were given through ~~a Melchisedec high priest~~ him—Moses the Prophet of God.[121] The Lord suffered all this to be because of the rebellion of Israel who were thus brought under tutors and governors until Christ "sprang out of Judah" [cf. Mic. 5:2] and broke their yoke.

9. The direct source or fountain of the Melchisedec priesthood was God, himself, but that of Aaron or[122] Levi was ordained by angels in the hand of a mediator. Those holding office never can rise higher than the power from whence they received it. No Levitical priest could ever possibly rise higher in spiritual privileges than the communion with angels. But the priest of the order of the Son of God could commune ~~with spirits~~ angels of ["]just men made perfect["] [Heb. 12:23],[123] with angels, with Jesus, and with his Father. Hence this holy order had the privilege to enjoy all the gifts, and powers, and blessings which God ever gave to man—and even like Enoch ~~and~~ Elijah and Moses[124] to rise by translation

---

117. "Aaronic" was added without deleting "Levitical."

118. "Aaronic" was added without deleting "Levitical."

119. McLellin added "and his sons."

120. McLellin added "Moses the Prophet and Seer of God, and then Aaron consecrated the Levites."

121. McLellin added "him—Moses the Prophet of God."

122. McLellin added "Aaron or."

123. McLellin added "angels of just men made perfect."

124. McLellin added "and Moses."

to eternal life in celestial glory, without ever tasting of death. But the Levitical order was circumscribed in all its powers both with God and among men. Its duties were mostly outward performances—ceremonial rights. It was typical, a mere shadow, but when the true order of the Son of God came it was the antitype and substance; and then there was of course no more use for the shadow or type.

10. Jethro, the ~~father in law brother in law~~ father in law[125] to Moses, was the priest of Midian. ~~And~~ He met Moses in the wilderness, and when Moses related to him how the Lord had delivered Israel, Jethro's heart leaped for joy, and he "rejoiced for all the goodness that the Lord had done to Israel. And Jethro took a burnt-offering and sa[page 69:] cr[i]fices for God["] [Ex. 18:9, 12]. And Moses & Aaron, and all the elders of Israel came and eat bread with Jethro. Thus showing that Moses & Jethro believed in and worshipped the same God, ~~and also held and officiated in the same order of priesthood~~. During Jethro's visit with Moses & Israel he recommended to them laws and regulations which they practiced as long as they had a national existance. Thus proving too his superior knowledge in the things of God. He at that time had more light and experience than Moses in some things.

11. By the authority of this royal or kingly priesthood, Abraham communed with his God in the land of Ur, of the Chaldees. By it Melchisedec lived and worshipped "under his own vine and fig tree" in the land of Salem. By it Jethro ministered in his own father-land of Media, and when he visited Moses at the mount of God, by it he directed and regulated all the camp of Israel. ~~By~~ Th[r]oug[h] ~~the authority of~~[126] it Moses overthrew and destroyed all the glory of Egypt, and triumphantly led Israel forty years in the wilderness. By its authority,[127] he communed with angels and with the Lord face to face. Israel rebelled against the authority of this priesthood, and refused to be sanctified by its "Law of Liberty" [James 1:25]; therefore the law of types & shadows was bound upon them until Jesus came and nailed it to his cross, and took it out of the way. It was because Korah, Dathan, and Abiram rebelled against ~~this~~ holy authority that the earth opened a wide mouth and swallowed them up.

12. This priesthood was Jesus Christ's authority while he went about manifesting such marvelous powers in doing good. And it was the

---

125. McLellin originally wrote "father in law," which he changed to "brother in law" and then changed back to "father in law."

126. McLellin added "Thoug [meaning "through"] the authority of" and then deleted "the authority of."

127. McLellin added an "s" to make "its" and also added the word "authority."

exercise of its power in him by wich he burst the bars of death, and thus triumphed over all his enemies. By its authority[128] the apostles and elders preached the gospel to all the world—"to every creature which is under heaven" [cf. Mark 16:15; Acts 2:5]. The declaration from the bosom of eternity was "Thou art a priest forever" [Heb. 5:6]. Thus signifying that when this holy authority is once [page 70:] received it is everlasting, it is endless, it is eternal, and it is even like the authority of God himself. The space of operations for one of this order is in all this world, and ~~also~~ in all worlds[129] throughout the universe of God during boundless eternity. Yes, its operations are in all climes and in all worlds. Its highest privileges are to hold converse with the Lord face to face in order to learn and know all things; and to rise by translation to Celestial glory, and[130] never taste of death. The Levitical order is not endless, nor eternal, ~~nor~~ but was limited, because all its operations were confined to this world, and to one people for a specified time, and to one tribe among that one people.[131]

13. When we thus contrast the two orders of priesthood we can see their vast differences and dissimilarities. The one filling boundless space with the sphere of its operations, the other confined to a tribe of the descendants of Abraham, and existing only for a limited period. The one endless and eternal; the other ever confined in its operations to time and external ordinances, and ending with death, or changing from father to son by pedigree.[132] The duty of one is to minister its blessings to both body and spirit—to the external and the internal man. The duty of the other was to minister in outward ceremonies for the external man only. The higher existed with God from all eternity and will to all eternity; but the lower began with Aaron and ended with John. The one is heavenly in its origin, in its power, and in its spirituality. The other (though derived from angels) was mostly earthly in its object, in its performances, and earthly also in its life and in its death.

14. Adam was the Lord's first Chief Ruler, Prophet,[133] and High Priest on earth. And that authority was vested in him because of Seniority: because he was the first—the Head and progenitor of the race of

---

128. McLellin added an "s" to make "its" and added the word "authority.

129. McLellin added "in all worlds."

130. McLellin added "rise by translation to Celestial glory, and."

131. The words "and to one tribe among that one people" appear to have been added later by McLellin.

132. McLellin added "by pedigree."

133. McLellin added "Prophet."

man: and because, after his fall he repented and exercised exceeding great faith before God. In the first organization of human society the order of God was that the oldest male should [page 71:] be the chief Ruler, Prophet,[134] and High priest of the whole race. For then ~~both~~ these most important offices were combined ~~to~~ in, and exercised by one person. And to keep this order perfect it was ordained that the first-born male child of the Ruler, Prophet,[135] and Priest should be the successor of his father, and have the undeniable right to those most important offices. But if the legal heir committed wilful murder i.e. shed innocent blood, or committed adultery, or dispised his birth-right[136] so as to sell it, then he lost all the rights, privileges, honors, and blessings pertaining to the first-born: and they fell of right to the next born. Cain, Japheth, Esau, and Reuben fell from their high estate, and hence lost their birth-rights. They were given to Seth, to Shem, to Jacob, and to Joseph. From Seth these offices passed down the line of the patriarchs or Royal Priests to Noah. The birth-right was then of great consequence, the one holding it having both[137] the temporal and spiritual[138] power to rule over and bless the race of man. And they held the promise too that the "Messiah should be born in their lineage."

15. He who then was king or chief ruler was also Prophet and[139] High priest of the "holy order of the Son of God." The priesthood being thus united to the chief dignity, and both given to the first-born, and because the chief ruler only performed the duties of the priesthood, it is therefore called by the inspired apostle "a royal i.e. kingly priesthood," and those who were blessed with it, "a chosen generation, a holy nation, a peculiar people" [1 Pet. 2:9].

16. From Noah the birth-right was confered upon Shem, and he was placed first, although younger than Japheth. Why it was so, or what crime he committed the historians of the sacred oricles have not informed us. And from Shem it passed in a regular line down to Abraham, to Isaac, and to Jacob. But among the sons of Jacob a difficulty occurs; and thereafter the <u>union</u> of authorities, as before, were never given to or exercised by one person among all the decendants of Jacob until ~~Moses, and not again until~~[140] Christ came. And in him was the embodiment of

134. McLellin added "Prophet."
135. McLellin added "Prophet."
136. McLellin added "birth-."
137. McLellin added "both."
138. McLellin added "and spiritual."
139. McLellin added "Prophet and."
140. McLellin first added and then deleted "Moses, and not again until."

all the holy authorities and powers which God had ever given to man. "For it pleased the Father that in him should all fulness dwell" [Col. 1:19]. [page 72:]

17. Reuben was Jacob's first-born, "The excellency of dignity: and ~~and~~ the excellency of power" [Gen. 49:3]. Yet by his base sin—"he defiled his father's couch"—he lost his birth-right [cf. Gen 49:4]. And afterward he and his nine brothers sold Joseph into bondage, and hence the Lord through Jacob[141] passed them all by and gave the blessing of birth-right to Joseph; because he had not sinned against his father's rights his dignity[142] or his honor. Judah "prevailed above his brethren," and of him came the chief ruler, judge, or king over all the tribes of Israel: but the birth-right of necessity had to go to Joseph, to be Prophet and priest.[143]

18. It is generally supposed by learned men that the rights of primogeniture were: 1. Authority and superiority over the rest of the family. 2. A double portion of the paternal inheritance. 3. The peculiar benedictions of the father. 4. The priesthood previous to the giving of the law. It at least appears, 1. That the first born were peculiarly consecrated to God, Ex. 22:29. 2. Were next to their fathers in dignity, ~~and~~ honor, and power.[144] Gen. 49:3. 3. Had a double portion of their father's goods. Deut. 21:17. 4. Succeeded him in the government of the family or kingdom, 2 Chron. 21:3. 5. Had the sole right of conducting the service of God; and hence the tribe of Levi, which was taken in lieu of the first-born, had the only right of administering in the service of God at the altar under the law. Num. 8:14-18.

19. After Jacob blessed Joseph's two sons Ephraim and Manassah we hear no more of such patriarchal birth-right blessings in Israel. Either it was not practiced among the tribes, or if so neither[145] their prophets or historians have ~~not~~ given us an account of it. The first born in lineal descent held the right of priesthood until Moses, with Israel, left Egypt for Canaan. Then the Lord chose and sanctified the first born males in all the families of Israel to be his—consecrated to him for holy purposes. And this order of things remained until the Mosaic law was given. Then the order was [page 73:] changed. The tribe of Levi was taken for priests instead of all the first born. And Aaron was taken for the High Priest in this order of things, and it was ordained that ~~the~~ his

141. McLellin added "through Jacob."

142. McLellin added "his dignity."

143. McLellin added "to be Prophet and priest."

144. McLellin added "and power."

145. McLellin added "neither."

oldest son was to be the successor in this ~~this~~ high and ~~most~~ very holy office. And this order of things was to continue among all that people while the law and its dispensation remained in force. Aaron was older than Moses, hence held the right to the priesthood because of precedence according to the great principles upon which the Lord had acted with the patriarchs.

20. Jesus was the first-born of Joseph and Mary, and therefore held the birth right. He was of the royal seed of David by both his parents: hence was a legal king, by linial descent. And God anointed him with the Holy Spirit and with power ~~at~~ after his baptism, and owned him by a voice from the most excellent glory to be his Son: ~~hence he became~~ and by an oath constituted him the[146] High Priest for the whole race of man–Gentile as well as Jew; and thus he was in his office like unto Adam & Melchisedec and Abraham:[147] and so he became the benefactor and Savior of men. He was no pretender or usurper, but was legally a King. Aaron was a high priest to all the tribes of Israel, but Jesus Christ was the High Priest to all the nations, tribes, and families of man. Aaron's priesthood at his death descended to his oldest son by right of birth and lineage. But Christ having no descendants "to declare his generation" [Acts 8:33], and having seen no corruption, and holding a higher order of Priesthood, therefore he abides the High Priest to his people forever.

21. But query, has there been a legal High Priest on earth since Christ? Does the Christian system require or acknowledge but one? ~ The office of high priest was first introduced among men to point them to Christ, and they offered sacr[i]fices for that object: and these offerings was one of their specific duties. The Aaronic or Levitical order of priesthood was given as a shadow, but not the very image of the Melchisedec. And it is noted, in the scriptures of truth, that the order of [page 74:] ministry given to Aaron and to his sons, and to all the tribes of Levi could have in it but ~~one~~ one High Priest at the same time. When he died the next in lineal pedigree received it. And so on until Christ came and changed the order. Now if there is no example, nor[148] shadow, nor image, nor pattern found in the law dispensation for more than one high priest at the same time, how is [it] that men can believe that more than one can legally exist in the gospel age? but one can exist, and that one is Christ.[149] "And having an High Priest over the

146. McLellin added "and by an oath constituted him the."

147. McLellin added "and Abraham."

148. McLellin added "example, nor."

149. McLellin added "but one can exist, and that one is Christ."

house of God, let us draw near with a true heart, in full assurance of faith" [Heb. 10:21-22].

22. Again, no where is it mentioned by the inspired Apostles that there was, or was to be any High priest in the church except Christ only. "But this man, after he had offered **one** sacrifice for sins, forever sat down on the right hand of God; to appear in his presence for us" [cf. Heb. 10:12; 9:24]. And in summing up the classes of ministers in their day, they speak of Apostles, prophets, elders, evangelists, pastors, teachers, ~~and~~ or deacons, "for the work of the ministry" [Eph. 4:12], but no where of High Priests. The last legal sacrifice ever offered was when Christ through the Eternal Spirit offered himself without spot to God. Inspiration says, "every high priest is ordained to offer gifts and sacrifices" [Heb. 8:3]. Now if a high priest could be appointed in the gospel day, what would be his duties? What could or would be his offering? What gift or sacrifice could he present that would be pleasing to God? And where would we find a rule of law regulating his conduct, and marking his specific duties, in the gospel plan, as was given relating to Aaron and to the precise duties of the High Priest's office under the law? And we answer, such could not be found in the revealments of God to man!

23. Aaron, in his office and duties, was a type of Christ. He and his successors[150] stood at the head of all the priestly authorities during the legal existance of the Jewish polity. Christ was &[151] is the anti-type of Aaron.[152] He stands at the head of all the ministry in the Christian system. "He <u>ever liveth</u> to make intercession for us. He abides a Priest continually" [cf. Heb. 7:3, 25]. While Aaron lived no other could hold his office, or act in his station as High Priest. Hence while Jesus lives no other can hold his office, or perform the duties of his calling. No one can act as High Priest in his stead, or hold that sacred authority vested solely in him. He is the "Captain of our salvation; [page 75:] the Apostle and High Priest of our profession" [cf. Heb. 2:10; 3:1]. In the Jewish system the[re] was but **one** high priest at the same time, and he could not continue "by reason of death." But in the glorious gospel system **we** have **one** High Priest of whom it is witnessed that "he lives forever," even Jesus of Nazereth And we neither need nor want another High Priest on earth.[153]

24. ~ "Therefore were they as polluted put from the priesthood.

150. McLellin added "and his successors."

151. McLellin added "was &."

152. McLellin added "of Aaron."

153. McLellin added "High Priest on earth."

They have defiled the priesthood, and the covenant of the priesthood." Ezra 2:62. Neh. 7:64. 13:29. ~

Among the Israelites all persons who were uncircumcised were considered unclean. Also all those who were not in the lineal descent of the covenant seed of Abraham Isaac & Jacob. Hence as the Jewish priesthood was counted to them because of their descent blood,[154] if their priests intermarried with any of the idolatrous or Gentile nations or people around them, they of course would be polluted. Their children would not be of the pure seed of Jacob. Any thing therefore that would hinder the floow, in their veins, of the pure blood of Levi, would of course defile their priesthood, as it depended upon that purity. In as much as Christ had made the last offering for sin, and forever sat down at the right hand of God, being the last and only High priest over the house of God for all future time, thereafter the inspired penman and their translators have generally used the word **minister** instead of priest for all those who held office under the New Covenant. Hence we hear them speak of "a faithful minister of the Lord; a good minister of Christ: minister of God: and an able minister of the new covenant: minister of Jesus: faithful minister in the Lord: faithful minister of Christ, a minister of the sanctuary."[155]

25. Now as there was a way in which the priests who administered the laws and rites of the Old Covenant could pollute their priesthood and thus defile the covenant made with them; so there is a way that the ministers of Christ can pollute themselves in[156] the holy authority given to them—through the spirit of prophecy and revelation. The whole order of the priesthood of the old covenant was established "after the law of a fleshly [page 76:] commandment" [cf. Heb. 7:16]. The whole order of the ministry of Christ was set up "after the power of an endless life" [Heb. 7:16]. Levi ministered in sacrifices. But Christ, his apostles, and Elders ministered in word and Spirit. One is called "the ministration of death" [2 Cor. 3:7]. The other the "ministration of life and peace." And in contrast with Aaron's, Christ's is called, "a more excellent ministry" [Heb. 8:6].

26. The preists who administered the old covenant with its rites and ceremonies had their authority because of the flesh. The ministers of Christ receive theirs by the Holy Spirit, because of true repentance, and

---

154. McLellin added "blood," probably intending to replace "descent."

155. McLellin added "minister of Jesus: faithful minister in the Lord: faithful minister of Christ, a minister of the sanctuary."

156. McLellin added "themselves in."

strong faith in God. It does not descend from one to another, but each individual receives the call and appointment direct from Heaven for himself.[157] The source of one is ~~Aaron~~ Levi.[158] The source of the other is Christ. One comes by blood. The other comes by Spirit. One ceases with death. The other is not only holy but everlasting. One could not bring perfection. But the ministers of the[159] other were commanded to be "perfect as their Father in Heaven was perfect"[160] [Matt. 5:48]. Then in order for an officer of Christ to pollute himself in[161] his holy ministry he must use his spiritual authority to commit sin with. He must use his ministerial power & place, not only to look upon sin with allowance, but to commit abomination himself, and to influance others to do so also. He must use his Christ-given authority to assist him to violate the laws of God, and thus to trample holy things under his feet. This pollutes his spirit and himself in[162] ~~and~~ his ministerial authority, and in his whole person. And when he does all this I know of no ~~law~~ principle, or rule of law, by which he can get the stain wiped away, or the sin blotted out. Hence a true and faithful **minister** of Jesus in order to salvation, in order "to save both himself and those who hear him," must live by every word that proceedeth out of the mouth of God. He must, ["]Preach the word, reprove, rebuke, and exhort with all long suffering & doctrine" [cf. 2 Tim. 4:2]. He must become like his Master, and be filled with godliness, & then strive for perfection. [page 77:]

27. In examining the institution of God with Israel as it was established among them in the wilderness we find that Moses stood in relation to them, as God stands to the intelligences of all the heavens. He was to God-ward, viz. as the mouth of God to all the people of Israel; and to Aaron he stood "instead of God." Aaron was mouth, and spokesman, and prophet for Moses, in the discharge of all their duties, as the representatives of God & Christ on earth.

The tribe of Levi were all taken for priests, and were to serve in the Tabernacle, for all the tribes of Israel, Num. 8:18, 19. They were ministers unto Aaron, Num. 3:6. The whole tribe of Levites was wholly "a gift to Aaron," and to his sons, to keep his charge, and the charge of the whole congregation, and to do the service of the tabernacle, Num. 3:9.

157. McLellin added "for himself."

158. McLellin added "Levi."

159. McLellin added "ministers of the."

160. McLellin added "was perfect."

161. McLellin added "himself in."

162. Mclellin added "and himself in."

8:19. The Levites were taken and cleansed and purified, and then Aaron—because they were his, a gift to him from the Highest—presented them before the Lord as an offering, and also made an atonement for them to cleanse them. Aaron was to preside over and direct them in all their official duties. He was a type of Christ, and the law was, with its ceremonies, a "**shadow** of good things to come" [Heb. 10:1]. ~ Christ came to put away sin, viz. sin offerings by the "sacrifise of himself." He fulfilled and then abolished all the ritual law of Moses. He was "the end of the law for righteousness to every one that believed" [Rom. 10:4]. He changed the whole order of priesthood, and of law relative to salvation. He now stands to the inhabitants of all the world, Jew and Gentile who believe in him, as Aaron stood to Israel. Aaron was the only High Priest of the Old Covenant, and all the priests and ministers of that dispensation were his servants, and the servants of his successors in office. Christ by the oath of his Father "abides a High Priest forever" [cf. Heb. 7:3], hence can have no successor. He, and he alone, as the great anti-type of Aaron, is the only High Priest of the glorious gospel dispensation. God gives to him all the ministry of the New Covenant, John 17:6. He calls, purifies, and then presents them before his Father that he may sanctify and endow them so that they may fill their ministry with joy. [page 78:] Christ stands at the head, presides over and directs all the Apostles and prophets, all the Elders and Deacons of the church of the first-born; and that too to a much fuller extent than ever Aaron presided over the Levitical priesthood during the reign of the law.

The conclusion then is inevitable: no high priest can legally exist in this church of ~~God on earth~~ Christ while Jesus lives, and performs the duties of his high and holy calling himself. Aaron stood at the head of the priesthood of the Mosaic institution, but by reason of death he had successors, who followed in the same office, until that order of things was abolished. But because Christ "ever liveth—hath an unchangeable Priesthood—abides a Priest continually" [Heb. 7:3, 24-25], therefore "God anointed the holy child Jesus" [cf. Acts 4:27], and appointed him to stand at the head of the whole gospel institution while it continues. Aaron stood at the head of the "shadow." But Jesus stands at the head of the substance. Yes, and will stand until he triumphs over all his enemies, and is crowned King of Kings and Lord of Lords, and my soul cries Amen and amen. ~

28. Aaron, because he was the High Priest of the law dispensation, had all the Levites given to him for the service of its rites and statutes. Jesus Christ, because he is the only High Priest of the gospel age, has all

the ministers of the New Covenant given to him as his servants; and hence he is the one who has a legal right to call, to qualify, to preside over, and to direct them in all their ministerial duties.

29. Aaron and his sons, and the whole tribe of Levi were called, chosen, appointed, consecrated, and then presented to the Lord, and an atonement made for them by the direct and express commandment of God. Aaron and his sons were first presented by Moses[163] and afterward the whole tribe of Levi by Aaron.[164] Jesus was constituted a [page 79:] High Priest forever by the "oath of his Father." Aaron was anointed with holy and consecrated oil. But Jesus was anointed with the Holy Ghost and with power from on high. The power, that made the anointing oil for Aaron holy, descended from heaven upon Jesus, and "the Spirit abode upon him." And his calling was announced to earth by the spirit of prophecy through Simeon and Anna when a babe[165] he was presented to the Lord in the Temple, and by John when a man[166] who said, "Behold the Lamb of God, who taketh away the sin of the world" [John 1:29]. By the rising star to the wise men of the east. By an angel visiting the Shepherds by night, and declaring, "Behold, I bring you good tidings of great joy, which shall be to all people. For unto you is born this day, in the city of David, a Savior, which is Christ the Lord" [Luke 2:10-11]. And a multitude of the heavenly hosts joined the angel, praising God, and saying, "Glory to God in the highest, on earth peace, and good will toward men" [Luke 2:14]. And the shepherds made known abroad the sayings of the angels concerning the Child Jesus. And by the voice from the most excellent glory, of the great eternal I am. Who declared at his baptism, "This is my beloved Son, in whom I am well pleased" [Matt. 3:17], and on the mount of transfiguration God said–hear ye him [Matt. 17:5].[167] And when He was put into that high position, by so many incontestible proofs, the Father gave him twelve Apostles, and seventy disciples to assist him in his ministry, to spread a knowledge of salvation to all the world, and to preach the gospel to every creature which is under heaven. ~~and on the mount of transfiguration hear ye him~~.

30. Each one of Christ's ministers was called, appointed, and ordained, and then presented to the Father on the memorable day of Pentecost, and received his sanction by "an endowment with power from on

163. McLellin added "by Moses."

164. McLellin added "by Aaron."

165. McLellin added "a babe."

166. McLellin added "when a man."

167. McLellin added "and on the mount of transfiguration God said–hear ye him."

high" [cf. Luke 24:49]. Thus were the Apostles of Jesus called, ordained, and then anointed with the Holy Ghost and with power, in order to qualify them to fill their ministry. It then was a concurrence or rather a concentration and union of all the spiritual powers of the Apostleship derived immediately & directly from [page 80:] the Father, the Son, and the Holy Spirit: instead of mearly receiving them of angels, or of their being "ordained by angels in the hands of a mediator" [Gal. 3:19] as was Aaron's authority. And as Aaron and his brethren ministered the statutes of the law, so Christ and his ambassadors administered the ordinances of the gospel. Both orders of priesthood were constituted by direct revelations from heaven.

31. Moses stood as mediator between the angels of God's presence, and Aaron and all the people of Israel in the organization of that priesthood: But after it was established Aaron and his Successors legally stood at its head. Moses was the mediator of that covenant. But Jesus is the mediator of the New and everlasting covenant. Moses dedicated the old covenant with the blood of beasts. But Jesus consecrated the new and living way by his own blood. The old covenant and priesthood and law were "ordained by the disposition of angels" [cf. Acts 7:53] through Moses as the mediator. Hence angels presided over that law dispensation. The New Covenant with its priesthood and Gospel was given to man by the eternal Father of all worlds and principalities and powers. It was ordained in the hands of Jesus as the mediator, but the Father presides over its destinies–and will until all enemies are put under his feet, and God is all, in all. So much is the new covenant, and priesthood, and gospel superior to the old, as God is higher than angels, and Jesus greater than Moses as mediator, and above Aaron as High Priest and as the Gospel is more resplendent than the law.

32. The Urim of judgement was placed in the Ephod and worn upon Aaron's heart continually when he went in before the Lord. Thus showing that the Lord intended to keep up a constant correspondence with his high priest, while that priesthood held the presidency of authority on earth. [page 81:] Showing too that the "priest's lips should keep knowledge, and the people should seek the law at his mouth: for he is the messenger of the Lord of hosts" [cf. Mal. 2:7]. Jesus gave Peter "the keys of the kingdom of heaven" [Matt. 16:19], and he promised his disciples another Comforter who should "teach them all things, yea, the deep things of God" [cf. John 14:26; 1 Cor. 2:10]. Thus showing that a constant intercourse must be kept up between the King in heaven and his ministry on earth, until he would come again "without sin unto salvation" [Heb.

9:28]. All the priests and Levites held a direct and constant intercourse with the High Priest during the long administration of that priesthood from Aaron until John, the Baptist. And according to the above pattern all the ministers of the New Covenant must be holy and spiritual minded enough to hold a direct and constant intercourse with Jesus the High Priest of our profession, or otherwise they are apostates from the faith of the Gospel.[168]

33. ~ All the ministers during the gospel reign must be called to the ministry by the spirit of revelation and prophecy, and then they must be set apart and ordained by the gift and power of the Holy Ghost which is in the one who ordains them. No man could legally minister at the altar during the reign of the law except he was a pure descendant of Levi–it descended to him because of his blood: except only when an inspired prophet was commanded of God so to do. So no man can legally administer the ordinances of the gospel unless he has been called by a direct "thus saith the Lord," and then been ordained by one who has the gift and power of the Holy Spirit. His authority then comes by the Spirit of revelation and by ordination.[169] Thus the Aaronic priesthood was constituted and continued after the law of carnal i.e. fleshly commandment. But the whole order of Christ was after the law of the spirit of life. [page 82:]

34. The order of Aaron required a victim, blood must be shed, hence it was called the "ministration of death" [2 Cor. 3:7]. But Jesus put an end to the shedding of blood in the worship of God by the "sacrafise of himself." He ["]through the eternal spirit offered himself without spot to God" [Heb. 9:14]. Hence instead of performing death, and offering blood, which could never bring perfection, but was imposed until the time of reformation; all the ministers ~~who hold~~ of Christ, who hold sacredly their God-given power, offer up "a pure offering," of "spiritual sacrifices, acceptable to God by Jesus Christ" [1 Pet. 2:5]. One deals in blood, the other deals in Spirit. One in the tragedies of death, the other in giving life, ~~and~~ peace, and perfection. Such a ministry could and would as truly build up a "spiritual house unto God, by the law of liberty" [cf. 1 Pet. 2:5; James 1:25], as Aaron and his servants would minister for Israel by the rites and statutes of the law of Moses.

35. The pattern then was for the Aaronic priesthood to possess the pure blood of Aaron and of Levi. The model or substance under Christ

168. McLellin added "of the Gospel."

169. McLellin added "and by ordination."

is, to be called of God, and then ordained, whether Jew or Gentile, by the direction and power of the Holy Spirit. Such and such only can preach the Gospel "with the Holy Ghost sent down from heaven" [1 Pet. 1:12]. Such only could go forth and build up the true church–baptize and confirm true believers, viz. lay hands upon them for the gift of the Holy Spirit in the name of the Lord, and bless them in the name of Jesus: and thus "minister the Spirit" to them so that they might be born from above. In this way true believers are born of water and born of the Spirit into the church and kingdom of Christ. Amen. ~ [page 83:]

Of Revelations.

"God, in divers manners, spake in time past to the fathers" [Heb. 1:1]. Paul.
"Holy men of God spake, moved by the Holy Ghost" [2 Pet. 1:21].[170] Peter.

1. A pure revelation is something made known from God to a holy man. In past ages the Lord has chosen "divers manners" in which to reveal his will to Adam's race. 1. By his own vocal[171] voice. 2. By the voice of the Holy Spirit. 3. By sending a holy angel, or angels. 4 By visions and trances. 5. By dreams. 6. By the Urim and Thummin. (For the use of Urim and Thummin we refer to page 56 under the head of "A seer of the Lord.")[172] ~ 7. By Jesus Christ.

2. 1. By his own vocal[173] voice. When God placed man in the garden of Eden he held familiar converse with him face to face "as a man talketh with a friend." And even after man had fallen he heard the voice of his Creator, while he was walking in the garden in the cool of the day. Moses near mount Sinai brought forth the whole camp of Israel to "meet with God" [Ex. 19:17]. ["]And when the trumpet sounded long, and waxed louder and louder, Moses spake, and God answered him by a voice" [cf. Ex. 19:19]. And both at the baptism and transfiguration of Jesus, there

---

170. The seventeenth-century King James Version is based on a later, corrupted Greek text, which is the result of a scribe accidentally dividing one letter (Π) into two separate letters (ΓΙ) and then intentionally adding another letter to produce the word "holy" (ΑΓΙΟΙ), producing the meaning "holy men of God." However the earlier and better attested reading has the word "from" (ΑΠΟ), which gives the original meaning as "men spake from God." See Nestle-Aland, *Novum Testamentum Graece*, 27th rev. ed. (Stuttgart: Deutsche Bibelgesellschaft, 2006).

171. McLellin added "vocal."

172. McLellin added the note referring to p. 56 at a later time.

173. McLellin added "vocal."

was heard a voice from the most excellent glory, declaring the mind of the Lord.[174]

3. 2. By the voice, and moving of the Holy Spirit. Gross matter coming in contact with matter can influence and act upon it. So spirit coming in ~~union or~~ contact or union with spirit can influence and act upon spirit. But all spirits being possessed of intelligence, then when they are in unison they can impart to each other that of which they are possessed. Spirit can search all things Yea, the deep things of God. And ~~man being~~ a component part of man being spirit, hence the Spirit of God can take spiritual things and show them unto man. [page 84:]

4. Thus men were and are inspired to speak forth the "Thus saith the Lord." And they may speak of things thus, whether they be things past, present or to come. When the Holy Spirit falls upon a man and inspires him to be a prophet he then sees, hears, and feels what is communicated, and hence delivers it with a certainty of confidence. The Holy Spirit is one in the Godhead with the Father and Son. They compose the highest court, council, or authority in heaven. They are the Head. They are the highest of all intelligences. They are in perfect unison, hence they are one God. One fountain, and one supreme Head. Hence all revelations derived directly by the voice or movings of the Holy Spirit, are as infalably the mind of God, as if he spoke them audibly from his throne. Whatever then a person speaks moved, guided, and directed by the Holy Spirit is scripture, is the will of the Lord, is the mind of the Lord, is the word of the Lord, is the voice of the Lord, and is the power of God unto salvation to all who hear and obey it.

5. Much is said of the work of the Holy Spirit among men in the living oracles of God. It is said of the Holy Spirit that he falls upon true believers, baptizes them, anoints them, fills them, ~~speaks~~ witnesses to them, speaks in them, to them, and through them. Makes them his Temple, dwells in them, communes with them, imparts to them spiritual gifts, and forbids them to run into evil. He inspires them to pray, seals them up unto the day of redemption, gives them spiritual power, takes of the things of God and shows it unto them, sanctifies them, and will finally raise them from death into immortality and eternal life. ~

6. 3. By sending a holy angel or angels to man. ~ The first mention in the scriptures of an angel of the Lord is in the days of Abraham. He visited Hagar by a "fountain of water in the wilderness" [Gen. 16:7], when she had fled from the face of her mistress. His predictions to

174. McLellin added "declaring the mind of the Lord."

Hagar have been fulfilling from that [page 85:] day to this, and are not all yet accomplished relative to Ishmael and to his descendants. But thereafter their visits are often spoken of throughout the divine volume. Paul says "And are they not all ministering spirits, sent forth to minister for them who shall be heirs of salvation" [Heb. 1:14]. The visitation of angels to man from the days of Abraham to the days of John the revelator was not looked upon as being out of character, illusory, or deceptive. They carried intelligence from Heaven to men and women for their instruction. They always brought messages from God to the "heirs of salvation." The visits, of the last angel whose appearance is mentioned in Holy Writ, are mentioned in the very last sayings in the Book; and are or ought to be of great worth unto the whole human family. It is certainly one of the highest privileges man can enjoy in this mortal state, to be visited by a being, clothed upon with immortality, bearing a message in his mouth from the highest Heavens.

7. 4. Of visions and trances. ~ Man has an interior sight, and when this inmost being becomes quickened and the mind and eyes opened to see, natural objects being lost to view, the man is said to be in a trance, or to see a vision. Almost all the prophets had visions from God. They were thus instructed in holy things. Sometimes they were caught away in the Spirit and heard and saw things until their souls would swell as it were, "wide as eternity." In the days of king Uzziah, it is said of Zechariah, that, "he had understanding in the visions of God" [2 Chr. 26:5]. And also "Daniel had understanding in all visions and dreams" [Dan. 1:17].

8. When a man or woman has a vision it is sometimes difficult for them to know, or at least to realize "whether they are in the body or out of the body" [cf. 2 Cor. 12:3]. The Spirit and [page 86:] prescience of the Almighty rests upon them opening their interior sight. And although it has been a query in the minds of many whether there was an interior being, which in vision, would leave the body and accompany the Holy Spirit or angel to the place of observation, or whether the body as well as soul accompanied them. Pure spirits have not to use locomotion in order to view and examine distant objects. They see them on the same principle as God looks at them. And hence all that is necessary is for them to look in order to see. That is, to turn their attention to an object, (if within their sphere,) in order to examine it. Hence it is only necessary for a sufficiency of the power of God to fall upon ~~a~~ seers to open their interior eyes or sight, and always the object to be presented seems to be near before them. But even then (at times,) it is impossible for them to explain whether they are "in the body or out of the body." But one thing

they do most assuredly know, they see. When the host of Assyrians had gathered around Elisha on the mount, his servant was affraid; but Elisha prayed, and said, "Lord open his eyes that he may see:—and he saw, and behold, the mountain was full of horses and chariots round about Elisha" [cf. 2 Kgs. 6:17]. Here, a glorious vision opened to the view of the young man—and to their deliverance! The host was first blinded so as to be led by Elisha into the midst of the city of Samaria; and then by the faith and prayr of Elisha their eyes were opened to see their position. ~

9. Sometimes persons in the visions of God "were carried away in the Spirit," to exceeding high mountains, to the banks of great rivers, or to the places which the Lord designed to show them, and even to Heaven itself, in order to see, to understand, to know. But one of the greatest benefits derived from this manner of seeing, aside from the importance of the intelligence communicated, is that the things seen are more indellibly impressed or printed upon the memory than could possibly be done by natural sight. When things are seen spiritually—seen in vision, they are as real to the person seeing as if seen with the natural eyes, i.e. the visionist does not realize generally but that it is natural sight, until the vision [page 87:] closes and they are ~~left~~ again left to themselves, to marvel, to be astonished, and to contemplate what passed before them; and to be troubled to know its interpretation. ~

10. Many times images, figures, and similitudes of very curious things are passed before the mind in visions and dreams, which require interpretation or explanation in order to get the intelligence designed: such as Jacob's ladder, Joseph's sheaf, and his sun, moon, and eleven stars; Pharaoh's fat and lean kine, and his good and withered ears; Ezekial's living creatures, each having four faces, one of a man, one of a lion, one of an ox, and one of an eagle; and also each having four wings; also his riddle and parable of "A great eagle, long winged, and full of divers coloured feathers." Nebuchadnezzar's night vision of a great image composed of gold, silver, brass, iron, and iron & clay. And Daniel's interpretation of his vision is a striking instance of God's prescience given to man. Daniel and John's visions of all the images, likenesses, and similitudes that passed in review before them shows to man that the gift of interpretation is even greater or more to be desired than the gift of vision—at least when such images & figures are presented to the holy man.

11. Visions seem to have been a favorite way in which to receive instruction from God, in all ages when he communicated with man. It may embrace within it every other mode; even the visitation of angels is called "a vision of angels." And Peter said, "In a trance I saw a vision"

[Acts 11:5]. When the Lord complained of Israel, he said, "I have multiplied visions, and used similitudes, by the ministry of the prophets" [Hosea 12:10]. They would sometimes become so corrupt that God would not be inquired of by them. Saul could get no answer from God "by dream or vision, nor by Urim, nor by prophets" [cf. 1 Sam. 28:6]. And in the days of Eli, the word of the Lord was precious, "for there was no open vision" [1 Sam 3:1]. And no truer saying can be found than the wise man's "Where there is no vision the people perish" [Prov. 29:18]. [page 88:]

12. Micaiah, Isaiah, Daniel, Paul, and John all had the heavens opened upon them in visions, and saw the Lord, sitting upon his great white throne, high and lifted up in the heaven of heavens, and all the host of heaven standing by him, on his right hand and on his left—holding a great general council together relative to the affairs of men, of kings, of kingdoms, of nations and of empires on this wide earth. They saw and heard things, which in their times, were "unlawful for them to utter" [cf. 2 Cor. 12:4]. They were commanded "to write them and seal them up unto the Lord" [cf. Ether 3:27].

13. O my soul! Could I but see, and read, and understand the visions of Enoch, of Gad, of Iddo, of Nathan, of Samuel, and of all of God's holy Seers, Patriarchs, prophets, apostles, and elders, which are lost—sealed up and hid away, to be brought to light for the benefit of the Lord's chosen people, during "the dispensation of the fulness of times" [Eph. 1:10]. In them is a fund of knowledge which will cause his children's hearts to rejoice and ~~to~~ continue to rejoice. Some of them are written in the pure language of Adam and of Noah. In them is pure wisdom, drawn from the highest source. In them is the unfolding of mysteries that the learned of the world are now searching for in vain. In them is set forth in plainness the pure word of God. In them is that native truth and clear light in which the holiest men that ever lived rejoiced with fulness of joy. In them are set forth the purest principles, rules, and laws of natural and spiritual life. In them are the ordinances and precepts of wisdom, knowledge, and spiritual understanding ~~by~~ in which Enoch, Elijah, and Moses lived and walked by which they triumphed over the world, over all the spiritual powers of darkness, and were "wafted to Heaven in chariots of fire," by translation without [page 89:] tasting of death. O God! hasten the day when those "sayings and visions of the Seers," shall begin to come to light, from their long resting places, for the instruction and salvation of the called, and chosen, and faithful ones "who will follow the Lamb whithersoever he goeth" [Rev. 14:4].

14.—5 Of Dreams.

There is a doubt whether the mind ever sleeps, or is at perfect rest in sleep. At times it may be that we repose so soundly that our memories may not be impressed so as to retain what passes in our minds during sleep, which is the only reason we do not always remember our dreams. Dreams are either **natural, sinful,** or Divine. They are natural when "they come through a multitude of business" [Eccl. 5:3]. And then Solomon says, "the multitude of dreams are vanities" [Eccl. 5:7]. They are **diabolical** when they are inspired from the Evil One. Deut. 13:1, 2. Jer. 23. "Behold I am against them that prophecy false dreams, saith the Lord. I have heard what the prophets said, who prophecy lies in my name, saying, I have dreamed, I have dreamed" [cf. Jer. 23:25, 32]. We also read of "filthy dreamers" [Jude 1:8].[175] But dreams are **divine** when they are inspired of God—when the prophets of the Lord are shown visions of the night in dreams. In spiritual dreams the mind is always peculiarly impressed with the extraordinary character of the night vision. They feel its importance, and strongly desire its interpretation.

15. The Lord talked with Abimelech in a dream relative to Sarah. Jacob saw the mysterious ladder in a dream. Joseph was early favoured with prophetic dreams: and he was noted for interpreting dreams for the Baker, and Butler, and king of Egypt. In Gibeon the Lord appeared to Solomon in a dream by night: and God said, "Ask what I shall give thee" [1 Kgs. 3:5]. And it was said of Daniel that "he had understanding in all visions and dreams" [Dan. 1:17]. In the New Testament we read that the angel of the Lord appeared unto Joseph in a dream, several times. And the prophet Joel, quoted by Peter, declared that in the last days God would pour out his Spirit upon all flesh, and, "Old men should dream dreams" [Acts 2:17]. Thus settling the principle that the [page 90:] Gospel dispensation should have spiritual visions and dreams of the night, as well as the Patriarchal or the Mosaic ages.

16. 7. "God hath, in these last days, spoken unto us by his Son" [Heb. 1:1-2].

When Jesus was on earth and tabernacled in flesh those who heard "his voice," and followed him, received pure wisdom flowing from his mouth, direct from the crystal fountain of truth. For it pleased the Father that in him "all fulness sh[o]uld dwell" [Col. 1:19]. He was the **way**, the **truth**, and the life. In him dwelt the fulness of the God-head bodily [cf. Col. 2:9]. Hence in him was concentrated, ~~all the~~ in perfection all

175. McLellin quoted this from the King James Version of Jude, but the adjective "filthy" is in italics, indicating that it is not found in the original Greek.

the spiritual gifts, authorities, and powers ever exercised by any and all the spiritual minded men who had ever lived on earth: for He was the Source from whence, or through whom they had all received things "only in part." After his resurrection he declared that, "All power is given unto me in heaven and in earth" [Matt. 28:18]. Well, then might it be said, "God has spoken to us by his Son" [cf. Heb. 1:1-2]. And, well might he say, "Come unto me all ye that labour, and I will give You rest" [cf. Matt. 11:28]. It would be impossible for the mind of intelligences "to rest," unless they were placed in direct union and communion with the very highest fountain of intelligence in the universe. Jesus held that position and relation to his Father, and promised to place all his true and faithful followers in that same state of elevated and perfect rest. Doubt & uncertainty produce anxiety, and where these exist quietude, peace, and perfect rest cannot dwell. But Jesus said "I will give you rest." Hence, the promise is to remove from them all fear, dubiety, and ignorance and settle upon them eternal tranquility. This however could not be done only upon one principle, and that is, to place man in a position to hold immediate and direct intercourse with the "Father of lights" [James 1:17], through the "voice of his Son, as he would reveal him" [cf. Matt. 11:27].

17. To know the Father and the Son is eternal life. And <u>to know</u> in spiritual things depends wholly on revelation directly to **us**. For if a revelation was given to others, and we only read or hear it read, then the intelligence it contains comes to us by faith and not by knowledge– [page 91:] we get it by learning, through faith or confidence in the testimony of others. True, the Same Spirit that first gave it, may bear witness to us of its truth, and then we have obtained a secondary knowledge. But when it comes to us by revelation direct from the fountain of intelligence, then we see, hear, and feel it, hence we can in truth say, <u>we know</u>. And when we reach this position in relation to Spirituality, we stand where we have power to gain eternal life in celestial glory—that glory in which God and all the church of the first-born reside. Here then is rest. Here is bliss. Here is perfection. Here is the highest glory of which intelligences are susseptible. In that state they will be perfectly happy, and perfectly willing to spend their eternity.

<u>Remarks</u>

18. The Lord in the formation of man seems to have so made him as to have designed to always keep up a direct intercourse with him. The position of man on this earth, and his necessities seem to demand it, because he is a being capable of developement to an almost infinite extent.

Many mysteries present themselves to man's view, which he is unable to solve, unless he could have access to the Head of all wisdom. All that he knows of his origin, and of his future destiny he has learned through the sources of direct intercourse with his Creator. Outside of that all is conjecture—all uncertanity. Hence, that man is so constituted, and that the avenues of light and intelligence are so opened to his view by his Creator, as that he can learn wisdom direct from his God, is one of the highest privileges that he could possibly enjoy. For more than 1,000 years of the world's first history men did exercise themselves in that faith and practice. And from their experience and observation, recorded in the Sacred Oracles, we of this age learn all we know of the past or future eternity relative to man's destiny—except we can act upon the same principles they did, and draw knowledge from the same source. All holy Oracles, the testimonies of all holy men, and all our own spiritual wants and aspirations invite us, & urge us to believe in and worship the same Creator, and to expect the same blessings and [page 92:] high privileges to flow to us which they enjoyed. God is unchangeable, and man, in his composition, in his capacities, and in his wants and necessities, is the same now as in the days of the prophets or apostles. Hence he may form the same union with his God, and derive the same, and even greater blessings from his liberal and bountiful hand.

19. "In human conversation we convey our thoughts one to another by such words as by the organs of hearing, make such a motion on the brain of those to whom we speak as gives them an idea of the words we utter, and by them of things which by their words are signified, and so it is the impression made on the brain which communicates our thoughts to them; So, when God reveals his will to a person, it seems only necessary to talk inwardly to them, that is, that he make such a motion on their brain as gives them a deep and clear idea of what he wished them to know: only the impression must be made in such a manner and degree, and with such circumstances, as may make it certain to the inspired person that it derives from God. When we hear the voice of any one, or receive a letter from him, we may be certain from the knowledge we have of his voice, or of his hand writing, that it is he indeed who speaks or writes to us; we may very well conceive that God can give such distinctive marks of what he inwardly speaks to us, or writes upon the tables of the heart [cf. 2 Cor. 3:3], as enables the one to whom he speaks to discern what he imprints upon it by the impressions that he gives."[176]

176. McLellin does not indicate the source of this lengthy quotation comprising all of section nineteen.

20. "We see natural objects by virtue of a light reflecting the species of things upon the retina of the eye, and thence deriving a peculiar motion to, and making a distinct impression on the brain; so, the holy man sees what God reveals to him, by a like motion of the Holy Spirit made upon his brain concerning it. And, as it is as easy to propose a material object to the view as to describe it by our words, so must it be as easy for God to dart such an impression or inward light upon the brain of the spiritual man, as shall give him a more bright and sensible idea of things than if he [page 93:] perceived them by the ear, or even viewed them by the eye. And as we more exactly discern a sensible object by the view, than we can know it by a description of it without that view, so the word of the Lord in vision is more excellent viz. more to be depended upon, than that which comes only by dream, or in a dream, in which we seem to hear one talking with us. Visions may be had either by day or by night. In open day Peter had a great and clear vision. And at noon-day Paul had a vision, and a voice said to him, 'I am Jesus whom thou persecutest' [Acts 9:5]. He also had a man speaking to him in a vision of the night."[177]

21. A revelation is the mind of God made known to, or impressed on the mind of an intelligent being. At times the great eternal Father makes known his mind to his Son, and he to an angel, and the angel to man. Hence pure truth in this manner passes through two mediums, after it leaves the Highest, before it reaches man. Spiritual truths have generally been first communicated to Seers, prophets, ~~and~~ or Apostles, and from them to the one or ones for whom they were first designed. Hence, the necessity of a pure influence or media surrounding as well as existing between[178] the intermediate ones through or by whom it passed from God to man. Such an influence and power is the Holy Spirit of God. It surrounds and pervades i.e. fills the atmosphere of all holy beings. Hence all the words of God to man are pure unadulterated truths. But when committed to man's keeping he may so alter and change them, and take away their plainness, as to cause much blindness and stumbling in the minds of even the honest in heart. So it is with the Bible, much of its plainness has been lost to the world, or[179] taken away by man.[180]

22. But all truths are not necessarily revelations from God. Man has it in his power, because he is man, to develop and declare truth. Were it

177. McLellin does not indicate the source of this lengthy quotation comprising all of section twenty.

178. McLellin added "as well as existing between."

179. McLellin added "lost to the world, or."

180. McLellin appears to have added this entire sentence at a later time.

not so he could not be a proper judge of truth. He could not be rewarded for embracing, nor condemned for rejecting God's truth. But having knowledge and capacity to judge of truth within himself; or rather having been constituted of body and spirit and his mind placed within such an organization, viz. being allied to a natural and a spiritual substance, which gives him power to examine and to determine [page 94:] relative to all natural and spiritual truths; and then to choose or to refuse; which constitutes his accountibility before God. He can determine natural truth by the laws of nature, but spiritual truth alone by the aid of the Holy Spirit. Here many make a fatal mistake by trying spiritual things by natural laws. That which is born or constituted of natural laws, is nature. That which is born or made new by spiritual laws, i.e. the laws which govern spirits, is spirit. Hence, to judge righteously, each should be judged by their own laws.

23. The laws of nature as far as known must be applied to natural objects in the investigation of truth, and the laws of spirituality as far as can be known must be applied in the investigation of spiritual truths. Man is invested with the natural and the spiritual combined into a close union, and then has a mind in the interior of both by which he can examine both kingdoms, and can learn and determine upon truth from either. Man then is truly the Lord of this lower creation.

24. No man can know the things of God by natural laws, because they are only spiritually discerned. And to a man who only judges of them by natural laws, spiritual things always appear simple and foolish. God is a spirit i.e. a spiritual being, not possessed of the grosser materials as man, hence if he communes with man, it must be with his interior being—his spiritual nature: hence he that learns of God must do so by the laws of spiritual intercourse. His spirit must attract the Spirit of God, and the two coming into contact and[181] union intelligence is imparted from the greater to the less. In order to [do] this, since the fall, man must be "born again, born from above, born of Spirit—renewed in spirit" [cf. John 3:3]. The "outer man" is thus put under the influence, direction, and control of the inner—the spiritual. Then it can be truly said of such a man, "He that is spiritual judges all things" [1 Cor. 2:15]. The pervading influence ~~then~~ at that time, which surrounds God and such a[182] man, is the same—it is Spirit. When man receives from God intelligence in this condition, it is as the <u>wise man</u> said, "Every word of God is pure." [page 95:]

181. McLellin added "contact and."

182. McLellin added "such a."

25. By the audible voice of the eternal Father, by the voice of his Son, by the voice of the Holy Spirit, by the voice of holy angels, by the voice of visions or trances, by the voice of dreams, and by the voice of Urim and Thummim, God has at sundry times and in divers manners spoken to men, during a period of more than 4000 years: he held familiar intercourse with holy men, and through them with the inhabitants of this earth. God has used seven voices, or rather a voice in seven manners in order to communicate his will to men. These are his "**seven eyes**, which are the seven Spirits of God sent forth into all the earth" [Rev. 5:6].

26. All the popular religionists of the nineteenth century deny to man the high moral or legal right to now hold direct intelligent intercourse with the Heavens by either of the preceding modes: alledging that "The Old and New Testaments alone are a sufficient rule of faith and practice for all Christians." I was taught this from youth to manhood, but do not now believe it, nor can I ever again. No more false or injurious belief could Satan, with all his aids, have instilled into the minds of men. The most wicked and also the most ruinous to the spiritual intelligence of mankind. What! to forever seal up all the avenues from God to man, and thus doom him to a kind of perpetual night, to a state of uncertainty and anxiety, without a sure hope, because all direct intercourse has thus forever ceased. Learned men have searched all the great libraries of the world, among all nations of men to gather up intelligence in order to settle some important points in spiritual matters. But still those disputed points are unsettled. Th[e]y now, after more than 1500~~0~~ years of searching, of study, of argumentation, of contentions and of Creed-making, are as widely separated in their principles, their forms of belief, and in their manners of worship as those who lived in the fourth century, before the New Testament books were canonized.

27. We attribute all the divisions and contentions among all denominations [page 96:] of professed Christians to four great evils. 1. To loosing the privilege and the power to hold intelligent intercourse with the Lord by direct revelations from Heaven. 2. To deny to man the inherent right to such intercourse. 3. To canonize the books we have in the old and[183] New Testament as the only rule of faith and practice. 4. To make human creeds to bind men's consciences, and to govern the church with during the Gospel age.

28. The principle of direct intercourse gradually died away during the first centuries of the Christian era; and since that period men in or-

183. McLellin added "old and."

der to strengthen themselves in their false positions have by their doctrines and creeds only been binding men tighter and still tighter with their human chains, so as to try to find reasonable excuses for their unutterable loss of the Spirit of revelation and prophecy. Notwithstanding all the canons of scripture, all the beliefs of men or of societies, all the controversies, all the creeds, of men, and all the doctrines of Devils, is it the privilege, the right, and the duty of men to expect more revelations from God, more light from Heaven, more unfolding of mysteries and truths from the Divine mind so as to prepare a people to enjoy the "faith once delivered to the saints" [Jude 1:3]? This is the great question we wish not only to examine, but to settle in this investigation.

29. In Deut. 4:2. 12:32. it is said, "What things soever I command you, observe to do it. Thou shalt not add unto the word which I command you, neither shall you diminish from it." In Revelations 22:18, 19. it is said, "If any man shall add to the words of the prophecy of this book, God shall add unto him the plagues that are written in it. And if any man shall take away from the words of the book of this prophecy, God shall take away his part out of the book of life, and out of the holy city." Although the Lord repeated the above injunction twice to Israel through Moses, yet, not even one man was ever found among that nation, or from that day to this in all the world, who was simple enough [page 97:] to suppose that rule or law ever applied to God, or to holy prophets: but they looked at it and understood it as it really was, that it was only intended to preser[ve] the purity of God's words of inspiration: To prevent men's alterations, additions or subtractions, to what God had revealed.[184]

30. The word book in the second case refers only to the 22 chapters of the Apocalypse, or to John's visions and revelations therein. No man properly informed could suppose that it refered to our New Testament, or that it was [in]tended to teach that God would no more reveal himself to man, or that man should no more write inspired truths. Chronologists generally agree that John wrote his three Epistles and his Gospel after he wrote his revelations. It can certainly mean no more here in John than it meant in Moses, as the intent, and meaning, and design seems to be the same. And at both times or periods it only taught that poor, weak, erring **man** must not presume to add to nor to diminish from the pure revelations of God. That right belonged exclusively to God. He had a perfect right to give more or less of his precious word. It would only be

184. McLellin added "to what God had revealed" in pencil.

vain inventions instead of pure revelations even if man should try it. It would only be imposition. The many false Gospels and epistles in the world show however that many men were found wicked enough to try their hand at making revelations to add to the Lord's words.

31. But that man has received and that he can **now** receive direct intelligence from his heavenly Father is the great foundation stone of Christianity. When a Christian lacks wisdom he may, Yes, he is commanded "to ask of God who giveth to all men liberally, and upbraideth not, and it shall be given him" [James 1:5]. This is one of the sweetest doctrines ever presented to my soul, or ever taught to mortal man. What! that man when he feels that he is in the dark [page 98:] or lacks wisdom upon any subject connected with his present, his past, or his future destiny, may, in the name of Jesus, approach his Creator and find "pure wisdom from above" [cf. James 3:17], instead of going to Priests–uninspired priests, or to creeds of Councils which would only corrupt and blind his mind. Blot this doctrine of intercommunion from the book of God, and take that highest privilege from man, and then that book with all its divine wisdom would be uninteresting to me.

32. Christ taught his disciples to pray, "Our Father who art in heaven" [Matt. 6:9]. Who ever heard of a father having a numerous family of dependant children with whom he never would converse upon any subject? He had had a first, a second, and a third family, and with them he had communed freely–talked familiarly. And some of those conversations were written out to show his manner of dealing with his children. But to his present offspring he is dumb. He opens not his mouth. They know not his will concerning them only as they can gather it in general principles from what he revealed to his former children. And although their numbers and circumstances are quite different–And although too the "would be wise ones," and teachers of his present family differ and quarrel about the meaning of his word to them of old, yet, in all that darkness, confusion, and uncertainty they are doomed to spend their lives. And all this because their father will not speak to them, or in any way let them hear his voice, in order to settle their difficulties. Such a course would be an anomily in the history of fathers ~~and~~ with their families. No such a father ever existed or ever will. The delight of earthly fathers is to communicate information to [page 99:] their children. And it is no less so with our heavenly Father. One of his principles of universal adaptation to all his children in all ages of the world is for them to "Ask and you shall receive."

33. The Psalmist said, "God is King of all the earth" [cf. Ps. 47:2].

Now, who ever heard of or knew an earthly king who would neither talk with his subjects, nor with his ministers; but leave them to plod through old records kept by by-gone ages in order to know how to build up, increase, and extend their kingdom? One important question here is how a man could be the minister or officer of a king without receiving a direct commission from him in order to give his acts authority in the Kingdom? In all the kingdoms of men on earth that have ever existed, the ministers approached their sovereign and held familiar converse with him. I ask, can the kingdom of God exist on earth on a different principle? And I answer no! distinctly no!!

34. Christ said to his disciples, "Ye are my friends" [John 15:14]. Now reader, think a moment; what is the usual course of friends? Is it not to have intimate converse and sociality together? If Jesus has friends now on earth where are the evidences of their intimacy? Where is the church, or minister, or conferences of ministers who now hold converse with Christ as with an intimate–yea, their best friend? O my soul, how plain these principles, and yet how few believe them! How pure, how holy, how good, and how well calculated to elevate man and to assimilate him into the likeness of his Creator. O how exceedingly happy the old Patriarchs, and Prophets, Apostles and Elders must have been when they could go to their heavenly Father, King, and true Friend and inquire and receive for answer a "Thus saith the Lord." Wisdom, knowledge, and spiritual understanding were thus received by them. Their stock of knowledge was thus improved, their hearts warmed, and their minds expanded. [page 100:]

35. Jesus revealed himself[185] by his own voice, ~~himself~~ by open vision, and by his angels to his first ministers and friends; but his most obedient children now, his most intimate friends in this age, must grope their way through all the mists and clouds and darkness of sectarian jargon, with all the uncertainty of their own fallible judgements in arriving at truth, and all this because they deny to Jesus the right to speak to his best and most intimate friends. Because they deny the gift of prophecy and revelation to be now necessary in order to "the work of the ministry, the edifying of the church, and the perfecting of the saints of God" [cf. Eph. 4:12].

36. Reader, what would you think of a kingdom governed by a king hid entirely behind a curtain? His ministers had never seen him, had never heard his voice, had never had any direct appointments or com-

185. McLellin deleted the word "himself" from later in the sentence and moved it to this position.

missions from him, nor had they any direct knowledge themselves of his existence. They had only heard that such a king once lived, once gave a set of ministers commissions, authority, and power to administer the "Law of liberty" [James 1:25] in his name, and therefore acting without knowledge upon a kind of belief, notion, or imagination that that old king was still alive they were trying to govern or rather to gull people into the belief or notion that they were his special favourites. But in doing so ambitious men saw that it was a matter of private judgement, and that they had just as good a right to form a party, become the Head of it, and thus gain "spoils" without the hard labour of tilling the earth; and so the kingdom being rent into factions, each leader or leaders would stand in the gate and halloo at the top of his voice, saying, Lo! this is the king's dominion, come ye and live ~~ye~~ in it. Such is a true picture of the present state of the world. O shame! shame!! on such a set of **men**. Truly they are "blind guides, leaders of the blind, and they all must fall into the ditch together" [cf. Matt. 15:14], unless they repent.

37. The only infallible rule of life which God ever gave to man to govern his [page 101:] actions, whether under the Patriarchal age, the law dispensation, or the Christian era, was that when he lacked wisdom, "he must ask of God in faith and get it." Get it then when he needed it. Get it immediately and directly from heaven. Get it because it was his privilege and duty to obtain it. Get it because the Lord holds the right, and is most willing to bestow it. Such always was, and such always will be man's high privilege in any and in all ages of the world's history; and will continue to be while even one man is left to have a probation on his earth.

March 10. 1857. Chester O[hio].

The call to the ministry.

1. Does it require a direct call from God in order for a man to preach the gospel, and to legally administer its ordinances? And if so, in what manner is such call given? No enlightened government in the world pretends to have ministers at home, or to send ambassadors abroad unless they have been called and legally appointed each to his particular station. And no such government would acknowledge the acts of a man pretending to be a minister unless he acted under the authority of credentials legally and regularly made out, signed, sealed, and delivered to him.[186]

2. Jesus Christ said of himself, "I came down from heaven not to do

186. McLellin added "to him."

mine own will, but the will of him that sent me. The Father which sent me he gave me a commission (commandment.)[187] what I should say, and what I should speak. Whom the Father sanctified and sent into the world" [cf. John 6:38-39; 10:36]. When Jesus entered upon his ministerial career he had the testimony and ministration of John the Baptist, the testimony of the holy scriptures,[188] the testimony and ministration of holy angels, the testimony of the baptism of fire and of the Holy Ghost, the testimony of the voice of the eternal I am, and the testimony of the authority and powers of the priesthood of the order of Melchisedec–which was the order of God,: and thus qualified he entered upon the duties of his high calling and ministry in the world. [page 102:]

3. Aaron was called to the High Priests' office, and then solemnly consecrated by special and direct revelations from heaven through Moses, and it is expressly declared by the Apostle, that, "No man taketh this honor unto himself but he that was called of God as was Aaron." Heb 5:4. His sons and the tribe of Levi were also called, appointed, and consecrated by very special orders or instructions from the Lord direct. Thus were the ministers of the law called, qualified, and organized each into his proper station. And their priesthood pertained to them thereafter because of lineal descent. They were not permitted to continue by reason of death. But Christ as a Priest "ever lives."

4. The first ministers of the Gospel received their call, their appointment, and their ordination direct from Jesus Christ–the Head of his church and kingdom. Each one was called by name and then ordained to his own special ministry, each for himself. Mar. 3:14. John 15:16. After Christ had risen from the dead he said to his faithful ministers, "As my Father hath sent me, even so I send you."

As I proceeded and came forth from the Father, so you proceed and go forth from me. As he gave me a commission to go into all the land of Judea and preach the gospel to Israel, and testify of him, even so I send you into all the world to testify of me, and to preach the Gospel to every creature which is under heaven.[189] As he sent holy angels to minister to and to comfort me, so I will send them with messages to console and build you up in the truth. As he anointed me with the Holy Ghost and with power, which abode upon me even so you must "tarry at Jerusalem, until you are endowed with power from on high" [Luke 24:49]. As he sent his loud voice from heaven, saying, "This is my beloved Son, hear ye

187. McLellin placed the word "commandment" within square brackets.

188. McLellin added "the testimony of the holy scriptures."

189. McLellin added "which is under heaven" in pencil.

him" [Matt. 3:17], so by my voice I send you into all the world to teach all nations. Those who receive your testimony and message shall be saved, but those who reject shall be damned.[190] [page 103:]

5. As the Father declared with an oath that I was the High Priest of the Gospel age forever, so I constitute you ministers in that royal priesthood with me forever. Hence by your testimony and ministry you shall condemn or save the world. To the one you shall prove "the savor of life unto life, & to the other of death unto death" [cf. 2 Cor. 2:16]. The Father was in me reconciling the world unto himself, so now I commit unto you the word of reconciliation. I was the ambassador from the court of heaven, so you are my ambassadors to beseech the world in my stead, "<u>to be reconciled to God</u>" [Rom. 5:10]. The Father sent me into the world as his Apostle, to bear witness to truth; to manifest his true character, and to show forth the express image of his person. For, "for this cause came I into the world that I should bear witness unto the truth" [John 18:37]. So you are my Apostles.[191]

6. An Apostle means a witness, one who bears testimony. And the word witness in Greek is Martyr, and signifies one who gives testimony to the truth at the peril of his life. Hence, it is said of Jesus that he witnessed before Pontius Pitale[192] a good profession. And he is called the "<u>faithful witness</u>" [Rev. 1:5].

Then as I have been the faithful Apostle of the Father to You, and in all Jewry, so I send You to be true apostles of me in Judea, in Samaria, and to the uttermost parts of the earth. Go then and teach the world righteousness. Publish my name with the gospel of peace to men. You now have full power to disciple all nations, and to bring them to learn of me that they may find rest to their souls.[193]

By the foregoing we see that the Apostles were appointed and sent forth, invested with full powers, and sustained by many infallible and incontestible proofs of familiar intercourse with him who is yet to become King of Kings, and Lord of Lords.

7. But no man believing in Christianity pretends to deny the call [page 104:] and inspiration of the Apostles of Christ. But whether it was the Lord's design that all the ministers of Jesus succeeding them should

---

190. McLellin writes as Jesus in first person in this paragraph, sections 4-5, and the middle part in section 6.

191. McLellin added "So you are my Apostles."

192. McLellin intended the spelling "Pilate" but unintentionally crossed the wrong letter.

193. In these four sentences, McLellin again uses the first person as if Jesus were speaking.

be called and sent of God, is a question about which they differ—widely differ. The Catholics claim an ordination and regular succession from the apostle Peter down through to Pope Pious ninth.[194] The head of the Greek church is the Patriarch of Constantinople. They too claim a succession of ordination from the Apostles. But Protestantism claims no one man as Head among all their multifarious divisions. And I know of no one sect or division of them which claims the one man Head. And none of them, so far as I know, believes that men now receive their call and ~~qualifications~~ appointment direct from God on the principle of new and direct revelations and prophecies, as in the days of the Apostles. Some of them profess to have a call from God, but it is difficult for them to intelligibly explain the manner of it, in as much as they at the same time profess to believe that immediate revelations from God ceased with the Apostles.

8. Probably all the books of the New Testament were written during the first century of the Christian era: and upon no subject were the Apostles less explicit than relative to the call, the ordination, and the duties of the officers of the church. To mark the specific duties of the ministry in that book is impossible. The qualifications which Bishops and Deacons should possess are laid down by Paul, but to note the official duties of even a deacon any where in that book cannot be done—even one distinctive duty. Thus clearly showing that the inspired writers never intended the books that we now have to be, or to ever become a rule of faith and practice for the church of God in after ages. ~
[page 105:]

9. "Now there were in the church at Antioch certain prophets and teachers, and as they ministered to the Lord and fasted, the Holy Ghost said, Separate me Barnabas and Saul for the work whereunto I have called them. And when they had fasted & prayed, and laid their hands upon them, they sent them away,["] Acts 13:1-3. "This charge I commit unto thee son Timothy, according to the prophecies which went before on thee, that thou by them mightest war a good warfare," 1 Tim 1:18. ["]Neglect not the gift that is in thee, which was given thee by prophecy, with the laying on of the hands of the presbytery, 1 Tim 4:14." Here it was expressly said that Paul, Barnabas and Timothy were specially pointed out by direct revelations from God through the gift of prophecy. And then the solemnities of fasting and prayr, and the laying on of hands followed, so as to thus consecrate them to God in their ministry.

---

194. Pope Pius IX (1792-1878) led the Roman Catholic Church from 1846 to his death in 1878.

Now if it required this immediate direction from God, then fasting, and prayr, & the imposition of hands in their being set apart to the ministry, is it not required in every instance? And if the above is not a pattern for the gospel age, we would ask, dear reader, when shall we find pure truth on this subject? Before Jesus left the world he promised his disciples another comforter, to abide with them forever, "to teach them all things" [cf. John 14:26]. Here we find him teaching them how ministers—Gospel ministers should be prepared for their ministry.

10. Here we can answer our first question. It does require a direct and immediate revelation from the Lord to call a man to the ministry of Christ, and no[195] man has a legal right to minister without such call. Now this being true what are we to think of the world of christendom who entirely deny to man the right to hold at the present day open communion with God? They must be such as the Apostle foresaw and described thus, "Having a form of godliness, but denying the power thereof: from such turn away. For the time will come [page 106:] that they will not endure sound doctrine; but after their own lusts shall they heap to themselves Teachers, having itching ears. And they shall turn away their ears from the truth, and shall be turned unto fables" [2 Tim. 3:5; 4:3-4]. No picture in prophetic vision could be more clearly drawn than the above. We will close this part of our subject with one more quotation, "For whosoever shall call upon the name of the Lord shall be saved. How then shall they call on him in whom they have not believed? And how shall they believe in him of whom they have not heard? And how shall they hear without a preacher? And how shall they preach, except they be sent?["] [Rom. 10:13-15.]

11. After long and close examination, observation, and experience in the investigation of this very important subject, and in trying to look at it unprejudiced in every possible point of view, we are perfectly satisfied that no man had a moral or legal right to administer the laws and ordinances of the Patriarchal epoch, or of the laws of Moses during the era of their legal existance, or more particularly the ordinances of the Gospel dispensation without in the first place he is a firm believer in the Spirit of revelation and of prophecy, and by that means and that only been pointed out and qualified to act in his office in the ministry. He must have his call direct from God, then his ordination by the imposition of hands to confirm upon him his ministerial qualifications. All done through the immediate act or work[196] [of] the Holy Spirit.

195. McLellin added "no" in order to make clear his original meaning.

196. McLellin added "the immediate act or work."

12. If a man only receives his call and ordination from the hands or authority of the Pope of Rome, then he is only the minister of Catholicism. If from under the hands or by the authority of the Patriarch of Constantinople, then he is only the minister of the Greek church, and is bound by the creeds that govern those sects and parties. But if he has joined himself to any particular sect of Protestantism and in that relation becomes a minister, he must of course pass the scrutiny of the uninspired judgements of men, and receive their sanction, in order to obtain an ordination. And when called and set apart in this way he becomes morally and legally bound [page 107:] to preach the doctrines and follow the practices of that church, or sect. He has placed himself within a kind of fold or pen, and cannot escape from it only at the peril of his ministerial life.

13. All sects and parties, who are not governed by immediate and direct intercourse with God, have Creeds relative to their church government, and most of them are written creeds. But if not written out in form, still they have them in precedents and former practices, in particular traits, and hence their ministers are required to square their lives and their ministerial labours by those views. And those who deny immediate and continued revelations for the government of the church, to a certain extent make the Scriptures a kind of Creed by declaring that "they contain all things necessary for salvation." Then the Book like a Creed is read, studied, and quoted to set forth and to prove their particular isms. All its plainness is twisted into a certain channel.

14. But, gentle reader, no man of the present day can trace his ordination in an unbroken line back to the Apostles of Jesus. And no man can show his call in the Book. And no Leader of a sect, who claims to be governed by piety and holiness, from Pope Pious 9th[197] down through all the ranks of party to Alexander Campbell[198] dare claim that he has been called and qualified by immediate directions from God through the Spirit of prophecy and revelation; hence the inevitable conclusion is that if any man among all those parties is pretending to preach the gospel and to administer its ordinances he is **man made**. Man has educated him, has called him, has judged him worthy, and then has given him the particular sanction of the ministerial authority of the church[199] to which he belongs. God has not been consulted in all the performance; because that would upset the fundamental principle of all their

197. For a summary of Pope Pius IX's life, see the Biographical Notes.

198. For a summary of Alexander Campbell's life, see the Biographical Notes.

199. McLellin added "of the church."

isms.—that is, that God does ~~not~~[200] reveal himself to man at the present day. The more I look at sectarianism the more dark and awful it looks to me. [page 108:]

15. We are aware that the above presents rather a dark looking picture, but it is no more dark than true. But now we have a more bright side at which to look. John the Revelator when wrapped in prophetic vision saw "an angel descend from heaven having great power, and the earth was lightened with his glory. And he said that Babylon, (the above confusion at which we have been looking,) the great is fallen, is fallen, and is become the habitation of Devils, and the hold of every foul spirit. And he heard a voice from heaven, saying, Come out of her my people, that ye be not partakers of her sins, and that ye receive not of her plagues" [cf. Rev. 18:1-2, 4].

16. The above assures us that notwithstanding all the wickedness of Babylon, and all the unbelief and opposition of sectarians, and all the rage of Devils, and all revealments through mediums of every kind of foul spirit, yet, the Lord will in the midst of all this send a holy angel from heaven and light up the earth with his glory. It teaches us that God has a people on the earth for whom he has a particular care, so much so that he sends a "voice from "heaven," to call them out of confusion, in order to secure them against all the evils of the last days.

17. John and his associate Apostles and evangelists preached the Gospel to all nations previous to his seeing those glorious visions on the isle of Patmos—yet, looking through the future vista of time, in vision he saw, "another angel fly in the midst of heaven, having the everlasting Gospel to preach to them that dwell on the earth, and to every nation, and kindred, and tongue, and people" [Rev. 14:6]. And soon followed that other angel proclaiming the downfall of Babylon. Showing [page 109:] clearly that if men have in their religious orders and parties forsaken the Lord and would have none of his direct council, yet his eye is upon the honest in heart, and he will "set his hand again the second time to recover a remnant of his people" [cf. Isa. 11:11]. He will send his angels and his voice from heaven, and will gather together his elect from the four corners of the earth and from the islands of the sea.

18. God then, by the ministry of his holy angels, and by his own voice from heaven, and by his own inspired ministry, ~~he~~ will again proclaim salvation to man—to Gentile and then to Jew. And this is to be done in the latter end of the Gospel dispensation, just before the "hour of his

---

200. Though McLellin deleted the "not," the meaning requires its presence.

judgement is come" [Rev. 14:7]. Reader, You will know whether You are honest in heart before God, and if You are, let us be ready. Let us be believers in the visits of angels, and in the voice of our Lord, in all the seven ways in which he ever communicated his will to man. Let us strive for all the spiritual gifts and powers of which "all the holy prophets have spoken since the world began" [Acts 3:21], or which God ever gave to man—for this is our high privilege. Let us begin to look up and to labour to see the church of Christ again reestablished. Let us look for and expect the organization of the kingdom of heaven which shall never again be thrown down or given to another people—for the time is soon at hand, Amen. Chester, O[hio]. March 4, 1857. [page 110:]

On man, spiritual existences, influences and powers.

1. Man is a compound being formed or organized of body, spirit, and mind. The body is composed or made up of the materials of the earth. The spirit and mind are from heaven. The spirit is a personal being possessing an intelligent existance either in or out of the body. The mind is the intelligent, active, moving principle or power of the spirit and body both. Through the medium of the organs of ~~the body~~ sense[201] man is or may be affected by objects peculiar to this earth. Through the medium of his spirit and mind he may be affected or acted upon by spirits and spiritual influences. Hence mankind are so constituted as to be allied to and acted upon both from the external material world, and also from the spiritual existances of the vast universe of God. To the external by means of the body, the frame, the tabernacle; and to the spiritual because of the spirit. Man then is the link which connects heaven and earth together. An intelligent being of heavenly spiritual existence, with the grosser particles of the materials of this earth in the form of a body, combined and united forms and constitutes man.

2. Atoms, corpustles, or particles of the materials of the earth in the form of dust, gathered together and formed by the creative power of God, constituted a body as a tabernacle for the immortal spirit from heaven, in order that man thus organized might have a state of trial or of probation[202] on the earth. Adam and Eve were the first, and all the progeny of mankind (except Jesus,) sprang or descended from them in the natural order of generation. Thus the body being formed of earthly materials could not have pre-existed[203] except in chaotic matter. It was

201. McLellin added "sense."

202. McLellin added "or of probation."

203. McLellin added "pre-."

the child of its mother earth, and the creative hand of its God and Father.

3. But various indeed have been the speculations of the wisest and strongest [page 111:] reasoners among the philosophers, lawgivers, and divines of the different nations and ages of men relative to the spirit and mind of man. Their origin, their capabilities, and their destiny. And no doubt Apostles, Seers, and Prophets of old "searched diligently by the spirit of Christ that was in them" to find out even more than is recorded in the inspired Scriptures on this important subject. Some sages held the opinion that the spirit of man was "a subtile air composed of atoms." Others maintained that it was "a flame or portion of heavenly light—a kind of emenation from the Deity."

4. Most men in reasoning about spirit in contradistinction to gross matter speak of it as immaterial or incorporeal. These words mean that which has neither form, substance, body, nor matter. But spirits are possessed of substance, form, intelligence, and locality. The essence of their existance is not the same in kind, in character, or in quality as that of which any of the exterior universe is organized. But it is a more subtle, transparent, and lucid substance peculiar to a spiritual and eternal state of being. Hence the spirit can and does exist in the body filling every part without increasing its dimentions. And at death the form is not lessoned until the grosser materials begin to dissolve so as to meet and assimilate with their kindred elements of earth.

5. All spirits exist in the four following classes, viz. unimbodied, imbodied, disimbodied, and glorified. The spirits in all worlds which have not as yet received or put on tenements of clay are of the first class. All those spirits which are now existing in mortal bodies are of the second class. Those which have existed in forms made of the "earth earthy" but have lost them by death, and not received them again by resurrection constitute class third. The fourth class is made up of all those which have received the "mortal coil," and then either by translation or by resurrection have gained "immortality and eternal life" at the right hand of God. Where all substances and intelligences are in affinity or unity with each other and with God. ~ [page 112:]

6. The God of all worlds and systems of worlds, the supreme cause of all organization, the father, the head, the protector, and the governor of all the spiritual existences of all the heavens and of the earth, is a pure perfect body of spirit, having substance, form, entity, individuality, and locality. His habitation or dwelling place is the heaven of heavens, in the center of all the systems of worlds which revolve around him

in the vastness and infinity of space. In his revealments to man he has said "I am God alone. There is no God with me. I am the first. I am the last. Before me there was no God. There is none like me. And there is none else besides me." ["]Yea, there is no God; I know not any besides me." [cf.] Isa 44:8.[204]

7. This Lord of Lords, this God of Gods, is the universally acknowledged supreme Head by common consent of all the superior intelligences in existance. He is the center and fountain of all good[205] authority and power. He is the embodiment of wisdom and perfection, and from him truth and knowledge flow through all the ranks and classes of beings who acknowledge his dominion. He exists from eternity to eternity without change of purpose.[206]

8. All spirits are possessed of form, individuality, and locality. A spirit is an uncreated, unbegotten, eternally existant, intelligent being. It has no beginning, hence it can have no end. All good spirits—except the Great God, are subject to change, to alter, to improve, and to progress until they arrive at perfection and in that state they will be willing to spend their future eternity.

9. God knows good and evil independently, but all other spirits can only know them by observation, by experience, and or[207] by comparison. The power i.e. the mind of pure spirit is superior to and above all other powers. It is the highest and consequently the controlling influance throughout, among, and over all other and lesser essences, powers and materials of the universe. It is the most [page 113:] translucent material existing, consequently it can penetrate, permeate, pervade, fill and control all other substances. Pure and perfect spirit changes not, but alteration, combination, and progression towards a common center, towards a state of perfection is the inevitable consequence of all the coarser materials.

10. Some suppose that mind and spirit are synonimous terms. That mind is spirit, and that spirit is mind. But mind is the manifestation and power of Spirit. Spirit cannot exist without mind nor mind out of spirit: neither can exist alone. Mind is the medium or vehicle through which spirit manifests itself and communicates to and with other spirits. Mind dwells in spirit as its tabernacle—or in other words all intelligence in spirits is their minds. Spirit is the dwelling place for mind as much so as the

204. McLellin added "Yea, there is no God; I know not any besides me.' Isa 44:8."

205. McLellin added "all good."

206. McLellin added "of purpose."

207. McLellin added "or" above the "and" but the "and" is not crossed out.

body is the tabernacle for the spirit: hence inspiration speaks of "the mind of the spirit" [Rom. 8:27]. Unimbodied ~~and~~ disimbodied and glorified[208] spirits have all the organs of sense as well as man, only they are adapted to spiritual beings in a spiritual state. They see, hear, taste, smell, and feel—reason, argue and contend, and exercise all the operations and offices peculiar to spiritual existances, to sociality, and to happiness. Indeed it is the spirit and the mind of the spirit which is the motive power of all the phenomina discovered in all the operations of nature. The body without the spirit exhibits no more phenomena than any other lump of inanimate matter.

11. We can speak truly of unimbodied and disimbodied spirits but not of unclothed minds, for mind cannot exist of itself separate from spirit; but spirit can exist out of an earthly tabernacle, and is itself always a habitation for the mind—and the operations of its mind are the manifestations of its intelligence. Then no form of substance can show forth intelligence, except a mind possessing faculties exist within that form. ~~In~~ [page 114:] In man the spirit is the connecting link between his body & mind. The mind is the highest power in existance, and is therefore the controlling influence of the universe. It acts on, moves and controls all existances, essences, and powers below it—for there are none above it. God is a pure and perfect body of spirit, which is the habitation of his infinite mind. The vastness of unbounded space contain the innumerable works of God, yet the infinitude of his mind can and does comprehend the whole.

12. The immensity of space is annihilated to the perceptions of a pure ~~and pure~~ and perfect spirit. That is, spirit has not to use locomotion in order to view distant objects, or to travel from place to place in order to search them out. The mind will look at, examine, and reflect upon objects millions of miles distant just as quickly and as easily as if only one mile distant. Hence we speak of the omnipresence of God. And although God's[209] tabernacle of spirit dwells in the h[e]aven of h[e]avens, yet his illimitable, infinite mind fills immensity, and comprehends all his works. "All things are plain and open before him."

13. God is possessed of all wisdom, knowledge, and power. He is the highest intelligence in all worlds within the ~~bounds~~ or vastness[210] of

---

208. McLellin added "and glorified."

209. Although McLellin has the plural spelling "Gods" followed by an apostrophe, it seems clear that he meant to write the possessive singular "God's."

210. McLellin added "or vastness" and then crossed out "bounds" but did not cross out the "or."

space. He has no superior to call him to account, or there is no tribunal above or beyond him before which he might appear in order to answer for his acts. His authority, his power, and his acts are independent—they are eternally perfect. He is always governed by benevolence, wisdom, and truth, therefore whatever he does is right. [page 115:] All that he does tends to the highest good of all other intelligences who "kept their first estate" [Jude 1:6], in order to raise them and so fill them with his own attributes as to bring them up into a state of perfection like himself, there to enjoy with him an eternity of bliss.

14. God does all things in heaven by consultation and by common consent. He has his courts or grand councils among his ministers in which all important matters relative to this world and its inhabitants are determined. And at times all the hosts of heaven are gathered in one vast general assemblage and stand on his right hand and on his left and cry amen, and clap their glad hands at his wise and righteous decisions. In this way heaven acts in perfect unity. And this is one of the grand reasons why it is a heaven of harmony of[211] peace and of felicity.

15. There are two classes of spiritual beings who can communicate with man, through the medium of inspiration, either by impression, or by vision, or by conversation. They are perfectly diverse in their characters, in their objects, and in their operations. The first class always incites man to do good—to obey God, to keep his commandments, and then to receive eternal life. The second class as assuredly urges man to do evil, to disobey God, to violate all his laws, and thus to receive eternal death. God is the head & ruler of the first class, but Satan of the other.

16. The Devil or Satan is a personage of spirit, is a fallen angel, is the prince of darkness, is the god of this world, is the prince of the power of the air, and is the king of the spirits of darkness—the prince of Devils. He is the first sinner, the greatest enemy of Christ, the adversary of all righteousness, the deceiver of woman, the tempter of man, the liar against the truth, the columniator of the good, the accuser of the faithful, the betrayer of the innocent, the destroyer of harmony, the author of death, the murderer [page 116:] of martyrs, and the final tormentor of all the sons of perdition. He was once near the throne of God, and in favour with him, for he was "in the truth." But he abode not there, he transgressed, was thrown out and cast down to hell, and all those angels or spirits with him "who kept not their first estate, but left their own habitation"—all, all those spiritual transgressors are "reserved in everlasting

211. Mclellin added "harmony of ."

chains, under darkness, unto the judgement of the great day" [Jude 1:6]. Satan is now, and ever has been since his fall the greatest opposer to Christ and enemy to mankind that exists within illimitable space. The center of his abode is hell, but this world seems to be the theator of his active exertions.

17. At the time of the sitting and deliberations of the general assembly of those heavenly intelligences who convened around the throne of God in order to determine about the creation of this world, Satan opposed himself to their decisions, and especially to Christ who was foremost in advocating them. A part of the angels joined with the Devil in his rebelion, but they all "fell like lightening from heaven" [cf. Luke 10:18]. And thus came the "Devil and his angels." They were cast out and "chains of darkness" thrown around them before the foundations of this earth were laid. Yes, before the decisions or decrees of God were made known relative to its creation and redemption. And their "chains" prevent or hinder them from seeing or knowing the future—hence Satan's opposition to Christ and to mankind. He seeks and labours diligently and unceasingly to people his dominions from the intelligences of this world. He seems to vainly think that he will ultimately conquer the Savior and his little band of "called and chosen and faithful," and thus continue to be "the god of this world." Thus to hold his illegal possessory or squatter's claim to it, to its "kingdoms and the glory of them." But he knows not the mind of God, for if he did he might dispair, for ~~Christ~~ God[212] will ultimately destroy all his works, and calculations of greatness, and will finally cast him into the bottomless pit, into torment forever and ever. [page 117:]

18. After man was created he had power to converse with his God and Father face to face, and learn from his mouth the principles and laws of truth. But after he had transgressed and was cast out of Eden—away from the tree of life, he was placed out on this broad earth in a state of trial, where he was subject to and acted upon by two kinds of spiritual influences. God and his angels, obedience, goodness, & happiness, and spiritual communion of a high and holy order on his right hand inviting him "to look and live." But on his left hand stood Satan and his angels inviting him to their converse and sociality. To disobedience, to enjoy the pleasures of sin for a season, which always led into bondage and misery and down, down to death, and finally to everlasting punishment. Herein is man's agency and accountability manifested. Standing upon earth between heaven and hell, subject to both classes of

212. McLellin added "God."

spiritual influences and powers, and having because of his present organism power or agency to choose or to refuse, and in consequence of his actions to receive rewards or punishments.

19. Because of man's nature derived from earth and earthly associations he could be easily approached and tempted with allurements and pleasures of momentary things, for he was surrounded with them on every side, and by yielding he gratified and pleased his carnal mind and fallen nature. And because by his fall he had lost the privilege of open communion with the Lord, and had to approach him "by faith and not by sight." And because too the Lord required man "to deny himself of all ungodliness and worldly lusts, and to live soberly, righteously, and godly" [cf. Titus 2:12] in order to obtain that faith which would entitle him to spiritual manifestations from above; and through that means and strict obedience to gain eternal life at the right hand of God.

20. But to hold immediate converse with spirits "under darkness" [Jude 1:6] required no "precious faith," no sacrafises of interest or ambition, no great struggles [page 118:] of soul, no obedience to divine laws, nor any change of life or character. No, a person might follow out those passions and earthly pleasures of life, and still obtain and hold converse with fallen or "familiar spirits." For Satan the ruler of all the inferior conclave of spirits would of course honor those with his communion, who would condescend to honor him or to receive honor at his hand.

21. All the inspired oracles of God recognize the doctrine of man's power and capability of holding converse with spirits, and of receiving direct intelligence from them. And that spirits either from above or below may come and take up their abode in man's tabernacle with his spirit and hold a kind of companionship with him in his body. It required however much experience in spiritual intercourse to become a proficient or renowned in spiritual powers. A few only from among the masses of mankind were chosen because of their peculiar faith, their organisms, their susseptabilities, their capabilities, their circumstances, or their earnest desires to become Leaders, or Teachers, or in some way distinguished in spiritual matters. And they were always put into classes in order that their influence might be greater either for good or for evil.

22. The ministers or messengers ~~from~~ of heaven were called Apostles, Seers, prophets, priests, Elders and Deacons &c. With them the Lord, his angels, and ["]the spirits of just men made perfect["] [Heb. 12:23] communed directly, and they were required to teach the lessons they had thus learned from those superior spiritual intelligences, to all men so far as it lay in their power. It devolved upon them to manifest and

to [page 119:] develop the true character of God, and to publish and to administer his special laws and ordinances to man. The ministers of Satan were called "dealers in familiar spirits," such as conjurers, charmers, diviners, incanters, inchanters, magicians, necromancers, observers of times, prognosticators, peepers, soothsayers, sorcerors, star-gazers, witches, and wizards. With these the devil and his angels communed directly. And others of mankind ~~sought to them~~ who believed in that class of influences sought to them in order to gain intelligence from beyond this sphere–from over on the other side of death, from the spirit world. And necromancy especially claimed to hold converse with the spirits of the dead–with near and dear departed relatives.

23. All unimbodied spirits both good and evil know all the past up to the present, but they do not all know all the future. Some things God has retained in his own mind alone. Hence it is said, "secret things belong unto the Lord our God, but those things which are revealed belong unto us and to our children forever" [Deut. 29:29]. Again, "but of that day and that hour knoweth no man, no, not the angels which are in heaven, neither the Son, but the Father only" [cf. Mark 13:32; Matt. 24:36].[213] The knowledge which Satan and his angels had prior to their fall they can still retain, but they left their "first estate" [Jude 1:6] before all the plan of redemption relative to this world and its inhabitants was completed. And since their fall their "chains of darkness" [2 Pet. 2:4] shut out the light of the future entirely from their eyes. All they know of it is what God has revealed to his servants the prophets, and what they have written.[214] Hence, when Satan or his angels reveal themselves to man it is always concerning the past or the present. They may speak of the future and it may come to pass or [page 120:] it may not, for they can only guess at it, they cannot see it.

24. The spiritual manifestations made within the present century in Mesmerism, clairvoyance, byology, spirit-rapping, miracles, healings, visions, trances, preaching, writing &c. indicate that an important era is upon us. No less important than "the revelation of the Man of Sin" [cf. 2 Thes. 2:3]. That there is both power and intelligence connected with this spiritual phenomina is admitted, but that it comes from God or from holy spirits is denied.

---

213. McLellin mainly follows Mark 13:32, but the word "only" is derived from the parallel at Matt. 24:36. Due to the doctrinal difficulty of the Son not knowing the time of the Second Coming, a few manuscripts of Mark and the majority of manuscripts of Matthew deleted the phrase "neither the Son." See Metzger, *Textual Commentary*, 62.

214. McLellin added "and what they have written."

25. Man from Adam till now has always been subject to superior and inferior spiritual influences. Different degrees of intelligence and miraculous power have been shown to man and through him both from above and from below, at various periods of the world's history. Miracles, actual counteractions of the known laws of nature, have been wrought by the servants of Satan as well as by the servants of God. At the court of Pharaoh the magicians turned rods to serpents, water to blood, and covered the land with innumerable frogs. The woman of Endor by the power of a "familiar spirit" called up Samuel the prophet from the dead, so that he talked with king Saul, and told him the time of his end. Satan opened up a vision to Jesus & showed him from the pinacle of a high mountain "all the kingdoms of the world and the glory of them in a moment of time" [cf. Matt. 4:8; Luke 4:5]. Jesus found a man in the country of the Gadarenes so possessed with the power of Satan that he could not be kept bound with fetters and chains. He could and did pluck them off at pleasure. [page 121:]

26. The more than natural strength to break fetters and chains, to draw away the curtain by vision and to show all kingdoms and their glory, to turn wood to flesh and then to fill it with animal life, to chan[ge] water to blood, to create myriads of frogs, and finally to enter the abode of death and there disturb the quiet of the tomb, to reach up as far as into the Paradise of the disimbodied spirits of the righteous and bring down the departed spirit of the old prophet, and then bring ~~him~~ up his body[215] ~~so~~ that he might portray the future to Saul–All these were certainly gigantic stretches of power from the inferior spirit world. But such and more too have been done in the past. Such po[we]rs have been exercised by men and women who received their spirit power direct from Sat[an] instead of from God.

27. The ancient Egyptians, Chaldeans and many other idolatrous nations but especially the Canaanites, previous to the days of Moses, had those Satan-i[ns]pired miracle-workers among them. They had lost the true knowledge of God, a[nd i]n that blinded state had not the faith, nor the wish to commune with him throu[gh] the medium of his angels, seers or prophets. But being unwilling to live without [s]piritual intercourse they sought to witches, wizzards, and magicians possess[ed] with the power to hold converse with "familiar spirits"–that is, fallen or unclean [de]mons, spirits of Devils who led them so far from God that they ceased entirely [to a]nswer the end of their creation. The Canaanites es-

215. McLellin added "his body."

pecially were renowned for th[eir D]evil-worship through the influence of diviners, necromancers, and witches. They d[id no]t like to retain God and his laws and his worship in their thoughts, and hence wer[e always] up to vile affections, to run with eagerness the downward road until Sat[an caught] them and [missing text] [page 122:] prepared them for literal destruction by the hand of the Israelites from off the face of the land of Canaan.

28. All that which has a tendency to lead man away from holding a direct intercourse with his Creator is wicked and calls for punishment. There are many and great degrees in crime and allurements in iniquity, but that which is the most opposed to God, and to man's highest and best interest, that which God th[e] most perfectly hates, which will ripen and prepare man the most speedily [f]or immediate, signal, and awful destruction, is for him to seek unto wizards [t]hat peep and mutter, to enchanters or necromances that disturb and profess to[216] call up departed [s]pirits, or to magicians who work miracles by Satanic power. It is the highest [si]n man individually or nationally can commit, of which he can be forgiven.[217] It is what the Lord has [c]alled "abomination in his sight."

29. The Lord said to Israel before they entered Canaan, "When thou art come [in]to the land which the Lord thy God giveth thee, thou shalt not learn to do after the [a]bominations of those nations. There shall not be found among you any one that [m]aketh his son or his daughter to pass through the fire, or that useth divination, or a[n en]chanter, or a witch, or a charmer, or a consulter with familiar spirits, or a wizard, [or] a necromancer. For all that do these things are an abomination unto the Lord. [A]nd because of these abominations the Lord thy God doth drive them out before thee. These nations which thou shalt possess, hearkened unto observers of times, an[d un]to diviners; but as for thee the Lord hath not suffered thee so to do. Thou shalt b[e per]fect with the Lord thy God" [cf. Deut. 18:9-13]. The Lord said to Israel through Moses, "Thou shalt not [su]ffer a witch to live" [Exod. 22:18]. King Saul in the days of his obedience to God was zealo[us about] that law, and consequently ordered his officers to slay the whole race. But [missing text] wit[h] h[im], he soug[ht] [page 123:] the woman of Endor, who had escaped with life, and was a proficient in the mysteries and powers of fallen spirits. And because of that deed it was recorded of him, "So Saul died for his transgression which he committed against the Lord, even against the word of the Lord, which he kept not, and also for asking

216. McLellin added "profess to."

217. McLellin added "of which he can be forgiven."

counsel of one that had a familiar spirit, to inquire of it. And inquired not of the Lord: therefore he slew him, and turned the kingdom unto David, the son of Jesse" [1 Chr. 10:13-14]. Thus the literal overthrow and entire destruction of the tribes or kingdoms of Canaan, and the signal and awful death of Saul were in consequence of their communing with fallen or foul spirits.

30. That man in this benighted world, during his state of probation, has both the capability and the power to hold intercourse with spirits either from heaven or from hell, is in our mind a settled ~~fact~~ point. When he was first created, his Creator first communed with him and familiarly taught him the pure principles of law and order, and the blessedness of obedience, and also the consequences of disobedience. But when he had left him or them Satan entered Eden and held a familiar converse with Eve. His object was to get her to violate law—to disobey her Creator. Afterward he tempted Cain who slew his brother Abel. And although the Lord had created but one woman for one man, and had given them a general and universal law regulating the union of the sexes, for he had said, "for this cause shall a man leave his father and his mother, and shall cleave unto his wife; and they twain shall be one flesh" [cf. Gen. 2:24; Matt. 19:5]. Yet, Satan soon entered again and tempted Lam[e]ch and he took to himself more wives than one [Gen. 4:18-19]. And we might continue the instances throughout the Lord's commandments to man. It would only be a series of God's laws, Satan's temptations, and man's violations and miseries.

31. When God delivers a law to man for a rule of action, it seems always [to] be a settled practice with Satan to tempt him to violate that law. [page 124:] In order for man to exercise his agency it is necessary for there to be "an opposition in all things" [2 Ne. 2:11], so far as man is concerned. Rewards and punishments are based upon the power of man to accept of influences from heaven or from hell, and to act according to their suggestions. Were there not an opposition inciting man to evil, there would be no justice in rewarding him for doing good. Were there no good there could be no evil, for evil can only exist or be so because it is in opposition to good. Good is so independently, but evil only exists as its opposite. If good and evil were not both placed before man he could not be an agent, or injustice be rewarded or punished. Man then has certain powers existing in him because he is man, because of his organism, because of his union of body spirit and mind: which powers are the foundation of his accountability.

32. All intelligences have certain inalienable rights and powers

dwelling in them because of their existance, each one according to the class or order of his being. Spirit could not exist without intelligence nor intelligence without power: so power could not exist or be exercised with out[218] mind and spirit both. Satan although a fallen spirit has his rights and powers, and no other intelligence has a right to infringe upon them. Hence it is said that "Michael, the archangel durst not bring against him a railing accusation" [Jude 1:9]. There are laws in the superior spirit world, as well as in the natural, regulating and governing their actions and their intercourse; and no spiritual being can entirely pass the bounds of those rules without doing as Satan did–rebell, transgress and fall. Hence, Michael dare not rail against or rebuke even the Devil but said, "The Lord rebuke thee Satan" [Jude 1:9]. [page 125:]

33. Satan uses all his power and influence in opposition to Christ, and to his policy, and his highest aim is to destroy. He can have no settled rules of policy because he knows not the future. But his very nature is enmity hate and opposition to all the intelligences of the universe who kept their first estate, or who live in harmony with God by keeping the perfect "law of liberty" [James 1:25]. In order to deceive, to decoy, and to lead astray Satan has power "to transform himself nigh into an angel of light" [cf. 2 Cor. 11:14]. So have his angels or fallen spirits, and so have also his ministers or false Apostles. Unclean spirits entering and inspiring men will have power in the last days "to show great signs and wonders, to work with all power, and signs and lying wonders, and with all deceivableness of unrighteousness–to make fire come down from heaven in the sight of men. There will be the spirits of Devils, working miracles, which go forth unto the kings of the earth and of the whole world, to gather them to the battle of the great day of God Almighty" [cf. 2 Thes. 2:9-10; Rev. 13:13; 16:14]. Such the Lord's holy prophets have declared will be the future. Such will be the powers and the miracle-working of Satan–inspired men and women in the "last times," that the whole world, (except "a few men left,") will run after them, and finally meet with a signal, literal, and awful destruction in being "burned up root & branch" [cf. Mal. 4:1].

34. There is no power but that of God which has a legal right to command, to govern, or to control spirits: and that right he holds because of his superiority, and because of the common consent of all othother superior intelligences. Even Christ during his ministry on earth said relative to his great powers, "The Father who dwelleth in me he doeth the work" [cf. John 14:10]. But when Jesus had risen from the dead he said,

218. McLellin added "out."

"All power is given unto me in heaven and in earth" [Matt. 28:18]. That is, among spirits and among men. Hence whatever man <u>now</u> does in spiritual matters; he must do in the name and by the authority of Jesus Christ in order to do it legally. The [rev]elations existing among and between unimbodied and disimbodied spirits below the Godhead [tea]ch that no one has independent control over the other, and can have no legal pow[er] [page 126:] to direct or to command them–only as they receive it from Jesus Christ.

35. When man tries to commune with, to call up, to direct, or to command spirits, (except he does it in the name and by the authority of of[219] Jesus Christ,) he steps out beyond his own rights and powers and hence Satan always takes advantage of him, and thereafter (except he repents,) influences, leads, and governs him in all his spiritual matters. Man then can only ~~deal~~ safely deal with or in spiritual affairs, and especially with spirits by faith in God, in and through the name of Jesus Christ. Only in Christ then is safety for man. In the days of the apostle Paul some Exorcists undertook to control and to command evil spirits without faith in God, and the result was they had to run for their lives "naked and wounded" [Acts 19:16]. But men without faith in God–by faith in Satan, or by the power of Magic can form such alliances with the "Devil and his host," as to perform marvelous things–things even astonishing and alarming! ~

36. There are two general laws which govern spiritual intercourse with man. One for the upper or superior world, and one for the lower or inferior world. Man can act according to or be governed by either law, hence can hold converse with either world. The first law is, Faith in God through the name and by the authority of Jesus Christ as the Savior of the world. The second law is, A passiveness of mind and spirit, that is, a yielding to the controlling influence or spirit which enters or comes upon the medium; without regard to its origin or source. The first requires purity of purpose, holiness of heart, and uprightness of character and life. The second requires only <u>passive obedience</u> without any regard to the character of the medium, or any knowledge of the source or origin of the controling spirit or influence. The ultimatum of all the communications from the inferior spirit world is to deny the divinity of Jesus Christ, to set aside all knowledge from the true God, and especially [to] deny the existance of Satan, as the great adversa[r]y of Christ. [page 127:]

37. God's laws governing and regulating intelligences in relation to

219. McLellin unintentionally doubled the word "of."

himself and to each other, are all based upon the eternally immutable and perfect principles of equity. To keep and to obey them would be for each being to rise higher and still[220] higher in progression, to reach nearer and nearer the center, to the likeness of God, to perfection; beyond which there is no improvement. And when all intelligences which pertain to this earth which abide law, which kept their first estate, become sanctified, glorified, and perfected by law—when all arrive at that highest point, then it will be truly said, "It is finished. It is done. God is all, and in all." ~

Chester. O[hio]. 1854.

Of Dispensations.

1. In this treatise we shall separate the world's history into five grand divisions, viz. epoch, era, dispensation, age, and period. In this way they wil[l] correspond with the five hours in the Lord's parable of the householder hiring ser[vants] to labour in his vineyard.

The first epoch is the morning hour of the world, reaching from Adam down through to Moses, containing about 2500 years of time according to Chronologists.[221] It had the Patriarchal form of government.

The third hour of the parable, was the one which was endured rather than enjoyed from Moses until Christ. It was the era of the ritual Law of images & shadows pointing to a substance. It remained about 1500 years.

The sixth hour is the noon time of the world, both as to its introduction, and also its termination. Its first season was the scattering time—of sowing the good seed, but its latter portion will be the accumulating, uniting, and concentrating space. Th[e g]eneral harvest time in which God will ga[ther] together in one all things in Chris[t] [page 128:] both of things which are in the heavens, and of things which are on the earth. It extends from Christ's first coming unto his second—to the Millennium. It exists for about 1900 years. It is the gospel dispensation—the center hour, two hours going before it and two to follow after it of the world's probation.

The ninth hour is the age of quiet, of perfect peace, of universal righteousness, for the earth shall be filled with the knowledge of the glory of the Lord, as the waters cover the sea. It embraces the one thousand years of Millennial rest.

---

220. McLellin added "still."

221. McLellin added "according to Chronologists."

The eleventh is the last hour of this world's natural existance. It continues from the close of the Millennium down through the little season of Satan's liberty, passes through the last resurrection, and the general judgement, and onward until the new heavens and the new earth are created, and finally forms its period [whe]n all things pertaining to this world are made new. It is emphatically [the] period of execution, of finishing by giving rewards and punishments to all [the] intelligences of this lowest world.

2. The above five principal divisions are characterized with some striking events each peculiar to itself. We have thus divided the world's existance into hours or times because each division has a body or code of laws particularly adapted to itself. The preceding order of things being in part abrogated, and new covenants and laws instituted more particularly appropriate to the development and happiness of the people[222] ~~of~~ for the incoming hour. These laws remained in full force during the era in which they were given, and the salvation of mankind depended upon their strict observance during their existance. But when set aside their salvation depended upon the observance of the new laws and institutions.[223]

3. Each time or hour (except the Millennium) begins and closes, with migh[ty d]isplays of Divine power—blessi[ngs] upon the righteous, but wrath upon the wicked. [page 129:] They close with a great and signal overthrow of those who oppose themselves to the change, or to the introduction of the new order of things: and each introduction is marked with eminent deliverance to those who embrace and carry on the preparatory work of the new order. All those five hours, times or seasons (except the last,) had a preparatory work to precede them, and in [the] first declaration of the message of preparation the light at first was ne[ither] clear nor dark, but at the evening time it became clear light. The prep[ara]tion was always begun under the laws of the preceding era, and thus carr[ied] on until all the characteristics of the incoming era were fully developed and established.[224]

4. The first hour, or the beginning epoch of the world, reaching fro[m] Adam to Moses, was governed by the Patriarchal laws and institutions. T[he] following are some of the noted events that characterized this period.

---

222. McLellin added "of the people."

223. It appears McLellin added this entire sentence at a later time, then even later added "and institutions" above the line.

224. McLellin added "and established."

1. The beginning of time with Adam
2. The temptation of the first pair, and their fall from innocence.
3. The first peopling of the earth by multiplication from Adam and E[ve].
4. The introduction of the plan of redemption through Christ by direct revelation
5. The offices of Chief Ruler & High Priest being given to the first-born.
6. A general degeneracy from the true knowledge of God.
7. By Enoch's great faith, perseverence, righteousness, and translation from earth to heaven without passing through death!
8. By a state of almost universal wickedness among men & their overthrow by a flood.
9. The building of the Ark and the preservation of Noah and family and of all manner of living creatures therein during the continuance of the flood.
10. The return of dry land when Noah and all living went forth upon it and beg[an] again to multi[ply and re]plenish the earth.
[page 130:]
11. The increase and spread of men again and their division into family and nations.
12. The division of the earth into Continents and islands, oceans & seas in Peleg's day.
13. The building of Babel, the confounding of the pure language, and the consequent confusion of tongues, and the spread of men from thence into all the earth.
14. The almost universal spread of idolatry among the nations.
15. The call of Abram and God's covenant with him and Isaac and Jacob relative to the land of Canaan.
16. The bondage of Israel in Egypt for four hundred and thirty years.

5. The third hour or the second era began at mount Sinai with Moses at the giving of the Law, and ended at the death of Christ. ~~It~~ [D]uring this era we have not to treat of the world as in the preceding epoch, [bu]t almost wholly of the Israelites–the descendants of Abraham. It [be]gins and ends with them. The laws which had governed the Patriarchs were [p]artly set aside, and a fiery law of rites & ceremonies was added at Sinai, [b]ecause of transgression. This era was characterized by the following.

1. By Israel's having in charge and keeping all the sacred records of the preceding Patriarchal epoch.
2. By their being led 40 years in the wilderness in going from Goshen to C[anaan].
3. By all the stupendous manifestations of miraculous power displayed in their behalf under their Leaders Moses & Joshua.
4. By their triumphantly entering Canaan their covenant land.
5. By their building a most magnificent Temple, and dedicatin[g] it to the true God, under the direct inspiration of the Lord, accordin[g] to the pattern of Heaven itself.
6. By their possessions of the Urim and Thummin, the sacred [page 131:] Ark of the covenant, the holy Tabernacle of witness, and the consecrated things kept in Holiest of holies in the Temple.
7. By the number and elevated bearing of inspired men Prophets[225] who prophesied among them and taught them the way of the true God.
8. By the division of the twelve tribes into two kingdoms of Judah and Israel, or of Jerusalem and Samaria.
9. By the overthrow and captivity of the **ten tribes** by the Assyria[ns] under Shalmaneser, after they had existed as a kingdom abo[ut] 254 years; and by their being hid from the world from that day to [this.]
10. By the destru[c]tion of imperial Jerusalem, and their beautiful Temple, and by the loss of all their sacred things kept in the Holi[est of holies.]
11. By 70 years captivity of the Jews in Babylon under the Chaldea[ns] and their return again to Palestine under Ezra & Nehemiah.
12. By their decline in true piety and their consequent subjugation [by] the Romans.
13. By their almost total loss of the spirit of prophecy & revelation from among them, and the consequent rise of differing sects and parties.
14. By the birth and ministry of John the Baptist, & his violent death.
15. By the birth and ministry of Jesus with all its circumstances.
16. By that unexampled people becoming so corrupt that their

225. McLellin added "Prophets" but did not delete the word "men."

highest ministerial authorities chose rather to have a notorious robber & murderer released among them than the innocent Jesus.
17. To cap the climax of their wickedness they crucified the Lord of glory.
18. In the death of Christ the law dispensation ended, and salvation thereafter depended upon obedience to the Gospel of Christ. ~ [page 132:]

6. The sixth hour or third general division is the Gospel dispensation. It began at the death of Christ, or more particularly at the day of Pentecost, at the descent of the Holy Spirit ~~Spirit~~, at the induement of the Apostles and Elders with power from on [hi]gh; and will end at the commencement of the Millennium. The great object of it manifested in its many striking events. It has a bright, a marvelous beginning, a [drear]y dark center, but a more wonderful and glorious ending. It is characterized by [the] following events.

[1.] By the resurrection of Jesus from the dead, and by his ascention to heaven.
[2.] The restoration of the priesthood of the order of the son of God, and by the qualification of his ministry with an endowment of power from on high, by the descent of the Holy Spirit, and by the miraculous manifestations of spiritual gifts & powers to the members of his church.[226]
[3.] The preaching of the Gospel, and the establishment of Christian churches in Jerusalem, in all Judea, in Samaria, and unto the uttermost parts of the earth.
4. The calamaties, the downfall, and the utter overthrow of the Jewish nation, and their wide-spread dispersion into all the countries of the world.
5. By ten severe persecutions against the Christians by the idolatrous Roman Emperors, and by the many Martyrs to their cruelty and fury.
6. The decline of true piety, of living faith, and of spiritual gifts & miraculous powers.
7. The difficulty of determining between the genuine and the spurious books claiming to be inspired–to have been written by the Apostles.
8. By the splits and divisions into sects and parties, and the con-

226. McLellin added "to the members of his church."

tentions among the professors of Christianity, after the spirit of revelation had ceased among th[em.]
9. By the calling of general councils to settle religious disputes, and the mak[ing] of human creeds for the government of the "Church of Christ."
10. The entire overthrow of that form of church government instituted by Christ & his Apostles. [page 133:]
[11]. The great division of the church into the Greek and Latin, or eastern and wester[n.]
[12]. By the rise of Mahomet,[227] and the spread of Moham[m]edanism by the power of the s[word.]
[1]3. By the loss of the true spirit of revelation, the blending of pagan rites and superstitions into their forms & ceremonies and then calling the mass Christianity.
[1]4. By the general spread of ignorance and superstition through what is sometimes term[ed] the dark ages, and the monstrous pretensions of the Pope of Rome.
[1]5. By the many Crusades made into the Holy land, professedly to redeem Chris[t's] sepulcher from the hands and dominion of infidels.
[1]6. By the invention of printing and the more general diffusion of books, an[d] the spread of what is called the knowledge of science.
17. By the rise of what is stiled the Reformation under Luther[228] & associates in [Europe.]
18. By the rise and spread of multitudes of religious sects, each governed by a [new] set of religious opinions peculiar to itself, but none claiming to be gov[erned] by direct revelations from God, as in the days of the Patriarchs, Prophets, or Apos[tles.]
19. By the commencement, the advance, and the completion of the preparatory work which is to precede the Millennium, which will be thus characterized.

> 1. By opening the fountains of light and truth from heaven to earth again, by the ministration of holy angels with messages to man.
> 2. The coming forth of ancient sacred records, & their translation for the salvation of the uprig[ht.]

227. For a summary of Muhammad's life, see the Biographical Notes.
228. For a summary of Martin Luther's life, see the Biographical Notes.

3. By the restoration of the priesthood according to the order of the Son of God to man.
[4.] By the re-organization of the church of Christ, and the establishment of the kingdom of heaven, through the spirit of prophecy and direct revelation.
5. By the endowment of the Lord's ministerial authorities with power from on high, [rathe]r than those in the days of Moses at the Tabernacle, or the Apostles at Pen[tecost.]
[6.] [By the prea]ching of the Gospel to [missing text] authority to Gent[iles] and then to Je[ws.] [page 134:]
[7.] For the restoration of all the spiritual gifts and powers ever enjoyed in all the prev[ious] dispensations, the Patriarchal, the Law, or the first part of the Christian, either among Jews & or G[entiles.]
[8.] For the great contrast between truth and righteousness, and all false religions. Betwee[n] power, and signs, and lying wonders of the **man of sin—anti-Christ**, through all his mediums, and the ministers of Christ in the discharge of their official duties.
[9.] For the fulness of the Gospel among the Gentiles, and its proclamation through them to all the branches, and families, and tribes of the house of Israel.
[10.] For the Deliverer's coming out of Zion, and turning away ungodliness from J[acob.] [cf. Rom. 11:26]
[11.] For the final restoration of the whole house of Israel from their long dispensions to covenant lands of their inheritance.
[12.] For the more marvelously miraculous displays of Divine power in their r[eturn] than were shown in their passage from Egypt to Canaan under Moses and J[oseph.]
13. For the general sound of war, and the universal crash and downfall of all th[e] nations and governments of men.
14. For the downfall of the <u>man of sin</u>, and of all anti-Christian power.
15. The awful distress and final overthrow of Babylon the great.
16. For the showing forth of all the signs and wonders which are to precede Christ's second[229] com[ing.]
17. The rolling back of the great oceans into a heap, into

229. McLellin added "second."

one place, and the marryin[g] of the continents and lands as they were before the days of Peleg, when they were div[ided.]
18. For the time when the kingdoms of this world shall become the kingdom of [Christ.]
19. For the sound of the trump and the resurrection of all the just to reign with [Christ.]
20. For the literal cleansing of the earth by fire as if it burned in an oven or furn[ace.]
21. The entire destruction of all the wicked of all the earth both root and branch.
22. For the de[s]cent of an angel with a great chain in his hand, and the [missing text] for one thousa[nd y]ears and cast [him into the bo]ttomless pit, and set [a seal upon him.] [cf. Rev. 20:1-3] [page 135:]
23. The entire removal of all the ills and ails that flesh is heir to, so that those who [missing] Christ to earth again may do it free from disease.
24. For the removal of the curse of the confusion of tongues and languages, and th[e] restoration of the pure language–the speech of Adam.
25. The descent of Jesus Christ, the second time, with all the hosts of heaven who pertai[n] to this earth, to marry the Bride & to reign universal King for 1000 years.

7. The ninth hour or the fourth grand division embraces the Millennial age [o]f one thousand years of rest. It will commence at the Second advent of Jesus, ~~and~~ at the binding of Satan, and will be noted by the following characteristics.

1. By the ratification and full enjoyment of the New Covenant with "the house of Israel and with the house of Judah," and with all their branches and families.
2. By the people all being righteous on the whole earth.
3. Their multiplying and replenishing the earth, and filling it with inhabitants, so that they will be as the sand upon the sea shore for multitude.
4. By all the children being born without pain or distress.
5. By all speaking one pure language as they did in the days of Adam & Noah.
6. By the whole world being governed by a perfect law, hence having universal peace.

7. All will know the Lord from the least unto the greatest, hence having no priestcraft.
8. By every man being ruler and priest in his own household.
9. By their building the holy cities [of] the New Jerusalem on the American land, and th[e] Jerusalem of old in the land of Palestine.
10. By their rising to as high a state of knowledge, and power, and perfection as it is possible for human beings to reach.
[11.] By their constant intercourse with Christ their King and Lord, and with glorifi[ed] beings who have either been translated or resurrected. [page 136:]
[12.] By there being no transgression, no sin, nor no death during the entire age.
[1]3. By living upon the fruits of the earth, instead tilling the soil for a subsistance.
14. By a state of perfect tranquility, having no strifes, no wars, nor any kind of trouble.
15. By a state of peace in government, in religious worship, in society, and in all the relations of life both physically and morally.

8. The eleventh hour is the fifth and last grand division. It is the judgement hour, the hour of execution, when all things pertaining to this planet will be judged. It is the finishing period relative to this earth and to its inhabitants. It will settle its state for all eternity. Some of its events will be the following.

1. The release of Satan from his imprisonment, and his goings forth to tempt man again.
2. The success he will have in turning men from holiness to vice, & from peace to war.
3. By the establishment of governments of men in opposition to that of Christ, by war & blood.
4. The ungodly gather up on the breadth of the earth, around the camp of the saints, to destroy them.
5. The last great struggle of Satan against Christ for the supremacy of this earth.
6. Satan is conquered and overthrown, and then cast into the bottomless pit.
7. The last trump sounds, all the dead small & great, from sea & land, rise and come to judgement.

8. God sits upon his great white throne, all the intelligences of this creation stand before him & are judg[ed.]
9. The decisions are passed, and all receive rewards or punishments, according to their deeds.
10. Every knee will bow, at the just & wise decisions of God, in the general Judgement.
11. The Sons of perdition will now pass through the second death, & forever thereafter[230] dwell with Satan.
12. By this world being melted or fused, & a new heaven & new earth formed[231] of the purified materials.
13. This world when thus made new will be taken to the center of all glorified worlds, to be thereafter the residence of God and the Lamb, & all the church of the first-born.
14. Here ends the work of the last period. Thence eternity will roll onward, but the enj[oy]ment of the glorified & the laws that will govern them, are matters in the mind of God un[til][232]

Fragment[†]

[continued from notebook p. 45] they should be superseded by the scripture.

This appears to be incorrect, because these gifts as they are laid [do]wn in the scripture, compose the Gospel ministry; and as this ministry is a part of the gospel plan, to say it was superseded by the gospel, would be the same as to say, the gospel has abolished the gospe[l.] [T]o say we must not look for such a ministry as the primitive Christ[ti]ans had, is the same as to say, we must not look for such a ministry as the New Testament directs us to, because it directs [us to] no other ministry than that of the apostolic church.

+++Those who oppose an apostolical ministry, a divine inspir[ation &] the restoration of miracles to the church, argue, that because these gifts were given to the church, before all the Scripture was writt[en ther]efore God did not intend them to be permanent. If this reasoning be correct, neither Baptism, the Lord's supper, nor the church itself, was designed to be permanent, because they were all instituted before any of the New Testament was written.

230. McLellin added "thereafter."

231. McLellin added "formed."

232. The rest of this thought and the end of Notebook 1 are missing.

†The following text appeared on the two leaves (four unnumbered pages) that were inserted between pages 44 and 45, which according to their placement in this volume following the bound pages, we have designated as notebook pages 137-40.

The commission for an apostolical ministry, is found in the same texts from which ministers derive their authority to baptize. "Go ye, therefore, teach all nations, baptizing them, &c. And lo, I am with you always, even unto the end of the world" [Matt. 28:19-20]. There are sundry texts in the New Testament, where people are exhorted to be baptized, but I believe none but those passages, that contain the apostles' commission, gives authority to any one to administer the ordinance. And as this authority is given only to an order of ministers acting under the apostles' commission, of course, those preachers, who say they do not act under that commission, have no authority to baptize, becaus[e] there is no text that authorizes any person, who may please to administer ~~B~~ baptism. [page 138:] This text proves, that Christ intended this order of ministers to continue till the end of the gospel dispensation. + + +

35. There is not a text in the Bible, that says God intended to take away those spiritual gifts from the church. On the contrary, that book exhorts us to "covet earnestly the best gifts." To "covet to prophesy, and forbid not to speak with tongues." To "follow after charity, and desire spiritual gifts, but rather that you may prophesy." 1 Cor. 12:31. Chap. 14:1, 39. Would God exhort us to follow after, covet, and earnestly seek those gifts, if he did not intend them for us? James says, "If any of You lack wisdom, let him ask of God, who giveth to all men liberally, and upbraideth not, [a]nd it shall be given to him" [James 1:5]. "If ye then being evil, know how to [g]ive good gifts unto your children, how much more shall your heavenly Father give the Holy Spirit to them that ask him" [Luke 11:13].

If God allows no person to be divinely inspired with wisdom, nor to receive the Holy Spirit in the present day, why do James and Jesus Christ exhort [u]s to ask God for these inestimable blessings? Would the blessed Jesus hold out [a] false hope to his people? To say these texts were confined to people [i]n the Apostles' days, and are not applicable to us in the present day, would be the same as to say, there can be no Christians in the present day, because if we do not follow after charity, seek wisdom of God, and pray to him for his Holy Spirit, we certainly cannot be Christians: then so sure as it is our privilege to be Christians in the present day, just so sure it is our privilege to enjoy a divine inspiration, and spiritual gifts. The two privileges must stand or fall together, the same scriptures promise and support both.

36. I will now try to answer such objections, as are most commonly brought against a restoration of the ancient order of things.

Objection 1. Miracles are not necessary in the present day; they were only wrought to confirm the gospel, and as soon as that was effected, their use was at an end.

[An]swer. If miracles, and the inspiration of the Holy Ghost were [page 139:] necessary to confirm the gospel among the Heathen in the apostles days, they are necessary to confirm it among them in the present day; because it is well known, that at least two thirds of mankind are still in Heathanism. It appears to me impossible, that partyism can be destroyed, prejudice and persecution exterminated, slavery abolished, wars done away, and the Jews, Mahometans, and Pagans, converted t[o] the gospel, without divine inspiration, and the gift of miracles. Ther[e] are as many evil spirits to dispossess, and as many sick people who need healing in the present day, as there were in the days of the apost[les.] As we have the same spiritual enemies to combat they had, we ne[ed] the same spiritual aid that they needed. And as the world labours un[der] the same moral diseases now, that it then did, the same remedies are necessary to remove them. Professors of Christianity at present are but poorly qualified to Christianize the world. The primitive church in possession of miracles and divine inspiration, did mor[e] towards evangelizing mankind in two centuries, than the chur[ch] has done without these gifts in sixteen.

37. Objection 2. If these miracles were continued, they would become so common that they would l[o]se their use.

Answer. We might as well say, that if we continue the ordinances of the gospel, they will become so common that they will loose their use. To say that a continual inspiration of the Holy Ghost, enlightening the minds and graciously affecting the hearts of Christians, would render such inspiration useless, would be as absurd as to say, that a continuation of the sun's shining daily on the earth, would render him useless to the world. It is as useful to a sinner to be regenerated; or to a sick person to be healed now, as it was in any former age of the world. [page 140:] If miracles were frequently wrought in the present day, and that by none but Christians, it would, no doubt, establish the publick mind in the faith of the gospel, and go far towards destroying partyism. From the days of Abraham, till a short time before the coming of Christ, the Jews had their divinely inspired prophets, prophetesses, and Priests, who foretold future events, and wrought miracles. Some of these prophets were Seers, who could see into the spiritual world, and converse with spirits, which is probably the gift Paul alludes to, when he speaks of discerning spirits. And from the history of the Jews, we find their [d]ays of inspiration and miracles, were alway[s] their best days. If God does not allow any of the spiritual gifts to his church in the [p]resent day, he does not admit his worshippers under the gospel [t]o as great an intimacy with himself, nor afford them as much [o]f his spirit, as he did those under the Law. If this be so, how can it be said of the gospel, that it excels the law in Glory? The Christian church at present, has less and fewer displays of divine glory, and power, and more partyism than the Jews had in the days of their prophets; but hardly as much piety. + + +

2.

ON THE TESTIMONY OF BOOK OF MORMON WITNESSES, 1871

W. E. McLellan's
Book
Jan. 4th 1871.

them in his hand, and showed as many of the leaves or plates as Joseph had ~~translated~~ to them. So that they saw, and looked upon them until they were entirely satisfied. And ~~he~~ the angel spoke to David Whitmer[1] and said, "David, blessed is the Lord, and he that keepeth his commandments." These men saw his form, saw his glorified appearance, heard his words, saw all that he showed them, and then saw him ascend to heaven again. This was no collusion. These men could not be mistaken They eith[er] told the truth [or] th[ey] wilfully lied. How [illegible] we know?[2]

This vision was in 1829. More than forty years ago, and what has been the conduct of those men since that day? Two of them are dead–and probably[3] two living. Those who are dead testified to the last hour of their lives ~~of~~ to the truth of their vision. Those who are still living are firm in their testimony. I visited David Whitmer after he was more than 65 years of age,[4] and he solemnly declared to me "I saw the Angel of God, I heard his voice, hence I know of a truth! Martin Harris[5] is some over 89 years of age,[6] and still he carries the book of Mormon under his arm, and testifies to all great and small, "I am Martin Harris in all

---

The title at the top of this page is ours, rather than McLellin's, and is meant as a general description of the notebook's contents. "W. E. McLellan's Book Jan. 4th 1871" is what McLellin himself wrote on the cover of Notebook 2.

1. For a summary of David D. Whitmer's life, see the Biographical Notes.

2. This paragraph is crossed out with a large X.

3. McLellin added the words "and probably" between the lines.

4. Whitmer's sixty-fifth birthday was 7 January 1870. The notebook date of January 1871 fits nicely with McLellin saying that Whitmer was "more than 65 years of age."

5. For a summary of Martin Harris's life, see the Biographical Notes.

6. Since Martin Harris was born on 18 May 1783, he would only be eighty-seven years old.

the world, and I know the book of Mormon to be verily true. And although all men should deny the truth of that book, I dare not do it. My hea[rt] is fixed. O god, my heart is fixed! I could not know more truly or certainly than I do."

12 In[7] 1833, when mobbing reigned triumphant in Jackson Co. Mo. I and O. Cowdery[8] [fled][9] from our homes, for fear of personal violence on Saturday the 20th day of July. The mob dispersed, agreeing to meet again on the next Tuesday. They offered eighty dollars reward for any one who would deliver Cowdery or McLellan in Independence on Tuesday. On Mond[ay] I slipped down into the Whitmer's settlement, and there in the lonely woods I met with David Whitmer and Oliver Cowdery. I said to them, "brethren I never have seen an open vision in my life, ...[10] [page 2:] Is that book of Mormon true"? Cowdery looked at me with solemnity depicted in his face, and said, "Brother William, God sent his holy Angel to declare the truth of the translation of it to us, and therefore we know. And though the mob kill us, yet we must die declaring its truth." David said, "Oliver has told you the solemn truth, for we could not be deceived. I most truly declare[11] ~~declare~~ to you its truth!!" Said I, boys I believe you. I can see no object for you to tell me falsehood[12] now, when our lives are endangered.[13] Eight men testify also to handling that sacred pile of plates, from which Joseph Smith, ~~translation~~ translated that heavenly work.

13. One circumstance I'll relate of one of these eight witnesses. While the mob was raging in Jackson Co. Mo. in 1833 some young men ran down Hiram Page[14] in the woods[15] one of the eight witnesses,[16] and

---

7. This is where Paul M. Hanson, "Unwavering Testimony," *Saints' Herald*, 9 Jan. 1929, 35, begins quoting the notebook.

8. For a summary of Oliver Cowdery's life, see the Biographical Notes.

9. Though the text is hard to read, the word "fled" is given in Hanson's transcript.

10. The extant photograph omits the rest of this page, but Hanson, "Unwavering Testimony," 35, provides the missing text:

> ... but you men say you have, and therefore you positively know. Now you know that our lives are in danger every hour, if the mob can only catch us. Tell me in the fear of God.

The text then continues with "Is that book of Mormon true?

11. McLellin's "I most truly declare" has been shortened (probably accidentally) by Hanson to "I must declare."

12. McLellin adds "hood" above the line.

13. Hanson, "Unwavering Testimony," 35, ends his quotation here.

14. For a summary of Hiram Page's life, see the Biographical Notes.

15. McLellin adds the words "in the woods" between the lines.

16. McLellin adds the word "witnesses" between the lines.

commenced beating and pounding him with whips and clubs. He begged, but there was no mercy. They said he was a damned Mormon, and they meant to beat him to death! But finally one [of] them said to him, if you will deny that damned book, we will let you go. Said he, how can I deny what I <u>know</u> to be true? Then they pounded him again. When they thought he was about to breathe his last they said to him Now what do you think of your God, when he dont save you: Will[17]

---

17. The extant fragment ends here.

3.

THE BLOOD OF ADAM AND OF CHRIST, 1877

W. E. McLellan. Jan 1877.

The blood of Adam and of Christ.

When Adam became a man he was an immortal being. He never would have died had he not transgressed in eating the forbidden fruit. And to never die or be subject to death is what I call immortality. The life that was in him must have been that eternal life principle that animates angels and all spiritual beings. Natural life or blood entered into Adam when he eat the forbidden fruit; and in consequence of his blood ~~life~~ his eyes were opened and he learned of his nakedness and also he come to know good and evil: hence mortal life[1] instead of immortal filled his veins. And because ~~of~~ the blood being[2] was of a corruptable nature death was the consequence. Immortality cannot have blood because blood always[3] has death in it.

Then human beings were generated or born in consequence of blood, it being that from which all the secretions of the body in mortality are derived. Had not Adam and Eve eaten the fruit, which made them mortal, gave them blood, then no progeny could have been born to

---

The title, "The Blood of Adam and of Christ," summarizes the contents of Notebook 3, drawing from McLellin's own initial subtitle. Larry C. Porter characterizes the notebook as a "discussion of blood as the vehicle through which the fall of Adam came and, reciprocally, through which the atonement of Christ will be efficacious in at least fifteen enumerated ways. McLellin argues for an elevated status for Adam before the Fall and promotes many LDS doctrines, for example translated beings, celestial glory, and the understanding of the Fall found in the Book of Mormon" ("The Odyssey of William Earl McLellin: Man of Diversity, 1806-83," in *The Journals of William E. McLellin, 1831-1836*, ed. Jan Shipps and John W. Welch [Provo and Urbana: BYU Studies and University of Illinois Press, 1994], 377n324). McLellin's inscription, "W. E. McLellan Jan 1877," was repeated twice on the cover.

1. McLellin added "life,"
2. McLellin added "was" but the word "being" is not crossed out.
3. McLellin added "always,"

them. No natural life could have been produced without the natural fluid. But Cain, Abel, and Seth were born by the natural process of generation. And in like manner the human family have all been produced. The blood is the life and fountain & cause of the production[4] of all flesh. It is the foundation and the source from whence all spring. And the blood being corruptible hence all must die. "In the day thou eatest thereof thou shalt surely die" [Gen. 2:17]; or fall from spiritual life, and take in the death fluid. This would be falling from immortality into mortality, into the death principle. Paul says, "by man came death" [1 Cor. 15:21], that is by transgression death entered our world. And so death passed upon all mankind in consequence of their taking in the corruptable, corroding life principle of blood.

Have immortal or resurrected beings any blood, or blood life by which they live or continue to exist? They have not! Angels that were once prophets certainly have material bodies, in which they appear to men. One said to John the revelator, "I am thy fellow servant, and of thy brethren the prophets" [Rev. 22:9]. And angels sometimes have eaten material food on earth which settles their identity and their individuality. Jesus said, "Handle me, and see; for a spirit hath not flesh and bones, as you see me have" [Luke 24:39]. And old Job speaking of his future hopes said, "Yet in my flesh shall I see God" [Job 19:26].[5] Immortals have flesh and bones, but do not have blood. The blood, the corruptable principle of life passes out after death before resurrection. But an objector might say, why then do they eat? The Psalmist says, "The Lord rained down manna upon Israel to eat, and had given them the corn of heaven. Man did eat angels food" [cf. Ps. 78:24-5]. If heaven has corn, and angels have manna to eat to sustain spiritual life, then all things whether natural or spiritual are kept in existence by some material substance. And because of [page 2:] this great principle Adam had given to him "all the seed of herbs and trees, the Lord said: to you it shall be for meat" [cf. Gen. 1:29]. This was said to Adam before he fell, while in his immortal—his bloodless state. Here we see that food is necessary in order to sustain angels and men. Hence food is the aliment [element] of all creation. Therefore the objector may turn his attention in some other way.

---

4. McLellin added "& cause of the production,"

5. There is controversy as to the meaning of Job 19:26, so that instead of a statement about a future resurrected body, modern translations provide various interpretations. For example, *The Holy Bible: New Living Translation* (Wheaton, Ill.: Tyndale House, 1997) has a marginal reading of "without my body I will see God."

The object of material food is not only for the purpose of making blood, but may also feed the eternal spiritual being or [illegible] fluid[6] in the veins of the redeemed. Hence Adam in his primevial immortal state did eat the seeds of earth, of herbs, and trees, in order to sustain him in his innocent sinless state. Adam eat natural food, so did the Lord and two angels eat of Abraham's repast of "Butter and milk, and the tender calf" [cf. Gen. 18:7-8]. The two angels may have once been prophets and been translated. But the Lord that was with them was at that time an unimbodied eternal[7] unclothed Spirit. It was before Christ's incarnation, before his birth of Mary, before it was said, "A body hast thou prepared me" [Heb. 10:5]. The Lord was at that time only a spiritual being, and his partaking of food shows conclusively that spiritual beings may eat natural food. Food is the substance and sustenance of all the living.

But the time came that Satan entered and induced the woman to violate God's law, and in consequence of that violation she fell into sin, fell from her innocent state, fell from spiritual union with God, fell from immortality into blood-life; and then she induced Adam to eat, to sin,[8] to fall, and to go with her in her rebellion.

They fell from their high innocent sinless state down, down so low as to put on mortality, and thus become subject to death. They eat the forbidden fruit and that changed the current of life. It planted in them the fluid ~~of~~ that tended to[9] corruption. It filled their veins with blood, the principle of death, and hence it was said, "In dying thou shalt die" [cf. Gen. 2:17]. Death was their only alternative, the inevitable result of their transgression. Thus Adam and Eve became dead to God, dead to spirituality, dead to all the enjoyment of spiritual ~~influences~~ life, dead to all the the[10] beauties and excellencies of spiritual existence or spiritual life.

Blood has in it the principle of death because of its cankering, corrosive, corruptable nature, but spirit has in it the power of life. Blood then is death, but spirit is life. There was no possible way for man to get out of this blood-life only to be changed[11] by translation or resurrection; and neither change could be accomplished by any exertion, or power, or

6. McLellin added "or [illegible] fluid,"

7. McLellin added "eternal,"

8. McLellin added an insertion caret here but placed "to sin" one line farther up, above the words "fell from immortality,"

9. McLellin added "that tended to,"

10. McLellin wrote two occurrences of "the," one at the end of the line and the other at the beginning of the next line.

11. McLellin added "to be changed,"

works of man. Divinity must come to his aid. One in the Godhead, far superior to man, must take upon him "flesh and blood," must condescend to come down to the level of men, to be born of a woman, (who was first in the transgression,) in order to redeem mankind; to [page 3:] take them out of their degredation, and place them back into immortality, the final state of all pure intelligences.

No intelligent spirit, no glorified personage, no exalted archangel, no translated man who lived in the third heaven in the immediate presence of God and Christ could have come down and redeem[ed] man. It must be one superior to them all. He must be a grade of spiritual intelligence, of spiritual organism identity[12] and power far in advance of any other personage in the vast universe, except Jehovah himself, and Christ was "One with him." Then it required one of the Godhead to leave heaven with all its riches and glories, and become poor, be veiled in flesh and blood, and dwell among men, in order to teach man the enobling principle of the Gospel by which he might rise to eternal life in celestial glory, the highest in the gift of God to man. In order that man might by obedience to the "law of liberty" rise to the enjoyment of the society and presence of God and the Lamb forever.

There was something about Adam, before he fell, that differed from pure spiritual or angelic nature, but I have no thoughts or[13] language that can reach or explain it or set it forth. Adam was a kind of medium between angels and men. He was not purely ~~human~~ divine nor was he altogether earthly. He possessed a heavenly spirit clothed in flesh and bones, and placed in a world of perfect peace without enmity or any death. The first pair were[14] placed there to have a probation, to have a free will, the power of choice, to have consciousness, to have judgement[15] to decide upon acts, hence when ~~he~~ they sinned ~~he~~ they "hid ~~himself~~ themselves from the presence of the Lord. ~~He~~ The man certainly knew something of his condition or otherwise he would not have been afraid so as to hide from his heavenly Father, with whom he had held open converse, after his creation. This was all in consequence of transgression in eating the forbidden fruit, and being thrown into a different state of existence. But the Lord called after him and told him his doom.

Adam with Eve were the representatives of the race of mankind, and

12. McLellin added "identity,"
13. McLellin added "thoughts or,"
14. McLellin added "first pair were,"
15. McLellin added "to have judgement,"

after they had fallen by sinning, they produced a progeny of fallen beings like themselves. All were brought into existence from the blood, "The life of all flesh" [Lev. 17:14], and hence were bound unto death the same as their parents, because blood the corruptable fluid coursed their veins. No being could ever be born without blood. Children then[16] were conceived and "born in sin" [cf. Ps. 51:5], that is born of sinful parents. The death fluid was the cause of their existence, and to death they were bound. There was no escape for the race only through translation or resurrection, and that could not be brought about only by one who had more spiritual authority and power than all men put together. Jesus alone had power given to him to redeem man from their fallen state. By his incarnation, his suffering, his death, and his resurrection he accomplished that great fete. [page 4:]

A little more about the food of immortals. "And out of the ground made the Lord God to grow every tree that is pleasant to the sight, and good for food; the tree of life also in the midst of the garden, and the tree ~~of the~~ of the knowledge of good and evil.["] Gen. 2:9. "And when the woman saw that the tree was good for food, and that it was pleasant to the eyes, and a tree to be desired to make one wise, she took of the fruit thereof, and did eat, and gave also unto her husband with her; and he did eat." Gen. 3:6. All these trees were created and planted for food, and were pleasant to the eye. Now all, all spiritualizing in the world by all those who follow Origen's lead, cant make it out but that the "tree of life, and of good and evil" were actual fruit trees, and that eating the fruit, or disobedience of God's command was the cause of their fall. The eating the fruit changed their natures so as to give them blood-life, instead of the eternal principle of spirit-life.

But the inspired prophets had a view of immortals needing food and drink and spoke of it in strains almost to[o] enobling for the human understanding; in describing the New Jerusalem or Millennial state. "And by the river upon the bank thereof, on this side and on that side, shall grow all trees for meat, whose leaf shall not fade, neither shall the fruit thereof be consumed: it shall bring forth new fruit according to his months, because their waters they issued out of the sanctuary: and the fruit thereof shall be for meat, and the leaf thereof for medicine." Ezekiel 47:12. But we will hear another prophet's voice, "And it shall be in that day, that living waters shall go out from Jerusalem; half of them toward the former sea, and half of them toward the hinder sea: in summer and winter shall it be. And the Lord shall be

16. McLellin added "then,"

King over all the earth: in that day there shall be one Lord, and his name one." Zech. 14:8, 9.

Here we may turn to John the Revelator, Seer, and prophet, who closed the Book of revelation so far as we have it. "And he showed me a pure river of the water of life, clear as crystal, proceeding out of the throne of God and the Lamb. In the midst of the street of the city, and on either side of the river, was there the tree of life, which bear[s] twelve manner of fruits, and yielded her fruits every month: and the leaves of the tree were for the healing of the nations." Rev. 22:1, 2. Ezekiel says, shall grow all trees for meat, and the fruit shall not be consumed, but bring forth new fruit according to his months, and the fruit shall be for meat, and the leaf for medicine. But John says, yielding her fruit every month, and the leaves were for the healing of the nations. And Zech. says, And the Lord shall be King over all the earth, in that day.

These prophecies show conclusively that there will be food and drink for all those resurrected, glorified and Millennial beings in the New Jerusalem. The righteous and the resurrected saints will live and reign with Christ on earth a thousand years in perfect peace, and will all eat the same food to sustain them. It will be the natural products of earth. They will not force nature in order to eat and live. Their food will be spontaneously produced. [page 5:]

<u>The blood of Christ</u>.

1. Washed from our sins in the blood of Christ. Rev. 1:5. 7:14.
2. The blood of Christ cleanses us from all sin. 1 John 1:7.
3. The blood of Christ purges the conscience. Heb 9:14.
4. Purchased the church of God with his own blood. Acts 20:28.
5. Prop[it]iation through faith in his blood. Rom 3:25.
6. Being now justified by his blood. Romans 5:9.
7. The communion of the blood of Christ. 1 Cor. 10:16.
8. Made nigh by the blood of Christ. Eph 2:13.
9. Sanctified by the blood of Christ. Heb 13:12.
10. Redemption through the blood of C[hrist]. Eph 1:7. Col 1:14. 1 Pet 1:18[-19].
11. Blood of N.T. in my blood for remission of sins. Matt 26:28.
12. This cup is the N. T. in my blood. Luke 22:20. 1 Cor 11:25.
13. Made peace through the blood of his cross. Col 1:20.
14. By his blood he obtained eternal redemption for us. Heb 9:12.
15. Almost all things are by the law purged with blood; and without the shedding of blood is no remission. Heb 9:22.

1. Washed.
2. Cleansed.
3. Purged.
4. Purchased.
5. Prop[i]tiated.
6. Justified.
7. Sanctified.
8. Redeemed.
9. Made peace.
10. And made nigh.

It is said, "The blood of Jesus Christ cleanseth us from all sin" [1 John 1:7]. I would ask how it is possible this should be? How can the blood of Christ be applied? We answer, by Christ taking blood, and through the eternal spirit offering himself without spot to God, and offering his blood upon the cross to make atonement for man's soul; thus offering the one sacrifise for the sins of all the world: and then taking the eternal life principle in his resurrection instead of blood, which gave him power to bring up all mankind, and plant ~~them~~ the righteous[17] in an eternal sinless state without blood.

But in order for Christ to redeem man from his fall, from his mortality and bring him back into immo[r]tality he had to be born of a woman, to partake of flesh and blood, and then have that blood offered as a sacrifise for sin on the tree, then take upon him the imortal[18] life principle to fill his veins, in order to give man by resurrection the endless principle of life also.

But we ask why it was necessary that the blood of Christ should be shed for the sins of the world? In Adam's fall he partook of blood, and became mortal, became a sinner, became unable to save himself, hence one of superior authority and power must act: a Savior was necessary in order to man's salvation. And he must partake of [page 6:] fallen nature, of blood life for man's redemption. "Christ was made flesh and dwelt among us" [cf. John 1:14]. He partook of corruptable blood, and being sinless, and One in the Godhead, he had power to redeem mankind from the fall. "For it is the blood that maketh an atonement for the soul." ~~Leviticus 17:11~~.

"For the life of the flesh is the blood; and I have given it upon the altar to make an atonement for your souls: for it is the blood that maketh an atonement for the soul." [cf.] Levi 17:11. This scripture is remarkably plain, and shows why Christ shed his blood to give life to the world. Adam fell and blood filled his veins and because of that he had to die. But Christ came and took flesh and blood and died, and rose again to atone for man and redeem him. He will redeem him by resurrection

17. McLellin added "the righteous,"

18. McLellin added a caret below the line after the letter "m" but never actually added a second "m" above the line to make the spelling "immortal."

from death into an endless state, without having blood in his veins. Redemption then means to be freed from blood. All the human family are brought into existence because of blood, and must all perish unless redeemed. Christ is the great Redeemer and sanctifier. "Then they also which are fallen asleep in Christ are perished, if Christ be not risen." So says Paul 1 C. 15:18 [cf. 1 Cor. 15:17-18].

Christ partook of blood, and being and remaining sinless and[19] innocent he had power to redeem mankind from the fall. But he had to take human nature, and thus be allied to man, be of his nature, be made as man ~~as man~~, in order by his own death and resurrection he might have authority and power to raise all mankind from the dead; so as to bring man back spiritually and temporally i.e. Spirit and body, into the presence of God. Blood is the life of all flesh and is that of which Adam partook when he or they eat the fruit. And in order for Christ to redeem man and bring him back unto God, he had to destroy in man the natural life principle–the blood. It is the blood that is corruptable; it is the spirit that gives life.

In order to rise Christ laid aside all his blood and was animated by the eternal life principle of spirit. In the resurrection to eternal life no being has a particle of blood in their veins, because flesh animated by blood "cannot inherit the kingdom of God" [1 Cor. 15:50]. The eternal principle of life animates every saint, and it is that by which he will be resurrected. All men that ever lived before Christ were sinners hence had not power to redeem themselves or others, therefore Satan had power over them when in death in order to keep their bodies and spirits apart. But Christ never having sinned, being perfectly innocent, therefore he had power "to lay down his life, and power to take it again" [cf. John 10:17], and hence had power to destroy him that had the <u>power of death</u>; and then power to resurrect all mankind!

What was Adam's fall? It was loosing the immortal principle of life, it was loosing open communion with heaven, [page 7:] and imbibing or taking into him corruptible blood. Thus he became spiritually dead to God, having lost his immortality. If Adam had not fallen then all things would have remained stationary continuing always[20] just as created. He never would have died, but remained endlessly in the world alone with Eve, without progeny; hence the world would have been created in vain: "but it was created to be inhabited" [cf. 1 Ne. 17:36].

In this arrangement I can see why and how Christ's blood cleanses

19. McLellin added "sinless and,"

20. McLellin added "always,"

our sin. It is that blood came because of sin, and when sin is finished blood will end also. In the resurrection all the righteous will then be immortal, eternal, and endless not having blood-life but animated by the principle of eternal life.

But how does Christ's blood cleanse us from our sin? It does it by being applied for our justification, by our obedience to the great gospel principle. Christ's blood stands as surity to his Father for us when we obey his law. It is only applyed by virtue of our yielding to its divine rights. And his blood will be the cause of our final redemption—our resurrection from death, and being taken back into immortality, into eternal, endless happiness—without blood or anything corrupting or[21] corroding. Then we will be tangible beings, because we shall have flesh and bones. Job said, "Yet in my flesh I shall see God" [Job 19:26]. And Jesus said, "For a spirit hath not flesh and bones as ye see me have" [Luke 24:39]. Therefore flesh and bones will be glorified in order for us to enjoy heaven in our immortalized bodies.[22]

Why did Abel shed blood and offer sacrifise? Because he was taught that it pointed to the great sacrifice of the Lamb of God, whose blood was to be shed that man might be justified by his blood; that is, that man might be finally redeemed, and brought back in the presence of God, into immortality without blood-life into the very nature of the Godhead themselves; to dwell with God, and be equal with the angels, and one with the Lord Jesus Christ, far up in celestial glory.

All the blood ever shed or sacrifices ever offered up pointing to Christ had direct reference to his one great sacrifise in offering himself upon the cross; shedding his blood to redeem man from his blood-life. But when he offered himself to his Father it was to be the last legal sacrifice ever offered by man. That ended sacrifice or offering ~~sacrifices~~ blood for ~~for~~ man's transgression. Christ's blood was a universal offering for the whole race, in order that through his death and resurrection he received authority and power to raise all mankind from the dead.

Christ partook of blood and entered into natural life among men in order to teach them that they might live forever, by obeying the great gospel truths which he taught. They might leave blood life and go back into immortality by a resurrection. It is not the cross but the blood shed there that gives it ist [its] virtue, that plants in it its saving power. O that man [page 8:] would learn the efficacy of the blood of the blessed Jesus! Man comes into existence and then lives because of blood, but Jesus

21. McLellin added "corrupting or,"

22. McLellin added "in our immortalized bodies,"

took the same in order to redeem man from blood and make him immortal, by spilling or laying aside his own blood he has power to cleanse all the righteous from blood, and bring them without blood into life eternal.

Blood, with the curse afterward attached to part of the race, is the colouring principle in all their natures. Take the curse and the blood all away and then all would be as white as snow flakes. White is the purest colour in existence. It is the celestial colour of all the church of the first born. White is the only pure colour that exists, and when we get to a state of perfect whiteness then we shall be pure, perfect and happy in the highest glory in heaven.

Objections answered. Some men think that because Adam had to eat to sustain life while in the garden, therefore he was mortal. But Jesus eat material food after his resurrection, and angels, probably in order to live. The Lord and two angels eat of Abraham's repast, so this argument falls. For Israel eat angels food, and the corn of heaven, and Jesus and the angels eating settles the matter in question.

I do not know the exact state of Adam before his fall, but the book says, "by one man sin entered into the world, and death by sin" [Rom. 5:12]. It says again, "For since by man came death" [1 Cor. 15:21]. If death came by Adam's eating the forbidden fruit, then it was not in the world until that fatal act. So this proves Adam's immortality without question. I mean he could not have died for death was not in the world.

Again the objector said, If blood is corruptible then Christ's blood was also, and hence it being so it could not cleanse man from sin. But it was poured out–shed for the sins of the world. It was necessary for Chr[i]st's life and character to be pure, but not his blood ~~not his blood~~ to be incorruptable in order to redeem man.

A preacher said to me after I had read to him the foregoing that when Adam was created he was only a babe, or as a babe without knowledge. But he knew enough to give names to all the animals of creation. "To all cattle, and to all the fowls of the air, and to every beast of the field; and whatsoever Adam called every living creature, that was the name thereof" [cf. Gen. 2:19-20]. When the breath of life was breathed into Adam, and his eternal spirit from heaven entered his body, he was then a full grown man, with all the capacities, strength, knowledge and attributes of a man. But he was not a natural or mortal man, because destitute of the life principle of blood, which is the foundation of all natural life. Talk not to me then about Adam's being a babe when he came from the hand of his Creator.

Adam was a whole man, an immortal man, a being who could and would live forever, because the death principle ~~had not entered the~~ [page 9:] had not entered the world until man sinned, and that brought in death. All this lower creation when first created were full grown also; but their progeny had to be born babes and grow up into life to full stature. As soon as evil and sin[23] entered it ran through all creation, setting all animated nature at variance, contention and war. War is the engine of Satan for destruction. It was the element in which he made himself ~~Satan~~ a Devil. He is both the instigater and promoter of all wars, and they are all in his interest first or last. And blood life will always tell in all difficulties, contentions and wars.

The preacher also said to me that death was in the world previous to Adam's sin. Paul says, "Death came by sin" [Rom. 5:12]. And also said, "Since by man came death" [1 Cor. 15:21]. And I cant think of it in any other light. There was nothing corruptable that would cause death before sin and blood entered the world. The Lord said of all things created, "Behold it was very good" [Gen. 1:31]. And hence no evil or death could possibly come in before sin entered. Sin and blood came, and hence death followed.

The blood of Christ, or the shedding of it is that which will redeem the world. He will bring up all mankind from the grave, because he shed his blood for their redemption from death. His blood atoned for the whole race of man. Had not Christ died and risen again then all creation (except those translated,) would have perished. Perished why? Because without bodies glorified they would never go and dwell in the presence of God, and hence must perish, being away from his presence. For without a resurrection they would remain naked spirits without bodies. Perish because they would be forever banished, and perpetual darkness reign around ~~them~~ and upon them. Talk not to me then that when persons die they go immediately to heaven. Those who died in Christ (of whom Paul speaks,) could not perish provided they were in heaven. When the righteous die they go to Paradise to dwell until their resurrection. Their resurrection and final redemption is all in consequence of the shed blood of the Lord Jesus Christ.

When Adam and Eve were created they were immortal, with no tendency to decay or death. They sinned and sin brought mortality, and mortality came by blood, and blood came by their eating the forbidden fruit, and death came as a consequence of mortality and transgression.

23. McLellin added "and sin,"

Christ came, took blood, and offered it on the cross for the race of mankind. Shed it that he might have power given him to resurrect ~~all~~ men from death into life without blood. Thus bringing ~~man~~ the righteous[24] in purity up to his Father. Blood is ~~the~~ life ~~of the~~ so far as to produce all the progeny ever born; but it always produced death in its consequences, in its results.

But Christ's redemption is to redeem man from blood, and bring him up into endless life without any corrosive, viscious, painful principle in his nature. Christ's blood then is the foundation and fountain of all happiness for all men. It washes, cleanses, purifies, justifies, sanctifies, and redeems mankind from all the consequences of their fall, and brings the righteous up to enjoy heaven, with all its glories. [page 10:]

During the last of October 1876, I went to hear a sermon and the preacher took for his text Matthew 12:38, "Master we would see a sign from thee." But his discourse was so foreign from what I conceived to be truth I came home and wrote the following.

The Gospel.[25]

There is a want of definite history to state the precise time when, where, and how the gospel of Christ was first introduced into the world. But from the fact that the first men were taught to sacrifice, to offer blood upon the altar, pointing to the Lord Jesus Christ, is evidence that they knew of Christ and of his gospel. Enoch the seventh Patriarch from Adam had such knowledge of the principles of truth and light that he walked with God, and was translated from earth to heaven. He knew of Christ, and even prophesied of his second coming and the destruction of all the wicked; when he would come to set up his kingdom for Millennial glory. He certainly knew of Jesus Christ and his gospel.

Noah was a perfect man in his generation. And he had direct intelligence from God, and no doubt he learned more or less of the gospel of Christ. He built an altar and offered sacrifices pointing to Christ. The Lord spok to Noah and to his sons, saying, "Behold, I establish my covenant with you and with your sons after you" [cf. Gen. 9:9]. Certainly with such intimacy between Noe and the Lord he must have learned of the

---

24. McLellin added "the righteous,"

25. Porter, "Odyssey of McLellin," 377n324, says that in this portion of the notebook, "McLellin argues that Adam, Enoch, Noah, and others knew about the gospel, the mortal condescension of God in Christ, and the infinite atonement. He explains that the purpose of the gospel in its fullness is to allow all believers to commune directly with heaven and to be delivered both in body and spirit."

gospel of Christ, which was the great principle of the wonderful salvation prepared for man.

When Abraham came into the land of Canaan, "He builded an Altar unto the Lord and called upon his name" [cf. Gen. 12:8]. Paul says, "Foreseeing that God would justify the heathen through faith, preached before the gospel unto Abraham["] [Gal. 3:8]. And ["]to Abraham and to his seed ~~were the~~ were the promises made.["] He says again, "And to thy seed, which is Christ" [Gal. 3:16]. Then Abraham knew of Christ and his gospel, because it was "preached to him." Abraham "saw the day of Christ, ~~and he saw it~~, and was glad." [cf.] John 8:56.[26]

Melchisidec was High Priest of the holy order of the Son of God; and hence he must have understood the gospel in plainness, because he held the same order of priesthood with the Lord Jesus Christ, and the same priesthood would be bound to preach the same Law or rule of salvation. Melchisedec must have been a great man and High Priest, and probably preached righteousness, and the gospel to his people, and established peace among them by his ministerial authority and power. He was the King of Salem, which is Prince of Peace.

Moses introduced into the Israelite camp the first born of all[27] the families of Israel, and they had authority and power, and they preached the gospel in plainness to all Israel. Paul says, "For unto us was the gospel [page 11:] preached, as well as unto them: but the word preached did not profit them, not being mixed with faith in them that heard it" [Heb. 4:2]. This was done before the Aaronic priesthood and law of Moses were instituted. Paul speaking of Israel says, "For they drank of that spiritual Rock that followed them: and that Rock was Christ" [1 Cor. 10:4]. Then all Israel knew of Christ. And before they reached Sinai they had the gospel preached to them in plainness by the priests of all the first born.

But when the priesthood of Aaron, and the law of Moses was introduced thereafter the religion of the Israelites became mostly ceremonial, had but little spirituality in it. It was a mere "shadow of good things to come" [Heb. 10:1]. Under that system or order of things there was a man inspired only occasionally to be a Prophet unto the people. But Moses looked at this great subject with very liberal views. When his seventy Elders were endowed at the tabernacle and prophesied,[28] Joshua was excited and said, "My Lord Moses forbid them. But Moses said, Enviest

26. McLellin added "Abraham 'saw the day of Christ, ~~and he saw it~~, and was glad.' John 8:56,"

27. McLellin added "all,"

28. McLellin added "and prophesied,"

thou for my sake? Would God that all the Lord's people were prophets, and that the Lord would put his Spirit upon them." [cf.] Num 11:[28-]29. The light in which Moses viewed this subject is precisely the same as that in which Christ and his apostles looked at it.

"And Jethro, Moses father in law, took a burnt offering and sacrifices for God: ~~A~~ and Aaron came, and all the Elders of Israel, to eat ~~bread~~ bread with Moses father in law before God." Ex. 18:12. Jethro came to Moses and Israel before they arrived at mount Sinai, while the first born priesthood was in authority among them; and that was the reason of his advice and liberality among them. He was the High Priest of the land of Median, and had a right to advise Moses, and regulate all Israel, as much so as Melchisedec had to bless Abraham, "who had the promises" [Heb. 7:6]. This meeting of Moses and Jethro was before what is called the law of Moses was given, hence they two acted jointly in ~~the High Priesthood of~~ regulating all the camp of Israel according to[29] the holy order of the Son of God.

Jethro worshipped the true God, the Lord of the Hebrews, and made offerings to him that were accepted. Aaron and all the authorities of Israel eat bread with Jethro, which showed conclusively that he believed in and worshipped the same God. Being the priest of Midian, and being older than Moses at that time in the Priesthood, hence he gave advice to him that the children of Israel practiced all their after lives, or as long as they existed as a nation. Jethro was of the same order of priesthood with Melchisedec who blessed Abraham. When he offered sacrifices he did so pointing directly to Christ. He was a Gentile priest, so was Melchisedec; which certainly shows that the knowledge of the true God, his worship, and his salvation by our Lord Jesus Christ, (who was to make the last great sacrifice for man,) was more wide spread over the world, in those olden times than many people suppose. The doctrine that Christ was and is, "The true [page 12:] Light which lighteth every man that cometh into the world" [John 1:9], is the only true principle of life. But Moses let Jethro depart, and he went to his own father land of Media.

More than a year after Israel started from Egypt for Canaan, Moses said to Hobab his brother in law, "Come thou with us, and we will do thee good: for the Lord has spoken good concerning Israel. But he said unto him I will not go; but I will depart unto my own land, and to my kindred. But Moses said, Leave us not, I pray thee; forasmuch as thou knowest how we are to encamp in the wilderness, and thou mayest be unto us as eyes. And it shall be, if thou go with us, that what goodness the Lord shall

29. McLellin added "regulating all the camp of Israel according to,"

do unto us, the same will we do unto thee." [cf.] Num 10:29-32. This shows evidently their unity of feeling, and rights of worship, according as their High Priests had taught them and dictated to them. Hobab lived under the rule of the priesthood of his father Jethro.

And many years afterward when Israel was at war with Jabin king of Canaan, Sisera captain of his host gathered his forces for war. Heber the Kenite lived in that country, who was of the children of Hobab. Jael the wife of Heber showed great kindness to Israel in the destruction of Sisera by driving a nail from the tent through his temples. This showed their fondness for the religion of the Hebrews. This people believed in and worshipped the true God, as well as the people of Melchisedec, and that singularly peculiar nation of Abraham's descendants. These people all must have known of the gospel, because of the ~~priesthood~~ priests of the order of the Son of God that lived and ruled among them. That ministry always had the gospel to some extent for its law or rule of action.

Ninevah, that great city of more than a hundred and twenty thousand people repented at the preaching of Jonah—one man warned them, and it is said, "So the people of Ninevah believed God, and repented in sackcloth and ashes, and God did not the evil he intended" [cf. Joel 3:5-6, 10]. So Ninevah an entire Gentile city seemed to know the character of God that he, "Was a gracious and merciful God, slow to anger and of great kindness" [Jonah 4:2]. Then Gentile Ninevah had some knowledge of the true God, and of his lovely character.

When the three Hebrews were cast into the fiery furnace, the king said, "Did we not cast three men bound into the midst of the fire? Lo, I see four men loose, walking in the midst of the fire, and they have no hurt; and the form of the fourth is like the Son of God" [cf. Dan. 3:24-25].[30] This King must have had special knowledge of God, and of his Son to thus speak; he had a great vision.

Tell me not them that the many nations of the earth in olden time had not the knowledge to some extent of the true God, and of his Son our Savior, and of his salvation. Christ was the true Light of every man that came into the world. Peter said, "I perceive of a truth that God is no respecter of persons, but in every nation he that feareth God and worketh righteousness is accepted of him" [cf. Acts 10:34-35]. These nations of whom I have been speaking all once had the true Light, but

---

30. McLellin quoted the King James Version, which is misleading since the Hebrew is literally "a son of God" or "son of the gods" and refers to an angel or divine person. The translation given by John J. Collins, *Daniel: A Commentary on the Book of Daniel* (Minneapolis: Fortress Press, 1993), 178, is: "the appearance of the fourth is like a divine being."

more or less departed from it, and hence their judgements. [page 13:]

Jesus said, ["]a man must be born again—born of water and the spirit, in order to be saved in the kingdom of God" [cf. John 3:3, 5]. Paul said, "Now if any man have not the spirit of Christ he is none of his" [Rom. 8:9]. Jesus promised his disciples another Comforter to abide with them forever. "To teach them all things, and show them things to come" [cf. John 14:26; 16:13]. But it is said that this promise only applied to the Apostles. Let us see. On the day of Pentecost Peter when filled with ~~with~~ the spirit of the gospel and of power, enlarged the promise. "For the promise is unto you and to your children, and to all that are afar off, even as many as the Lord our God shall call" [Acts 2:39]. This promise was co-extensive with creation both then and now. And a little farther on speaking of Christ he says, "Him hath God exalted with his own right hand to be a Prince and a Savior, and we (apostles,) are witnesses of these things; and so is also the Holy Ghost, whom God hath given to all them that obey him." [cf.] Acts 5:[31-]32. This settles one point that was not only a gift of the Holy Spirit, but it was the Holy Spirit itself, given to and received by believers. Peter takes a very wide scope in his view of this matter.

Joel and Peter both say, "It shall come to pass in the last days, saith God, I will pour out of my Spirit upon all flesh: and your sons and your daughters shall prophesy, and your young men shall see visions, and your old men shall dream dreams" [Acts 2:17]. Here we have a very large calculation, a wide spread diffusion of the Holy Spirit in gifts and blessings to men and to women. It would seem as though we had jumped over and got beyond the Last Days, and lost all the spiritual gifts and blessings and powers that belong to the gospel dispensation. But these spiritual gifts and their enjoyment would look like what Moses prayed for, "For all the Lord's people to be prophets" [cf. Num. 11:29]. And Paul had the same view exactly. He said, "For ye may all prophesy, one by one, that all may learn, and all be comforted" [1 Cor. 14:31]. And Paul goes far enough to command all believers in his day, "To covet earnestly the best gifts" [1 Cor. 12:31]. Yes, "To covet to prophecy, and forbid not to speak with tongues" [1 Cor. 14:39]. To ["]follow after charity, and desire spiritual gifts, but rather that you may prophecy" [1 Cor. 14:1]. This is the gospel in its enjoyment. This is some of its fulness among believers. This is pure gospel possessed in truth and verity.

If all this is not enlarging the sphere of Christianity—of the gospel into a wide field of spiritual things, then I must say I cant understand the king's English. This is what I call the gospel in its fulness, and in its blessed effects, and glorious results. This would be not only believing the truth of the gospel, but living in it and enjoying it. This would be the wide extended influence which Christ and his apostles intended by the gospel sweep in the world. The church bearing all the gospel fruits of the Spirit, and then enjoying all the nine spiritual gifts and powers. The objects of the gospel plan ~~plan~~ was to make men and women spiritual beings. Have them taught by the spirit, led by it, guided by it, and so inspired by it as to speak a "Thus saith the Lord." This would be the church, Yes, all believers holding spiritual communion direct with Heaven.

The law of Moses was designed only for Israel as a nation. The gospel was designed for the whole world, for all mankind, both Jew and Gentile. It had no respect [page 14:] of persons, but in every nation whosoever fears and loves God is accepted of him. The law of Moses was confined to Israel, but the gospel was unconfined, was universal pardon and peace to all the world. Jesus said, "Go, preach the gospel to every creature, and signs shall follow the believers of this free gospel" [cf. Mark 16:15, 17]. And the apostles went every where preaching, "The Lord working with them with signs following" [Mark 16:20].[31] Not going before to produce faith, but the signs followed.

O how plain the gospel principles are, but in Catholocism and all Protestantism how few believe them! O how few!! All the professors of the world have mostly failed to obtain spiritual gifts, and then signs to follow. They have them not, therefore they contend strenuously against their being enjoyed; saying they are not necessary now in as much as we have a New Testament; and they are satisfied with mere outside show, and with hollow forms and ceremonies. Pleased with the tinsel and show of the world.

The gospel came into the world with power—spiritual power, and it was intended to always continue in power, provided men continued to believe and practice its truths. I believe in a gospel with power in it, and without that belief I am not religious at all! If the sick cannot be healed, without Doctors, by anointing with oil, with fervent prayr, and then the "Laying on of hands," the gospel with all its forms and ceremonies would be uninteresting to me.

The gospel system was intended to be a universal principle of deliv-

---

31. The earliest and best Greek manuscripts of Mark conclude the gospel at 16:8. Some manuscripts have a shorter ending, while the great majority of later manuscripts have verses 9-20. See J. Lee Magness, *Sense and Absence: Structure and Suspension in the Ending of Mark's Gospel* (Atlanta, Ga.: Scholars Press, 1986).

erance for both body and spirit. It was to be spiritually born, and then the body to be healed when sick. It was intended for all its members to be spiritual minded, to be prophets of God. It was for all to rise to a high degree of light, and then to walk in it, so as to hold direct communion with the heavens. Paul said to a church of believers, "When you come together, every one of you hath a psalm, hath a doctrine, hath a tongue, hath a revelation, hath an interpretation. Let all things be done unto edifying" [1 Cor. 14:26]. Here the Spirit's power is positively set forth among the members of the church. They were to have the spiritual gifts and enjoy them.

The gifts were not confined as in olden time to a few individual prophets, but they were intended to be universally possessed by all believers. They were to be a common inheritance of both men and women. This was the gospel system preached by Christ and by the Apostles, and ought to be enjoyed now. This would be faith with power and demonstration of the spirit in it. It would be Christianity with faith and spiritual gifts and blessings in it. It would be the possession of powers more than the Patriarchal or law ages guaranteed to its professors. It would in reality be what Moses wished "That all the Lord's people might be prophets" [cf. Num. 11:29]. Then visions and revelations would be common with believers, so that it would be that the honest in heart would not perish. The wise man said, "Where there is no vision the people perish" [Prov. 29:18], for the want of spiritual intelligence. [page 15:] Paul said, "I am not ashamed of the gospel of Christ; for it is the power of God unto salvation to every one that believeth" [Rom. 1:16]. To believe the gospel is to believe the truth, it is faith in God, it is repentance for all past sin, it is baptism for the remission of sin, and then the reception of the Holy Spirit by the laying on of hands, of the Elders of the church, and then a new spiritual life in Christ unto the end; "when all the saints shall dwell with God" [Moro. 8:26]. This is the gospel as believed and practised by the Apostles of Christ; and it ought to be believed in an[d] practised at this day. O my Lord, how long until people will come to the light of this glorious gospel? How long until the church of Christ will rise with all these spiritual gifts and powers in it, and be blessed with visions and revelations from the Lord Jesus Christ, the great Head of the true church of Christ?

Priesthood.[32]

Priesthood is the holy authority and power from God to enable a

32. Porter, "Odyssey of McLellin," 377n324, says this portion of the notebook "is a

man to minister in holy things. Two orders of priesthood, or authority from God have legally ministered in the world, since its creation, viz. the Melchisedec and the Aaronic. All the ministerial authority that man ever received from God from Adam to Moses was given to them in the order of Melchisedec. All those who were denominated the first-born were of that order. And during the Adamic religion the birth right was of great consequence. They stood at the head of the race of mankind. The consecration to the birth right made them Prophet, Priest, and King, or at least it gave them a legal right to that most important station; and also to a double portion of their father's estate (Deut. 21:17). The oldest male heir of the ruling family held the legal right to those most important offices. But if the legal heir committed wilful murder, sold his birth right, or violated his father's rights or his honor then the birth-right of course went to the next born. Cain, Japheth, Esau, and Reuben—and the ten older brethren of Joseph lost this peculiar right and blessing. It went to Seth, to Shem, to Jacob, and to Joseph.

But little is said of birth right blessings or priestly authority from the time Jacob blessed the sons of Joseph until Moses and Israel started from Egypt to go to Canan. And after the first-born of Egypt were all slain, then Moses appointed that the first born of the families of Israel should be the priests of that nation. This order of priesthood remained with them some months, until they reached mount Sinai. The priests of this order preached the pure Gospel of the Christ to all Israel in plainness. It is said in Heb. 4:2 "For unto us was the gospel preached as well as unto them: but the word preached did not profit them, not being mixed with faith in them that heard it." If those priests had the pure principles of the Gospel and preached them unto Israel then they must have been of the order of Melchisedec Priests, for the gospel always was the law of that order. But this order as that of prophet, priests, and king was entirely abolished—set aside forever, and the establishment of an entire new order was instituted for Israel. One never ~~before~~ heard of before in the world. [page 16:]

The Aaronic priesthood was specially set up and solemnly consecrated for all Israel, to administer the law, and attend to the service of the tabernacle, and afterward of the Temple; throughout all their generations, to be to them an everlasting priesthood. Aaron was made High

---

short undated essay about the orders of priesthood—patriarchal, Melchizedek, Aaronic, Christian—revealed by God in different eras. Contrary to this preaching in the 1830s about two priesthoods, McLellin here argues that only one priesthood order can exist on earth at a time."

Priest, and his sons chief priests, and all the rest of Levi were given to Aaron and his sons as their servants. But the order of the Levites was never constituted or called priests during ~~during~~ the reign of the law. This priesthood was confined to Israel, but never passed out among the Gentiles.

When Christ came into the world he set up his own priesthood, of the order of Melchisedec. His priesthood embraced all the world in its preachings and in its administrations. It was truly the order of the Son of God. It embraced without distinction of nation or tribe, love to all men. It was a universal priesthood for all men—for every creature which is under heaven. Christ in setting up his own priesthood abolished and set aside the priesthood that preceded it, as much as the first born was set aside in order to introduce the Aaronic. Two orders could not exist at the same time and be in full force among one and the same people; for the stronger would naturally abolish or overrule the weaker. The weaker would certainly become null and void. No history or hint is given in any inspired book of two priesthoods acting among any one people at the same time. ~ The order of the Son of God was never mixed up with any other order whatever. It stood by itself alone. It was not in "part only," but was perfect in itself. It needed no help nor additions. It was impossible to combine it with the Aaronic; because the duties of that order was specifically to administer the law of Moses; and that had its fulfilment in Christ, and was then set aside, with all its rights and its priesthood—all were abrogated. Hence no mention is made in any inspired book of the New Dispensation of Aaronic priests ministering in any ordinance of the Gospel[33] before Christ came—Except John the Baptist.

Again, Aaronic priests were all solemnly consecrated with ordination, and sacred oil poured upon their heads. Now if one could exist in the gospel dispensation he must certainly be set apart in the same manner as the law directs in order that his acts might be legal. And a more serious ~~t~~ difficulty is that no Gentile or stranger could hold the office or administer its rites in any case, for it is stated positively five times in the Bible that he should die if he did. Num 3:9, 10, 38. 1:51. 18:3, 7, 22, 32. 16:40.[34]

And then I would ask how a high Priest of the law age, and one of the Gospel dispensation could both exist and operate together at the same time? One would assuredly minister the law of Moses, (he would know nothing else,) but the other's ministrations would certainly be the gos-

33. McLellin added "of the Gospel,"

34. Originally McLellin listed only five verses, but later added Num. 3:9; 18:3, 22, 32.

pel ordinances. Another difficulty would be the law of Moses could not be operative or be in force among the Gentiles, because it was confined alone to Israel. Again, no priesthood after being rightly set up can exist "in part only," but must have all its orders in their proper places in order to properly perform all its functions.

The Aaronic priesthood had three orders viz. High Priest, Chief priests, & Levites. Christ's order must be as perfect, it too must have three orders viz. Elders, Priests, and Teachers, or Elders, Bishops, and Deacon. The Aronic was a type of Christ's order. But again, if any priesthood exists it must have all its orders. The hood in Moses' day [page 17:] embraced three orders, and if the three orders do not exist then the hood is incomplete. It is in vain to pretend to have any priesthood without all its regular orders in it, and for any people to pretend to have the Aaronic priesthood among them and not have the three orders in working order is simply null and void.

The law of Moses points out precisely how the Aaronic ministry must be consecrated and set apart. Now every priest of that order must be so ordained & and[35] placed in their office as the law directs or otherwise their acts are illegal. And if the three orders do not exist then the priesthood is incomplete, hence cannot minister in all the laws of the order, or of the dispensation in which they live.

Priesthood means authority and power from God, and it includes a set of ministers to perform its duties. In Christ's order there are Apostles, Prophets, Elders, Bishops, and Deacons. All the ministers have their specific stations and duties, each one in his own office. An Apostle is a witness. His duty is to preach the gospel, to bear testimony of Christ and of his system of salvation. To tell what he knows. His evidence is of what he has seen, heard, and felt. His knowledge is within himself–not second handed. He stands in the most important relation to God of any minister in the priesthood. His office contains within it all the authority of all the other offices, whose duties are not so honorous as his. He may legally act in either or any of them. But the other ministers cannot act legally in any office superior to their own.

The Prophetic calling is to see the future and describe it. Tell of coming events. To give the people a "Thus saith the Lord." They were held responsible to do the mandates of the Lord, and it mattered not as to circumstances they must act as bidden; and all their acts legally performed were valid. ~~Eldrs~~ Elders, Bishops, and Deacon's duties were to

---

35. McLellin wrote an "&" at the end of one line and "and" at the beginning of the next.

minister the gospel, and attend to its ordinances, and to all the duties of church service.

Priesthood, knighthood, and brotherhood always means more than one in order to constitute a hood. Hence priesthood must have an order of ministers in it in order to be such. Hood is condition, quality, or character. It means fixedness and totality. When the word is applied to Priests it means an order or company of them. No hood can exist without an association to constitute it. It must have a number of individuals in it. One man cant be an association; because it requires an order of ministers to establish it as such. Aaron's priesthood had three specific orders in it, and no more. Christ's ministry had just three orders in it and no more. So the law ministry was a shadow, a semblance, or a figure of the true order of Christ's.

Such words as less, lesser, or greater is never used in inspired language in reference to priesthood, because ~~the~~ two priesthoods[36] cannot exist together any more than the firstborn and the Aaronic could. When the Levitical or Aaronic order was set up all the first born were offset and paired off by the Levites, and the overplus of the first born paid five sheckels a piece to Aaron or rather into the treasury and that redeemed them. And that order of the first born was never introduced among any peole thereafter, any more than the Patriarchal authority remained in force after Moses set up the [page 18:] first born of all the families of Israel.

Whenever a new or a different priesthood was set up then the old or former one was always set aside, while the incoming one was in existence. Such has always been the Lord's course when dealing with priesthood. Hence when Christ introduced his order the Aaronic was entirely set aside—abrogated forever. No existence of its legal ministrations can thereafter be found in any inspired book. The law being fulfilled and set aside that priesthood had to die also.

First then we have the Patriarchal priesthood viz. the first born of the reigning family, who received the birth right from his father. Then we have the first born of the families of all Israel. Then the Aaronic came in, which terminated when Christ's order was set up. Each order ended when the new one was established. It was so with the Patriarchal, and with Moses' first born; and if it was not so with the Aaronic then the Lord must have established a new precedent and law in his dealing among men. I boldly assert that the Lord never had two priesthoods in

36. McLellin added "priesthoods,"

operation in his Church of God or Church of Christ at one and the same time since the world began, as evidenced by any inspired book. Such thing as two priesthoods existing at one time[37] would be an anomily in God's kingdom.

Priesthood is divine authority given directly to its possessor from God, and, it was always bestowed, in all past time by direct revelation. No priesthood was ever established but in that way. Any man or set of men who claim to be ministers of the Lord without their ministerial authority [being] derived directly from God is simply assumption and a nulity. He is only man educated, man called, man ordained, and man sent out to preach and to minister; hence it is all manism and nothing more. All the churches they build up and rule over are only man-made, but no power from God shown forth among them; it is all ceremony and simple performence of men and nothing more.

But after a true priesthood is established among a people they may fall from it, and l[o]se all its powers. It was thus with the Patriarchal authority. It seems to have been done away long before Moses' day. The priesthood of Jesus was rightly and properly set up by him and his apostles, but in Catholicism [page 19:] its authority ~~its authority~~ has been lost to the world by "Transgressing the laws, changing the ordinances, and breaking the everlasting covenant" [cf. Isa. 24:5].

As Catholic religion exists today with all its ceremonies and mummeries, it has fallen from the original pattern of the gospel plan and is only trickery of men. They have introduced nine orders of ministers among them, instead of three, ~~wlch~~ which was Christ's number; and they officially changed the ordinance of baptism from immersion to sprinkling, by their assumed authority. And they have many performances among them that is pure foolery, mearly to fascinate their followers. And they have mixed up the doctrine of Christianity with Paganism that a man could scarcely find or pick out the pure truth of heaven.

And Protestantism has improved but little on their old Mother! All their authority is derived directly from the Catholics, or it is assumed. God has not authorised their priestly authority, or in fact not any authority in Protesta[n]tism. Their preachers dont seem to know or care any thing about priesthood, or the true order of heaven. I do not know of any popular sect among them all that claims direct authority from God, by any new revelation. God is mum relative to all their ministry or priestly authority. They claim their call and authority as ministers be-

37. McLellin added "as two priesthoods existing at one time,"

cause of impression. But impression gives no direct knowledge from God. Without some kind of language no intelligence can be given or received. Impression without signs of some kind gives no sense. All men think or form ideas by means of words or images; so that God nor man can think or speak without words or symbols of some sort. Language must be used in order to give any instruction. And any language from God would be a new revelation. And to claim that would spoil their religion; because they say the Bible contains all things ~~all things~~ nescessary for man's salvation; and that God will never reveal to man any thing more than is in that Book. This is Protestantism. This is sectarianism. They all worship a dumb God! For if God cannot nor will not speak, he certainly is not the God of the Bible. [page 20:]

But the Catholics claim infallibility for the Ecumenical councils, and also for their Popes. If the Lord has ministerial authority on the earth he can and will reveal himself to them, as in olden times, and let them know the truth, and also open up the future to them and "Show them things to come" [cf. John 16:13]. He told Noah there was a flood coming; he told Abram to "Get thee out of thy country, and from thy kindred +++ unto a land that I will show thee" [Gen. 12:1]. He said to Lot by his angels, "Escape for thy life" [Gen. 19:17]. And Lot fled to Zoar. Jesus said, "As it was in the days of Noah and of Lot, even thus shall it be in the day when the Son of man is revealed" [cf. Luke 17:26, 28, 30]. These men were warned by the Lord and his angels and escaped. Now if before Christ's second coming he does not warn the world by immediate revelation, by his own vocal voice, and by his glorified angels it will not be as it was with Abram with Noah, and with Lot. To all such as do not have direct communion Jesus will come to them as a thief in the night.

Before Christ makes his second appearance in the world he will establish a order[38] priesthood with whom he will hold direct converse as with Noah and Lot, and they will warn the world of the coming calamities and judgements that will overtake the wicked; and all the wicked will be burned with fire and brimstone as the people of Sodom and Gomorrow was, and there will be no escape. The Psamist says, "The Lord forsaketh not his saints; they are preserved forever: but the seed of the wicked shall be cut off" [Ps. 37:28]. And Moses prophesied that "all the wicked should be cut off from among the people" [cf. Lev. 20:17]. And Malachi said "And the day that cometh shall burn them up, saith the Lord of hosts" [Mal. 4:1]. All this destruction and burning

38. McLellin added "order,"

will be because man lost the Priesthood of Jesus Christ, and went about to establish their own righteousness, and did not submit to the righteousness of God—ceased to commune direct with him. Wo to the world because they have lost the true priesthood, and hence communion with our Father in heaven. O that man would learn his best interest! ~ Go to page 28.[39] [page 28:]

Moses neglected or set aside the Patriarchal priesthood or authority entirely in his setting up of the first-born priesthood among the Israelites. Ex 13:2. This first-born priesthood preached the gospel to all Israel, as well as it was preached in the day of the Apostles. Heb. 4:2. And then when Israel rebelled this first-born priesthood was set aside—carried off with the Levites and was never heard of any more in the world among any people. The Aaronic was set up and established in Israel, and remained in full authority until Christ came, then he introduced his own order, the order of the Son of God, and entirely set aside the Aaronic order, as much so as Moses did the Patriarchal and the first-born. ~ Two priesthoods could not exist and be in force at one and the same time among any people; any more than the first-born and the Aaronic could exist together. No priesthood was ever an appendage to another, as they could [not] exist together. Each hood while it existed was always independent in its authority. No such words as greater or less is used in inspired language in reference to priesthood, hence I discard them. Each priesthood while it existed held direct authority from God, and was not under any control from any other source. It was the highest authority from God while it existed, hence none other could exist with it. The Patriarchal dw[elled] alone, the first-born was alone, and so was the Aaronic. But when Christ set up his order it was independent. It was the order of the Son of God, and needed no help. It had all the [illegible]. Nothing in spiritual things need exist when there is no necessity [illegible] its existence. Hence no necessity for the Aaronic order of Priests. [Return to] Page 20. [page 21:]

Spiritual gifts and powers.[40]

"Now there are diversities of gifts, but the same Spirit—dividing to every man severally as he will. To one is given by the Spirit the word of

39. McLellin wrote "Go to page 28" because he had more thoughts on the subject and the nearest available space was the bottom third of page 28, the content of which is added here.

40. Porter, "Odyssey of McLellin," 377n324, says this portion of the notebook "is an undated explication of the gifts of wisdom, knowledge, faith, healing, miracles, prophecy,

wisdom; to another the word of knowledge by the same Spirit" [cf. 1 Cor. 12:4, 8, 11].

[Noah] Webster says, "Wisdom is the capacity of making the best use of knowledge. It is discernment and judgement, so as to use the best means and the best ends to accomplish an object. It is to use knowledge to the best purpose." There is such a thing as the direct gift of wisdom by the Spirit of God. And that gift is to enable the saints to understand all things. Solomon says, "The Lord layeth up sound wisdom for the righteous" [Prov. 2:7]. It would seem from this that the righteous only can have pure wisdom, because he says the fear of Lord is the beginning of knowledge and wisdom. He says again, "I wisdom dwell with prudence, and find out knowledge["] [Prov. 8:12]. Wisdom and knowledge are so intimately connected that I will treat of them together.

When we accumulate knowledge we want wisdom to know how to use it properly. Knowledge is the accumulation of facts in the mind, then we want wisdom to know how to put those facts to a good proper purpose. There is much said in the Scriptures of wisdom, knowledge, and understanding. The Lord planted the tree of knowledge in midst of the garden of Eden, the eating the fruit of which, was the cause of our first parents fall. Still the eating that fruit gave them some knowledge. It is said of Solomon, "And the Lord gave Solomon wisdom and understanding exceeding much, and largeness of heart even as the sand that is upon the sea shore; for he was wiser than all men" [cf. 1 Kgs. 4:29, 31]. This was saying a great deal of any one man, but in the first part of his reign he surely manifested it. Again it is said, "Wise men lay up knowledge" [Prov. 10:14]. That is, they accumulate it in abundence. "Wisdom excelleth folly, as far as light excelleth darkness" [Eccl. 2:13]. "Man's wisdom maketh his face to shine" [Eccl. 8:1], like Moses face did when he came down from the mountain, and had to put a veil over his face, that the Israelites could look upon him. If a man is filled with wisdom, knowledge, and spiritual understanding he is prepared for all the changes of this inconstant world.

Paul said to the Romans, "Ye are filled with all knowledge" [Rom. 15:14]. And to the Corinthians he said, "That in every thing ye are enriched by Christ, in all utterance, and in all knowledge" [cf. 1 Cor. 1:5]. Knowledge and wisdom seem to have been great and grand motives,

---

discerning spirits, speaking in tongues (which he here claims should be used only if persons present do not understand the tongue spoken), and beholding angels. McLellin emphasizes the need for direct ministration of the Father, the Son, the Holy Spirit, or other intelligences in heaven."

placed before the minds of believers to induce them to rigorous action in the Christian life to obtain them. But the teaching of the preachers (of what is called,) the Christian world today deny to man the right or privilege to obtain knowledge or wisdom direct from God, by any mode by which the ancients obtained it. Although the apostle said to true believers in his day, "If any of you lack wisdom, let him ask of God, that giveth to all men liberally, and upbraideth not; and it shall be given him" [James 1:5]. No plainer scripture can be found in all God's [page 22:] word. It says "it shall be." And who is stronger than the Lord? Or who is mightyer than the Spirit of truth? Or who may turn aside his councils, and say, it shall not be? No plainer promise can be given than is given here, and why true believers may not obtain that for which they should plead I cannot see.

3. <u>To another the gift of faith by the same Spirit</u> [cf. 1 Cor. 12:9].[41]

The gift of faith is something peculiar. It cannot be exercised only upon one principle, only in one way, and that is, by a direct immediate vision or revelation from the Lord. It comes in no other way. It comes right at the end of that view. The believing man waits, stands still until the Lord speaks–until the Lord directs, then and not till then does the power of the "gift of faith" spring up in the soul. Its immediate, its direct; therefore it is called "the gift of faith." The angel of the Lord said to Philip, "Arise, and go toward the south–and he arose and went" [Acts 8:26-27]. But why go? Because he had the gift of faith in the word spoken. And ["]the Spirit said to Philip, Go near, and join thyself to this chariot. And Philip ran thither["] [Acts 8:29-30]. Because he strongly believed. He had the gift of faith in the Spirit's word. This was an immediate exercise of faith because of immediate revelation to him. But without a Thus saith the Lord, no man ever yet had the "gift of faith."

No Catholic or Sectarian can ever possibly possess or exercise the gift of faith, who believes that the Bible contains all things necessary for life and salvation. Because it requires a new revelation to every one who can exercise that gift. And without that gift in the full exercise of it, when Christ makes his second appearance, no flesh will or can be saved to enter the Millennium. This gift of faith is different from the common exercise of faith upon [im]mediate testimony. It springs up only on immediate evidence, conveyed to the mind directly from God.

41. Though he does not specifically number them, McLellin intended the first two gifts to be wisdom and knowledge.

4. To another the gift of healing, by the same Spirit [cf. 1 Cor. 12:9].

This gift was marvelously bestowed on the Lord Jesus Christ. No afflicted person ever came to him and went away without being restored.[42] It also rested on the Apostles and Elders of the Church of Christ to a wonderful extent. Stephen and Philip did great healings as well as the Apostles. The religion of the Lord Jesus was intended to bless both the bodies and the souls of men. The bodies when sick, and the souls when sorrowful. Hence the object was to bless man kind temporally and spiritually. ~~Jesus~~ James says, "Is any among you afflicted? let him pray" [James 5:13]. O yes, say professed Christians all believe when afflicted they ought to pray. That's a duty specially enjoined, certainly commanded. Again, ["]is any merry? let him sing Psalms["] [James 5:13]–Paul says, ["]singing and making melody in your hearts to the Lord" [cf. Eph. 5:19]. O say professors, we love to sing the songs of Zion. But again, "Is any sick among you? let him call for the Elders of the Church; and let them pray over him, anointing him with oil in the name of the [page 23:] Lord: and the prayr of faith shall save the sick, and the Lord shall raise him up; and if he have committed sins, they shall be forgiven him. Confess your faults one to another, and pray one for another, that you may be healed. The effectual fervent prayr of a righteous man availeth much" [James 5:14-16]. Jesus said in speaking of believers in the gospel, "They shall lay hands on the sick, and they shall recover" [Mark 16:18]. Now for the life of me I cant see why this mandate of heaven is not obeyed in the churches today, provided they are really Christians. No language could be plainer, or more positive. He shall pray if afflicted–Sing if merry–send for the Elders if sick: and do all in the name of the Lord Jesus Christ, and by his direct authority in his word; and then get well by the simple means used.

5. To another the working of miracles [1 Cor. 12:10].

Webster says, ["]A miracle is an effect contrary to the established course of things, or a deviation from the known laws of nature; a supernatural effect. A thing effected by a direct agency of Almighty power, and not by natural causes." This definition suits us very well.

A miracle is something performed by some intelligent being by the power of his faith in some other personage. There are two sources of miracles. One from good and the other from evil power. Satanic power

42. McLellin ignored the statement in Mark that Jesus was not able to perform any miracles (evidently due to the unbelief of the people): "And he could there do no mighty work, save that he laid his hands upon a few sick folk, and healed them" (Mark 6:5). This revealing passage was omitted by Luke and toned down in Matt. 13:58.

has worked miracles, and will in the future, with great strides of evil power. Paul in speaking of the second coming of Christ, says, The evil One "shall work with all power" [cf. 2 Thes. 2:9]. That is with all the power that is within his grasp, with all that he has ever exercised in the world. His power will be so great in performing wonders that the world will be enamored with the displays; and even the Kings of earth will run after Satanic ministers on account of their prodigies.

I have heard it declared lately by a very popular preacher that God would bring in and establish the Millennium mearly by the proclamation and force of the gospel truths without any supernatural agency. But if so I cant understand the prophets. Isaiah says, "The Lord shall utterly destroy the tongue of the Egyptian sea; and with his mighty ~~hand~~ wind shall he shake his hand over the river, and shall smite it in the seven streams, and make men go over dry shod. And there shall be a highway for the remnant of his people." 11:15[-16]. Also 35:[4,] 5, 6. He says, "The Lord will come and save you["]—evidently speaking of his second coming. ["]Then the eyes of the blind shall be opened, and the ears of the deaf shall be unstopped. Then shall the lame man leap as a hart, and the tongue of the dumb sing: for in the wilderness shall waters break out, and streams in the desert."

Jeremiah says, "Behold, the days come saith the Lord, that it shall no more be said, The Lord liveth, that brought up the children of Israel out of the land of Egypt; but the Lord liveth, that brought them up from the land of the north, and from all countries whither I had driven them; and they shall dwell in their own land, that I gave unto their fathers." [cf.] Jer. 16:14, 15. [page 24:]

When Israel came from Egypt there were great displays of power. Great miracles were performed, but the displays in bringing Israel from their long home will so far eclipse all the displays and miracles wrought on their way from Egypt to Canaan, that it will not even be mentioned in comparison. Talk about miracles then in the wonderful displays in Israel's coming from their northern land back to the land of their fathers. There will be miraculous wonders displayed beyond any thing the world has ever yet seen. All these marvelous works will be performed in order to fit the world for Millennial rest.

Jesus said, "These signs shall follow them that believe; In my name shall they cast out Devils; they shall speak with new tongues; they shall take up serpents and if they drink any deadly thing, it shall not hurt them; they shall lay hands on the sick, and they shall recover." Mar[k]. 16:17, 18. This Scripture is to[o] plain to need comment. I will only refer to one more miracle, to Elisha making iron to swim upon the water. 2 Kings 6:6. But there were hundreds of miracles performed by Patriarchs, by Seers, by Prophets, by Jesus Christ, by Apostles, and by Elders. And an important question is by what power were they done? The answer is, "To another the working of miracles, by the Spirit of God" [cf. 1 Cor. 12:9-10]. The Spirit was the direct agent, the direct power in the performance of all miracles the world has ever ~~saw~~ seen.

6. To another the gift of prophecy [cf. 1 Cor. 12:10].

Webster says, "A prophet, is one who prophesies, or foretells events; a predicter; a foreteller. Prophecy. To utter predictions, a declaration of something to come; a foretelling; a prediction; especially, an inspired foretelling." This is the light I think in which all enlightened men ought to look at it, to look at a prophet as a man who can "tell of things to come." Bring up unborn events, and tell them plainly. Such were Moses, Elijah, Isaiah, and Daniel. It is said, "Prophecy came not in olden time by the will of man; but holy men of God spake as they were moved by the Holy Ghost" [2 Pet. 1:21]. This is the clearest declaration to be found in Holy Writ relative to the nature of prophecy. Men of God moved to speak, and what they spoke was the Word of God. No man can recive and deliver prophecy mearly of his own will, he in order to know the future must be moved by the Holy Ghost. He must have the knowledge of the Most High in visions and revelations. "He must see the vision of the Almighty, falling into a trance, but having his eyes open." [cf.] Num 24:16.

If a person has no experience in visions and revelations he can only imagine respecting the manner of the prophets, but his imagination may run at random without certainty. But true prophets always knew when God moved them. But to understand all the spirits that rankled in the wor[l]d, and to know true prophets from false ones, required experience, and deep knowledge in the things of God. They must have a knowledge of the spiritual gifts of the Gospel themselves. Must get into a frame of mind to see, hear, and feel spiritual things. I look upon the gift of prophecy to be the most important of any gift ~~of any~~ God has to bestow on man. Paul said, "For greater is he that prohesieth, than he that speaketh in tongues" [1 Cor. 14:5]. [page 25:]

The gift of prophecy was in the world with holy men, from the days of Adam until the days of Christ. And when Jesus Christ established his system of religion among men, the intention was to make all believers prophets, both men and women. Joel's prophesy rehearsed by Peter said, "And on my servants and on my handmaidens I will pour out in those days of my Spirit; and they shall prophesy." Acts 2:18. And Paul said to a Church of believers, "For ye may all prophecy one by one, that all may learn, and all may be comforted." 1 Cor. 14:31. John the apostle said, or rather an angel said to John, "For the testimony of Jesus is the Spirit of prophecy." Rev 19:10. Joel said, men and women shall prophesy, and Paul said all believers might prophecy, and the holy angel said, the testimony of Jesus is the true spirit of prophecy. And Jesus said, the Comforter "should show them things to come." John 16:13. Now with all this before me, I cant but believe in the gift of prophecy now—in my day to believers. Hence well might Paul say, "To another the gift of prophecy, and all may prophecy" [cf. 1 Cor. 12:10; 14:31].

7. To another the gift of discerning spirits [cf. 1 Cor. 12:10].

We apply to Webster again. "To discern is to perceive with the mind; to apprehend with distinctness. To perceive; to distinguish; discover; penetrate; discriminate; espy; descry. The power or faculty of the mind by which it distinguishes one thing from another. Discernment is accuracy and keenness of mental vision."

It is the prescience of the Almighty resting on the man, to cause him to see and discern between truth and error, between light and darkness. To see by the true, pure Spirit of discernment, as the Lord sees into the mind of a person, into his spirit, to know what exists there; as Peter saw the heart, spirit, and mind of Ananias, then of Sapphira, his wife, to know they lied to the Holy Ghost. It is for a man to be so inspired of the Spirit as to not be deceived by hypocrites. It is to see the interior workings of the spirits and minds of persons, who come before the inspired man, so as to know and declare their fate for good or for evil. This gift of discernment is a very important gift in the house of God, in the "true Church of Christ," to enable the Lord's ministers to see and know what is before them in their ministry. It is said of Jesus that he "perceived and discerned the thoughts of their hearts." [cf.] Luke 9:47. This was prescience in him, this was God given, this was the true discerning of spirits, this way seeing even the thoughts, and their interior workings.

When Elisha was in Dothan and the king of Syria had sent his army and surrounded Dothan in the night[43] Elisha's young man, very early in the morning, saw this host; he was frightened and said, Alas, my master! how shall we do? But Elisha said, Fear not: and he ["]prayed and said, Lord I pray thee open his eyes that he may see. And the Lord opened his eyes; and he saw: and Behold, the mountain was full of horses and chari-

43. McLellin added "in the night,"

ots of fire round about Elisha.["] [cf.] 2 K[gs.] 6:17. This was pure discernment, pure seeing by the gift of the Spirit. When Elisha came to Damascus and saw Hazael, he settled his countenance upon him [page 26:] and wept, seeing, yes, discerning the evil that Hazael would do to Israel in the future. Elisha stood and viewed him and was so grieved that he could not restrain his tears; discerning by the gift of the Spirit the wickedness that lay deep in Hazael's heart. This was looking deeply not only into man's spirit and heart, but into his future life, and discerning his acts, perceiving truly what was to be the man's future course. This was the gift of discernment of Spirit in truth and verity.

8. <u>To another the gift of divers kinds of tongues</u> [cf. 1 Cor. 12:10].

For long ages after the world was created the human family had only one tongue, one language, one lip; and that was what we call the <u>pure language</u>. This tongue was used from Adam down to the tower of Babel. There confusion of language commenced. Thereafter different languages or tongues were spoken; and they still continue to be spoken at the present day. When language was confounded and tongues were introduced it was then as it is now, no one could understand one another's speech. All was confusion, all was jargon among the people. It must have been to them a strange medley of things. And the people [were] awfully disappointed about their great Town they were erecting in order to reach heaven, or in order to escape another flood. From this place they emigrated to different countries, and built up separate communities or kingdoms.

But the time will come when as Paul said, "Whether there be tongues, they shall cease" [1 Cor. 13:8]. And Zephaniah says, "Therefore wait ye upon me, saith the Lord, until the day that I rise up to the prey: for my determination is to gather the nations, that I may assemble the kingdoms, to pour upon them mine indignation, even all my fierce anger: for all the earth shall be devoured with the fire of my jealousy. For then will I turn to the people a pure language, that they may all call upon the name of the Lord, to serve him with one consent." Zeph 3:8, 9.

But while tongues remain, and are spoken it will be necessary to spend much time in schools to learn them, and then there are hundreds of tongues that cannot be learned in schools. Then there must be a direct "gift of tongues" from the Spirit of the Lord in order to understand or speak them. Hence in looking at this subject Paul said, "to another is given the gift of tongues" [cf. 1 Cor. 12:10], that these people may hear the gospel—the glad sound of salvation. This gift would enable persons to "preach the gospel with the Holy Ghost sent down from heaven" [cf. 1 Pet. 1:12]. Then the gospel would take effect among the heathen, because it would be preached in power, in demonstration by inspired ministers. The gift of tongues would be all important to all missionaries.

On the day of Pentecost when the apostles and disciples were endowed with power from on high, "the gift of tongues" was given to them in a marvelous degree. [page 27:] They spoke to the assembled multitude in some sixteen different dialects. "They were all filled with the Holy Ghost, and began to speak with other tongues, as the Spirit gave them utterence. The people being amazed said one to another; How hear we every man in our own tongue, wherein we were born, speak the wonderful works of God. And they were all amazed, and were in doubt, saying, one to another, What meaneth this?["] [cf. Acts 2:4, 7-8, 11-12.]

This was about as great a display as was seen at Babel when the language was confused. Jesus in some of his last words speaking to believers said, "They shall speak with new tongues" [Mark 16:17]. And Paul said, "God hath set in the church, diversities of tongues" [1 Cor. 12:28]. He said again, "I would that ye all spake with tongues" [1 Cor. 14:5]. And also that, "Tongues are for a sign to unbelievers" [cf. 1 Cor. 14:22]. I have one thing to say about the gift of tongues. No man ought to speak in tongues unless there is a person or persons present who do not understand the tongue spoken. Even then he should not speak unless there is an interpreter present. The object of tongues is to have all instructed who are present.

9. To another the gift of interpretation of tongues [cf. 1 Cor. 12:10].

"To translate into intelligible or familiar terms. To make clear.["] So says Webster. An interpretation expresses a thing in the vernacular tong[u]e, that is spoken in another speech or tongue. Instance, a man speaks in German or French to an English audience, and a man is present who knows the three languages, and speaks or interprets what is spoken to the audience. This is called interpretation. But this is not what Paul calls the gift of interpretation. This gift was and is by a direct power of the Spirit of God upon the mind of the interpreter, revealing to him precisely what was said, so that he unfolds to those present what is spoken. But all this must be under the immediate inspiration of the Holy Spirit. Must be by immediate divine communication.

All the gifts of the Spirit were supernatural operations by a direct influance, a direct gift. They come immeddiately from God at the time needed, at the time they are used. And unless the minister is holy enough to have the Spirit in his own heart no effect follows. Hence hypocrites and ungodly persons have no control over the spiritual gifts. They are designed for believers only. Jesus said, "These signs shall follow them that believe" [Mark 16:17]. Believers are the persons benefitted.

Interpretation is a wonderful gift of the Spirit, so as to enable a man to understand any tongue, language, or speech spoken so as to change or translate it into the tongue or language that is usually spoken, or used by those present in the church or assembly; and to do so without stopping to learn it, but do so by an immediate direct impulse of that unseen Spirit. When a man speaks in an unknown tongue, the interpreter listens then he speaks by the power of the same Spirit in interpreted language to those present. Its all done by the direct inspiration of the Spirit of truth. Hence interpretation is as great or greater gift than for an inspired Prophet to receive and deliver a "Thus saith the Lord." [page 28:]

And again to another the beholding of Angels, & ministering Spirits [Moro. 10:14].

There are three classes of intelligences in heaven. 1. The Father, the Son, and the Holy Spirit; constituting the Godhead. 2. Eternal unimbodied Spirits; constituting intelligences, entities, and identities. 3. Angels or ["]Spirits of just men made perfect["] [Heb. 12:23]. Angels are beings that have been translated or resurrected from earth, and glorified in heaven. When they visit the earth they always come with some message for mortals. When that is deliverd they return to their home in heaven. They then wait until another mandate is given, then with swiftness they pass out to deliver it. Much is said about angels in holy Writ, and they always appear as tangible beings; so that they eat and drank material food on earth with men; thus showing that they were once men.

An angel messenger said to Hag[a]r in the wilderness, "I will multiply thy seed exceedingly, that it shall not be numbered for multitude." Here the names angel, Lord, and God are given to this messenger. Gen. 16:10. When Joshua was at Jeric[h]o, a messenger appeared to him, with a drawn sword in his hand, and ["]Joshua said to him, Art thou for us, or for our adversaries? And he said, Nay; but as captain of the Lord's host am I now come.["] [cf.] Jos 5:[13-]14. Angels are ["]all ministering spirits, sent forth to minister for them who shall be heirs of salvation.["] Heb. 1:14. Multitudes of angels have left the shining courts above and came to earth to visit men and women, and deliver intelligent messages. A multitude of the heavenly host once sang on the hills of Judea, "Glory to God in the highest, and on earth peace, good will toward men" [Luke 2:14]. The book speaks of an "innumerable company of Angels" [Heb. 12:22]. [page 10a:]

The Lord Jesus Christ.[44]

Christ from eternity possessed or existed in a spirit-form, but he laid aside his glory to be veiled in flesh—to be born of a woman, or for his body to be born. By taking a body he allied himself very nearly unto man's nature. He took upon him a part of mortality, hence subject unto death. I am aware that many religionists say and profess to believe that Jesus Christ had two whole and perfect spirits existing in his body. A whole man and a whole Christ. The God and a whole man united—that is, that the man took in the Christ, and hence that he had a human spirit and body and then Christ inherited that perfect man as a tenant at will. But if so the man in which Christ dwelt could have lived alone without him entirely; because he was a perfect man without Christ: this being so, I can see nothing but a human sacrifice in the Savior's death. They say again that God did not nor could not suffer.

But if the divine Deity did not suffer then the atonement was not infinite nor meritorious! Hence the world will need another Redeemer. But if Jesus Christ had two spirits—the human and the divine, man must have the same likewise, for our Lord "took on him the form of a servant, and was made in the likeness of men. He was found in fashion as a man" [Philip. 2:7-8], and still further, "Wherefore in all things it behooved him to be made like unto his brethren" [Heb. 2:17]. Man has but one spirit and one natural body, and Jesus Christ had just the same. Christ, the Word, the Anointed was the soul, the spirit, the divine, the living principle, the intelligent inner man that dwelt in and animated the body of Jesus. He had not two souls or spirits for that would be an anomily. [page 10b:]

Jesus Christ had but one spirit and one body, and when he died he said, "Father into thy hands I commend my spirit: and having said this he gave up the ghost" [Luke 23:46]. He did not have two spirits to commend, nor two ghosts i.e. spirits to yield up. But the body of Jesus gave or yielded up the Christ. The spirit of Jesus left his body as our spirits leave our bodies in dying i.e. the spirit leaves the body as I would leave a

44. This four-page essay, entitled "The Lord Jesus Christ," is actually located in the middle of Notebook Three between pages 10 and 11. The four pages, made from one folded sheet, were numbered 10a-10d by the LDS Historical Department, but the text is placed here for continuity.

house in which I had dwelt. The body gave up the Word, the Messiah; who had glory with his Father in vast eternity.

When Christ came into the world he said, "A body hast thou prepared me" [Heb. 10:5]. Prepared for the Word that was God. The body held the intelligent interior man, the Christ placed within. But not a body and a spirit for him to dwell in. His body was the tabernacle of the Christ. The three, the body, the soul or spirit containing a mind co[n]stituted the man Christ Jesus. No double meaning here. No blending of human and divine spirits in one person, so as to constitute life in order to make a Savior. There is no mystery in all this, but deep and abiding mysteries attend all other theories on this important subject. There is no such thing as a human spirit; all spirits are divine.

Jesus had no more spirits than man because he was made precisely as man, "He was found in fashion as a man, he humbled himself and became obedient unto death, even the death of the cross" [Philip. 2:8]. He humbled himself because he was made in the likeness of men.

"And the Word was God. Jesus thought it not robbery to be equal with God" [cf. John 1:1; Philip. 2:6], but ~~made~~ became obedient unto death. I ask who died? Did the Word who was God–equal with God die? Did the divine being die? What is death except a separation of body and spirit? Did Christ, the Word pass through death, pass through all the agonies and pains of death in the seperation of spirit and body in dying? Then it follows that God, the Son suffered in dying. It was the Christ the[45] spirit and mind that suffered. [page 10c:] Jesus said, "My soul is exceeding sorrowful, even unto death: and his sweat was as it were great drops of blood falling down to the ground" [Matt. 26:38; Luke 22:44]. It was the agony and keen suffering of the inner man, the Christ the spirit of Jesus that caused "bloody sweat to fall down."

John said, "The Word was made flesh and dwelt among us" [John 1:14]. And Paul said, "God was manifest in the flesh" [1 Tim. 3:16].[46] Now I want to know something of this indwelling, whether that that was made flesh, or manifest in the flesh dwelt in a body and spirit or a body only? The apostle says, "Wherefore, when he cometh into the world he sayeth, a body hast thou prepared me" [Heb. 10:5]. But not a body and a

45. McLellin added "Christ the,"

46. McLellin correctly quoted the King James Version, but most biblical scholars and modern translations follow the earliest available Greek, "he who was manifest in the flesh." Though it turns on a single horizontal mark, the KJV changed the personal pronoun, ΟΣ, to a reference to God, θΣ. See Leon Vaganay, *An Introduction to New Testament Textual Criticism*, 2d ed. rev., ed. Christian-Bernard Amphoux and Jenny Heimerdinger (Cambridge: Cambridge University Press, 1991), 56.

spirit—a whole man, because Christ was the spirit which inhabited and animated that body of flesh and bones. I conceive of Christ in his body precisely in the same sense as my spirit exists in, inhabits and animates my body.

When Jesus said I, me, and mine I conceive only the interior person of the body speaking. I do not think of two distinct, intelligent spirits talking, one human and the other divine. There are no human spirits in existence. A human body in life possesses a spirit but it is a divine being, and can be tempted because it has a mortal body with passions and appetites. I think of Christ personally just as I do of man possessing only one spirit and one body.

I cant conceive or think of a pair of double spirits in Christ when he went to Paradise—going to Paradise together as only one person. In that case Christ must have been two persons if there was two intelligent spirits. How he[47] could ~~he~~ be but one being in that case I cant see. How a human spirit and divine spirit could constitute but one person. Again, if Jesus Christ had two spirits those spirits had two minds, for all spirits have minds. Hence he was not one Christ but two. The human spirit had a mind and the divine spirit also, hence I must think Christ was a double being in spirit and mind both, altogether different from man. [page 10d:]

Christ went to Paradise as only one spiritual being, not accompanied unaccompanied or rather unassociated[48] by a human spirit. As Christ existed before he took a human body, so he lived in Paradise, when separated from his body. He was a whole Christ in Heaven, he was a whole Christ in Paradise, and then he was a whole Christ as the Mediator after his resurrection, and now lives in heaven in his body of flesh and bones, but has no human spirit with him or in his person[49] there. This idea of Jesus Christ possessing a human and a divine spirit[50] is the greatest vagary of which the mind can conceive. It destroys my Savior entirely for me. It destroys his life in the flesh, it destroys his atonement, it destroys his redemption for man, and his existence and enjoyment in heaven.

But if Christ existed in a separate and perfectly formed man, with a body and a spirit, and that man thus formed could have existed alone without Christ in him, then that man or being must either be saved or

47. McLellin added "he,"

48. McLellin added "unaccompanied or rather unassociated" but his original wording "not accompanied" was not deleted.

49. McLellin added "or in his person,"

50. McLellin added "spirit,"

lost, by obeying the gospel, as any other man. Jesus could not, by proxy, be saved for him. His salvation was an individual thing; unless by Christ dwelling in him gave him a right to heaven. And if he was a perfect man without Christ in him, then he must have had all the attributes and faculties of a man; could talk, eat, drink, and sleep: but is it the theory that Jesus Christ did all this by proxy for him?

Does he and Christ both live together in heaven now as a double being, or is he a single Christ? And if the man, in whom he dwelt, and Christ are both saved, is Christ saved in the man, or is the man saved in Christ; and do they now dwell together in heaven? Does the body that was prepared for Christ still exist in glory as the Christ, or has it (what is called,) a human spirit and body[51] glorified with him, and are they living in heaven double? They could as easily live double there as here. This double dealing I cant understand, I cant get it into my mind endwise nor edgewise. But I can think of Christ taking a body as my spirit took my body, and then living in it, and dying in it, and resurrect in it, and ascended in it; and now lives in it in heaven. This is my Lord Jesus Christ, my Savior and my Redeemer. There is no double dealing in all my theory of my Savior. An old Methodist preacher told that Christ lived in a perfect man while he lived on earth, but my reasons are all given in this treatise!![52]

---

51. McLellin added "and body,"

52. The last sentence, which was written later, appears in a different color ink.

4.

VIEWS ON THE BIBLE, 1877

The Bible
Queries respecting it
In 1877

9. The books copied by uninspired men.

Malachi is said to have lived abut 400 years before Christ, and more than 100 years ~~after~~ before Simon the Just completed the canon and it is said he put the book together very much as we now have them. But there are just as wise, learned, and conscientious men in the Catholic Church, who have some seven more books in the canon of the Douay Bible, than there is in [the] King James translation. Now we ask how an illiterate man can tell who is right or wrong in the make up of books for a canon? [page 31:]

After inspired men, with their inspired word of revelation, had ceased among the Jews, how can we know for a certainty that we or they are right in the collection, or in any collection of inspired books? It is all conjecture! Its all a may be so!! There is much said about Ezra's making up a canon, but it is all conjecture. It is left to us in uncertainty as to

---

Notebook 4 consists mostly of excerpts from other works, while the current presentation is limited to those passages that are most likely original to McLellin, followed by John L. Traughber's comments in a concluding footnote. The title, "Views on the Bible, 1877," is ours. "The Bible: Queries respecting it In 1877" is McLellin's inscription on the cover.

Larry C. Porter summarized the contents of Notebook 4 as "a lengthy 1877 essay about the inspiration, composition, compilation, and translation of the Bible, blaming uninspired scribes and copyists for the many omissions, errors, and discrepancies in this sacred volume of scripture" ("The Odyssey of William Earl McLellin: Man of Diversity, 1806-83," in *The Journals of William E. McLellin, 1831-1836,* ed. Jan Shipps and John W. Welch [Provo and Urbana: BYU Studies and University of Illinois Press, 1994], 377n324). In one instance, on page 104, after quoting Ephraim Chambers's *Cyclopaedia* on "the idea of inspiration[,] it is now admitted by the most enlightened theologians, was progressively developed," McLellin added his own comment: "(It is not true.)"

For more recent scholarship, against which to compare the sources McLellin relies on, we recommend Bart D. Ehrman, *The New Testament: A Historical Introduction to the Early Christian Writings* (New York: Oxford University Press, 1997), and C. Dennis McKinsey, *Encyclopedia of Biblical Errancy* (Amherst, New York: Prometheus Books, 1995).

Ezra's work, or his inspiration either. I am willing to admit that Ezra was a good man, and did much in restoring the Jews back to their promised land again, after their 70 years of captivity, aided very much by Nehemiah. But that he was inspired in gathering together their sacred books; and not only to collect, but as some would vainly imagine re-write them, and bring to light all those misplaced or lost. I cant even imagine, let alone believe from all the testimonies of history and circumstances, and learned men's investigations, that Ezra was inspired to re-write the sacred books i.e. those that were lost, or to collect and put together all king James canon.

And the materials of the men of that age for writing were scanty, especially just after their long captivity, they had not time to make brass or gold plates, on which Jahn[1] says they kept their most sacred records. How they could at that time put papyrus leaves, rolls, of parchment, plates of lead, stones, bricks, Ivory, wood, brass, or gold together so as to form a connected volume, as large as [page 32:] the Bible, is mysterious to me, unless as Jahn says, the plates were put together with rings in the back by which to carry them.[2]

Writing or inscribing with an incision tool, or painting on such materials was very slow and tedious, laborious and expensive. The making of any thing that could be called a book or volume in Ezra's time took a long and tedious time. Still they did have what was called books long prior to the days of Ezra or Simon either. The learned say <u>those men</u> collected and arranged, each in his place, the sacred inspired documents into a volume. But I think those accounts [are] very doubtful, on account of the many difficulties in the way. ~

But after all the labour and expence of gathering up MSS. for the Septuagint, the translators were, no doubt, Alexandrine, but not Palestinian Jews. The internal character of the entire version, particularly of the Penteteuch, sufficiently attests the fact. The division into verses and chapters is much later than the age of the translators. Our present editions have been printed in conformity with the division into chapters made in the 12th C. After the general reception of the Septuagint version, numerous mistakes were made in the transcription and multiplica-

1. For a summary of Johann Jahn's life, see the Biographical Notes.

2. Johann Jahn, *Jahn's Biblical Archaeology,* trans. Thomas C. Upham (New York: Mark H. Newman, 1849), 95-96: "Those books, which were inscribed on tablets of wood, lead, brass, or ivory, were connected together by rings at the back, through which a rod was passed to carry them by." The first English translation of *Jahn's Biblical Archaeology* appeared in 1823.

tion of copies. Origin undertook to regulate all these differences and difficulties, but utterly failed! [page 33:]

We have no substantial reason to believe that either of these men, Ezra or Simon were divinely inspired; hence we say, "The Bible was copied out by uninspired men." And many inspired books and writings of Seers and prophets had been lost or destroyed at the burning of their magnificent Temple by Nebuchadnezzer; and during their long stay in an enemies land, as the following treatise will set forth.

10. The lost inspired books refered to in the Bible.

Here we wish our readers to patiently read and examine the passages refered to, and be satisfied that we are right not only in our quotations, but also in our conclusions....[3] [page 35:]

We will say a few words about the lost books. If we only had all the lost books and inspired writings that were had among the Jews there we would have a fund of knowledge of which we are now deprived. The Jews as a nation were idolaters from the days of Solomon unto the days of Josiah, which was about 400 years; and then again until they were carried away into Babylon; hence they must have been more or less careless about preserving any documents pertaining to the true God, to his true religion, or to his true worship. And when the Jews and their sacred temple were plundered, and [page 36:] their temple burned with its sacred treasures, that had not been robbed, and hundreds of them destroyed, and no doubt many of their sacred records, books and writing were destroyed also.

And during their long captivity in Babylon many of their annals and sacred writings were lost! Hence I am more astonished that we have so many of their writings preserved through all their mishaps and troubles than that we have so few. We are very thankful that we have what we have. Had we the inspired writings as they were declared and written out by prophets and Seers, we would have a fund of intelligence of which we are now deprived. O that God would hasten the time that Jesus saying will be fulfilled, he said, "For there is nothing hid, which shall not be manifested; neither was any thing kept secret, but shall come abroad." Mark 4:22. There are many records lost, and some precious ones hid up unto the Lord, that I verily believe will surely soon come to light!! [page 37:]

---

3. On pages 33-35, McLellin lists forty-nine lost books or writings referred to in the Old Testament, along with the appropriate scriptural references.

11. "Book of the Law" found by Hilkiah in the Temple.

A very peculiar and curius story is told in 2 Kings 22:8 about the High Priest Hilkiah's finding "The book of the Law," in the Temple in the days of Josiah; probably among the rubbish, as the workmen were repairing the house of the Lord. It seems that the king, nor any of his nobles, his trained servants, his priests, nor any of his prophets had ever seen the "Book of the Law." How long it had lain hid is a secret. But most probably from the days of Solomon–the great idolater of all Israel.

Solomon introduced and practiced idolatry among all the Israelites. It is said of him that "The the[4] high places that were before Jerusalem, which were on the right hand of the mount of corruption, which Solomon the king of Israel had builded for Ashtoreth the abomination of the Zidonians, and for Chemosh the abomination of the Mohabites, and for Milcom the abomination of the children of Ammon; did king Josiah defile. And he [did] break in pieces the images, and cut down the groves, and filled their places with the bones of men" [2 Kgs. 23:13-14].

But Josiah reads the "Book of the Law," found by Hilkiah in the temple. ["]And the king went up into the house of the Lord, ~~and~~ and all the men of Judah and all the inhabitants of Jerusalem with him, and the priests, and the prophets, and all the people, both small and great: and he read in their ears all the words of the Book of the covenant which was found in the house of the Lord" [2 Kgs. 23:2]. ~ [page 38:]

["]And the king stood by a pillar, and made a covenant before the Lord, to walk after the Lord, and to keep his commandments and his testimonies and his statutes with all their heart and their soul, to perform the words of this covenant that were written in this book. All the people stood to the covenant." [cf.] 2 Kings 23:2, 3.

It was some over 640 years before the Christian era that Hilkiah found this treasure, the long lost "Law of the Lord" in the holy and dedicated house of God. And to the astonishment of all Israel it was read by the young king, by a pillar. It seems from this statement that their sacred writings had all been lost during their idolatries. We have said this was a curious story and so it is. To think of a people, who once communed with God through the prophets and Seers, and that unerring instrument–the Urim and Thummim, to have fallen off so far into idolatry as not only to l[o]se their communion, but also to l[o]se their sacred law–the covenant. And seemingly all their inspired writings; so that the

4. McLellin wrote "the" twice, neither occurrence marked for deletion.

whole people assembled in Jerusalem to hear that holy book of the Law read by the king as he stood by "a pillar." And this was not more than forty years before they were carried into captivity to Babylon. And during that long captivity, they could have made but few books; hence all this accounts for the loss of so many inspired books refered to in the preceding section. [page 53:][5]

Some of our own thoughts.

We want to know the peculiar power under which the prophets and apostles received their prophecies, visions, and revelations?

Inspiration came to man by a certain influx into his soul from God. Sometimes we go and find thoughts; sometimes thoughts come and find us. In an inspired moment we do not bring up thoughts to our memory but we see them in all their own fresh life and reality. We do not first think them out by any effort of the will; we stand still and see them. Thoughts flash upon our inward eye, and take possession of us.

The Lord has seven eyes, voices, spirits, ways, modes, or manners in which he has revealed to man his will in past times. His voice was heard by Adam in the garden when God said to him, "Adam where art thou?" [cf. Gen. 3:9.] At mount Sinai, when he spoke to Moses, "And God answered him by a voice" [Ex. 19:19]. "At the baptism of Jesus, and on the mount of transfiguration." This voice was vocal, and the Father spoke words audibly to the ears of those who heard.

There is no dispute as to the voice of Jesus of Nazareth while on earth, both in his natural life and in his resurrected and glorified state, his voice was truly heard. It is said, "Holy men of God spake as they were moved by the Holy Ghost" [2 Pet. 1:21]. It moved the prophets at Antioch to point out Barnabas and Saul [page 54:] for the ministry of Christ [Acts 13:1-2]. It spoke to them audibly in plain language. In Timothy it is said, "The Spirit speaks expressly" [1 Tim. 4:1]. Angels frequently appeared to persons and spoke to them verbally, and brought messages to them from the Lord. A vision is the supernatural rep[re]sentation of an object to a person when awake. It is seeing with the eyes of the mind. It is interior or spiritual sight. It is looking at things by the inner man. "The hidden man of the heart" [1 Pet. 3:4]. It is seeing spiritual things in the spirit. A man in vision cannot tell whether he is in the body or not, but he knows he sees, and the impression left upon the

5. Pages 39-52 consist of quotations from various sources on "The ways and maner of inspiration." Then McLellin presents his own views.

mind or memory is more clear, permanent, and lasting than any thing ever seen with the natural eyes. ~

Dreams are from three sources, from vanity, evil, or Satan; from a multitude of business; or they come direct from the Lord. When the body sleeps the mind is still active. It sees objects as definitely as if seen with the natural eye. This shows conclusively that there is in man[6] an "eye of the mind." The mind has powers whether we are asleep or awake. Dreams, however, are mysterious things. It seems, however, that dreams ~~are~~ given of God are a kind of definite certainty. They give direct knowledge—they always give superior confidence to the mind. The individual who has a spiritual or divine dream feels no hesitancy in following out the intelligence it gives. The same power that gives them can unfold their meaning. Joseph of old in the Egyptian prison [page 55:] said to the Baker and Butler, "Do not interpretations belong to God?" [Gen. 40:8.] But he distinctly affirmed, "It is not me, but God shall give the answer." The Lord only causes true spiritual dreams, and he alone can interpret them.

I have consulted many authors relative to Urim and Thummim with but little success or profit. I have talked with numbers in relation to Peep-Stones, and with others relative to those stones called Interpreters or Directors. And I have seen many peep-stones, but could not see any thing in them. Some have said to me that words or writing would appear on the stone, and when written off would disappear, and a new writing would come, and so on until a communication would be received of much intelligence. Candid men have told me this. Some learned men, so far as the learning of the world is concerned, have supposed the Urim & Thummim was the twelve precious stones of the High Priests' breastplate, but if so the Urim could not be put into the breastplate. The first mention of this instrument is in Ex 28:30. "And thou shalt put into the brea[s]tplate of judgement the Urim and the Thummim." Next it is mentioned in Levi 8:8. "And he put the breastplate upon him: also he put in the breastplate the U. & T.["] Whatever may be said of this instrument it seems to have been a power with God for good. It was used to inquire of God and get answers. Whether the answers were verbal or written [page 56:] is an unsettled question. But that the answers were perfectly true and reliable is undoubted. They were as true as if God had spoken in vocal words by a voice to the inquirer. Hence I consider the answers spoken by that sacred, unique instrument the most sure, reliable, and perfect of

6. McLellin added "in man."

any that God ever gave or could give to man; because God was its light, and true light, knowledge, and wisdom and truth[7] were its answers to man. 1 Sam 30:7, 8.

Now I would say all true Prophets were verbally inspired, and if we had their prophecies as they delivered them, then we should have infallible truth and certainty, so far as they unfolded truth to man, touching any subject upon which they wrote. But there is no evidence, any where, that we have the Scriptures as originally written by inspired men. To[o] many uninspired copyi[s]ts, scribes, & transcribers, have had hold of the originals and their copies. And then translators are numerous, and hence the many discrepencies and contradictions to be found in the Book, of what is called divine truth—the revelations of God, as we now have them. No doubt the ~~copists~~ copyists had original annals or manuscripts out of which to write one Bible. But no learned man will say that we have autograph or original copies now. No original copy of the books of the Bible can now be found in the world. We are forced to depend upon uninspired scribes and translators for our Scriptures. The cop[y]ists may have had originals, but they are lost! lost to us at present!! Gone, hid up to God. [page 57:]

In seeing by the Urim and Thummim, the thing communicated always comes in language, in words, or such representation as gives a clear idea to the mind, so that the word spoken or thing seen is infallible evidence to the mind. The Lord is the One who gives the instrument its power to tell or shew things. And if the one inquiring is unworthy,[8] then it gives no light—no answer comes, as in the case of Saul. 1 Sam 28:6.

"Holy men of God spake as they were moved by the Holy Ghost" [2 Pet. 1:21]. Now the manner of this speaking and moving is what we want to ascertain, what we want to look at. Peter says again, "The prophets have inquired and searched diligently, what manner of time the Spirit of Christ which was in them did signify, when it testified beforehand the sufferings of Christ, and the glory that should follow." 1 Peter 1:11. This "inquiring and searching," is just what we want to understand. The prophets said relative to their inspiration that it came by a "Thus saith the Lord, or the word of the Lord came to me saying." The prophet inquired of the Lord, and a voice came and spoke to his mind as to what he wished to know. And it came in intelligent language, in a sure word impressed on his heart, and even printed on his mind, so that there could be no mistake in the inspiration.

7. McLellin added "and truth."

8. McLellin added "un" before the word "worthy."

And if we had the original words of the prophets, delivered in our language, just as they spoke them in their own language without copying, transcribing, or translating then their utterances [page 58:] would be pure—could be depended upon. Then such inspiration would give knowledge to the possessor, and certainty to those who read or heard; and the writers of the Bible being thus inspired, then they did more than believe or think what they said about God, duty, and immortality—they most positively did know! This is the reason why inspired men speak with authority, and philosophers speak without it. But knowledge, though it gives authority, does not give infallibility. The idea of inspiration in the days of Adam, of Enoch, of Noah, of Abraham, of Moses, and of Daniel was pure, unalloyed, and genuinely true; without admixture of error, falsehood, or wrong. It existed down near to Abraham's time in the pure language taught to Adam. It had no double meaning. It said what it meant, and meant what it said. It was the very essence of purity in all its ideas, words, language, principles, and sentiments. Thus ~~this~~ there[9] was pure inspiration, delivered by holy prophets of God.

I look upon inspiration as being one of the most important principles in pure religion. (And I dont know how pure religion can exist without it.)[10] It is the foundation of all the difference between natural and revealed truth. If there can be no such thing as inspiration from God, then man is utterly and entirely in the dark ~~and~~ in[11] perfect uncertainty. Inspiration is the only medium by or through which spiritual knowledge can be obtained. It opens up communion between [page 59:] heaven and earth. It gives man the power to know his origin, his source from whence he came, and his destiny, whither he is going. Shut out the light of inspiration and man knows nothing spiritually. Then it is that which opens up all the fountains of light to man, relative to his soul! to his personality.

If so much is in inspiration as a principle, and more in its practice, it certainly behooves us to properly understand it. It is a direct gift from God to man. If a man has not that gift from God, and pretends to deliver revealments he is only an imposter, or a revelator ~~of~~ from his own heart, or from[12] Satan. Satan may tell some truth, but always has a lie mixed up in it. Pure truth comes from God only relative to all spiritual

9. McLellin added "there."

10. McLellin added the parenthetical statement "(And I dont know how pure religion can exist without it)."

11. McLellin added "in."

12. McLellin added "from his own heart, or from."

things. The Lord always speaks to man in one of his seven appointed ways. Most of the Lord's revealments have been by or through the divine power and energy of the Holy Spirit; but sometimes in some of his other ways. I conceive that nothing in the universe can use intelligent language unless that thing has a form and a mind within that form; except it is an actual personality. The Holy Spirit has both a form and a mind within it. He has spoken, has used intelligent language to man. This then is immediate and direct inspiration from the highest source. From one in the Godhead.

The Lord will condemn and overthrow the inhabitants of the [page 60:] whole earth, because they have ceased to commune with him by direct revelation–by true inspiration. They have lost the direct knowledge of God, and even their <u>ministers</u> deny to man the right to hold such communion as the prophets and apostles enjoyed; to now hold such direct intercourse and power with God. They say the Bible is all the revealments[13] that God will ever give to man–say it is enough for his salvation. And then they even say they cant understand nor comprehend its mysterious pages. Such is the doleful condition in which men have placed themselves. O! the folly of mankind. But few mortal men know, at the present day, the sweetness, the joy, the elevation, and the glorious privilege of direct intercourse with God. It is the most enobling principle, and practice, and enjoyment that man can possibly reach or receive. O that man would consult his best interest! That he would come to the enjoyment of direct inspiration from God; and thus escape the great judgements that are now falling upon mankind, and that will grow worse and worse "to the time of the end" [cf. Dan. 11:35, 40]. Amen!! ~ [page 83:]

<u>**Remarks**</u>.

It is contended that Moses wrote the first five books of the Bible. But if he did he wrote of his own death, in the 34th chapter of Deuteronomy; which would be impossible to believe. It would have been very unnatural for him to use such expressions as the following, "And there arose not a prophet since in Israel, like unto Moses, whom the Lord knew face to face." Deut. 34:10. "Now, the man Moses was very meek above all the men which were upon the face of the earth." Num. 12:3. It would be very inappropriate for Moses to write such sentiments. These words must have been written by some after scribe or copiest.

---

13. McLellin added "the revealments."

Mention is made of Og, king of Bashan, and his iron bed-stead[14] which was then at Rabbah, the capital of the Amorites in the days of David, but not in Moses time. It was David that took Rabbah. 2 Sam. 12:29. It seems that the writer must have lived after Rabbah was taken.

Jair took several cities and their coasts, and called them the "cities of Jair unto this day." This last sentence clearly implies that considerable time had elapse[d] since these towns were so named after the time of the writer. This expression "unto this day," occurs about thirty times in the Bible history, and must have been made by copiests instead of the original writers. [page 84:]

In Deut. 2:12. it is said, "The Horims also dwelt in Seir beforetime, but the children of Esau succeeded them, when they had destroyed them from before them, and dwelt in their stead; as Israel <u>did</u> unto the land of his possession, which the Lord gave unto them." This could not have been written by Moses, because Israel had not taken possession of that land, nor yet destroyed its former inhabitants in Moses lifetime. There are evidences from the first to the last of Deut. that will not admit of Moses being its author or writer; but as a book it must have been written much later than his time. But it is clear that the law which is recited in this book, and in Exodus, was originally written by Moses. It was written and placed in the side of the Ark, under the oversight of the Priests, and occasionally read to the people by them.

In Ex. 16:35, it is said, "The children of Israel did eat manna forty years, until they came to a land inhabited: they did eat manna, until they came into the borders of the land of Canaan." Now the 16th chapter was written before the last chapter of the book, and it is certain that this chapter could not have been written until after Moses' death; for the forty years[15] had not yet expired, nor had they come into the land at the death of Moses, and he therefore could not have written the above.

In Genesis 36:31, it is written, "These are the kings that reigned in Edom, before there reigned any king over the children of Israel." This writer or scribe must have lived after there was a "King over Israel.["] [page 85:] He describes certain events reaching from the time of Esau to the times of the children of Israel; so that the writer must have lived in, or subsequent to Saul's time. Then follows a list of the kings of Esau to

14. According to Moshe Weinfeld, *Deuteronomy 1-11,* Anchor Bible Series (New York: Doubleday, 1991), 184, the Hebrew word ereś ("couch, bedstead") is used figuratively for a sarcophagus, 9 x 4 cubits or 13.5 x 6 feet wide.

15. McLellin added "years."

the first king over Israel, and counts eight generations, which corresponds to the genealogy from Jacob, the twin brother of Esau, reaching to Obed, the grandfather of David; whereas, to Moses it is but four generations. And still farther, in that same place mention is also made of the Dukes that succeeded the eight kings, who did not complete their reign till long after. This points to a still later period when this book of Genesis was written, or rather copied out as it now stands.

Ninevah is mentioned in Gen. 10:11, so called from Ninus,[16] who must have lived more than than[17] 200 years after Moses. Ur of the Chaldees is mentioned in Gen. 11:28. It is very doubtful if the name of Chaldees was known in the days of Moses, much less in Abraham's time. It was then called Padan Aram. Dan mentioned in Gen. 14:14, is without doubt, the place so named by the six hundred Danites from Laish, which they took and named after their father Dan[,] Judges 18:29, long after Joshua's time. Hebron is mentioned in Gen. 37:14, the name is of a city of the Anakim's, called Kirjath Arba until given to Caleb; after which it was called Hebron, as is shown in Joshua 14:14, 15. This shows [page 86.] Conclusively that these names were altered and written out by after scribes or copiests. ~ Joseph is made to say in Gen. 40:15, that he "was stolen away out of the land of the Hebrews." How could it be so called until the Hebrews succeeded the former inhabitants, and they did not [do] this till long after Joseph and Moses?

The foregoing examples, taken from the several books of the Penteteuch demonstrate that Moses did not write as a whole, or either passage as cited; but they were written, or copied and compiled long afterwards. But there are writings of Moses in them. The expressions in the books point to some body beside Moses as their author; and some of the foregoing references make it clear that the Penteteuch lived not in its present shape previous to the captivity. Considerable of the writings and sayings and doings [of Moses] is found in the Penteteuch; just as the writings sayings and doings of Luther are found in the history of the Reformation, but he is not the author of that history.

In the discourses of Balaam in Num. 23:21 he says "The shout of a king is among them"; and Num 24:7, he says that "his king shall be higher than Agag, <u>and his kingdom shall be exalted</u>." This points also to a time not earlier than David when this was written. The words

16. John Kitto, *A Cyclopaedia of Biblical Literature* (New York: Mark H. Newman, 1845), 2:422, said Nineveh meant "the dwelling of Ninus."

17. McLellin wrote "than" twice, neither marked for deletion.

italicised[18] above are found in 2 Sam. 5:12 and applied to David after the complete overthrow of those hereditary [page 87:] enemies, the Amalekites, and the killing [of] their last king Agag, as is found in 1 Sam. 15. The writer of Num. 24:7 was acquainted with the kingdom of Israel first established in Saul's day, and with its old enemy, the unfortunate Agag; which req[u]ired him to live at least 450 years after Moses' death.

In Joshua 4:9 we are told that a monument was erected in Jordan to commemorate the passage of Israel, the writer says, "And they are there unto this day." This implies that considerable time had elapsed since the time of its erection and the writers day. Gilgal in Canaan was so called, "Unto this day" [Josh. 5:9]. Again [in] Josh. 9:23 it is said that Joshua appointed the Gibeonites "hewers of wood and drawers of water for the house of God." Now there was no house of God until one was built by Solomon; so that this writer was not earlier than Solomon. And in verse 27 there is a clear distinction made between the time of this event and the time of the writer, the first is denoted by "that day," and the latter by "this day."

In Josh. 19:27 in giving a description of the lot which fell to Asher, it says, "It goeth out to Cabul on the left hand." And in 1 Kings 9:13 we learn [h]ow, when, and where, and by whom this land of Cabul was so named. Solomon had given this land containing 20 cities to king Hyram of Tyre, in payment for timber for the Temple, and for his own house; and when Hiram came to see it, he did ~~did~~ not like it, "And he called them the land of Cabul [page 88:] (That is dirty,) unto this day." Which implies that considerable time had elapsed since it was so named, until this writing, and this points to a time later than Solomon, when both this account and the reference to it in Joshua was written.

In Joshua 19:29, mention is made of the "Strong city of Tyre," which chronology informs us was built about 240 years before the Temple in Jerusalem, and more than 200 years after Moses' death, and Joshua seems not to have survived him long. Again in the 47th V[erse]. Is related the fete of the Danites in taking Leshem or Laish, which did not occur for many generations after. The same account, more in detail, is given in Judges 18th as an event succeeding the death of Samson: in the 1st V. it says that it was when "There was no king in Israel"; which indicates that the writer lived after there was a king in Israel. But in V. 30 are events refered to reaching "unto the day of the captivity of the land." This points to a day still later, when Shalmanezar carried away

18. By "italicised," McLellin means the underlined words.

the ten tribes. Dan being among them, about 115 years previously to Judah's captivity B.C. 606. This account credited to Jo[s]hua could not have been written until after the captivity; but how long after must be inferred from circumstances.

The book of Joshua concludes with the account of the death and burial of Eleazar who it seems outlived him. When and by whom the Penteteuch and Joshua were written is entirely uncertain. And who wrote or transcribed and filled them out is equally uncertain. [page 89:] They show conclusively that Moses and Joshua were not the authors of those books accredited to them. No clue is given as to who were the writers or scribes or copiests. Hence we are left in the dark, in uncertainty!

The next historicle book of the Jews is the book of Judges. It claims no one as its author, nor is there any good ground for conjecture as to who wrote it, or when. But from numerous expressions, such as we find in chapters 17:6. 18:1. 21:25. to the effect that the thing related took place when "There was no king in Israel," determines the time of the writer to be after there were kings in Israel. In Judges 1:21 mention is made that "the Jebusites dwelt[19] with the children of Benjamin in Jerusalem unto this day." This would imply that this book or circumstance described, was written while David reigned in Hebron, for he drove out the Jebusites before he began to reign in Jerusalem, as we learn in 2 Sam. 5:5-9.

Next is the book of Ruth claiming no author, and from the last chapter, which contains a genealogy reaching down to David shows it was not written before his time, although the scene of the book is laid in the time of the Judges. Ruth 11 [?]. The next two books are attributed to Samuel, and called 1st and 2nd Sam. These books contain 55 chapters, and at the beginning of the 25th chapter [of 1 Sam.] is related the death of Samuel, and the following thirty contain the history of events that transpired after [page 90:] his death. In 2 Sam. 23:1 it is stated, "Now these be the last words of David"; thus overlapping the book of 1 Kings, where chapter 2:1-10 recites David's last words and his death; just as the genealogy of Ruth overlapps the history of Samuel.

Now of course Samuel did not write those books containing the history up to "David's last words," which occurred over forty years after his death. And furthermore, the compilers of the Jewish history, when they put Samuel's name to these books did not intend that authorship should be attributed to him. These books are in the Septuagint called "Books of Reigns."

---

19. The King James Version text has the present tense "dwell."

Thus we must conclude that, as in the case of all the preceding books, the author of the books of Samuel is unknown. And the same may be said of the two books of Kings and the two books of Chronicles, as no man appears as their author, and no one pretends to know any thing about it, whether Jews or Greeks; and these comprise the great body of the Jewish sacred history. Hence we conclude, that so far as we have examined, the Jewish history was not written by any one whose name is a guarantee of its truthfulness as a whole; and that it was not written or copied by the actors in the events recorded, or by any who were co[n]temporary with them. But here we think we have presented sufficient proof that the Bible, as a book was copied out by uninspired men; hence its many contradictions, want of correct history, and its many discrepencies. ~ [page 94:]

Here we have more than 25 different calculations, of learned men, and no two of them agree in their numbers.[20] We then can see the perfect unreliability and uncertainty of all human ch[r]onological calculations as to the age of the world.

...[21] The examination of this subject shows but to[o] plainly the uncertainty of all human calculation relative to time from the Bible. Learned men differ so widely on the subject that an illiterate man stands appaled! Years gone by we undertook to study the chronology of the Bible; but we failed in any favourable result; and from that day till now we have been satisfied to let the matter rest in uncertainty to our mind. And in after years in examining learned men's efforts to find out the age of[22] [the] world from the Bible, or from the calculations of heathen nations, or their wise men among them, we find all uncertainty, hence we cease to hope for a solution on Chronology. ~ [page 95:]

Remarks

On close examination we find there is great uncertainty relative to who wrote the books that are now in our Protestant Bible. We know not who gathered them up and put them together into their present condition in book form. But it was done by uninspired men so far as we now know. We do not know how many books ought to have been put into the canon. Nor do we know whether the English Bible has been translated

20. McLellin quoted from Kitto's *Cyclopaedia* for calculations regarding the time elapsed from the creation of the world to the birth of Christ: 6,174 years of Indian chronology, Rabbi Lipman's 3,616-year time line, and other sources.

21. McLellin here made a seven-line quotation from Kitto.

22. McLellin added "age of."

correctly, inasmuch as it was done by learned but not inspired men. And then when gathered up by those men and a book made, there were more inspired books left out than we now find in our canon—called lost books. And at one time their sacred law was—entirely lost for a great while; but finally was found by the High Priest Hilkiah, in the Temple, and presented to the young king Josiah, and to the whole nation of the Jewish people. And in the book as now presented to the world we have so many **mistakes** that its hard to put entire confidence in <u>all</u> its history.

We find also some near forty books refered to by the writers and compilers of the Bible, which have been "<u>totally lost</u>." Not only the originals, but all the copies from them are gone! Those too, written by Seers, prophets, scribes, and secretaries of that singularly peculiar people or race of Abraham—eye witnesses of the things about which they wrote. They not only left histories but they also obtained and wrote the "Thus saith the Lord," direct from his mouth. But they are gone!! ~ [page 96:]

I am of opinion that registries or records were kept by Adam and by his immediate descendants, and also by Noah and his posterity: and that from these memoirs Moses and his scribes abridged their histories, and learned and recorded their genealogies, aided by divine inspiration. These books or memories kept by Patriarchs and Priests, Seers and Prophets, which have either been "<u>Hid up</u>" or <u>lost</u>, were those from which the recorders, historians, and compilers of our Bible, viz. Moses, Ezra, and Simon the just, drew their book knowledge. Moses and probably Ezra, and Simon had the originals to consult, especially when the first copies were made. But after their captivity, in Ezra and Simon's day the lights were more dim. Yet the great misfortune of after ages when the abridgements were made, the originals were lost—probably destroyed! We have not now the direct sayings of the Lord, through the mouth of his holy Priests, Seers and Prophets, but we have only abridged accounts by those who lived in after ages.

"And Moses wrote all the words of the Lord, and he took the book of the Covenent, and read it in the audience of the people and they said, All that the Lord hath said will we do and be obedient. And Moses took blood, and sprinkled both the book, and all the people" [cf. Heb. 9:19]. Thus the Covenent was dedicated and ratified. But what or how much that sacred "Book of the covenant["] contained, which was afterward put in the side of the **Ark** with the "tables of stone," and all delivered into the care of [page 97] the Priests to be kept in the "Holiest of ~~all~~ holies," cannot at present be determined by any books or records now known.

It was not the book or writing which God wrote on the tables of stone, for the covenant had been written and dedicated by Moses before he went up on the mount to receive the "Law on tables." This book! this important record, then must be lost? And where are the sacred laws written by the finger of God himself on the <u>two tables</u>? It surely was not the whole Penteteuch. For the <u>two tables of stone</u> were only about four feet long and two wide, which could only have contained a small part of the five books of the Penteteuch. Adam Clark[23] says, "A roll written on vellum lies before me, it is two feet two inches in breadth, and one hundred and two feet long. This contains the Penteteuch only." Then if it requires so much surface to hold the <u>five books</u>, who knows what was written on the two tables; or in the book of the covenant, laid up with them in the Ark or on what material it was written?[24]

And whether we have the whole or only a part written out in our present Bible? We can certainly have only extracts. I should really like to know what book it was, or rather the contents of the book, found by the High Priest Hilkiah in the Temple, during the reign of Josiah. It was called the book of the law. This book seems to have been the only canonical book among the Hebrews until after the Babylonish [page 98:] captivity. Their Seers, Prophets, and scribes wrote records of ordinances, covenants, genealogies, rites, ceremonies, commandments, laws, judgements, and even commentaries; but there had been no compilation, or the making of one general book ~~book~~ of faith, or code, or canon until after their great long and tedious captivity in Babylon.

While the Jews retained among them their Urim and Thummim, and had inspired prophets and Seers they were never commanded to make a Bible. True, they had scribes and kept records, but they did not so far as we are informed so compile or combine them as to hold them canonical. But the Chaldeans besieged and finally sacked their empire city, burned the Temple, killed many of their people, and no doubt destroyed many valuable books in the general wreck. They put out king Zedekiah's eyes, and took him captive to Babylon. They killed Jeraiah the high Priest, and after his death no mention is made that any of their high Priests ever held, or had the great privilege of holding and using the Urim & Thummim from that day down through till their final dispers[i]on by the Romans, after the ministry of Christ among them.

After their return from Babylon, Ezra their Leader and scribe probably gathered up all their sacred books and records that he could find, and wrote or copied out an abridgement from them [page 99:] from the

23. For a summary of Adam Clarke's life, see the Biographical Notes.

24. McLellin added "or on what material it was written."

beginning, even from Adam, containing the history as far along down as his own time. The Hebrews rebuilt their Temple–or rather they built a temple, and endeavored to re-establish their ancient worship, but the tabernacle, the ark of the covenant, the altar of incense, the heavenly fir, the pot of manna, Aaron's rod that budded, the mercy seat, the Urim and Thummim, and the divine Shekinah were never again seen or known in Israel, after their return to Jerusalem from their long captivity. The Temple built by order of Cyrus and his successors never contained those Holy Things.

From Malachi down to Christ, some four hundred years there seems to have been no "open vision." At least the canon of the Bible closes with Malachi. Thereafter all enquiries after truth, and a true history of that singular and peculiar people have to grope their way in their researches among "Apocryphal books," or profane histories.[25] The "Spurious books," if we could only credit them, lifts the curtain a little, and gives us some curious details. One tells us the reason that Hebrews, after their captivity, never had the contents of the "Holiest of all," which were kept in Solomon's temple. 2 Macabees 2:1-8. "It is also found in the records that Jeremy, the prophet, being warned of God, commanded the tabernacle, and the Ark to go with him, as he went forth into the mountain [page 100:] where Moses climbed up to view the heritage of God. And ... he found a hollow cave wherein he laid the tabernacle, and the ark, and the altar of incense; and he stopped the door, and said, "As for that place, it shall be unknown until the time that God shall gather his people again together, and receive them to mercy. Then shall the Lord show them these things, and the glory of the Lord shall appear."

But I am very thankful that we have so much of the sacred writings as we have to read and consult in our Bible.[26] I learn more from them than from all other sources. I learn of the creation. I learn of the fall of man. I then learn by those inspired writings of ~~his~~ man's redemption: and can find many precepts of wisdom showing how mankind should regulate their conduct, which I never could learn outside of inspiration. Then I say again I am pleased to consult the divine Oracles. [page 101:]

The New Testament.

We will write a few things about the New Testament. It is the most singularly unique book in existence. It is the most esteemed of any book,

25. See Michael David Coogan, ed., *The New Oxford Annotated Apocrypha,* 3d ed. (New York: Oxford University Press, 2001).

26. McLellin added "in our Bible."

among all the enlightened nations in Christendom. I have searched much to find out all concerning it, but I have failed! Yet, I have learned much and I will now present the result in as succinct or condensed a form as it is possible for me to do....[27]

1. Who were the writers of the books of the New Testament?

The writings of the New Testament were probably written by three of the original twelve apostles, and by the apostle Paul; and the four evangelists Mark, Luke, James and Jude. Learned men differ in the matter whether James and Jude were of the twelve apostles, who wrote the records bearing their names; and many of them incline to the opinion that they did not. [page 102:] Great minds have argued against the canonical[28] authority of both James and Jude, Hebrews, 2 Peter, 2 and 3 John, and also the Revelations of St. John.

Thus seven books of the New Testament are warmly disputed, claimed not to be genuine by learned men. We know not then who wrote them, however our belief may be. We suppose from the evidence of antiquity, of writers of eminence, that the books of the New Testament were written by those whose names are attached to them. But those evangelists seem to have written as they knew themselves, or as they were dictated by apostles. And Luke (if he wrote the Acts of Apostles,) by no means gives us even a succinct history of most of the apostles; but from the 13th chapter onward confines his narative mostly to Paul and his labours. [page 109:]

3. Of the lost books left out when it was compiled.

1. Many ~~gospels and~~ biographies of Christ. Luke 1:1, 2.
2. Paul's first letter to the Corinthians. 1 Cor. 5:9.
3. Paul's few words written to the Ephesians. Eph. 3:3.
4. Read the epistle from the Laodiceans. Col. 4:16.
5. The epistle of the common salvation. Jude. 3.
6. Prophecy from the book of Enoch. Jude. 14
7. Commandments to the Colossians relative to Marcus. Col. 4:10.
8. Commandments to the Thessalonians. 1 Thess. 4:2.
9. And I went up by revelation. Gal. 2:2.
10. The books and parchments of Paul. 2 Tim. 4:13.

"Many have taken in hand." Yes many, many had written, and Luke speaks not in condemnation of those writers, but seems to want to add

27. McLellin here listed the seven sections on the New Testament and relevant page numbers in his notebook.

28. McLellin added "canonical."

his mite too in the matter, and his testimony also, "having had a perfect understanding of all things from the very first." Here we have the declaration that "Many had taken in hand to set forth a declaration of those things most surely believed among us" [Luke 1:1-2]. And no censure for their praisworthy understanding. We in all candor and sincerity look where–O! where are those manuscripts of those of honest hearts and good intentions? Where, Oh where are they? Lost! lost entirely, and we are left in ignorance as to their contents, and to mourn, in our day, for the want of the knowl[page 110:]edge they contained of Christ and his ministry on earth, and of the many glorious principles they would have given us.

If we had Paul's first letter to the Corinthians then we might know more about fornication; what it was really considered in the apostle's day. "I wrote to you in an epistle not to company with fornicators." No, "not so much as to eat with them." I should like to see this master stroke from the pen of the noble apostle of the Gentiles on fornication. But it likewise is lost! All its intelligence lost to Jew and to Gentile. Hence in those lost writings a fund of knowledge is gone, with the disappearance of that important document, which was written or dictated to his scrib[e], by his truly great–inspired mind.

"As I wrote afore in few words." If we only had those few words of heavenly flame, written to the Ephesians, we would then understand some of Paul's "knowledge in the mystery of Christ." But they are mislaid and lost entirely! I should like to dig into this precious document of Paul's knowledge of mistery, down into some of the depths left unexplained in all his other Epistles. Some commentators think this does not refer to an epistle going before, but it is strange logic to me. I think there is no doubt of his referring to an epistle he had previously written to the Ephesians. But is like much that was written by the true, genuine spirit of inspired revelation–lost; gone forever, unless some man would rise with the old Urim and Thummim, and bring it back to light. [page 111:]

An apocryphal epistle can be seen in Adam Clark's commentary to the Colossians,[29] but that there was a true epistle written them by an apostle cannot be reasonably disputed, but it comes not to light in our day.[30] I hate the idea of not having all the inspired writings of those holy

29. Adam Clarke, *The Holy Bible, Containing the Old and New Testaments ... with a Commentary and Critical Notes* (New York: Methodist Episcopal Church, 1831), 6:509-10, reproduces the apocryphal letter of Paul to the Laodiceans in Latin, along with an English translation, as found in some late manuscripts of the Vulgate.

30. Col. 4:16 refers to a now-lost letter from Laodicea, which may have been written

apostles because their souls were set on fire when they wrote by the living principle of the divine direction of the Holy Spirit. But that epistle too is gone with all its superior searching knowledge in the wisdom of Christ.

"Of the common Salvation." "Of which salvation the Prophets have inquired and searched diligently ... Searching what, or what manner of time the Spirit of Christ which was in them did signify ... Which things the Angels desire to look into." Jude had written to them concerning this peculiar salvation, and then for them "to earnestly contend for the faith which was once delivered to the saints." There has been much controversy and speculation about Jude, among the learned, whether he was once of the 12 apostles and also about his epistle. It was for a long time considered doubtful, held somewhat as apocryphal. But after reading their arguments I can see no valid reason why this epistle should be thrown away among the rubbish. I see no incorrect principles advocated in it. It is to me rather a precious document, tells of "the angels [page 112:] who kept not their first estate, and of the archangel contending with the Devil, about the body of Moses; and of Enoch's prophecies about the second coming of Christ." Such are its pure teachings, an[d] I love them; they give me great intelligence. And I presume Jude had seen the prophecies of Enoch as they were at first delivered by that Patriarch. I do not believe that he quoted from a spurious book. I had much rather believe the true one was lost since Jude's day. The prophecy is true whether it comes from a genuine or spurious one. There were many genuine scraps or rolls, or books lost from the first to the fifteenth century. Probably the papyrus was worn out and laid away or destroyed without a copy left.

"You know what commandments you received concerning Marcus." [cf.] 1 Thess. 4:2. Col. 4:10. I presume those mandates were written, and ought to have been preserved, so that we might know what was commanded of the Lord to his saints. Revelations of the Lord were usually written and carefully kept for their future use. I wish I could see those pure words of the Lord, in those commandments, no man would be more pleased to consult those sacred revealments than I, for they contained pure wisdom from the highest source.

Paul says, "And I went up by revelation." Here he positively [page 113:] declares that a revelation had been given, giving special directions for him to go up to Jerusalem; but if recorded it has failed to come down to our day. And I have no doubt but that many **visions** and revelations

---

by Paul or Epaphras. See Eduard Lohse, *A Commentary on the Epistles to the Colossians and to Philemon* (Philadelphia: Fortress, Press, 1971), 174-75.

were given to men, as Eusebius says, "Of approved piety," in that golden age. A great deal of light might have been shed upon our minds relative to spiritual things if we only possessed them. They would show us the doctrine, the government, and the general building up of the "true Church of Christ."

How I would like to see the "Books and parchments" of St Paul. A fund of "Wisdom, knowledge, and spiritual understanding," no doubt, was crowded into those documents. His "knowledge in the mystery of Christ," probably, was plainly set forth, as far as it was "Lawful to utter." O my soul! when I think of the blindness and darkness of all ages since the first centuries, because they have run away from God–the God of revelation, and tried to build up creeds, forms, and ceremonies–without any power or the true principle of faith in God so as to get revelations from him direct to themselves to enlighten and guide them into all truth. Although the children of Israel had the law of Moses, yet God never ceased to give them prophets and revelations as far down as they would heed his voice. The Bible or book of revelations was not closed for ages and generations. So it would have been with the Christian era provided they had kept the faith "once delivered to the saints." They then would have continued to receive visions and revelations all the way through the gospel dispensation. But wo! the world because they have rejected God and revelations and visions from him and try to [page 114:] be content with their "cistern that will hold no water," no visions and revelations direct from God. It is not as in the days of Noah and of Lot, for Noah was taught direct by God himself, to save him from the flood; and Lot had the visitation of angels to save him from the flames of "fire and brimstone.["] Again I say, Wo be the present inhabitants of earth, because they commune not with God!

4. How many inspired books ought to be in the canon? [page 115:]

Instead of 27 books in the canon, we ought to have at least 37, to order to have the inspired writings that are mentioned. But I do not believe in a collected or an established canon at all. Now why? Because I believe that if Christians had lived their religion they never would have ceased to have pure visions and revelations to guide them. This would have superseded a canon!

5. The book was compiled by uninspired men.

It is said Malachi lived four hundred years before the first coming of Christ, and that he was the last of the divinely inspired prophets. So the Jews were 400 years without a "Thus saith the Lord." No wonder they became so hardened and wicked as to be willing to kill the "Lamb of

God." They had become obdurately dark, after they ceased to commune directly with Heaven. Shortly after Christianity had spread through the world, in the days of the Apostles, and "Was preached to every creature which is under heaven" Col. 1:23. Then soon men began to depend on themselves or on councils or conferences of men, assembled in order to dig out of mens brains [page 116:] intelligence which they ought to have obtained from the great Head of the church. A few centuries had not passed before no men of "Approved piety" were found who had visions and revelations from God to direct and guide them in their work of salvation.

The whole plan of the gospel system was intended to make men and women true prophets of the Lord. Paul said, "For by one Spirit are we all baptized into one body ... and have been all made to drink into one Spirit" [1 Cor. 12:13]. And then he commands the Corinthian brethren and sisters "To covet earnestly the best gifts" [1 Cor. 12:31]; after describing nine spiritual powers. And above all to "Follow after charity, and desire spiritual gifts, but rather that ye may prophecy." 1 Cor 14:1. This would be a very high state of communion with their Heavenly Father. If this gift and practice had been kept up, it would have superceded the necessity of opinions and councils of men getting together to make church rules, regulations, or laws. The Head of the church would have given them all the intelligence needed, through their men "of approved piety," by their inquiring of God and getting immediately and directly a "Thus saith the Lord."

Thus the church would have been led if they had lived in the spirit and practice of the gospel. It contains a system of direct intercourse with God. John says to believers, "But ye have an unction from the holy One, and ye <u>know</u> all things." 1 John 2:20. Jesus said to his followers, "Unto you it is given to <u>know</u> the mysteries of the kingdom of God." Luke 8:10. "If any man will do his will, he shall <u>know</u> of the doctrine, whether it be of God." John 7:17. Again, "The Comforter shall teach you all things." John 14:26. [page 117:]

It was because believers ran away from these glorious principles and practices, and soon began to trust to men and to councils of men, and finally soon ran into priestcraft, which for ages has blinded and bewildered the inhabitants of earth; and finally broken them into fragments and parties. When the New Testament canon was settled the Christian churches or its ministers were in a furious contention about the Sonship of Christ, so that men were banished for their opinions and beliefs. This was done soon after the Nicean Council held in 325. Hence none but uninspired men handled the MSS. of the New Testament, or compiled them into their present canon.

And from that time to this men have run to and fro in order to settle difficulties, and get mankind into more of a oneness in Church matters, but instead of union and oneness divisions and splits gro[w] [wo]rse and still worse. All the collections or canons of inspired or uninspired books has not saved them from "Confusion worse confounded."

Printing was entirely unknown when the books of our N. Testament was first written, either among the Jews Greeks, or Romans, and our modern [book binding] was unknown also; hence all their scraps or books must have been inscribed on metal of some kind, or written on papyrus or parchment, and must therefore have been many times copied or transcribed before those documents reached the days of printing. They were many times copied during the first centuries, after the apostles were all gone, that too by uninspired men. [page 118:]

When the books were compiled it was certainly by uninspired men. Then it was the judgement or mere opinion of such men who gave us our New Testament. It was men uninspired too, men who were quarreling and wrangling with each other about their religious principles and beliefs, who sat in judgement upon the various book[s] that now compose our New Testament, and which we esteem so highly. Still men who lived nearest the apostolic age seriously doubted some seven books that we now hold sacred!

I am like the Gove[r]nor among the Jews who returned to Jerusalem from their long captivity in Babylon. I want to see some man rise with the old Urim and Thummim, to tell us which book is canonical and genuinely inspired, and which is not. He could see in that holy Instrument and tell us precisely all about what we would want to know [concerning] our books.

But uninspired men copied out the books, and then they put them together into a volume; but they left out many sacred writings that we ought to have to enlighten our minds. Not even one name of all the copies of ancient time has come down to us. Their names are in oblivion, and at this day we cannot tell who compiled their labours in making books, and then putting them into a volume. [page 131:]

Remarks

We do not present these discrepencies thinking or expecting that they are from the pens of inspired men, but we lay the blame where we think it belongs, viz. among the cop[y]ists, scribes, manipulators, and translators of the manuscripts of the New Testament books. True inspiration gives no faults or contradictions. Whatever comes from men of God is unmixed truth—truth without alloy, or any alterations. I candidly believe in the Christianity that I find taught in the New Testament Scriptures, notwithstanding its discrepancies.

Besides the lost books which were not put into the canon of the New Testament, there is quite a large collection of books in what is called the "Apocryphal New Testament."[31] Some of which bear evident marks of being spurious. But as many learned men have said, "No doubt the Apostles wrote many books or epistles which have been lost"; so I most fully believe.

Eight men wrote the twenty seven books constituting our present New Testament. It is only positively certain that three of the eight were of the twelve apostles, viz. Matthew, Peter, and John. Mark and Luke were only Evangelists. Paul was an apostle, but not one of the Twelve. As to who James and Jude were learned men disagree. Some believe that they were of the Twelve, but others think they were only Evangelists.

Chronologists too differ widely as to the dates of the writing of the books. But all believe that they were all written within the first century, or rather between the years 37, and 106.

As to when, where, and by whom the books of the New Testament were collected together and compiled, as they now stand in our code or canon, is a question that learned men have not settled. But it is pretty generally admitted and agreed that the canon was completed some time between the 3rd and 7th C[enturies]. Neil[32] says, "The first canonical mention of the books as they now stand, was by the Laodicean council about the year 363.["] P. 333. [page 132:]

7. The copies and the translations of the N.T. [page 133:]

In examining this subject of the writing and compiling of the sacred or inspired books, so as to make a Bible, one thing especially impressed my mind with a great deal of force—The books both of the Old and the New Testaments were gathered together and combined into volumes by uninspired men; and that too many years and even centuries after they were written. Over one hundred years elapsed between Malachi, the last

---

31. For a modern translation, see J. K. Elliott, *The Apocryphal New Testament: A Collection of Apocryphal Christian Literature in an English Translation* (Oxford: Clarendon Press, 1993).

32. This is probably William Neill, who wrote *Lectures on Biblical History* in 1846 and *The Divine Origin and Authority of the Christian Religion* in 1854. For a summary of his life, see the Biographical Notes.

of the Jewish prophets, and Simon the just; who is supposed to have completed the Canon of the Old Testament. And more than 250 years after John had his visions on the isle of Patmos before a New Testament appeared, as a compiled book.

After the Jews had killed their prophets, and stoned them that were sent unto them, and there was "no answer from God," then without being directed by prophet or Seer, the High Priest Simon arrogated to himself the authority to s[i]t in judgement upon "the word of God," and say which shall be admitted into the canon, and which shall be set aside as spurious. His being assisted by the Great Synagogue does not mend the matter in my mind.

About the commencement of the 4th C., the Christian world had got into a contention—a great and lasting, a furious and wicked contention about the Sonship of Christ. So that Constantine the Great assembled what is generally called, "The first general Co[u]ncil." He issued letters to the Bishops of the several provinces of his empire, enjoining them to assemble together at Nice, in Bythinia, which was accordingly done in A.D. 325. The number of Bishops was 318, besides a multitude of presbyters, deacons, and others amounting in the whole to 2048 persons. One great object of their assembling was to establish a rule of faith as it respected the Arian controversy. This thing they thought they did, by making what is commonly called the "Nicene Creed." This council was in session about 67 days.[33]

But instead of quelling or quieting the contentions, this Creed seemed to arouse new energies, and bring out new arguments, and hence a greater amount of talent into the field; and the controversy was carried on until bitterness, wrangling, persecution, banishment, and death followed—with all its horrid evils.

During this state of things the canon of the New Testament was determined in part. As among the Jews inspiration had ceased [page 134:] among them viz. Direct and immediate intercourse from God to them. Then was a trying time. A great work must be done: All the books which have claims must be gathered together, and learned, not inspired men must sit in judgement upon them. This one is received, but that one is thrown aside; until at the end of their labours we have 27 books considered canonical; but numerous ones set aside as Apocryphal.

Historians are very silent about who, where, or when this work was done. Who composed the court, or by what rules their decisions were

33. See Marvin M. Arnold, *Nicaea and the Nicene Council of A.D. 325* (Washington, Mich.: Arno Publications, 1987).

made, or how they determined between the genuine and the spurious, we are left mearly to conjecture. However little confidence we may have in the writings of the Apocryphal N.T., yet there is one thing certain, some inspired—divinely inspired books written by Apostles, Evangelists, and prophets during the first century of the Christian era have been lost, which ought to be in our established canon of the New Testament. We learn by our preceding notes that Ezra and Simon are generally supposed the abridgers, arrangers and compilers of the Bible. This however is only guesswork. But who did so for the books of our N.T.? What deliberative council, or body of learned men, or indeed what assembly of any kind ever convened, who assumed authority and did construct or compile our valuable New Testament?

Here by all the examination I have been able to make I find all uncertainty—all in mystery! Still I have unlimited confidence that divinely inspired men wrote the original manuscripts or books of our New Testament, yet I most firmly believe[34] that all the discrepencies now found in them were not made by inspired men, but by uninspired men who copied and re-wrote them over and over after first written.†

---

34. McLellin added "believe."

†On the bottom of p. 134, John L. Traughber wrote: "I received this [note]book from the Express Office at Norborne, Mo., Nov. 10, 1884. It was sent to me as a present by Mrs. Emeline McLellan now of Troy, Mo. J. L. Traughber, Jr. Nov. 11th, 1884." Then Traughber wrote the following observations within the notebook beginning on pages 135-38 and continuing onto two pages McLellin had left blank except for the page number 123, which we number as 123a-b. [page 135:]

Of Inspired Books
By J. L. Traughber, Jr.

In the foregoing work Dr. McLellan has done what most believers in the Bible will not do; that is, admit discrepancies and imperfections in the Bible as it now stands; although he does not want it thought that such imperfections as he so explicitly points out militate against the purity of the original writings, or the infallible nature of the inspiration that actuated the first writers. But from my standpoint he has shown that there is no reliability in the so called "inspired writings["]; for if the Bible comes to us the only representative of that pure inspiration which the Doctor believes influenced the ancient apostles and prophets, and is manifestly full of errors and improprieties, what ground have we for assuming that infallible inspiration originally dictated the "sacred writings," if we can not find such infallible inspiration in the world in our own day? It appears to me, that with no such inspiration among men now, and no way to prove that it ever existed except by writings whose imperfections would be enough, if once divested of the assumed sacredness of absoslute perfection in their present mutilated shape, to stamp them as human productions, there is absolutely no ground for believing that any class of men ever existed who were possessed of such inspiration.

I think the Doctor very clearly shows that, even admitting that the originals of the Bible were inspired as claimed, there is now no means of determining what part of it is true and correct. [page 136:]

As to the New Testament, I think from the showing of its own adherents, it is the result of centuries of patching up and working over by the early Christian church. It was established by force and perpetuated by tradition. Is it [at] all reasonable to suppose that the Christian religion rose up from obscurity to the dignity of an absolute despotism without any notice being taken of it by opposing systems of religion? Without being contested by strong and able arguments from those whose faith and living was to be annihilated by its successful establishment? Yet, where are those opposing arguments of the first centuries of the Christian era? Echo answers, "where?" If Christian arguments were able to overcome the arguments of the opposers of Christianity why were not the arguments of the opposition preserved, and their inferiority insisted upon by the leaders and teachers of the Christian church? To my mind their [absence] stands unanswerably against the oft repeated Christian boast the Christian faith was established [page 137:] by its own intrinsic merit, while others were overcome because of their weakness and inconsistencies.

All that now remain of the arguments of the opposers of Christianity, are a few quotations in the works of early church Fathers from works which they attempted to answer. The reasons why this is so, is very clear to my mind. When the Christian church became the dominant power of Europe and parts of Asia and Africa, it set itself the task of gathering together the literature of the world, and everything which tended to the discredit of the Christian religion was destroyed except such as men incorporated in Christian literature.

Judging the New Testament by its present form and status, and considering that its adherents have had it in their hands to carefully revise and correct, if it is as poor a thing as we now find it, we are reasonably warranted in believing that it was a much poorer thing to begin with; for reason will teach us that the believers in that book would use their powers to improve rather than deteriorate it. [page 138:]

The reason why the ordinary Christian argues so strongly for the absolute purity and perfection of the Bible writings, is that they instinctively see that if they concede as much as Dr. McLellan has proved, they yield the claim of infinite superiority of the "sacred writings" to all other writings.

Dr. McLellan clearly proves that the Old Testament, as a history is utterly unreliable, though he seems not to have realized the crushing weight of his own deductions against the integrity of Bible writers. When he proves that the great prophecy of Balaam was written as late as the time of David, he destroys ~~at~~ in one fell blow both the fabricated prophecy and the non-integrity of the writer who pretends to record it. The same is true of other points elaborated by him.

It seems that the utter stupidity of that story of Hilkiah's finding the law in the Temple did not dawn upon the Doctor. If the King of Judah knew nothing of the Law of Moses, nor the priests who ministered under the law knew nothing of it, it would be an anomalous state of affairs.

If such a thing were to be sprung on a people now, instead of being revolutionized by it, when it was unknown to all their accredited history, they would without exception denounce it as a fraud, fabricated by the pretended finder or some other. Suppose that some clerk in the government employ at Washington should come out of some room in the Capitol with a manuscript containing what purported to be the constitution of the United States, yet was so utterly at variance with the known historical constitution that its adoption would cause the destruction of the Congressional Library and several goverment buildings in Washington and the butchery of several thousand goverment officials, could any person now living be induced to believe that it had ever been the constitution of the United States, and that our whole national history is a falsehood? Yet something similar is what the Bible tells us was actually done in the reign of Josiah. Hilkiah, it is stated, was a priest. What kind of priest was he? The Bible would evidently have us to infer that he was an Aaronic priest; one whose duties were defined only in the law of Moses, which he knew nothing about until Shaphan, the writer, gave it to him. A likely story, is it not? [page 123a:]

I have speculated a good deal as to about how much reliance ~~was~~ is to be placed in the so cal[l]ed historical writings of the Old Testament. There may have been such a man as Moses. If so, he was the orig[in]ator of the Israelites, in all probability; they being mostly ignorant slaves who knew nothing of their own history, and thus were fit dupes of any fraud he chose to foist upon them.

There may have been nothing of it until after the Babylonian captivity. It may be that the Jews were some kind of people before the captivity, but it seems probable to me that the Jewish history now in existence was all forged after that time; in which case we have no warrant that there is any truth in it. From the frequent references of the books of Kings and Chronicles to each other, it is evident that they were written simultaneously or nearly so; or else that the original books were interpolated with these references by some later scribe. As the references stand in the book as a part of the body of the text, if they are interpolations, we have [no] means of knowing how much of the books are interpolations, nor whether we can place any reliance on the work of a copyist who was so unscrupulous in handling the writings of another.

The Law may have been invented first, fabricated and antedated, then the history may have been fabricated to sustain it. No matter how it was done, there is no sense in making the future welfare of a single soul dependent on a faith in the divine inspiration of the law or the moral integrity of the Old Testament writers.

As to the New Testament, laying aside the objections which I have already presented, it is self condemned, and unworthy of a moments serious thought, as to whether it is true or not. There is no need to write an elaborate treatise to prove that Christianity is a fraud. Fifteen minutes examanination [examination] of the references I shall give should be enough to convince every sensible person, who is honest, that it is not and can not be true.

In the first place, it is conditioned on the truth of the Old Testament; that is to say, the Law of Moses. If the Law of Moses was not inspired of [God], Christianity, founded upon it, is of [page 123b:] necessity false; but this is only one side of the question. The other side is this: If the Law of Moses was inspired of God, and God is not a liar, then there is no room for Christianity, for it comes in contact with plain provisions of the law.

Eternity of the Law of Moses and the sacrificial offerings of beasts is proved by the following: Ex. 28:43; Ex. 29:9, 28, 42, 45; Ex. 30:21, 30, 31; Ex. 31:13, 16, 17; Lev. 3:17; Lev. 6:18; Lev. 7:36; Lev. 10:9, 16; Lev. 16:29, 31, 34; Lev. 17:7; Lev. 23:14, 21, 31, 41; Lev. 24:3, 9, 10; Lev. 26:32-45; Num. 10:8; Num. 18:8, 19, 23; Num. 19:10, 21; Num. 27:11; Num. 28:3, 6, 10, 15; Num. 29:14, 15, 29; Deut. 6:1, 2, 7, 24; Deut. 4:9, 10, 23, 31; Deut. 5:29; Deut. 8:11; Deut. 11:1, 8, 9, 10, 11, 12; Deut. 12, whole; Deut. 13:1-5; Deut. 27:26; Deut. 29:14, 15, 29; Deut. 30:2-20; Deut. 32:46.

The Eternity of the Aaronic Priesthood and its everlasting authority to minister and offer sacrifices under the law is proved by the following: Ex. 19:21, 25; Ex. 28:43; Ex. 29:9, 28, 42, 45; Ex. 40:13; Lev. 6:18; Lev. 7:34; Lev. 10:9, 15; Lev. 16:29, 31, 34; Lev. 17:6, 7; Num. 3:10; Num. ~~8:10~~ 10:8; Num. 18:8, 19, 23; Num. 25:11, 13; Deut. 18:5.

If God spoke these promises and commandments Christianity has no warrant in the law of Moses. If God did not speak them, Christianity is false because it pretends that God did speak them.

J. L. Traughber.

5.

WHY I AM NOT A LATTER DAY SAINT, 1878

Wm E McLellan
Some of my thoughts
in 1878.
Why I am not an L. D. Saint of
any click or party

Some principles and practices of the Church of Christ.

Now I want to write plainly and candidly—unprejudiced. There were five great and wrong principles established and acted upon when Joseph Smith and Oliver Cowdery organized their church on the 6th day of April 1830; which principles and their practice arising therefrom with other things[1] caused its ultimate overthrow;

1st Smith required Oliver to ordain him a Prophet, Seer, Revelator, and Translator on that 6th of April. 2nd J. Smith declared by his revelation that the church should receive, "His word, as from the mouth of God" [cf. D&C 21:5; RLDS 19:2b]. 3rd Joseph claimed on that day that he and Cowdery were Apostles of the Lord Jesus Christ. 4th J. Smith said to Oliver, "Thou shalt not command him who is at thy head, and at the Head of the church" [D&C 28:6; RLDS 27:2d]. 5th Again, in 1830

McLellin neglected to paginate Notebook 5. While LDS Church archivists had numbered the obverse of each leaf 1-6, we have identified each page, 1-12. The title ("Why I Am Not a Latter Day Saint") is condensed from McLellin's own inscription on the cover: "Wm E McLellan Some of my thoughts in 1878. Why I am not an L. D. Saint of any click or party." Larry C. Porter identified the contents as "an 1878 statement that accepts Joseph Smith's gift to translate the Book of Mormon but objects to several aspects of Joseph Smith's ordination, titles, and prominence in the organization of the Church in 1830. [McLellin specifically] criticizes Zion's Camp for renouncing peace, and rejects the plurality of Gods, two priesthoods, baptism for the dead, tithing, and the restoration of the priesthood by John the Baptist" ("The Odyssey of William Earl McLellin: Man of Diversity, 1806-83," in *The Journals of William E. McLellin, 1831-1836*, ed. Jan Shipps and John W. Welch [Provo and Urbana: BYU Studies and University of Illinois Press, 1994], 377n324).

1. McLellin added "with other things."

Joseph set himself up above all others, in the matter of receiving and giving off revelations for the church.

1st As to the ordination of a Prophet or Seer, I know of no place in the word of God where a Seer, or inspired Prophet was ever ordained by man. It is not a ministerial office, but is a direct gift from God. It is neither confered or confirmed by ordination. And the man or men who pretend to confer such office or state upon any man only act from the suggestion of their own hearts, or from the promptings of Satan. Hence the ordination of Joseph Smith by O. Cowdery on the 6th of April 1830; and Smith's ordination of David Whitmer Prophet & Seer[2] on the 8th day of July 1834 were all without authority from God, all wrong, null & void.

Hence all claims to that office, or to that station is simply fallacious and silly. True Aaron was consecrated High [page 2:] Priest by Moses, and the Urim and Thummim was placed in the breast-plate, and that in the Ephod which was worn by Aaron as a service or gift; so that he could inquire of God through or by that instrument and get answers for the people. But Aaron was never ordained either Prophet or Seer. High Priests both of the order of Melchisedec and of Aaron were either consecrated or ordained, but never Prophets or Seers.

2nd As to receiving any mortal man's word as we would the voice of God is simply preposterous. No man ever did or ever could. Hence that command was perfectly vain. It would be a perfect impossibility. God's voice is the highest evidence that can be presented to man's mind; but the word of fallible man is to a great degree uncertain, and consequently must be received with some doubts until his revealment is proved by revelations going before.[3] J. Smith delivered a revelation in 1830 positively contradicting a declaration in the book of Mormon, saying, "Teachers have not authority to baptize" [cf. D&C 20:58; RLDS 17:11e]. I prefer the book of M[ormon]., hence his "word" cannot be relied on as being positively certain. His statement relative to the tares also contradicts the sayings in the New Testament.[4] If I should follow up this subject I would not know where to stop, as to his discrepancies.[5]

2. McLellin added "Whitmer Prophet & Seer."

3. McLellin added "until his revealment is proved by revelations going before."

4. What McLellin refers to is that in the New Testament, the Son of Man sows the seed, the tares are bound in bundles, and the wheat is gathered into the barn (Matt. 13:30, 37, 41), while Joseph Smith has the apostles sowing the seed, the wheat gathered first, and then the tares bundled for burning (D&C 86:2, 7; RLDS 84:1b, 2d). In the Joseph Smith Translation of the Bible, the order of the wheat and tares is reversed to fit the D&C version.

5. After the sentence had already been finished with the words "where to stop" and a

3rd An Apostle of Christ must have knowledge within himself. All the Apostles of Christ in Jerusalem, and all the Disciples in America saw, heard, and felt, hence they could bear a firm testimony and witness that they most positively ~~knw~~ knew what they declared. Did Smith and Cowdery thus know? They did not. They never in the early part of the church so professed or declared. They were Apostles of the true translation of the book of M[ormon]., but not Apostles of Jesus Christ. Paul was called [page 3:] after the ascention of Christ. He saw, heard, and felt, hence was a genuine, true Apostle, having knowledge within himself. Smith should not have made so false a claim for himself & Cowdery.

4th The Lord Jesus Christ is certainly Head of his Church as much so as a man is head of the woman. Paul says, "God gave Christ to head over all things to the Church, which is his body" [cf. Eph. 1:22-23]. It was a wretchedly false claim for Smith or any man in the world to claim to be head of the church. If Christ is Head and any man on earth is head also then the church would be an anomily, having two heads on the one[0] body.

5th One of the most unchristian and ruinous principles that Smith or any man ever did or could lay down was the one ~~one~~ that he alone was to receive and cause to be written revelations and com[mandments][7] for the church. He revelated thus "Behold, verily, verily I say unto you, no one shall be appointed to receive commandments and revelations in the church, excepting my servant Joseph,[8] for he receiveth them even as Moses" [cf. BofC 30:2; D&C 28:2; RLDS 27:2a]. Moses declared, when Joshua wanted him to forbid prophesying in the tents of Israel, "Would to God all the Lord's people were prophets, and that the Lord would put his spirit upon them" [cf. Num. 11:29]. This declaration was made under the law age, in the darkness of ceremonies and rights [rites], by the distinguished law giver ~~of~~ in that age of sacrafises. And Joel and Peter said, "God will pour out his spirit upon all flesh" [Joel 2:28; Acts 2:17], which spirit the angel said to John, "For the testimony of Jesus is the Spirit of prophecy" [Rev. 19:10]. And Paul said to "All that in every place call on the name of Jesus Christ our Lord–For ye may all prophecy one by one, that all may learn, and all may be comforted" [cf. 1 Cor. 1:2;

---

period placed at the end, McLellin appears to have added "as to his discrepancies."

6. McLellin added "one."

7. McLellin added "and com."

8. McLellin quoted from the 1833 Book of Commandments, which has "my servant Joseph," rather than the expanded "my servant Joseph Smith Jr" of the 1835 edition of the Doctrine and Covenants.

14:31]. The wish and design of Moses and of the three distinguished Apostles was [page 4:] that in the law age and also during the whole gospel dispensation men should receive and deliver off a "Thus saith the Lord," for the benefit of other men. Yes, to "comfort and edify them" [cf. 1 Cor. 14:3].

But this practice of receiving God's word would violate J. Smith's rule of assuming to himself the exclusive right, and would place him down upon a level with his brethren. It would set up the great liberal gospel principle that "All might receive the Spirit["] [cf. Gal. 3:14] and by it "show forth things to come" [cf. John 16:13], to enlighten all the honest hearted in all the world.

These five great principles and practices being wrong at the origin of the church of Christ, it is not wonderful that many other wrongs would enter into it, and so destroy its usefulness in the world. If we persue it a few years longer we will find other miserable, wretched wrong principles and and[9] worse practices, started up by the <u>Leaders</u> of the movement; and finally worked its entire ruin, and it ceased to be the Church of Christ, and turned to be a new <u>thing</u> under the sun, governed by an entire different set of principles & practices.

We will pass on a few years and see if the above remark is not true in detail. 1st The Church at first was taught and practiced the principle of non-resistance for some years. Would not return evil for evil or railing for railing[10] or smite when smitten. They trusted in God's word which says "vengence is mine and I'll repay" [cf. Rom. 12:19]. In 1833 in August ~~they~~ Smith professed to receive this word from the Lord, "Renounce War, and proclaim peace" [D&C 98:16; RLDS 95:3d]. But in less than two month[s] the Leaders renounced peace and proclaimed war. In July 1833 the church was mobbed in Jackson Co. Mo., what they then[11] called "The Zion of God." [page 5:] They were set upon by the old inhabitants of the country. The leading men in Ohio, receiving news of the mobbing, held a council and determined ~~to send~~ and sent Orson Hyde[12] and John Gould[13] all the way, near a thousand miles, from Kirtland to Zion to tell the members of the church to stand in their own defence—to fight if oppressed. This was contrary to all revelation, and to the best interests of

9. McLellin accidentally doubled the word "and" at the end of one line and beginning of the next.

10. McLellin added "or railing for railing."

11. McLellin added "then."

12. For a summary of Orson Hyde's life, see the Biographical Notes.

13. For a summary of John Gould's life, see the Biographical Notes.

the church, and was the prime cause of the entire church being driven from the county, over the Missouri river into Clay Co.

In January 1834 the scattered, persecuted Elders held a consultation together in council[14] in their forlorn condition and sent Lyman Wight[15] and P. P. Pratt[16] to Kirtland, O. to see the first Presidency of the entire church, in order to consult with them, to learn and know what the church must do in her ~~forlorn~~ condition distressed situation.[17] Wight was fully imbued with the war spirit, and inspired Smith and company with the idea of redeeming Zion, viz the Church of Zion, with <u>men of War</u>!! The Leaders issue[d] a proclamation to the entire church in the eastern states, to gather up their munitions of war material, and assemble at Kirtland the first of May. About a hundred men gathered, and the 4th day of May was set to start for upper Missouri. But, as in the days of Ahab and Mic~~h~~aiah,[18] "There came forth a lying spirit, and stood before the Lord" [cf. 1 Kgs. 22:21]. So it was with J. Smith an evil spirit whispered in his ear to call a council of all his first ministers. They assembled on the 3rd day of May, and deliberated relative to names and ap pel[l]ations. They concluded that Christ was not the name to go to war in, hence they threw the name of the Church of Christ entirely [page 6:] away, and adopted the non-descript name of the <u>Church of Latterday saints</u>. And in that name on the next day they set out for Missouri, gathering numbers by the way, until when they reached Clay Co. Mo. they had about 400 men in their army of veterans, with Joseph Smith at their head as their great Generalissimo–their Prophet and Leader!

Now in this warrior raid they imbibed four great leading doctrines and practices that were eminently and miserably wrong. 1st They took a wrong doctrine or principle in imbibing the disposition to fight for their religious belief! 2nd Then it was an evil spirit dwelling in them in order to make them carry out their design. 3rd Then they had to take a false, fictitious **name** in or under which to carry out their War doctrine and spirit. 4th Then their practice was war–~~like~~ was to resist evil by evil, was to smite when smitten, was to take vengence into their own hands. All this was contrary to the peaceable and glorious doctrines of the Lord Jesus Christ,[19] to cease to do evil, and cease to resist evil. I cant

14. McLellin added "in council."

15. For a summary of Lyman Wight's life, see the Biographical Notes.

16. For a summary of Parley Parker Pratt's life, see the Biographical Notes.

17. McLellin added "distressed situation" above the words "forlorn condition." He crossed out "forlorn" but clearly intended to do the same to "condition."

18. McLellin changed "Michaiah" to the correct "Micaiah" by deleting the extra "h."

19. McLellin added "Christ."

see or know how intelligent men could be so blindly led only that their minds were holden and inspired by the power and persuasions of the Devil and Satan.

There were some very good and intelligent men in that camp, led on by their confidence in Joseph Smith's inspiration, until they were led to death by that awful scourge of the human race viz. Cholera. For when they had reached near Liberty, Clay Co. Mo., the cholera seized about seventy of their number, and fourteen died of it! This was fatal to all their great calculations of conquering [page 7:] the mobbers by war and fighting. They had no living faith in God to stop the ravages of that curse upon them for lifting their swords in the name of pure religion. But numbers of them had to die! Fall by the dread monster!! O my soul[20] when I look back at that singular scene, I cant but marvel and wonder at those men who were actors in that ~~scene~~ tragedy. That a professed prophet should be so deceived and led to desolation and ruin by as ambitious ~~a man~~ men as Lyman Wight and J. Smith![21] This to me looks dark and dismal.

But they failed entirely failed in their hopes and expectations of their declared object to take their brethren and reinstate them back upon their land, in Jackson Co. from which they had been forcibly driven in 1833, the year before. But not even one stone was turned over towards the redemption of Zion, nor of their brethren, but evil and only evil [was] produced by that warrior raid into upper Mo. It roused and embittered all the country round about in all the upper Counties. And much precious time, thousands in money squandered—wasted foolishly, and many most excellent lives lost, worse than wasted. Wo! be to all war feeling and practice in the church of Christ where it commenced, or in the Church of Latter Day Saints where it was carried out.

On[e] thing I have to say after looking at all this folly, I pitty men that get into the meshes of such a delusion, as to believe that a Prophet or Seer could be legally[22] ordained by man; also to think any man's word was as true & certain [as] God's voice to them;[23] or that a man [page 8:] or men could be Apostles of Jesus Christ without seeing, hearing, and feeling him, as the Apostles of old did is to me the mearest nonsense; and for a man to claim to be Head of the church while Christ lives to be Head

20. McLellin added "my soul."

21. McLellin added "and J. Smith." However, he forgot the subject of the sentence was "a professed prophet" in revising it to refer to both Wight and Smith.

22. McLellin added "legally."

23. McLellin added both "true & certain" and "voice to them."

himself, simply shows a great want of honesty and a knowledge of the gospel system; but above all to claim the only power with God to receive and write communications–inspired mandates for all true believers, is simply monstrous. Here I leave the claims of Joseph Smith in the hands of the honest searchers after truth + + +

That he was the medium through whom the book of Mormon was brought to light ~~must be admitted~~ I am willing to admit and most firmly believe[24] but then and there his mission and work ended. Here I will give a quotation from his own revelation, given in March 1829, more than a year before he set up his Church of six members: "He has a gift to translate the book, and I have commanded him that he should pretend to no other gift, for I will grant him no other gift" [BofC 4:2].[25] With this quotation I will cease with this matter. [page 9:]

[Reasons Why I Do Not Believe in the Reorganized Church][26]

I will tell some of the reasons why I do not believe in the "Reorganized church of Jesus Christ of Latterday Saints"; presided over, taught, and led by Joseph Smith, the second.[27]

1st It is contrary to the gospel system for any **one man** to hold the stations of President and Head of the church. Christ on both continents set ~~first~~ in the church first Apostles–twelve men to establish and lead the church onward to triumph. No one man power was seen among them, after Peter opened the door to the Jews at Pentecost, and to the Gentiles at the house of Cornelius. Thereafter the gospel door was wide open for all the world both Jew and Gentile. Prophets were set second in the church, [they] were under the direction and government of the Apostles, so far as all their ministerial duties were co[n]cerned. And whenever people put one prophet at the Head they violate the great gospel principle. They set God's ~~ways~~ rules at defiance and try to establish their own ways.

2nd I do not believe in a plurality of Gods. But this is the doctrine of the Josephites.[28] To believe in and worship more Gods than one is

24. McLellin added "and most firmly believe."

25. McLellin quoted from the 1833 Book of Commandments (except for "should" in place of "shall"). The 1835 Doctrine and Covenants (32:1) made a number of significant changes to this passage: "*you* have a gift to translate the *plates; and this is the first gift that I bestowed upon you*; and I have commanded that *you* should pretend to no other gift *until my purpose is fulfilled in this*; for I will grant *unto you* no other gift *until it is finished*" (D&C 5:4; RLDS D&C 5:1d).

26. The title of this otherwise untitled essay is drawn from the first sentence.

27. For a summary of Joseph Smith III's life, see the Biographical Notes.

28. The plurality of gods in LDS and early RLDS (Community of Christ) belief is de-

idolitry, one of the wickedest sins mortal man can commit: and why any men in the 19th century could originate or hatch up that idea is most surprising to me. All the Scriptures testify that "There is but **one** God." God himself says, "Yea, there is no God besides me? Yea[29] I know not any." [cf.] Isa. 44:8. And if God's knowledge, which extends to all worlds throughout all space knows no God but himself, then where will we find room for another God? I know the book says, "As there be gods many, and Lords many" [1 Cor. 8:5]. It says also, "But to us there is but one God, the Father" [1 Cor 8:6]. Thus the whole point and matter is settled, firmly fixed. God's word is true when it says, "There is but one God, of whom are all things" [1 Cor. 8:6]. [page 10:]

3rd. I do not believe in two priesthoods existing in the church of Christ at one and the same time. There never were two priesthoods at the same time in the church of God, or the church of Christ since the world began. Whenever a new priesthood came into existence then the preceding one was done away–set aside entirely as useless. When Moses introduced the first-born ~~priests~~ ministers in the camp of Israel, for all that race of Abraham, the Patriarchal Priests[30] was set aside, it is never more mentioned as existing in Israel, or in the wide world afterwards. When the Aaronic was introduced and set up in Israel then the first-born were all paired off by the Levites, and by a few of them paying five sheckels each into the treasury. Then the first-born priests are never more heard of in Israel, or in the world. The Patriarchal reigned alone until the first-born was set up, then disappeared. The first-born operated alone until set asidide [aside] by the Levites. The Aaronic existed alone, until Christ came and set it aside and introduced his own Melchisedec order of Apostles, Elders, Bishops, and Deacons;[31] or as on this land, of Elders, Priests, and Teachers.[32] And his order reigns alone as much as the Patriarchal, the first-born, or the Aaronic did, while they ministered before the Lord in their priestly authority.

---

rived from the 1840s Nauvoo period. See *The True Latter Day Saints' Herald,* Dec. 1860, 280-83.

29. McLellin added "besides me? Yea," mistakenly punctuating the addition with a question mark.

30. McLellin added "Priests" but did not change the verb to the plural "were."

31. The term "apostles" occurs sixty-four times in the New Testament, ranging from Matt. 10:2 to Rev. 21:14; "elders" sixty times, though often in reference to Jews rather than Christians; and "bishop(s)" and "deacon(s) five times each at Phil. 1:1; 1 Tim. 3:1-2, 8, 10, 12-13; Tit. 1:7; 1 Pet. 2:25.

32. The phrase "on this land" refers to the Americas and draws from the Book of Mormon, which mentions "elders" seven times at Alma 4:7, 16; 6:1 (RLDS 2:11, 23; 4:1)

4th I do not believe in lineal rights to priesthood. The gospel system knows nothing of lineal rights. It is trying to combine all former dispensations into the gospel system. No Apostle or priest after Christ ever had a successor by lineage. Each minister received his authority by faith and obedience in himself. I am aware that the Patriarchs, and Aaron and his sons had successors by lineage, but Christ introduced a free gospel system, with no hereditary followers on either continent. All had to act and minister from their own individual faith in God [page 11:] for themselves. Not even a hint is found in the New Testament or in the book of Mormon of any hereditary claims by even any one individual.

5th I do not believe in baptizing for the dead![33] It destroys the principle of man's accountability. All men are to be judged according to the deeds done in the body. And if I could be baptized for a person and bring him up in the resurrection, and thus save him, it must be done without his agency, thus destroying his accountability. I save him being proxy for him. Proxy salvation is no salvation at all. Away then with this doctrine. Let every person be saved by their own faith and righteousness; but not by proxy! ~~And~~ But if they are saved in that way then their salvation would not be theirs, but the one who stood surety for them. Nonsense and worse! Proxy never saved a soul since the world began, nor never will, except Christ's proxy for us.[34]

6th I dont believe in tithing one tenth. Not a hint of tithing is found in all the New Testament, or book of Mormon, in ~~its~~ their gospel parts.[35] Its advocates have to go back into the old obsolete law age in order to find tithing. And then there would be a great difficulty having no priest according to the law. It is said, "And the priest the son of Aaron shall be with the Levites, when the Levites take tithing." Nehemi[ah] 10:38. Who is authorised to take or to receive and distribute tithing according to any gospel principle. There is no law or hint given in the gospel system about tithing in any one instance.

---

and Moro. 3:1; 4:1; 6:1, 7 (both editions); "priests" seventy-nine times, and "teachers" thirty times, ranging from 2 Nephi to Moroni.

33. Based on Joseph Smith's teachings in Nauvoo, early RLDS members supported this practice. See Robert B. Madison, "Baptism for the Dead: One RLDS Perspective," *Restoration: The Journal of Latter Day Saint History* 7 (Apr. 1988): 18-23; Roger D. Launius, "An Ambivalent Rejection: Baptism for the Dead and the Reorganized Church Experience," *Dialogue: A Journal of Mormon Thought* 23 (Summer 1990): 61-84.

34. McLellin added "except Christ's proxy for us."

35. McLellin is correct in this. The only mention of "tithes" in the New Testament is where Jesus condemns the Pharisees for the practice (Matt. 23:23; Luke 11:42). In the Book of Mormon, Alma 13:5 refers to Abraham paying tithes and 3 Ne. 24:8, 10 quotes Mal. 3:8, 10.

The doctrine and practice among the Apostles was donations for the benefit of the poor saints, but never any tithing. This again is trying to blend the Law and Gospel ages together. This all L.D. Saints are bound to do, for they try to have the old obsolete priesthood of the law age combined with the Melchisedec order of Priesthood of the Son [page 12:] of God. And thus have two pri[e]sthoods existing at the same time in the church, which was never the case in any former age of the world. Each priesthood while it existed legally in the church or world was head in spiritual affairs, hence could have no partners, or another existing with it, to be an appendage to it.[36]

7th I do not believe John the baptist came and ordained J. Smith and O. Cowdery on the banks of the Susquehannah in 1829. John at that time must have been either a disimbodied Spirit, or an Angel clothed in a material body. No disimbodied spirit can ever visit this earth. And no angel ever ordained a man to any ministerial office since the world began, trusting to the books. Even Christ, after his resurrection into a glorified body, as the angels have, did not at his appearance to Paul ordain him, but said to him, "Arise, and go into the city, and it shall be told thee what thou must do" [Acts 9:6]. This to my mind shows the rule or law by which such things are governed. It is said John confered the Aaronic priesthood upon them at that visit. John was only a chief priest, and did not[37] possess the [priest]hood to give. No Aaronic priest ever ordained any man to any office since they were consecrated themselves. Levi[ticus] 8. Hence that professed ordination was a myth—a nullity. A falsehood! A wicked wrong!!

I never saw such an amount of egregious folly as is manifest in trying to introduce a dead priesthood into the church of Christ, ~~and~~ and[38] then continued in all the parties of L. D. Saintism. Its a perfect impossibility that the old law priesthood should be revived into existence again. And then a priest of that order would be bound to administer the laws of Moses, but not the gospel of Jesus. He would only know the law, but would not know the gospel of Christ, hence could not administer it. Again I say O the folly of otherwise good men!!

---

36. McLellin added "to be an appendage to it."

37. McLellin added "not."

38. The doubling of "and" occurred at the end of one line and beginning of the next.

6.

ON ORIGINAL SIN, 1878

Some of my history
and
also about peep-stones

<u>Original Sin, or Total depravity.</u>[1]

What is original sin? It was the sin of the first sinner. It was the first violation of law and order; the first transgression of an intelligent being. It was the original evil One, who transgressed far up in eternity—It was at creation's dawn. It was when the grand council of the intelligences of heavn was sitting to determine relative to creation.

Then and there when a proposition was made to create and redeem a world, Christ expressed his opinion relative to the subject; but Lucifer delivered a diverse opinion. The intelligent spirits of heaven deliberated upon the two sentiments of those two Mighty Ones. And finally when the vote was reached, and the decision given, two thirds of those spiritual beings voted with Christ, but the other third voted with Satan. But Satan rebelled against that decision. That rebellion was sin, and for that sin he was cast out into outer darkness, with all those who transgressed with him. Thus came Satan and his angels. Jesus says, "Satan abode not in the truth" [cf. John 8:44]. ~

He was not tempted so to do by any other being, but originated the

---

Even though McLellin wrote "Some of my history and also about peep-stones" on the cover of Notebook 6, he ultimately never mentioned either peep-stones or anything about his personal history. Rather, he composed eleven essays, seven of which (the first and third through eighth) were written in response to an article by *Southern Review* editor Albert Taylor Bledsoe, a Methodist. While sometimes McLellin quotes the article verbatim, other times he appears to be either paraphrasing or summarizing it or simply making his own comments on the subject at hand. For these reasons, all seven essays are reproduced here. Borrowing from the lead essay, "On Original Sin," our assigned title better reflects the contents of the notebook than McLellin's own misnomer. In addition to the eleven complete essays, the notebook contains fragments of topics McLellin intended to address but left unfinished.

1. Compare Bledsoe's "Augustinism: Original Sin," *The Southern Review* 22 (1877): 5-61.

thought in his own mind; hence he alone was responsible for his act. He was the original, the first sinner. Original sin then began with the Devil and Satan, and his unruly spirits or demons that were cast out of heaven with him.

Eve and Adam became sinners by rebelling agains[t] the mandate of heaven, but was tempted so to do by the great Son of Perdition, the bitter adversary of Christ. By their sin they brought death into the world. The decree for the offence was, "Thou shalt surely die" [Gen. 2:17]. But what was this death? Previous to this death they were immortal beings, the principle of eternal life coursed in their veins; and gave them activity. But their transgressing God's law by eating the forbidden fruit changed the current of life and caused them to have or take in[2] blood. And blood being corruptible they must end in death. Here they lost the immortal principle of life that hitherto had given them life, and hence fell into mortality or blood-life, and became subject to all the ills and ails consequent thereupon.

And this mortality they communicated to all their offspring–this death principle; because progeny could not be born into the world without blood, for "blood is the life of all flesh" [cf. Gen. 9:4]. And because of blood comes all the ills, the temptations and troubles of life. It was the sin of our parents that brought in blood, and blood brought in the death of the body. It is blood that gives mortal life, and is also the cause of death. Hence all who possess blood must die, or be translated. This is what we call natural death.

This death passed upon all Adam's ~~family~~ posterity. They are all "conceived in sin" [cf. James 1:15], that is, they are conceived in blood, or because of blood, and therefore because of that fluid they must die. For "In Adam all die" [1 Cor. 15:22]. They die [page 2:] because they are partakers of the death fluid. And this is one of the consequences of our first parents transgression.

But as to spiritual death. Adam and Eve died spiritually when they sinned; that is, they were seperated from spiritual intercourse and union with God. They lost that and became dead in their "trespasses and sins" [Eph. 2:1]. They saw they were exposed to temporal death, to be cut off from the earth, and in this present state they could have no converse with their Creator. This was an awful condition. Here God interposed in wisdom, in love, and in condescention to the first pair, and made known to them the plan of redemption; evidenced by his teaching them to offer

2. McLellin added "or take in."

sacrifices, pointing to Jesus, who would be the last l[e]gal[3] sacrifise ever offered up for man's sin. Hence Adam & Eve became spiritually alive by faith in God, through obedince to Christ. They then offered "acceptable sacrifices" [cf. 1 Pet. 2:5] to their Father in heaven.

But as to the eternal death of their posterity is a question we wish to look at. Did Adam and Eve die temporally, spiritually, and eternally when they eat the forbidden fruit? They did not. True, they lost their spiritual union with God, and was sentenced to death; and they would have died eternally, had not the plan of redemption in Christ been made known to them. By transgression they became sinners, and their sin must either be forgiven or punished. "Sin is the actual, voluntary transgression of the law" [cf. 1 Jn. 3:4]. They transgressed law and they sinned. But Paul says, "For where no law is there is no tran[s]gression" [Rom. 4:15]. Infants can be under no law therefore[4] they can be under no sin. And the Book says, "Children shall not be put to death for the fathers" [cf. Deut. 24:16]. But "Every man shall be put to death for his own sin." Deut 24:16.

Adam was a representative of the race, but only so far as he was their natural[5] progenitor. If his sin in his fall could pass to his posterity, then he must have been the father of both their spirits and their bodies. Then his progeny must receive their spirits different from what he did his. He had his direct from God, but theirs in that case, would have come from mortal beings or parents.[6] A mortal being or thing can not produce an immortal. And if our spirits did not come from God they could not go back to him. The Book says, "And the spirit shall return unto God who gave it" [Eccl. 12:7]. Our spirits did not exist in our first parents either before or after their fall. They came from God right out of heaven. Moses said, "God was the God of the spirits of all flesh" [Num. 16:22]. And Zechariah says, "The Lord formeth the spirit of man within him" [Zech.] 12:1. Now God and Adam can not both be the father of our spirits. Hence our spirits could not sin in Adam. Adam's sin brought mortality, and mortality brought blood, and blood being corruptible hence all must die. It is blood that gives mortal life, and also is the cause of death.

And the spirit with its mind being encased in a corruptable body therefore disease, pain, trouble, and death comes upon all who are so

3. McLellin added a word in a different color ink that appears to be "lgal" for the word "legal."

4. McLellin added "therefore."

5. McLellin added "natural."

6. McLellin added "or parents."

clothed in clay. If the sin of the fall could pass to posterity in any other light, then the children would have to die eternally for the sin of their parents, contradicting plain Scripture truth. [page 3:]

Children are all alive in Christ until they arive to the years of accountability. They are not responsable until they are capable of sinning. But says Orthodoxy "All are born under the guilt of Adam's sin." No. Condemnation does not attach until actual sin is committed. "The child shall not die for the father's sin." No stain of Adam adheres to children only the stain of mortality in blood-life. The sin then of our first parents has nothing to do with the damnation or salvation of their offspring. Each must be saved or lost according to his or her faith and conduct in this life. To talk then of Adam's offence standing against us temporally, spiritually, and eternally is mere rubbish to be thrown into the waste basket.

Some of the orthodox hold that Adam's sentence includes the whole of his posterity, that they must die eternally. The sentence of our first parents had no reference to eternal damnation, only to their temporal and spiritual exclusion. ~ Augustine[7] in [the] 5th century invented the dogma of the guilt of Original sin. He did so in order to justify the "eternal damnation of all unbaptized infants." Before his day it was only called the "disease, the depravity, the disorder, or the corruption of our nature." We have an original infection of our nature from Adam, because we partake of blood. Moses said, "For the life of all flesh is the blood thereof" [cf. Gen. 9:4]. In Augustine's controversy with Pelagius[8] he contended for the awful doctrine of the moral guilt of infants. The fathers called what we inherit from Adam "natural evil, corruption, but not sin,—not a moral evil. They regarded it as the misfortune, not as the fault of sin of newly-born infants; that they inherited a corrupt nature from corrupt parents. Blood is the life, for out of it sprang all life of all the human family. And blood being corruptable, that is, in consequence of blood comes mortality, wrong passion, desires, and feelings. All these originate in consequence of our being possessed of blood-life. Hence the saying of the Psalmist "Behold, I was shapen in iniquity; in sin did my mother conceive (or warm) me" [cf. Ps. 51:5]. My mother being a sinner of course she warmed me in her mortal blood. Not that I was a sinner, or in any sense under condemnation. I was inn[o]c[e]nt and only a sinner when I had transgressed God's law, because all sin is a sin against law.

That the new-born infant deserves God's wrath and condemnation

7. For a summary of St. Augustine's life, see the Biographical Notes.

8. For a summary of Pelagius's life, see the Biographical Notes.

is monstrously abhorrent. This misshapen thing ought to be expelled and banished into the limbus of human inventions and gross errors.

There is in man a tendency to natural evil, in consequence of his blood-life with its corrodings, but not a moral evil; corruption but not sin. The early fathers of the church expressly rejected the doctrine of "Original sin." They held it is true, the universality of human corruption, or the original infection of our nature from Adam, but they denied that this corruption or infection is sin. They regarded it as the misfortune, not as the fault or sin of newly born infants, but that they inherited a corrupt nature from corrupt parents.

Chrysostom[9] says, "Infants are corrupt descendants of Adam, though they are not defiled with sin." Infants inherit from Adam blood which lays the [page 4:] foundation of disease, and the corruption of our nature, and finally sometimes leads to death; but not in consequence of their sin in any sense. Infants have disease and death because of the corrupting, corroding material in them.

Augustine is the very first writer who used the terrible word "Original sin," and stamped it with the seal of orthodoxy. None of the fathers pretend that natural depravity in the abstract, or in itself is imputed to man as sin, or unpunished as such. There is a bias to sin found in all men, or a disposition to do what is forbidden by the divine law. Augustine was the father, not of the church, but of Romanism, and Calvanism, and Jesuitism; these three isms have spawned an infinity of lesser isms.

But how comes it, that any word should be employed to designate "natural depravity," as a disease or a sickly moral disease of man, and not be applied to his action; and since man has no guilty agency, (or agency of any kind,) in bringing it upon himself? The state of depravity, or corruption in which all men are born, is not their sin, because it is not a voluntary transgression of the law of God.

The sin of Adam gave man a probation in which he might so act as to gain an eternal reward. Had Adam not sinned then man would not have been. But his sin gave him blood, and the human race came because of blood. And man has the noble freedom of choice between good and evil; to gain rewards or to suffer punishments. It is said "the sin of Adam laid a world in ruins." At the time he sinned no human beings existed to be ruined except the two—Adam and his partner. And as a consequence of his transgression men were produced, and "men are that they might have joy" [2 Ne. 2:25]. That they might be endowed with all the attrib-

9. For a summary of St. John Chrysostom's life, see the Biographical Notes.

utes of their Maker, only in a finite degree; to have ability to see and embrace truth. To have a Savior pointed out to them to redeem them from all their troubles.

The speculations of gifted minds on this all important subject have been multiform. Calvanists, Arminians, and Pelagians have laboured hard to solve the difficulty, but it is unillucidated. They seem to dig into mysteries instead of plain truth. To cover up truth by a verbiage of words. Man exists that he may have the freedom of choice, the freedom of will. To stand looking at good and evil, and then freely choosing which to follow. "Christ is the true Light, which lighteth every man that cometh into the world" [cf. John 1:9]. And by following that Light he may gain eternal life. Sin is a voluntary transgression of law, and holiness is a voluntary obedience to law.

The Jesuits plan[n]ed and cultivated the two great principles from which afterwards innumerable and immense evils resulted. Viz. "That to deceive and lie is a virtue when religion can be promoted by it.["] The other was, that ["]errors in religion, when maintained and adhered to after proper admonition ought to be visited with penalties and punishments." The first gave rise to false reasonings pious frauds, and lying wonders. The other found its fullest [page 5:] and most fatal expression in the horrors of the inquisition. Yet the abhorrent principles were generly held by historians and leaders in the church, of that day and long thereafter. And were especially held by Augustine.

The first sin which Adam committed, in which each one of us bore a part, is accounted to us for "Original sin"; and for this sin we must be punished. But when persons are baptized they need no longer pray for the pardon of original sin, but only for those sins which they daily continue to commit, either in thought, word, or deed. Augustine says, ["]There cannot be sin without will, because it takes by the will. That sin is in such a sense a voluntary evil, that it is in no way sin unless it is voluntary. Sin has its origin in the will of the creature and not in God, or in fate." These statements being true then his theory of Original sin is false.

But to go back a little in order to get the marrow of the subject. In order to get in Original sin Augustine says, "Adults were baptized for the forgiveness of sins.["] So those same words must be used in the baptism of infants. But as they have no sins of their own, so they must needs have Original sin to be forgiven in baptism. Little infants were declared to be miserable little sinners. They were fallen, depraved, and ruined creatures; and therefore needed redemption, regeneration, sanctification, and holiness, ere they could be admitted into the kindom of God. Thus the doctrine of natural or total[10] depravity as a hell-deserving sin was invented to uphold the doctrine of baptizing infants to save them from hell.

Augustine endeavoured to show, that infants incurred the guilt of original sin, because it was their own voluntary sin! He contends that ["]when Adam sinned, all his posterity was in him, and the individual will of each and every one, concurred with his will in the first transgression. This it is which makes their sin voluntary; and, consequently truly sin, even in the new-born infants. They sinned voluntarily in Adam. If one soul was made from which are derived the souls of all men who are born, who can say that he did not sin when the first one sinned? In respect to the origin of the seed from which all were to spring, all were that one individual, and all these were **he**; none of whom as yet existed individually." Thus is Original sin all in the dark fogs of worse than bigoted priest-craft.–It is wo[e]ful blindness, unintelligible jargon. He calls ["]the question of the guilt of original sin, most vexatious, most dangerous; and full of breakers." And well he might.

The historians, writing of the fourth century, (about the middle of which Augustine was born,) say:–The first of those two horrid principles of lying and murder, had been embraced in the preceding century; and what a host of pious falsehoods, have through all the centuries grown out of it, to the great detriment of religion. The most pious teachers of this century were infected with this leprosy. I cannot except Ambrose,[11] nor Hilary,[12] nor Augustine, nor Gregory Nazianzen,[13] nor Jerome[14] ... The other principle, from the time [page 6:] when Constantine gave peace and security to the Christians, was approved by many; and in the conflicts with the Priscil[l]ianists and Donatists it was corroborated by examples, and unequivocally sanctioned by the authority of A[u]gustine, and thus transmitted to succeeding ages.

Augustine held that baptism was the absolute condition of pardon and salvation: if so it follows that the unbaptized cannot be saved, or escape the punishment of the future world. Hence all Christians' children, dying without baptism, as well as the heathen, even those most highly valued for their virtues, must be eternally doomed. He maintained that

10. McLellin added "or total."

11. For a summary of St. Ambrose's life, see the Biographical Notes.

12. For a summary of St. Hilary's life, see the Biographical Notes.

13. For a summary of Gregory Nazianzen's life, see the Biographical Notes.

14. For a summary of Jerome's life, see the Biographical Notes.

there was no middle place, so that he who is not with Christ, must be with the Devil. He says that infants are doomed to eternal misery, not merely for the loss of baptism, but for "Original sin." It was for this sin, that they deserved God's wrath and damnation."

He says again, "unless infants receive the benefits of the sacrament of baptism they must be damned. But damned they cannot be without sin. Hence, since they have no sin of their own in their proper person, it is necessary for us to credit them with Original sin." Historians say of him that "He stamped his image on all succeeding ages." But one of the features of this image, be it forever remembered, was stamped on the annals of the church in characters of blood, and in the grim terror of the Inquisition! The spirit, not of Christ, but of Cain, reigned in their mortal bodies. Protestantism owes to him only the dark Calvinistic scheme of Predestination.

The fathers taught that death (depravity,) is in consequence of Adam's sin, and yet that is not, in itself, to be regarded as sin, and punished accordingly. God punishes us only for our own sins, and not for Adam's.[15] That the flaw of wickedness is not nature, but contrary to nature, and has its origin, not in the Creator, but in the will of the creature, and not in God, or in fate. Sin is no way sin unless it is <u>voluntary</u>. If sin be natural it is not sin at all: It must be voluntary. Wickedness is not nature, but contrary to nature, and has its origin not in the Creator, but in the will; that is, in the will of the creature. Sin takes by the person whose sin it is, and not by the will of another. He says ["]the fallen Angels and men fell by their own free-will."

He expressly says, "That God foreknows, but does not predetermine them: God foresaw, but did not predetermine, the fall of some angels and men ... On account of that which he has not received, no one is guilty; but on account of that which he ought to do and does not, he is justly guilty. No one is compelled by his nature to sin. Nor does any other nature ~~compell~~ compel him. For one does not sin when he suffers that which he does not will. If sin cannot be avoided there are no sins; for who sins in that which cannot in any way be avoided. But sin [page 7:] is committed, therefore it can be avoided.[16]

---

15. McLellin wrote and then deleted the following because he had already written it at the beginning of the previous paragraph: "Augustine says, unless infants receive the benefit of the sacrament of baptism they must be damned. But damned they cannot be without sin. Hence since they have no sin of their own, in their proper person, it is necessary for us to credit them with Original sin.—" This error indicates that he is copying from someone else's work.

16. McLellin wrote and then deleted the following redundancy from the previous

But Augustine himself it seems began to doubt. He says, "When we approach the question of the punishment of infants, believe me, I am pressed by perplexeties, nor can I find out at all what answer is to be given to it." Then he ought to have kept silence, and not penned the nonsense that all mankind sinned in Adam. It is certain that if all sinned in common, then death came by the sin of all. But it is the doctrine of Paul, that "by one man, not by all, sin entered into the world, and death by sin" [cf. Rom. 5:12]. But there can be no participation of an infant in an act of the free-will of Adam, unless his will is identified with Adam's will.

The dogma of Original sin of Augustine, came down through the dark and troubled stream of the Middle Ages, and finally, in spite of all the shocks of time, deposited it securely in all the great creeds of Christendom–Romish, Lutheran, Calvinistic, and Anglican. If Pelagius had admitted the fall (says Bledsoe,)[17] and ruin of the race, the depravity of mankind as a fatal disease, but denied its sinfulness, he would have occupied ground from which he could not have been dislodged. I have drawn much of this from his "Southern Review,["][18] and I am thankful for the privilege.

But once more. Why baptize infants at all? They answer ["]for saintship, righteousness, adoption, inheritance, and brotherhood with Christ, and be made members of him." Theodoret[19] says, "It is a pledge of future blessings, a type of the resurrection, a communication of Christ's passion." &c. Isodorius[20] says, "Infants obtain redemption, regenera-

---

two pages: "The fathers taught that death (depravity,) is in consequence of Adam's sin, and yet that is not, in itself, to be regarded as sin, and punished accordingly. God punishes us for our own sins only, and not for Adam's. But Augustine contended that when Adam sinned, all his posterity was in him, and the individual will of each, and every one, concurred with his will in the first transgression. This it is which makes their sin voluntary; and consequently truly sin, even in the new-born infants. They sinned voluntarily in Adam. If one soul was made, from which are derived the souls of all men who are born, who can say that he did not sin when the first one sinned? In Adam all have sinned, as all were that one man. Those are not condemned who have not sinned, since that sin has not passed from one to all, in which <u>one</u> all have sinned in common, previously to the personal sins of each as an individual. In respect to the origin of the seed from which all were to spring, all were that one individual, and all these were **he**; none of whom as yet existed individually." The second to last sentence was not a part of the previously written material.

17. For a summary of Albert Taylor Bledsoe's life, see the Biographical Notes.

18. Albert Taylor Bledsoe founded the *Southern Review* in January 1867 and was its editor until his death in December 1877, assisted by his daughter Sophia Bledsoe Herrick beginning in 1875. Sophia continued as editor through its final issue in July 1879, with sponsorship from the Methodist Episcopal Church South since 1870.

19. For a summary of Theodoret's life, see the Biographical Notes.

20. McLellin has misspelled his name as "Isodorius." Bledsoe's "Augustinism," 11, gives the Latin name correctly given as "Isidorus Pelusiota," meaning Isidore of Pelusium. For a summary of Isidore's life, see the Biographical Notes.

tion, and adoption.["] But never freed from Original or birth-sin. It was left for the controversalist Augustine, to bring up from the deep of his imagination the awful doctrine of Original sin, and the more horrible stain on Christianity of infant damnation, in the hell prepared for the Devil and his angels. [page 8:][21]

We want now to say a few words on this much discussed and debated subject of Original sin. As we said in the beginning Satan was the first sinner, and Eve was the second, and Adam was the third in transgression. But after Eve and Adam had both sinned, they were cast out of their beautiful garden, and away from the "tree of life," and driven away in order to labour in the wide earth, to gain their living by the "sweat of their brow" [cf. Gen. 3:19]. Their natures were made mortal—made corruptable in that of taking in blood-life by their fall. Then because of blood children were born, and the question arises whether their little ones were sinners? Or were they only born of sinful parents? "Born into trouble as the sparks are to fly upwards." "In sin did my mother conceive me" [Ps. 51:5]. Now the question is whether the mother or child was the sinner? The child could not transgress law by being conceived by its mother. In no sense could it be said that the infant sinned in conception, because sin is disobedience of law, and the conceived child had no volition, was unable to obey or disobey, hence could not be accountable, had no will of its own in conception, was not an agent in any sense. It had nothing but its origin because of blood from its parents. And its blood-life was not its fault, it had no agency in the matter of its being born of sinful parents.

An infant in conception has no will, all its powers of mind come afterward. It is an unfinished thing, only part of a being; and no unfinished thing can think—can meditate—can reason, has no mind as yet, cant possibly act; therefore cant be a sinner, because sin is an act—an intelligent act. Then the mother must be the one who "warms and feeds the living fire." She nourishes the child in gestation. A little helpless, innocent child a sinner! It is one of the most outrageous, infamous sentiments of which the human mind can conceive. The most unworthy of an enlightened age. Then all the iniquity and sin must be in and of the mother, and not the child.

Christ said of infant children, "For of such is the kingdom of heaven" [Matt. 19:14]. ["]Little children are not capable of committing sin; wherefore the curse of Adam is taken from them in Christ. They are

---

21. At this point McLellin appears to present his own ideas on Original Sin.

alive in Christ from the first one born, until the last one that will ever be brought forth. For the power of redemption comes on all them that have no law" [cf. Moro. 8:8, 22].[22] This is the spirit of inspiration–it is sacred truth. Original sin has been shaped in the work shops of human folly, and not stamped in[23] the mint of Divine Wisdom.

Until a law was given sin was not in the world. Sin cannot exist without law, because sin is a transgression of law. What human, or divine, or morral law could an infant transgress? It is not capable of obeying or disobeying of law, but is perfectly innocent. And what it has to look back to our first parents for is its natural blood-life, and in consequence of that it has to suffer all the "ills flesh is heir to," even while in infancy, and finally sometimes even suffers death. It partakes of the fallen or mortal nature of our first parents and must be redeemed in Christ. If not redeemed it could never rise from the dead–[page 9:] could not get a glorified body, so as to live in heaven; hence would have to be left out of the glory of that upper world. But the redemption of Christ passes upon and resurrects all infants, because they are not condemned by law.

No being can go and dwell in that upper glory without a body glorified. Christ did not go there while he was disimbodied. He went to Paradise, the place of the departed spirits of the righteous. Infants are all alive in Christ, and will be alive in him by their resurrection during all eternity. Sin! They have no sin, neither moral or spiritual. Infants are under no law–have no sin, consequently no condemnation. I say again, "Of such is the kingdom of heaven" [Matt. 19:14]. Christ came into the world with the object to make men as good and innocent as little children. He said, "Except ye be converted, and become as little children, ye shall not enter into the kingdom of heaven" [Matt. 18:3]. The question is how are children saved, and from what are they saved? First then, they are saved by the app[l]ication of the merits of Christ; and they are saved from an eternity away from him by their resurrection. Had not Christ risen from the dead all this lower creation would have been lost. But how lost! A decree or vote was passed in the grand council of intelligent spirits in heaven when they agreed to come into the world and take bodies, and have a probation on this earth; to never return back to heaven unless they could go there in their bodies glorified. That was the reason why Christ did not ascend up "to his Father" in his disimbodied state. He said

22. This Book of Mormon quotation is another clear indication of McLellin's authorship here.

23. McLellin accidentally doubles the word "in" at the end of one line and beginning of the next–neither instance having been marked for deletion.

to Mary, "I have not yet ascended to my Father and your Father" [cf. John 20:17].

When persons die their spirits, "return unto God who gave them" [cf. Eccl. 12:7]. And then the righteous are sent to Paradise, but the wicked are consigned to Prison. When persons die their spirits do not go immed[i]ately to heaven, to dwell with the Lord Jesus Christ, but they go where disembodied spirits dwell, while in their naked state. An unclothed or disimbodied spirit is not fit for heaven or hell, but dwells in a place prepared for it, there to remain until their resurrection. And when they get their bodies they will go to their final abode.

I dont know the precise state of infants, either on earth, or in heaven. Whether, when in heaven they will remain in their condensed form as infants, or whether in their glorified state they will be enlarged as men and women? Fully capable of enjoyment as intelligent men. Whether their spirits when freed from infant-bodies will assume the full size of men to enjoy glory? Or whether their spirits have to grow or can grow as their bodies do in order for their enjoyment in heaven. But of one thing I feel sure, all who die in infancy are not damned, as Augustine's theory would have them, but they are everlastingly saved. Saved because Jesus Christ is the Savior of all the innocent. And as infants are perfectly innocent, neither subject to law, nor in any sense under law, therefore ~~therefore~~[24] they are under no condemnation and consequently they must be saved. Satan has no claim upon them in any sense, any more than he had on the innocent Jesus of Nazareth. [page 10:]

The ninth clause of the Articles of faith of the church of England has a clause respecting Original sin. That clause teaches, that even the new-born infant, mearly on account of what it brought into the world with it "dese[r]veth God's wrath and damnation." From the time of A[u]gustine down to the Reformation, the sentiment of that clause was used to justify the damnation of unbaptized infants, dying in infancy. The wrath and damnation of God is turned ~~away~~ aside from the poor, little, helpless creatures, by the ablution of water from priestly fingers!

Original sin standeth not in the following of Adam, but it is the fault and the corruption of nature of every man that naturally is engendered of the offspring of Adam; whereby man is very far gone from Original Righteousness, and is of his own nature inclined to evil, so that the flesh lusteth always contrary to the Spirit; and therefore in every person, born into this world, it deserveth God's wrath and damnation.

---

24. McLellin unintentionally wrote "therefore" twice, then deleted the second occurrence.

[If a Person Exercises Faith][25]

If a person exercises faith in an object today that is no reason why he should have faith tomorrow, because faith always has an object, and the object of today may not be the object of tomorrow. And every object has its own faith, and it requires immedate faith to produce a result. The oftener a man exercises faith the easier it becomes. Confidence increases the oftener faith is exercised. A person can add to his faith, and thus strengthen it. And by its continual exercise it grows stronger—more firm.

Moses believed in God, and also had faith in him. He and the children of Israel were besieged on the bank of the Red Sea by the Egyptians. He firmly believed in God, but did not then know what to do, until the Lord told him to stretch his rod over the Sea. But still he had no faith until the Lord said, "Stretch out thine hand over the sea, and divide it." The moment the word "divide" ~~it~~ struck his ear living faith sprung into his heart and power followed. He first had belief, then the immediate gift of faith, and then the Holy Spirit produced the power of dividing the Sea, which stood in heaps or walls of water on either side while Israel passed through on dry land.[26] This was the divine gift of faith. [page 11:]

~~In Hebrews it is said, "Faith is the evidence of things not seen." According to the above faith is evidence in the mind of unseen things. Its [the] operation of mind and Spirit.~~[27] [page 12:]

Knowledge[28] and free-~~Will~~ Agency

Thus says Mr Stewart,[29] "On this point I must decline offering any opinion of my own, because I conceive it as placed far beyond the reach of our faculties." Dr Campbell[30] says, "The subject is what I have never yet seen achieved by any, and indeed dispair of seeing." And Locke[31] declares, "I have long since given off the consideration of that subject, re-

25. This essay, which has been assigned a title from its initial words, was written upside down from the previous text.

26. McLellin added "while Israel passed through on dry land."

27. These three sentences were written upside down on the page and later crossed out.

28. McLellin has miscopied the title, writing "Knowledge" instead of "Foreknowledge." The title of Bledsoe's essay is "Foreknowledge and Free Will," *The Southern Review* 15 (1874): 91-109.

29. For a summary of Dugald Stewart's life, see the Biographical Notes.

30. For a summary of George Campbell's life, see the Biographical Notes.

31. For a summary of John Locke's life, see the Biographical Notes.

solving all into this short conclusion, that if it is possible for God to make a free-agent, then man is free, though I see not the way of it." But A. T. Bledsoe writes[32] ~

Why should it be thought impossible to reconcile the free-agency of man with the foreknowledge of God? No one pretends that there is any disagreement between the things themselves, as they really exist; if there is any discrepancy in the case, it must exist only between our ideas of foreknowledge and free agency. What shall we do then? Shall we set to work to reform our ideas? Shall we explain away the free-agency of man, or deny the foreknowledge of God? No. We may retain both.

The great doctrine of moral necessity is that volitions are brought to pass by the infuence of motives, and that it is impossible in any case but[33] that a volition must come[34] from the influence of the strongest motive. I think this argument does not prove anything in relation to the causation of choice. The great doctrine of free-will which is clear and unquestionable, is overshadowed and obscured by an imperfect and ambiguous phraseology, rather than by the[35] inherent difficulties of the subject.

When the existence of a thing is infallibly and indissolubly connected with something else, which has already had existence, then its existence is necessary; but the future volitions of moral agents are infallibly and indisolubly connected with the foreknowledge of God; and therefore they are necessary. True. But what does it prove? Does it prove that they are necessary with a moral necessity? Does it prove that they are brought to pass by the influence of moral causes? Foreknowledge exerts no influence on the thing known to make it necessary. But no moral arrangement is shown to exist in the above arrangement. The infallible connection it shows to exist, is admitted to be entirely different from the infallible connection between moral causes and volitions.

The foreknowledge of a future event proves it to be[36] necessary in precisely the same manner that the knowledge of a present event shows it to be necessary. In what sense does the knowledge of a present event prove it to be necessary? It is necessary because it is indisolubly connected with the knowledge of it. It could not possibly be known to exist, unless it did exist, hence it is said to be necessary.

---

32. McLellin later inserted "But A. T. Bledsoe writes" in a different color ink. This indicates where this particular quotation begins, but we can not be sure where it ends.

33. McLellin added "but" above the line in brown ink.

34. McLellin added "must come" above the line in brown ink.

35. McLellin originally wrote "by their."

36. McLellin added "be" above the line in brown ink.

I know a thing exists; and therefore it does exist. This is to reason from effect to cause. But what does it prove? Why, it proves that the thing does exist–it proves the bare fact of its existence. The indisoluble connection, or the necessity, in this case, exists between the foreknowledge and the event known; and it has no relation to the question how the event came to exist. We admit that volitions [page 13:] are efficient causes, and that they have effects, with which they are connected.

For the sake of distinctness in our language, as well as in our thoughts, I shall call one a logical, and the other an axiomatical necessity. A thing then, which does exist, is said to be necessary with an axiomatical necessity; because it is impossible for it not to exist while it does exist; and it is[37] said to be necessary, with a logical necessity, because it is indissolubly connected with the knowledge of it. The thing which now exists, having already made sure of existence, it is impossible they should not exist, or in other words, it is impossible they should not exist while they do exist. In like manner, if the future existence of any thing is foreknown, it is impossible it should be otherwise than true, that it should exist, or come to pass–that is to say, if it will exist, it will be impossible for it not to exist at the time of its existence.

Foreknowledge I admit, infers this kind of necessity. All the above is perfectly true, without the least reference[38] to the question, how it came to exist, or how it will come to exist? But this does not prove that it is necess[a]rily produced. For, supposing it to exist, its existence would be necessary in the above sense, even if it had no cause of its existence. The necessity here refered to is a necessity in the order of our ideas, and in the course of events. And it has no reference whatever to the causation of anything: it is a fundamental law of belief, and not a causal necessity.

There is an indissoluble connection between the existence of a thing, and the certain and infallible knowledge of its existence; or between the effect of a thing and the thing itself, or that it is imposible for a thing to not exist[39] while it does exist. In this sense human volitions are necessary. If it can be truly said, that a thing is foreknown, it follows that it will come to pass, or the proposition which it affirms the future existence of it, is necessarily true.

It is freely conceded, that whatever God foreknows will most certainly and infallibly come to pass. He foresees all human volitions; and

37. McLellin added "is" above the line in brown ink.

38. McLellin originally wrote "influence," which he corrected to "reference."

39. McLellin originally wrote "to exist," which he corrected to the wording "to not exist."

therefore, they will most certainly and infallibly come to pass, in some manner or other: the bare fact of their future is clearly established by God's foreknowledge of them. And if all human volitions will be brought to pass, by the operation of moral causes, then this manner of their existence is foreknown to God, and all will come to pass in this way. We have just as much right to suppose that God foreknows that the volitions of moral agents are not necessitated, as the necessitarian has to suppose that He foreknows the contrary; and then it would follow that our volitions are necessarily free, or without any producing causes. If God foreknows that our actions will come to pass in the way we call freely, then, as foreknowledge infers necessity, our actions are neces-s[a]rily free.

Every advocate of free-agency contends that volition proceeds from the mind, acting in view of motives, and therefore, is not destitute of a sufficient ground and reason of its existence, and denies that volition is necessarily brought to pass by the operation of motives. [page 14:]

The necessitarian contends that with God "there is no time" but that to his view all things are seen as if they were present. His knowledge is without succession, and there is no before nor after with him; all things are intimately present to his mind from all eternity. Dr. Dick[40] believes that "God sees all things at a glance." Now, present things are not known[41] to exist because they are implied by known causes, but because they are present and seen. And hence, if God sees all things as present, there is not the shadow of a foundation whereon to rest the proof of "moral necessity" from his foreknowledge. It is all taken away by their own doctrine, and their argument is left without the least support from it.

Indeed there is no need of lugging the foreknowledge of God into the present controversy, except it be to deceive the mind. For all future events will certainly and infallibly come to pass, whether they are foreknown or not; and foreknowledge cannot make the matter any more certain than it is without it. We may say that God foreknows all things, and we may mix this up with all possible propositions; but this will never help the conclusion, that "all future things will certainly and infallibly come to pass." It is just as much a contradiction in terms to say that what is future will not come to pass, as it is to say, that what God foreknows will never take place! This whole argument, from the foreknowledge of God, is indeed, a grand specimen of undesigned metaphysical jugglery,

40. For a summary of John Dick's life, see the Biographical Notes.

41. McLellin originally wrote "are known," which he corrected to "are not known."

by which the mind is called off in one direction, whilst it is deceived, perplexed, and confounded by not seeing what takes place in another.

And how unreasonable are those who have imagined that we are free-agents, because God has chosen not to foresee our free actions; as if the supposition that he might have foreseen them, does not infer necessity just as much as the fact that he does foresee them. Indeed these reasoners seem to have expected to see one truth by shutting their eyes upon another. This then is the conclusion of the whole matter. The prescience of God does not make our volitions necessary; it only proves them to be certain. It proves them to be certain, just as present knowledge proves them to be certain. It proves it to be certain, because it is impossible for a volition, or any thing else, not to exist at the time of its existence, and not because it is imposible for it to come to pass without being necessitated. In short, it proves an axiomatical and a logical necessity, but not a causal necessity—that is to say, it proves nothing to the point.

And besides, the bringing in of the divine prescience only serves to blind and not to illuminate. For God foreknows only what is future; and all future things will come to pass just as infallibly without being foreknown as they will with it. If we assume them to be future, it is just as much a contradiction to deny that they will come to pass, as it is to assume [page 15:] that they are foreknown, and yet deny it. Nothing can be proved in this way, except what is assumed or taken for granted.

In conclusion, the necessitarian takes the wrong course in his inquiries and lays his premises in the dark. To illustrate this point: I know that I act, hence I conclude that God foreknew that I would act. Again, I know that my act is not necessitated, that it does necessarily proce[e]d from the action or influence of causes, and hence I conclude that God foreknew that I would thus act freely, in precisely this manner, and not otherwise. Thus I reason from what I know to what I do not know, from my knowledge of the actual world as it is up to God's foreknowledge respecting it.

The necessitarian persues the opposite course. He reasons from what he does not know—that is, from the particulars of the divine foreknowledge, about which he absolutely knows nothing, down to the facts of the actual world. Thus quitting the light which shines so brightly within us and round us, he seeks for light in the midst of impenetrable darkness. he endeavors to determine the phenomena of the world, not by looking at them and seeing what they are, by deducing conclusions from God's infinite foreknowledge respecting them!

God foresees all our actions, and also all about them. He foresees that our volitions will come to pass, and also how they will come to pass. If the argument from foreknowledge proves any thing, it just as well proves the necessity of freedom as any thing else. It seems strange to me that so many bright thinkers, with superior intellects should so long have endeavored to draw conclusions from "The dark unknown" of God's foreknowledge, without perceiving that no powers, however great, that no genius, however exalted, can possibly extort from such a method any thing but the dark, and confused, and perplexing exhibitions of an ingenious war of words.

Of Action and passion.

There are no two things in nature which are more perfectly distinct than action and passion; the one necessarily excludes the other. An act of the mind cannot be a produced effect; that the ideas of action and passion, of cause and effect, are opposite and contrary the one to the other; And Hence it is absurd to assert that the mind may be caused to act, or that a volition can be produced by any thing acting upon the mind. This is a self evident truth.

We freely admit that a body may be caused to move. Body is perfectly passive in motion, and hence its motion may be caused. But the mind is not passive in volition, and hence the difference in the two cases. It is an error of the necessitarian in confounding the action of the mind with the motion of body. Body is said to act when it only moves, and mind is said to move when it really acts. When a body moves it simply passes from one place to another; and when the mind acts or chooses, it simply [page 16:] prefers one thing to another. The body suffers a change; the mind itself acts. The one is pure passion or passiveness; the other is pure action–the very opposite to passivity. The one is a suffering, and the other is a doing.

No one means to assert, that there are no conditions or antecedents on which the action of the mind depends. No free-agent will contend the mind can choose a thing, unless there is a thing to be chosen; or can read a book unless there is a book to be read. The question is, can the mind be efficiently caused to act? We do not at all confound action and passion. The necessitarian confounds motion with volition, passion with action. The only cause in every case of motion is force, which acts upon the body moved, and puts it in motion. All the rest is pure passion or passiveness. We do not at all confound action and passion. Living and being are not acting. We are not passive in regard to volition. This is an act of the mind itself. The action of the mind is different, in nature and in kind, from a passive impression made upon the mind from without. Action itself is opposite in its nature to passion—to a produced effect.

We are conscious of a volition or choice; and hence we infer that we have a power of acting, or putting forth volition. This power we call the will. No man can show, that the sensibility and the will are one and the same faculty of the soul. The passive impression, the state of the sensibility, is produced; but this is not a volition. The passive impression exists in the sensibility; the volition exists in the will. The first is a produced effect; the last is an act of the mind. The mind is active in regard to or in its volition; and hence these cannot be produced by the action of any thing upon the mind. If the mind cannot be caused to act, it is not true, that an action or volition does or can result from the necessitating action or influence of motion.

Of Cause and Effect

Of the axiom that every effect must have a cause. In order to lay it open to clear light, it will be necessary to consider the nature and the use of the maxim, that every effect must have a cause. Cause and effect are correlative terms; and when we speak of an effect, we mean something that is produced by a cause; and hence the famous proposition, that every effect has a cause amounts only to this, that every effect is only an effect.

It is common now to say, there is no change in nature without a cause. But it does not mend the matter in the least: it may disguise, but does not alter the nature or real import of the maxim in question. Change and effect must mean the same. The axiom or maxim, that every effect must have a cause, is a self evident and universal proposition. In this respect it is like the axioms of geometry. An effect is that which is produced by a cause. The very idea of an effect implies its relation to a cause, and to say that it has one is only to say that an effect is an effect. [page 17:] For if it were not produced by a cause, it would not be an effect. It is impossible for the imagination of man to conceive, that an effect or that which is produced by a cause, should be without a cause. It has no reputation in reason.

In what sense does every act of the mind come under the idea and definition of an effect? This is the question. Is it brought to pass by the prior action of motive? Is it necessitated? The maxim in question is applied to volition; every change in nature, even the voluntary acts of the mind must have a cause. This is a proposition which, I venture to say no man in his right mind ever ventured to deny. Did any man in his right mind ever contend that a "volition could produce itself," can arise out of nothing, and bring itself into existence? Universally libertarians maintain with one consent that the mind is the cause of volition. Is the mind nothing? Is motion the efficient or producing cause of volition? This is the question.

If the necessitarian means to assert that nothing, whether it be an entity, or an attribute, or a mode, can bring itself into existence, no one disputes his doctrine. It is most true, that there can be no choice without a mind that chooses; a mind, an object, and a desire, are the indispensable prerequisites. The invariable antecedents to volition; but there is an immense chasm between this position and the doctrine that the mind cannot put forth a volition, unless it is made to do so by the action of something else upon it.

Whence do we derive the ideas of cause and effect, and of the necessary connection between them? The only way in which the mind ever comes to be furnished with the ideas of cause and effect at all is this: we are conscious that we will a certain motion of the body, and we discover that the motion follows the volition. It is this act of the mind, this exertion of the will, that gives us the idea of a cause; and the change which it produces in the body, is that from which we derive the idea of an effect. If we had never experienced a volition, we should never have formed the idea of causation. The idea of positive efficiency, or active power, would never have entered our minds.

The two terms of sequence and consequence, with which we are thus furnished by an actual experience, is an act of the mind, or a volition, on the one hand, which we call an efficient cause, and a modification or change in inert passive matter, on the other, which we call an effect. We have really no idea of an efficient cause, except that which we have derived from the phemomena of action. When we see any change or effect in the material world, we should conclude that it proceeds from an action of Spirit. Whenever we see a change in matter, we should infer an act by which it is produced; and thus, through all the changes and modifications of the material universe, we shall behold the sublime manifestations of an un[ending] ever-present and all-pervading agency of Spirit. [page 18:]

We have no experience that an act of the mind is produced by a preceding act of the mind, or by the prior action of anything else. A change in body necessarily implies the prior action of something else by which it is produced; an act of the mind only implies the existence of an agent that is capable of acting. The question is, whether every cause is an effect? Or, in other words, whether an act of the mind can exist without being produced by the prior action of something else; just as the motion of body is produced by the prior action of mind? We say it can exist without any such producing cause.

Of the Will and the Feelings[42]

If every state of the Will bears the same relation to some feeling–such as appetite or desire–which an effect sustains to its cause, it seems impossible to regard it as possessing the characteristic of freedom. On the contrary it must evidently appear to be bound fast in the mechanism of cause and effect, and therefore not a free act of the mind. The will is the only self-active power of the soul. The will is the master and not the slave, of the passive susseptabilities of the soul. Our feelings possess no real strength by which they act upon and control the will. If our desires, affections &c., operate to influence the will, how can it be free in putting forth volitions? Thus we are supposed to be free, because we have a power to resist, in some cases at least, the influence of desire. But this is not always the case. Our desires or passons may be so strong as entirely to overcome us–and what then? Why we cease to be free-agents, and it is only when the storm of passion subsides, that we are restored to the rank of accountable beings. [John] Locke thinks we frequently cease to be free agents, in consequence of the irresistable power of our desires and passions.

To talk of liberty, or the contrary, as belonging to the will itself, is not to speak with good. For the will itself is not an agent that has a will: the power of choosing itself has not a power of choosing. That which has the power of volition is the inner soul, and not the power of volition itself. To be free is the property of an agent, who is possessed of powers and faculties, as much as being cunning, valiant, bountiful, or zealous. But these qualities are the properties of persons, and not the properties of properties. For power is a property of the person, or the soul; and not the property of a property.

The free acts of the will are determined by the will itself. Power is a property of the mind itself, and is ascribed to our desires, or passions, or affections which are likewise properties of the mind. Desires do not impel the will to act, but desire, feeling &c, are merely the conditions necessary to volition, and not its producing cause. But what do we mean by a

42. Cf. Bledsoe's "The Relation of the Will to the Feelings," *The Southern Review* 23 (1878): 339-51.

will, if it is not the faculty by which the mind acts, by which it exerts a real force?

The truth is, that in feeling the mind is passive; and it is absurd to ~~to~~ make a passive impression, the active cause of any thing. The feeling or sensibility does not act, it mearly suffers. The appetites and passions, which have always been called "the active powers," "the moving principles," s[h]ould be called the passive susseptabilities. [page 19:]

Inclination and previous bias, and appetite and disposition are distinct from volition—our desires and affections are also different—neither is feeling volition. The feelings do not act upon and control the will. The will is independent of their influences.

The will—the only self-active power of the soul—the mind, is not under the dominion of causes over which it has no control. Or, in other words, that the will is master and not the slave, of the passive susseptabilities of the soul. This distinction made between the power of a principle and its authority enables us to form a precise estimate of the place which conscience naturally and rightly holds in man's constitution. We cannot form a notion of the faculty of conscience, without taking in judgement, direction, and superintendency. This is a constituent part of the idea, that is of the faculty itself; used to preside and govern, f[or] the very economy and constitution of man, belongs to it. Had it might, as well as right; had it power, as it has manifest authority, it would absolutely govern the world.

If our desires, affections, &c., operate to influence the will, how can it be free in putting forth volitions? The desires by which volitions are supposed to be determined, are in reality nothing more than the conditions or occasions on which the mind acts; and that they themselves can exert no positive influence or efficiency. The necessitarian asserts, that "we know that the feelings do exert an influence in the production of volition." At first view this may appear very evident to the mind; and yet, after all, it may be only "an idol of the tribe."

He might have supposed, that our desires and affections are produced by the action of external objects; and yet on the supposition that these exerted no positive or causal influence, the doctrine of liberty might have been most successfully maintained. For, after all, the desires and affections produced in the mind would not be the cause of our volitions. They would mearly be the occasions on which we act. There would be no necessary causel connection between motive and their corresponding actions. Our volitions would be perfectly free from all preceding influences whatever. Our volitions might depend on certain conditions, it is true, such as the possession of certain desires or affections but they would not result from the influence or action of them.

They would be absolutely free and uncontrolled. The fact that a desire or affection is the indispensable condition, the invariable antecedent of an act of the will. Nothing is more common than for men to mistake an invariable antecedent for an efficient cause–the will is the faculty by which the mind acts, by which it exerts a real force. The necessitarian asserts that the will is determined by the "strongest appetite, disposition, or inclination." He also says, moral necessity may be as absolute as natural necessity. But in some cases, a previous bias or inclination or the motive presented may be so powerful that the act of the will may be certainly and indissolubly connected therewith. But it is wrong to suppose that our feelings possess a real strength, by which they act upon and control the will. [page 20:]

The Mind and Will.[43]

The great point is, What determines the will? What is meant by determining the Will? The necessitarian says, "it is not[44] to learn whether the mind acts at all. This no one can doubt. Nor is it to determine why we will act[45] at all." The very nature of the faculty of the will implies that we put forth volitions. But the real point of inquiry is, why we will one way rather than another; why we choose one thing rather than its opposite? What is it that determines not only that there shall be volitions, but what shall they be, and how shall the mind put forth volitions at all? And how a Spirit comes to act, and why its action has such a particular direction and determination?

Can there be one cause of volition, and another cause of its particular direction? There cannot. No such distinction can be shown to exist by a reference to the cause of motion. All motion and the direction of the object is caused by force. Choice always has an object. It is of the very nature and essence of a choice to have some particular direction and determination. The activity of the soul, is the cause of its acting; yet motive may be the indispensable condition of its acting; and in this sense, may be the reason why a volition is one way rather than another. There are not two causes in the case, one to produce volition, and another to deter-

---

43. Cf. Bledsoe's "Of the Application of the Maxim That Every Effect Must Have a Cause," *The Southern Review* 23 (1878): 26-33.

44. McLellin added "not."

45. McLellin added "act."

mine its object. That which produces a thing is its efficient cause. Does not every cause of volition include the efficient cause thereof?

The necessitarian and libertarian are directly opposed to each other about motive and volition. When we reason from those things which begin to be up to God, we clearly reason from effects to their efficient causes. The necessitarian holds that volitions are necessarily connected with the influence of motives; they are brought to pass by the prevailing and effectual influence of motives. Motive is the effectual power and efficacy by which they are produced. They are not merely caused to be thus, and not otherwise, by motive; they are caused to rise and come forth into existence. This is the doctrine which I deny. Can this system be reconciled with the reality of virtue, with the moral agency and accountability of man, and with the purity of God; then I shall lay aside my objections.

What determines the will? The necessitarian replies, it is the strongest motive. To be determined by the strongest motive, to follow the greatest apparent good, to do what is most agreeable, or what pleases most; these forms of expression set forth the same fundamental doctrine.

A volition does not proceed from the mind, or from motive, or from any thing else in the same manner that an effect, properly so called, proceeds from its efficient cause. If we mean by an effect every thing that [page 21:] comes to pass, of course a volition is an effect; for no one can deny that it comes to pass. Or, if we include in the definition of the term every thing which has a sufficient reason and ground of its existence, we cannot deny that it embraces the idea of a volition. For under certain circumstances, the free mind will furnish a sufficient reason and ground of ~~a volition~~ the existence of a volition. A volition does not proceed from the mind, or from motive, or from any thing else, in the same manner that ~~that~~ an effect, properly so called, proceds from its efficient cause.

I put forth a volition to move my hand. The motion of my hand follows. Now, here I observe the action of the mind, and also the motion of the hand. The effect exists in the body, in that which is by nature passive; the cause in that which is active in the mind. The effect produced in the body, in the hand, is the passive result of the prior direct action of the mind. It is in this restricted sense that I use the term in question, when I deny that a volition is an effect. Action is the invariable antecedent of bodily motion; but not of volition; that whatever may be its relations to other things, a volition does not sustain the same relation to any thing in the universe, that an effect sustains to its efficient cause, that a passive result [has] to the direct prior action of which it is produced.

A volition is mearly a state of the mind, which does not sustain the same relation to the mind that an effect does to its efficient cause. If an act of the mind is an effect, surely we may say, that the act or productive influence of motive, or of any thing else, is likewise an effect; and so on ad infinitum. The truth is if we take it for granted, that a volition is an effect, and as such must proceed from a prior action of something else, we cannot escape the ad infinitum absurdity.

Whether we ascend through the self-determining power of the mind, or through the determining power of motives, or through the joint action of both, we cannot save ourselves from such an absurd consequence only by a glarring act of inconsistency. Hence we are forced back upon the conclusion that action may, and actually does arise in the world of mind without any efficient or producing cause of its existence, without resulting from the prior action of any thing whatever.

Action must take its rise somewhere in the world, without being caused by prior action; or else there must be an infinite series of acts. It takes its rise in the mind, in that which is essentially ~~acti~~ active, and not in matter. The action of volition may take its rise in the world, spontaneously proceeding from mind itself, without being made to do so by the action of any thing upon it.

The necessitarian says, the act of creation, not the mere purpose to create, but the real causative act of creation, existed in the divine mind from all eternity. Why then did the world spring up and come [page 22:] into existence at one point of time rather than another? How happened it that so many ages rolled away, and this mighty creative act produced no effect? How can this be, if a causative act of the Almighty may exist, and yet, for millions of ages its omnipotent energy produce no effect? Indeed, such a doctrine destroys all notions of cause and effect; it overthrows the "great principle of common sense" that cause and effect necessarily imply each other; and involves all our reasoning from cause to effect, and vice versa, in the utmost perplexity and confusion. It throws clouds and darkness over the whole field of inquiry. The necessitarian involves the whole scheme of moral necessity in a great absurdity of an infinite series of causes.

The self-determining power of the mind cannot be sent out into the absurdity of an infinite series of volitions. Is volition brought into existence, like the motion of the body, by the prior action of any thing else? We answer No. Is volition an effect, in the same sense, that the motion of the body is an effect? What is a volition just as it is revealed to us in the light of consciousness? Is it an effect, as the motion of body is an effect? We always conceive of the subject in which such an effect resides as being wholy passive—passive as to its production; and just in so far as it is in itself active, it is not the subject of an effect, but the author of an action.

Is volition produced in the mind, and is the mind passive as to its production? Is it, like the motion of a body, the passive result of the action of something else? No. It is not the result of action; it is action itself. The mind is not passive as to its production; it is in and of itself an action of the mind. It is not determined; it is a determination. It is not a produced effect, like the motion of body; it is itself an original producing cause. There is a manifest difference between an act and an effect. It is not in the nature of the human mind to keep itself always dead to the voice of consciousness. It is not in the power of any system always to counteract the spontaneous workings of nature. The stern and unrelenting features of fatalism cannot always be so intimately present to the mind, as entirely to exclude it from the contemplation of a milder and more captivating system of philosophy.

To the mind of the necessitarian one fixed idea shuts out the light of observation. Even when he contemplates that living source of action, that bubbling fountain of volitions, the immortal mind of man itself, he only beholds a thing, which is made to act by the action of something else upon it; just as a body is made to move by the action of force upon it. This philosophy is, therefore, an essentially shallow and superficial philosophy.

For if a volition is an effect, properly speaking, the only question is as to its efficient cause: it is necessarily produced by its cause. [page 23:] A cause is said to imply its effect: it is not the mind, but an act of of[46] the mind, that implies motion in the body. Now, if volition is an effect, it has an efficient cause, what is that cause? By the action of what is it produced? The mind has a self determining power.

But does the mind act at all? It does, and this no one can doubt. But why do we will at all? The very nature of the faculty of will implies that we put forth volitions. But why do we will one way rather than an other; why do we choose one thing rather than its opposite? Why the act of the will should be thus, and not otherwise?

Can there be one cause of volition, and another cause of its particular direction? I answer, there cannot. No such distinction can be shown

46. McLellin has accidentally doubled the word "of" at the end of one line and beginning of the next—neither marked for deletion.

to exist by a reference to the cause of motion. Force is the cause of motion and without it motion does not exist. So if a choice exist at all, it must be a choice of some particular thing. Hence whatever causes a volition to exist, must cause it to have a particular determination. The "activity of the soul" is the cause of its acting; yet motive may be the indispensable condition of its acting; and in this sense, may be the reason why a volition is one way rather than another. But it is denied that there can be two causes in the case; one to produce volition, and another to determine its object. The activities of the soul are the causes why its acts are thus and thus limited, directed, and determined. A mind endowed with activity always gives rise to its own acts. That which produces a thing is its efficient, producing cause.

I deny that a volition does proceed from the mind or from motive. Whatever may be its relations to other things, a volition does not sustain the same relation to any thing in the universe, that an effect sustains to its efficient cause, that a passive result sustains to the direct prior action by which it is produced. The subject in which an effect is produced is always passive as to its production; and just in so far as it is itself active, it is not the subject of an effect, but rather of an action. Such is the idea of an effect in the true and proper sense of the word.

Volition is not the result of action; it is action itself. The mind is not passive, as to its production; it is in and of itself an act of the mind. It is not determined; it is a determination. It is not a produced effect, like the motion of the body; it is itself an original producing cause. There is a clear and manifest difference between an act and an effect. In motion there is always causality in the production of action. All our consciousness recognizes this principle. It is not in the nature of the human mind to keep itself always deaf to the voice of consciousness. It is not in the power of any system of theology to always counteract the spontaneous workings of nature. What then is a volition just as it is revealed to us in the light of consciousness? Does it result from the prior action of the mind, or from motive, or from any thing else? In other words, is it an effect, [page 24:] as the motion of body is an effect?

Effects always proceed from their causes. The subject in which an effect resides or proceeds is always wholy passive, as to its production; it is the author of actions; it is action itself. It is not a produced effect, like the motion of the body; it is itself an original producing cause. Acts and effects are very different things. The mind is alway[s] active. It is never still or dormant. It never sleeps or rests. The body sleeps and takes rest in sleep. But the mind is ever awake, and has power because it is mind that puts forth volitions. Choice is a natural result of the immortal mind. The mind can originate thought, and can send out volitions, and cause the will to act this way or that, as circumstances may demand. The mind has a self-determining power in and of itself.

Volition is mearly a state of the mind, which does not sustain the same relation to the mind that an effect does to its efficient cause. Then the doctrine of liberty stands firm. Mind just exerts its own influence of itself. Action actually does arise in the wo[r]ld of mind, without any efficient or prod[u]cing cause of its existence, without resulting from the prior action of any thing whatever. Action takes its rise in the mind, in that which is essentially active and not in matter. Volition may take its rise in the world spontaneously proceeding from the mind itself, without being made to do so by the action of any thing upon it. A volition cannot rise out of nothing, but the mind is its producing cause itself, which is not passive, does not likewise imply a preceding act by which it is produced. It only implies the existence of an agent that is capable of acting, and the circumstances necessary to action as conditions, not as causes.

But the question is, whether every cause is an effect? Or, in other words, whether an act of the mind can exist without being produced by the prior action of something else; just as the motion of body is produced by[47] the prior action of mind? We say that it can exist without any such producing cause. An act is not an effect. All intelligent beings are capable of acting without being compelled to act. We believe in action which is uncaused by any prior action; and hence, we can reason from effect up to Cause, and then find a resting place.

We do not look beyond that which is uncaused. We think there is action somewhere uncaused by preceding action: if not God himself would not be the first Cause.[48] If not there would be an infinite series of causes, which would destroy the idea of a first Cause; hence destroy our ideas of God entirely. Every advocate of free-agency contends that volition proceeds from the mind, acting in view of motives, and therefore is not destitute of a sufficient ground and reason of its existence. The mind of man is more nearly allied to the nature and infinity of God, than any power in the vast universe. It possesses attributes as God, though in a finite degree. [page 25:]

---

47. McLellin wrote "by" twice, then deleted the second occurrence.

48. See Orson Pratt, *Great First Cause or the Self-Moving Forces of the Universe* (Liverpool, Eng.: R. James, 1851); Gary James Bergera, *Conflict in the Quorum: Orson Pratt, Brigham Young, Joseph Smith* (Salt Lake City: Signature Books, 2002).

President Edwards[49] of the presbyterian church maintained that volitions were effects in the proper sense of cause and effect. He supposes motive to be the producing[50] cause of volition. But Mr. A. T. Bledsoe, one of the most thorough thinkers of the Methodist connection; from whom I have made many extracts, and whose thoughts I esteem highly; maintains that volitions are caused or produced in or by the mind—originate in the mind; or flow out from it, without any other producing cause. We ought to clearly see between action and its relation to the mind, and motion and its relation to matter. Motion is always passive. It is always a result. It possesses no self-acting principle. Action is not passive. It is not a result in its strict sense. And it is self-acting. The foreknowledge of any future event proves the necessity of that event. In other words, an event cannot be foreknown unless it be actually and necessarily <u>certain</u> that the event will take place.

Foreknowledge always implies the necessity of the event; but implies nothing as to its cause. It is as present knowledge of a present event, that as that as[51] that can exist without any reference to the cause of the event, so divine foreknowledge of a future event may exist without any reference to its cause. There is no contingency in the foreknowledge of God. To God, all things past, present, or to come are distinct in God's view. There is no process of reasoning with God. All events are before him. All causes and effects are also present to his omnicient sight. God sees all things past, present, and future, just as we see that which is before us. It is no[t] faith in him, but sight. It is not inference but experience.

Liberty and necessity are diametrically opposite; and to say a thing is necessary, and at the same time free, is a contradiction in terms. Certainty and necessity are not the same; for, although every thing necessary is certain, every thing certain is not necessary. Volitions are free, in their very nature. A necessary volition is an absurdity, a thing inconceivable. We know no such thing in the world as a negative cause. It is a contradiction in terms. The very essence of Causality is positiveness. Darkness and cold are states or conditions of being. The sun which is a positive cause, producing light and heat. When the cause of light and heat is withdrawn the effects cease. There is a difference between a produced effect and an induced act. It is the <u>mind</u> which wills, and not the ground

49. For a summary of Jonathan Edwards's life, see the Biographical Notes.

50. McLellin added "producing."

51. McLellin doubled the words "that as" at the end of one line and beginning of the next and crossed out the second instance.

or reason presented to it. It is the man who acts, and not the occasion which is offered for acting.

M.[52] Victor Cousin[53] on the mind.[54]

There is a three fold distinction of the attributes of the mind into the intelligence, the sensibility, and the will. This furnishes a transparent medium through which the facts, the laws, and the relations of the spiritual world may be clearly discerned, instead of being distorted, as they usually are, by the knotty obscurities of false psychology. Philosophers have used different words to [page 26:] express these divisions of the mind, such as the Cogn[i]tive faculties, or the intelligence,—the Feelings, or the sensibility, and the Co[g]n[i]tive Powers, or the will. In the soul, says Aristotle,[55] there are three qualities, or three great divisions. If we ask in which of them is the seat of moral virtue or goodnes[s]. First, it is not in the intelligence, or the cogn[i]tive powers. The intellectual virtues, and not moral virtue, are seated in the intelligence.

Toward a possession of the virtues, knowledge has little or no weight; but the other qualifications are not small, but rather of infinite importance, since they arise from the frequent practice of just and temperate actions. In other words, real virtue consists, not in knowledge, nor in going over the theory of virtue in the mind, but in the practice of virtuous actions.

Secondly, the seat of moral virtue is not in the passions, By the passions, I mean desire, anger, fear, confidence, envy, joy, love and hatred. In a word, those ~~those~~ feelings which are followed by pleasure or pain. But thusly, since virtue is not in the intelligence, nor in feeling or the sensibility, it necessarily follows, that it must reside in the will. Then moral virtue is voluntary in its origin, and consists not in thinking, nor in feeling, but in the performance of virtuous actions by the Will. Or more properly speaking, in the habits which result from a repitition of such voluntary acts. Here then we have the distinction between the intelligence, the sensibility or feelings, and the will clearly given.

Modes of thinking are obvious states of intelligence, and is defined to be "that by which we think." The will is the purest type of active power within the range of human knowledge. The clearest idea of active power,

52. The "M" represents "Monsieur" or "Mister."

53. For a summary of Victor Cousin's life, see the Biographical Notes.

54. Cf. Bledsoe's review of Cousin's *Course of the History of Modern Philosophy* in *The Southern Review* 20 (1876): 196-210.

55. For a summary of Aristotle's life, see the Biographical Notes.

says [John] Locke, is had from Spirit. Taking a survey of the mental modifications, or phenomena, of which we are conscious, these are seen to divide themselves into three great classes. In the first place, there is the phenomena of knowledge; in the second place, there is the phenomena of feeling, or of Pleasure and Pain; and in the third place, there is the phenomena of will. Will and desire ought not to be confounded. Desire is a feeling of sensibility; and not an executive volition or act of the will.

We may passively desire that it should rain, or that a fortune might be left to us, &c.—without putting forth any volition, or act of the will, to secure the result. This distinction between will and desire appears to us so very clear, is so distinctly seen in the light of consciousness, that we cannot but wonder that they have been confounded by Hamilton[56] and Kant.[57] A simple act of the will, or a volition, can indeed be seen and understood only in the pure light of consciousness. We must distinguish between will and desire, between executive acts of the soul and its passive susseptabilities.

M. Cousin, lays the foundation of the scheme of free-agency, as over against the doctrine of philosophical necessity; a doctrine on which, [page 27:] as Bishop Butler[58] says, "infidelity bases itself," or erects its batteries; and on which, also the great Reformation of the 16th century erected that appalling dogma of Predestination. There are three facts which are all important, which must stand in the mind ~~solitary~~ distinct[59] and unimpeached. These facts are: to feel, to think, and to act.

We are conscious of an act, of an effort of the mind. Is the mind passive in this act? No; we venture to answer for the universal intelligence of man. If this act had been produced in us by a necessitating cause, would not the mind have been passive in it? In other words, would it not have been a passive impression, and not an act, not an effort of the mind at all? Yes; we again venture to answer for the unbiased reason of man. But it is not, as we have seen, a passive impression; it is an act of the mind, and hence it is not necessitated because it is not stamped with the characteristic of necessity. The will has not necessarily yielded like the intelligence and sensibility, to motives over which it had no control. It does not bear upon its face the mark of any such subjection "to the power and action" of a cause. It is marked with the characteristics not of necessity but of liberty.

56. For a summary of William Hamilton's life, see the Biographical Notes.

57. For a summary of Immanuel Kant's life, see the Biographical Notes.

58. For a summary of Joseph Butler's life, see the Biographical Notes.

59. McLellin deleted "solitary" and added "distinct."

We carry about with us the irresistable conclusion or conviction that we are free; that our wills are not absolutely to be forced under[60] the dominion of causes over which we have no control. Hence we see and know we are self-active. In willing, and in willing alone, the mind is self-active and free. In thinking, and in feeling, it is passive and necessitated. For the will,–the one and only self-active power of the mind or soul,–is at once the seat of personality, by which we are distinguished from a thing or a machine, and the center of all responsability. If we were not free in the act of willing, we could not be accountable beings or resposable moral agents.

All virtue and moral goodness consists in acts of the will and in habits formed by the repetition of such acts. The intelligence or reason furnishes, or rather receives, the rule of moral action; the sensibility, or heart, supplies the motives of moral action; but the will–the free, the self-active, the responsible will–puts forth or exerts the moral act itself. Virtue consists in acts of the will. Conscience, says Butler, is a perception of the understanding, and a sentiment of the heart. Virtue, or holiness, is, then, a practical habit of the will, voluntary in its origin, in as much as it results from a repetition of voluntary acts. [page 28:]

The Holy Ghost.[61]

Has the Holy Ghost–the Holy Spirit an existence as an individual person? Is he a personal identity? He is named with[62] the Father and the Son as a person with them. "Baptizing them in the name of the Father, and in the name of the Son, and in the name of the Holy Ghost." Here he is named as a person, as much so as the Father or Son either is so named. Why always call the Holy Spirit he his him or himself[63] and not she or it, if he is not a person. ~~"He shall teach you all things."~~ Six times is the word **he**, applied to the Holy Spirit in John 16:13. He is usually thus denominated.

I am aware that nothing can use language–can use speech, unless that something has a personal form and mind within said form. Intelligent voice cannot be uttered without an identity. The Holy Spirit has

60. In a different color ink, McLellin added "be forced under."

61. This essay (notebook pages 28-38) was certainly written by McLellin, as evidenced by the abrupt change in literary style and quotation of 2 Ne. 2:28, which he introduces "And the Book says."

62. Mclellin wrote "with" twice and then deleted the second occurrence.

63. McLellin originally wrote "the Holy Spirit he or him," then added above the line, in two stages, "his" and "or himself," resulting in the reading "the Holy spirit he his him or himself."

spoken, has used his voice to give intelligence. Through the prophets at Antioch, he said, "Seperate me Barnabas and Saul" [Acts 13:2]. He said to Philip relative to the Ethiopian eunuch, "Go near and join thy[s]elf to his chariot" [cf. Acts 8:29].

No man or being can be a Teacher unless he possesses intelligence, and nothing can possess that without a form and mind within that form to manifest forth its ideas. Intelligence and teaching can only exist in sentient beings. No person can be a teacher without faculties with intellect. And those cannot exist outside of personality–outside of spirit form containing mind.

Spirit has power in influence. Influence of spirit[64] is that celestial aspect which can operate in all things below it, for there is nothing above it. Influence is thrown out from spirit and mind, as light is thrown out from the sun. Spirit is one thing and its influence is another. Spirit form has an abode somewhere in space, but its influence may exist [page 29:] every where, in all space. Space is illimitable. All spiritual and material beings dwell within space, and occupy a part of it. All spirits have minds, and exist as seperate identities.

"Wherefore[65] the Holy Ghost also is a witness to us." Heb 10:15. A witness must have knowledge within himself. Knowledge does not dwell in any thing except **mind**, and mind does not exist in any[66] thing but spirit: so spirit and mind is the Holy Ghost; and is as much a person as the great eternal Father or the Son either.

"There are three that bear record in heaven, the Father, the Word, and the Holy Ghost" [1 John 5:7].[67] The Father, and the Son bear record or witness, so also does the Holy Ghost, hence he is one with them, as much a personality as either. He has a voice by which to give testimony, and hence the Holy Ghost can produce a sure record of truth. If the Holy Spirit is not a personal being he cannot speak, can not bear record, cannot bear witness in giving testimony.

The Spirit is ~~possessed of~~ spirit-substance, and can only exist in one place at one time; but spirit's influence can be every where present; it reaches out in all existence–in all eternity. Inspiration says, "I said unto

64. McLellin added "of spirit."

65. The King James Version has "whereof," though it is printed in italics.

66. McLellin added "any."

67. The verse 1 John 5:7 is absent from the Greek manuscript tradition except for a few late minuscules. It was not in Erasmus's first published Greek New Testament of 1516 but was added to the third edition of 1522, leading to its inclusion in the King James Version. See Jaroslav Pelikan, *The Reformation of the Bible: The Bible of the Reformation* (New Haven, Conn.: Yale University Press, 1996), 102.

the spirit, I behold thou hast shown unto me the tree which is precious above all. And he said unto me, what desirest thou? And I said unto him, to know the interpretation thereof; for I spake unto him as a man speaketh; for I beheld that he was in the form of a man; yet nevertheless I knew that it was the Spirit of the Lord; and he spake unto me as a man speaketh with another" [1 Ne. 11:9-11]. This is plain and definite so that no man of intelligence can mistake it.

Paul says, "Now the spirit speaketh expressly" [1 Tim. 4:1]. And Peter says, "Holy men of God spake as they were moved by the Holy Ghost" [2 Pet. 1:21]. If the Holy Spirit moved the prophets of old to speak the word of God; and spoke expressly to the Apostles, "To teach them all things, and show them [page 30:] things to come" [cf. John 14:26; 16:13], then he must be a personal being which can be[68] seen, heard, and and ~~its~~ his influence can be[69] felt.

The Apostles said, "We are witnesses of these things; and so is also this Holy Ghost, whom God hath given to all those that obey him" [cf. Acts 5:32]. No one can be a true witness without knowledge within himself; and no being or personality can have knowledge, or be a witness either without a spirit form and a mind in which for knowledge to dwell. Knowledge dwells not in influence, in either[70] electricity, or in wild wind; but must have a tabernacle, a special form, or a mind to inhabit in order to manifest or show itself, ~~or speak either.~~ or be known to exist.

The Apostle [Paul] says, "God hath revealed them to us by his spirit" [1 Cor. 2:10]. No revelation can be given or received either, only in signs or words; and if words are used they can only be used by an intelligent personality—such is the Holy Spirit. If the Spirit is a person~~ality~~ which can only be in one place at one time, how can he operate upon or dwell in thousands of persons at one and the same time?[71] It is only ~~the only~~ the influence or power of the spirit that thus rests upon them, but not its person~~ality~~. The difficulty is for mortals to understand Spirit existence. For there is nothing &c[72] They can see and understand some material or natural things,[73] but to see and comprehend spirit, a person must be

---

68. McLellin added "which can be."

69. McLellin added "and its influence can be" to "and felt," thus unintentionally doubling the word "and." Then he deleted "its" and replaced it with "his."

70. McLellin added "either."

71. McLellin had two question marks in this sentence, the first one where we have substituted a comma: "If the Spirit is a person~~ality~~ which can only be in one place at one time? how can he operate upon or dwell in thousands of persons at one and the same time?"

72. McLellin added "existence. For there is nothing &c."

73. McLellin added "or natural things."

spiritual minded—must be thrown into the spirit, or have its influence powerfully upon them. "Jesus saw the Spirit of God descending like a dove, and lighting upon him" [Matt. 3:16]. And Job says, "Then a spirit passed before my ~~eyes~~ face" [Job 4:15]. To see a spirit a person must be thrown into a visionary state. Elisha prayed for his servant and said, "Lord open his eyes." And when his eyes were opened "he saw and behold,[74] the mountain was full of horses and chariots of fire round about Elisha" [2 Kgs. 6:17]. This was a wonderful vision seen while in the spirit.

The Holy Spirit is one thing, and its fruits and spiritual gifts is another thing. The fruit is something that grows in us, [page 31:] planted there by the Holy Spirit and[75] lifting us up toward heaven. Each believer in Christ must bear good fruit in order to be a good disciple of Christ. But the gifts of the spirit are diffused among the saints, one gift to one, and then another to another, as the spirit dictates and directs; so that all believers may be edified and comforted together.

Some thinkers suppose that God has a material body, as the Son has a glorified body. They cant conceive of him as pure Spirit or spiritual being. They must think of him as a material being, possessed of bodily[76] organs and faculties of life as mortals have. But I look upon the great God the eternal Father as a being possessed only[77] of spirit and mind. John says, "God is a spirit: and they that worship him must worship him in spirit and in truth" [John 4:24]. Then away with all your materialization in God! My God is spirit; so also is the holy Spirit: neither of them has a material, or even a glorified form.

The Father, the Son, and the Holy Spirit constitute the Godhead in heaven, and have so constituted it from eternity, and will to all eternity. They are one God, one in unity, one in council; constitute one court—one tribunal; and they reign independent of all other powers in the vastness of eternity. There is no tribunal above them or round about them of equal decision and power.[78] They are the highest—the uppermost in all worlds. This is the kind of a God I wo[r]ship and adore.

I know it is said, "Christ is the image of God—the express image of his person" [cf. 2 Cor. 4:4; Heb. 1:3]. God has a likeness and image, and Jesus Christ was in that express likeness in spirit and in person~~ality~~. He could be this without the eternal Father having flesh and

74. McLellin added "and behold."

75. McLellin added "planted there by the Holy Spirit and."

76. McLellin added "bodily."

77. McLellin added "only."

78. McLellin added "of equal decision and power."

bones. I cant conceive of a spirit~~ual~~ being material, Though It may take on a natural body.[79] Was not Christ as much in the image of his Father before he was born of Mary as afterward? I believe he was. Hence his being born of a woman added nothing to his likeness or image. The body is the express image and likeness of the spirit within, in all mortal beings. [page 32:]

The saying in Genesis relative to man's creation is, "And God said, Let us make man in our image, after our likeness" [Gen. 1:26]. It is evident that Christ[80] at that time had no material body, hence to say our image, and our[81] likeness, and us, would have been inappropriate, provided the Father only had a material body, and the Son had not. The truth is, the Father, the Son, and the Holy Spirit each only had a spirit-form in eternity,[82] hence ~~they~~ each of them[83] had an image and likeness, and made man exactly after it.

When Jesus Christ died his naked spirit—the tabernacle of his mind, went to Paradise and then to Prisen. He certainly had at that time a spirit-substance, a spirit-form in which his intelligent mind dwelt. Then God could create man in or after that spirit-form, and thus make him a material being, and place his spirit within a[84] material body. Thus God created man in his image and in the likeness of his[85] spirit-~~ual likeness.~~ form.[86]

The argument is, the Holy Spirit is one in the Godhead, but he could not be thus if he were not a person, if it was only an influence.[87] He has a distinct characteristic name as a person, with the Father and the Son. He is always spoken of as he his[88] ~~or~~ him, or himself[89] and not as it. He is called a Comforter, a Teacher, a witness, and bears record or testimony to all true, firm believers. "I beheld that he was in the form of a

---

79. McLellin added "It may take on a natural body" and then later added "Though."

80. McLellin added "Christ."

81. McLellin added "our."

82. McLellin added "in eternity."

83. McLellin added "each of them."

84. McLellin accidentally doubled the word "a" at the end of one line and beginning of the next—neither marked for deletion.

85. McLellin added "in the likeness of his."

86. McLellin originally wrote "and spiritual likeness," which he revised as "and spirit-form." The hyphen was already there because he had divided "spiritual" at the end of the line.

87. McLellin added "if it was only an influence."

88. McLellin added "his."

89. McLellin added "or himself."

man, nevertheless I knew it was the spirit of the Lord" [1 Ne. 11:11]. Then he has ~~a~~ the[90] definite form of a person.

He speaks with a spiritual voice, and urges Prophets to speak by his power. He can open up the future to the honest in heart, and "show them things to come" [cf. John 16:13]. He can throw out great influence from his person. Jesus could not see the spirit descending upon him provided it had no form, no substance, if it was not a personality. Revelations can only be given by a person who can articulate sounds. Job could not see a spirit pass before his face if it had no spirit[91] substance, had no personality. No being can see ether,[92] electricity, or wild wind. ~ [page 33:] Then we say the Holy Spirit is a personal being. An intelligence seperate and distinct from every other person in existence. And yet in unity in the Godhead. He is one in all their official acts. He is in perfect accord in that highest council in all things, and in all worlds.

When Jesus ascended to heaven he sent down the Holy Spirit, and he it is who reigns in and among all true believers in Christ. He causes them to bear fruits—holy fruits of the Spirit: and then gives them "spiritual gifts," in order to bring them up on the highest plane, and plant them near to God. Thousands of professed believers mistake Christianity because they do not believe in, nor enjoy the Holy Spirit's fruits and spiritual gifts. They live on a plane far below.

O! that mankind would come up to a the[93] point of believing in the personalaity of the Holy Spirit, and also in his special gifts and powers, and then enjoy them in all their fulness. Then we would have a world fitted for the second coming of the Lord Jesus Christ, to reign in glorious majesty for one thousand years; while all wickedness would end, during that reign of peace.

But again, the three could not be **one**, provided two were persons and the other only an influence. In this sense there could be no oneness of persons,[94] nor unity either. Then there could not be three in one; there would be only two, and an influence joined with them, but not a person. To me, this distroys the idea of the Godhead. I must have three persons or none, according to the Books.

The Godhead are not independent identities of each other, but are in unity and oneness. The Father is an identity, so is the Son, and so is

90. McLellin deleted "a" and added "the."

91. McLellin added "spirit."

92. McLellin added "ether."

93. McLellin deleted "a" and added "the."

94. McLellin added "of persons."

also the Holy Spirit, or there cannot be a oneness of the three. If one is a person so each must be or they could not have one voice, could not each be one in the Godhead. [page 34:]

Paul says, "And he that searcheth the hearts knoweth what is the mind of the Spirit" [Rom. 8:27]. And the Book [of Mormon] says, "According to the will of his Holy Spirit" [2 Ne. 2:28]. If the Holy Spirit has a mind, and a will, and a voice, and can be lied unto and tempted, then it must be an individual person. Nothing has a mind, or a will, or a v[o]ice unless it has a form of its own. And all forms with minds possess intelligence, and can manifest it to other minds. Intelligence dwells in nothing but mind, and mind always dwells in living animate forms. And will is always a power of mind, so that it cant exist out of mind. To say that the Holy Spirit has a mind and will is to say it has a seperate, and distinct,[95] individual existence as any other personal being.

Mere influence has no mind or will either. A spirit with mind can throw out an influence, and it will operate as directed by the power of the mind; but without mind no influence can be exerted. Hence mere ~~spirit or~~ influence ~~from it~~ cannot manifest intelligence, any more than wild wind. But in divine Writ the Holy Spirit is represented as possessing both mind and will, hence can show forth intelligence, then it must be an individual person.

The promise by Peter was, "And ye shall receive the gift of the Holy Ghost" [Acts 2:38]. Intelligent persons only have gifts to bestow as rewards of merit. Mere influence has no gifts to present to its votaries. It can use no words, has no will, has no voice, has no choice between good and evil; but is merely an element of power thrown out from intelligent mind.

The Holy Spirit can bear witness. Jesus said, "He shall testify of me." John 15:26. He can bear record, "There are three that bear record in heaven." 1 John 5:7. He can, "Show things to come." John 16:13. He can teach, "He shall teach you all things." John 14:26. He can speak and forbid, "We[96] were forbidden of the Holy Ghost to preach the word in Asia." [page 35:] Acts 16:6. He can bear fruit, "The fruit of the Spirit is love." Gal. 5:22. He can give gifts, "For to one is given by the Spirit the word of wisdom." 1 Cor 12:8. He can use stamp or seal, "Ye are sealed with the Holy Spirit of promise." Eph 1:13. He can be grieved, "Grieve not the Holy Spirit of ~~promise~~ God, whereby ye are sealed unto the day of redemption." Eph 4:30. He can use, "The sword of the Spirit, which is the

95. McLellin added "distinct."

96. In the King James Version, the subject of the sentence is "they" not "we."

word of God." Eph 6:17. He can be lied unto, "Why hath Satan filled thine heart to lie to the Holy Ghost." Acts 5:3. He can be tempted, "Ye have agreed together to tempt the Spirit of the Lord." Acts 5:9. Finally, "The Spirit itself maketh intercession for us with groanings which cannot be uttered." Rom 8:26.

It would be an impossibility for the Holy Spirit to pray for us if [he] is not an individual person. A person cannot pray without using words either in thought or vocally. The Holy Spirit cannot use intercession or prayer without thoughts or language, if he is not a person so as to have thoughts. But if he has a mind and will then he is a personality.

From eternity Christ had a Spirit and a mind as well as the Father; then why not speak of the Holy Spirit as Christ's spirit, as well as to speak of him as the Father's only. The Holy Spirit is never called Christ's Spirit. He is always spoken of as coming from the Father.

In speaking of the Comforter—the Holy Ghost, Jesus said, "I send the promise of my Father upon you." Luke 24:49. "But when the Comforter is come, whom I will send unto you from the Father he shall testify of me" [cf. John 15:26]. "How be it when he, the Spirit of truth, is come, he will guide you into all truth: for he shall not speak of himself; but whatsoever he shall hear, that shall he speak." J[ohn] 16:13. Now if the Holy Spirit is only an influence, and has no ears he cannot hear, and if he has no mouth he cannot speak. But if he has [page 36:] ears to hear, and a mouth and voice with which to speak, then he must be a distinct personality. This position is incontrovertable. He could not hear, nor pray, nor teach, bear record, give witness or testimony, bring things to remembrance, nor guide into all truth, if he were not a person distinct from every other personality in existence.

All spirits have intelligence and influence. And each one throws out influence from its union of spirit-substance with mind. Thus, the Father, the Son, and the Holy Spirit each exist in spirit, and power and influence can proceed from each one or either of them. Each one of these persons has a mind and will of his ~~or his~~ own, and can throw out its own influences. True, the Holy Spirit is called the spirit of God, so is also the Son called the Son of God. The Book says,[97] "The Son proceeded forth and came from God" [cf. John 8:42]. ~~"The Holy Spirit~~ it also says, ["]The spirit of truth[98] also proceedeth from the Father" [cf. John 15:26]. The one came or proceeded from the Father as well as the other. Hence ~~The~~

97. McLellin added "The Book says."

98. McLellin added "It also says, The spirit of truth."

"proceeding" of each[99] ~~con each~~ alike constitutes one as well as the other a personality.

The word God is translated from a plural noun in Hebrew, and hence may embrace three persons in the Godhead, each one having a distinct spirit and mind ~~within~~ constituting[100] himself, and a seperate existence from each other, and yet in unity and oneness.

All spirit-forms are in the image of God, and they all have three great leading attributes. 1st There is understanding, intelligence, or reason. 2nd Heart, sensibility, or affections. 3rd Will or power. By the first we think; by the second we feel; and by the third we act, or put forth the volitions of power.

The argument is the Holy Spirit is one in the Godhead, he is named as such. The Book says, "In the name of the Holy Ghost" [cf. Matt. 28:19]. He would not have a name with the Father and the Son—they being persons, if he were not a person. An influence is not called he, his, or him as the Holy [page 37:] Spirit is. The Holy Spirit has a distinct char[ac]t[er]istic[101] name as a person, and not mearly as an influence. He is called a Comforter, a Teacher, a Witness, and can a[nd] does make a record and can bear testimony; he has a voice and can and does speak; he can and does exert an influence from his person; He has a Spirit-substance and has been seen; he has a Spirit-form and can pass up and down; he can give gifts and nothing can do so without intelligence; he exists in space and is not diffused every where; he exists as a seperate identity; he has knowledge within himself and communicates it to other persons; he can give revelations, and has done so often in past time, and influenced others to do so.

His influence or power can operate upon all mankind at one time; he dictates and directs all Christians in all lands; he is a person with the Father and Son, always was and always will be to all eternity; he is the express image and likeness of the Father and the Son; he has a Spirit-form and man was made precisely like it; he is not an emanation or mere influence but an actual form and personality; he can show things to come—future things; he can articulate sounds and can thus give off revelations; he as a person is one in the highest council in heaven; he was sent into the world by Jesus Christ as Christ was sent by his Father; he is not an independant person but in unity in the highest tribunal in heav-

99. McLellin added "of each."

100. McLellin added "constituting."

101. McLellin originally wrote "charistic," to which he inserted the "t" for "chartistic," evidently in an effort to create "characteristic."

en; he has a mind and will and voice and can think and speak by his mind, and determine by his will, and communicate ~~by~~ intelligence by his voice; he can determine between good and evil; he can forbid to do evil or go wrong; he can be tempted and lied unto; he **can** bear fruits and give gifts or be grieved; he can pray for the honest in in[102] heart and groan for their relief; he has ears ~~and~~ to[103] hear and understand the mind of the Father and the Son; he has a mind, a will, and intelligence and an influence.

Now if all this does not prove the identity and personality of the Holy Spirit I must confess my wo[e]ful ignorance in all spiritual things!

August 15 / - 78 ~ W. E. McLellan ~ [page 38:]

But again, there is an influence or emanation thrown out from the Spirit of the Father, from the Spirit of the Son, and from the Spirit of the Holy ~~Spirit~~ Ghost.[104] Each one has an influence, and ~~can~~ exerts it in space.[105] "~~And~~ The Spirit of God moved upon the face of the waters." Gen. 1:2.[106] "And Jesus sighed deeply in his Spirit" [cf. Mark 8:12]. And, "He rejoiced in Spirit" [Luke 10:21]. "Now if any man have not the Spirit of Christ he is none of his" [Rom. 8:9]. The influence of the Holy Spirit is shown in his fruits and spiritual gifts in believers. Its influence and power is ~~is~~[107] shown in all its works among mankind. So that each one of the three being a person throws out his own emanation; and they throw it out in unity, or each for himself, and its operation may always produce power. Paul says, "By the power of the Holy Spirit of God" [cf. Rom. 15:13]. Then the Holy Spirit has power and if he[108] can exert it then he is certainly a distinct person.

Of faith. ~ [109]

The gift of faith rests on testimony and that evidence must be immediately produced, with the influence of the Holy Spirit combin[e]d,

102. McLellin accidentally doubled the word "in" at the end of one line and beginning of the next—neither marked for deletion.

103. McLellin added "to."

104. McLellin deleted "Spirit" and added "Ghost."

105. McLellin originally wrote "and can exert it in space," which he revised as "and exerts it in space."

106. McLellin added this scriptural reference between the lines.

107. McLellin wrote "is" twice and deleted the second occurrence.

108. McLellin added "if he."

109. The essay, "On faith," covers the bottom half of page 38 and almost all of page 39. The writing for this section is smaller, with more words per line and less space between lines. It is a later version of the following essay, "Faith."

which always produces power. Faith is not power neither is power faith. Man has no power with himself. "For there is no power but of God" [Rom. 13:1]. So says Paul. Faith is the direct gift of God, because of an immediate communication from him. God commands, and man's faith is fixed in that mandate, then the Holy Spirit produces the result. The gift of faith always depends on an immediate act of God. The Lord ~~speak~~ speaks man hears and obeys by faith, and the result is power is produced by the combination of the Holy Spirit of God and faith in man. It is thus the union of the Spirit with faith that always produces the result of power. Faith and the Holy Spirit is always the producing cause of power.

The fruit of faith grows in the mind because of the written word of God. It is not an immediate [act] but is produced gradually—it grows like fruit. It depends entirely on testimony without any direct influence from the Spirit. It is only a high degree or state of belief, produced in the mind from the weight of evidence. But living active faith is a different principle. It is the medium through which power is given from God. Faith is the concentration of the powers of the mind or it is the focal point of power. Faith is always an act of the mind, but spiritual power comes only from God. He is the giver of both faith and power, and power comes through faith as a medium. [page 39:]

Belief and Faith are different degrees of the act of the mind. Belief accumulates gradually upon the strength of evidence. But faith is a gift and is an immediate act of God in the mind, which is exercised in or on some object and producing a result according to the power of faith exercised.

People are apt to blend belief and faith together—that is use one as synonomous with the other; but they are widely different. Belief is an act of the mind giving full assent in a gradual manner to the force of evidence. And can be exercised without any direct influence of the Holy Spirit. Man has the power within himself to believe or disbelieve, and can firmly believe a falsehood as well as the truth. But faith must be true to itself; it is never exercised in a falsehood, because the Holy Spirit which is always combined with true faith receives things just as they are, truth for truth and falsehood for falsehood. A person in belief may be deceived, but true faith never. The act of faith and the result of faith combined with the Holy Spirit of God, as it always is, is always true to itself, becaus it can not be deceived or led astray. But be[lie]f is often false, because the object about which the evidence is given may not exist.

Paul says, "There is no power but of God" [Rom. 13:1]. And Micah says, "I am full of power by the Spirit of the Lord" [Micah 3:8]. And Paul says again, "God hath given us the Spirit of power" [cf. 2 Tim. 1:7]. In all this we see the source and medium of power, it is the Holy Spirit, and that Spirit is the incitement to faith always. It is always united with faith in producing power. It is the channel of power, or the producing cause of power. The combination of faith and Spirit always precedes power, and brings it forth to view.

When I have read 1 Cor 12:9. Eph 2:8. Matt 9:22, 29. Mark 5:34. 10:52. Luke 7:50. 8:48. 18:42. And scanned them closely I am led to consider more firmly that man's salvation is all because first of belief and then faith. They in unity with the Holy Spirit is the foundation of all power from God, and of all salvation in the world to come.

["]Daughter, thy faith hath saved thee" [cf. Luke 7:50; 8:48]. That is, the faith and confidence exercised in me has drawn the power from me that's made you whole. The Spirit-power from me joined with your faith has removed the disease. Paul says, "Perceiving that he had faith to be healed" [Acts 14:9].[110] This young man of Lystria [Lystra] heard Paul and Barnabas preach Jesus and the gospel of power and demonstration, and believed with all his heart, and hence the Spirit's power was manifest in his case.

No where is it said, "By the power of faith," because faith has no power. Faith is an act of the mind, which brings power from God. It has no[111] [page 40:] power, but is the medium of power. Its that through which power comes. Now I will give some quotations about faith. Great F[aith]. Little F[aith]. Weak F[aith]. Have no F[aith]. Increase of F[aith]. Full of F[aith]. Revealed from F[aith]. to F[aith]. Righteousness of F[aith]. F[aith]. made void. The word of F[aith]. Faith comes by hearing. Measure of F[aith]. Proportion of F[aith]. Obedience of F[aith]. Household of F[aith]. Fruit of the Spirit of F[aith]. One F[aith]. unity of F[aith]. Shield of F[aith]. Joy of F[aith]. F[aith]. of the gospel. Work of F[aith]. Breastplate of F[aith]. Unfeigned F[aith]. Mystery of F[aith]. Fight of

---

110. McLellin should say, "Luke, the author of Acts, says concerning Paul."

111. At the bottom of page 39, the following is written upside down:

A~~a~~aronic Priesthood

> Joseph Smith in his history, and Oliver Cowdery in his letters to W. W. Phelps, both declare that John the Baptist came and ordained them to the Aaronic Priesthood on the bank of the Susquehannah river at the time of their baptism.

This short paragraph was then crossed out with a large "x." Because the regular text surrounds and avoids hitting these four lines, they must have been written previous to the regular text on this page.

F[aith]. Faith of God's elect. Common F[aith]. Foundation of F[aith]. Full assurance of F[aith]. Faith a substance. Author and finisher of F[aith]. Dead F[aith]. Works make F[aith]. perfect. Prayr of F[aith]. Precious F[aith]. F[aith]. overcomes the world. Holy F[aith]. Justified by F[aith]. e[s]tablished in the F[aith]. F[aith]. grows exceedingly. The Spirit is power, and faith draws it to man. ~

Faith[112]

Through which power is[113]
is given from God.

Faith rests on evidence but that evidence must be immediately produced[114] with the influence of the H[oly].[115] Spirit combined, which always produces power. Faith is not power, neither is power faith. Faith is the direct gift of God because of an immediate communication from him. God commands and man's faith [is] fixed in that then the Spirit[116] produces the result. Then the gift of faith in man[117] always depends upon an immediate act of God. The Lord speaks man hears and obeys by faith, and the result is power ~~is~~ produced, by the combination of the Spirit of God and faith in man and Spirit in man.[118] It is then the union of Spirit with faith that always produces the result of power. Faith[119] is alway the producing cause of power.

The fruit of faith grows in the mind because of the written word of God. It is not an immediate act of the mind but is produced gradually—it grows like fruit.[120] It depends entirely on testimony without any immediate influence from the Spirit. It is only a high[121] state of belief produced in the mind from the weight of evidence. But living active faith is a dif-

---

112. This essay covers three-fourths of a page but is written upside down from the regular text. It is an earlier version of the preceding essay, "Of Faith."

113. McLellin accidentally doubled "is" at the end of one line and beginning of the next—neither marked for deletion.

114. McLellin added "but that evidence must be immediately produced."

115. McLellin added "H."

116. Mclellin added "then the Spirit."

117. McLellin added "in man."

118. McLellin added above the line the words "and Spirit in man," but there is no indication as to where these words are to be added.

119. McLellin added a caret after the word "Faith," but without anything above the line. At this same point, the other version of the essay has "Faith and the Holy Spirit."

120. McLellin added "like fruit."

121. McLellin added "high."

ferent principle. It[']s the medium ~~of power with God~~. Faith is the concentration of[122] or the focal point[123] of power.

Faith is always[124] an act of the mind of man,[125] but ~~power~~ spiritual power ~~always~~[126] comes only from God. God is the giver of both[127] faith and power, and power is exercised or comes through the medium of[128] faith. Belief and faith are different degrees of the[129] acts of the mind. Belief accumulates gradually upon the strenght of testimony. But faith is a gift ~~of God~~ and is an immediate act of God in[130] the mind, exercised in or on some object and producing a result, according to the power of faith exercised.

People are apt to blend belief and faith together—that is use one as synonomous with [the] other; but they are widely different. Belief is an act of the mind giving full assent to evidence. And can be exercised without any direct influence of the Holy Spirit. Man has power within himself to believe, or refuse his assent; and can firmly believe a falsehood ~~as well as a truth~~.[131] But faith must be true to itself; it never believes fa[l]schoods, because the Holy Spirit which is always combined with true faith receive~~d~~s things just as they are, truth for truth and falsehood for falsehood. Belief may be deceived, but true faith never. The act of faith and the result of faith combined as it is ~~always~~ with the Holy Spirit of God is always true, because it cant be deceived. But belief is often false.

122. McLellin added "of." In the other version of the essay, McLellin has "of the powers of the mind."

123. McLellin added "point."

124. McLellin added "always."

125. McLellin added "of man."

126. McLellin added, then deleted, "always."

127. McLellin added "both."

128. McLellin added "the medium of."

129. McLellin added "degrees of the."

130. McLellin added "God in."

131. McLellin added, then deleted, "as well as a truth."

7.

REASONS WHY I AM NOT A "MORMON," CA. 1880

I will here give some of the reasons why I am not (what is called,) a Mormon, or a Latter Day Saint of any of its various parties. L.D.S.ism has broke into pieces and organized more than thirty differing factions since sometime ~~about the~~[1] the death of Joseph Smith, their Prophet and Leader. And each party has claimed that they were the only true and living church among them all, to the exclusion of all the others. And each party claimed that they had the "spiritual gifts" among them, and much of the power of God displayed among them. And some of these have gathered hundreds of converts, and seemed to prosper for a season. But most of the factions among them have fallen into decay, and some to entirely disappear. Many of them in the various parties usually declare that they knew they were in the true work of the Lord—in the true church of God or of Christ[2] organized of the Lord in these Latter Days; in order to bring in the "rest of God." But this great knowledge has failed in hundreds of instances, and many of those who thus testified have gone to their long home, and their testimony failed entirely. It is astonishing to hear and see the confidence with which men and women would testify, as to their faith in their church organizations. And it does not seem after their many failures that they are discouraged, for there are some boldly declaring that they know they are right now and no mistake. But their failure will soon tell upon them, as it has those parties in the past. Now I want to write plainly, candidly, and unprejudiced in presenting the following matters—as I think matters of fact. I would much rather write of good things than evil things. But there have been so many wrong principles and doctrines introduced and practiced upon in the church (pro-

---

In the absence of a title from McLellin, we have constructed one for this essay, drawn from wording in the first sentence. The composition can be dated to approximately 1880 based on McLellin's reference to the "nearly fifty years" that had passed since Oliver Cowdery's commission to preach to the Lamanites (American Indians), which occurred in September 1830.

1. McLellin added "sometime ~~about the~~."

2. McLellin added "or of Christ."

fessing to be,) the church of God, or the church of Christ, and then the church of Latter Day Saints, that I am bound by duty and strong obligation to set them forth, in order to warn others and keep them from running into falsehood, and into ruinous speculations in religious matters. When I have accomplished this task[3] I shall be content on this subject. [page 2:]

Things which I do not believe that is generally believed by Latter Day Saints most firmly.

1. I do not believe, that Joseph tran[s]lated the book of Mormon. He only read the translation as it appeard before him. The Lord translated it for him. so says the book "Wherefore, thou shalt read the words which I shall give unto thee" Page 111, of the Palmyra edition [2 Ne. 27:20].
2. I do not believe, he ever possessed the Urim and Thummim during his whole life.
3. I do not believe, he ever possessed the Interpreters after he lost the 116 pages first translated.
4. I do not believe, that he ever received authority to gather the Gentiles to a Zion.
5. I do not believe, that he or any man ever had authority to appoint and ordain Apostles of Christ.
6. I dont believe, that an Angel ever ordained a man to any ministerial office in the church of Christ.
7. I dont believe, the church was ever established by Joseph, it was only organized. Set up by man's authority.
8. I do not believe, in receiving J. Smith's word[4] as from the mouth of God as we are commanded on the 6th of April -/30 [1830].
9. I dont believe, in holding general[5] conferences to make rules and laws for the government of the church of Christ.
10. I do not believe, in disimbodied spirits communing with man, as Angels do.
11. I dont believe, In a Prophet being placed at the Head of the church as Leader and sole Dictator. Sep. 1830.

---

3. McLellin added "task."
4. McLellin added "word."
5. McLellin added "general."

12. I dont believe, ~~I dont believe~~ in nine officers as ministers placed in the church, instead of three.

13. I dont believe, in two Priesthoods existing in the church of Christ at one and the same time, as Smith planted them.

14. I dont believe, in Aaronic or Melchisedec high Priests existing in the true church of Christ in this dispensation.

15. I dont believe, in altering (said to be,) true revelations from God, as Smith did in a miserable manner in 1831.

16. I dont believe, in the order of Enoch, and false names, as was set up and practiced in Zion in the spring of 1832.

17. I dont believe, in an entire change of name of the church to that of the church of Latter Day Saints on the 3 of May 1834.

18. I dont believe, in setting up three men as first Presidents of the church, instead of twelve Apostles at the Head.

19. I dont believe, in a council of 15 men as the highest court in the church to try transgressors, when three could do better.

20. I dont believe, in the spirit and practice of War, as practiced or acted[6] by J. Smith and army in 1834, in their tramp to Missouri.

21. I dont believe, in the word sent by O[rson]. Hyde and J[ohn]. Gould, from Smith and council, for the church to fight in their own defence.

22. I dont believe, in revelating and ordaining a Bishop, to take charge of Church property as his business.

23. I dont believe, in ordaining a Patriarch to give patriarchal blessings to the whole church. [page 3:]

24. I dont believe, in pretending to dedicate Zion, and the Temple in Kirtland, and no power from God to assist them.

25. I do not believe, in pretending to translate with Urim and Thummim when only a small Stone was used.

26. I dont believe, in only one man to receive and give off revelations for the whole church. Its unch[r]istian.

27. I do not believe, in Moroni's revealing the place of the plates to Joseph Smith in 1823,[7] again in 1827.

---

6. McLellin added "practiced or acted."

7. McLellin appears to have originally written the date 1822, then crossed out the second "2" and added a "3" above the line to make the date 1823.

28. I dont believe, in John the Baptist, or Peter, James, and John ordaining J. Smith and Oliver Cowdery.[8]
29. I dont believe, in the Tithing law, it is opposed to the consecration law, and sets it aside. One was all, the other one 10th.
30. I dont believe, in driving the witnesses from Far West by his Danites at the peril of their lives, as was done in 1838. ~
31. I dont believe, in robbing the Gentiles in Davis Co. in 1838 of quantities of household good[s], as the L. D. Saints did do.
32. I dont believe, in the doctrine of hereditary rights of priesthood in the Gospel sy[s]tem.
33. I dont believe, in the doctrine of plurality of Gods, and God making, as J. Smith taught in Nauvoo; in a sermon there.
34. I dont believe, in the doctrine of baptizing for the dead by proxy as was taught and practiced in Nauvoo.
35. I dont believe, that God himself was once a man as men are now, and that he rose by exaltation to be a God.
36. I dont believe, that men can or will ever by any system of exaltation become Gods and reign over world glorified.
37. I dont believe, in polygamy[9] as taught and practiced by Joseph Smith in Kirtland, in Far West, and in Nauvoo.

---

8. According to church chronicler John Whitmer, the first mention of a higher priesthood was in June 1831 when "the Lord made manifest to Joseph that it was necessary that such of the elders as were considered worthy, should be ordained to the high priesthood" (Bruce N. Westergren, ed., *From Historian to Dissident: The Book of John Whitmer* [Salt Lake City: Signature Books, 1995], 69). When the Doctrine and Covenants was published in 1835, it included a new revelation, dated September 1830, referring to a previously unmentioned ordination to this priesthood: "And also Peter, James, and John, whom I have sent unto you, by whom I have ordained you and confirmed you to be apostles and special witnesses of my name, and to bear the keys of your ministry" (cf. LDS D&C 27:12; RLDS D&C 26:3a). This text was absent from the 1833 version of the Doctrine and Covenants, known as the Book of Commandments. Richard L. Bushman, *Joseph Smith and the Beginnings of Mormonism* (Urbana: University of Illinois Press, 1984), 162-63, 240-41n55, suggests that Peter, James, and John may have ordained Joseph Smith to the high priesthood in the summer of 1830, rather than prior to the church's founding. Dan Vogel finds the idea advanced by William McLellin and David Whitmer that "angelic ordinations were late additions to Mormonism [to be] supported by considerable circumstantial evidence" (Dan Vogel, *Religious Seekers and the Advent of Mormonism* [Salt Lake City: Signature Books, 1988], 218). McLellin, in this notebook and elsewhere, gives his opinion that "two priesthoods cannot exist legally in the 'church of Christ'" and that the hereditary priesthood of Joseph Smith III is equally unwarranted (Letter 9).

9. See Richard S. Van Wagoner, *Mormon Polygamy: A History*, 3d ed. (Salt Lake City: Signature Books, 1992); Todd Compton, *In Sacred Loneliness: The Plural Wives of Joseph Smith* (Salt Lake City: Signature Books, 1997).

38. I dont believe, in the book of Abraham[10] translated (pretended to be)[11] from Papyrus taken from the bosom of an Egyptian Mummy.

39. I dont believe, in Joseph's savage[12] abuse of Elders who hapened to differ with him in their opinions.

40. I dont believe, in giving false and fictitious names as Smith gave to nine Elders in Zion in the year 1832. ~

41. I dont believe, in the attempted endowment in the Temple in Kirtland in 1836. It was an entire failure.

42. I do not believe, in giving false revelations as Oliver's to the Lamanites, that Teachers have no authority to baptize, & as to the tares.

43. I dont believe, that any man has any authority to ordain or consecrate a Seer or Prophet of the Lord. Its a gift from God.

44. I dont believe, in ordaining or having high Priests, or Aaronic Priests[13] in the true Church of Christ in the gospel dispensation.

45. I dont believe, ~~his~~ Smith's revelations ought to have been printed in 1833, and the Lord suffered a **mob** to destroy them.

46. I dont believe, Smith's everlasting orders of Enoch, set up in Zion, and then[14] in Kirtland in 1832 ever accomplished any good.

47. I dont believe, in altering his revelations three times before they were printed in the book of Doctrine and Covenants.

48. I dont believe, in Smith's plans of gathering in Zion, in Kirtland, in Far West, in Diamon, and in Nauvoo, all failed.

49. I dont believe, in building a great Temple in Kirtland, and going in debt there for $30,000 dollars, but it went to decay. [page 4:]

50. I dont believe, in going in debt $40.000 in New York for goods, then sell them out and never pay for them afterward.

---

10. There is a pencil line through the words "I dont believe, in the book of" and the letters "Abrah" in "Abraham," but the line was probably not drawn by McLellin. On the Book of Abraham, see H. Donl Peterson, *The Story of the Book of Abraham: Mummies, Manuscripts, and Mormonism* (Salt Lake City: Deseret Book Co., 1995); Charles M. Larson, *By His Own Hand upon Papyrus: A New Look at the Joseph Smith Papyri,* rev. ed. (Grand Rapids, Mich.: Institute for Religious Research, 1992).

11. McLellin added "(pretended to be)."

12. There is a pencil line through "39" and "I dont believe, in Joseph's savage," but probably not drawn by McLellin.

13. McLellin added "Priests."

14. McLellin added "then."

51. I dont believe, in setting up a Bank in Kirtland, without a charter, then break down to the ruin of a many good men.

52. I dont believe, in running away from debts in the night, hid in a wagon, to keep people from knowing, as Smith and Rigdon[15] did do.

53. I dont believe, in combining temporal and spiritual power together, as when Smith became "trustee in trust for the Temple lot" in K[irtland]. in 1834.[16]

54. I do not believe, in Danite bands or Destroying Angels as set up by Joseph Smith in Far West in 1838. They drove the Witnesses away.

55. I do not believe, Martin Harris ever ought to have been one of the three witnesses to the book of Mormon.

56. I dont believe,[†] [page 5:]

Webster says, "A translator is one who renders into another lan-

---

15. For a summary of Sidney Rigdon's life, see the Biographical Notes.

16. McLellin added "in 1834."

[†]McLellin left this sentence unfinished and more than three-fourths of the page blank. John L. Traughber utilized this space to write the following about McLellin's view of Martin Harris:

Observations by J. L. Traughber, Jr.

It is important in this connection to note the fact that Dr. McLellan did not believe that Martin Harris ought to have been one of the three witnesses to the Book of Mormon. It may well be asked, why did the Doctor hold such a view as this? It must be that, in his long and intimate acquaintance with Smith and Harris, he saw in their conduct evidence that they were not to be relied on as men of truth. While it would be enough to cause an apposer of the Book of Mormon to deny its truth, to believe of Harris as Doctor McLellan, with him it was different. He had settled down on the thought that the Book of Mormon was true, and nothing that he might learn of the immoral characters of the men who were responsible for the existence of that book, ~~nothing~~ could shake his faith in its divinity. To an ordinary mind it would be sufficient to stamp the whole Mormon schem[e] as a fraud to believe that Harris signed the testimony just [to] be one of the witnesses, and that Smith took him in order to get his money; but to the mind of Dr. McLellan that was only an error of Smith's, and did not in any way affect the truth of the Book of Mormon. While there can be no doubt that Dr. McLellan was a firm and honest believer of the Book of Mormon, he has left enough on record to show the falsity of nearly all Mormon claims and pretensions, and to his indefatigable labors and researches is due the knowledge of much of the folly of Mormons.

I believe that if Dr. McLellan could have been freed from the idea that the Book of Mormon was a divine revelation, he would have made it hot for the Mormons, more so than he ever did. [The last sentence was added later by Traughber in purple ink. At the same time he wrote this last sentence, he underlined the word "error" in the previous paragraph.]

guage; one who expresses the sense of words in one language by equivalent words in another.[17] ~

1. Joseph Smith found in 1827 in a little box with the plates the Interpreters or Directors with which he brought 116 pages of[18] the book of Mormon to light. He would place the Interpreter in his hat, and then place his face[19] in it so as to ex[c]lude the light, then the appearance of a piece of parchment would come before his eyes. The characters of the plates would appear on a line on the parchment before his eyes, and then the translation would appear inmediately under it in English. And all J. Smith had to do was to read the English to his scribe; then that would disappear, and other lines would come. And so he continued until the translation was completed. Thus the Lord translated it and not man, and man was only the medium through which it was done. A translator must understand both languages, and express the same ideas of the one into the other. So Smith was not the translator.

2[-3].[20] The Urim and Thummin was never on the American continen[t]. It was never used to translate language in any one instance. It was always used to inquire of God and get answers. Num. 27:21. It was probably hid by Jeremiah before the Babylonish captivity, when he hid the other sacred things of the Holy of holies. With the Interpreters Joseph read the translation of 116 pages which Martin Harris lost. He then used a small black or brown stone by which the entire book was brought to light, and printed in 1830. In 1829 the plates and other sacred things were hid up in a cave until the Lord sees fit to bring them forth to light.

4. Joseph Smith's gatherings were unfortunate at least. Those who believed in his revelations, who had gathered, were driven from his Zion in 1833, from Clay Co. in 1836, from Far West and Diammon in 1838, from Kirtland in 1838, and from Nauvoo in 1846. It is not said in revelation any where that the Gentiles shall ever gather or be in a gathered condition at Christ's second coming. Nephi ~~saw~~ in vision, "saw the church of the Lamb of God +++ upon all the face of the earth" [cf. 1 Ne. 14:12]. This is as Christ said when sp[e]aking of his second coming, His angels "shall gather together his elect from the four winds, from one end of heaven to the other" [Matt. 24:31]. They could not be "upon all the

17. McLellin inserted this sentence at a later time than the rest of this section.

18. McLellin added "116 pages of."

19. McLellin added "his face."

20. This entry combines two numbered topics, 2-3, from the preceding list, with which McLellin intended to match the current numbers, although the correlation broke down as the second list progressed. In any case, McLellin identified the subsequent paragraph as number 4.

face of the earth," as Nephi saw them. Or at the "four winds, from one end of heaven to the other," as Christ declared, if they were to be gathered into a Zion for safety.

5. The appointment and ordination of Apostles was always only in the hands of the Lord Jesus Christ, but never in the hands of man. J. Smith and his associates, the three witnesses, called, appointed, and ordained his twelve Apostles. Of course, they were man made, and not apostles of Christ. A man to be an apostle of Jesus must see, hear, and feel him, must be true witnesses. A witness must have knowledge within himself or he is not nor cannot be a true Apostle of the Lord Jesus Christ. [page 6:]

6. No instance can be found in any inspired volume where angels ever officiated in ordinations. They brought messages to holy men, but never ordained them to any ministerial office. Christ did not even ordain Paul, after his own glorification, because the Apostolic authority was on the earth. True he ordained the twelves Nephites as disciples or Apostles, because that authority was not among them when he appeared among them. Then angel ordinations are a nulity—outside of all inspired books. J. Smith and O. Cowdery professed to be ordained by an Angel or Angels.

7. Of organization. To organize means to ~~counteract~~ construct so as that one part co-operates with another. To gather up various parts and plant them together. Establish is to settle firmly; to fix unalterably. To make firm. Thirty two times is establish used relating to the church, but organize is not once so used in the book of Mormon. I believe in talking and acting according to the language of the books. Then it is not organize at all, but establish.[21]

8. Man's word as God's. To receive mortal man's word as God's word from his own mouth is simply an impossibility. No intelligent man can do it. Even if he received all his words by direct inspiration; we then must examine and compare them with previous inspirations, and see their agreement or disagreement, and receive or reject according to their truth thus determined. Hence Joseph assumed a position to[o] high for mortal man.

9. Conferences. Holding general conferences of ministers to settle church matters may do for sectarians, but not for the church of Christ. Such conferences never assembled, so far as we know, during the times of the writing of the New Testament. Nor did the Nephites ever so meet

21. McLellin added "but establish."

for more than a thousand years of their history. When the people of God on both continents wanted knowledge they would not go to conferences, but they would go direct to the Lord and get it pure from the eternal fountain. Church history tells us of conferences held frequently during the third century. Conferences were held ~~frequently during the third century~~ in order to dig out of men's brains what God was willing to reveal. The whole object of Conferences was and is to supplant the true church government of heaven. Hence I cant beleive in holding general conferences. Its Catholic out and out.

10. An unimbodied or disimbodied spirit[22] was never seen by mortal man, except in vision. They could see God just as easy, "Whom no man hath seen nor can see" [cf. John 1:18]. But embodied angels have been frequently seen. Its passing strange to me that men natural men profess to see spirits. Its only spiritualism. Moroni being a disimbodied spirit could not have been the angel who visited Joseph Smith, to tell him of the treasures of Cumorah. Angels can visit and give messages to men but disimboidicd spirits cannot. -- [page 7.]

11. A Prophet, or three Presidents at the Head of the church. Jesus Christ planted twelve Aposles as the first authorities in his church, but not three men to be the Heads of the church of Christ. To place one man or three men as the prophet or prophets at its Head is priest-craft, and nothing else but the worst form of priestcraft and actual tyrany. Its man placing confidence in his fellow man—trusting in the arm of flesh. The gospel designed for "all to prophesy." Twelve Apostles were placed "first in the church. Secondly, prophets" [cf. 1 Cor. 12:28]. Not a prophet first and apostles second, as J. Smith finally organized his church. He claimed to be head of man, and of the church also. It was not [a] Christian~~ity~~ system.[23]

12. Orders of ministers. Jesus Christ set three ~~orders~~ offices of ministers in his church, upon both continents. At Jerusalem it was Elder, Bishop, and Deacon. In America it was Elder, Priest, and Teacher. Not first President, Patriarch, Apostles, High Priests, Elders, Bishop, Priest, Teacher, and Deacon. Such an order savors more of Catholocism than Protestantism or Christianity. It is not the gospel system—nay verily.

13. Two Priesthoods. Priesthood means an order of ministry. Neither Melchisedec or Aaronic priesthood ever had but three ~~orders~~ offices in it. And there never existed but one order at any one time in the church of God, or in the church of Christ since the world began. One

22. McLellin added "spirit."

23. McLellin added "system."

never was an appendage to another. It was three officers in the hood under the law age, and three only since Christ came. Two orders could not exist together. One would override the other. J. Smith declared that two priesthoods belonged to the church. Such is an impossibility, it never was so on earth.

14. High Priests. The office of high Priest ceased in the church when Christ came and took and exercised[24] that office himself. No mention is made of it in inspiration, as existing in the church after Christ came into the world, and chose his Apostles and set them to work. The book of Mormon is silent in all its New Testament part of such office. And the Latter day Saints never claimed to have high Priests of the Aaronic order, hence they had not the Aaronic Priesthood.[25]

15. J. Smith's revelations. He and his advisers altered and changed, throwed away and added to his revelations so as to make them read quite differently. They altered them three [or rather] several times before they printed and published them in the book of Covenants. They did this to my individual knowledge. They took out, and also added whole paragraphs. Now if the Lord said what he meant, and meant what he said why alter and change what he did say. I must say when I contemplate this thing I am astonished to think men should so trifle with their own revealments. And that to[o] in the direct face of what they considered God's word telling them "To not add nor diminish on pain of destruction and horrid plagues." David says "I God[26] will not alter the thing that is gone out of my lips." [cf.] Ps 89:34. [page 8:]

16. False names. False names and secret orders do not belong to any true church in any age or country, and all such things are of the Devil. Zion was cursed with both of them in setting up the order of Enoch in the spring of 1832. But the order (of what the heads of the church or Leaders[27] called the order of Enoch,) was instituted consisting of nine members. But the low dirty thing never accomplished any good for the church nor themselves either. They gave to each member a fictitious name, but although they called it an everlasting order yet it failed entirely in two years! and ought to have failed.[28]

17. The change of name. The first authorities of the church of Christ on the 3rd day of May 1834 made an entire change of the name of

---

24. McLellin added "and exercised."

25. McLellin added "Aaronic Priest" to his original "hood."

26. McLellin added "God."

27. McLellin added "church or Leaders."

28. It appears the words "and ought to have failed" were added later by McLellin.

the church from that of the church of Christ to that of the church of Latter Day Saints! Then again in 1837 to the church of Christ of Latter day Saints; then in 1838 they changed again to the church of Jesus Christ of L.D.S. And thus it stands to day. Seven times in the book of Mormon the name is clearly stated to be the church of Christ, or the true church of Christ. And when men profess to firmly believe that book, and then contend for any other name, I know not their end.[29] Its the characteristic name, and no other should be used.

18. ~~Three~~ One ~~men~~ man as President. The one man power in the church is not of God, but is priestcraft of the deepest die. The doctrine of a church and a one man President of the whole church is unknown in the gospel system. The doctrine of Paul was that all the members of the church, both male and female "might prophecy" [1 Cor. 14:31]. To prophesy is to deliver a "Thus saith the Lord," and all such deliverances would be sacred truth; and be for edification and comfort. Christ set in his church[30] first Apostles–not a first president, and after that Apostles. J. Smith's system turned the thing up side down–wrong end first. I love the gospel system, it is a beautiful plan for man's salvation. Let Christ be the Head of the church, but no Prophet or President however exalted in spiritual knowledge. Jesus Christ established twelve men on both continents to be his first ministers–not first a Prophet.

19. High council. This council set up by Joseph Smith in Feb. 1834 had no pattern in all the word of God, and was entirely unnecessary. Three Elders could have done the business much better and much cheaper. It was an entire new thing, unheard of in all revelation. It was an anomaly! This court was set up to try transgressors, and much valuable time spent in its sessions, and no real advantage gained.

20. War. War is always of the Devil, and no man ever engages in it, except in self defence, and still be in the service of God. J. Smith and a band of soldiers traveled near a thousand miles in 1834 in order to redeem Zion, and to prove them on a fools errand the Asiatic Cholera knocked down about sixty of their number, and 14 died of it! Awful to contemplate. Some of his first and best Elders fell and died!! ~ [page 9:] And not one particle of good, but thousands of evil, worked out because of that warrier raid!!! And all was done and suffered by following a professed prophet to their wo[e]ful ruin. I cant contemplate that whole proceeding from first to last without a shudder of horror! Let it sleep in the past!!

---

29. McLellin added "their end."

30. McLellin added "church."

21. O. Hyde and J. Gould. These men were sent from a council of the first authorities in Kirtland, Ohio, to Jackson Co. Mo. to tell their brethren to fight in their own defence. They obeyed council and fought, and that was the great reason why the entire church was driven from the county. O tell not about the sins of the church in Zion, it was iniquity in the Leaders in sending the cursed word of War, war. Let the Leaders get out of the road and then they draw all those who follow after them unavoidably. Thousands of misery and wretchedness followed this unwise council from J. Smith and his unwise advisers!

22. A Bishop appointed. It is not found in inspiration, nor in church history either for in[31] the first centuries of the Christian era that ever Bishops took charge of church property. No such office was known among the Christians of the first centuries on either continent. Among the ancients[,] Bishops or Priests which is the same, took the oversight of the church, and that was their business, but not to dabble in property. Smith in this set up an entire new office ~~entirely~~, never heard of before ~~in~~ among any church or people. Hence it was a nulity, and in its workings proved a curse to the church in Zion, and in Far West.

23. A Patriarch. No Patriarch is heard of during the law age, nor in any part of the gospel dispensation. We cant see the authority for such an office in the church. Its throwing the church back into the days of the patriarchs before Moses. It finally became a system in the church of L.D.S. of "grab game for money." But Joseph Smith by having a Patriarch and Aaronic priests in his church thus combined the three dispensations into one whole. He united the Adamic, the law, and the gospel all together, thus destroying the whole. Because each dispensation ought to and does stand alone. There cant be a combination, because each age has to be governed by its own specific laws, and priesthood[32] suited to its age, and they can not be blended together. It would be an anomily!

24. Of dedications. I do not believe in the authority that dedicated Zion or the Temple in Kirtland. There was no power from God shown forth in those pretended dedications; as was seen and known when Solomon's Temple was dedicated in Jerusalem. If ceremony and nothing but form was seen in Joseph's dedications then we are prepared to say they were not of God; but only manism and nothing more. O deliver me from such folly as was practiced in the church of Latter Day Saints all the way through their history. [page 10:]

---

31. McLellin added "in" without deleting his original "for."

32. McLellin added "and priesthood."

25. Urim and Thummin. I have the testimonies of Martin Harris, Elizabeth Cowdery, and Emma Smith[33] saying that J. Smith used a small stone in reading off the translation as it appeared before him, of the entire[34] book of Mormon. He only used the Interpreters until he had finished the 116 pages that M. Harris lost. The ~~entire~~ book that we have was brought to light by the use of a small stone which he possessed before he obtained the ~~the~~ plates. He never possessed any Urim and Thummim in his life. It was never used to translate languages. And the Interpreters were never used to get revelations from God. They were never used interchangeably. The L.D.S. use the name in order to find some foundation for the Interpreters in the Bible.[35] They nicname them. ~

26. One man power. In the gospel dispensation no one man can stand at the Head as Prophet and Leader, and be the only one to receive and deliver revelations for the whole church. Yet Joseph Smith claimed that right and power. He said by revelation, "No one shall be appointed to receive commandments and revelations in this church[36] excepting my servant Joseph" [BofC 30:2; LDS D&C 28:2; RLDS D&C 27:2a]. This was contrary to the spirit actuating of[37] Moses, of Jesus, and of the Apostles. Moses said, "Would to God all the Lords people were prophets" [cf. Num. 11:29]. Jesus said, "The Comforter shall teach all things" [John 14:26]. And Paul said, "For ye may all prophesy one by one" [1 Cor. 14:31]. And the Angel said to John, "The testimony of Jesus is the spirit of prophesy" [Rev. 19:10]. These statements being true then Joseph's system was anti-law, and outside of Christianity. It was pure priestcraft! It was placing him at the head of the church, and at the head of **man**. He revealed to Oliver thus, "Thou shalt not command him who is at thy head, and at the head of the church" [LDS D&C 28:6; RLDS D&C 27:2d]. Then we have a man standing as God-ward to the whole church in this free and glorious gospel dispensation. But I say away with all your man Heads!!

27. Moroni. He was a disimbodied spirit, and hence could not appear unto man to give him any manifestation. Therefore the statement of his appearing unto Joseph to reveal the place of the deposit of the plates was false. Angels can minister to man, but disimbodied spirits

33. For a summary of Emma Hale Smith's life, see the Biographical Notes.

34. McLellin added "entire."

35. McLellin added "in the Bible."

36. McLellin added "in this church" to make the text correspond to the 1833 Book of Commandments, which also remained the same in all editions of the Doctrine and Covenants.

37. McLellin added "of."

cannot, except they garb themselves in forms.[38] I have no doubt an angel ministered to Joseph, but it was not Moroni. Old Lehi said, "From the grave no traveler can return" [cf. 2 Ne. 1:14]. And Job said, "I go whence I shall not return" [Job 10:21]. I cant see why a man so well acquainted with things should make so false a claim as this is. I dont think he ever made it for some ~~years~~ months or years[39] after his church was organized.

28. Angel ordininations. There is no[40] inspired record of any angel ordination. No man was ever set apart to any ministerial office according to any inspired[41] record extant by angels.[42] Therefore for Joseph and Oliver to make such a false claim, was in every point of view wrong in the extreme. Angels minister to men, but not to ordain them. John the baptist [page 11:] could not ordain Joseph and Oliver to the Aaronic priesthood, because he did not[43] hold the hood himself. And no chief priest ever consecrated or ordained any man, and when an angel they would not do what they could not do when alive. Peter and James both died, and hence are disimbodied spirits, and hence prohibited from coming back to earth again. Smith held that John never died, but remains on earth in a kind of sem~~mi~~ immortalized state. Then according to their statement two disimbodied spirits, and an imbodied man came and ordained them. In 1831 I heard Jose~~p~~ph tell his experience ~~some twenty times probably~~, many times[44] about angels visits, and about finding the plates, and their contents coming to light, but I never heard one word of John the baptist, or of Peter, James, and John's visit and ordination. Till[45] It was told some ~~year~~ years ~~or two~~[46] afterward in Ohio.[47] But I cant believe the story for the above reasons.

29. The tithing law. Consecration of property to the Bishop was taught for eight years in the church before the tithing law was delivered by Joseph. The two are directly opposed to each other. One required all,

38. McLellin added "except they garb themselves in forms."

39. McLellin added "months or years."

40. McLellin added "no."

41. McLellin added "inspired."

42. McLellin added "by angels."

43. McLellin added "not."

44. McLellin first added "some twenty times probably," then deleted these four words and substituted "many times."

45. McLellin added "Till" as the new beginning of this sentence.

46. The original statement appears to have been "It was told some year or two afterward." Then, perhaps when the words "in Ohio" were tacked onto the end, McLellin added the "s" after "year" and deleted "or two," which made the resultant wording "some years afterward."

47. McLellin added "in Ohio."

but the other required only one tenth. Both could not be obeyed by any man. If all is consecrated, then one tenth would only be a part. Two such opposites could not come from a God of consistency. Hence I throw both of them away as contradictions, and not from a just being.

30. The witnesses driven. The witnesses to the Book were hunted and houn[d]ed and driven from Far West in 1838, at the peril of their lives, because they would not uphold Joseph and Sidney in their oppressions and false doctrines. They fled and their property was confiscated. And their wives had to leave Far West with only what clothing they could wear away. Armed bands of L.D.S. entered their houses and gave the women their orders. But mobs were soon after the Leaders, and they were taken and imprisoned in Clay Co. jail for months; and they took a change of venue to another county, and while on their way they eluded their guards, and fled the state, and passed on to Quincy, Illinois. But were never privileged to enter Far West again, or any part of the state of Missouri.

31. The Gentiles robbed. During their wars about 60 men went into Davis Co. well armed, and scared away the inhabitants from their homes, then robbed their houses and farms of all they wished, and hauled their plundered goods into Far West, and there kept them until the Missouri militia came near the town, they then became alarmed for fear the goods would be found in their possession. They hauled them a few hundred yards N.W. near the stone quarry and ~~throwed~~ threw them in a little bottom. I myself went [page 12:] down to see them. They lay in piles, and while I walked around among them, knowing they were robbed and plundered, I could not help thinking, Said I, O the false and miserable religion under which this people of the Latter day Saints are acting, and the wickedly ruinous Spirit by which they are possessed!! I think there was as much as ten wagon loads of every thing that could be gathered in and round about farmers' houses; from a fine bureau down to a little kitchen chair. Said I O fatal fanaticism, ruinous policy, direful, awful delusion! I know not words that will express the feelings I had while I walked round among those goods. But such ware Latter Day Saints at that day. P. P. Pratt took a few men and went to Galatin, the county seat of Davis Co. drove away the keepers and robbed the store of what they wished, and took the goods up to what was called DiAmmon. Pratt took a keg of nails on his horse before him and when he reached DiAammon he threw them down saying "Nails are cheaper here than in Boston." This was told to me by a respectable man who stood and saw the transaction. But I cant tell it as bad as it was. But in justice I must say

it was a state of warfare, and the old setlers–the Missourians[–]robbed the L.D.S., and burned down their houses, and destroyed their thousands. It was a scene of murder and bloodshed all around.

32. Hereditary priesthood. Hereditary rights would do for the Patriarchal and Law ages, but it does ~~they do~~[48] not belong to the gospel dispensation, any more than the Patriarchal or Law ministry does, or sacrifices, or circumcision, or Patriarchal blessings do. The gospel is an independent principle or doctrine, and cannot be united with any other age or doctrine. Can not unite it with the Patriarchs or with Moses and his laws. It stands alone. It has its own priesthood, and its own laws, independent of all other epochs, ages, or dispensations. It is a perfect system, and needs no combination with any other. And why J. Smith should try to unite it with the Patriarchal and Law ages I cant conceive if he remained a true Seer of the Lord. Not a word or hint about hereditary rights in the gospel system–not a word!!

33. Plurality of Gods. The doctrine of the plurality of Gods, and God making is the most ruinous of pure religion, of any that could be introduced. When God spoke from heaven he said, "Beside me there is no God; I know not any" [cf. Isa. 44:6, 8]. Tell me about a God being higher than Jehovah, and you tell falsehood. The Godhead in heaven is the only God in the unlimited universe. 35 and [3]6.[49] God making then by exaltation or in any other way is ruinous to Christianity. That man can ever be exalted or in any other way become a God to me is monstrous–is an absurdity of the deepest die. Man become a God and reign over a glorified world with his numerous progeny by many wives and concubines. Plurality of Gods is connected with plurality of women. They cant be seperated. [page 13:]

34. Baptizing for the dead. The scripture they refer to to[50] prove this unseemly thing they take from 1 Cor 15: 29. "Else what shall they do which are baptized for the dead, if the dead rise not at all? why are they then baptized for the dead?" There is no doubt in my mind that this refers to Christ as the one dead, and that baptism was for him, or in his name.[51] To me it upsets the whole Christian system, to baptiz for the dead by proxy. It destroys man's agency. In truth there is no proxy except Jesus Christ. He is the one who died for us, and cleanses our sins by

---

48. McLellin added "they do" above the line, then deleted it.

49. These numbers indicate that McLellin is combining them here with number 33 to retain a correlation to his initial list of numbered topics.

50. McLellin added the second "to."

51. The Greek original has the plural *huper ton nekron,* "for the dead ones."

his own blood. He is the one who satisfied all the demands against us. And will, if we have strong ~~faith~~ belief and faithful obedience sanctify us and receive us to himself. Then away with all your proxy baptisms. I want every man to stand for himself; and be judged according to his own deeds, and then saved by his own faith.

35. Polygamy. Mrs. Joseph Smith, the widow of the Prophet, told me in 1847 that she knew her husband the Prophet practiced both adultery and polygamy. I am aware that polygamy was practiced in Israel from Abraham until Christ. And if there is a blot on the Bible, I consider that practice one of the foulest! One thing is certain when God created Adam, he then made one woman for him. He could have put him to sleep again, and then took another ~~another~~ rib from his other side and made him another woman, so that the world could have been peopled the sooner. Again when the world was drowned Noah could have taken more women than one to have repeopled the world in quicker time. But God gave but one woman as a wife to Adam, and Noah and his three sons had in the ark but one wife each. This shows me the beauty and wisdom of God in pairing off the man with only one mate.

Jesus said, "He that made them at the beginning made them male and female, and said, For this cause shall a man leave father and mother, and shall cleave unto his wife: and they twain shall be one flesh" [Matt. 19:4-5]. He said farther, "Moses because of the hardness of your hearts suffered you to put away your wives: but from the beginning it was not so" [Matt. 19:8]. Here the doctrine is plainly taught that one woman was designed for one man, and no more. "Of twain they shall be one flesh." Plurality then of wives is not to be mentioned as belonging to pure Christianity. We are to[o] plainly taught the doctrine of oneness in and among the sexes. One man for one woman, "and it was so from the beginning." The doctrine and practice of polygamy is subversive of the great principle of unity. No unity can exist in polygamy. But when two hearts are joined there is agreement and union. Then "They two can become one flesh." They are mated, but man cant mate with many wives.
[page 14:]

36. The book of Abraham.[†]

[†]McLellin left a fourth-page blank space here to fill in later. John L. Traughber utilized the space to write the following in purple ink: "Why the Doctor failed to write about the Book of Abraham, I do not know. One reason probably was that it was ~~dor~~ translated (?) at Nauvoo, long after the Doctor had withdrawn from the fellowship of Joseph Smith. (Since I come to think it, I am not sure that the Book of Abraham was not translated (?) while Smith was at Kirtland; at any rate, he purchased the mummies and the papyrus parchment found in the bosom of one of them, from which parchment the Book of Abraham was

37. Joseph's abuse of Elders. When an Elder differed with Smith in opinion; or if he had committed any fault or crime (as ~~they~~ he thought,) he would use all the language and epithets he could command to set them in a ridiculous or false light. And S. Rigdon was worse than he. No wonder that about seventy of his first Elders quit him and strenuously opposed him in Kirtland, in 1837; and finally prevailed and drove him and Rigdon out of Kirtland: and they [Smith and Rigdon] went to Far West, Mo. Men that fell under their ban was to be pitied. I dont conceive that by any means [to be] the best way to treat men, and especially brethren. Harshness would never gain me. "Love is the fulfilling of the Law" [Rom. 13:10].

38. The endowment. The endowment was sought for in Kirtland, O. on April 6th 1836, but was not received, and was an entire failure. The church had built a large Temple and only partly finished it, and in it assembled at sunrise, and remained fasting until the next morning sunrise. Then about five hundred ministers began to wend their way home from that noble building, many of them disappointed and dispirited. The scene through which they had passed was one long to be remembered. No display of power from God was given. All the power given was the power of man. It was manifested in ordinations, in washing and anointing, and blessings by the authority of men. The Heads or Leaders claimed that by laying on their hands in their ordinations and ordinances "The whole power of the church rested on each one of those of the assembly, and that was their endowment."

They had a little bread, sent in by the sisters, ~~and some went~~ in the evening, The Twelve as servants[52] carried round to them on servers a little bread and wine,[53] and some of them partook of the wine so freely so as to become badly intoxicated! But when I look back upon those times and scenes I feel a kind of shudder, to think that intelligent good men could be so infatuated and blindly led. But such is human nature. False prophets have led multitudes of men into the most outragious falsehoods, and even into wo[e]ful crimes and many misdemeanors. ~ [page 15:]

39. Ordination of Prophet or Seer. The command cant in any inspired volume be found to ordain a Prophet or Seer. No where is it found

---

translated (?), while he lived in Kirtland, but he might not have translated (?) it till got settled in Nauvoo.) I have never read the book of Abraham further than what is given in the Pearl of Great Price; whether that is all of it, I dont know. –J. L. Traughber, Jr.–"

52. McLellin added "The Twelve as servants."

53. McLellin added "a little bread and wine."

where ever a Prophet or Seer was ever ordained by man. The station or office is a gift from God, and neither confered or confirmed by ordination from man. A Seer is a kind of independant man. He sees or can see the past, the present, or the future, by his gift from God. He can see natural or spiritual things, and then describe them just as they are or were or will be. A Seer's gift is the highest station and greatest gift God ever bestowed on man. He possessed all the power that God ever gave to man on earth, and lifts him up so as that he may be as near to God as man ever gets while in mortality. A Prophet or Seer is always bound to deliver to mankind whatever mandate is given to him, without fear of consequences. They can always detail a, "Thus saith the Lord."

40. High Priests. The gospel dispensation knows nothing of high Priests of the order of Melchisedec, or of the order of Aaron; except Christ only. The order of the Son of God which Christ held himself possessed or[54] held all the offices of the gospel age in it. They were all in the Priesthood and Jesus Christ held the Hood himself alone. Man does not hold priesthood, but holds office in it, and power and authority ~~is~~ comes in the office that a man holds in the priesthood. Man holds no priesthood, but when legally ordained he holds authority according to his station in the hood. The Latter Day Saints, so far as I know, never claimed to have Aaronic High Priests in or belonging to their church: hence they did not have that priesthood; they only had a part of it. In order to have the Aaronic priesthood they must have High priest[s], chief priests, and then Levites, or otherwise it would be incomple[te] consequently imperfect. It would be an impossibility for an Aaronic priest to exist in the gospel day, for that priesthood and law was done away in Christ. Paul speaking of the priesthoods says, "For the priesthood being changed, there is made of necessity a change also of the law" [Heb. 7:12]. If the priesthood and law was both changed I cant see why they should exist now.

41. Printing revelations. In Joseph's revelations it was said often "Keep these things from the world"; but in the last of November 1831, in a council of some dozen Elders it was determined to print them, notwithstanding the prohibition. Joseph, Sidney, and Oliver were appointed a committee to examine them and prepare them for the press. They did so by taking those expressions to "keep them from the world" entirely out.[55] And they made ~~them~~ many other serious alterations in them taking out whole parag[ra]phs and adding others. In this condition they were carried to Mo. by Oliver Cowdery and John Witmer, and

54. McLellin added "possessed or."

55. McLellin added "entirely out."

partly printed in a little "book of Commandments" in 1833. But Mobs hindered them from being [page 15a:][56] published to the world in full. It was singular about their destruction, for if the work was done according to the mind of the Lord why should sacred things be so destroyed? But in their mutilated and altered condition they could have been of but little worth to the church or to the world, hence their destruction. But there are many things about their printing and their destruction that is marvelous to me. And also about the Leading men setting up two Priesthoods in the church. But evil principles and practices accumulated fast when they began to go astray. So matters went until 1834, the Leading men set aside the name of the church of Christ entirely, and took another name and another character also. They named it the church of latter day saints, and so have run in that name with its alterations until the present day. But how long they will be permitted to go on I know not. Their revelations were altered three times to my knowledge[57] before they were printed in the book of Doctrine and Covenants.

42. Building a Temple. A magnificent large Temple was built in Kirtland, O. in 1834, 5 and 6. The latter day saints built one also in Nauvoo, Ill. from about 1840—to 1846. But the Ohio Temple partly went to decay, and the Nauvoo house was burned. If Elder [Russell] Huntley had not had ~~it~~ the K. Temple[58] repaired, in about 1850, it too would have gone to entire decay. It is kept now by an old lady to show to visitors, as a curiosity. Thousands and thousands of dollars were expended and thousands of indebtedness incurred in thus building those Temples, and but little good ever accomplished. They were truly latter day Saint structures, prepared with stands in each end in order to seat their two orders of priesthood. In those they held a kind of mock, false, and foolish endowments; contrary to every principle of goodness or holiness. They professed to build those Temples by inspiration, but it must have been from an evil sourse.

43. Going in debt. Joseph Smith professed that in May 1829, the Lord said to him, "Seek to bring forth and establish the cause of Zion. Seek not for riches but for wisdom" [LDS D&C 11:6-7; RLDS D&C 10:3a-3b]. Again in July 1830 he delivered this, saying, if[59] it came from the Lord, "In temporal labours thou shalt not have strength, for this is not

56. McLellin numbered two consecutive pages "15," then crossed out the second "15" but kept "16" as the next page. Accordingly, the current page has been numbered "15a."

57. McLellin added "to my knowledge."

58. McLellin added "the K. Temple."

thy calling. Attend to thy calling, and thou shalt have wherewith to magnify thine office" [D&C 24:9; RLDS 23:4c-4d]. But in the face of all this, and in defiance of what he called the Lord's word, in 1836 Joseph, Sidney, and Oliver went to New York and run into debt 40 thousand dollars for merchant's goods, brought them into Kirtland, sold them out and never paid for them. Mrs. Emma Smith told me in 1847 that over two hundred thousand dollars[60] were proven in the probate court in Carthage, Hancock Co. Ill. against the estate of Joseph Smith and not a dollar to pay it with. O deliver me from such ruinous speculation of a Prophet!!
~ [page 16:]

44. Smith's Bank speculation. In the end of 1836 or the beginning of 1837 Smith and Co. set up a Bank in Kirtland, O., and run it for a while without a state charter, but it broke down to the ruin of many men. It was a regular swindling concern, and how intelligent men could uphold a man as a "true Prophet" I cannot see, one who engaged in so much ruinous speculation is inconceivable to me–it is certainly incomprehensible. But Joseph and Sidney soon had to leave Ohio and flee to Far West, where they even did worse than they did in O. Because here [in Missouri] they warred and fought and caused a number of deaths; But they were finally taken by the Missouri militia and taken to Clay Co. Jail and confined for several months. But they got out and fled to Quincy, Ill., thence to Commerce–changed its name, and built up a large city called Nauvoo. There they were taken by the Illinois militia, and confined in Carthage jail. Here a blackened **mob** killed both Joseph and Hyrum Smith.[61]

45. Combining temporal and spiritual power. Before J. Smith left Kirtland on his warrior tramp to Mo. in 1834, he took a deed as "trustee in trust for for ~~of~~ the church of the Temple lot."[62] Thus setting up the two powers of temporal and spiritual[63] together, like the Popes of Rome. If J. Smith had obeyed the commandments of God from the time he finished the translation of the book of Mormon, he would have been alive today. But his enemies had power over him because he dabbled in tem-

59. McLellin added "if."

60. During the four decades after hearing this information from Emma Smith, McLellin's memory may have multiplied the amount. D. Michael Quinn, *The Mormon Hierarchy: Origins of Power* (Salt Lake City: Signature Books and Smith Research Associates, 1994), 591, gives the debt as $25,023.95.

61. For a summary of Hyrum Smith's life, see the Biographical Notes.

62. McLellin originally wrote "trustee in trust for the Temple," though there could be a previous word underneath "Temple." Next he added "of the church of" before and "lot" after "the Temple," then deleted "of" and added "for," unintentionally doubling the word "for."

63. McLellin added "of temporal and spiritual."

poral things. He should have solely given himself to his ministry, to his spiritual calling.

46. Of the Dissenters.[64] This was a secret band with oaths and imprecations, binding them to obey all the orders of the Presidency. In conclave they passed a resolution to kill some of the Dissenters. And Oliver Cowdery, David and John Whitmer,[65] and L. E. Johnson[66] were especially obnoxious to them. But these men heard of their resolution, and by fleeing from the city saved their lives. But those Presidents of the church of latter day saints had to lie[67] a long time in prison to reflect over their folly in driving those special witnesses to the book of Mormon from their midst. The three witnesses to the book of Mormon never united with the ~~the~~ church of latter day saints after that cold blooded driving them from among them.

47. Martin Harris. He was not with Joseph, Oliver, and David when they received their vision and testimony of the Angel's visit. He came afterward, and the four went into the woods and prayed that Martin might see. And after strugling in prayr for a while Martin quit them and went off by himself and staid so long that Joseph went to find him and found him and joined with him, when they ceased praying[68] Martin said he was willing [to] sign the required testimony of the book, and he did so. I think in this Joseph erred ~~as~~ as he did often. He ought to have had the three together–when the two had their vision and gave their testimony. But I think that Martin's money had much to do in his and Joseph's intimacy. Martin was considered wealthy. [page 17:][†] [page 18:]

---

64. Traughber used his characteristic purple ink to change "Dissenters" to "Danites," assuming McLellin intended to name the "secret band" here, as he did in the short list above. In fact, the paragraph is about both.

65. For a summary of John Whitmer's life, see the Biographical Notes.

66. For a summary of Lyman Eugene Johnson's life, see the Biographical Notes.

67. McLellin added "to lie."

68. McLellin added "praying."

[†]Page 17 was left blank, and Traughber used the space to write the following:

> The Secret of Mormonism. – The one great secret of Mormonism, the one that the originator of the fraud tried hardest to envelop in impenetrable mystery, was the precise manner in which the great first fraud, the Book of Mormon was contrived and foisted on the earliest Mormon dupes as a translation from ancient plates by the power of God. It will be seen by reading the following page [i.e., page 18] that my late friend, Dr. McLellin, accepted the story told by Smith and others about the loss of all the writings on the B. of M. which Smith had in his possession at the time Martin Harris took the 116 pages and lost them. I will prove that Smith and Cowdery lied when they pretended that such was the case.
>
> To be in harmony with Smith and Cowdery's stories, 1st, Smith should have let Harris take all that he had translated up to the time in question. 2nd, There

Joseph Smith's errors and wrongs

1. His finding the plates of the book of Mormon.

The 21st of September 1823, he went to a little hill lying between Palmyra and Canindagua, New York State, and in a small stone box or chest, by prying up the top stone, he discovered a pile of gold plates, and said in his heart and with his mouth, "It will make me and my father's family rich"; but a superior power removed him from the spot imediately; and he did not obtain the plates for about four years. Riches was not the object of the contents of those plates coming to light. But he begged and plead with the Lord and solemnly promised to be faithful, so that finally the plates and the Interpreters, ~~delivered~~ found with the plates were delivered to him in 1827. And then he went forward and succeeded in bringing the book of Mormon to light in 1830.

2. One hundred and sixteen pages lost.

After J. Smith obtained the plates he was much persecuted, because he declared that a holy angel had revealed all this matter to him. This as it were set people crazy, and some evil men even sought his life. So his relations, as well as he ha[s] declared to me. But he fled to his father in Law in Pennsylvania. Here he read off the translation of 116 pages from the plates, and Martin Harris was mostly his scribe. Harris' wife[69] was an en-

---

should not have been any part of the present book of Mormon in existence in the English language till Smith commenced to translate in the early part of 1829. 3d, Smith should have commenced at the first of the book of Mosiah and gone through with the whole book.

It is a lie for the following reasons: 1st, The B. of M. was finished before the end of June, 1829, and the time between the commencement of the work in 1829 and its completion was too short for so much writing to have been crowded into it. 2nd, The fore part of the B. of M. was the part last worked on, as is evidenced by the wording of a pretended revelation in May, 1829, which gives Smith directions for making a new fore part to the book. 3d, The pretended revelation says that Smith had retained that part of the book which includes and follows the reign of King Benjamin.

No Mormon can dodge this issue. The revelations in which he pretends to believe show that there was deep, dark, damnable plotting in the contrivance of the Book of Mormon. It makes no difference whether a man receives much or little of the Mormon fraud as divine revelation [because] as much as he does receive is based on lies, if he believes in any part of Smith's pretensions.

I can find no ground of apology in all that I know of Mormon claims: I have no faith in anything savoring of Mormonism. I have no use for, nor patience with any pretense that there was divinity or even honesty in the work of Smith or Cowdery from the beginning. Their words convict them of lying; their acts convict them of hypo[c]ri[s]y; their ends show them ~~then~~ to have been wicked impostors who had had lost all self respect and forfieted the respect of all others.

J. L. Traughber, Feb. 26th, 1889.

69. For a summary of Lucy Harris's life, see the Biographical Notes.

tire unbeliever, and a great opposer to her husband's course. He plead with Smith to let him have those 116 pages to read to his wife, she knowing that Smith was a very illiterate person. Martin thought by that means he would be sure of his wife's conversion. But instead M. Harris lost the 116 pages entirely, and never found them again. In this Joseph committed a grevious error, and in consequence the plates were taken from him, he lost his gift of reading the translation, and he also lost his Interpreters, by which he could read the translation as it appeared before him. He was some months in deep repentance; finally the Lord, or rather his guardian Angel, delivered the plates to him again, but not the sacred Interpreters. He never possessed them again in his life. But the Lord gave him light and power in a seer-stone in his possession before he received the plates, to finish the translation, which was completed in 1829, and the book printed in 1830. Had the people called Mormons lived according to the precepts and principles of that Book to the present day, then the opprobium, which now attaches to the name would never have been. Its doctrine is pure and its principles correct. ~ [page 19:]

3. His ordination by John the Baptist, in 1829, the 15th of May

Joseph Smith says in his history, "A messenger from heaven descended in a cloud of light, and having laid his hand upon us, he ordained us, saying unto us, 'Upon you, my fellow servants, in the name of Messiah, I confer the Priesthood of Aaron, which holds the keys of the ministering of angels, and of the gospel of repentence, and of baptism by immersion for the remission of sins; and this shall never be taken again[70] from the earth, until the sons of Levi do offer again an offering unto the Lord in righteousness[']" [cf. JS-H 1:68-69].

Oliver Cowdery describes this scene as follows.

"The angel of God came down clothed with glory, and delivered to us +++ the keys of the gospel of repentance +++ We listened—we gazed—we admired! 'Twas the voice of the angel ~~of God~~ from glory. +++ We received under his hand the holy priesthood, as he said, 'Upon you my fellow servants, in the name of Messiah, I confer this priesthood, and this authority, which shall remain upon earth, that the sons of Levi may yet offer an offering unto the Lord in righteousness[']" [cf. JS-H 1:71n].

We have this to say, no angel ever ordained any man to any office in[71] priesthood, since the world began; as any inspired record extant will inform us. No Aaronic chief priest ever ordained any body. The Aronic priesthood had three ~~orders~~ offices in it, High Priest, Chief priests, and

70. McLellin added "again."

71. McLellin added "office in."

Levites. It must exist in all its ~~orders~~ offices, or otherwise it is only a part of the priesthood. John was only a Chief priest hence could ~~could~~ not appoint or ordain a High Priest, and hence the hood would be deficient. It would be less than the whole order, therefore null and void. Ordinations only confer office in the priesthood, but not the hood itself. The Aaronic priesthood belonged to the tribe of Levi exclusively, but could not go into any other tribe, or under any circumstances go among the Gentiles, or to any stranger. Num 1:51. J. Smith claimed that he was of the tribe of Joseph, hence could not hold the Aronic priesthood at all. Now, an Angel never ordained, Chief priests never ordained. They did not hold the hood, hence could not confer it. The whole[72] priesthood was the order of it. Joseph said, "I have sent u[n]to you John[,] my servants Joseph and Oliver, to ordain you unto this first priesthood which you have received, that you be called and ordained even as Aaron." Laying on hands did not ordain them as Aaron. Aaron had much ceremony. Levi. 8. Exodus 28. Not ordained as Aaron at all. [page 20:]

4. Relative to Peter, James, and John's ordination.

Joseph Smith declared in his revelation thus, "And also Peter, James, and John, whom I have sent unto you, by whom I have ordained you and confirmed you to be appostles and special witnesses of my name, and to bear the keys of your ministry" [cf. LDS D&C 27:12; RLDS D&C 26:3a].[73] Now the same objection obtains here as relates to John the baptist's ordination. It cant be found in any of the inspired books where an angel ever performed an ordination. J. Smith declared by revelation that John the Apostle[74] never died, but underwent such a change as to be preserved on earth, to bring souls unto Christ until he would come the second time. James and Peter both died, and hence were disimbodied spirits. Now if so, would a **man** and two naked spirits come to these men and jointly ordain men to some high office? I say no, distinctly **no!**

Their profession to have been ordained by angels or spirits to either the Aaronic or Melchisedec priesthood was false, hence nugatory and void! There is no such thing as ordain[in]g[75] a man to Priesthood. He can only be ordained to some office in it. No man ever held the whole order of priesthood; that pertained only to the Lord Jesus Christ. The

72. McLellin added "whole."

73. McLellin's statement in Letter 9 shows he knew this verse was not in the 1833 Book of Commandments and was added to the 1835 Doctrine and Covenants.

74. McLellin added "the Apostle."

75. McLellin wrote "ordaing," then placed a caret under the "n," probably intending to add "in."

more I have looked at J. Smith's system of things, or his order of ministry, the more I disbelieve it to be in accordance with the gospel order, according to Christ's sy[s]tem.

5. <u>Joseph claimed that he and Oliver were Apostles of Christ</u>.

The Apostles of Christ all saw, heard, and handled him. No person can be an apostle without such an acquaintance. An Apostle is a witness, and no person can witness or testify to that which they do not individually know. No hearsay testimony will do, it must be actual knowledge in himself. So Smith and Cowdery were only witnesses of the true translation from the plates—the book of Mormon; but not of Jesus Christ in any sense. For them to make such a profession was simply false in every sense of the word. They could not be apostles of Jesus unless they had seen him. Paul says, "Last of all he w[as] [s]een of me" [1 Cor. 15:8]. [page 21:]

6. <u>Joseph's principle of exaltation for himself</u>

His revelation on the 6th of April says, "For his word ye shall receive, as if from mine own mouth" [LDS D&C 21:5; RLDS D&C 19:2b]. No mortal man on earth could do such a thing as to receive any man's word as a direct revealment or voice[76] from God. The Lord's voice to man is the most infallible evidence that any man ever received. But we receive man's word with some doubts until we have time to prove them. Man's word is not equal to the voice of God, that is infallible certainty. This revelation was giving Smith power over the consciences of men entirely. It was making him a God to them. It was exalting him above every other man in the world. It was contrary to every principle of gospel liberty. It was one of the many things[77] that finally ruined the church. It was hoisting him up on a pole to be looked up to and worshipped.

7 <u>Joseph's Canada revelation</u>

Sometime in 1829 he professed to receive a revelation from the Lord directing Oliver and others to go to Kingston in Canada in order to obtain a copy-right in that dominion, for the book of Mormon. They went but failed, and returned without it. The revelation proved so perfectly false that it was never put with his other revelations, or ever printed either. Riches was not the object of that wonderful, and singular book's coming to light. Joseph wanted to sell the book in the Cannadian dominion in order to raise money. When Joseph first saw the plates the thoughts of riches spring into his heart, but he was removed from the place, and it was some four years before he obtained them. But now he

76. McLellin added "or voice."

77. McLellin added "things."

imagined that the sale of his book in Canada would bring him in funds; but in this he was failed.

Now if he as revelator delivered a false revelation so near his beginning, out of his own heart or from Satan, what confidence can any intelligent man have in his after productions? They are bound (as I am,) to receive them with many doubts. Joseph wanted this revealment of his to die, and never be remembered by any mortal man. But I have seen and read a copy of it my individual self. Hence all his book of Covenants must be received with many doubts!! This revealment of his was a miserable piece of [page 22:] wickedness. It was trying to seek riches out of sacred things; hence it[,] to a great meaure[,] for good destroyed his usefulness for ~~good~~ spirituality[78] in all his after life. It was delivering a "Thus saith the Lord," when the Lord had not spoken.

8. As to Joseph's being ordained a Seer.

"A Seer is a revelator, and a prophet also; and a gift which is greator can no man have" [Mosiah 8:16]. A Seer must have the Urim and Thummim, the Interpreters or Directors, or a Seer-stone of some kind in which to see, or he is not an inspired Seer of the Lord. After Joseph Smith finished the book of Mormon he never used a Seer-stone in which to see: hence was not a Seer. But he required O. Cowdery on the day he organized his church to ordain him a Seer. The Lord did not direct it, hence there was no authority or power in the performence. It was mere speculation, it was manism, and nothing but ceremony. I say again that there is no place in inspired Writ where a prophet or Seer was ever ordained by man. A Seer was a very peculiar man, he always had great power with God, and authority among men. He could learn the past, the present, or the future; and he could deliver the mind of the Lord for the benefit or use of mankind. But Joseph Smith, by transgression, lost the power and the means to see, hence was not an inspired Seer of the Lord after he finished the Book. All ordinations would not make him a Seer. It is a gift direct from God, not from man by ordination.[79]

9. As to holding general Conferences.

Conferences are assemblies of men for the purpose of doing some church business. During the days of inspiration among men, no mention is made of a general conference. Whenever any one wanted knowledge from God on some important matter, he went to some one who had authority, and power with the Lord, to some Prophet or Seer, and there re-

78. McLellin added "destroyed his usefulness for ~~good~~ spirituality."

79. McLellin added "by ordination."

ceived direct intelligence from the Highest, and thus the matter was settled, and that was an end of all controversy relating to all spiritual subjects. No conference of men or ministers in order to dig out of the brains of each other, ever got together in a general conclave during all past time, while they had inspired men among them, on either continent or in any country. All spiritual subjects were determined and settled by direct inspiration. Such a thing as a general conference of men meeting to settle [page 23:] spiritual questions was never thought of or acted upon during the Patriarchal age, the era of the law, or in the gospel dispensation.

The one who held the birth-right before Moses, and the High Priest after him until Jesus Christ were the ones who had this inestimable gift from God. And after Christ a "spiritual gift" was within the reach and power of every believer who received the gift of the Holy Ghost. Paul said, "For ye may all prophecy one by one, that all may learn, and all may be comforted" [1 Cor. 14:31]. The gospel plan was a system of liberty. No tyrants could live in it and enjoy it. It was so ordered that every honest faithful member could hold communion with God for himself, and learn what he needed. If all could prophesy, then all could foresee, and foreseeing the Spiritual things of God is one of the greatest, highest, and most blessed gifts of God ever given to man.

Hence conferences would be an infringement of that gift. Away then with such assemblies to do the Lord's own business, especially during the ages of inspiration among men. But when men or the church l[o]se inspiration or inspired men from among them, they must invent something else to govern them. The learning and wisdom of the world, or of learned men must be called in to aid to govern the (what ought to be,) entire spiritual kingdom of God. But all such wisdom was folly and worse than nonsen[s]e. In Asia conferences became frequent during the third century, after they had lost the blessed gift of inspired men among them. No greater evidence of the folly and weakness of Joseph Smith than his appointing conferences. His revelation is, "The Elders composing this church of Christ, are to meet in Conference once in three months + + + to do church business" [LDS D&C 20:61-62; RLDS D&C 17:13]. No greater sectarian notion could ever have got into Joseph's brain. All rules, laws, and regulations for sentiment, principle, doctrine and government ought to and could come through the medium of direct revelation, provided inspired men lived among them—then Conferences are a violation of the Lord's manner of Government. Away then with all general[80] Conferences!! ~ [page 24:]

80. McLellin added "general."

10. O. Cowdery's revelation to the Lamanites.

"And now behold I the Lord say unto you, that you shall go unto the Lamanites, (Indians) and preach my gospel unto them, and[81] cause my church to be established among them" [cf. BofC 30:7]. Cowdery and four others viz. P. P. Pratt, Peter Whitmore,[82] Ziba Peterson,[83] and Dr F. G. Williams[84] went to the Indians in N.W. Ohio, but they would not hear, they then went to them west of Missouri, but they would not hear, not one was ever converted hence no church could be set up among them, and the revelation proved entirely false. It says "cause my church to be established among them." No church was ever established among the Indians by either Cowdery or any of his immediate friends of the church of Christ. The Lamanites are yet roaming and fighting among themselves, and against the forces of the United States. Where they are converted they will "beat their swords into plowshares, and there spears into pruning hooks, and learn war no more" [cf. Isa. 2:4]. Poor Indian now roams in the wil[d]s of America from the straits of Magellan in the south to near the North pole, and are mostly[85] ignorant idolaters. Dying without a knowledge of Jesus, or his saving gospel. Nearly fifty years have passed since that revelation was given, and yet the Indians are wild and blood-thirsty. No pure gospel among them. Then I say that no more false revelation could have been delivered from man's heart or from the Devil than that one concerning Cowdery and the distressed Indians.

11. The head of the Church.

Joseph revealed to Oliver thus,[86] "Thou shalt not command him who is at thy head, and at the head of of the church" [LDS D&C 28:6; RLDS D&C 27:2d]. No man o[n] earth can be Head of the Church while Jesus lives to be Head himself. Paul said, "And hath put all things under his feet, and gave him to be Head over all things to the church" [Eph. 1:22]. Again, "he is the head of the body, the church" [Col. 1:18]. "For the husband is the head of the wife, even as Christ is the Head of the church, and he is the Savior of the body" [Eph. 5:23]. The church does not need nor can have two heads, one of them would be superfluous, be

81. McLellin quotes the 1833 Book of Commandments; the 1835 Doctrine and Covenants (51:3) and current editions (LDS D&C 28:8; RLDS D&C 27:3a-3b) have an added conditional statement: "inasmuch as they receive thy teachings thou shalt."

82. For a summary of Peter Whitmer's life, see the Biographical Notes.

83. For a summary of Ziba Peterson's life, see the Biographical Notes.

84. For a summary of Frederick Granger Williams's life, see the Biographical Notes.

85. McLellin added "mostly."

86. McLellin added "thus."

unnecessary. Christ is the only legal head of the church for all time. It was [page 25:] wicked in the extreme for any mortal man to make such a claim as to be head of the church, it was assuming Christ's legal position, it was blasphemous folly, for Joseph Smith to claim to be head of both man and the church. It was impossible for him to maintain himself in that position, hence he was slain in the middle of his life, meanly and unlawfully by mob violence! It is really awful for a man to make such great claims as J. Smith did if the Lord did[87] not authorise him to do so, nor qualify him therefor—which would have been an impossibility. There are two spirit worlds[88] that can commune with man, and Joseph's revelations contained to[o] many falsehoods to have come from the Lord, or from his superior spiritual beings, hence they must have come from his own heart, or from the nether world—from the spirits of evil. We admit there is much truth in some of his professed revelations, but occasionally great falsehoods! That was always Satan's plan to tell a great deal of truth with a little falsehood mixed up with it. Now I affirm Christ to be the only legal Head of the church for man, and Joseph Smith's revelation on that subject[89] to be false in theory, principle, and practice.

12. The translation of the Bible.

To Sidney Rigdon it is said, "And a commandment I give u[n]to thee, that thou shalt write for him (Joseph,), and the scriptures shall be given even as they are in mine own bosom, to the salvation of mine own elect" [LDS D&C 35:20; RLDS D&C 34:5a-5b]. I was intimately acquainted with the manner of this (said to be) translation. Smith would seat himself, with his scribe at the desk, and his big Bible spread out before him, and then he would read and correct whatever he thought was amiss, Hence it was not a translation, but simply only a correction. Joseph had no knowledge of the language in ~~the~~ which the scriptures were originally written, therefore he had no power to translate, but only to correct. It was a misnomer to call it a translation. He altered and changed its reading a great deal, and sometimes for the worse. Translation is to take a thing expressed in one language and express the same in another language or tongue; but Smith did not do this, hence it was no translation in any sense of the word. ~~It is then in no sense a translation~~. [page 26:]

13. A bishop of the church ordained.

"I have called my servant Edward Partridge,[90] and give him a com-

87. McLellin added "if the Lord did."

88. McLellin added "worlds."

89. McLellin added "on that subject."

90. For a summary of Edward Partridge's life, see the Biographical Notes.

mandment, that he s[h]ould be appointed by the voice of the church, and ordained a Bishop unto the church +++ to take care of church property" [cf. D&C 41:9; RLDS 41:3c]. There is no parallel in the word of God for any such officer, either in Asia or in America; It was an entire new office under the sun. There is no warrant or parallel for it in the word of God, or church history either. Then it likewise was a false get up. It was entirely unnecessary, as well as unheard of. And E. Partridge never accomplished any good in his office in his life, or on account of his station. A Bishop in the apostolic age was ordained to take charge of a branch of the one universal church, in spiritual matters, but not in temporal. They were Priests to teach in spiritual things. Their character were particularly pointed out by Paul, but not their ministerial duties, only to teach and[91] take the "rule over the church" [cf. 1 Tim. 3:5], among the true[92] believers.

14. A Gentile gathering of the church in this age.

"Men shall be appointed to purchase the lands, and to make a commencement, to lay the foundation of a city, and then ye shall begin to be gathered with your families, every man according to his family and his circumstances" [cf. LDS D&C 48:6; RLDS D&C 48:2c-2d]. No men were ever appointed to purchase lands or sent to do so either. The gathering of those who believed that Joseph Smith was a prophet and revelator were in such a hurry that they did not wait for men to be appointed to have things prepared before them. This gathering to a Zion was an unfortunate thing for the church. They gathered by hundreds into Jackson Co. Mo., from the summer of 1831 until the fall of 1833, then they were driven pel mell from the Co., from their lands and from much of their property by mobs.[93] They stopped one or two years in Clay Co. but was forced to leave there and they settled in a kind of wilderness, intersperced with timber and prairie; which they got laid off into a county afterward[94] named Caldwell, and they soon made the wilderness blossom as the rose. But they and the Missourians could not dwell as neighbors, in the same region. In the fall and winter[95] of 1838 they had again to leave their beautiful region of country, their homes, their firesides, and their cultivated lands, and flee for life. This time they left the State and went to Illinois. [page 27:]

Here in a free state they found an assylum from the peltings of mobs

92. McLellin added "true."

93. McLellin added "by mobs."

94. McLellin added "afterward."

95. McLellin added "and winter."

for a season. They first stopped in Quincy, but soon removed up to Commerce which name they changed to Nauvoo. Their leading men, with J. Smith were taken prisoners in Far West, and confined for months in Clay Co. Jail. But finally took a change of venue to another Co. and slipped their guards, and they too went to Illinois. In Nauvoo they built up a large city and community. Their numbers were thousands, but mobocracy prevailed again. Their Prophet and Leader Joseph Smith, and their Patriarch Hyrum Smith were murdered in Carthage Jail, ~~and whole~~ Hancock Co, Illinois, June 27th 1844. And the believers in their church establis[h]ment had to leave their renowned City and again flee for life!

This time they bend their course to the Rocky mountains, beyond the abodes of civil[iz]ation, away to the region of the great Salt Lake; and they are there to day—reveling in their many wives, and probably concubines. I have one thing to say about a Gentile gathering, before Jesus makes his second appearance. I know of no place in the Word of God where such a thing is predicted. I believe in ~~a Jewish~~ an Israilite gathering first, and then the Gentiles may come in and <u>assist</u> them to build cities for safety and convenience; but not to first gather ~~gather~~ and call in the Israelites to a gathered place. Hence we can see plainly why Smith and his devoted followers were never prospered in trying to gather together in a Zion or any of its stakes. I think Smith's ~~entire~~ course was entirely premature—was hurried beyond its time. Hence he never really prospered in any thing only in gathering numbers into his fold. Thousands and thousands united with him in church fellowship, and many thousands of human sufferings followed their many dispersions from their gathering places! I said thousands of human suffering. Tongue cant tell the heart rending scenes that that people have under gone, in their peltings by mobs, and mob outrages. Many were killed—butchered in an outrageous manner. And women and children suffered untold hardships. But a just God will finally give every mobocrat his just ~~reward~~ punishment in the bitterest **<u>hell</u>!!** [page 28:]

15. <u>Joseph Smith's consecration Law</u>.

Edward Partridge being ordained Bishop of the church, the revelation and Law said to the members,[96] "And behold, thou shalt consecrate all thy properties that which thou hast unto me, (saith the Lord,) with a covenant and deed which cannot be broken; and they shall be laid before the bishop of my church +++ so that it cannot be taken from the church. +++ And he that sinneth and repenteth not shall be cast out,

96. McLellin added "to the members."

and shall not receive again that which he has consecrated unto me" [BofC 44:26-27, 31].[97] This law or rule could not be carried out in any state in this nation; and I dont know that it could in any nation or country in the world.

This was an entirely new thing under the sun. No such law can be found like this in all this lower creation, for a man to give up all he has into the hands of any man. Consecrate here means to give up all control of ones own earnings of his properties. No sane man could do so and still be satisfied. Every man wants to control his own business.

The bishop and his two councillors, as honest men I think as I ever knew, tried to put this law in force in Jackson Co. Mo. in the years 1832 and 3, but entirely failed. They worked at it for months in and among the faithful, but effected no good whatever. They were to build a storehouse and keep all the surplus in that, but none was ever built, and the thing fell through entirely and was given up. J. Smith then was at great fault to make or declare such an unheard of law. He must have thought so too for he entirely changed it in a few years. and in a few years more he throwed it entirely away, and then introduced the "Tithing law," of one tenth instead of all. The disciples on both continents had their goods in common stock, but his system was entirely different from that. They must first consecrate all their property, and build a storehouse to hold the surplus. It was the most mixed up law or system that I ever contemplated. It had no parallel in all past time, it has no precedent in the present, and I can find no place for it in the future. So I will cast it away into the waste-basket among other useless r[u]bbish, to be given "to the moles and the bats" [Isa. 2:20]. [page 29:]

16. Two priesthoods in and for the church of Christ.

Priesthood is authority and power in the Lord Jesus Christ, but office in it is authority to act in the various stations to which men are ordained, whether as Apostles, Elders, Priests, or Teachers. Priesthood is in Christ, and men receive authority to act in it because of call, appointment, and ordination. One man is placed in the apostolic office sta-

97. The passage McLellin quotes is from the 1833 Book of Commandments, to which a number of significant changes were made in the 1835 Doctrine and Covenants (13:8-9, 11): "And behold, thou wilt *remember the poor*, and consecrate *of* thy properties *for their support* that which thou hast *to impart* unto *them*, with a covenant and a deed which cannot be broken. *And inasmuch as ye impart of your substance unto the poor, ye will do it unto me*; and they shall be laid before the bishop of my church ... that they cannot be taken from the church.... And ... he that sinneth and repenteth not shall be cast out *of the church*, and shall not receive again that which he has consecrated *unto the poor and the needy of my church, or in other words*, unto me" (D&C 42:30-32, 37; RLDS 42:8b-9a, 11a, modern editions).

tion,[98] but another takes a different office, each must act[99] according to his station, or the authority of his office.

J. Smith in his book of Covenants says, "There are in the church two priesthoods, namely, the Melchisedec, and the Aaronic, including the Levitical priesthood" [LDS D&C 107:1; RLDS D&C 104:1a]. The Melchisedec priesthood is all right for the Christian dispensation when properly understood. Christ is the only High Priest of the gospel dispensation. No other can exist in heaven or on earth while he lives. But one high Priest could live at the same time under Moses' law, ~~and he was a type of Christ~~; hence but one can exist in the gospel age, and that one is Christ.

And as to Aaronic or Levitical priesthood, it died when the law was abolished. It cannot exist where the gospel lives. It was only intermediate, existing and officiating between Moses and Christ. The law ministry was only a shadow made by the true substance or order of Christ. There were but ~~the~~ three officers or ministers in the Aaronic order of their priesthood or of their ministry, viz. High Priest, Chief priests, and Levites; hence the substance—the ministry of Christ, which made the shadow, can have but three offices in it viz. Elders, Priests and Teachers: because the shadow must be similar to the substance. No person except he is of the tribe of Levi can possibly hold office in the Aaronic priesthood under any circumstances. The book says, "And the stranger (Gentile or Jew,) that cometh nigh shall be put to death." Num 18:7. "And thou shalt appoint Aaron and his sons, and they shall wait on their priest's office: and the stranger that cometh nigh shall be put to death.["] Num 3:10.

The Levites were a service of gift—"they were wholy a gift to Aaron, and to his sons; out of the children of Israel." [cf.] Num 3:9. The ministers of Christ were wholy a gift to him from his Father. "I have manifested thy name unto the men which thou gavest me out of the world." John 17:6. [page 30:] Both Aaron and Christ were High Priests. Aaron stood at the head of the ministry of the Law age, and Jesus at the Head of all the ministry of the gospel age: and both had all the ministry of their respective ages given to them to preside over and direct. Aaron for the law, and Jesus for the gospel. There is no power in heaven or on earth that can now legally appoint and consecrate a priest of Levi—of the law age to any office in the gospel dispensation. That authority is dead since the gospel ministry was established. Moses set aside the Patriarchal authority of

98. McLellin added "station," but his original "office" was not deleted.

99. McLellin added "must act."

one man's being Priest for the whole race of man, and set up a ministry of all the first born of ~~all~~ the families of all Israel.

But Israel rebelled at Sinai and the first-born ministry was set aside—paired off with the Levites, and they as a ministry ~~was~~ were never heard of again afterward as officiating among men. The Levitical priesthood was entirely set aside when the gospel ministry was established. It was abolished, abrogated forever; just as the birth-right, or Patriarchal ministry, and the first-born ministry was set aside by Moses; so Jesus Christ set aside the Aaronic or Levitical. Hence J. Smith's Aaronic priesthood was without divine authority, and was a perfect void.

It was an impossibility for John the baptist to confer the priesthood of Aaron, (as J. Smith claimed,) from the fact that he was only a Chief priest, and had no authority or power in or over the high priest's office. And without a high priest the hood was not complete. And no Chief priest could consecrate any Levite; so that in Smith's church they could have had but one ~~order~~ office of priests, allowing his claim of ordination by John to be correct. No order of Priests could be set up without some one holding authority to set it up; and we see that John had not that authority. By this we see Smith's whole system of priesthood was and is "the ba[s]eless fabrick of a vision"! Got up mearly in order to have some office to pretend to confer on his particular friends. The more we look at J. Smith's orders of priesthoods and ministry, and his church establishment the more we see it differing from the true order of Christ and his Apostles and Disciples. Hence I lay it away as a "dream of a false night vision." I cant believe in but one order of priesthood in the "true church of Christ." They can do all the ministrations of that church, then we have no use for another. Give me the Melchisedec order and I am perfectly satisfied! [page 31:]

17. J. Smith materially altered his own revelations.

In November 1831, Joseph Smith assembled a council in Hiram, Portage Co. O. and during its sittings it was determined to have all his revelations printed, and he, O. Cowdery, and S. Rigdon were appointed a committee to read over, and prepare them for the press. But they seemed to think themselves authorized to alter and change what they claimed to be the revelations of the Lord, to an alarming extent. They altered words, sentences and paragraphs. They took out passages and added others so as to entirely change the sentiment, and thus made them read very different.

Now if as they said and professed to believe that these revelations were from the Lord direct, then if so their alterations would bring a curse instead of a blessing. Moses said to Israel, "Ye shall not add unto the word which I command you, neither shall you diminish ought from it." Deut 4:2. Again, "What thing soever I command you, observe to do it; thou shalt not add thereto, nor diminish from it." Deut 12:32. We will hear Solomon, "Add thou not unto his words, lest he reprove thee, and thou be found a liar." Prov. 30:6. Jesus said, "Till heaven and earth pass away, one jot or one tittle shall in no wise pass from the law, till all be fulfilled." Matt 5:18.

I am astonished that sane men should dare do as those men did with what they considered the Lord's word. They must have believed as I now do that Smith's revealments were from evil spiritualistic influence. It was spiritualism condensed. There is some truth in his revelations, but mixed with much error and falsehood. And the revelations were sent to Jackson Co. Mo. by O. Cowdery and John Whitmer, during the winter of 1831 and 2, for publication. J. Smith visited Mo. in the spring of 1832, and in council it was agreed that the printers Phelps,[100] Cowdery, and Whitmer should examine, alter and correct them again before printing them. They printed 160 pages, in a small book, called "Book of Commandments."

But in the summer of 1833 a **mob** destroyed their building, their press, their bookwork, and the printers had to flee for their lives. I have a copy gathered up among the rubbish by one of the printer boys, and roughly bound.

The revelations were then taken back to Ohio, and in Kirtland they formed [page 32:] another committee by adding ~~adding~~ Dr. F. G. Williams to the former one. Here the said to be revelations underwent another awful scathing and alteration, and was published in a book ~~of~~ called "Doctrine and Covenants." If any man had the original as first given and there read the alterations, he could not help being surprised at their changes. And why sane men should act so I cant conceive. ~ Now if these revelations were from God, and he spoke what he meant and meant what he spoke how could any man or men alter them for the better? I think to change the Lord's word is a great crime! John says that awful plagues shall fall upon the man who tampers with the word of God, and the Lord "will take his part out of the book of life" [Rev. 22:19]. Then if J. Smith's revelations were sacred I pity the men who altered them. We only have to refer to the manner [of] Joseph Smith, Oliver Cowdery, and Sidney Rigdon's deaths in order to see their fates! Sidney

100. For a summary of William Wines Phelps's life, see the Biographical Notes.

Rigdon died a monomaniac, Oliver Cowdery did not live out half his days, and Joseph Smith was miserably butchered by blackened mob! Wo be the men who destroyed the revelations of the Lord (or those pretended to be) by their ~~their~~ changes and alterations!

18. The order of Enoch set up in Zion.

On the 26th of April 1832, Joseph Smith, S. Rigdon, and N. K. Whitney,[101] and some Elders in Zion organized the order of Enoch, with nine members, and gave to each a fictitious name, as Gazelam, for Joseph, Pelagoram for Sidney, Ahashdah for Whitney, Olihah for Cowdery, Shederlaomach for Williams, Mahalaleel for Harris,[102] Zombra [Zombre] for Johnson[103] &c. This was directly contrary to what they had previously professed to believe, and to be opposed to all secret societies or combinations of all kinds. But the Enoch's order was private when first set up. It was giving a certain number of men privileges above their brethren. There was no equality here. It was a privileged order. None others were admitted into their councils. This was exalting some and degrading others. This was the start of odious distinctions among that confiding people. There was a great amount of folly and wickedness. Fictitious names never came by inspiration from God, neither a secret order in the church of Christ. The true church is full of liberty and confidence. No fictitious or false names or principles or theories in the church is at all allowable. Joseph said in his revelation, "This order I have appointed unto you to be an everlasting order, and unto your successors" [cf. LDS D&C 82:20; RLDS D&C 81:5a]. But March 1833 in [page 33:] Kirtland, O., another revelation is given setting aside their brethren in Zion, and setting up another band of men; it says, "You shall no longer be bound as a united order to your brethren in Zion, but shall be called the united order of the stake of Zion, in the city of Shinehah (Kirtland,) +++You are dissolved as a united order with your brethren" [cf. LDS D&C 104:47-48, 53; RLDS D&C 101:9a, 9d]. Altho the first order was to be an "Everlasting order," yet that everlasting order only lasted two years! I never saw a greater amount of nonsense in any documents and conduct in all my reading in life. Its enough to blast ~~the~~ J. Smith's[104] whole system of government.

101. For a summary of Newell Kimball Whitney's life, see the Biographical Notes.

102. Six of McLellin's identifications are confirmed by other sources, while William W. Phelps equated "Mahalaleel" with Algernon S. Gilbert. See David J. Whittaker, "Substituted Names in the Published Revelations of Joseph Smith," *Brigham Young University Studies* 23 (Winter 1983): 111-12.

103. For a summary of John Johnson's life, see the Biographical Notes.

104. McLellin added "J. Smith's."

19. Ordained president of the whole church.

On the 25th of January 1832, Joseph Smith was ordained to the presidency of the whole church, in Amherst, Lorain Co. O., in a general conference by Sidney Rigdon. I was present and know what I say. Then in March 18, 1833, Joseph's history says Dr. F. G. Williams and Sidney Rigdon were ordained Councillors with Smith in the Presidency. I fail to find in the New Testament or book of Mormon any pattern or direction for any such presiding power, or authority. Hence it was a get up of Joseph's own brain. It was placing Smith up on a pole to be looked up to, feared and worshipped, as some of his followers did do before his death. His system was somewhat of a counterpart of Popery. J. Smith was head of all his followers, and the Pope of Rome is head of all under his authority. The Pope claims infallibility, and J. Smith claimed that his followers should, "Receive his word as from the mouth of God" [cf. LDS D&C 21:5; RLDS D&C 19:2d].

The Apostles in Asia, and the Disciples in America were all equal in their official capacity, and in their ministrations; had no president among or over them. They were free and equal in their offices and ministrations, and esteemed each other as brethren of the same common church government. They all administered as Elders in the ["]Church of Christ," each one according to his ability, not esteeming any as masters but as servants of all. There were not great I's and little U's among them. They were truly ~~brethren~~ brethren together. [page 34:]

20. A Patriarch of the church appointed.

This office pertained to the patriarchal age but not to the gospel dispensation. But Joseph sought to blend the patriarchal age, the law era, and the gospel dispensation into his system of church government; which was an impossibility. The patriarchal ministry was set aside by Moses. He then set up the first-born of all the families of Israel as ~~That~~ their ministry; and that order was paired off by the Levites, in setting up the Aaronic priesthood; and that lived and legally ministered until Christ, it was then abolished entirely, and the gospel ministry established to minister until Christ's second coming.

There were no patriarchal or law ministers in Christ's system of ministry. There is no need of any. Jesus Christ's ministry can alone perform all the duties of the dispensation. There can be no legally appointed patriarchs or high priests or Aaronic priests either holding legal authority in Christ's plan. Jesus established a w[h]ole ministry of his own, unmixed with any other order, of Elders, Bishops, and Deacons, viz. Elders, priests and Teachers.

Christ's order of ministry was entirely distinct from the Patriarchal, the First-born, or the Aaronic. It was truly the order of the Son of God. It was above them, held a superior authority, and had more power, and held very much higher aims, and more responsibilities. Their doctrine and ministry[105] could lift people higher up in perfection and true Christian dignity.

21. Hyde and Gould sent to Zion.

They came in the time of **mobbing** in Zion, the church members prior to that had not ~~not~~ lifted a hand to opose or smite their enemies. But those two men said the orders from head quarters, f[ro]m a council of the highest authorities was for the members of the church to stand in their own defence, raise weapons and defend themselves. Fight when opposed and oppressed. This the members were quick to do. Hitch ten yoke of cattle to a wagon and let the forward yoke run into a ditch and they will drag all the others in. Such was the case here. The Heads advised fight and fight it was. A battle was soon fought, some were killed, which roused the whole country. A general gathering on both sides, and the result was the members of the[106] church surrendered [page 35:] their arms, and were soon driven from the county. But during the melee [Orson] Hyde & [John] Gould fled for their homes in O. like hireling shepherds! But it was the most unwise council that ever could have been sent from J. Smith and council. Some were killed on both sides, which so enraged the people of the country–the old inhabitants, and their numbers being so far superior to the members of the church, of course the weaker portion had to flee to save their lives. And out of the County they hurled them in haste, over the Mo. river into Clay Co. If the members of the church of Christ had stood fast and never lifted their arms to fight, then the Missourians, would have punished only a few in their opposition. But to fight just suited their enemies, and it was a most wicked policy for the peacible followers of Christ. To fight for their religion or rights just suited the Missourians and ~~suited~~ the[107] the Devil and Satan.

22. High Council of the church.

Joseph Smith and friends on the 17th day of February 1834 organized, what they denominated a High Council with 15 members to compose it, as a kind of church court, to try transgressors. But no example or pattern can be found in any of the Lord's dealings with men on earth. It

105. McLellin added "and ministry."

106. McLellin added "members of the."

107. McLellin added "the Missourians and ~~suited~~ the."

was entirely without precedent or rule. Three men could do the business much better, much cheaper, and save much valuable time. Hence the setting up of this council was consumate folly. It was mearly intended to find some special office for J. Smith's particular favourites. This too was false and nugatory—unheard of in inspiration and was silly.

23. The dreadful spirit of war.

The inflamable War Spirit that Hyde and Gould brought to Zion soon spread itself throughout the whole church eastward and westward. In January 1st 1834 at a conference of all the authorities of Zion Lyman Wight and. P. P. Pratt were appointed and sent[108] to Kirtland, O. ~~and~~ to see the Presidency to try to devise means for our relief in our destitute condition. Because we felt lonesome and forlorn. Wight being fully imbued with the war spirit he soon got an order issued by the Presidency to the entire church to gather up their munitions of war, and come up to Kirtland the first of May.

And then prepare sword in hand, to go up to Zion, and redeem it by the sword. [page 36:] They gathered some hundred men, and the 4th day of May is set for them to start and travel some 1000 miles to Zion to reinstate their brethren back upon their hands from which they had been ruthlessly expelled by **mob** violence. This army of vet[e]rans—of Elders and Priests set out with J. Smith, their Prophet at their head as Generalissimo. On the last of June 1834 about 400 able bodied men reached Clay Co. Mo., and camped near Liberty.

Here the Asiatic Cholera broke out among them, about sixty or 70[109] of their number had it and fourteen died with it. Smith caused them to disperse into different parts of the county. But on the 8th day of July he assembled his camp followers into a general conference, and giving them a lecture dismissed them. Some wended their way homeward, but others remained. Now in all the past history of nations or individuals I have never seen so much folly and weakness displayed as in this warrior raid to upper Mo., by Smith and followers. Thousands of dollars paid out—worse than wasted; and most valuable time ~~and lost~~ wasted, as well as many lives lost, and much human suffering endured; and not one particle of good accomplished, but ~~myriades~~ myriads of evil to all concerned in following a prophet who did not nor could not see what was before him; but all his teachings relating to this war ~~were~~ ended in "evil and only evil["] and that continually! I can but say O the folly and weakness of **men!!** Not one particle of good resulted toward the redemption

108. McLellin added "and sent."

109. McLellin added "or 70."

of Zion. But the Missouri inhabitants became more exasperated, and more determined to keep the church out of Jackson Co. Not one stone was turned toward the redemption. Talk not to me that J. Smith was one particle inspired of God in all this[110] war spirit. If any inspiration guided him it was the inspiration of the Devil. Because not one particle of wisdom dictated or governed the whole proceeding first or last.

24. The **name** was changed.

On the 3rd day of May 1834 assembled a select council of a few of ~~his~~ J. Smith's[111] leading men and intimate friends and high dignitaries of his church in Kirtland, O., and made an entire change of the characteristic, God given, beautiful name of the Church to that [of] the "church of the Latter day Saints." Up to this moment, from its organization it was called "The Church of Christ." But now takes a fictitious, false, and nondiscript name, no where else found in the world. [page 37:]

But this is in accordance with all J. Smith's history after he finished the Book. He altered and changed every thing he touched for the worse.[112] He altered and changed what he called his sacred revelations. He altered the divine volume of the book of Mormon, and he corrected and altered the scriptures of the Old and New Testaments. It seemed as though he never knew when to quit altering. The more I examine his course and history the worse and worse it apears until his awful death June 27th 1844. They changed the name of the church again in 1837. That year a great difficulty occurred in the church, after their Kirtland bank broke down, and about 70 of his Elders quit him ~~and S. Rigdon, and~~ the three witnesses to the book, and like myself, they never united with the church presided over by Joseph again. They then after wearing the name L.D.S. four years changed to the church of Christ of L.D.S. In one year more they changed again and called it the church of Jesus Christ of Latter Day Saints. Thus they wear it today. I want no other name but the true Church of Christ, nor will accept or live under any other, nor admit of any[113] change.

25. Sylvester Smith's downfall.

Joseph Smith and Silvester Smith[114] had a serious difficulty while on their warrior raid to Mo., over an old dog, and would have fought but their brethren interfered and prevented. They organized their army

110. McLellin added "this."

111. McLellin added "J. Smith's."

112. McLellin added "for the worse."

113. McLellin added "any."

114. For a summary of Sylvester Smith's life, see the Biographical Notes.

with Genls Col's, Majors, Captains &c. Sylvester was their Adjutant Genl. And after they had returned to Kirtland, a charge was presented against J. Smith by Sylvester to the High Council,[115] and after two days and evenings were occupied in its investigation. The result was J. Smith is cleared, and Sy[l]vester condemned for daring to bring a charge against a person as the Head of all Latter day Saintism. Sylvester had proved his charges, but it was argued that it would ruin the church to condemn Joseph, and have him publicly confess before this august council, and them before the church. Sylvester is required to sign a document that the p[e]ople called a lie bill! He refused to do it. His older brother took him out of doors and advised and begged him to sign it. A though[t] struck him that he would go into the house and propose to the council [page 38:] that if they would agree to bear all the blame before God for his act of signing, he would bear all the blame and stigma of the world. They voted to do so. I heard a prophesy delivered in Kirtland in meeting "that those men who passed that enormously wicked vote, should not live out half their days; or if they did they should die a most miserable death." And so far as I know of their deaths it has proved literally true. Joseph Coe[116] was killed by a bull. S. Rigdon died a monomaniac. Roger Orton[117] died of delerium tremans. John Johnson died of an entire stoppage of urine. Hyrum and Joseph Smith were miserably murderd. Luke Johnson[118] died by starvation from poisoning his stomach. Saml. H. Smith died before he was forty. And Oliver Cowdery did not live out half his days. Lyman E. Johnson broke through the ice and the fishes nibbled at him. I have not heard how others passed away. But one thing I do know it was one of the most wicked <u>votes</u> that ever men passed as the sequel has abundently proved.

26. <u>J. Smith ordained his Successor</u>.

In a general conferance or assembly in Clay Co. Mo.; called on the 8th day of July 1834, by Joseph Smith. He organized ~~the~~ a high council for Zion, then after making many remarks that the time had come for him to appoint his Successor in office. He said many had said and believed that it would be Oliver Cowdery, but said he Oliver has lost that privilege by transgression. The Lord has shown me that David Whitmer is the man. Then he and Dr. Williams stepped forward to David and or-

115. McLellin added "to the High Council."

116. For a summary of Joseph Coe's life, see the Biographical Notes.

117. For a summary of Roger Orton's life, see the Biographical Notes.

118. For a summary of Luke Samuel Johnson's life, see the Biographical Notes.

dained him Prophet, Seer, Revelator, Translator, and President of the church, to stand in his stead, provided any thing befel him.

Ten years ago when visiting David I asked him if he believed that J. Smith ordained him legally, and whether he still retained that authority? After reflecting a little he answerd, **I do!** But no man ever ordained a Seer in this world so far as inspiration informs us, hence I have no confidence in the procedure. Smith was not[119] dictated of God in that transaction. Something must rise diferent from Smithism to bring in "the rest of God," and universal peace to the world. [page 39:]

27. <u>Twelve Apostles chosen and ordained</u>.

On Feb 14th 1835, J. Smith called a conference of all the Elders in Kirtland, O., and the three witnesses of the book chose twelve, whom they called Apostles of Jesus Christ. No man can be an Apostle of Jesus unless he has seen, heard, and felt, and has a personal acquaintance with him, and knowledge of him. So this appointment and ordination was a perfect nulity! They were Apostles that Joseph Smith lived, but not that Jesus lived. Hence this was only ceremony without authority or power either.

All Christ's apostles in Asia and his Disciples in America were chosen personally by himself, hence they had perfect knowledge of him, and we hold that all apostles of Jesus must have just such knowledge, or otherwise they are false Apostles.

28. <u>The long promised endowment</u>.

In January 1831 a long revelation was given by Joseph to the church in Colesville N.Y. saying, "I give you a commandment that you shall go to the Ohio: and there you shall be endowed with power from on high, and from thence whomsoever I, the Lord will shall go forth among all nations" [cf. LDS D&C 38:32-33; RLDS D&C 38:7b-7c]. This raised great expectations among the Elders, and finally a Temple is commenced in, Kirtland, O., and becomes partly finished, and on the 6th day of April 1836 is the day set for the great endowment to be given. All is anxiety and preparation. Washings and anointings were attended to in great solemnity. The morning arrived and some five hundred ministers assembled in the Temple at sunrise. Tubs of water were in readiness, and also towels, and each others feet were washed, which was said to be the last gospel ordinance to be performed before the expected endowment. Then a scene of exortation, prophesying, and in speaking in (what they called,) tongues, and pretended interpretations followed. We remained

119. McLellin added "not."

until sunrise next morning fasting, excepting a little bread and wine furnished us in the evening. Some partook of the wine so freely on an empty stomach, that they actually became drunken! And a scene ensued that would be hard to describe. One thing I state candidly, I saw no one man in that assembly that was endowed with [page 40:] super-human power—no not one. This wonderful enduement then was only a farce—a very great failure. After washing, fasting, and praying for 24 long hours it was a signal failure to obtain even a moiety of supernatural power. O said I this is the baseless fabric of a vision, it is mear vanity! Farewell to Joseph Smith's Latter Day Saintism forever. The foregoing are some of the reasons why I do not believe in J. Smith's system of religion† [page 41:]

Some principles and practices of the church of Christ.

Now I want to write plainly, candidly, and in an unprejudiced man-

†The following was written by John L. Traughber in purple ink:

Remarks by J. L. Traughber, Jr., Feb. 11,1887.

From page 18 to this page, Dr. McLellan tells enough to forever damn the claims and pretensions of Joseph Smith and his followers, even if this were all that could be known of Mormonism outside the statements of Mormons.

Let it be borne in mind that the writer of the foregoing pages was one of apostles who were appointed and ordained as set forth on page 39. He was personally present in many of the important councils of the Mormon church, prior to his withdrawal from it, in 1836.

Compare the brief account here given, and on page 14, with the accounts given by Smith and others in Mormon books. It is claimed by Smith and the Mormons that great power from God was manifest in the "Endowment." Here, we find Dr. McLellan testifying that "prophecies, pretended tongues and interpretations" was the only pretense of divine power that he witnessed, and that was no endowment at all, as they had been prophesying, speaking tongues and interpretations for years.

In April, 1881, I visited Dr. McLellan at Independence, Mo, and while we were talking one day about the Endowment, the Doctor told me several items connected with it which are not recorded in this book, but some of which he had given me in letters before I saw him. He said that sometime during the night of April 6th, 1836, some of those "holy saints" (?) who were fasting, made up a purse and sent to Painesville, 9 miles away, and purchased a keg of wine, which was brought into the temple to them, and of which they drank so freely that some of them became beastly drunk, among whom was Samuel H. Smith, a brother to Joseph, and one of the eight witnesses of the Book of Mormon. He said that before Samuel became entirely helpless, he staggered up into the stand of the first Presidency and delivered a prophecy in the name of the Lord, and soon after become entirely helpless and vomited [into] a spittoon several times full, which Dr. McLellan emptied out of one of the temple windows, after which the Doctor had him and several others removed from the temple, and spent the balance of the night taking care of Samuel.

Mrs. McLellan, who was present while the Doctor was talking remarked: "The Latter Day Saints talked about it, seeming to think that was nothing wrong in Samuel's being drunk; and that it was a wonderful proof of the power of God that one so drunk could deliver a prophecy."

ner on this subject. There were six great, leading and wrong principles set up and acted upon when at and near their start, that Joseph Smith and Oliver Cowdery acted upon when they organized their church on the 6th day of April 1830: which principles and their practices arising therefrom, with many other things, caused its ultimate overthrow and downfal and final ruin.

1st Joseph Smith required Oliver Cowdery to ordain him a Prophet, Seer, Revelator, and Translator on the 6th of April 1830. 2nd J. Smith declared by his revelation that the church should receive, "His word as from the mouth of God" [cf. LDS D&C 21:5; RLDS D&C 19:2b]. 3rd Joseph claimed on the 6th of April that he and Cowdery were Apostles of the Lord Jesus Christ. 4th J. Smith said to Oliver, "Thou shalt not command him who is at thy head, and at the Head of the church" [LDS D&C 28:6; RLDS D&C 27:2d]. 5th In 1830 Joseph set up himself above all others, in the matter of giving and receiving revelations for the church. 6th Joseph claimed that the Angel John the Baptist ordained him and Oliver in 1829 on the banks of the Susquehannah river to the Priesthood of Aaron.

1st As to the ordination of a Prophet or Seer, I know of no place in the word of God where a Seer, or inspired Prophet was ever ordained by man. It is not a ministerial office, but it is a direct gift from God. It is neither confered or confirmed by ordination. And the man or men who pretend to confer such office or state upon any man only act from the suggestion of their own hearts, or from the promptings of Satan. Hence the ordination of Joseph by Oliver on the 6th of April 1830 was illegal null and void. And Joseph's ordination of David Whitmer on the 8th day of July 1834 had no value in it either. Both ordinations were valueless to those two men. Neither had any authority from God, hence no authority was in them, and no power from God followed them.

Hence all claims to that office or to that station by ordination[120] is simply fallacious and silly. True Aaron was consecrated High Priest by Moses, and the Urim and Thummim was placed in the breast-plate, and that in the Ephod which was worn by Aaron as a service of gift; so that he could inquire of God through or by that instrument and get answers from God[121] for the people. But Aaron was never ordained either Prophet or Seer. [page 42:] High Priests both of the order of Melchisedec and of Aaron were either consecrated or ordained, but never Prophets or Seers.

---

120. McLellin added "by ordination."

121. McLellin added "from God."

2nd As to receiving any mortal man's word as we would the voice of God is simply preposterous. No man ever did or ever could do so. Hence that command was perfectly vain. It would be a perfect impossibility for any sane man to even try to do so. God's voice is the highest evidence that can be presented to man's mind; but the word of fallible man is to a great degree uncertain, and consequently must be received with some doubts, until his revealments are proved by comparing with revelations going before. J. Smith delivered a revelation in 1830 positively contradicting a[122] declaration in the book of Mormon, saying, "Teachers have not authority to baptize" [cf. LDS D&C 20:58; RLDS D&C 17:11e]. But the Book says, "Alma consecrated Teachers in the land of Sidom to baptize unto the Lord" [cf. Alma 15:13]. I prefer the book, hence Smith's word and revelation were spurious, and can not be relied on as being certain. His statement relative to the tares sowed in the field also contradicts the book of the New Testament. If I should follow up this subject I would not know where to stop, as to his discrepencies.

3rd An Apostle of Christ must have knowledge within himself. All the Apostles of Christ at Jerusalem, and all his Disciples in America saw, heard, and felt, hence they could bear a firm witness and testimony that they most positively knew what they declared. Did Smith & Cowdery thus know? They did not. They never in the early days of the church so professed or declared. They were Apostles of the true translation of the book of Mormon, but not Apostles of Jesus Christ. Paul was called after the ascention of Jesus. He saw, heard, and felt, hence was a genuine, true Apostle, having knowledge within himself. Smith should not have made so false a claim for himself and Cowdery.

4th The Lord Jesus Christ is certainly Head of his Church as much so as the man is head of the woman. Paul says, "God gave Christ to be Head over all things to the church, which is his body" [cf. Eph. 1:22-23]. It was a wretchedly false claim for J. Smith or any man in the world to claim to be head of the church. If Christ is Head and any man on earth is head also, then the church would be an anomily having two heads on the one body. Again, "And he is the Head of the body, the church." Col. 1:18. [page 43:]

5th One of the most unchristian and ruinous principles that Smith or any man ever did or could lay down in this gospel dispensation[123] was the one that he alone was to receive, and cause to be written revelations

122. The doubling of "a" occurred because the first was written at the end of one line and the second at the beginning of the next.

123. McLellin added "in this gospel dispensation."

and commandments for the church. He revealed thus, "Behold, verily, verily I say unto you, no one shall be appointed to receive commandments and revelations in this church, excepting my servant Joseph, for he receiveth them even as Moses" [BofC 30:2; cf. LDS D&C 28:2; RLDS D&C 27:2a]. Moses declared when Joshua wanted him to forbid prophesying in the tents of Israel, "Would to God all the Lord's people were prophets, and that the Lord would put his spirit upon them" [cf. Num. 11:29]. This declaration was made under the Law age, in the darkness of ceremonies and rights [rites], by the distinguished Law giver of that age of sacrafices.

And Joel and Peter said, "God will pour out of his spirit upon all flesh" [Joel 2:28; Acts 2:17]. Which spirit the angel said to John, "For the testimony of Jesus is the spirit of prophecy" [Rev. 19:10]. And Paul said, "To all that in every place call on the name of Jesus Christ our Lord–For ye may all prophecy on[e] by one, that all may learn, and all may be comforted" [cf. 1 Cor. 1:2; 14:31]. The wish and design of Moses, and of the three distinguished Apostles was that in the law age, and also during the whole gospel dispensation men could and should receive and deliver a "Thus saith the Lord," for the benefit of mankind. Yes, "to comfort and edify them" [cf. 1 Cor. 14:3].

But this practice of receiving God's word would violate J. Smith's rule of assuming to himself the exclusive right to give off the Lord's word, and would place him upon a level with his brethren. It would set up and put in practice the great liberal Gospel principle that "All might receive the Spirit["] [cf. Gal. 3:14] and by it, "show forth things to come" [cf. John 16:13], to enlighten all the honest hearted in all the world.

6th As to the angel ordination of Joseph and Oliver, I am surprised that they should make so false a claim, because no angel ever ordained any man, so far as the inspired books inform us. Again seven times it is said in the Bible–in the Lord's word that if one of any tribe in Israel, or any stranger touch that priesthood except the tribe of Levi only[124] he should die. Num 1:51. 3:10, 38. 16:40. 17:13. 18:~~3~~, 7, 22, ~~32~~. Joseph claimed to be of the tribe of Ephraim, consequently could not hold the Aaronic priesthood in any sense. No chief priest ever consecrated or ordained any man in any ministerial office, in all past time. Then four or more things were wrong with Smith and Cowdery's ordination, which rendered it nugatory, null and void!! [page 44:]

1st Angels never ordained. 2nd Chief priests never ordained. 3rd

124. McLellin added "only."

No tribe could hold Aaronic priestly office in Israel, or in the world, except the Levites only. 4th No chief priest could give the **hood**. It would be illegal and acting above himself. The Hood pertained exclusively to Aaron—the high priest. And even Aaron had no authority or power to ordain or consecrate a High Priest of his order.[125] All after Aaron received the high Priest's office by birth-right.

All the above important principles and practices, being wrong at the origin of the church of Christ, it is not wonderful that many other wrongs would enter into it, and so destroy its usefulness in the world. If we persue it a few years longer we will find other miserable, wretched wrong principles and worse practices started up by the **Leaders** of the movement; and they finally worked the church's entire ruin. It ceased to be the original church of Christ, and turned to be a new thing under the sun; It claimed to be the church of Latter Day saints;[126] governed by an entire different set of principles and practices.

We will pass on a few years and see if the above remark is not true in detail. 1st The Church of Christ at first was taught and practiced the principle of non-resistance for some years. Would not return evil for evil, or railing for railing, or smite when smitten. They trusted in God's word which says, "Vengence is mine and I'll repay" [cf. Rom. 12:19]. In 1833, in August J. Smith (professed) to receive this word from the Lord, "Renounce War, and proclaim peace" [LDS D&C 98:16; RLDS D&C 95:3d]. But in less than two months the Leaders or presidency of the church renounce "peace and proclaime War"! In July 1833 the church was mobbed in Jackson Co. Mo., what was by the church called the Zion of God. They were set upon by the old inhabitants of the country. The Leaders in Kirtland Ohio, receiving news of the mobbing held a council and determined on resistance and sent John Gould and Orson Hyde all the way, near a thousand miles, to tell the church in Zion to stand in their own defence—to fight ~~in their~~ when oppressed! This was contrary to all revelation of the gospel age[127] and the best interest of the church, and was the prime cause of the entire church being driven from the county over the Missouri into Clay Co.

In January 1834 the scattered and persecuted Elders held a consultation together [page 45:] in council, in their forlorn condition, and sent Elders Lyman Wight and P. P. Pratt to Kirtland, O. to see the (what was

125. McLellin added "of his order."

126. McLellin added "It claimed to be the church of Latter Day saints," which he enclosed in square brackets.

127. McLellin added "of the gospel age."

called) first Presidency of the entire church, in order to consult with them, in order to learn and know what the church must do in her distressed situation. Wight was fully imbued with the war spirit, and by his representations and influence inspired J. Smith and council with the idea of redeeming Zion, viz. the Church that was driven from Zion, with one hundred men of War!! The Leaders issue a proclamation to the entire church in the eastern states to gather up their munitions of war material, and assemble at Kirtland the first of May. About a hundred men gathered, and the 4th day of May was set to start for upper Missouri. But, as in the days of Ahab and Micaiah, "There ~~came~~ came forth a lying spirit, and stood before the Lord" [cf. 1 Kgs. 22:21]. So it was with Joseph Smith and spirits. An evil spirit came from the Lord and whispered in Joseph's ear to call a council of all his first ministers. They assembled on the 3rd day of May, and deliberated relative to names and appelations. They concluded that the church of Christ was not the name in which to go to war, hence they throwed the name of Christ entirely away, and adopted the wrong, the useless, the non-descript name for their church and people of the Church of Latter Day saints.

In that name they set out next day for Mo., gathering numbers of brethren by the way until when they reached Clay Co. Mo., they had some 400 men, mostly ministers in their army of veterans; with Joseph Smith at their head, as their great Generalissimo—their Prophet and Leader!

Now in this warrior raid they imbibed four great leading doctrines and practices that were eminently and miserably wrong. 1st They took a wrong doctrine and principle in starting on that miserable warrior raid to fight for their religious belief. 2nd Then it was an evil spirit dwelling in them in order to make them carry out their design. 3rd Then they had to take a false, fictitious name in or under which to carry out their war doctrine and spirit. 4th Then their practice was war, War, War. They meant to resist evil by evil; was[128] to smite when smitten; was[129] to take vengeance into their own hands. All this was contrary to the peaceable and glorious doctrine of the Lord Jesus Christ. I cant see or know how intelligent men could be so [page 46:] blindly led only that their minds were "holden," and inspired by the power and persuasions of the Devil and Satan.

There were some very good and intelligent men in that camp, led on by their confidence in Joseph's inspiration, until they were led to death

128. McLellin added "were" above "was."

129. McLellin added "were" above "was."

by that awful sco[u]rge of the human race viz. the Asiatic Cholera. For when they had reached near Liberty, Clay Co. Mo., the cholera seized about seventy of their number, and fourteen died of it! This was fatal to all their great calculations of conquering the mobbers by war and fighting. They had no living faith in God to stop the ravages of that curse upon them for lifting their swords in the name of pure religion. But numbers of them had to die. Fall by that dread monster! O my soul! when I look back at that singular scene I cant help but marvel and wonder at those men who were principal actors in that tragedy. That a professed inspired prophet should be so deceived and many led to desolation and ruin by as ambitious and blood thirsty ~~a man~~ men as Lyman Wight and Joseph Smith.[130] This to me looks dark and dismal.

But they failed entirely failed in their hopes and expectations of their declared object to take their brethren and reinstate them back upon their lands in Jackson Co. Mo. from which they had been forcibly driven by a ruthless mob in 1833, the year before. But not even one stone ~~stone~~ was turned over towards the redemption of Zion; but evil and only evil was produced by that warrior tramp into upper Mo. It roused and embittered all the region of country in all the upper Counties. And much precious time thousands in money squandered—wasted foolishly, and many most excellent lives lost worse than wasted. Wo be to all war feeling and practice in the Church of Christ where it commenced, or in the church of Latter Day Saints where it was carried out in practice

One thing I have to say after looking at all this history of folly, I pity mankind who get into the mishap of such a bewilderment and delusion. For any one to believe that a Propet or Seer could be legally ordained by man, or to receive any man's word a[s] true and certain as God's voice to them, or that any man could be an Apostle of [page 47:] Jesus Christ without seeing, hearing, and feeling him, as the Apostles of old did do, is to me the silliest nonsense; or for a man to claim to be Head of the church while Christ lives to be Head himself; This simply shows a great want either of knowledge or honesty, or of both, of the Gospel system; but above all to claim the only privilege, and authority, and power with God to receive and give off communications—inspired mandates for the church is simply monstrous, as Joseph Smith did do.

But when we follow Joseph Smith a few years we find him setting war ablaze in all the church, and taking false doctrine and principles, and false spirits also, and a false name for the church; then a miserable

130. McLellin added "and Joseph Smith," then inserted "many" to complete the compound passive subject.

false practice for the whole church; here I drop him and I leave the claims of Joseph Smith as a true Prophet and man of God in the hands of all the honest searchers after pure truth, and true men.

That he was the medium through and by whom the Book of Mormon was brought to light I admit and fully believe. But that he committed grievous faults—official faults afterward[131] I as firmly believe, as the foregoing treatise will show. Here I will give one quotation from one of his revelations, taken from the old book of Commandments printed in 1833, in Independence, Mo., relative to himself: "He has a gift to translate the Book, and I have commanded him that he should pretend to no other gift, for I will grant him no other gift" [BofC 4:2].[132] With this quotation I will cease with this treatise and matter.[†]

---

131. McLellin added "afterward."

132. McLellin quoted from the 1833 Book of Commandments, except for "should" in place of "shall," but the 1835 Doctrine and Covenants (32:1) made a number of significant changes to this passages: "*you* have a gift to translate the *plates; and this is the first gift that I bestowed upon you;* and I have commanded that *you* should pretend to no other gift *until my purpose is fulfilled in this*; for I will grant *unto you* no other gift *until it is finished*" (LDS D&C 5:4; RLDS D&C 5:1d, modern editions).

[†]At the bottom of page 47, Traughber added the following in purple ink:

Kinderhook Plates.

> In 1843, some plates were dug out of a mound near Kinderhook, Ill. Finally they fell into the hands of J. Smith. In his history in the Millennial Star, Vol xxi, No.3, Smith says that he translated some of them. Wilber Fugate and Robert Wiley testify that they made those plates and the "engravings thereon" to perpetiate a practical joke on the Mormons. J.L.T., Jr.

For more on this, see Stanley B. Kimball, "Kinderhook Plates Brought to Joseph Smith Appear To Be a Nineteenth-Century Hoax," *Ensign* 11 (Aug. 1981): 66-74.

Letters
1854-1880

1.

TO ORSON PRATT, 29 APRIL 1854

Chester + roads,[1] O. April 29th 1854.

Prof. Orson Pratt,[2]

Dear Sir,

Yours, bearing the Baltimore post-mark, of the 21th inst, lies before me; and I feel gratified at the **earnest** spirit, and **warm** manner in which your letter was written. It called to my mind afresh reminisances both pleasing and painful. You say "Do not be affraid to tell me your **feelings** and your **desires**. Be frank and open as we used to be; and let us renew and strengthen our friendship upon the great principles of righteousness. +++Let me hear from you often." In the first place I am not the least affraid. In the next place, You Sir know me well enough to know, that it is my very nature to be frank & open in my intercourse with mankind. And nothing would be more pleasing to me than to renew and strengthen our friendship **upon the great principles of righteousness**—provided it was possible for us to do so. And in the next place I am willing to hold a free and friendly intercourse with you. And I can do so without ill feelings, although we might diffir widely in our opinions, in our belief, and in our faith. But my dear Sir, the **causes** which led me to peaceably withdraw from the church in 1836 are unremoved, and still have their bearing upon my mind. And since that day many other causes have been added, which together form ins[e]p[a]rable barriers to my acting in unison with the church of Latter Day Saints. And as to my going all the **tedious way** to Utah to learn the will of God concerning myself,—my duty, or my privileges—At present I would respectfully decline. Notwithstanding all your sympathies and anxieties expressed in your letter for me. I am Sir as much surprised at your course in remaining with **that church**, advocating its doctrines and following its practices, as you possibly can be at my

1. McLellin refers to Chester Crossroads, where he lived from March 1853 through September 1859, about five miles south of Kirtland, Ohio. See Larry C. Porter, "The Odyssey of William Earl McLellin: Man of Destiny, 1806-83," in *The Journals of William E. McLellin: 1831-1836,* eds. Jan Shipps and John W. Welch (Provo and Urbana: BYU Studies and University of Illinois Press, 1994), 346-47.

2. For a summary of Orson Pratt's life, see the Biographical Notes.

remaining out of it. But could I believe that salvation for **me** was to be obtained only by taking your **warm** advice "to go to Salt Lake city, and throw myself and energies into the bosom of that church," (which at present would be a **sin** for me,) then Sir, no sacrifice would be to[o] great for me to make—For I desire salvation more tha[n] all other things within the gift of God to man. There are many, very many reasons why I decline to follow your advice at present. On the 18th of Jan. 1832, Joseph Smith Jr. and I were alone in his translating room. I was writing a letter to a friend, and desired brother Joseph to inquire of the Lord for me relative to an important matter, but he said to me "Do you inquire of God and I will pray for you that you may obtain." I did receive and write it. And when I read it to him he shed tears of joy, and said to me, "Brother William, that is the mind and the will of God, and as much a revelation as I ever received in my life. You have written it by the true spirit of inspiration." But from this circumstance I never was vain enough to suppose that "I was planted in Joseph's stead." Nor that it was my duty or privilege to receive by revelation laws or regulations for the whole church. I knew better. But at that time I saw, heard, and felt what I wrote. T[h]ere and then I learned a principle, and was put in possession of a power that I never shall forget. I learned to **know** the voice of the Spirit of God clothed in words. And if I had heeded its voice from that day to this, I should have missed many—very many difficulties through which I have passed. On the 29th day of April 1844, while engaged in fasting and prayr, I had a **vision** from the Lord of great things. Since that time I have had other visions and revelations. And hence **I know** I am not cast off for ever. I only need to bring my heart right before God, and exercise great faith in him, and humble prayr before him, (which is my high privilege,) in order to obtain "Wisdom from God, and knowledge from heaven" [cf. James 1:5]. Then even were I convinced and thoroughly satisfied that the Latter Day Saints in the wilderness, in their constituted authority, held the **unpolluted Priesthood** of Christ [page 2:] yet I do not feel that it could be my duty **to travel** so far to learn the "**mind** of God" concerning **me**. Nay, verily. If I lack wisdom—I ask of God—Hence, I do not feel to go so far, to consult **men**—nor councils of men, relative to my salvation. Why Sir, it is impossible for me to believe that right is wrong, or that wrong is right. That people, whom You recommend to me so strongly, believe and practice many things which I could not either **honestly** believe or practice. Hence a membership, or even very high **authority** among them would not be pleasing to me. If I could be freely chosen, by the voice of the whole church as their Leader, Seer, & Head, spiritual and temporal, and then have millions of California gold at my command, and then be assured that I could have long life and enjoy continued good health, and a continuation of their united and universal confidence unto the end—Yet Sir, all **this** would be no inducement to **me** to go to that church and preach and practice their **doctrines**. No! No!! verily **No!!!** ~ For me then to go with my present views would be to ensure damnation instead of salvation. You wrote to me in your letter "I hope you will bear with me in my plainness." I answer, I will Sir. Will you do so with me? For I never saw, read, or heard of doctrines and practices so repugnant to my faith, and to my feelings as some now taught and practiced among that people in Utah. I should have to sacrifice every holy principle that I have ever learned from God, if I were to take your advice. Aside from the principles you learned in the first three years of Joseph Smith's public ministry I know of no principle or practice of **that people** now, which they have learned since that I believe or admire. Hence you see your home among the mountains would be no **home** for me. "Your people could not be my people, nor your God my God" [cf. Ruth 1:16]. The doctrine of Christ as it was first taught and practiced in the church organized [in] 1830, is scarcely now known among you, or if known is not esteemed or heeded.—Here let me refer to a sentence of yours relative to your "**shudder**," because in an evil hour you spoke against the **prophet**. When a man is placed in a public position, all have a right to see his official **acts**, to examine them, to judge of them, and to talk about them. When therefor I speak about men or measures, I shall do so plainly although those men may have held, or may now hold high positions. ~ But I will now give you a few of the reasons why I left that people and remain from them, and do not even have a desire to return to them. Although many of them I held personally and officially in high esteem, (yourself among the first.) Their doctrine was in 1833 "to renounce war and proclaim peace" [cf. LDS D&C 98:16; RLDS D&C 95: 3d]. Their practice was in 1834, to proclaim war,[3] and gather up a troop, and travel from Kirtland, O. to Clay Co. Mo. with arms and munitions of war in hand. But it was a failure, so far as good was concerned. And in order to go to war they changed the name of the church, as well as its spirit, and in doing so became a **sect** in all its bearings. In 1836 they sought an endowment from on high. But I have no fears to say, they made a perfect failure. And in looking back upon that event I feel ashamed of conduct that I witnessed in the "Heads of the Church." From there after they

3. McLellin added the word "war" above the line.

went into many ruinous speculations–into pride, into fine and expensive dressing, (while the families of the Elders, who were traveling were in actual want,) into expensive rides in parties, into drinking spirits to excess, into feasting parties. They went largely into debt, (which they never paid,) and largely into merchandizing, and then into banking–ruinous–rotten banking. And finally fled from Kirtland between two days–when no man persued them. When they commenced their excess of merchandizing I quit them. I left them because I could not uphold them as men of God, while they practiced such things. Orson, you cannot have forgotten the scenes of drunkenness during the pretended enduement in Kirtland in 1836. I shall never forget them, nor the hundreds of false prophecies delivered in the Temple on that occasion. I am not speaking [page 3:] from hearsay, or in order to find fault where none existed. But you strongly advise me to go and humble myself in confession before **that church**, who upheld and practiced these things. You say "I know there is no salvation for those acquainted with this work, out of this Church." Now Sir your Knowledge and mine differs, widely differs in this matter. I know that no man can be saved in celestial glory, who practices such things, or who advocates and upholds men in such practices. While I was in Nauvoo in 1847, Mrs Emma Smith told me that there were debts proven in court against the estate of Joseph Smith deceased, of over two hundred thousand dollars. Speculation, ruinous speculation brought that immense debt upon his bankrupt estate. I shudder not to speak of such wickedness. I marvel not at many of the troubles through which the L. D. Saints have passed. And yet I feel sorry to the bottom of my heart that Joseph Smith and his brethren, (for I once loved them,) had not lived the pure principles of the doctrine of Christ. Then he would have been alive to day, and I would have been standing shoulder to shoulder and heart to heart with **him**, and with the thousands of the faithful. But now "The Lord will have to set his hand **again** the second time, to recover the remnant of his people" [cf. Isa. 11:11]. That people commenced their evil doctrines and practices in Kirtland, they grew worse in Far West, and still a great deal worse in Nauvoo, but they have, and will cap the climax in the Valley. In Kirtland it was cheat and defraud, in Far West it was rob and plunder, and in Nauvoo it was cheat, defraud, rob, plunder, and murder; and in the Valley, they even shoot a man dead, without Judge or jury at their Tabernacle door, and all the congregation say, Amen.[4] As they–the Latter Day Saints have

4. This is a reference to Madison Hambleton's murder of Dr. John M. Vaughn at Manti on 9 February 1851. See David L. Bigler, ed., *A Winter with the Mormons: The 1851*

meted out to others, "so it will be measured to them again—heaped together and shaken down" [cf. Luke 6:38]. Let me say to you, that your hardest troubles are awaiting you as a people in those vallies of the mountains. A judgement, speedy, sore, and awful awaits that people in their far off retreat. Do not understand me to justify the mobs that have persecuted you, and laid your former inheritances waste. For I think they acted as much like Devils as men could. But their bad conduct did not, nor could not justify the church in their course. But again, at present I do not believe in the following doctrines as held by the Latter Day Saints. viz: The tithing of the members of one tenth of all their prosperity. Their baptisms for the dead. Their spirit and practice of war. Their Popishly combining the spiritual and temporal power in the Head of the church. Their doctrine of the generation of spirits. Their system of plurality of Gods—and God making. Their doctrine of poligamy—The plurality of wives and concubines. And their exaltations consequent upon the foregoing. And I might continue, for I know not where our differences would end. But O! if it were possible for that people to be brought to repentance, that they might be spared. I have but little hope that many of them will be spared. You and all the leading ones, when speaking of the church say "I know." Knowledge is beyond hope and faith. Hence you could not be made to **believe** you are wrong when You know (that is, think) you are right. I know something of the feelings and actions of that people towards those whom they call Apostates. And when you read this letter you may say, well—truly he who was once our brother William is an apostate in very deed. My confidence and faith is in God, but not much in men. I care but little about epithets, or curses that men may heap upon me. I mean to serve God according to the highest degree of light I can obtain. But says you we are marvelously prospered. We are gathering our thousands; while all the parties who have come out opposed [page 4:] to **us** have sunk into insignificance. I am aware that your numbers increase, and that you are gathering your your[5] thousands in wealth, and in numbers in the Vallies. But the greater will be the sorrow—and the crash when your **sore** troubles come. But you would say I have no fears. So it was said to **me** on the Square at Far West during the summer of 1838. I told them that great calamities were at their doors. Then the church there was in great prosperity. But that very fall[,] troubles quick

---

Letters of Jotham Goodell (Salt Lake City: Tanner Trust Fund and J. Willard Marriott Library, University of Utah, 2001), 74-75, 82-84, 170-71, 216.

5. McLellin accidentally wrote "your" at the end of one line and repeated it at the beginning of the next line.

and sudden fell upon them. In 1845, I traveled on the same steam boat from St Louis to Cincinnatti with Orson Hyde. I told him that Nauvoo would soon fall. He said no, that the church never before was in so prosperous a condition. But soon the City was—as it were—a waste. Mind ye now, what I say, Your afflictions and sorer trials than the Latter Day saints ever yet have passed through are close upon you. But say You, **Mobs** hitherto, of the Gentiles, have been our scourge, but now we are out of their reach. God has a scourge and a judgement in store, and feel it you must, suffer it you will. And as one of the revelations says "But few of you will remain to receive your inheritances" [cf. LDS D&C 63:31; RLDS D&C 63:8e]. It is not pleasant for me to contemplate these scenes, but duty requires **me** to write thus plainly to you. Since 1831 I have been familiar with the history of many of those in the Valley. Once I loved them and their society so dearly, (that even since I have not acted with them yet,) I cannot forget my former feelings. Hence, I have sought their publications of books, pamphlets &c. But I have watched their history since 1836 with deep anxiety. But still I cannot as you say, "Put on my hat and say, I will arise and go back to them." And I have stated in this letter a few of my reasons as plainly as under the circumstances I could do. But Sir, I cannot do justice to the subject with pen, ink, and paper. You say, "I most earnestly[6] desire to see you repent, if repentance is for You; of this I cannot judge." I care not for the judgement that men pass upon **me** in this matter. But I have not in this letter called upon **You**, or upon **that church** to repent. For I do not believe that they as a people can repent.—Even though they, like Ninevah, should set in sackcloth and ashes; or like Esau, should seek it earnestly and carefully with tears. For they have **polluted** every holy thing ever committed to their charge, and have committed all manner of abominations in the sight of the Heavens. Therefore destruction, but not salvation awaits them.

You will please to take this letter ~~letter~~ to the Valley, and show it to the Leading **men** in the church; especially those of the original council of the "Twelve." There is not one of them as men for whom I entertain the least personal ill feeling. Please to give my respects to your Lady.[7] (I do not say ladies—for I do not know that you have a plurality of **wives** or **concubines**.)[8] And if You have I am not probably acquainted with any but

6. McLellin added the word "earnestly" above the line.

7. For a summary of Sarah Marinda Bates Pratt's life, see the Biographical Notes.

8. Pratt had married six women by this time: the sisters Adelia Ann and Charlotte Bishop in late 1844, though Charlotte left him a few months later; Mary Ann Merrill on 27 March 1845; Sarah Louisa Chandler in February 1846, though she died in June 1846; Marian Ross on 19 February 1852; and Sarah Louise Lewis in June 1853.

the **first**. I well remember the night You immersed her in lake Ontario. Will You Sir answer this letter before You leave St Louis for the far off West. I shall anxiously look for another letter from You. I received Your Seers[9]—and intend to have them bound. I also received your "Volume" some year ago. I feel under obligations to You Sir for those writings. Mrs Kent[10] and Bond[11] &c. have had the satisfaction of their perusal.

Please receive these lines from your old friend and sincere well wisher. ~

I am as ever, W. E. McLellin.

9. McLellin refers to copies of *The Seer,* a periodical Pratt published in Washington, D.C., beginning in January 1853.

10. Mrs. Kent is unidentified.

11. This appears to be Charlotte W. Bond, living in Kirtland, Ohio. For a summary of her life, see the Biographical Notes.

2.

TO JOSEPH SMITH III, 10 JANUARY 1861

Linden, Genesee Co. Mich. Jan, 10. 1861.

Joseph Smith Esq.

For a length of time I have contemplated addressing a letter to You, relative the position You have taken at the **Head** of an organization of many scattered Latter Day Saints. I read your speech delivered at the last April Conference in Amboy, Ill.[1] I have also read what has been published in the "Herald," over your signature. I have admired your manner of both speaking and writing–the candor you express. Now Sir, in this letter I shall write frankly, freely, and plainly. But at the outset let me say that in matters of mind, men may differ widely, and may express their views freely, and at the same time remain friends–allowing to each other the inalienable right to think for **him**self. Our motives are known to God, and he will be our Judge. Hence I set not[2] myself up to judge your conscience, or to condemn your motives. But some of the positions you have taken, and some of the principles advocated I propose to examin[e.] First, giving a little of my own history. I became in[tim]ately acquainted with your Father in the fall of 1831, and was a minister in the church over which he presided until August 1836. Since which I have taken some pains to **watch** the course of events among that "peculiar people." But for some dozen years past I have been retired from all religious organizations–following my professional business. The positions I occupied during my union with your Father gave me great opportunities to know the doctrines advocated, and the practices persued. ~

The two Priesthoods–which is the boast of that church–never, no never should have been instituted there. The Aaronic or Levitical priesthood was instituted, consecrated, & organized to administer the "fiery law of Moses"–and for that <u>alone</u>. When that law was fulfilled and abrogated the priesthood went with it–it was entirely set aside also. No Levitical priest has ever held legal authority on earth since the ascent of

1. See "The Mormon Conference," *The True Latter-Day-Saints' Herald*, May 1860, 102-04.

2. The "not" is added above the line.

Christ, and the de[s]cent of the Holy Spirit. The New Testament, or book of Mormon knows not an Aaronic priest after that date—Please examine. There is no law prescribing the calling, or duties of a Levitical priest outside of Moses rituel. So surely then as one should live, his duty would require him to administer the Law.

The Law, with its accompanyments, was a "shadow of things to come" [Col. 2:17]—viz. the Gospel dispensation. Under the Law but one **High** Priest could legally exist at the same time. So if that was a shadow or type, then the substance and anti-type ~~can have~~ the Gospel dispensation, can have but **One High** Priest—Christ Jesus!—As ~~the~~ their office changed from father to Son—"by reason of death" [Heb. 7:23]—But Christ "ever lives to make intercession for his people["] [cf. Heb. 7:25]—Hence no change from him to another. [page 2:] The high, or royal priesthood is the priesthood of the gospel age, and Christ is its only High Priest. The highest office in it for man on earth now or ~~since~~ in the Apostolic age is the Apostleship. Christ set in his church "**First**, Apostles." [1 Cor. 12.28] &c.—and so on to the Deacons.

I have in my possession (in manuscript) a copy of the Articles and Covenants of the church given in June 1830—and drawn from their unprinted book of revelations during the year 1831. I also have a copy of the book of Commandments—as far as printed in Jackson Co. Mo. in 1832 [1833].—but which was afterward altered and printed in the book of Doctrine & Covenants. In it (as at first given) there is no mention of High Priests or of Lesser Priests. Hence I am no believer in High Priests, or Levitical Priests either in this age or dispensation. High Priests were first ordained at the June Conference, in Kirtland, in 1831, after S. Rigdon had joined the church. Your Father presided in that assembly. During the winter following they got up the idea of Priests being of the Livitical order. All this was contrary to the New Testament, the book of Mormon, & the first Articles of the church, hence all **wrong!** And if I am right in this, (and I know I am) then all Elder Sheen's[3] ideas about your hereditary priesthood are worse than vain! In your speech at Amboy you said "I believe my Father was a good man." And in the same speech you go strongly to condemn the principle and practice of Polygamy. I do not wish to say hard things to You of your Father, but Joseph, if You will only go to your own dear **mother**, she can tell you that he believed in Polygamy and practiced it long before his violent death! That he delivered a revelation sanctioning, regulating, and establishing it—and that he finally burned the

3. For a summary of Isaac Sheen's life, see the Biographical Notes.

Awful document before her eyes. Elder Marks[4] can tell You that (before its conflagration) it was read in the High council of Nauvoo, over which he presided. Your Mother told me these items when I was in Nauvoo. I am not dealing in fictions, nor in ill founded slanders—and would now feel glad if these things had never been enacted. But Sir, I have felt it a solemn duty to lay these items before You. And Sir, Your Mother (if she feels disposed) can give You a rather black catalogue reaching back as far as the date of your birth. Then Sir, if You are honest before the Heavens yourself, never, no never proclaim again publickly or privatily that "I believe my father was a good man," whilst the means to know his real character lies so near You—even in the bosom & memory of your **Mother!** I write this to You because You are now in a responsible, public position: Now Sir, if your Father was a "good man," and You are his legal Successor, then You are legally & morally bound to carry out his measures ~ [page 3:] Hence I saw in the phrase "good man," a great deal of meaning. And when I read your speech (taking you to be **honest**) I felt a pang wring my old aching heart. Joseph, You are but a youth, Do be admonished by one who has grown old, Take not your own dear Father for a pattern in your religious career. Altho he might have had some good traits, Yet in all that constitutes pure-God-like goodness he was wo[e]- fully lacking! If You have determined to be **Great** in the eyes of God, then do carve out your own course, but not pattern after his. My heart aches when I look at your position. I am aware that you have taken your position at the **Head** of a body of religionists. They had taken their position and had published it to the world—I know of no rule by which You can keep up that organization, and materially alter or change it.

I was with your Father & his friends when he tried to organize the Church according to the Doctrine & Covenants. I positively know that he signally failed—failed in Kirtland in 1836. They got the ministry into a difficulty from which, or out of which they never recovered. Something near a hundred of his Elders soon thereafter left him, (myself also) and in consequence he had to leave Kirtland for Far West. I left because the Heads went into ruinous Speculations—and other reasons.

I feel a deep anxiety about the work, which is ~~the~~ to precede & to usher in the Millennium. I firmly believe it will be accomplished during this century. I hope in my day. I have not an objection that You should head the work! But I want it be **the work**—the very work itself. I can have no faith, at present, in what You are **now** trying to do. Nay, verily! Let me

4. The word "Marks" is added above the line. For a summary of William Marks's life, see the Biographical Notes.

tell You that perils await You, not for truth's sake, but because You are laboring to build up and establish a Priesthood, yes, priesthoods founded in error. Because You are trying to walk—as a Successor—to one who fell out by the way—To one who died in debt (from ruinous speculations) more than <u>two hundred thousand dollars</u>! But its no use, for when men take their positions, they wont listen to reason, in opposition. For say they "**he**'s an old Apostate." The Lord Knows that I want to <u>know</u> and to <u>do</u> the truth in all matters pertaining to my salvation. Had Your Father been advised—taken different counsels from some of that which immediately surrounded **him**, I have no doubt he might have been <u>alive</u> to day. But he is gone, and You profess to stand in "**his** stead," take heed lest a mighty fall awaits You also. I am sure, if a vision from God, should show You the future, You would stop run[n]ing the race you are now traveling. [page 4:]

I have no doubts (after long investigation & reflection) but that your Father translated the book of Mormon—and on the 6th of April 1830 organized the "Church of Christ." Did both by the teachings & inspiration of the Heavens. But **they** soon began to go astray, and the further they went the wider from the **true path** they went, until he fell by his wickedly violent death in Carthage! From the highest testimony I've had, and the best light I've seen I think the Twelvites are, as nearly as they can, carrying out Joseph's measures—more nearly than You propose to do. And I think that they are the wickedest people now on this wide earth. If You live to be as old as I now am, You will not believe **Two** Priesthoods legally belong in the Church of Christ. That whilst Jesus holds his High Priesthood in heaven, High Priests can legally hold that office in his church on earth. You will not believe in any name for the church but that given so distinctly in the book of Mormon—"the Church of Christ." Nor will you believe in "Baptism for the dead," as held by your Father, and the church of Latter Day Saints over which he presided. Neither will you receive as of divine authority all that which is called revelations in the book of "Doctrine & covenants." Finally You will not believe that your Father lived and died a "good man." There will be such overturns in the world, and especially in all (**now**) existing churches—and especially among those over whom You now preside that You will see your present mistakes. That power, and intelligence, and inspiration which caused the book of Mormon to come into the world is not now among the Latter Day Saints—no, nor never will be!! By the position you now hold, You deprive yourself of the influences of the Celestial Heavens! My dear Sir, place & preferment—and the praise or honor given by mortals have no charms for me. What I most desire, and what I've most looked for for years past, is to see some man or men clothed with God-given Apostolic power, and then see them organize and set in order "the kingdom of heaven," according to the "pattern of heavenly things" [cf. Heb. 9:23].—until which, I must still be a looker on. I have seen nothing in what You have said or written which gives me to understand that You are clothed with the qualifications of an Apostle. I should be glad to have You in reply, inform me what are the evidences to You of your Call to stand in your present position. I wish You to understand that I have no personal ill will to any one in Your Society—but for some of them I have entertained a very high regard. Still I believe they are now much mistaken. I saw and personally examined the Organization under your Father—under Sidney Rigdon—under J. J. Strang[5]—under David Whitmer—under Brigham Young[6]—and I have closely examined the "Herald" of your organization. I have lived to see the fall and the ruin of the four first. They all professed to be governed by direct Visions & revelations. And in each I heard men and women testify & say "I know the Lord is with us"!!!! Among You men are not scarce who profess to be led & governed by visions, by Angels, and by immediate revelations. If others failed who knew so much—where are your evidences above theirs? But my sheet is full—but the subject is yet full also—Yours—W. E. McLellin M.D.

My best respects to your Mother and the family[7] ~

I have written to four of five of the leading men in the "New organization" but up to the present hour I have received no reply, except only James Blakesley. Will You be pleased to let me hear from You at your earliest convenience. Our family are well ~ W. E. M.

---

5. For a summary of James Jesse Strang's life, see the Biographical Notes.

6. For a summary of Brigham Young's life, see the Biographical Notes.

7. This two-part postscript was added upside-down in the top margin of the first page of the letter.

3.

TO GRANVILLE HEDRICK, CA. 1864

Union Corners, Genesee Co., Mich.
Dear Friend:–

Of late I have been retrospecting my past life, and my religious experiences. I have read the historic part of the Bible through to "Psalms" carefully! I have read the book of Mormon attentively, and I have earnestly prayed for TRUE light and understanding; to know things just as they WERE, ARE, and WILL BE. There are certain fixed laws and principles in Spirituality, as well as in Science, and those laws govern wherever intelligence exists, and God's dominion is acknowledged. The World's history is divided into five HOURS or great dispensations, viz: Patriarchal, the Mosaic, the Gospel, the Millennial, and the judgment hour. Each era has laws for the salvation of mankind, adopted to its own peculiar epoch, and by the observance of which, during the time of authority, salvation is, was, and will be obtained. However, in observing, we find one universal, immutable LAW existing and governing the whole in all ages of man, on this earth–of constant and unalterable adaption, in and under all the vicissitudes of life, viz.: Both God and man's right to direct intercourse. The Lord's right to speak, and men's right to hear and his duty to obey. God never did nor never will give revelations enough in any age to take away or to preclude man from that right. This right for man to commune with his Creator is the key-stone to the whole fabric of intelligence upon earth. It is the foundation and cap stone of all pure religion; of all true wisdom, knowledge, and spiritual understanding among intelligence. God himself, and all holy Prophets and Apostles always maintained this doctrine. Every Prophet and witness of Jesus, lived upon intercourse with God. The Lord is the fountain of intelligence, and all obedient intelligent beings have a right to that pure source to gain wisdom.

The histories of previous revealments show the mind of God concerning those to whom, or about whom he spoke, and by reading those

---

This letter is available only in its published form as it appeared in Granville Hedrick's Bloomington, Illinois, publication, *The Truth Teller*, Oct. 1864, 57-58. For a summary of Granville Hedrick's life, see the Biographical Notes.

histories in after ages men can learn great and important truths, but not the immediate will of God about themselves. Knowledge relative to their own immediate duty must come direct. More especially is this the case when there has been any falling away from the right way. When men are in the dark—have lost their way, then an immediate guide is necessary in order to lead them into the light, in other words, when in past ages, men had strayed from God, he always, (when he called at all) called after them either by Prophets or Apostles, who received their message at his mouth, and without such message the Prophet could not have told them what to do to be saved. The messages given to former Prophets would not reach their case, it must be one directed to them especially in order to lead them from darkness to light.

It is because of the rejection of this great principle and practice of "Direct intercourse with the Heavens," that the world of professed believers are in such an awful state of confusion—so many Churches "crying lo! here, and lo! there" [cf. Matt. 24:23]. It will be by the close application of the great rule of "direct intercourse," that "any flesh shall be saved at the last day" [cf. Matt. 24:22]. Some man or men must gain faith and power enough with God, to gain "direct intercourse" with Him, and then go to work and "set in order the things of God among men" [cf. Titus 1:5].

The study of the dealings of God with man in all of the inspired revealments of past ages, is important and necessary, but living faith, and "direct intercourse" saved all the ancient Saints, and its that only that will save any in this generation or any other. It was this "faith in God, and direct intercourse" with him, which the Ancients exercised, that has given to the world any Holy Scriptures to read; that has ever produced any miraculous powers among men, and that has ever saved any in Heaven, even of the "Church of the first born" [Heb. 12:23]. It was that by which all the Saints during the Patriarchal and Mosaic ages were saved, and also all during the first of the Christian era. In truth, without the exercise of "direct intercourse with God," no one can know whether he is to be saved or [page 58:] lost, because without it there is NO KNOWLEDGE in spiritual things. Without it the faith we exercise is faith in other men's faith, instead of faith in God. Laws or ordinances delivered from God at the beginning of a dispensation are always intended to be in force during that era, and salvation and an "intercourse with God" are only obtained by obedience to those principles delivered. Adam lived in the beginning of the first epoch, and Moses lived at its end. Both held "direct communion" with their Creator. Joshua lived in the first of the Law era, and John the Baptist and Christ lived near its end. All of them held "direct communion." Peter and the Apostles lived in the commencement of the Gospel dispensation, and some man or men must live at its end, and they, like as the Apostles must hold a like "direct familiar intercourse with God," in order to fill the pattern, and be as in former dispensations, i.e. and the era with and in the same precious "i[n]tercouse." The same priestly authority, and political power which exists at the commencement of a dispensation in the founders must also characterize the leaders at its winding up or close. Adam was the first Ruler and Chief Minister of the Patriarchal age, and Moses held the same legal authority at its close. Moses introduced the Law era, and Jesus closed it. Jesus was a "Prophet like unto Moses" [cf. Deut. 18:18]. Both were legally Chief Rulers and High Priests of the Order "of the Son of God" [LDS D&C 107:3; RLDS D&C 104:16]. Apostles introduced the gospel dispensation, and Apostles must close it. The Apostolship was the highest legal ministerial authority ever exercised in the "Church of Christ," at its commencement, and in the great work of the last days, the Apostles will be looked up to as the "mouth-piece of God" to all true believers. Hence, the priesthood which begins and establishes a dispensation, always governs it throughout its continuance, and also winds it up at its end.

The ministry of the Nephites was all of the order of Melchisedec. They had no Levitical Priests, because there were none of the Sons or descendants of Levi among them, and none others could legally officiate in the Levitical Priesthood. And because of that order they had more knowledge of Christ and his gospel, than even the Jews at Jerusalem had, until his personal appearance among them. And because it was always the business and duty of the Priest of the order of Melchisedec, i.e. the order of the Son of God, to preach the Gospel, although they might be bound to a certain extent, (as being of Israel) to live according to the Law of Moses, until it was "fulfilled and taken out of the way" [cf. Matt. 5:18; Col. 2:14]. Still the great truth stands out throughout all the oracles of God, and that truth is, that the Lord never had a minister called and chosen to declare his councils, but that was an inspired man. Were it otherwise his ministry could not be legal, because a minister must always hold the credentials of his superior, that is, of the one who sends him. The Lord always has, and always will hold "direct intercourse" with all his ministers, and such ministers are always enabled to "preach the Gospel with the Holy Ghost sent down from Heaven" [cf. 1 Pet. 1:12]. And the holy spirit "searches all things, yea, the deep things of God" [1 Cor. 2:10], &c., &c.

W. E. McLellan.

4.

LETTER FRAGMENT, CA. MAY 1869

at 3½ P.M. Their principal Elders would not take no for an answer, but that I must speak to them again. I spoke an hour and a quarter, and when I closed I dont think there was a dry face in the house. Well, I have struggled, and fasted and prayed [page 2:]

forgiven me. Tuesday eve I reached Richmond and called on my old friend and brother David Whitmer. I found him just recovering from a hard fall—pretty much well. In the first place he is wealthy, in the next place he is a perfect gentleman, in dress, manners, &c [page 3:] Jacob Whitmer's[1] and O. Cowdery's[2] widows live there. Their children are grown and married. Jacob's oldest son[3] married his cousin, Vashti,[4] W's youngest daughter He is very popular, and wealthy. He is ~~judge~~ a lawyer and judge, of two courts. David's wife had but two children. They are widow & widower, and both live at home. David Jun[5] is also quite wealthy. Oliver's wife had but one child—a daughter, married well to a Doctor, and the widow lives with them. ~ But n[ow] as to my visit with David. I staid with him two nights and one day—talked a great deal. I found him a man of God, with clear, clean, unfeigned faith in God. He most firmly believes the great truths of the Latter Day work. he still firmly holds to his appointment under the hands of Joseph Smith. He thinks the time soon at hand when he must be Active.

The surviving portion of this letter, written to an unknown recipient, contains a few lines at the bottom of page 1, a similar number of lines at the bottom of page 2, and two complete pages, 3-4. According to internal clues, McLellin wrote it immediately following his visit to Richmond, Missouri, making it possible to tentatively date it to May 1869, which is more or less confirmed by the postscript.

1. Elizabeth Ann Schott was Jacob Whitmer's widow. For a summary of her life, see the Biographical Notes.

2. Elizabeth Ann Whitmer Cowdery was Oliver Cowdery's widow. For a summary of her life, see the Biographical Notes.

3. For a summary of David P. Whitmer's life, see the Biographical Notes.

4. Vashti P. Whitmer was the daughter of Peter Whitmer Jr. For a summary of her life, see the Biographical Notes.

5. Actually, this son was not identically named and not known as "Junior." For a summary of David J. Whitmer's life, see the Biographical Notes.

On Wednesday we retired to an upper chamber of his great two story white house, and there had a long talk together alone. We bowed and prayed together, and then he laid his hands upon me, and reordained or confirmed upon me all the Authority which I ever held legally in the "church of Christ." Give glory to God O! my soul for the pure mercy of the good Lord. O rejoice! I dont know whether Headrick is on the sure foundation but if he aint we will try to get him there. All acquainted with him say h[e] is an honest man, and it may be that God is in it preparing the way! I hope it is so. [page 4:]

At least I shall go to his conference, and be a looker on. And then I will write a few lines to you again, and let you know my course. I have decreed to spend the remainder of my days in active service—trying to do the will of God, according to the highest light which shines upon my mind. All I have to do now is to take care of my wife and myself temporally. The friends were so anxious to have me come to conference that they wanted to give me money to pay my way up and back on the rail road, after they ~~they~~ had heard me preach on Sunday.

Now You talk of going to [blank] land and to Iowa, but I advise You if you want to hear pure truth go to Zion—go to Independen[ce.] Go to where God will build up a Holy people. Because if I live I mean to hold forth nothing but purity in doctrine, in principle and in practice; and I feel as tho I knew I will have friends. O dont run away to that miserable spirit brineland![6]

Nor dont go among the Jo'ites, because they are much divided, and some are leaving them. The Temple lot is laid out in city lots, and houses all over it, except a square or about a square right where the Temple was to Stand, is vacant, and our friends have purchased three lots so as to secure the site &c. I wonder if Martin [Harris] still has the deed to that lot. Please to let me know. Ask him & write to me. Tell if he is still alive, and able to go round among folks? I wish I knew now. But I must stop. May the good Lord direct you to go to Zion. I intend to move there just as soon as I can sell here. I have an offer for my place, and I think I'll sell. I feel that Zion is my future home! May God preserve You and keep you until his coming and kingdom

Most truly yours
W. E. McLellan

This is Monday night 24th. I intend to start in the morn for Independence[7]

---

6. This is a derogatory reference to the Salt Lake Valley.

7. This postscript was written upside down at the top of this page.

5.

TO DEAR FRIENDS, 12 JULY 1869

Brownsville, Mo. July 12th 1869. Monday morn

Our very dear friends,

Yours of July 1st came in by last Tuesday's mail, and in the first place I will go to work to answer your questions. I am willing you shall read my letters to any friend who believes the truth. I will do as you say if I wish any thing kept I'll p[u]t in on slips &c. You say "I was a little surprised at your uniting with Headrick, but not sorry." I'll try to tell you why I united with him. In the first place he delivered a number of prophecies which have already come to pass. So his friends who heard him declare. I could tell you what they were—but no matter now. One he declared that in 1867. Some should begin to gather to Zion. Which they did in that year. Again he declared that in 1868 the Lamanites should begin to hear and receive the Gospel. Two E[l]ders went down to the Creek nation and built up a church among them of over forty members, who are now strong in the faith, and are rejoicing in the truth. Two of those Indians came up and was with us in our conference on the 4th of June. One was ordained and sent back to them. I might go on, but let this suffise. They go back on the original principles as taught at first in 1830 and up to 1834 when they declare Joseph fell. Dont You know that I published in the "Ensign" in 1847 that Jos. fell in 1834. Please read on page 77.[1] We set aside all extras as doctrine or principle which cannot be sustained by the New Testament, and that inestimable inspired book of Mormon. [page 2:]

I went up to Independence to attend their conference which was to have been the 28 of May, but was put off until the 4th of June. They had meetings every ~~every~~ day between the 28th & the 4th. So I had a good opportunity to investigate. And I set and said nothing during the meeting & conference, but on the 5th I stated to them precisely my position,

1. McLellin, in "The Successor of Joseph, the Seer," *The Ensign of Liberty of the Church of Christ1,* Mar. 1848, 77, says: "He [David Whitmer] is [the] only President in and over the true church of Christ, organized on the 6th day of April, 1830, and which fell in 1834, but which has been re-organized again the 'second time' in 1847."

that I was willing to believe Hedrick was a Prophet, and the church had chosen him to preside over the whole church, and I was willing to take him to preside. I hea[r]d, after he got there on the 1st, a great deal of his teaching, and of his decisions, I was willing to admit I could see wisdom in them. Hence I united with them. But mind you, I did not say that I believed him a Seer or Translator. He has never given proof of having those gifts in his possession. We started home on the 7th. I found all well. I soon sold my place for $1,700 in cash, and started again in a few days to Zion in order to purchase a home. I examined 13 different houses and lots for sale, then bought one near the square for $1500, a good frame building—just suiting us. And we calculate to move in a few weeks. As I went to Independence the last time I went through Richmond, and reported to David my experience in the matter of uniting with Hedrick, also a bro. Frisby[2] came home with me, and he had great anxiety to see David so we again came by to see him. Its only about two miles out of the way, only we have to cross the river twice. We had remarkably pleasant visits with David & family, and while there we received a revelation through him. I tell you my soul rejoiced in God! John Whitmer visited David between the times that I was there, and [page 3:] they had familiar talks all about it; and John declared that he was going to sell out and move to Zion. That will stir up the balance of them. John has become wealthy in Far West. David was perfectly satisfied with my course, and even justified it. I tell You I feel as though I was in my element, only I want to be among my brethren and sisters in Zion. If prospered I'll soon be there. O if You could only go to Zion your whole soul ~~soul~~ would be filled to hear the burning eloquence fall from the lips of God's Elders. O how I wish you could come, even if it was only to make a visit. It does seem to me that You must come. It certainly cant be that You have lived so long in the faith, and then never enjoy the great blessings resulting from being and meeting with people of the Lord. I commenced corresponding with Hedrick I think in 1864 and had some dozen letters from him, so that I pretty well understood his positions. He declared publickly in conference that he was not successor to Joseph Smith he stood not in Joseph's place. He said he stood in his own place, and he must do his own work.[3] And I fully believed him. For I most firmly believe that David will yet act in his station. I tell you I have as much confidence in David, as in any man in this wide world. Still I be-

---

2. For a summary of George Pack Frisbey's life, see the Biographical Notes.

3. The words "He said he stood in his own place, and he must do his own work" are added above the line.

lieve that Hedrick has a glorious gift, and if faithful in it he will do a great work. He has done a great work now to commence the gathering, and the work of the Lord among the Lamanites! The people in Independence are not only willing we shall come back, but many are anxious for us to do so. They are very friendly with us. Hedrick preached at 11 on the 6th of June and I in the afternoon at 3. We had a [page 4:] brick church, but the house was joined, and some said ¼ of the people were out doors round the windows. How do you suppose I must have felt to again have the privilege of proclaiming in Zion, when I had stood more than 30 yrs ago to preach[4] the same everlasting gospel. Hedrick came to where I was that evening and catched me by the shoulders and gave me a good shaking. Said he, "we did not know there was so much in you." I tell You my soul has warmed and burned within me many times since I preached first to this people in Zion. For during my first discourse to them I knew the gracious and Long suffering, and good Lord forgave me all my past sins. When I came to that point it powerfully affected me so that I could not utter for a while, but my tears soon relieved me so that I went on[.] If ever there was a man happy, since the world began, I feel that I am that man. The remainder of my time be ~~they~~ my days [torn paper] which shall be devoted to God. We have enough of the good of this world to support and sustain my wife, and I'll depend on the Lord. I had fasted and prayed much during the winter to learn and know my duty, and now thank God I feel sure that I know it certain. My wife[5] says say to sister Bond I'll write to her some of these times. She says give my love to Mrs Bond and Mary.[6] But she has seen so many start ups that she is discouraged. She is not very pious, or spiritual minded. But is willing to go with me to Zion. Mr Clark[7]—Helen's[8] husband will move with us. He has sold his farm, and intends to go there in order to go into business. He is an entire unbeliever in any thing, but rather a noble hearted fellow. Good to Helen and his children, which makes me think more of him. All our children are entire unbelievers. But I dont believe that any of my blood will still remain in unbelief. My faith is that they will all come in finally—altho it may be by judgements—some judgement! C Wm[9] still lives in one

---

4. The words "to preach" are added above the line.

5. For a summary of Emeline Miller McLellin's life, see the Biographical Notes.

6. This is Mary E. Bond, daughter of Ira and Charlotte W. Bond. For a summary of Mary's life, see the Biographical Notes.

7. For a summary of Lafayette W. Clarke's life, see the Biographical Notes.

8. For a summary of Helen Rebecca McLellin Clarke's life, see the Biographical Notes.

9. For a summary of Charles William McLellin's life, see the Biographical Notes.

part of our house. But is as near an infidel as may be. I want to know if Martin's deed was ever recorded in Jackson Co. Please to ask him and then write to me. 14 No. of the T. T.[10] were published, but it is not now printed. and will not be for sometime to come. Some things I find in it are not true, but mostly its good. Give my love to my dear old sister Daton.[11] Tell her I hope to see her yet in Zion among the saints. What's become of Old Mr. Parmer?[12] and his son Gid?[13] If I kn[e]w any thing more to say that I think would be interesting I would write it. Ask me all the questions you can think of, and I'll try to answer them. Be sure to keep up your correspondence, and dont fail me.

I am most sinc[e]rely yours in the new and everlasting covenant, and in Christ. ~ ~

W. E. McLellan M.D.

---

10. Granville Hedrick's publication, *The Truth Teller,* ran from July 1864 through December 1868, first from Bloomington, Illinois, and then from Independence, Missouri, through a total of fourteen issues.

11. The identity of Sister Daton is unknown.

12. Mr. Parmer remains unidentified.

13. Gid Parmer remains unidentified.

6.

TO DAVIS H. BAYS, 23 NOVEMBER 1869

Independence, Missouri,
November 23, 1869.

Elder D. H. Bays:[1]

Yours of the 16th inst. is before me, and I read it with interest. You say that "pure and unadulterated truth" is all you want–and you say, "may the Lord help us to get it." But you are anxious that I should state the difference of opinion between us, so as to compare notes in writing. Well, I would do so willingly, but you say you are going to Ray County sometime during the ensuing month, and if I will give you special directions, you will visit me, and at least call and see me, and then have opportunity to "compare notes." Well, I prefer that course in that visit. I feel sure that you will not regret a visit with me.

I joined the church on the 29th day of August, 1831, was baptized by Hyrum Smith, and, on the 24th, was ordained an Elder, by the spirit of prophecy and revelation.[2] So the elders present testified. It was about ten miles west of Independence, among the Colesville Branch, who had just moved [page 291:] to the land of Zion, and a special conference of some fifteen elders when I was set apart to the ministry. I remained with the church until August, 1836, although sometimes much tried because of the conduct of her leading authorities. But when I saw them go into drunkenness and into ruinous speculation, pride and folly, I peaceably withdrew from them; merely writing back to them "it was because I had lost confidence in the HEADS of the church." I have never operated with Joseph Smith or his party from that day to this!! As to Brigham-ism, Young Joseph-ism, or G. Hedrick-ism, I have no use for either of them. Nay, verily!!

But, say you, "Do tell what you believe." Well, I believe in the "church of Christ." But have no use for the name of L. D. Saints in any of

1. For a summary of Davis H. Bays's life, see the Biographical Notes.

2. Of course, McLellin was not ordained before he was baptized. His actual baptismal date was the 20th, rather than the 29th, of August. Either McLellin or the RLDS *True Latter Day Saints' Herald*, from which the text of this letter is preserved, introduced this error.

its parties or factions. I believe David Whitmer was legally and properly appointed and ordained on the 8th day of July, 1834, by Joseph Smith, in a kind of general assembly of all his camp followers, and all the ministerial authorities in the land of Zion, [who] met together three miles west of Liberty, Clay Co., Mo.; and that he holds that authority sacred to-day. You say, "Why then does he not come forward to lead the people?" I answer, When Moses was legally appointed of God to go and lead Israel, he presented himself; but his life was sought, he fled and was away forty years, while Israel suffered all manner of hardships. At any time when David would have taken the presidency of the church of "Latter Day Saints," and gone with them, he would have lost his power to do good, and establish the true "church of Christ" on earth. You may think this strange reasoning–nevertheless it is true. I do not believe in plurality of Gods or women; in baptism for the dead; in two priesthoods in the gospel church. Not I; and many other things which you are bound to believe, if you go with young Joseph. I tell you I am well posted as to beliefs and doctrine of men and devils. And I am not going [with] any of them. Be sure to come and see me. I live near the Square, in Independence. But be sure to answer as soon as you can.

Yours in the love of pure truth,

W. E. McLellan.

7.

TO DEAR FRIENDS, FEBRUARY 1870

Independence, Mo. Feb 1870

My dear Friends,

Your last came in several days ago, and I will now answer. Last Tuesday I went to visit David [Whitmer] again in Richmond I found them as well as usual for them. David has got to be an old man with all the infirmities of age. He is quite feeble–still smart for an old man. He is one year older than I. I found him just as strong in faith as he ever was. But he says the Lord tells him, "when I want You I will call You." "Be still therefore and know that I am God" [cf. Ps. 46:10]. He says he's not able to get beyond that. I dont think there would be much object of his acting much without he can obtain the Interpreters. Altho he and I do not differ in sentiment except about the time to set up the church, and establish it permanently. I staid in Richmond two days and nights. I had a great deal of talk with widow Cowdry,[1] and her amiable daughter.[2] She is married to a Dr Johnson,[3] but has no children. She gave me a certificate And this is the copy. "Richmond, Ray Co., Mo. Feb 15th 1870[”] ~

> I cheerfully certify that I was familiar with the manner of Joseph Smith's translating the book of Mormon. He translated the most of it at my Father's house. And I often sat by and saw and heard them translate and write for hours together. Joseph never had a curtain drawn between him and his scribe while he was translating. He would place the director in his hat, and then place ~~in~~ his face in his[4] hat, so as to exclude the light, and then [illegible] the word[s][5] (he said) as they appeared before him [page 2:]

I tell you it was very interesting to me to talk to those old veterans

1. This refers to Elizabeth A. Whitmer Cowdery, Oliver Cowdery's widow.

2. For a summary of Maria Louise Cowdery Johnson's life, see the Biographical Notes.

3. For a summary of Charles Johnson's life, see the Biographical Notes.

4. McLellin adds the words "face in his" above the line.

5. In 1982 Robert F. Smith made a conjectural emendation suggesting the passage should read: "_i____ to his scribe the words"; see Richard S. Van Wagoner Collection, Ms 597, Bx 11, Fd 6, Manuscripts Division, Marriott Library. The 1985 transcript in the Community of Christ Archives has a handwritten addition: "[give] off to his scribe the words."

who had Knowledge of the beginning of the work. She was perfectly frank and familiar! I had hours and hours of conversation with David. I tell you he is posted in doctrine and principle, and says he is ready whenever the Lord says go—said he, I will go, and gladly go too! I am now looking for some **man** to rise with the Interpreters or Directors—Those ancient eyes by which hidden treasures can and will come to light. (Joseph in his history and all L.D.S.ism call those Interpreters the Urim & Thummim) But I prefer calling it by its proper name—It never was Urim nor Thummim But L.D.S.ism nicknamed almost every holy thing which it touched. I have less and Less patience with its unholy doings, the more I see of it. David promised to come and see us just as soon as the weather got warm so he could venture out. There are some fifteen or twenty of us here who cannot go with the Hedrick party. They are in reality nothing but Latter Day Saints. True they dont hold to polygamy, but they hold to many wild notions of that infamous ism.

Now you may inquire what I am going to do. I answer there is much to do. I read a document to David while there advocating his position just as I consider it. I asked him whether I should publish it or not? He said yes, if I would publish it under my own signature. As soon as I have means I calculate to have it printed to send abroad. I have selected some 60 hymns and songs. I mean to keep on until I have enough for a book. And I calculate to keep storing my mind with all the wisdom and knowledge which I can reach by faith and prayrs and searching. I feel and have felt as though the time was **now**. It must come soon or we shall all be gone—"die without the sight." Altho we have had such confidence that it would come in our day!!![6]

6. Robert F. Smith, ibid., also guessed that a word written in an illegible line at the bottom of the second page reads "David."

8.

TO DAVIS H. BAYS, 24 MAY 1870

Independence, Mo.,
May 24th, 1870

Elder D. H. Bays:

I find in the *Herald* of to-day, two letters of our correspondence. I did not write that letter for publication, and think I ought to have been consulted. But I am not sorry they are published. In this I will be a little more particular.

I joined the "Church of Christ," August 20th. On the 24th, I was ordained an elder. On the 25th, I and Elder Hyrum Smith started for Kirtland, Ohio. On Tuesday, the 25th of October, I attended a General Conference in the town of Orange, Cuyahoga Co., Ohio, where I was first introduced to Elder Joseph Smith. During its sittings, I, with nine others, was nominated to be ordained to the priesthood by Joseph. He asked if we were wiling to take upon us the office? I arose and said that I was willing to do anything that was the will of God, but I did not understand the duties of the office, and asked an explanation. Bro. Joseph said we were to take upon us the office, and it would explain its duties. We were ordained to the priesthood by Oliver Cowdery. On the 14th of February, 1835, I was chosen as one of Joseph's twelve apostles. On the same day we were ordained to our new stations. Now I have given you my ordinations. Think of them as you please.

I was clerk of the conference in which the twelve were chosen, and I was appointed by the twelve as a scribe among them. And I now have our apostolic record, as we first made it up. On the 26th of April we received our solemn charge by Bro. Joseph, in a [page 554:] large congregation. On the 4th of May, we started east on a mission. We returned the last of September; and the next April was appointed for our endowment. We passed through it; but I, in all candor say, we were most egregiously mistaken or disappointed! In a few days I said to Joseph:

The original letter having disappeared, the text is derived from the *Saints Herald*, 15 Sept. 1870, 553-57.

"I am disappointed! I supposed—yes, I believed that during the endowment, I should get *knowledge*; but I have not."

He said to me, "What do you want?"

I said, "I want to *know* for myself."

He laid his hands upon my head, and prophesied thus: "If you will take a mission to the south, and pray fervently upon the hills and in the deep valleys, before you return you shall have your soul's desires."

On the 9th of April I started on my southern tour, but did not realize what had been promised. I returned to Kirtland the last of June, but only returned to see speculation, pride and folly, drinking to excess by the leaders, &c., &c. I made up my mind to leave.

But now I will try to answer some of your statements and arguments.

Query.—"Why should an elder, to whom God revealed his will; after having remained in the 'church of Christ' five years, 'peaceably' withdraw from it?"

I did not withdraw from the "Church of Christ." That church had ceased to exist. It was not the Church of Christ of L. D. Saints, or of Jesus Christ of Latter Day Saints, but simply the "Church of L. D. S." They set aside the name of Christ entirely, by authority of a council in which J. Smith was *moderator*, and took the silly, non-descript name of the "Church of Latter Day Saints." The church—the whole church—wore this name for three years, then the Joseph party—whom the dissenters called "Lick Skillets"—had a furious and serious difficulty. They had a regular "set to," or fight, in the Temple. About seventy of Joseph's first elders quit him. Among them, the three "witnesses;" David, Oliver and Martin, his scribe and church recorder his private secretary, a member of the twelve, and a number of his high councilors, &c., &c. The *name* was a matter of contention.

The dissenters took for their church the original name of the "Church of Christ," and Martin Harris furnished the money, and Leonard Rich[1] went to Chardon, and got that name recorded. This alarmed the "Lick Skillets," and they got together, and changed the name to the "Church of Christ of L. D. S." Thus it remained until in Far West they added to it, "Jesus," and so they have worn that name ever since.

Leave the "Church of Christ"? No, sir. I left that sect called L. D. S.—that nondescript.

Now, sir, in the Book of Mormon, after Christ's appearance, the church was called "the Church of Christ," and no additions or alter-

1. For a summary of Leonard Rich's life, see the Biographical Notes.

ations in that book. And all the revelations given to or through Joseph Smith up to the 3d of May, 1834, were given to the "Church of Christ." Tell me, will you, who had authority to alter the name? Now, I ask you, could it be the "Church of Christ," and the church of the Latter Day Saints at the same time? And I answer, No! No, never!! I could say much more on the *name*, but this will do.

As to "Joseph Smith's party," it is answered in the above. Now, sir, they went on in their speculations in Kirtland, until the winter of 1837. Joseph and Sidney had to run away from there between two days, hid in a wagon. The dissenters carried the day. But you say "legal grounds for this trifling objection." Well, if I have not given reasons, judge ye!

But again:

"All the spiritual authorities of the church, in its *early* and prosperous days *** confirmed all baptized believers members of the 'Church of Jesus Christ of Latter Day Saints.'" [page 555:]

I don't want to charge you with want of understanding. But that name never was known in the church (I believe) until 1838. Talk about L. D. S-ism then to some other man.

"If the church which was organized in 1830, and continued to flourish till its rejection in 1841."

Who told you it was not rejected until 1841? It was rejected, sir, when they took the spirit of *war* for the entire church in the winter of 1833-4. They then suffered Satan to give them an entire "false name," on the 3d of May, 1834. And the Lord to show his disapproval of their entire course suffered the cholera to afflict about sixty of the number of Joseph's "braves," and some fourteen died in their warrior tramp—starting from Kirtland on the next day after their *name* was altered! Do you want "pure and unadulterated truth"? I can enlighten you as far as I *know*. Joseph Smith transgressed so as to be rejected in 1834. He then had one privilege left him to legally perform—that was to appoint and ordain his successor. The "choice seer" was called to preside over the "Church of Christ," but when it had changed its *name*, its nature, its spirit, and its doctrine, it was no longer the "Church of Christ," but it was in reality the "Church of Latter Day Saints." Yes, I peaceably withdrew from that ism, but not from the "body of Christ."

Now, in relation to the ordination of David Whitmer. You say I have "too much ambiguity." Well, I'll try to be plain, so that you shan't misunderstand me. Although you misrepresent me in saying "David was ordained in a kind of general assembly of all Joseph's camp followers." I definitely stated, "and all the ministerial authorities of the land of Zion met together." Do my sayings justice. Joseph called a General Conference of the authorities of Zion, his camp followers were present, and in that he organized a High Council for Zion. David Whitmer was constituted president of it, and John Whitmer and W. W. Phelps ordained to be his counsellors, and twelve others placed with him. I was one of the Twelve. Then Joseph Smith arose and said, "The time has come when I must appoint my successor in office; some have supposed it would be Oliver Cowdery, but," said he, "Oliver has lost that privilege by transgression. The Lord has made it known to me that DAVID WHITMER IS THE MAN." Joseph, and his counsellors then laid hands upon him, and ordained him to be Prophet, Seer, Revelator, Translator, and President of the Church. Joseph then gave David a charge to be faithful, in the hearing of the assembly. He then said, "Now, brethren, if any thing should befall me, the work of God will roll on with more power than it ever has done hitherto."

As to your "Presidency of the High Priesthood," I do not hold that such an office exists in the true "Church of Christ."

You say a revelation was given in 1829, "respecting ordinations." It was not given in 1829, nor until 1835, when the first book of Doctrine and Covenants was compiled. I know what I say.

But now I will say a few things about the Book of D. & C. No revelation given to the church was printed until June, 1832. And the Book of Commandments was not printed (in part) until 1833. I presided in council in Joseph's translating room where and when it was first agreed upon to print them. A committee of Joseph, Sidney, Oliver &c., were appointed to prepare them for publication. They altered and changed, took out whole sentences and paragraphs, and *added* others; and in that altered and mutilated condition, Oliver Cowdery and John Whitmer were appointed to carry them to Zion–Independence–and print [page 556:] them. They printed some, but a mob tore down their office, destroyed their book-work, &c. I hired a printer boy to gather up the numbers, as far as printed, and tempora[ri]ly bind it for me. I have it now:– Thank God!

But I say, Joseph, with the church, fell in 1834, and thereafter had not power with God to do right. In 1835, (in Kirtland), another committee was appointed to *fix up* the revelations for print again. I was teaching their High School in the lower room–the printing office being overhead. And I as often in Joseph's office, and know positively that some of the revelations were so altered, mutilated and changed, that a good scholar would scarcely know them. In one revelation I have counted more than twenty alterations!! Hence, who can depend upon them? I cannot. I will not. Those quotations you make from those given in 1829, I know were made out of whole cloth, and *added*. What will you do with them? Swallow them like a man would swallow a toad, toe nails and all? I for one cant do it!! You of course have your agency and must do as you think best, and I want you to do so freely, without compulsion. But you must let me have my freedom too.

"I am led to conclude that I am either lamentably ignorant of the law of God, or Bro. David has never been 'legally and properly appointed and ordained.' I charge you with a great want of intelligence on this point. If you only understood it right, it is as straight as a nail in a sure place."

I will leave some points of your letter to another time to answer. I have yet to see a point of argument adduced that cannot be very reasonably answered.

You say: "To deny two priesthoods in the church, is virtually and substantialy a denial of the whole latter day work,—and a base delusion."

I am well aware that the history of Joseph does say he was ordained to the Aaronic priesthood by John the Baptist; I don't believe it. Don't startle! I'll tell you why. No angel or spirit ever ordained a man to any office since the world began! Search the Bible and Book of Mormon. I heard Joseph tell his experience of his ordination and the *organization* of the church, probably, more than twenty times, to persons who, near the rise of the church, wished to know and hear about it. I never heard of Moroni, John, or Peter, James and John. It was after he *fell* from God that these things were put in, in order to sustain the falsehood of these two priesthoods. I do not say but angels conversed with him, and gave him much instruction how to proceed. But that they ever ordained him *I deny*. His history was gotten up after he fell from God!

But now as to the two priesthoods. One order of priesthood existed from Adam down to Moses. It was the birth-right priesthood. One priesthood existed from the time Moses left Egypt until Israel rebelled. Then those priesthoods were set aside. The birth-right was given to the oldest son of the race of man, and also the oldest son in all the families of Israel, which Moses set up in order to "sanctify Israel." But Israel rebelled, and the "law was added because of transgression" [cf. Gal. 3:19]. Then all previous priesthoods were set aside, and the Aaronic set up. That with high priest, chief priests and Levites, remained in full force until Christ came. Then the law and the *priesthood* were all set aside by Christ and his ministry. Jesus became High Priest of the race of man. All former priesthoods were set aside. Jesus stood in Aaron's stead; he was anti-type to Aaron. He is the only High Priest of the gospel age. For his ministry, there are in his priesthood apostles, bishops, elders, deacons, &c.; but not high priests. Jesus set no such office in his church. Nephi and his brethren laid down or away their priesthood; went forward and was baptized into [page 557:] Christ, and took his ministry, and went forward and converted their whole race to the gospel system. A Levitical priest never lived or ministered among the Nephites from Lehi to Moroni. And from the day Jesus set up his kingdom, no high priest ever lived among them on either continent.

All your trouble arises from your taking that mutilated and altered Book of D. & C. Set it aside, as I have done, until some man arises with urim and thummim, or the directors or interpreters, and then we shall know what to receive, and what to set aside. The revelations will be corrected, and all will be well!

Now, sir, you may print this if you choose, and your strictures on it also,—I am content. I am just as certain that all Latter Day-isms is doomed to run a false road, as I am that I breathe the air of heaven. I am not satisfied. I have not answered all the points I wished; but my space is filled, and I'll cease for the present.

I am yours in the strongest feelings of friendship,

W. E. McLellan, M.D.

9.

TO OLD FRIENDS, 21-25 OCTOBER 1870

Independence, Mo. Oct. 21 1870
My dear old friends,

Your kind letter post marked the 1st inst. came to hand in due time, but I have delayed answering it, because I was contemplating a visit to see bro. David, hence I concluded to wait until my return, so that I might have something to communicate that would be interesting to you. Tomorrow morning I intend to leave for his residence. We are very well at present. Helen R.[1] Has a babe [paper torn] on next Sunday. She has done remarkably well for her. Its a Daughter. They still live with us or imme[diat]ely ajoining. Mr. Clark[e] is at present in the saw mill business. Marcus N.[2] has gone to Troy, Lincoln Co. to follow his profession. He writes that he is doing very well. Our other children live where they have for some time and so far as we know are well. So far as religious matters are concerned here, Hedricites are doing about as usual. They generally have meetings on Sunday. But their leading ones have difficulty frequently, jars and discords. And such is L. D. S.ism every where. Two men have come here from the Bluffs, one was a Josephite, but left them, the other lived at Salt Lake some seven years. They cant go Hedrickism, but we have a little prayr-meeting frequently. Another young man here has occasionally been with me for a few weeks. He has read the book of Mormon once through regularly. Says he cant condemn it. I guess he is some over thirty years old, but has no family. He meets with us, and seems to be much interested. Last night we were together at my house until after ten Oclock, and had a very spiritual time. But the Hedric-ites are very jealous of us. But we pay no attention to them, but simply attend to our own business. We are in earnest, and I believe the time is near–now when the "kingdom of heaven," will be set up and established–no more to be thrown down. I have been reading and writing most of the summer and fall so far I have quite a book of manuscript, I expect to publish it some day but shall not until I get spiri-

1. The words "Helen R." were added above the line.
2. For a summary of Marcus Nelson McLellin's life, see the Biographical Notes.

tual minded brethren around me to read and scan each treatise. I want it to contain pure truth and nothing else. I have five foolscap pages, reviewing [Davis H.] Bays and [Isaac] Sheen. And I have not spared! I perfectly dispise their **miserable** misrepresentations. I cant believe them honest, or that they want to know the **truth**. I tell You[3] I know Josephism is built on a flimsy, sandy foundation, and God's truth will wash all the sand from under it! All Latter Day-ism is nothing on earth but sectarianism!! Now with all the close investigations I have been able to make I have not been able to change my views about Priesthood. I know that **two** priesthoods cannot exist legally in the "church of Christ." All L.D.S.ism claimes them. And while they are under them they cant avoid running wrong. They cant help themselves! They must run into error. Pure truth alone is going to stand when Christ comes. O my Lord look at the world!!! Wo be the inhabitants of earth they will be burned literally. The "church of Christ" will, it must[,] become the "joy and the Deliverer," of the whole earth—the righteous in all parts of the world. I had rather be a member of the true church, than to have all the riches, honors, or pleasures of earth. I feel just so! Hence I have retired from the world [paper torn] to earn money! Devote myself exclusively to the Lord's business ~ [page 2:]

I am here at the Center of Zion. If—I say if the Lord has ever appointed a place in this age for a place of gathering, this is the one. I know that in 1847, I—yes I was commanded of the Lord to go and bow on that lot, and offer up my prayers. I was not disobedient, but did as told to do. I felt a clearness and peace that no tongue can describe, when I had done my duty. I know then as to this place being the Center. To talk about hereditary rights in the gospel age is hereditary nonsense—simply vanity. Hence all young Joseph's claims founded on that principle is worse than vain. The truth says "old things are all done away, and behold all things are become new" [cf. 2 Cor. 5:17]. Then to talk about the law of Moses, or the Aaron[ic] [Pr]iesthood either remaining in force is simply nonsense. And there has been no hereditary rights since these "old [things"] were all done away!! All priestly auth[or]ity in the gospel age comes by direct faith in God, but not in consequence of pedigree, lineage, or birth-right in any sense. Hence the claim of young Joseph, (because he was his father's seed,) is simply non-sense. All those revelations, and silly items of doctrine were got up after Joseph's fall, hence fictitious & silly. Tues morn Oct. 25th I went down to David last Satur-

3. The word "You" is written above the line.

day, and remained with him until yesterday morning. We were together all day Sundy &c. We had much talk together. There was not a jar between us. And I came home yesterday perfectly satisfied. I was happy, because of what was manifest. The word of God came, and set me at rest! I have felt to rejoice in spirit ever since. There is a burden thrown off my mind that weighed heavily upon it. The Lord said, "Did You not once officially ~~th—w~~ throw away all names but the name of the "Church of Christ." I said yes, Were you not then baptized into Christ, and **his** church? I said in my heart yes. Then why not now go forward and build up my church? I said I'll do so with all my heart. Did I not say to you through my servant David that I required you to fulfil all the **ministry** to which I the Lord had caused you to be ordained in in[4] my church; and also to fulfil all the special revelations which I had ever given you." Yes O yes, then I am willing to go forward. O Lord stand by me in all my duties!! I have not given it in the words, but I have endeavored to give the ideas. We shall get together and organize, and then go forward–right here at the Center of Zion!! Then we want all the honest in heart in all the world to unite with us. But we shall not[5] strive so much for numbers but for "holiness to the Lord." O I feel happy this morning! I have no doubts!!! I feel sure the Lord is at the helm. My old heart has burned within me ever since I received that glorious intelligence from Heaven. Now I feel sure that we shall prevail, because I have lost the love of money, the love of riches, honors, or pleasures. I have no object before me only to serve and only God. I mean to be humble, meek and Lowly; and not have contention with any. If any comes, and wishes to unite with us, who have not shed innocent blood, who have not been polygamists, nor run so far into abominations that they cant be forgiven, we will receive them, but polygamists will have to wait until some man rises with the Interpreters or Urim in order to tell their fate. This word from the Lord came opposed to some of my previous notions, but all was so plain to my mind that I bowed willingly to Light! When we get things regulated–I will write to you again. But if you want to know any thing, just ask your questions. I am glad indeed that you still feel to write to me. You ought to know how I esteem your letters. I tell you a number of times David was so filled with the Spirit on Sunday he would spring to his feet & lay it down in earnest. He is deeply interested in the work! May the good Lord direc[t] [you] all aright.

---

4. The word "in" was unintentionally repeated at the end of one line and beginning of the next.

5. The word "not" is added above the line.

I am as ever
W. E. McLellan M.D.

Let me hear from You, with all the questions you want answered, and I'll try.[6] I tell You again I am happy. I feel that evidence in my Soul. O that You could feel it, it is so sweet and consoling. I have a divine testimony that all who now take hold of this work shall feel the same testimony. O how I wish I could see you. But it seems as though I was present with you in Spirit.

6. This postscript was added upside down in the top margin of the first page of the letter.

10.

TO MARK H. FORSCUTT, 1 OCTOBER 1871

(Originally to Isaac Sheen, October 1870)

Independence, Mo.,

October, 1870.

Herald Office, Plano, Ill., Elder M. H. Forscutt:[1]

The most of this letter was addressed to Elder [Isaac] Sheen for publication at its date, but it failed to come to light. I now send it to you for publication; this 1st of Oct. 1871, hoping that I may see it in the *Herald*.

Elder I. Sheen:–

Your long treatise, or rather strictures, relative to my letter to Elder [Davis H.] Bays came to hand a few days since. I have discovered no argument in its lengthy production but that might be easily answered. It contains much misrepresentation. In this letter I will be more particular. I think the name of the church, the two priesthoods, and the book of Doctrine and Covenants, are some of the most important items in our controversy. First then as to the NAME. It is said in the Book of Mormon, "And now, it shall come to pass that whosoever shall not take upon them the name of Christ, must be called by some other name, therefore he findeth himself on the left hand of God" [cf. Mosiah 5:10]. This is plain and definite. In the *Evening and Morning Star,* as re-published in Kirtland, O., in October, 1836, may be found the minutes of a council in which J. Smith Jr. was moderator, and O. Cowdery clerk. There we find the highest official authority of the church throwing away the name of Christ entirely f[rom] the church, and the introduction of that silly, fictitious, false, [page 154:] and non-descript name of the "Church of Latter Day"–save the name of Saints! Mind you this is not as Elder Bays has expressed it, "It is the Church of Christ, composed of Latter Day Saints."

The *Saints' Herald* published this letter in four parts and prefaced each installment: "The following letter is inserted in the *HERALD* for the following reasons: It is seemingly wrong for a man to be attacked and not permitted to defend himself, and that the saints may see the spirit of the writer, which is easily discovered. We do not endorse it by any means" (1 Mar. 1872, 153-55; 1 June 1872, 341-42; 15 July 1872, 435-37; 1 Aug. 1872, 472-74).

1. For a summary of Mark Hill Forscutt's life, see the Biographical Notes.

This is only a dodge to get rid of argument or true reasoning. I do not have opposition to the individuals who believe in the great work of the last days being called saints, believers, disciples, christians, or brethren and sisters. But I persistently, seriously, and sincerely object to the "Church of Christ" taking any other specific name except its own beautiful, distinctive, characteristic NAME. Again, I say, no more can the "Church of Latter Day Saints," and the "Church of Christ," be the same church at the same time? And I say No! distinctly No!! And I want it distinctly understood that the entire church, with Joseph Smith at its head, wore this specific cognomen for more than three years, before Jesus Christ was added to it! When a legislative body passes an act, or makes a law, it requires the same or a higher amount of authority to repeal it. No council being called after the one on the 3d of May 1834, where it was officially changed, then all the after alterations were without authority, hence null and void.

D. H. Bays says, "Joseph Smith, and I might with propriety say *all* the spiritual authorities of the church, in its early and prosperous days, in confirming all baptized believers by the laying on of hands, confirmed them members of the 'Church of Jesus Christ of Latter Day Saints.'" This is unqua[l]ifiedly untrue! That name was never known in the church for seven or eight years after its first organization; and it was then fixed up and given in Far West. It is curious to me that he should make such an assertion; because it is utterly untrue!

But when persons are baptized by a minister of Latter Day-ism, and confirmed a member of any of the parties of that body, they are then as properly sectarian—confirmed not in Christ's Church, but into a sect or party just as much as if confirmed into the Baptist or Campbellite church. I consider the Latter Day-ite churches just as much sectarian as any Catholic or Protestant churches whatever. Ah! but say you, we have the gifts of God among us. So say the Brighamites. So say the Rigdonites. So say the Hedrickites and all the ites of Latter Day-ism. Is it an evidence that your organization is right? If so it proves all the others right also. Again, you might say we are prospering wonderfully, we are making converts all over the United States, and in Canada, and away in old England. Have you prospered equal to or beyond the Catholics or Protestants either? Then say nothing to me about numbers as an evidence, or of gifts either.

Always after Christ visited this continent the church was called the "Church of Christ," or the "True Church of Christ." It is so called *nine* times in that book [of Mormon]. All the revelations given to or through

Joseph Smith until the 3d of May 1834, were given to the "Church of Christ." Latter Day-ism never was even mentioned in the church until the day the official authorities set Christ's name aside, and took that non-descript name under which so much wickedness has been perpetrated. I am aware that in the Book of Mormon the church was specifically called the "Church of God" as many as thirty-four times. But all this was before Christ ministered among them in person. The Nephites enquired particularly about the name by which the church should be called. They said to Christ, "Tell us the name whereby we shall call this church?" [LDS 3 Ne. 27:3; RLDS 3 Ne. 12:16]. He said to them, "Ye must take upon you the name of Christ, which is my name. For by this name ye shall be called at the last day. *** Therefore ye shall call the church in my name. But if it is built upon the works of men, or upon the works of the Devil, verily I say unto you, they have joy in their works for a season" [LDS 3 Ne. 27:5, 7, 11; RLDS 3 Ne. 12:18, 19, 23]. I am not at all surprised that the Latter Day-ites rejoice in the works of men and devils. When the authorities throwed away the name of Christ for the church entirely, and took the name of the "Church of Latter Day Saints," they were inspired to do so by the Devil. Hence it was the works of men and of devils, as Jesus said to the Nephites. The authorities had no revelation (except from Satan) to alter that beautiful, significant, characteristic, God-given name of the "Church of Christ," to any other name under heaven. Moroni describes three states of mankind in the 4th chapter of Mormon. First, the sectarian churches. Second, the holy church of God. Third, the entire unbelievers, those who do not believe in Christ. When he speaks of the true church, he says: "Why have ye polluted the holy church of God? Why are ye ashamed to take upon you the *name* of Christ?" I tell you Christ is the name, the nature, the spirit, the life, the light, and the power of all Christians, in all lands.

The word *latter day* does not apply to [page 155:] the gospel dispensation at all. We do not live in the latter day, but we live in the last days. Late is a comparative word in grammar. After the flood was late, from Moses till Christ was later or latter, and from Christ till now was last. Peter, rehearsing Joel said, "It shall come to pass in the *last days*" [Acts 2:17]. Old Jacob said to his sons, "Gather yourselves together that I may tell you that which shall befall you in the *last days*" [Gen. 49:1]. Paul said, "In the *last days* perilous times shall come" [2 Tim. 3:1]. Again, "Hath in these *last days* spoken to us by his Son" [Heb. 1:2]. Peter said, "There shall come in the *last days* scoffers" [2 Pet. 3:3]. John is definite and settles the point, "Little children, it is the *last time*" [1 John 2:18]. But now we turn to the Book of Mormon, Nephi 11th chap.: "But behold, I prophesy unto you concerning the *last days*; concerning the days when the Lord God shall bring these things forth unto the children of men" [LDS 2 Ne. 26:14; RLDS 2 Ne. 11:80].[2] Again, in the same chapter, "But behold, in the *last days,* or in the days of the Gentiles" [LDS 2 Ne. 27:1; RLDS 2 Ne. 11:116]. Book of Jacob, chap. 4th: "And in the day that he shall set his hand the second time to recover his people, is the day, yea, even the *last time,* that the servants of the Lord shall go forth in his power" [cf. LDS Jacob 6:2; RLDS Jacob 4:3]. But the prophet Haggai, when speaking of the second temple, built a way down under the law, designates it properly as "The *latter house*" [Hag. 2:9]; because it was built under the law times, or latter times. Moses looked at it just as I do, he said, Deut. 31:29, "For I know that after my death ye will utterly corrupt yourselves, and turn aside from the way which I have commanded you; and evil will befall you in the latter days." Now I have the books to harmonize with my views. I believe the Lord knew enough to give the correct NAME to his church. He named it just right, and I am unwilling to wear any other distinctive name for the church only the "True Church of Christ," lest I stand among the goats on the *left* hand at the Last Day. This will do as it respects name. Argue against it as you please. [page 341:]

All the government of the Church of Latter Day Saints is thrown under *two* priesthoods, and it must be governed by them in order to be what they call right. And the doctrine of two priesthoods being false, then its whole government is false also. I reiterate that it is an impossibility for the Aaronic or Levitical priesthood to exist legally in the gospel age. I will give you a few reasons here why.

1st. The Book of Mormon nor New Testament knows nothing of Aaronic priests in their government or administration.

2nd. If the Aaronic priesthood must exist in the gospel age, then High Priests, Chief Priests, and Levites must also. It must be a whole ministry and not a part only.

3rd. Aaronic Levitical priests were all consecrated by Moses and Aaron. Can any man legally act in that office without a solemn consecration?

4th. Then we ask who has authority to consecrate and set them apart in their office or station as Aaron and the Levites were?

5th. There are two covenants, one from Mount Sinai which is the Law—which gendereth to bondage. But the other is the Gospel, and

2. The disparity between the LDS and RLDS versions results from Orson Pratt's shortening and versifying the chapters for the 1879 LDS edition.

makes us free as Jerusalem is free, which is the mother of us all. Choose under which you will live.

6th. The Levitical priesthood could not carry the people to perfection, but was mostly temporal in its object.

7th. The anointing oil was poured upon Aaron and his sons in their consecration. Can a priest act unless thus consecrated?

8th. Can a stranger or a Gentile hold [page 342:] this priesthood, in any sense, or under any condition whatever?

9th. No priest of the order of Aaron ever ministered in spiritual things, except John, the forerunner of Christ.

10th. The Aaronic priest's whole duty was to attend to altars, to the tabernacle, and to the Temple, and as the gospel system has none, what would a priest of that order do now?

11th. It was death for any Israelite of any tribe but Levi, or any Gentile to officiate in the Levite priest's office. Num. 1:51; 16:40; 18:3, 7, 22, 32; 3:51, 53; 16:40;[3] Deut. 11:6.

12th. Some were killed—smitten with leprosy, etc., because they sought unlawfully to minister in the priesthood contrary to God's law. Deut. 11:6; Num. 16:31-34; Ps. 106:16, 17; Num. 26:9, 11; 2 Chron. 26:18.

13th. No Aaronic or Levitical priest was ever consecrated or set apart after their first ordination. They acted because of birthright. Because they were of the pure blood of Levi, by lineage or pedigree.

14th. From 25 to 50 [years of age], the priests of Aaron or Levi were to be active in the priest's office—then retire and live among their brethren. Num. 8:24, [2]5, [2]6. Must Latter Dayites do likewise?

15th. Aaron and all Levi are made after the law of a carnal commandment, but all Jesus' ministry are made after the power of an endless life. [cf.] Heb. 7:16.

16th. Will priests of the Aaronic order have successors now by lineage or pedigree as during the law age?

17th. Any one baptized by an Aaronic priest is baptized into the law, or rather under the law, but not into Christ, nor into the Church of Christ. Hence, he is bound to keep the law of Moses.

18th. He that is least in the kingdom of heaven, is greater than any Aaronic priest. John was one of the greatest.

19th. The Levites were wholly a gift to Aaron. Num. 3:9, 12; 18:6.

3. If McLellin had better ordered his references, he would have avoided this repetition of "16:40."

But all Jesus' ministry were wholly a gift to him, for the purpose of preaching the gospel to all the world. John 17:6.

20th. The Levites were taken for the first-born or redeemed. Num. 3:12, 45; 8:18; 13:2; 22:29; 34:20; 3:39-51.

I might give more queries on this subject, but I'll quit. But you have entirely failed to prove that High Priests, or Aaronic priests either, should exist in the Church of Christ in the gospel day. Because you have made no quotations from documents printed before the church went into darkness. You and Elder Bays, and all Latter Dayism, claim that *two* prie[st]hoods ought and must exist in the chur[ch]. The word lesser priest, Aaronic priest, or Levitical priest, is not found in the Book of Mormon. The word High Priest or Priesthood is not found in the Book of Mormon, after Jesus personally ministered on this continent.[4] The word priesthood is not found in the Book of Commandments, as far as printed in this city in 1833. Then all the support you have for two priesthoods in the church in the gospel age you have to take from that altered, mutilated, changed, mixed up, and bungled Book of Doctrine and Covenants. And the documents in it were twice, if not three times *altered* and changed before they came to light in that book. No man can be a High Priest or Aaronic or lesser priest either, in the gospel church in this age. No man can sustain the doctrine of two priesthoods in the church at one and the same time by the Bible, or Book of Mormon, and by those books I am willing to be judged. [page 435:]

Now I will examine the claims to validity of the Book of Doctrine and Covenants. None of Joseph Smith's revelations were ever printed or published until June, 1832. Some of them were printed in the *Evening and Morning Star,* edited and published by W. W. Phelps & Co., in Independence, Mo. It was published from June, 1832, until July, 1833. Then it was destroyed by mob violence. They also printed in the "Book of Commandments," *some* of the revelations in regular course, as far as they were given, until September, 1831. Now I have in my possession a copy of the old "Stars," and also the Book of Commandments, as far as printed here. The *Star,* re-published in Kirtland, was commenced in January, 1835. All its numbers, until October, 1836, were printed in the interest of the church of Latter Dayites. In November, 1831, I presided in a council in Joseph's translating room, in which it was first determined to print the revelations at all. It was often said in those given before to

4. "High priest" occurs at Mos. 23:16; 26:7; 29:42; the heading of Alma 1; Alma 4:4, 18; the heading of Alma 5; Alma 5:3; 8:11, 23; 13:14; 16:5; 30:20-22, 29; 3 Ne. 6:22; Eth. 14:9; "high priesthood" occurs at Alma 4:20; 13:6-8, 10, 14, 18.

"Keep these things from the [page 436:] world." But in this council it was determined the time had come for them to be printed, and go to the world, contrary to the Lord's directions! The council lasted one evening, and the next day and evening. J. Smith, O. Cowdery, and S. Rigdon, were appointed a committee to prepare the revelations for the press. In doing so they took out of them, added to them, and altered them just to suit their then supposed enlightened view. Thus altered and changed, O. Cowdery and J. Whitmer were appointed a committee to carry them to Zion, in order for them to be published in the "Book of Commandments." J. Smith, S. Rigdon, and N. K. Whitney visited Zion in April, 1832. W. W. Phelps, O. Cowdery, and J. Whitmer are the committee of publication. And they were still to examine said altered revelations before publication, and alter again when necessary. Many councils were held by these men, while here in Zion. The Order of Enoch was set up by them, and to all nine members of it, false names were given; such as Gazelam, Pelagoram, Ohihah, &c.! O shame on such nonsense! The committee of publication commenced the work.

In 1831, I wrote off a number of the revelations as originally given, and have them now. They were materially altered, (seen by comparison), before printed at all. After the meeting, O. Cowdery was sent to Kirtland to consult with the leading authorities of the church, and then soon sent on to New York, and purchased another press and fixtures, and set them to work in Kirtland. They professed to reprint the *Stars,* but did so in a very altered condition. In September, 1834, J. Smith, O. Cowdery and F. G. Williams were appointed a committee to fix up the revelations again in order to have them printed. And in August, 1835, they had completed their labors, and submitted them to a general assembly. I think there is scarcely a revelation printed in that book but that is altered and changed. I have counted more than twenty material alterations in one revelation, by comparing it as printed here and in Kirtland. Now if the Lord gave these revelations he said what he meant, and meant what he said. And no additions or subtractions could make it plainer. Man's additions would only bring the curse of God sooner or later, as it did do. But they had to alter or to fix them up to suit their advanced views. The idea conveyed to our minds is that the Lord grew in wisdom and knowledge, so that his revealments must be [ms. page 1:][5] altered to suit the advanced intelligence. Thus they come to us in their mutilated

5. Here the extant portion of McLellin's letter to Forscutt begins (Miscellany Collection, P13, f36, Community of Christ Archives, Independence, Missouri). The holograph is missing the top half of the page for pp. 1-2 but has survived in whole for pp. 3-4.

condition, three times altered and changed, and fixed. In their present condition who can have confidence in them? But I'll drop this part of my subject.

I say J. Smith transgressed many times from 1827 till 1834. But in 1834 was his fall. Thereafter he had not power with God to officially[6] act in accordance with the mind and will of the Lord. He commenced his history on ~~on~~ the second day of May 1838. O. Cowdery wrote his first letter on history Sep. 7th 1834, to W. W. Phelps. In it he says "April 5th 1829 my natural eyes first saw Joseph Smith." Joseph says in his history, "that on the 15th day of April O. Cowdery ~~Cowdery~~ came to my house until which time I never had seen him." Here is a difference of ten days. Their memories were at fault.[7] John Whitmore who was church recorder and historian, had quit the church, and took his history with him, and keeps it carefully yet; and hence Joseph was compelled to depend upon his treacherous memory for items or facts. Hence his mistakes. All the writings of the "Church of Christ," and of the church of Latter Day-ism, were made out after the leading authorities had fallen from God, therefore we can't depend upon them; except those only which were printed in this city in 1832 & 3. And even not entirely in them. We can't have[8] full confidence in Oliver's letters, nor in Joseph's history either. To my knowledge there are some things wrong in both! But is there such a thing on record as a prophet ever writing his own history? Oliver wrote his letters after he had gone teeth and toe nails into the spirit of WAR, which is the spirit of hell. He had assisted to change the name of the church. He had assisted for two days and evenings in the high council in Kirtland in August 23rd and 24th, 1834, to screen J. Smith from deserved punishment for great crimes which he had committed while on his way to Mo. with his "braves and veterans," in order to redeem Zion. The church of Latter Day-ites, they argued, was going to suffer if J. Smith was condemned; hence they made a scape goat of Sylvester Smith to bear the sin away. It killed Sylvester so far as the world was concerned. And in its results, it entirely broke down the council. No man who be-

6. The *Saints' Herald* does not reproduce McLellin's underlining.

7. The dates, cited from "History of Joseph Smith," *Times and Seasons,* 1 July 1842, 832, are typographical errors. Brigham H. Roberts noticed that the Manuscript History of Joseph Smith has the 5th and 7th, rather than the 15th and 17th, of April (B. H. Roberts, ed., *History of the Church of Jesus Christ of Latter-day Saints* [Salt Lake City: Deseret News, 1902-1912], 1:32n).

8. Here ends the available portion of the first page of the letter. Because the top half of page 2 is similarly missing, the text now returns to the published version in the *Saints' Herald.*

longed to that council has lived out half his days, or otherwise, so far as he has died it has been a most miserable death! And such will be the [page 437:] end of all those who composed that noted council, who are alive to-day. After all this misdoing, Oliver and Joseph wrote their histories. They were written at a time when the church had run wo[e]fully into falsehood and error, as to doctrine, government and practice.

Elder Bays says I refer to my ordination in 1835 as valid. I did not so state, nor do I now so hold. As to the endowment in Kirtland, I state positively, it was no endowment from God. Not only myself was not endowed but no other man of the five hundred who was present—except it was with wine! "THE CHURCH OF CHRIST CEASED TO EXIST." I assert that the Church of Christ did cease to exist when the authorities throwed away its name, its spirit and some of its doctrine. I again repeat that the Church of Christ fell in 1834, and J. Smith also fell, and was thereafter only president of that new church of Latter Day-ites. It matters not to me if all men on earth should say as Bays, "I unhesitatingly and persistently deny." I have the Book of Covenants as first printed in Kirtland, and I also have the minutes of the council when the name was first changed; they said, "Resolved that this conference recommend to the conferences and churches abroad, that in making out and transmitting of their proceedings, such minutes and proceedings be made out under the above tittle, of the church of Latter Day Saints." My book of Covenants, in the title page, has "Doctrine and Covenants of the church of [the] Latter day Saints: carefully selected from the revelations [ms. page 2:][9] of God, and compiled by Joseph Smith &c. presiding Elders[10] of s'd [said] church." The name of the church is several times given in that book as the church of Latter Day Saints. You wanted testimony, will this do you?

So far as the testimony of the Twelve published in that book is concerned it was a base forgery. The Twelve left Kirtland in May proceding on an eastern tour. They were ~~either~~ in the state of Maine, ~~or on their way homeward~~ or at least in the east.[11] They held their last conference in Farmington, Maine Oct. 2. 1835. ~ So their testimony could not in truth be in that assembly in Sep. 24, 1835. So much for that item. The ~~quotation~~ quotation from Jeremiah is not in point at all. His prophesy was

9. The text of the original letter is again available here and continues to the end of the letter.

10. The presiding elders are listed on the 1835 Doctrine and Covenants title page as Joseph Smith, Oliver Cowdery, Sidney Rigdon, and Frederick G. Williams. The *Saints' Herald* changes McLellin's "Elders" to "elder," which is incorrect.

11. McLellin adds "or at least in the east" between the lines.

burnt, but Joseph's was before him. Jeremiah did not alter, nor take out whole revelations or parts, but only added. He says the changes were made in June, 1832, which is not true. He says again, "A stream cannot rise above ~~the~~ its fountain." That's true. And in order to have Joseph and Oliver ordained legally he must have an Angel do it. An Angel never ordained a man to any ministerial office since the world began. Then say you how did Joseph and Oliver get authority to start? I answer, that a revelation from the Lord gives a man both power and authority to do whatever it commands. The Lord commanded Joseph to baptize, confirm, and ordain Oliver, then Oliver to do the same for him. This was legal and valid. [page 3:] Samuel anointed Saul & David kings. That was legal, altho Saml was no king himself. You say, "either accept the whole history, or throw it all away." No Sir, I will sift it and receive truth, but reject error. ~

Now Elder Sheen your first statement is simply untrue. You say the Star and Messenger and Advocate were published from June 1832 till Sep. 1836. The first No. of the re-printed Star is dated Jan. 1835. You thought Elder Bays was not equal to his task, and hence you wanted to help him. I am willing all the talent of your church shall take hold. Truth is mighty, and figures and dates wont lie. I have all Oliver's letters and I simply say they were all written after he had lost power to officially act according to the mind of the Lord. They were all written in the interest of Latter Day-ism; and hence cannot be depended upon. From the decision of that high council in Kirtland, on the 23rd of Aug., 1834, when they voted officially[12] to take upon them all the responsibility before God if Sylvester Smith would commit an unjustifiable act, by signing a document to excuse Joseph Smith. Wo be the spiritual power of the church from the 3rd of May 1834, when the name was changed, and after that wicked decision!

No such statement is in the book of Commandments as that John was ordained by an Angel when eight days old, as you stated. I know the paragraph relative to "Traveling Bishops, high Priests &c," never was printed until 1835, in the book of Covenants. Harp on it as you please. Such expression is not found either in the book of Commandments, or Star as printed in Zion. You speak of 1829. 32 & 3 thus, "This was the second time that these paragraphs were so published before the book of Commandments was published." The above is not true in any sense. Those things were not reprinted, or not printed at all until 1835. You say, "Will Mr McL. assert that Joseph was not so ordained." I myself attended

12. McLellin added "officially" above the line.

the Amherst Conference, and know positively that he was only ordained President of the church. Priesthood was not mentioned in his ordination at that time and place. You say, "I was to be High Priest, when I was ordained an Apostle." That's not true. No law of God defines such a rule. You speak again of an item "published in Jan. 1833.["] I want you to be correctly informed relative to dates before you write again. Its unfortunate for you that I have the original Stars as printed here, and also the reprint of Kirtland. You quote from a revelation given [in] 1830. Now after the word "I will drink of the fruit of the vine with you on the earth" [LDS D&C 27:5; RLDS D&C 26:2a], all after is not found in the Star or Commandments as printed here.[13] Hence away goes your Angel ordinations. This revelation[14] was got up in 1835, in order to sustain them in their dark views about angel ordinations.[15] You have failed entirely to prove that High Priests, or Aaronic priests either should exist in the "Church of Christ["] in the gospel day. Because you have made no quotations from documents printed before the church went into darkness, and altered and changed their revelations.

Your long quotations from the reprinted Star relative to David and my signatures to documents[16] adds nothing to your cause, but to mine. As to your statement about <u>name</u> I refer you to what I have already said. You say, the Star of 1832 and 3 contains many revelations which was afterward published in the "book of Commandments." This is simply not true. That book was not published after 1833. The additions were made to the revelations in 1835, and published in the Doctrine & Covenants. You say again, "That assertion is erronious, and I will wait for more definite charges, instead of undefined defamations." I state truths and facts, but its you that misrepresent. You state things, well, I'll say erroneous about the reprint of the Stars, about the priesthoods,[17] about the name, about the ordination of Joseph & Oliver, about Joseph's ordination in 1832, about a Seer being not ordained, In representing [page 4:] that Joseph ordained his seed or son[18] <u>legally</u>,[19] and I might go on but I'll stop in order [to] hear from you again. In the editorial of the May No. of the re-

13. The part introduced into the 1835 Doctrine and Covenants consists of D&C 27:5b-13; RLDS 26:2b-3b.

14. McLellin adds the word "revelation" above the line.

15. McLellin's wording, "their dark views about angel ordinations," is printed in the *Saints' Herald* as "their darkness about angel ordinations."

16. The *Saints' Herald* does not print the words "to documents."

17. The *Saints' Herald* prints McLellin's plural "priesthoods" as "priesthood."

18. McLellin adds "or son" above the line.

19. The *Saints' Herald* does not reproduce McLellin's underlining.

printed Stars we find for the first time in the world's history, "Progress of the church of Latter Day Saints." And in the same No. we find four columns ~~of~~ written on the change of name, headed, "To Saints." But the editor does not use the words Latter Day in that article. And in the next No. ~~and other~~ another is written of seven columns on the name. But in that lengthy article the word Latter Day does not yet appear. The editor must have been ashamed of the adopted name. O the folly of man.

In the reprinted Stars, (from which you quote,) all the revelations (I believe,) printed there, taken from, or professed to be taken from the old Stars printed in this city, are altered and changed. And when put in the book of Covenants were jumbled together in confusion. As I said whole revelations were made up (out of men's[20] brains) and added, and whole paragraphs also, relative to priesthood & Presidency. If you have the Stars as printed here, and as reprinted in Kirtland, by comparison it is plain. You say "the Stars reprinted in K[irtland]. was done from June 1832, until Sep. 1836." You ought to have known this is not true. The Stars from which you quote were not printed until Jan. 1835, and afterward. Not until the church had changed its Spirit, its name, and many of its doctrines, government & practice. Throwing all under false priesthoods.[21] I do know, (because I was personally there,) that most of the revelations in the book of Doctrine & Covenants were altered and changed from their original as first given, before they were printed in that book. The revelations given by or through J. Smith after he ceased to give them by the use of the Interpreter, by which ~~he~~ the book of Mormon was translated, cannot be altogether depended upon, after he ceased to give them in that way.

I had a long talk with Oliver Cowdery in Elkhorn, Wis. in 1847. I asked him to what did you ordain J. Smith on the 6th of April 1830? Said he "I ordained him Prophet, Seer, Revelator, and Translator just as the revelation says." All your remarks then on that subject amount to simply nothing provided they acted by divine appointment.

Now I have written a few things on the name,[22] on the two priesthoods, and on the Covenants. But much more could be written on these important subjects. I hope to see my strictures and reasonings in print, and acco[r]ding to your promise as an editor I shall certainly expect it. Great pains were taken to publish my former letters to Elder Bays, and the first one without my knowledge or consent. But this letter

20. The *Saints' Herald* prints McLellin's "men's brains" as "man's brains."

21. The *Saints' Herald* prints McLellin's plural "priesthoods" as "priesthood."

22. The *Saints' Herald* does not reproduce McLellin's underlining.

was refused the light,[23] but the reasons I know not. Accept my best respects.

I am as ever a lover of pure and unadulterated truth.

W. E. McLELLAN M. D.

23. The *Saints' Herald* does not reproduce McLellin's underlining.

11.

TO OLD FRIENDS, 22 FEBRUARY 1872

Independence, Mo Feb. 22, 1872

My old friends,

Yours of Feb. 1st came to hand, and I have just read it over again. I was born on the 18th of Jan. 1806., so you can answer enquirers. I calculate to live until I am 85, if I can. We too have had extremely cold weather this winter, but it is very pleasant to day. We have had but little rain, for a good while. We have had no serious accidents in our city this winter, except two small fires. We have good health. Grace C.[1] has been with us most of the winter. She attends School. Otherwise we are alone. I have no faith in J. Smith's criticisms. As to Urim, I say again it never was on this continent. I have learned more about it and the Interpreters lately. The Urim was used specially to inquire of God and get answers. The Directors were only used to translate languages, but never used to get revelations. Hence all the gam[m]on about getting revelations by or through the Interpreters is baseless. If you have the first edition of the Book [of Mormon], consult Pages 173, 216, [21]7, 328, 545-6. &c.[2] Also see Bible, Num 27:21. 1 Sam, 28:6. 1 Sam, 23:9. 30:7, 8. These pages and passages will explain what I mean. Joseph truly only read off the translation as it was translated and shown on the appearance of parchment before him, when his face was in darkness. True, he was the instrument through whom it was done! We ought to be properly informed, and so speak and write upon all subjects. [page 2:]

Young Joseph said when he assumed his place that he "believed his Father was a good man." "I never can believe my father taught Polygamy." Now his own Mother told me that "She knew he did." He also said, at that gathering, that "the Book of Covenant[s], was auxiliary to the Bible." They also publish in all their papers that he was a "martyred Prophet." If he died a martyr then wickedness was metamorphosed into righteousness. Tell me then if they are not bound to carry out his mea-

---

1. For a summary of Grace Clarke's life, see the Biographical Notes.

2. The page numbers correspond to Mosiah 8:13-9:1; 28:7-29:11; Alma 37:21-30; Ether 3:17-4:12 in the 1830 Book of Mormon.

sures—Polygamy and all. Or back square out of their position of a martyred Prophet! I think some of going to St Louis to attend the 6th of April Conference. I dont know yet. [Mark] Froscutt wrote me that the first half of my letter should come out the 1st of March. I talk about good Polygamists! provided there are any good in that class. "If hell is not partly full of such beings, then there is no kind of a hell![")]—J. B. Noble![3] I dont wish for any patience to talk about that "abomination." I had Mr Lee[4] here with me this winter—a rank Polygamist. I dont think the suits in Utah will amount to much—they can prove anything that they want. I should like to have Grace's picture, but have not means to spare. We have plenty, but live close. Today I have been to see that house about which I wrote to Mr Miller.[5] It is a good cabin, 16 feet square, with a good roof, and two large lots, one set to nice fruit, for $300. dollars—Tell me if he intends to come? You want me to come and see you—I think it doubtful! Had I means to spare I would travel some. The Headrickit[e]s here have brok[en] in two. One party assumes to be church of Christ, the other holds with Granville, I am doing but little only writing. I have my book almost finished, but have no means to print it. Tell your mother there are many—to me—mysteries in the words of the Books, and her inquiry about "the Balls in the net is one." My very best respects to all inquiring friends. As ever, W. E. McLellan ~

Altho this is one of the prettyest cities in the world, still times are very dull here, money is very scarce. There are three houses here selling out at cost, and three or four houses on the square empty and shut up. Kansas City—only nine miles away kills this place. It is a good time now to buy property here. A ~~house and~~ brick house on the next lot west [a group] of men bought a year ago at $24 hundred ~~a year ago~~, sold the other day for $15 hundred. I am as much in favour of Independence to day as I ever was. I have no disposition to leave Zion until the end comes. More judgements in [18]71 than for 20 years past.[6]

---

3. Joseph Bates Noble, a Utah polygamist, was called on a mission to the states in October 1871 and returned home to Utah Territory in March 1872. He must have met with Forscutt or McLellin in late 1871. If not, they were at least aware of his missionary endeavors in the Midwest. For a summary of Noble's life, see the Biographical Notes.

4. This is probably the polygamist Thomas LaFlesh Lee, who was called on a mission to the Midwest in November 1871 and returned home in April 1872. For a summary of Lee's life, see the Biographical Notes.

5. The identity of Mr. Miller is unknown.

6. This postscript was added upside-down in the top margin of the first page of the letter.

12.

TO JOSEPH SMITH III, JULY 1872

Independence, Jackson Co. Mo. July 1872

To President Joseph Smith.

I have thought for a great while I would address a letter to you. I want [that] you should read it carefully over before you lay it away as useless. I will try to write nothing but truth. I was very intimate and familiar with your Father from Oct. 1831 until Aug 1836. I certainly knew him well, for he attended my High School during the winter of 1834, and the winter of 1835 we learned Hebrew together in the same class. Here I had good opportunity to know his make and strength of mind. I was with him in many councils, and a number of general conferences when I was usually clerk. I traveled with him hundreds of miles, eat with him, slept with him etc. He attended with me two days while I debated with a Campbelite preacher. It seems to me but few men had better opportunities to know J. Smith for five years than I, except those who were with him all the time. ~ He professed to be Prophet, Seer, Revelator, and Translator. I firmly believe he was, Translator until he finished the Book of Mormon. But he delivered a revelation in March 1829 with these remarkable words in it, "And he has a gift to translate the book, and I have commanded him that he shall pretend to no other gift, for I will grant him no other gift." Book of Commandments, page 10.[1] Now if that was true it settles the whole matter. When the Book of Commandments was printed in this city in 1832 and 3, the printers would print off a form and sen[d] it to Kirtland to the Presidency, and if anything was wrong it was marked and sent back. I presided in a council in Hiram, Portage Co. O[hio]. In Nov. 1831 in which J. Smith, O. Cowdery, and S. Rigdon were appointed a committee to read over and prepare the revelations for the press. Thus Joseph had two chances to know if they were correct. I am aware that those important documents

---

1. BofC 4:2; cf. D&C 32:1, published two years later and significantly revised: "*you* have a gift to translate the *plates; and this is the first gift that I bestowed upon you;* and I have commanded that *you* should pretend to no other gift *until my purpose is fulfilled in this;* for I will grant *unto you* no other gift *until it is finished*" (LDS D&C 5:4; RLDS D&C 5:1d, modern editions).

were altered **three** times before they appeared in the Doctrine and Covenants. And there were many other great changes made in the Church. But more of this hereafter.

When Joseph delivered the 116 pages of the translation to Martin Harris, his plates, his interpreters, and his gift were taken from him for some two months. The plates and gift of translation was restored to him, but not the interpreters. He translated the entire book of Mormon by the use of a little stone he had in his possession before he obtained the plates. His deliverance of those pages was a great blunder! I had a long talk with O. Cowdery in Wisconsin in 1847. I asked him this question, "To what did you ordain J. Smith on the 6th of April 1830." He said, "I ordained him Prophet, Seer &c. Just as the revelation said to me." When he finished the translation of the Book thereafter he did not see—that is he did not use his stone. So say all those who were intimate with him at the time. In Oct. 1831 I wrote a revelation as he delivered it. And I know he used no stone to see then. I set by hours and heard him (what you call) translate the Bible. I know that he used no stone then. But I only call that production a correction of the Bible!! Instead of a translation. I have seen the stone by which he translated often. But I ask was he a Seer on the day the church was organized? Did he have the Interpreters. I say no! distinctly no!! No man can be a Seer without the means. He did not possess the means hence was not, nor could not be Seer. Because he once possessed the gift, and finished what the Lord gave him to do, it does not follow that he must always keep seeing and translating. And that without the Directors!!

I know the claim is made for You that you are a Seer. But I ask you candidly do you yourself believe you are a Seer? When you have no means to see or translate with either. But if you have I should be extremely glad to learn it. I am very anxious to find and see a Seer of the Lord. But again, Joseph had a revelation for Oliver and friends to go to Canada to get a copy-right secured in that Dominion to the Book of Mormon. It proved so false that he never would have it recorded, printed or published. I have seen and made a copy of it, so that I know it existed. So do all those connected with him at the time. Oliver's revelation to go to the Indians proved untrue. It says, "You shall go unto the Lamanites and preach my gospel unto them, and[2] cause my church to be established among them. Book of Com. page 67." Utterly false. His system of confer-

2. BofC 30:7; the 1835 D&C (51:3) and current editions (28:8; RLDS 27:3a-3b) have the added conditional statement at this point: "inasmuch as they receive thy teachings thou shalt."

ences was without foundation in God's word. It was Catholic and Protestant. In Nov. 1831 he or rather they–the committee altered his own revelations materially–so as to take out whole paragraphs and add others. This was eminently wrong. In the first place God spoke what he meant, and meant what he spoke, if he spoke at all. In April 1832 Joseph set up the "order of Enoch" in the land of Zion–as this was called–and gave to the nine members each a false name, as Gazelam, Palagoram &c. Wrong again. He established that every man that joined the church might be ordained. Miserable. His appointing and ordaining Edward Partridge a Bishop to take care of church property has no warrant in the word of God, nor in church history either. His consecration law (as at first revealed) could not be put in force in any state in this nation, and I don't know as it could in any place in the world. It and the tithing law is directly in opposition to each other, hence both could not be true or from God!! His word to Zion by Orson Hyde and John Gould for the men of the church to stand in their own defence, caused the church to be driven out of the county! It was contrary to the pure principles or precepts of the Gospel of Christ, and the best interests of man. There was no precept, or pattern, similitude or parallel in the Lord's revealed word for his High Council set up or established on the 17th of Feb. 1834. It was a great blunder and an anomily. Three Elders could have done the business better, and much cheaper, and saved much valuable time. ~ His spirit of **war** scattered and diffused in all the church in 1834, to go and gather up "the strength of the Lord's house" to go up to Mo. To try to reinstate the church back upon their lands in Jackson Co. was extremely wrong and wicked. Evidenced by the Cholera's taking ~~taking~~ some of their best men. Some sixty had it, and 14 died!! O my soul[,] think of hundreds of men traveling more than a thousand miles and accomplish a solemn nothing!! And during their journey to Mo. in their "warrior camp" Joseph had a furious quarrel with Sylvester Smith–his adjutant General. And they would have fought, but was prevented by their brethren. This was over an old dog!![3] And when they had got back

3. After logging many miles with Zion's Camp, Sylvester Smith threatened to kill Joseph Smith's dog because it had been harassing Sylvester for several days. As the story goes, Joseph replied: "If you kill him, I will whip you!" to which Sylvester replied that he would defend himself. Thereupon Joseph announced a revelation that the Lord would punish those who murmured or were contentious. The camp soon succumbed to cholera and several men and animals died. Among the casualties was Sylvester's horse, which was seen by some as fulfillment of prophecy. On their return to Kirtland, Joseph moved to have Sylvester censured; Sylvester responded by bringing a complaint before the Kirtland High Council claiming Joseph had been abusive and was unjustified in censuring him. The council, siding with Joseph, ordered Sylvester to confess that he had "wickedly and maliciously

to Kirtland, a charge was preferred, and two days and evenings was spent by the High Council in its investigation. The result was that Sylvester is required to sign a document—usually since called a lie bill[4] — S. Smith had proved his charges, but the argument was "that it would ruin the church for J. Smith to be condemned and have to confess." So the decision and judgement was given against Sylvester. He refused to sign the document. [page 2:]

But his older brother took him out and persuaded him to sign it and thus save the church and Joseph. A thought struck him. He went in and told the council, "If you will take all the responsibility before God for the act of signing: I will take the responsibility before the world." They voted to do so, and the fatal deed was perpetrated! This deed entirely killed Sylvester in the eyes of the world; and in its results broke down the council!! All those who composed that council, who have died[,] died an untimely, miserable death! Or did not live out half their days. Witness uncle J. Johnson,[5] L. E. Johnson, Joseph Coe, (he was pummeled to death by a bull), Joseph and Hyrum Smith, and Roger Orton. Then those not living out their days. Saml. H. Smith, Luke Johnson, and Oliver Cowdery. I know not how some have passed away. But I do know there was never a more wicked official business performed on this wide earth.

His appointment and ordination of a Patriarch to bless the church, has no precedent in God's word, hence null and void. It was trying to combine the Patriarchal age with the Gospel era. It cannot be done in truth and verity. He set aside his "order of Enoch" in Zion, and established one in Kirtland with much nonsense and many false names. And it never accomplished even one good object. It was entirely foreign from the order of heaven. Away then with such foolish nonsense. His calling and ordination of Apostles in Feb. 1835, instead of having Christ personally to call, and appoint, and ordain them was wrong in the extreme. They could not be Apostles of Jesus, but they were only Apostles of Jo-

---

accused our brother Joseph Smith, Jr. with prophesying lies in the name of the Lord." According to McLellin, Sylvester signed the statement under pressure and "fear of punishment." See Fred C. Collier and William S. Harwell, eds., *Kirtland Council Minute Book,* 2nd ed. (Collier's Publishing: Salt Lake City, 2002), 41-58; also discussed in Roger D. Launius, *Zion's Camp: Expedition to Missouri, 1834* (Independence, Mo.: Herald Publishing House, 1984); James LeBrande Bradley, *Zion's Camp: Prelude to the Civil War* (Logan, Utah: By the author, 1990).

4. By calling the confession as a "lie bill," McLellin emphasized that it had been coerced and was unreliable.

5. The reason McLellin lists John Johnson as his uncle is that his wife's mother was sister to John Johnson's wife. See the Biographical Notes for Emeline Miller McLellin and John Johnson.

seph Smith. An Apostle is witness, and he (as Paul) must see Jesus in order to be his witness. His appointment of more seventies than **one** has no precedent or pattern. Moses had one Seventy, and Jesus had one Seventy as a patter[n] after Moses. On the 3rd of May 1834 he assembled a council in Kirtland of the first authorities[,] entirely throwed away the "name of Christ" for the church, and named it the "church of Latter Day Saints." This was in violation of every principle of sacred truth in the book of Mormon on that subject. Finally, on the 8th of July 1834 he assembled a kind of general assembly of all the Elders of Zion, and all his "camp following," then living, at Elder L. Wights and organized another highest council or court of fifteen men. Then ordained David Whitmer President of it. Then ordained him to be his Successor, to stand as Prophet, Seer, Revelator, and Translator in his stead for the church. ~ But before he left Kirtland on his "warrior tramp" he took a deed to the Temple lot as "trustee in trust" for the church. Thus combining temporal and spiritual power together, like the Popes of Rome.

But now I ask, had Joseph the right to gather the Gentiles to Zion? I want to look at this subject in the light of the book of Mormon. 1st edition. Take pages 32, 85, 117, 488, 499, 501, and 514.[6] Take page 501 Chap. 10 Nephi. And no subject can be plainer. "If the Gentiles will repent I will establish my church among them, and they shall come into the covenant, and be numbered among this the remnant of Jacob & they shall assist my people, the remnant of Jacob; and also, as many of the house of Israel as shall come, that they may build a city, which shall be called the New Jerusalem; and then shall they assist my people that they may be gathered in, which are scattered upon all the face of the land, in unto the New Jerusalem. And then shall the powers of heaven come down among them; and I also will be in the midst" [cf. LDS 3 Ne. 21:22-25; RLDS 3 Ne. 10:1-4]. At every place you will find it said, "Behold they (the Gentiles,) shall be numbered among my people, O house of Israel." But it is never found that the Gentiles are gathered and then the house of Israel to come in among them. No wonder the inhabitants of Zion were driven out, for they had no business to be gathered! There is no warrant for a Gentile gathering in the Book, until after the Lamanites and Is[r]ael are gathered.

Yes, Christ intends to establish the "Church of Christ" among the Gentiles that ["]through their mercy Israel may obtain mercy." He will then as the Book says, "And I also will be in the midst" [3 Ne. 21:25]. He

6. The page numbers correspond to 1 Ne. 13:39-14:4; 2 Ne. 10:15-25, 20:2-14; 3 Ne. 16:12-17:5, 20:42-21:7, 21:22-22:5, 30:2-4 Ne. 1:7 in the 1830 Book of Mormon.

will be there to call, appoint, and ordain his own Apostles. "And then shall the powers of heaven come down among them. Then shall the work of the Father commence among all the dispersed of my people" [3 Ne. 21:25-26]. Glorious day! Happy hour!! Not as formerly with Joseph or his son Joseph either in calling their Apostles when nothing but ceremony, sectarian ceremony was manifested. I am aware of what I say, and am responsible to God for my views. That gathering will be the Lord's—not man's, and it will be with power, and the saints will never be driven from their possessions. But they "shall build the waste cities and inhabit them; and they shall plant vineyards, and drink the wine thereof; and they shall make gardens and eat the fruit of them. And I will plant them upon their own land, and they shall no more be pulled up, saith the Lord God. Amos 9:14."

Now in as much as you are a candid man, you will look at these things honestly and fairly. I have spent about two years since I retired from active business persuits in carefully, studiously, and prayerfully reading, writing and reflecting upon the great work of the Last Days. My motto was and is "I will without prejudice or preconceived opinions embrace truth, and only truth." I have tried to see why so many thousands ran with Joseph into so many errors, and then followed Brigham Young to Salt Lake, and ran greedily into so many abominations!! And I think I've found the cause.

Now Joseph I will relate to you some history, and refer you to your own dear Mother for the truth. You will probably remember that I visited your Mother and family in 1847, and held a lengthy conversation with her, retired in the Mansion House in Nauvoo. I did not ask her to tell, but I told her some stories I had heard. And she told me whether I was properly informed. Dr. F. G. Williams practiced with me in Clay Co. Mo. during the latter part of 1838. And he told me that at your birth your father committed an act with a Miss Hill[7]—a hired girl. Emma saw him, and spoke to him. He desisted, but Mrs. Smith refused to be satisfied. He called in Dr. Williams, O. Cowdery, and S. Rigdon to reconcile Emma. But she told them just as the circumstances took place. He found

7. The identity of "Miss Hill" is unknown unless Linda King Newell and Valeen Tippetts Avery are correct that McLellin erred here, confusing the protagonist of John Cleland's 1749 novel, *Fanny Hill,* with the real individual McLellin mentions a few lines later, Fanny Alger (*Mormon Enigma: Emma Hale Smith, Prophet's Wife, "Elect Lady," Polygamy's Foe, 1804-1879* [Garden City, New York: Doubleday, 1984]: 66). By comparison, Richard S. Van Wagoner (*Mormon Polygamy: A History,* 3d ed. [Salt Lake City: Signature Books, 1992], 6-8, 21n7) found a distinction in the narrative between two separate episodes, the earlier of which would have occurred near the birth of Joseph Smith III in November 1832.

he was caught. He confessed humbly, and begged forgiveness. Emma and all forgave him. She told me this story was true!! Again I told her I heard that one night she missed Joseph and Fanny Alger.[8] she went to the barn and saw him and Fanny in the barn together alone. She looked through a crack and saw the transaction!!![9] She told me this story too was verily true. Now I would not have told you this had it not been for one thing. You said in your speech at Amboy April 6th 1860, "I believe my father was a good man, and a good man never could have promulgated such doctrines." You referred to Polygamy. Now let me tell you my dear Sir. I asked your Mother particularly upon this point. She said, one night after she and Joseph had retired for the night, he told her that the doctrine and practice of Polygamy was going to ruin the church. He wished her to get up and burn the revelation. She refused to touch it even with tong[s]. He rose from his bed and pulled open the fire with his fingers, and put the revealment in and burned it up. But copies of it were extant, so it was preserved. You say, "I have never believed it and never can believe it." Can you dispute your dear Mother? She related this to me, and will if you ask her tell you the same thing. It made a powerful impression on my mind at the time, and I've often reflected on it since. Now Sir suppose you could be convinced that your father not only believed in Polygamy but actually practiced it his individual self, then what would you say—and then do about it? Was he an <u>Adulterer</u> so long ago, and still a "good man." You say, "I believe in the doctrines of honesty and truth." So do I. But I can't believe your father continued to be a religiously honest man. No sir. I can't for if I should I would have to believe your Mother a liar, and that would be hard for me to do, considering my acquaintance with her. [page 3:]

You say again, "It is my determination to do right and let heaven take care of the result." What a glorious determination! I advise you to stick to it. That's been my mind for years past. I feel that I <u>know</u> I love the Lord Jesus, and the glorious principles of the Gospel. But I dont—I cant love falsehood, hypocracy, and wrong doing. And I see so much wrong-doing in Joseph's official cases, I could not go with him, nor could I go with **ONE** who takes up <u>the work</u> where he left it. They prac-

8. For a summary of Fanny Alger's life, see the Biographical Notes.

9. Todd Compton, *In Sacred Loneliness: The Plural Wives of Joseph Smith* (Salt Lake City: Signature Books, 1997), 35, acknowledges differences between this account and Chauncey Webb's statement that "Emma was furious, and drove the girl, who was unable to conceal the consequences of her celestial relation with the prophet, out of her house." Compton resolves the discrepancy by pointing out that "whether Emma saw her husband in the barn or discovered evidence of Fanny's pregnancy, her reaction was the same."

ticed so much wrong that I quit them in 1836. And even now in looking back over the matter I am not sorry! only for the cause. In the spring of 1836 I took a mission south and returned the last of June; but only returned to find the Presidency to a great extent absolved in temporal things. They had gone to New York and run into debt about forty thousand dollars for goods—which was never paid!!! They brought on a kind of stuff they called French Cordial. It would intoxicate. I myself saw your father so much under its influence that he could not **walk strait!** You may doubt what I say, but it matters not. They formed a kind of an association and kept it up until they went into that swindling Kirtland banking concern, about which so many lies were prophesied. Popularity, and drinking, feasting and hilarity was the order of the day. The Presidency and leading men got up a ride to Cleveland, some 15 couple[s]. Fine dressing, fine carriages, fine harness and horses as the country produced were hired, and they set out. They drove into Cleveland and through the streets round and round to show Big. People inquired who is this? O its Joseph Smith—the Mormon Prophet! They put up at a first class hotel, called in the wine &c. Some of them became high, and smashed up things generally. Next morning their bill was over two hundred dollars. No matter—we are Big-merchant-men of Kirtland. Next day on their way home they took dinner at Euclid, and imbibed so freely that when they started home they commenced running horses, turned over and smashed up one buggy so they had to haul it home in a wagon. But no confessions were ever required or made. All seemed to go swimingly!! But I sickened! I left!! I could tell much more.

But now what I know about Joseph's revelations. In Nov 1831 in council in O[hio]. Joseph, Oliver, and Sidney were appointed a committee to prepare them for being printed in the book of Commandments. I know because I was present, that they were materially altered, then sent to this City for publication. In the spring of 1832 Joseph &c. came to this place and in council it was determined—Here I'll give an item from your father's history. "W. W. Phelps, O. Cowdery, and J. Whitmer be appointed to review and prepare the revelations for publication." This was their second alteration. Sep 24th, 1834 more than twenty material alterations in one revelation. Remember that altered, mutilated thing is what you now have in the book of Doctrine & Covenants. And you claim authority according to it. You seem to base your authority to act as Prophet, Seer &c according to it. What! dont you think God could speak plainly without alteration? Then why change the sentiment? My dear Sir, let me tell you that you stand on a slippery foundation, and the floods will sweep you away. But say you I have thousands with me, and we are prospering greatly in numbers being added. Do you prosper more than the Latter Day Saints did from [18]40 to [18]45? And where are those thousands today? They are mostly with Brigham, sunk into the lowest degradation of crime. What do you think your end will be?

Disappointment, wo[e]ful disappointment!!! I feel sorry that you took the position you did. Had you come out squarely on original principles then you would have been right. But my hopes are now very slim. That old book of Covenants–is not true, and to stand upon it "the hail will swap away the refuge of lies." I know I write plain but I cant write otherwise about all Latter Day Saintism. But now as to the two priesthoods claimed by the church. How an intelligent man can hold them as the L.D.S. do, with the plainness of the books before him I cant see. Such a word as priesthood is not used in the book of M[ormon]. in its Gospel history. The word is not found but twice in the New Testament outside of the 7th of Hebrews. The words minister, ministers, or ministering is usually used in the inspired books instead of priesthood. It is an impossibility for a High Priest to exist legally in the "Church of Christ" in the gospel dispensation, except Christ only. But one High Priest could exist under the law era at one time. Christ is the anti-type to that one, or to Aaron. He and he alone is now High Priest. But as to the story of John, the Baptist ordaining Joseph and Oliver on the day they were baptized: I never heard of it in the church for years, altho I carefully noticed things that were said. And today I do not believe the story. Now why? The law with its ministry was only a "shadow of things to come" [Heb. 10:1]. When the substance came[,] the "shadow," was done away. There is not a word said in both the books the N.T. and book of M[ormon][10] about Aaronic, or Levitical, or Lesser priests as existing in the Gospel age. All the testimony must be drawn from the Book of D. and C. But three orders of ministry existed under the law. It was a shadow. Now there must have been a substance that made the shadow. That substance could not have more than three orders. Elders, Priests or Bishops, Teachers or Deacons was the substance. But says you they had a High Priest, Elders, Priests, and Teachers in the book of M[ormon]. So the "church of Christ" has a High Priest, Elders, Priests, and Teachers.

I believe in a high Priesthood. In an order of ministry. In all the ministry mentioned in the Books. High Priest, Elders, Bishops, and Deacons; or High Priest, Elders, Priests, and Teachers–which is the same

10. In the manuscript McLellin later added "the N.T. and book of M" above the line.

thing. But says you what will you do with Apostles, Prophets, Evangelists, and Pastors? I answer, an Apostle is not an administrative officer. When they ministered they did it as Elders. Prophets were not administrative officers either. And Evangelists were traveling Elders merely; and Pastors were Bishops, or Priests. In this way the book of M[ormon]. and the New Testament are reconciled and harmonized. I can see no earthly use for Lesser priests. I can find nothing for them to do, that the ministry of the "church of Christ" could not do better. I hold that Apostles, Elders, Bishops, and Deacons are all in the Melchesidick Priesthood with Jesus as the High Priest—holding different stations only. ~ Moses personally appointed his twelve Num 13. Jesus personally called and ordained his twelve at Jerusalem Mark 3:14. And he called and ordained his twelve Disciples on this continent. Mind you Moses and Jesus personally did this work. No man can be a true Apostle of Jesus without personally knowing him. Those chosen were Apostles but not High Priests. If a man is an Apostle he always acts as an Elder in administering ordinances. An Apostle hold[s] this position in the Priesthood. An Elder is an Elder in the Mechesidic priesthood—and so on. Priesthood is not an office but an order of ministry.

An Aaronic priest's whole duty was pointed out by the law, and when the law was abolished then the rule by which they should act, which defined their duties, was all set aside also, and hence there was nothing for them to do. The whole order was set aside also. All the ministers of the first-born who started from Goshen to Canaan with Moses, were all set aside when the law priesthood was established—offset by the Levites, and the remainder redeemed by paying five shekels into the treasury Num 8:18. 3:47. Then if the law priesthood was set entirely aside, we have an example of the same or similar transaction in the numbers of the first-born. We have not a hint of the Aaronic or law priesthood's ever acting [page 4:] after the Gospel ministry was instituted by Jesus Christ. I say no hint in the New Testament or book of Mormon.

But it supposeth me that I am writing much for nought. Because Joseph Smith has taken his position and will not probably alter. But I will touch a few more points. Now all L.D.Sism claims that Joseph Smith translated the Book with Urim and Thummim, when he did not even have or retain the Nephite or Jaredite Interpreters, but translated the entire Book of M[ormon]. by means of a small stone. I have certificates to that effect from E. A. Cowdery (Oliver's widow,) Martin Harris, and Emma Bidamon. And I have the testimony of John and David Whitmer. The Urim was never on this Continent. Its use was to inquire and receive the word of the Lord direct. Num 27:21. I Sam 28:6. 30:7, 8. But was never used to translate languages. The Directors or Interpreters seem to have been prepared for the special purpose of interpreting or translating languages, but not to inquire and get revelations from God. The Book says, "Now these things were prepared from the beginning, and were handed down from generation to generation, for the purpose of interpreting languages + + + and whosoever has these things is called Seer, after the manner of old times. Page 216" ["]I will cause that these stones shall magnify to the eyes of men, these things which ye shall write Page 545." ["]I can assuredly tell thee, O King, of a man that can translate the records: for he hath wherewith he can look, and translate all records that are of ancient date Page 172." The Urim was used alone for the purpose of inquiring of God. The Interpreters were used alone for the purpose of interpreting languages. They were not used interchangeably. Now by this we see how all L.D. Saints have been deceived, and beli[e]ved erroneously in this item.

Now I will write a few things about dedications. When Solomon dedicated his Temple at Jerusalem power was manifested and displayed. God sent down fire from heaven and burned up the sacrifise, and filled the house with his glory. When Jesus was dedicated in his ministry, after his baptism the heavens were opened upon him, and the Holy Spirit came down, and abode upon him; and a voice from the excellent glory, saying, "This is my beloved Son" [Matt. 3:17]. When the Apostles were dedicated for their ministry on the day of Pentecost, the whole room was filled with the power of God. And "sat upon each of them" [Acts 2:3]. When the Disciples on this land were dedicated to carry out their mission on earth, they were so filled with the power of God that even their garments, as well as their countenances shined with the glory of God until they were whiter than the driven snow." But when the land of Zion was dedicated by J. Smith and his Elders in 1831, it was done as sectarians would do it by ceremony, and ceremony only, without any power being shown forth. The great God did not acknowledge its performance by any of his displays or foot steps. The Lord kept entire silence because he did not acknowledge it by any act of his power. When that noble structure the Temple in Kirtland was dedicated, after only being partly finished, it was done without any power being sent forth, or manifested in any degree to the large congregation assembled in it. I was present and know what I say. In 1836 when they undertook to get an endowment in the Kirtland Temple. All washed and with oil anointed themselves, and appeared in the Temple at sunrise, then all feet were washed, and about five hundred ministers took their places, and solem[n]ly prayed. We remained there fasting until sunrise next morning. We however partook of some bread and wine in the evening. And some partook so freely, on their empty stomachs, that they became **drunk!** I took care of S. H. Smith in one of the stands, so deeply intoxicated that he could not nor did sense anything. I kept him hid from the crowd in the stand, but he vomited the spit-box five times full, and his dear brother Carlos[11] would empty it out of the window. But I would prefer to draw a curtain over the awful scene! Other[s] imbibed to[o] much also. But let the curtain fall!! ~

This was a dedication with a vengeance to it, instead of pure power from the Lord. Take Solomon's Temple, Jesus consecration, the Apostles at Jerusalem, and the twelve disciples on this land and power was displayed in each case. But no power in any of Jos. Smith's dedications. Please to make the contrast and tell why! If it was not transgression, what was the cause of so much disappointment?

I think now on carefully reading this over, that every sentence and sentiment in this letter will bear strict scrutiny and investigation. I want you should read it carefully over. I send it to you and wish you to show it to Elders [Isaac] Sheen, Rogers,[12] Banta[13] and as many others as you may feel disposed. I am content to present the truth to you, and others. And I know I have prayrfully endeavored to do so—unmixed with any falsehood. If in any matter I was convinced I was wrong I would retract gladly. You may think me an enemy. But I assure You I have kindly feelings for yourself, and the family of the Smiths. You may say, "Well the old Dr is a great Apostate!" But I firmly believe in God, and in the sacred book of Mormon—with it wide open, and not shut up. And I do know I am a lover of pure truth.

Now I wish you to direct your particular attention to the revelation of March 1829. "For I will grant him no other gift."[14] The gift of translation was ~~was~~ his particular gift—or rather the reading off the translation as it appeared before him. God's word (if he spoke it) was verily true. Hence all his pretensions to other gifts were untrue. But in the spring of 1830 the revelation relative to the Canada mission was certainly untrue. Now if he delivered a word by pretended revelation which was positively

11. For a summary of Don Carlos Smith's life, see the Biographical Notes.

12. For a summary of Israel Lewis Rogers's life, see the Biographical Notes.

13. For a summary of Elijah Banta's life, see the Biographical Notes.

14. BofC 4:2; two years later D&C 32:1 amplified this passage to: "for I will grant *unto you* no other gift *until it is finished*" (LDS D&C 5:4; RLDS D&C 5:1d in modern editions).

false, then I ask you how we can depend upon any of his future predictions. How could we tell as to their truth or falsehood? Now, I cant help but stand in doubt. Especially as it was said to him that he should not have "those gifts." But there is no accounting for the credulity in man! I have a copy of this letter, and if you give it to your friends it will be well—but if not I can send it to them.

I am most respectfully yours. I am as ever,

[signed] W. E. McLellan M.D.

I received the 1st Aug. Herald
this morning. Sep. 8th/72[15] ~

N.B. Now if you want the truth consult this letter closely. You may go on in your course, but I will not bid you God-speed in miserable L.D.S.ism. If a man has opinions or beliefs different from mine, I dont discard him for that reason. Opinions and beliefs are free to enjoy, and I am willing to have them freely expressed and still have no malise or prejudice against the man. All I ask is for a man to be candid and honest. And now Joseph I feel and know I wish for pure truth in all my religious views and feelings. I would not intentionally speak or write to injure the character or feeling of any man living or dead. But I have to look at things with my own eyes, and according to my own judgement. And I try to realize that I will have to be judged according to the "deeds done in the body." I do not write this for publication, but for your own eyes. Will You please to answer some of the points in this letter, and very much ob[l]ige me. You can tell me what you think of it. I want you to know one thing, I feel no e[n]mity at any man for differing with me in views, on religious matters. Nor for the expression of those views. I have read this letter to a number of my friends in order to have them criticize it. And I have thought much about the propriety of sending it. I send it in order that you may be properly informed as to matters while I was intimate with your Father, and the Church. But I'll close ~

Prosperity to You in all righteous undertakings. W.E.M. ~

15. This dated comment is written upside down, probably after the *nota bene* statement that follows.

13.

TO DEAR MARY, 30 AUGUST 1872

Independence, Mo. Aug. 30th 1872.

Dear Mary,[1] and all the friends,

Yours of the 27th inst. came in this morning. I had began to think I was either forgotten or then You must all be dead or dying!! But finally the silence was broken, and I find you all alive; and I think You must be much improved, in order to wait on company as you did while Elder Froscutt was with You. I consider him a gentleman, but <u>much</u> in the dark on many points in religion. My letter has finally come to light in the Herald, altho it took 4 papers to publish 12 columns of matter.[2] But they could or did afford 16 columns all in <u>one</u> paper to publish [Isaac] Sheen's long article in the examination of my letter to Elder Bays.[3] I was glad to see my letter in print altho it had to be divided, and come to light in papers so far apart. I think I was <u>meanly</u> treated, for it took me more than a year to get it in their columns at all. They divided my letter so as to neuteralize the effect. If any man can get fairness or honesty in L.D.S.ism he can do more than I. It requires trickery to carry out that dark, and condemned, and damning ism, in any and all its parties. But most miserable thing let it die! You can read that letter in confidence, for it contains truth!

Moses waited forty years in the land of Midian, keeping the flocks of Jethro, But how long the Lord will wait <u>now</u> before the <u>great work</u> of the <u>Last Days</u>, will commence, and he will establish his church among the Gentiles I have been unable so far to learn. I am seeking to know daily, and feel just as though I should know soon. Yet how long I know not.

[page 2:]

I have been writing a long letter to Joseph Smith—a large foolscap sheet full—double lined—as I am writing this letter. In it I have many

---

1. Although someone, most likely an RLDS archivist as a cataloging note, wrote "McClellands letter to Aunt Mary" in the top margin of the letter, the recipient's identity remains unknown.

2. McLellin's letter was published in *The True Latter Day Saints' Herald,* Mar.-Aug. 1872, represented in the current collection as Letter 10.

3. See Letter 6 in the current collection.

things of importance to him. Still my hopes are very slim as to his profiting by them. I think his course is fixed, and he is determined not to alter or change. But I say wo betide his cause, for it will sink, and never be heard of in Celestial glory. All the power there is manifested among them arises from Spiritualism. Or is Spiritualistic. The Lord never has given to the Church with his Father's work or his either the gift of tongues as to the Apostles on the day of Pentecost. Now I know this is a big sweep, but it is not to[o] big to be true. I could give you some strong reasons, but I prefer to let you think. I may tell hereafter.

But now I ask had Joseph the right to gather the Gentiles to a Zion? I want to look at this subject in the light of the Book of Mormon. 1st Edition. Take pages 32, 85, 117, 488, 499, 501, and 514. Take page 501 in last Nephi, chap. 10. And no subject can be plainer. "If the Gentiles will repent +++I will establish my church among them, and they shall come into the covenant, and be numbered among this the remnant of Jacob +++and they shall assist my people the remnant of Jacob; and also, as many of the house of Israel as shall come, that they may build a city which shall be called the New Jerusalem; and ~~then~~ then shall they assist my people that they may be gathered in, +++unto the New Jerusalem. And then shall the power of heaven come down among them, and I also will be in the midst" [cf. 3 Ne. 21:22-25]. At every place you will find it said, "Behold, they (the Gentiles,) shall be numbered among my people, O house of Israel" [3 Ne. 16:13]. But it is never found that the Gentiles are gathered, and then the house of Israel to come in among them. No wonder the inhabitants of Zion were driven out, for they had no business to be gathered!! Yes, Christ intends to establish the church (not organize it.) among the Gentiles that "through their mercy Israel may obtain mercy." He will then as the book says, "And I also Will be in the midst" [LDS 3 Ne. 21:25; RLDS 3 Ne. 10:4]. He will be there to call, appoint, and [page 3:] ordain his own Apostles. "And then shall the power of heaven come down among them. Then shall the work of the Father commence among all the dispersed of my people" [cf. LDS 3 Ne. 21:25-26; RLDS 3 Ne. 10:4]. Glorious day! happy hour!! Not as formerly with Joseph or his Son Joseph either in calling their apostles, when nothing but ceremony, sectarian ceremony was manifested. I am aware of what I say, and am responsible to God for my views. That gathering will be the Lord's–not man's, and it will be with power. And the Saints will never be driven from their possessions. But they "shall build the waste cities, and inhabit them. ~~And I will plant them upon their own land~~, they shall plant vineyards, and drink the wine thereof, and they shall make gardens and eat the fruit of them.

And I will plant them upon their own land, and they shall no more be pulled up, saith the Lord God." [cf.] Amos 9:14[-15]. A few things about dedications. When Solomon dedicated his Temple in Jerusalem power was manifested and displayed. God sent down fire from heaven and burned up the sacrafise and filled the house with his glory. When Jesus was dedicated in his ministry, after his baptism, the heavens were opened upon him, and the Holy Spirit came down and abode upon him; and a voice from the excellent glory, saying, "This is my beloved Son" [Matt. 3:17]. When the Apostles were dedicated for their ministry on the day of Pentecost, the whole room was filled with the power of God. And it "sat upon each of them" [Acts 2:1]. When the Deciples on this land were dedicated, to carry out their mission, they were so filled with power that even their garments, as well as their countenances shined with the glory of God, until they were whiter than the driven snow" [cf 3 Ne. 19:25]. But when the land of Zion was dedicated by Joseph Smith, and his Elders in 1831, it was done as sectarians would do it, by ceremony! and ceremony only!! without any power being shown forth. The Lord did not acknowledge its performance by any of his displays or foot-prints. He kept entire silence because he did not acknowledge it by any act of his power. When [page 4:] that noble structure the Temple in Kirtland was dedicated–after only being partly finished, it was done without any power being sent forth or manifested in any degree to the large congregation assembled in it. In 1836 when they undertook to get an endowment in the Temple. All washed, and with oil anointed themselves, and appeared in the Temple at sun rise, then all their feet were washed, and about ~~about~~ five hundred ministers dedicated themselves by solemn prayr. We remained there fasting until sun rise next morning. We however partook of some bread and wine in the evening. And some partook so freely, on their empty stomachs, that they became **drunk!** I took care of S. H. Smith, in one of the stands, so deeply intoxicated that he could not nor did not sense any thing. I kept him hid from the company but he vomited the spit-box full five times, and his dear brother Carlos would empty it out at the window. But I would prefer to draw a curtain over the awful drunken scene! Others imbibed to[o] much also. But let the curtain fall!! This was a dedication with a vengeance to it, instead of pure power from God. Take Solomon's Temple, Jesus consecration, the Apostles at Jerusalem, and the twelve Disciples on this land, and power was displayed in each case. But no power in any of Jos. Smith's dedications. Please to make the contrast and tell me why! If it was not transgression, what was the cause of so much disappointment?

The Urim & Thummim was never on this continent. Its object or use[4] was to to[5] inquire and receive the word of the Lord direct. Num. 27:21. 1 Saml. 28:6. 30:7, 8. But it was never used to translate languages. The Directors or Interpreters was used for the special purpose of interpreting or translating languages; but not to inquire and get revelations from the Lord. The book says, "Now these things were prepared from the beginning, and were handed down from generation to generation, for the purpose of interpreting languages +++and whosoever has these things is called Seer, after the manner of old times.["] Page 216 [LDS Mosiah 28:14, 16; RLDS Mosiah 12:19, 21]. ["]I will cause that these stones shall magnify to the eyes of men, these things which ye shall write.["] Page 545 [LDS Ether 3:24; RLDS Ether 1:89]. ["]I can assuredly tell thee O king of a man that can translate the records: for he hath wherewith he can look, and translate all records that are of anci[e]nt date[."] P. 172 [cf. LDS Mosiah 8:13; RLDS Mosiah 5:72]. The Urim was used <u>alone</u> for the purpose of inquiring of God. The Interpreters were used <u>alone</u> to interpret languages. They were never used interchangeably. Now by this we can see how[6]

4. The words "or use" were added above the line.

5. McLellin accidentally doubled the word "to."

6. The extant document—a sheet of paper folded to make four pages—ends here at the bottom of page 4. The letter continues, but the remaining portion has not been preserved.

14.

TO JOHN L. TRAUGHBER, 11 MARCH 1875

I imagine there is not a man living that has taken the pains that I have, and that has had my opportunities to form correct intelligence concerning that is[s]ue.[1] I commenced my acquaintance in 1831. I first was ordained an elder, then a high priest, then a councillor in the High Council, then an apostle; but left them in 1836, and never held any connection with Joseph Smith until the day of his death.

Joseph's widow,[2] told me in Nauvoo, in 1847, that she knew that Joseph practiced it[3] himself; and I believed her then, and so I do now. She said she knew that Joseph did have the Polygamic revelation. No doubt they carried it to an alarming extent in Nauvoo before they were killed. Young Joseph knows better than to hold or publish that his father was not a polygamist. I wrote the facts to him, and referred him to his own mother; but still he publishes abominable falsehoods on that subject.

This short extract from Letter 14 is from John L. Traughber, "Some Statements by Dr. W. E. McLellan," 1. Traughber's quote marks around each paragraph have been removed and his bracketed comments placed in the notes. This same approach will apply to the display of subsequent letters to Traughber.

1. John L. Traughber added: "[He refers to Mormonism]."
2. Traughber added "[Emma Smith]."
3. Traughber added "[polygamy]."

15.

TO JOHN L. TRAUGHBER, 6 DECEMBER 1875

I visited Mrs. Emma Smith in Nauvoo, in 1847. She told me plainly and frankly that her husband did receive and deliver the Polygamic revelation himself, and she knew he practiced its provisions. And she said she knew he had committed adultery with girls previous to that.

I wrote several letters that were published in the Herald, but they never tried nor pretended to answer the last one they published. They did well to be silent, for what I wrote was plain truth and unanswerable. In the March No., 1872, June 1st, 1872, July 15th, and August 1st, 1872–scattered in the four numbers may be found some of my arguments; but I admitted more then than I could conscientiously do now, after my own mature deliberations and investigations.

Relative to my abuse of the Smiths, I have this to say: At Far West, in 1838, seven or eight of the leading men were taken prisoners late in the evening. Next morning it rained a little, but Capt. Guest[1] wanted to see Smith. He was about the middle of the encampment of some three thousand men, closely guarded by a Captain's company, who stood about three feet apart, with their faces turned inward toward the prisoners. They allowed no man to approach nearer than five feet. I stood back with those who wished to see. Joseph observed me and said, "Come up and shake hands with me." Said I, "The guard will not let me." Said he, "Come in here." Capt. Searcy[2] was well acquainted with me, and said to me, "You can go in, Sir." I went in and talked with him an hour or two. Nothing unpleasant happened there. But when they were taken to Richmond, Ray Co., and confined and chained together in a cabin and guarded, I went to Mr. G. Robinson[3] on business; but Smith

---

This short extract of Letter 15 is from John L. Traughber, "Some Statements by Dr. W. E. McLellan," 1-2.

1. Captain Guest has not been identified.

2. The identity of Captain Searcy is unknown, though he could be the Colonel Searcy of Ray County mentioned in Heber C. Kimball's June 1834 journal (Stanley B. Kimball, ed., *On the Potter's Wheel: The Diaries of Heber C. Kimball* [Signature Books and Smith Research Associates, 1987], 192-93).

3. For a summary of George W. Robinson's life, see the Biographical Notes.

would not suffer me to do any business, but railed on me fearfully! Until the Captain who went with me, said to me, "D__m him, knock him down!" I said, "No, he is a prisoner; I will not hurt him." He[4] sent up a charge to the General commanding. I was sent for. I took the Captain who heard Smith's railing, who stated facts. I was released. I have been a little particular in this matter because Latter Day Saints love to bat me, but I fear them not. In those matters I have a conscience, (like Paul), void of offense.

4. Traughber added "[Smith]."

16.

TO JOHN L. TRAUGHBER, 19 FEBRUARY 1877

When the Book[1] was translated, and at the printer's with the copy-right secured, Joseph delivered a long revelation for O. Cowdery and others to go to Kingston in Canada, and get a copy-right secured in that dominion, to the book, in order to sell it and make money out of its sale. They went, but did not succeed; and the revelation proved so false that Joseph never would have it printed or put [it] with his other revelations either.

This short extract of Letter 16 is from John L. Traughber, "Some Statements by Dr. W. E. McLellan," 2-3.

1. John L. Traughber added "[of Mormon]."

17.

TO JOHN L. TRAUGHBER, 7 MAY 1877

•

As to Joseph Smith's revealing: He would usually seat himself, and seem to be in deep contemplation for a few moments, then commence and deliver a sentence or a part of a sentence to his scribe, who would write it down, then read it vocally, then J. S. would deliver more–and so on till the communication was finished. Smith never wrote any himself; he always had a scribe to write for him.

J. Smith's revelation for Cowdery to go to Canada was never printed. M. Harris had the copy that I read, in manuscript.

This short extract of Letter 17 is from John L. Traughber, "Some Statements by Dr. W. E. McLellan," 3.

18.

TO JOHN L. TRAUGHBER, 22 JUNE 1877

I felt determined to visit Richmond. I went there on the first of June, on Friday, and stayed among the Whitmers until Monday morning, then came home with a heavy heart, and remained so until the next Saturday—fasting and praying. Finally, on Saturday I received light, and that was that that peep-stone by which they professed to receive communications by John Whitmer's little son[1] of ten years old, was not of God. I was very much impressed to return and make known my knowledge on that special point; and on the 16th, I went down to the neighborhood. +++ Thence I passed on to Richmond two miles to consult David. Our interview ended without any profit or satisfaction to me. I finally told him that I knew that peep-stone seeing was not of God. He said [page 23:] he knew it was: so our Knowledge clashed. +++ I had hoped to see the Church of Christ arise with David Whitmer as its principal prophet; +++ but when I found that David and all hands were under the guidance of a peep-stone in the hands of a little ten year old boy, my old heart sickened and I turned from it and them with no ordinary feelings."[†]

This short extract of Letter 18 is from John L. Traughber, "David Whitmer: 'The Last Witness' of the Book of Mormon," 22-23.

1. This ten-year-old could not have been a son of John Whitmer. Of Whitmer's three sons, John Oliver was born in 1835 and died in 1846; Jacob was born in 1844, married in 1871, and would have been thirty-three at the time; and Alexander was born in 1849 and was killed in the Civil War. However, Whitmer's grandson, John Edward Johnson, was thirteen at the time—the son of Whitmer's daughter, Sarah Elizabeth. For a summary of John Edward Johnson's life, see the Biographical Notes.

[†]"In other letters, the Doctor expatiates on the matter thus," continued John L. Traughber, who quoted McLellin as follows:

> Little John sees cave beyond cave in which sacred records are deposited. Sees the Temple being built, the stones of white marble having been prepared by the Nephites of old, and all the blocks of stone numbered, and will be raised to their places without the sound of a hammer; the stones are now buried near the spot. Sees large numbers of Israelites near the north pole, and they are soon to come in large ships, by way of California. They are a kind of giant race. Sees also a small dwarfish race on that continent near the north pole. Sees also large, curious animals with three horns upon their heads, on that land. Sees the unfaithful saints with black spots upon their garments at the present time. As to David

Whitmer and his ism, I am perfectly satisfied it is not of the Lord's direction. +++I once had great confidence in David; I must say I have lost much of it. Still I can't help but like the man, although when I was at Richmond last, he really abused me and said to me that if I did not repent I must "go to hell." I told him I had nothing in that matter to repent of. +++I don't like going to hell where David wanted to send me for telling the truth. I think he had spirits in him at the time he was talking to me.

19.

TO JOHN L. TRAUGHBER, JULY 1877

Smith called a general conference on the 8th of July.[1] In that conference he organized the "High Council of Zion," and ordained David Whitmer as its First President. He then ordained David as Prophet, Seer, Revelator and Translator. Then gave him a most thorough charge to be faithful in his station."[2]

This short extract of Letter 19 is from John L. Traughber, "Some Statements by Dr. W. E. McLellan," 3.

1. John L. Traughber added "[1834]."

2. Traughber added: "[This was done in Clay Co., Mo., July 8th, 1834.–J.L.T.]"

20.

TO JOHN L. TRAUGHBER 25 AUGUST 1877

I joined the church in 1831. For years I never heard of John the Baptist's ordaining Joseph and Oliver. I heard not of James, Peter and John doing so. These things were gotten up in after years in order to sustain them in their false Priesthoods. Nothing was said about Aaronic priesthood, (at least I never heard of it), until in the year 1832. I heard S. Rigdon preach (he [Rigdon] said) his first sermon relative to Aaronic priesthood that year. At first there was nothing said in the church about priesthood. It was an after "get up." There was nothing said, according to my recollection, about Urim and Thummim for some years. The two priesthoods were not fixed up for some years after the church started. A Patriarch was not set up (I think) until 1834. The 18th of March, 1833, S. Rigdon and F. G. Williams were ordained counsellors in the Presidency. On the 6th of June, 1831, in a conference in Kirtland, several elders were ordained to the High Priesthood ([as] Joseph says) "for the first time."

This short extract of Letter 20 is from John L. Traughber, "Some Statements by Dr. W. E. McLellan," 3-4.

21.

TO THOMAS FULLER, 1877

I found that Smith did not always tell the truth. He would drink to excess. He and others of the Presidency went to New York and run in debt Forty thousand dollars, (which was never paid.) The leading men went into pride, fine dress for themselves and their women. Took expensive rides, costing them hundreds of dollars, while the poor among them were suffering for the necessaries of life. He materially altered his own revelations before they were ever printed.

This short extract of Letter 21 is from Charles W. Lamb, brother-in-law of the recipient, in Lamb's letter to the editor of *The Return*, Nov. 1890, 364.

22.

TO JOHN L. TRAUGHBER, 14 DECEMBER 1878

J. Smith and S. Rigdon came to Zion (here) in April, 1832, and set up a secret order of nine men, and gave to each one a fictitious or false name. The order was called the "Order of Enoch." I came here as a high priest, according to their system, in May, 1832. I was very familiar with their leading men, and was with them in their open councils; but I never heard of this secret council till I went to Kirtland, in 1834. It was set up as an "everlasting order," but two years afterward it was set aside and another "Everlasting Order" set up in Kirtland, Ohio. Deliver one from such folly! But my eyes were holden in those days, because I had confidence in J. Smith.

The first of November, 1831, a council was called in Joseph's translating room. I presided, and of course would notice and know all that passed in that council. The object of the council was to determine relative to printing Joseph's revelations. Hours were spent in talking the matter over, and it was finally decided to have them printed. Joseph, Oliver and Sidney were appointed a committee to read them over and prepare them for the press. In the revelations it was often said, "Keep these things from the world." These expressions were taken out, and many other alterations–material alterations–[were] made in their reading. I stood by hours and saw them do this work. In this condition they were sent to Mo. by O. Cowdery and John Whitmer, in a bound blank book. But in April, Joseph and Sidney came to Mo., and held another council, and appointed Phelps, Cowdery and [John] Whitmer a committee to read over the revelations and alter them again, when they thought they could better the language. Thus, they were twice altered before they were printed. Then when the printing establishment was destroyed here by a mob, we sent O. Cowdery to Kirtland with the book of revelations. He went to New York and bought another press and [page 5:] set it to work in Kirtland. Another committee is formed by adding Dr. [Frederick] Williams to the former one. This committee revised all the revelations,

---

This extant portion of Letter 22 is from John L. Traughber, "Some Statements by Dr. W. E. McLellan," 4-10.

and changed them so much that a man would scarcely know them to meet them in a brush-heap! This is the book out of which Latter Day Saints have to read and learn doctrine and government for their church! Deliver me from such altered and bungled (said to be) revelations. I have no use for that book of Doctrine and Covenants only as a relic of folly.

After the mobbing here in 1833, Joseph delivered a revelation containing these words, "Renounce war and proclaim peace" [LDS D&C 98:16; RLDS D&C 95:3d]; but in about two months they held a council in Kirtland, comprising the highest authorities of the church, and determined on war; and sent Orson Hyde and John Gould all the way to Zion to tell the men to stand up and fight if oppressed by a mob. "Fight in defense of pure religion." We did fight; and that was the great reason why the church was driven from this county and never allowed to return again. But January 1st,[1] we held a council in Clay Co., and sent Lyman Wight and P. P. Pratt to Kirtland in order to consult the first authorities of the church, relative to our forlorn condition. Wight told Joseph that if he had an hundred men, he could redeem Zion. A proclamation was issued to the Eastern churches to gather up their war material and come to Kirtland by the first of May. About an hundred men came, and the 4th of May was set to start for Zion. But on the 3d. was the important council called to deliberate concerning the change of name. In this, the name of the "Church of Christ" was set aside, and S. Rigdon made a motion, and N. K. Whitney seconded it, to call it the church of "Latter Day Saints." They wore this name for three years, then changed again, and called it "The church of Christ of Latter Day Saints[.]"[2] Then in Far West[3] they started a little paper called the "Elder's Journal," in which they dubbed it as it stands today, "The church of Jesus Christ of [page 6:] Jesus Christ of[4] Latter Day Saints." I am only giving you history. Latter Day Saintism was born in war, and it will die in war! Joseph left Kirtland at the head of his braves, and as he advanced he gathered forces, until when he reached Clay Co., Mo., he had some four hundred men well armed. But the day

1. John L. Traughber added "[1834]."

2. The name of the church at its organization in April 1830, the Church of Christ, was changed in May 1834 to the Church of the Latter Day Saints, then by revelation in April 1838 to the Church of Jesus Christ of Latter-day Saints. There is little support for McLellin's suggestion regarding another intermediate name, the "Church of Christ of Latter Day Saints." See Susan Easton Black, "Name of the Church," in *Encyclopedia of Mormonism: The History, Scripture, Doctrine, and Procedure of the Church of Jesus Christ of Latter-day Saints,* ed. Daniel H. Ludlow (New York: Macmillan, 1992), 3:979.

3. Traughber added "[1838]."

4. In starting a new page of the transcript, Traughber accidentally doubled the words "Jesus Christ of."

they reached Clay Co., about seventy were taken with Asiatic Cholera, and fourteen died. Joseph disbanded his men, and most of them returned home. Thus all their calculations of redeeming Zion by the <u>sword</u> were blasted; and evil, and only evil, attended that warrior tramp of some one thousand miles, on a fool's errand; and, yet, this is not all.

Joseph returned to Kirtland, and they continued to build a Temple of some 80 feet by 65. And when it was dedicated, (being only partly finished), the committee of three, who superintended its erection, were in debt some $30.000. On March 29th, 1836, that great house was dedicated with a great deal of <u>ceremony</u>. On the 6th of April, 1836, the ministerial authorities, about five hundred in number, entered that house at sun-rise, and remained fasting until next morning, sun-rise, in order to receive an <u>endowment</u>, but utterly failed in their endeavor! It was more an endowment with <u>wine</u> than power from God. In a day or two, I, individually, went to Joseph and told him plainly that I was disappointed. Said he, "What do you want?" I told him I wanted knowledge and power from God; that as an Apostle I might go forth to the nations of the earth, and preach to them in their own <u>lip</u> the pure gospel of the Lord. He rose and laid his hands upon my head and prophesied: "Go South on a mission. Go to the tops of the highest hills, and to the bottom of the lowest valleys, or ravines, and call fervently on God, and before you return, you shall receive all that you desire." I hesitated not; but started on the 9th of April, and wended my way to the Ohio River, and down that to Cincinnati, then out into Kentucky, and preached and built up some branches and strengthened others. But far in the woods, [page 7:] the last of June, in a deep ravine, I was praying–full length on my face–when a still, small voice said to me, "Get up and go home." But I said, "No; for I was sent here by a prophet of the Lord," (as I supposed). I continued to pray, but the voice spoke to me again, and I could not mistake it. It went through me with a shock. I prepared, and the second day I sat out for home; but reached there the last of June to find that the Presidency of all the church had gone to New York and bought $40.000 worth of goods; and next morning after I returned home, six wagon loads of these goods rolled into Kirtland, and they filled two stores and set to work. Mind you, these were the leading men–the Presidency.

Soon fine dressing and fine parties were the go; and soon a fine ride was determined upon. Some fifteen couples hired fine carriages, [with] fine harness[5] and fine horses and when all was in readiness, they sat out

5. Wilhelm Wyl, *Mormon Portraits; or, The Truth about the Mormon Leaders from 1830 to 1886* (Salt Lake City: Tribune Printing, 1886), 309, has "with fine harness and fine horses."

for Cleveland, some 19 miles distant. They drove round and round through the streets. People gazed and inquired: "Who's all this?" "O, it's Joe Smith, the Mormon prophet, and his company." They put up at a first class tavern; called for a room, refreshments, and something to drink. Some of them became intoxicated and they broke up about $200 worth[6] of dishes and furniture. Next morning they paid their bill, and sat out for home. They stopped at Euclid–half-way–and took dinner, and again drank freely; and after they sat out for home, they commenced running horses and turned over a buggy and broke it up so they had to haul it home on a wagon. But all went swimmingly. We are great merchantmen, money plenty! But no confessions were ever required or made in the church for this wild goose chase. My lady was not in condition, so I did not go on this ride; but two of the men who did go told me about it.

They still continued their parties and their drinking to excess, until I sickened, and, with a heavy heart, left the place and church, and wended [page 8:] my way to Illinois, with my companion and two little children.[7] I wrote a letter to J. Smith, and sent him my license; but they returned it to me two years afterward, and I have it yet. I said in my letter: "Suffice it to say, when any one wants to know why I left you, I tell them, 'It was because I lost faith in the Heads of the church.'["] And from that day to this, I have not regained it! Could any rational man blame me for thus leaving a people who were running after riches and pleasures of a wor[l]dly kind, instead of seeking the welfare of Zion? The leaders left spirituality and ran full tilt after worldly things. I never united with Joseph after I then quit him, although they sent me back my license; but this was through the influence of the Twelve. They could not bear the idea of having one leave their number and company. They almost perfectly knew me, and I now think they loved me.

They still carried sail, till in 1837, they set up a Kirtland Bank, without a charter from the state. It ran awhile–long enough to get monied men of the church to take stock in it; but it broke down to the financial

---

6. In ibid., 309, Wyl has "about twenty dollars' worth," which seems more reasonable.

7. In ibid., Wyl quoted the previous paragraph and opening sentence of this paragraph. In doing so, he corrected "sat out for" to "set out for" in all instances, changed "miles distant" to "miles away," and omitted the sentence "My lady was not in condition, so I did not go on this ride; but two of the men who did go told me about it." For emphasis, he placed nine words in italics. He may have correctly transcribed the letter in two instances where Traughber likely miscopied it: (1) Wyl has "with fine harness and horses," Traughber "fine harness and fine horses"; (2) Wyl has "twenty dollars' worth of dishes," Traughber "$200 worth of dishes."

ruin of many confidential men. The state authorities fined Smith and Rigdon $1.000 each, and they ran away from Kirtland in the night, hidden away in a wagon! They went to Far West in the winter of 1837-8. On the 4th of July,[8] the inhabitants of Far West had raised a tall liberty pole on their square, with a flag floating from its top; and S. Rigdon made a tremendious speech at its base. In a few days a cloud arose in the West, and hovered over that pole. A vivid flash of lightning struck it at its summit and literally shivered it to its base. After the shower, men gathered, marvelling at what had happened to their liberty pole. Joseph came and walked over the splinters and prophesied: "If our enemies come upon us, they shall be shivered to splinters, as this pole has been torn." But the sequel proved the entire reverse. The Latter Day Saints were required to give up their arms, and soon leave the state. Smith and [page 9:] four or five others were taken and confined in Liberty jail for several mo[n]ths. Thus the shivering was on the other foot.

The Witnesses had quit Smith during their bank troubles in Kirtland, in 1837, and Cowdery and David Whitmer had removed to Far West. But when Joseph and Sidney came there, they soon set up a band of Danites, and swore them to obey the Presidency of Joseph and Sidney. In their deliberations they passed a decree to kill the "Dissenters," as they called all who would not go with the Presidency, or who would oppose them in their measures. They[9] heard of this decree, and about sunset pretended to be going to hunt their cows, but in reality to get away. They met about a mile away, and determined to go about twenty-five miles to Dr. McLellan's. They did well for about nine miles, but in the darkness of the night lost their way, and wandered all night in a twelve mile pra[i]rie. Next morning they reached my house, and I entertained them for about a week, until they got their wives away from Far West. These men were O. Cowdery, D. Whitmer, John Whitmer and L. E. Johnson. In a few days Jacob Whitmer brought them their coats, as they had come away without them. The Danites went to their houses and required their wives to leave without anything only the clothes they had on, and they did so; and their goods were confiscated. But woe was the doom of that Presidency and their Danites in a few weeks. Thousands of men marched to Far West and inflicted untold hardships on those wicked men. But I must give one more piece of history. During the wars, back and forth, J. Smith took about sixty men, well armed, and went out into Davis Co., as much as 60 miles, and scared away the inhabitants and

8. Traughber added "[1838]."

9. Traughber added "[Dissenters]."

gathered their household and farm goods and hauled them in wagons into Far West. But when ~~they~~ the army came near Far West, they hauled those goods out about half a mile N.W., near the stone quarry, and threw them in piles in a little bottom. I, myself, went to [page 10:] see them, and saw an old man who said he came about 60 miles for his goods. I think there were as many as ten wagon loads of goods scattered in that little bottom. I marvelled greatly to see them. P. P. Pratt took a number of men from Adam-Ondi-Ahman, and went down to Kingston, the county seat of Davis county, and scared away the keepers and robbed the stores of what they wanted; and Pratt took a keg of nails on his horse before him. When he reached home, he threw down the nails, declaring: "Nails are cheaper here than in Boston." But I'll quit on evils and wrongs in the West. I was never in Nauvoo until 1847; but from reliable men's stor[ies], I believe things grew worse and worse until the death of the Smiths.

The Josephites take up the work where old Joseph left it, and are trying to pack it onward; but it is a heavy load and will finally break their backs. I will now give you reasons why I cannot believe in the doctrines and practices of the Young-Josephites, and will try to be candid and unprejudiced.

I don't believe in carrying so much iniquity and wrong doing as Joseph's father introduced. Such, for example as milking the Gentiles; such as killing Dissenters, or even bitter persecutors; in running into debt thousands of dollars. Emma Smith told me in Nauvoo, in 1847, that there was proved against the estate of Joseph Smith, in probate court in Carthage, Hancock Co., Ill., over $200.000, but not a dollar to pay the debt! The $40.000 for goods in New York, nor their fines for banking without a charter were ~~never~~ ever paid. +++Mrs. Smith told me that she knew her husband practiced both adultery and Spiritual Wifery! And that she also knew that he had the Polygamic revelation. I say, again, Oh! deliver me from so much false doctrines and all the practices growing out of them. Go into such things I cannot. I would have to be made over; my mind would have to be "holden" again.

23.

TO JOHN L. TRAUGHBER, 5 JANUARY 1879

As to the means, or Interpreter, or stone by the use of which J. Smith read off the translation, or the words as they apeared before him: I have the written certificates of Martin Harris Emma Smith and Elizabeth Cowdery, Oliver's widow; besides, the statements of David and John Whitmer, all agreeing substantially in one. I always understood from the first that J. S. read off the 116 pages by means of the Interpreters found with the plates, and thereafter used a small stone. I have many times seen that peculiar stone; but I could not see anything with it. It would not, when put in a dark place, give any light to my eyes.

"It was more an endowment with wine than power from God."[1] About five hundred ministers entered that great Temple about sunrise, and remained fasting until next morning sunrise, except a little bread and wine in the evening. The Twelve were required to take large servers, and set glasses of wine and lumps of bread, and go through the house and serve the brethren. I did my part of the serving. During the night, a purse was made up, and a wagon sent nine miles to Painesville, and a barrel of wine procured, and then it was a time. All the latter part of the night I took care of Samuel H. Smith,[2] perfectly unable to help himself. And I had others removed from the house, because they were unfit to be in decent company.[3] I am sorry that candor and truth requires me to say so much. +++As to E. Robinson,[4] I am not astonished at his statements, since his awful race with S. Rigdon. I could tell you things about that man that would sicken your stomach, even if you do have strong digestive powers! After I heard of their performance, I wrote this couplet:

This short extract of Letter 23 is from John L. Traughber, "Some Statements by Dr. W. E. McLellan," 11-12.

1. McLellin quotes his own statement from Letter 22 in response to Traughber's presumed question about it.

2. For a summary of Samuel Harrison Smith's life, see the Biographical Notes.

3. This paragraph, from "About five hundred ministers entered" to this point, is quoted in Wilhelm Wyl, *Mormon Portraits; or, The Truth about the Mormon Leaders from 1830 to 1886* (Salt Lake City: Tribune Printing, 1886), 308-09, the only variance being the omission of "nine miles." For emphasis, Wyl placed eleven words in italics.

4. For a summary of Ebenezer Jay Robinson's life, see the Biographical Notes.

So sickish is the theme, that from it
The muse must turn awhile to vomit: [page 12:]
With heaven made nerves and filthy hunks,
It would physic more than a million of skunks.

That will do for Ebenezer. I know that a great many statements made in that little "Advocate,"[5] are wholesale falsehoods; because I was there, and was a close observer of matters and things. I left the old church for less causes than I see in this late uprising.[6] As I said in a former letter my mind was then "holden," so that I did not see the false doctrines that they believed and advocated. I left them because of the conduct of the leading men—the Presidency. Standing where I did, as one of Joseph's Apostles I was bound to uphold the first authorities. As an honest man I could not, hence I peaceably withdrew, and when I settled in Illinois, I wrote to Joseph a letter, enclosing my license, and merely said: "Suffice it to say, when any one asks me why I left you, I say to them, It was because I lost confidence in the Heads of the church."

5. Traughber added "[Blair's Saints' Advocate]." For more on William Wallace Blair, see the Biographical Notes.

6. Traughber added "[Reorganization]."

24.

TO JOHN L. TRAUGHBER, 1 OCTOBER 1879

He[1] submitted willingly to be ordained President of the High Council of Zion by J. Smith, in 1834, when no such council could be instituted or set up in the church of Christ, hence, illegal and void. He submitted to be ordained President of the whole church, also Prophet, Seer, Revelator and Translator by Joseph Smith on the 8th day of July, 1834. This whole proceedure was outside of the revelations of God to man. No man was ever ordained by man Prophet, Seer, or President of the whole church, since the world began, so far as inspiration informs us.[†]

This short extract of Letter 24 is from John L. Traughber, "Some Statements by Dr. W. E. McLellan," 12.

1. Preceding his extract from this letter, John L. Traughber wrote, "Speaking of David Whitmer, Dr. McLellan says."

[†]After transcribing extracts from Letters 22-24, John L. Traughber wrote the following:

> The foregoing extracts are taken from letters written to me by Doctor McLellan. The letters were all written at Independence, Mo., where the Doctor resided from 1869 until the time of his death, March 14, 1883. I visited Dr. McLellan in April, 1881, and walked with him over the "Temple Lot" lying west of the court house in Independence. He showed me the spot of the temple and related the farce of consecrating first the whole land of Zion, then the temple lot, and lastly the spot of the temple. He said that the laying of the cornerstone of the temple, which is spoken of in Mormon works as something great, consisted of a ceremony over a rock which Martin Harris picked up in a little hollow which is on the temple lot.
>
> As it may be a matter of question in the minds of some people why the Doctor's name in Mormon works is spelled differently from the manner in which he spelled it in later years, I will state the explanation which he gave me. He said that he spelled his name McLellin till a son of his went from home to attend school, when his son got to spelling it McLellan, when he adop[t]ed and retained that form of spelling it.
>
> I talked with Dr. McLellan and his wife about the endowment at the Kirtland temple, 1836. They stated that before Samuel H. Smith became dead drunk, he staggered up on the stand of the First Presidency and delivered a prophecy. Mrs. McLellan remarked that the Latter Day Saints seemed to think that it was all right for Samuel to be drunk, and spoke of it as almost a miracle that he could deliver a prophecy when he was so drunk he could hardly stand.
>
> In 1879, I asked David Whitmer, at Richmond, Mo., if he was along with that party who rode to Cleveland, mentioned in one of Dr. McLellan's letters to

me. He said he was not, but that Oliver Cowdery was, and that Cowdery told him that it would have been a disgrace to worldlings [i.e., mortals], to have acted as some of the party did; and that Hyrum Smith becoming intoxicated by drinking at the table said: "While we are having a spree, let us have one that is worth something," and thereupon raised his cane and broke up the dishes on the table.

Believing that these extracts and statements are true, as they came from persons who would rather have spoken in favor of Joseph Smith than against him, and deeming them important as showing the character of Joseph Smith and others to be inconsistent with their profession, I submit them to the consideration of thoughtful people.

J. L. Traughber, Jr.

Mandeville, Mo., May 23, 1884.

Four days later Traughber swore in an affidavit before a notary public that these extracts from McLellin's letters were accurate.

25.

TO UNIDENTIFIED RECIPIENT, CA. 1878-1879

On the 6th of July, 1834,[1] in Clay County, Mo., Joseph Smith and Frederick G. Williams ordained David Whitmer President of the Stake of Zion.[2] Then Joe said the time had come when he must point out and ordain his successor. Said he: "Some have supposed that Oliver Cowdery would be the man, but the Lord has made known to me that David Whitmer is the man." Joe and Williams then stepped out and ordained David to be "Prophet, Seer, Revelator and Translator["] and "President of the whole Church" to be Joe's successor.

This extract was published in Wilhelm Wyl, *Mormon Portraits; or, The Truth about the Mormon Leaders from 1830 to 1886* (Salt Lake City: Tribune Printing, 1886), 295, the only existing source for this letter. Since Wyl quoted from two additional McLellin letters (Letters 22, 23), for which John L. Traughber left extracts, we know that Wyl corrected for punctuation and spelling, added italics for emphasis, and omitted some phrases without adding ellipses but was otherwise a reliable copyist. The same level of accuracy and license may be assumed for the current text. Wyl failed to mention the name of the recipient or date of composition for any of the three letters he cited.

1. Since McLellin consistently gives the date as 8 July 1834 (see Letters 6, 12, 19, 24), the "6th of July" was probably an error on Wyl's part. For support of the 8 July date, see Max H. Parkin, "A History of the Latter-day Saints in Clay County, Missouri, from 1833 to 1837," Ph.D. diss., Brigham Young University, 1976, 232n25.

2. Wyl added "[Missouri]."

26.

TO JAMES T. COBB, 14 AUGUST 1880

Independence Mo. Aug. 14th 1880. ~

Mr. J. T. Cobb.[1]

Yours of Aug. 9th lies before me, and has been carefully read and considered. I did not answer your former letter, because I did not think I could do any good by it, and I now have doubts as to any good resulting, but I'll comply with your request.

I am "opinionated." When I thoroughly examine a subject and settle my mind, then higher evidence must be produced[2] before I change. I have set to my seal that the book of Mormon is a true, divine record and it will require more evidence than I have ever seen to ever shake me relative to its purity. I have read many "Exposes." I have seen all their arguments. But my evidences are above them all!

I have no faith in Mormonism, as an ism, even from its start, neither have I in Latter day Saintism from its start—through all its developments. I have no confidence that the church organized by J. Smith and O. Cowdery was set up or established as it ought to have been. And the further its run[,] its run [is] still farther from the true way—farther from the plain simplicity of that **Divine** record, the Book of M[ormon]. I dont know that I am surprised at a thinking man for rejecting L.D.S.ism as its now developed in any and all branches of what is called Mormonism ~

But when a man goes at the Book of M. he touches the apple of my eye. He fights against truth—against purity—against light—against the the[3] purist, or one of the truest, purist books on earth. I have more confidence in the Book of Mormon than any book of this wide earth! And its not because I dont know its contents, for I probably have read it through

1. For a summary of James T. Cobb's life, see the Biographical Notes.

2. Larry C. Porter has "introduced" instead of "produced" ("William E. McLellan's Testimony of the Book of Mormon," *Brigham Young University Studies* 10 [Summer 1970]: 486; "McLellin Expresses Feelings in Letter," *Church News* insert, *Deseret News,* 8 Dec. 1985, 6).

3. The word "the" was unintentionally repeated at the end of one line and beginning of the next.

20 times. I have read it carefully three times[4] within a year, and made many notes on it. It must be that a man does not love purity when he finds fa[u]lt with the Book of Mormon!! Fight the wrongs of L.D.S.ism as much as you please, but let that unique, that inimitable book alone. I have but little confidence in the purity of a man's life or in his principles of action after becoming acquainted with that Book, and then fight or oppose its divine excellency! Hence, you may know what I think of your course!!

When I first joined the church in 1831, soon I became acquainted with all the Smith family and the Whitmer family, and I heard all their testimonies, which agreed in the main points; and I believed them then and I believe them yet. But I dont believe the many stories (contradictory) got up since, for I individually know many of them are false.

My advice to you is cease Your opposition and strife against the Book, and fight against wrong doing in **professors**: for you might just as well fight against the rocky mountains as the Book!

David Whitmer has lost his thumb of his right hand several years ago, and cannot write. And he would not be willing to write much to a man who fights the Book of M. which he knows to be true. I saw him June 1879, and heard him bear his solemn testimony to the truth of the book–as sincerely and solemnly as when he bore it to me in Paris, Ill. in July 1831.[5] I believed him then and still believe him. You seem to think he and I ought to come out and tell something–some darkness relative to that book. We should lie if we did, for we know nothing against its credibility or divine truth.

I can but hope you will alter your course and use your talents ~~and~~ energy and all your exertions in behalf of the truthfulness of that glorious volume!!

With profound respect for truth, purity & holiness I subscribe myself a lover of all that is true and wholesome.

I as ever. W. E. McLellan M.D.

P.S. Like you I want to add a few words. I never had but one letter from you until this one. You seem to think S. Rigdon the bottom of all

4. Porter has "through" instead of "three times" ("McLellan's Testimony," 486; "McLellin Expresses Feelings," 6).

5. In the first entry of his earliest journal, McLellin wrote: "D[avid] Whitmer then arose and bore testimony to having seen an Holy Angel who had made known the truth of this record [Book of Mormon] to him" (Jan Shipps and John W. Welch, eds. *The Journals of William E. McLellin, 1831-1836* [Provo and Urbana: BYU Studies and University of Illinois Press, 1994], 29).

M.ism. Many people know better. He never heard of the work of Smith & Cowdery, until C[owdery]. and P. P. Pratt brought the Book to him in Mentor, O. True enough, I have but little confidence in S. Rigdon, but I know he was more the tool of J. Smith than his Teacher and director. He was docile in J. S. hands to my knowledge ~

I left the church in Aug. 1836, not because I disbelieved the Book [of Mormon] or the (then) doctrine[6] preached or held by the Church, but because the Leading men to a great extent left their religion and run into and after speculation, pride, and popularity! Just like the Israelites and the Nephites often did. I quit because I could not uphold the Presidency as men of God; and I never united with Joseph and party afterward!! I have often examined all the reasons You assign, but they have but little bearing on my mind. ~ I know a man can sit down and find crookedness in almost any thing by prying closely into[7] it. In that light you are to work at the Book, and M.ism. Your life like all other **exposers** will be spent in vain, and worse than in vain. Then spend your time and energies at something more worthy of a lover of truth. Great events are just a little ahead of us. Great things are on hand today, but they will increase. Again I say I have no faith in any party or faction of L.D.S.ism any where in the world. I live alone outside all churches. I most firmly believe that the Lord will establish the Church of Christ shortly, and then (if they will accept of me) I'll unite with them!!! Thus I look for power from God to be displayed among his mini[s]ters. And then the Book of M. will be a kind of **standard** for the faithful. But I'll close hoping you may yet come to see the truth.

Give my [re]spects to J. F. Smith.[8] W.E.M. ~

6. Porter has the plural "doctrines" instead of singular "doctrine" ("McLellan's Testimony," 487; "McLellin Expresses Feelings," 10).

7. Porter has "with" instead of "into" ("McLellan's Testimony," 487; "McLellin Expresses Feelings," 10).

8. This sentence is written upside down. For a summary of Joseph F. Smith's life, see the Biographical Notes.

Appendixes

A.

McLELLIN'S PUBLISHED ARTICLES & LETTERS, 1832-1849

Letter to "Beloved Relatives," 4 Aug. 1832. In *The Journals of William E. McLellin, 1831-1836,* edited by Jan Shipps and John W. Welch. Provo and Urbana: BYU Studies and University of Illinois Press, 1994.

Letter to "My dear old [Quorum of Twelve] Friends," 24 Jan. 1837. In *Journals of William E. McLellin,* eds. Shipps and Welch, 1994.

Response to S. M. M'Corkle's "Conversion of the World." *The Ensign,* 15 July 1844, 5.

Response to B. W. S.'s "Startling Facts." *The Ensign,* 15 July 1844, 6.

"On Faith." *The Ensign,* 15 July, Sept. 1844, 8-11, 38-40.

"History of the Rise and Progress of This Church." *The Ensign,* 15 July 1844, 13-14.

"Baptism." *The Ensign,* Aug., Sept. 1844, 21-23, 40-41.

"Our Politics." *The Ensign,* Aug. 1844, 29-30.

Response to an essay on Matthew 5:48. *The Ensign,* Sept. 1844, 36.

"Buffalo, Scott County, Iowa." *The Ensign,* Sept. 1844, 36-38.

"The Work of the Holy Spirit among Men." *The Ensign,* Sept. 1844, 41-45.

"Farewell Address." *The Ensign,* Oct. 1844, 58-59.

Letter to Sidney Rigdon, 23 Dec. 1844. In *Latter Day Saint's Messenger and Advocate,* 15 Jan. 1845, 91-93; *Gospel Herald,* 4 Nov. 1847, 141.

Letter to Brother [Samuel] Bennett, 15 Mar. 1845. In *Latter Day Saint's Messenger and Advocate,* 15 Mar. 1845, 149-51.

Letter to Sidney Rigdon and Ebenezer Robinson, 28 May 1845. In *Messenger and Advocate of the Church of Christ,* 1 July 1845, 251-54.

Letter to Sidney Rigdon, 18 June 1845. In *Messenger and Advocate of the Church of Christ,* 15 July 1845, 267-68.

Letter to Sidney Rigdon, 21 August 1845. In *Messenger and Advocate of the Church of Christ,* 15 Aug. 1845, 302-03.

Letter to Elder Leonard Story. In *Messenger and Advocate of the Church of Christ,* Mar. 1846, 464.

Letter to Elder Richards. In *Messenger and Advocate of the Church of Christ,* Mar. 1846, 464.

Letter to John C. Bennett, 13 Aug. 1846. Extract in *Zion's Reveille,* 28 Jan. 1847, 11.

Letter to John C. Bennett, 14 Aug. 1846. In *Zion's Reveille,* 28 Jan. 1847, 11; *Gospel Herald,* 2 Dec. 1847, 164.

Letter to John C. Bennett, 18 Aug. 1846. In *Gospel Herald,* 2 Dec. 1847, 164.

Letter to James J. Strang, 27 Sept. 1846. In *Zion's Reveille,* 28 Jan. 1847, 11; *Gospel Herald,* 2 Dec. 1847, 165-66.

Letter to John C. Bennett, 30 Sept. 1846. In *Zion's Reveille,* Nov. 1846, 2; *Gospel Herald,* 2 Dec. 1847, 165.

"Our Address." *The Ensign of Liberty of the Church of Christ,* Mar. 1847, 14.

"The Endowment from on High." *The Ensign of Liberty of the Church of Christ,* Mar., Apr. 1847, 15-16, 57-60.

Letter to "My old, well tried, and beloved friend, David Whitmer," 2 Dec. 1846. In *The Ensign of Liberty of the Church of Christ,* Apr. 1847, 17-20.

"The Name of the Church." *The Ensign of Liberty of the Church of Christ,* Apr. 1847, 20-24.

"The Places of Gathering." *The Ensign of Liberty of the Church of Christ,* Apr. 1847, 24-29.

"James J. Strang, of Voree, Wis." *The Ensign of Liberty of the Church of Christ,* Apr. 1847, 29-32.

Letter to James J. Strang, 19 Oct. 1847. In *Gospel Herald,* 28 Oct. 1847, 129.

Debate with James J. Strang. In *Gospel Herald,* 28 Oct., 25 Nov. 1847, 130-31, 153-55.

"Our Apology–And Our Tours." *The Ensign of Liberty of the Church of Christ,* Dec. 1847, 33-36.

"A Seer of the Lord." *The Ensign of Liberty of the Church of Christ,* Dec. 1847, 36-41.

"The Successor of Joseph, the Seer." *The Ensign of Liberty of the Church of Christ,* Dec. 1847, Mar. 1848, 41-47, 76-79.

"Signs of the Times." *The Ensign of Liberty of the Church of Christ,* Dec. 1847, 47-49.

"Treatise on Priesthood." *The Ensign of Liberty of the Church of Christ,* Jan. 1848, 49-54.

"Things in Kirtland." *The Ensign of Liberty of the Church of Christ,* Jan. 1848, 54-57.

Comments on legal successor of Joseph Smith. *The Ensign of Liberty of the Church of Christ,* Jan. 1848, 60-62.

Comments on father and family. *The Ensign of Liberty of the Church of Christ,* Jan. 1848, 63.

"Our Principles in Kirtland." *The Ensign of Liberty of the Church of Christ,* Mar. 1848, 65-71.

"The Covenant Lands." *The Ensign of Liberty of the Church of Christ,* Mar. 1848, 71-76.

"The Kingdom of Heaven." *The Ensign of Liberty of the Church of Christ,* May 1848, 81-87.

"Latter Day Saintism." *The Ensign of Liberty of the Church of Christ,* May 1848, 89-91, with sections on Young, Rigdon, Strang, and Brewster.

"Peculiar Omens." *The Ensign of Liberty of the Church of Christ,* May 1848, 95-96.

"Our Prospects." *The Ensign of Liberty,* Aug. 1849, 97-98.

"Revelations." *The Ensign of Liberty,* Aug. 1849, 97-98.

"Our Tour West in 1847." *The Ensign of Liberty,* Aug. 1849, 99-104.

"Remarks on the Above." *The Ensign of Liberty,* Aug. 1849, 105.

"The Work of the Holy Spirit among Men." *The Ensign of Liberty,* Aug. 1849, 105-12.

"Latter Day Saintism." *The Ensign of Liberty,* Aug. 1849, 112.

B.

McLELLIN'S "RUINS OF CENTRAL AMERICA AND YUCATAN"

This fifty-one-page notebook, located at the LDS Church Archives, Salt Lake City, consists entirely of extracted quotations from John L. Stephens's book, *Incidents of Travel in Central America, Chiapas, and Yucatan*. Stephens's book was published in 1841 and went through numerous editions and printings.

The title, "Ruins of Central America and Yucatan," is McLellin's from the cover of his notebook. On the page facing page 1, John Traughber made the following comments: "The contents of this little book consist mainly of extracts from the account of [Frederick] Catherwood and Stephens' explorations [of] ancient American ruins, with a few remarks of Dr. McLellan here and there. The Doctor supposed that these extracts greatly coroborated the pretended history of the Book of Mormon. As I see it, nothing more would be required to prove the utter unreliability of the Book of Mormon than a careful and critical reading of these extracts in connection with the Book in question."

Contrary to Traughber's remark that McLellin made "a few remarks ... here and there," there appear to be no statements actually made by McLellin. On the back cover of this notebook, Traughber wrote: "Received from the Express Office at Norborne, Mo., Nov. 20, 1884. J. L. Traughber, Jr."

C.

BIOGRAPHICAL NOTES

This register lists every personal name mentioned in McLellin's notebooks and letters. Each entry begins with the surname as McLellin wrote it, followed by the correct spelling in brackets if McLellin misspelled it. Where he spelled a name correctly and incorrectly, the incorrect spelling is given in parentheses. If available, birth and death dates are listed in parentheses following a name. Where we were unable to find outside information, we simply mention what role the individual plays within the notebooks and letters. Biblical characters are not included. Full citations for sources used in compiling these notes are found in the bibliography.

Adrian [Hadrian] (76-138) was born Publius Aelius Hadrianus on 24 January 76 at Rome, son of senator Aelius Hadrianus Afer and Domitia Paulina. Married Sabina in 100, though later had a homosexual relationship with a Bithynian boy named Antinous. Became emperor of Rome in 117. Built Hadrian's Wall, 120-23, across northern England in defense against the Picts. Died on 10 July 138. See Birley, *Hadrian.*

Alger, Fanny (1816-ca.1890) was born on 20 September 1816 in Rehoboth, Massachusetts, daughter of Samuel Alger and Clarissa Hancock. Married Joseph Smith Jr. about February or March 1833, Smith dictating words of ceremony to Levi Hancock, who repeated them to the couple. Married Solomon Custer in November 1836 and had nine children. Died sometime after 1885. See Compton, *Sacred Loneliness*, 25-42, 641-68; Tinney, *Fanny Alger*; Van Wagoner, *Mormon Polygamy*, 7-8.

Ambrose, St. (ca. 339-397) was born in Trier (modern Germany), son of the praetorian prefect of Gaul. When Auxentius, bishop of Milan, died in 374, Ambrose was a popular choice as bishop even though not baptized. He accepted, was baptized, and ordained bishop. Wrote *De fide (On the Faith)* about 378 to 380, a refutation of Arianism. Wrote *De officiis ministrorum (On the Duties of Ministers)* probably in the 380s. Wrote *De sacramentis (On the Sacraments)* about 390, six liturgical treatises on sacraments given during Easter to catechumens. See Ramsey, *Ambrose.*

Aristotle (384-322 B.C.) was born in Stagira in northern Greece, son of Nicomachus and Phaestis. Became a pupil of Plato at the Academy in Athens about 367 B.C. Married Pythias about 347 B.C. and had one daughter, though wife was tortured to death by the Persians. Lived with common-law wife, Herpyllis, and had one son. Established the Lyceum in Athens in 335 B.C. Wrote *Metaphysics*, *Nicomachean Ethics*, *Politics*, *Poetics*, *De anima (On the Soul)*, and *Organon* (treatises on logic). Died at Chalcis on the island of Euboea. Barnes, *Aristotle*.

Augustine, St. (354-430) was born at Tagaste (modern Algeria), son of Patricius, a pagan, and Monica, a Christian. Began fifteen-year affair in 372 with mistress, by whom he had a son, Adeodatus. Studied at University of Carthage. Converted to Manichaeism for nine years, 374-83. Appointed professor of rhetoric in Milan in 384. Baptized in 387 by Ambrose. Ordained a priest in 391. Became co-adjutor bishop to Valerius at Hippo in north Africa in 395 and sole bishop in 396. Wrote *Confessions*, 397-401, a candid autobiography. Wrote *De civitate Dei (City of God)*, 413-26, a Christian philosophy of history. Taught doctrines of predestination and original sin. Died on 28 August 430 in Hippo. See Brown, *Augustine*.

Banta, Elijah (1823-1889) was born on 5 January 1823 in Kentucky, son of Peter Banta and Mary Voris. Married Emeline Campbell in October 1846. Baptized into Reorganized Church in April 1863. Ordained an elder in April 1865. Served as a bishop, 1873-74; 1882-89. Married Hattie Crosby in 1877. Died on 19 March 1889. See Black, *RLDS Members*, 1:277; Christoph, *Van Voorhees*, 565.

Bays, Davis Henry (1839-1905) was born on 5 March 1839 in Colorado County, Texas, son of Henry L. Bays. His parents associated with Lyman Wight's group in Texas in late 1840s and James J. Strang's church at Beaver Island in 1850s. Married Elizabeth about 1860. Baptized into Reorganized Church in May 1861 and ordained an elder the next month. Ordained a seventy in September 1878. Resigned from Reorganized Church in 1892. Joined Baptists and then Campbellites in mid-1890s. Published *The Doctrines and Dogmas of Mormonism Examined and Refuted* in 1897. See Black, *RLDS Members*; Smith, *Truth Defended*, 3-9.

Blair, William Wallace (1828-1896) was born on 11 October 1828 in Holley, New York, son of James Blair and Fanny Hamilton. Married Elizabeth J. Doty in December 1849 and had seven children. Baptized in October 1851 into William Smith's church. Investigated Baneemyism in 1852, the year he joined with Charles B. Thompson to found the New Organization. United with John E. Page's church in 1855. Baptized in April 1857 by Zenos H. Gurley Sr. into the New Organization (later Reorganized Church) and ordained an elder and then high priest that month. Ordained an apostle in October 1858 by Jason W. Briggs and Zenos H. Gurley Sr. Appointed church recorder in June 1859. Called to be first counselor to RLDS President Joseph Smith III in April 1873. Died on 18 April 1896 in Lamoni, Iowa. See Black, *RLDS Members*, 1:478-80; Knisley, *Biographical Dictionary*.

Bledsoe, Albert Taylor (1809-1877) was born on 9 November 1809 in Frankfort, Kentucky, son of Moses Bledsoe and Sophia Taylor. Graduated from West Point Military Academy in 1830. Married Harriet Coxe in April 1836 and had seven children. Served as assistant to Episcopal bishop of Kentucky in 1836. From 1845 to 1867, published *A[n] Examination of President Edwards' Inquiry into the Freedom of the Will*; *A Theodicy; or, Vindication of the Divine Glory; An Essay on Liberty and Slavery;* and *The Philosophy of Mathematics*. Founded, edited, and published *The Southern Review,* 1867-77, which from 1870 was sponsored by Methodist Episcopal Church South. Died on 8 December 1877 in Alexandria, Virginia. See Hays, "Polemics and Philosophy"; Woodworth, "Bledsoe."

Bond, Charlotte Wilcox (1803-1882) was born on 17 December 1803, in Honeoye Falls, New York. Married Ira Bond and had six children. Baptized into Church of Christ in April 1833. Joined Reorganized Church in 1860s. Became blind in 1871. Died on 17 December 1882 in Kirtland, Ohio. See Black, *RLDS Members*, 1:516; Porter, "Odyssey of McLellin," 375n301.

Bond, Mary E. (1828-1899) was born on 24 July 1828 in Mendon, New York, daughter of Ira Bond and Charlotte Wilcox. Joined Reorganized Church in 1860s. Died on 4 February 1899 in Kirtland, Ohio. See Black, *RLDS Members*, 1:517-18; Porter, "Odyssey of McLellin," 375n301.

Brown, John (1722-1787) was born in Carpow, near Abernethy, Perthshire, Scotland, son of John and Catherine Brown. Received first Greek New Testament in 1738 at age sixteen. Ordained minister of church in Haddington in 1751. Married Janet Thomson in 1753 and had eight children, though she died in 1771. Published *A Dictionary of the Holy Bi-*

ble in 1769, revised and updated for a hundred years. Married Violet Croumbie in 1773. Published *The Self-Interpreting Bible* in 1778, with twenty-six editions through 1909. Published *The Christian, The Student, and Pastor, Exemplified in the Lives of Nine Eminent Ministers of Scotland, England, and America* in 1781. Died on 19 June 1787 in Haddington, East Lothian, Scotland. See Mackenzie, *John Brown*.

Buck, Charles (1771-1815) was born in Hillsley, Gloucestershire, England. Married in 1795. Ordained minister of independent church at Sheerness, Kent, England, in 1795. From 1799 published *Anecdotes, Religious, Moral, and Entertaining; A Theological Dictionary; A Treatise on Religious Experience; The Young Christian's Guide;* and *The Practical Expositor; or, Scripture Illustrated by Facts, and Arranged for Every Day of the Year.* Died on 11 August 1815. See Styles, *Memoirs and Remains.*

Butler, Joseph (1692-1752) was born on 18 May 1692 in Wantage, Berkshire, England. Reared a Presbyterian, became an Anglican, published *Fifteen Sermons Prepared at the Rolls Chapel* and *The Analogy of Religion, Natural and Revealed, to the Constitution and Course of Nature* in 1726, 1736. Appointed bishop of Bristol in 1738, bishop of Durham in 1750. Died on 16 June 1752 in Bath, Somerset, England.

Campbell, Alexander (1788-1866) was born on 12 September 1788 near Shane's Castle, County Antrim, Ireland, son of Thomas Campbell and Jane Corneigle. Married Margaret Brown in March 1811 and had eight children, but wife died in 1827. Became minister of newly organized Brush Run Church, 1812. Immersed by a Baptist minister that year and converted his church to immersion. Published debate with Presbyterian John Walker in 1820, *Infant Sprinkling Proved To Be a Human Tradition.* Co-founded with father in early 1830s the Christian Church or Disciples of Christ, also known as Campbellites. Founded and edited *The Christian Baptist,* 1823-30, changed name to *The Millennial Harbinger,* continued editing, 1830-64. Published translation of New Testament, *The Sacred Writings of the Apostles and Evangelists of Jesus Christ,* 1826. Married Selina Bakewell in 1828 and had six children. Published *Delusions: An Analysis of the Book of Mormon* in 1832, *Christianity Restored,* 1835; *The Christian System,* 1839. Founded Bethany College in Bethany, Virginia (now West Virginia), 1840. Published the *Memoirs of Elder Thomas Campbell* in 1861. Died on 4 March 1866 in Bethany, West Virginia. See Humble, *Alexander Campbell.*

Campbell, George (1719-1796) was born on 25 December 1719 in Aberdeen, Scotland, son of Colin Campbell and Margaret Walker. Ordained a minister in Church of Scotland, 1748. Married Grace Farquharson in June 1755. Helped found Aberdeen Philosophical Society, 1758. Published *A Dissertation on Miracles* in 1762 responding to David Hume's essay "Of Miracles." Became professor of divinity of Marischal College in Aberdeen, 1771. Published *The Philosophy of Rhetoric* in 1776, then a two-volume book, *The Four Gospels, Translated from the Greek*, in 1789, including notes on proper translation of ancient documents. Died on 6 April 1796 in Aberdeen. See Suderman, *Orthodoxy*.

Chrysostom, St. John (ca. 349-407) was born in Antioch. Ordained a priest in 386. Excelled in oratory, thus Chrysostom ("golden-mouthed"). Wrote "On the Priesthood." Became patriarch of Constantinople in 398. Condemned by synod of the Oak (convened by rival Theophilus of Alexandria) in 403 and removed from his see. Exiled to Cucusus in Lesser Armenia, then to village of Pityus near the Black Sea. Killed in Comana by guards who forced him to march in ill health. See Kelly, *Golden Mouth*.

Clark [Clarke], Adam (ca. 1762-1832) was born in Moybeg, Londonderry, Ireland, son of John Clarke and Miss M'Lean. Became a Methodist circuit preacher in England in 1783. Married Mary Cooke in April 1788 and had twelve children. Published *A Dissertation on the Use and Abuse of Tobacco*, 1797; *A Letter to a Methodist Preacher on His Entrance into the Work of the Ministry,* 1800; and the six-volume *Bibliographical Dictionary,* 1802-04. Elected Methodist conference president, 1806, 1814, 1822. Published eight-volume commentary on Bible from 1810 to 1826. Published *Clavis Biblica* and *The Preacher's Manual* in 1820, *Memoirs of the Wesley Family* in 1823. Died on 26 August 1832 in London. See Etheridge, *Adam Clarke*.

Clarke, Grace (1864-) was born on 2 November 1864 in Genesee County, Michigan, daughter of Lafayette Clarke and Helen McLellin. See Porter, "Odyssey," 347.

Clarke, Helen Rebecca McLellin (1843-) was born on 11 February 1843 in Hampton, Illinois, daughter of William McLellin and Emeline Miller. Married Lafayette W. Clarke in December 1863. See Porter, "Odyssey," 329, 347.

Clark [Clarke], Lafayette W. Married Helen McLellin in December 1863. See Porter, "Odyssey," 347.

Cobb, James Thornton (1833-1910) was born on 15 December 1833 in Beverly, Massachusetts, son of Henry Cobb and Augusta Adams. Educated at Dartmouth College. Baptized into LDS Church in October 1863. Married Camilla Clara Mieth in November 1864. Married Mary Van Cott. Collected information on history of Mormonism in late 1870s. Died on 31 January 1910 in Salt Lake City, Utah.

Coe, Joseph (1784-1854) was born on 12 November 1784, in Genoa, New York, son of Joel Coe and Huldah Horton. Married Pallas Wales in January 1816, but she died in 1822. Later married Sophia Harwood. Baptized into Church of Christ and ordained an elder before June 1831 when he traveled with Joseph Smith to Missouri. Ordained a high priest in October 1832. Appointed to Kirtland high council in February 1834. Gave $800 (one-third of cost) to purchase Egyptian mummies and papyri for Smith in 1835. Rejected as high councilor in September 1837. Excommunicated in December 1837. Died on 17 October 1854 in Kirtland, Ohio. See Cook, *Revelations*, 86-87; Black, *Who's Who*, 62-64.

Constantine the Great (ca. 280-337) was born in Naissus (modern Yugoslavia), son of emperor Flavius Valerius Constantius and St. Helena. Proclaimed emperor at York in 306. Escaped detention at court of Diocletian and returned to Rome as conqueror in 311. Granted official status to Christian church in Edict of Constantine, 313. Convened council of Arles in 314, condemning Donatism. Ordered Sunday a public holiday in 321. Convened and presided over council of Nicaea in 325, condemning Arianism. Rebuilt Byzantium and established it as capital, Constantinople, dedicated in 330. Baptized just before death in Nocomedia. See Grant, *Constantine*.

Cousin, Victor (1792-1867) was born on 28 November 1792 in Paris, France. Began lecturing at Sorbonne in 1815. Published *Cours de l'historie de la philosophie moderne* in 1828. Became member of Académie Française in 1830. Drafted French education bill of 1833. Published *De vrai, du beau, et du bien* in 1836. Served as minister of public instruction in 1840. Died on 13 January 1867 in Cannes, France. See Leopold, "Cousin"; Simon, *Victor Cousin*.

Cowdery (Cowdry), Elizabeth Ann Whitmer (1815-1892) was born on

22 January 1815 in Fayette, New York, daughter of Peter Whitmer Sr. and Mary Elsa Musselman. Baptized into Church of Christ on 11 April 1830 by Oliver Cowdery and married him in December 1832; they had six children. Died on 7 January 1892 in Southwest City, Missouri. See Gunn, *Oliver Cowdery*, 219-23; Dear, *Whitmer Family*, 48.

Cowdery, Oliver (1806-1850) was born on 3 October 1806 in Wells, Vermont, son of William Cowdery and Rebecca Fuller. Served as Joseph Smith's scribe for Book of Mormon translation and one of three witnesses in 1829. Baptized by Joseph Smith in May 1829, received revelation next month on how to organize Church of Christ and became a charter member ("second elder") on 6 April 1830. Called "into the wilderness among the Lamanites" (D&C 32) in October 1830. Ordained to high priesthood in August 1831. Married Elizabeth Ann Whitmer in December 1832 and had six children; alleged to have polygamously married Mary Ann Lyman the following year. Edited *The Evening and the Morning Star,* 1833-34; *Latter Day Saints' Messenger and Advocate,* 1834-37; *Northern Times,* 1835. Ordained assistant president of High Priesthood, December 1834. Assisted Martin Harris and David Whitmer in choosing and ordaining twelve apostles in 1835. Threatened with excommunication and demoted to assistant counselor in First Presidency in September 1837; excommunicated in April 1838 for initiating lawsuits, accusing Joseph Smith of adultery, neglecting calling due to law practice, counterfeiting, and keeping paid notes. Joined Methodist church in Tiffin, Ohio, in January 1844. Became publication agent for George Hinkle's "Church of Jesus Christ, the Bride the Lamb's Wife" in 1845. Re-baptized by Orson Hyde in November 1848 in Kanesville, Iowa. Died on 3 March 1850 in Richmond, Missouri. See Gunn, *Oliver Cowdery*; Quinn, *Origins*, 544-45; Vogel, *Mormon Documents*, 2:397-401; 409-12.

Dick, John (1764-1833) was born on 10 October 1764 in Aberdeen, Scotland. He was a Scottish Presbyterian minister (United Secession Church) and professor of theology; published *The Conduct and Doom of False Teachers,* 1788; *An Essay on the Inspiration of the Holy Scriptures,* 1800; *Sermons,* 1816; and *Lectures on the Acts of the Apostles,* 1822.

Dyonisius [Dionysius], St. (d. 268) was presbyter of Rome during 250s. Elected Bishop of Rome in 259, he convened a Roman synod in 260 demanding that Dionysius of Alexandria answer a charge of tritheism. Died in Rome.

Dyonisius [Dionysius] the Great (ca. 190-265) was a disciple of Origen. Became head of catechetical school in early 230s, bishop of Alexandria in 247. Went into hiding during Decian persecution of 250-51 and exiled to Libya in Valerian persecution of 257-60. Wrote *Refutations and Defense* to Bishop Dionysius of Rome, defending orthodoxy of trinitarian doctrine. Wrote *On the Promises*, rejecting John as author of book of Revelation. Attacked Sabellianism, accusing him of separating persons of the Trinity (tritheism). Died in Alexandria. See Attwater, *Saints*.

Edwards, Jonathan (1703-1758) was born on 5 October 1703 in East Windsor, Connecticut, son of Timothy Edwards and Esther Stoddard. Married Sarah Pierrepont in July 1727 and had eleven children. Became minister of church in Northampton, Massachusetts, in 1729. Published *A Faithful Narrative of the Surprising Work of God* in 1737 describing how evangelical preaching resulted in a revival. Published *Treatise concerning Religious Affections*, 1746; *An Humble Inquiry concerning Communion*, 1749. Dismissed by Northampton Church in 1750; became minister at an Indian missionary outpost in Stockbridge, Massachusetts, 1752; published *Freedom of the Will*, 1754. Became president of College of New Jersey (now Princeton University) in 1758. Died on 22 March 1758 in Princeton, New Jersey. See Nichols, *Jonathan Edwards*.

Eusebius (ca. 260-ca. 340), a pupil of Pamphilus, was baptized as an adult at Caesarea and became bishop there about 313. Wrote *Praeparatio*, refuting pagan mythology and offering a Christian interpretation of the Old Testament; *Historia Ecclesiastica (History of the Church)*, the main source for early Christian history with long passages from earlier works; *Demonstratio Evangelica*, showing fulfillment of prophecy in life of Christ; and panegyrical *Life of Constantine*, 337-39. See Grant, *Eusebius*.

Forscutt, Mark Hill (1834-1905) was born on 19 June 1834 in Little Bolton, Lancashire, England, son of Robert Forscutt and Amy Hill. Married Elizabeth Unsworth in 1860 and had three children. Joined Morrisites (followers of Joseph Morris), 1861-62, serving as clerk of the first council. Baptized into Reorganized Church in January 1865 while living in Salt Lake City. Worked as assistant editor of *Saints' Herald* in 1870s. Compiled *The Saints' Harmony* in 1889, a selection of music for Reorganized Church. Died in October 1903 in Nebraska City, Nebraska. See Black, *RLDS Members*, 2:810-11.

Frisby [Frisbey], George Pack (1834-1919) was born on 17 March 1834 in Marrietta, Ohio, son of George P. Frisbey and Sarah Ann Byram. Married Lucinda A. Ary in October 1853 and had six children, though she died in 1868. Married Evaline Bradley in 1869 or 1870 and had nine children. Joined Church of Christ (Temple Lot) in 1867 and moved to Independence, Missouri, same year. Served on board of publication for *The Search Light* in 1890s. Discussed with Joseph Smith III differences between Temple Lot and Reorganized Church in 1897. Died on 14 February 1919 in Independence. See Anderson, *Memoirs of President*, 338.

Gould, John (1808-1851) was born on 11 May 1808 in Ontario, Canada, son of Seth Gould and Hannah Sager. Married Olivia Abigail Harrington about 1832 and had nine children. Presided over a Free Will Baptist Church in Spafford, New York, in 1831. Baptized into Church of Christ about 1832 and ordained an elder and seventy in 1836, president of First Council of Seventy in April 1837. Released from office in September 1837 because predecessor became eligible again. Excommunicated in January 1838, re-baptized and reinstated as Seventy about 1841. Received temple endowment in February 1846. Died on 9 May 1851 in Cooley's Mill, Iowa. See Cook, *Revelations*, 204; Black, *Who's Who*, 104-107; Quinn, *Origins*, 548.

Gregory Nazianzen, St. (ca. 330-ca. 391) was born in Arianzum near Nazianzus in Cappadocia, son of Gregory, bishop of Nazianzus, and Nonna. Studied at University of Athens. Baptized in 358. Forcibly ordained a priest by father in 361. Preached "Five Theological Orations" at Church of Anastasis in Constantinople in 380, leading to acceptance of Nicene creed at council of Constantinople. Made bishop of Constantinople in 380, forced to resign in 381. Compiled with St. Basil of Caesarea *Philocalia*, an anthology of the writings of Origen. Died in Arianzum. See McGuckin, *Gregory of Nazianzus*.

Hadrian. *See McLellin's spelling* Adrian

Hamilton, Sir William (1788-1856) was born on 8 March 1788 in Glasgow, Scotland, son of William Hamilton and Elizabeth Stirling. Became member of Scottish bar in 1813. Married Janet Marshall in 1829 and had three children. Appointed chair of logic and metaphysics at Edinburgh University in 1836. Published *Discussions on Philosophy and Literature, Education and University Reform* in 1852. Died on 6 May 1856 in Edinburgh. See Mounce, "Hamilton"; Bowen, *William Hamilton*.

Harris, Lucy (1792-1836) was born on 1 May 1792 in Palmyra, New York, daughter of Rufus and Lucy Harris. Married cousin Martin Harris in March 1808 and had five children. Reportedly burned 116 pages of Book of Mormon manuscript. Separated from husband about 1831 and died in summer of 1836. See James, "Lucy Harris."

Harris, Martin (1783-1875) was born on 18 May 1783 in Easttown, New York, son of Nathan Harris and Rhoda Lapham. Married cousin Lucy Harris in March 1808 and had five children, but Lucy died in 1836. Book of Mormon scribe (the first), April-June 1828, then lost 116 manuscript pages. Next year became one of three witnesses of Book of Mormon, also mortgaging 240-acre farm to raise $3,000 for first 5,000 copies. Baptized into Church of Christ by Oliver Cowdery on 6 April 1830, ordained a priest in June 1830, ordained a high priest in June 1831. Separated from wife, Lucy, about 1831. Appointed member of first high council in Kirtland in 1834, dropped from high council in 1837. Participated in paramilitary campaign, Zion's Camp, in 1834. Assisted Oliver Cowdery and David Whitmer in choosing and ordaining twelve apostles in 1835. Married Caroline Young in November 1836 and had eight children. Excommunicated in December 1837. Declared in 1838 "he never saw the [Book of Mormon] plates with his natural eyes[,] only in vision or imagination." Reconnected with Joseph Smith before May 1841 and was re-baptized in November 1842. Confessed belief in Shakerism in 1844. Proselytized in England for James J. Strang, 1846-47; organized new Church of Christ with William E. McLellin, January 1847; helped William Smith and Leonard Rich organize new church, 1855-57; and helped form another church with Leonard Rich in 1860. In September 1870 traveled to Utah and was rebaptized into LDS Church. Died on 10 July 1875 in Clarkston, Utah Territory. See Vogel, *Mormon Documents*, 2:253-59, 291; Quinn, *Origins*, 551-52, 596.

Hedrick, Granville (1814-1881) was born on 28 September 1814 in Clark County, Indiana, son of George and Elizabeth Hedrick. Married Eliza Ann Jones and had one son. Baptized into LDS Church in 1843. Published *The Spiritual Wife System Proven False* in 1856. Ordained an apostle by John E. Page in May 1863. Ordained president of High Priesthood of Church of Christ by John E. Page, July 1863. Received revelations, 1863-64, about church returning to Independence, Missouri. Edited *The Truth Teller,* 1864-68. Moved to Independence, Missouri, in 1867. Purchased part of original temple lot in 1869 for what was called

Church of Christ (Temple Lot). Died on 22 August 1881 in Gardner, Kansas. See Shields, *Divergent Paths*, 76-77; Davis, *Story*, 431-35.

Hilary, St. (ca. 315-367) was born at Poitiers, married and had a daughter named Abra before converting to Christianity. Became bishop of Poitiers about 353. Condemned at synod of Biterrae in 356 and exiled to Phrygia for four years. Defended orthodox position at council of Seleucia in 359. Wrote in 350s *De Trinitate*, first extensive study of Trinity in Latin. See McBrien, *Catholicism*, 614-15; Glazier and Hellurg, *Catholic Encyclopedia*, 382.

Hill, Miss, is mentioned in McLellin's July 1872 letter to Joseph Smith III. Based on an 1847 interview with Emma Smith, McLellin referred to Joseph's Smith's involvement with (1) a servant girl named Hill and (2) a servant girl named Fanny Alger. Historians wonder if McLellin erred by writing "Hill" or if there was, in fact, another young woman before Alger. The latter conjecture comes from McLellin's mention of a time period near Joseph Smith III's birth (1832), which would have predated Alger's arrival in the Smith home. If there were a Miss Hill, any further information about her has been lost to history. See Newell and Avery, *Mormon Enigma*, 66; Van Wagoner, *Mormon Polygamy*, 6-8, 21n7.

Hooker, Richard (1554-1600) was born in Heavitree, near Exeter, Devon, England, son of Roger and Joan Hooker. Studied at Oxford and was ordained a clergyman in Church of England in 1581. Married Joan Churchman in February 1588. Made rector of Boscombe, Wiltshire, in 1591. Wrote eight-volume defense of Church of England, *Of the Laws of Ecclesiastical Polity*, five volumes from 1593 to 1597 and the rest posthumously. Died on 2 November 1600 in Bishopsbourne near Canterbury, Kent, England. See Secor, *Hooker*.

Hyde, Orson (1805-1878) was born on 8 January 1805 in Oxford, Connecticut, son of Nathan Hyde and Sally Thorpe. Joined Methodist church in 1827, served as Campbellite minister from late 1820s to 1831, and was baptized a member of Church of Christ and ordained an elder, then a high priest, in October 1831. Called as clerk to First Presidency in June 1833. Participated in paramilitary expedition, Zion's Camp, in 1834. Married Marinda Nancy Johnson in September 1834 and had ten children. Ordained one of original twelve apostles in February 1835, disfellowshipped in August but reinstated the next month. Served with

Heber C. Kimball in England, 1837-38. Apostatized in October 1838, was disfellowshipped in January 1839 and dropped from Quorum of Twelve in May but was re-baptized and reinstated into quorum the next month. Dedicated Palestine in October 1841 for gathering of Jews. Edited *The Latter-Day Saints' Millennial Star,* 1846-47. From 1843 polygamously married (1) Mary Ann Price, (2) Ann Eliza Vickers, (3) Julia Thomene Reinert, (4) Elisabeth Josephine Gallier, and (5) Sophia Margaret Lyon. Served on Nauvoo city council, 1843-45; appointed to Council of Fifty, March 1844. Sustained as president of Quorum of Twelve, December 1847, but demoted in 1875, resulting in John Taylor becoming president at Brigham Young's death. Published *Frontier Guardian*, 1849-52. Died on 28 November 1878 in Spring City, Utah Territory. See Barron, *Orson Hyde*; Hyde, *Orson Hyde*; Quinn, *Origins*, 552-54.

Irenius [Irenaeus] (ca. 130-ca. 200) was probably a native of Smyrna (modern Turkey), where he became a disciple of Polycarp. Studied at Rome. Became bishop of Lyons in 178. Wrote in late 180s *Adversus Haereses (Against Heresies)* against Gnosticism and millenarianism—especially of Valentinus and the Montanists. Wrote *The Demonstration of the Apostolic Teaching*, an apologia on Christian principles from Old Testament texts. See Osborn, *Irenaeus*; Grant, *Irenaeus*.

Isodorius [Isidore], St. (ca. 360-450) was probably born in Alexandria. Became a monk and retired to monastery of Lychnos, which is near Pelusium, Egypt. Wrote about 2,000 letters dealing with church dogma, monastic discipline, and practical morality.

Jahn, Johann (1750-1816) was born on 18 June 1750 in Tasswitz, Moravia. Took monastic vows at convent in Bruck in 1774, ordained to priesthood in 1775, and became canon of St. Stephens in Vienna in 1806. Authored works on biblical archaeology, Hebrew grammar, and readings in Aramaic and Arabic: *Biblische Archäologie* in three volumes, 1797-1805; *Elementarbuch der hebräischen Sprache,* 1799; *Chaldäische Chrestomathie,* 1800; *Arabische Chrestomathie,* 1802; *Grammatica Linguae Hebraicae,* 1809; *Archaeologia Biblica,* 1814. Died on 16 August 1816 in Vienna.

Jerome, St. (ca. 345-420) was born Eusebius Hieronymus in Dalmatia (modern Slovenia), of Christian parents. Ordained a priest in 379. Became secretary to Pope Damasus I in 382. Established a monastery at

Bethlehem about 389. Revised Old Latin gospels and made new Latin translation of Old Testament, 391-406, the resultant Vulgate becoming the standard of Roman Catholic Church. Died in Bethlehem, Palestine. See Kelly, *Jerome*; Rice, *Saint Jerome*.

Johnson, Charles (1826-) was born on 24 June 1826 in Richmond, Missouri. Became a medical doctor. Married Maria Louise Cowdery in September 1856 at Richmond, Missouri. See Gunn, *Oliver Cowdery*, 219.

Johnson, John (1778-1843) was born on 11 April 1778 in Chesterfield, New Hampshire, son of Israel Johnson and Abigail Higgins. Married Elsa Mary Jacobs in June 1800 and had fifteen children. Joined Methodist Church in 1826 or 1827. Baptized into Church of Christ in early 1831. Hosted Joseph Smith and family in home, 1831-32. Ordained an elder in February 1833, high priest in June, and appointed to Kirtland high council in February 1834. Became charter member and stockholder in Kirtland Safety Society in January 1837. Rejected as high councilor in September 1837, left church in 1838. Died on 30 July 1843 in Kirtland, Ohio. See Black, *Who's Who*, 152-54; Cook, *Revelations*, 199.

Johnson, John Edward (1863-1921) was born on 26 November 1863, son of James Edward Johnson and Sarah Elizabeth Whitmer, Sarah being a daughter of John Whitmer. Married Stella Smith and had three children. Died on 5 August 1921. See Dear, *Whitmer Family*, 40.

Johnson, Luke Samuel (1807-1861) was born on 3 November 1807 in Pomfret, Vermont, son of John Johnson and Elsa Jacobs. Baptized into Church of Christ in May 1831 by Joseph Smith, ordained a priest soon after and a high priest in October. Married Susan Poteet in November 1832 and had ten children, though she died in 1846. Appointed to Kirtland high council in February 1834 and participated in paramilitary campaign, Zion's Camp, that year. Ordained one of original twelve apostles in February 1835. Attended Hebrew school, 1835-36. Became a charter member and stockholder in Kirtland Safety Society, January 1837. Filed charge in May 1837 against Joseph Smith for speaking disrespectfully against brethren. Disfellowshipped in September 1837, again in October, reinstated the next month, then excommunicated in December and again in April 1838. By 1843 served as Methodist Episcopal minister. Re-baptized in March 1846 in Nauvoo. Married America Morgan Clark in March 1847 and had eight children. Migrated to Utah in

1847, polygamously married Margaret Eliot in 1854, and was endowed in April 1854. Appointed a bishop in St. John's, Tooele County, in 1858. Died on 9 December 1861 in Salt Lake City, Utah Territory. See Flake, *Prophets*, 363-65; Cook, *Revelations*, 110-11; Black, *Who's Who*, 154-57.

Johnson, Lyman Eugene (1811-1859) was born on 24 October 1811 in Pomfret, Vermont, son of John Johnson and Elsa Jacobs. Baptized into Church of Christ in February 1831, ordained an elder in October and high priest the next month. Participated in paramilitary expedition, Zion's Camp, in 1834. Married Sarah Susan Lang in September and had two children. Ordained one of original twelve apostles in February 1835. Became charter member of Kirtland Safety Society in January 1837. Disfellowshipped in September 1837, again in October, reinstated the next month, then excommunicated in April 1838 for "bringing distress to the innocent," assaulting Phineas Young, not attending church, failing to observe Word of Wisdom, and unrighteous conduct. Drowned in Mississippi River on 20 December 1859 at Prairie du Chien, Wisconsin. See Flake, *Prophets*, 377-78; Cook, *Revelations*, 111; Black, *Who's Who*, 158-59.

Johnson, Maria Louise Cowdery (1835-1892) was born on 11 August 1835 in Kirtland, Ohio, daughter of Oliver Cowdery and Elizabeth Whitmer. Married Charles Johnson in September 1856 at Richmond, Missouri. Died on 9 January 1892 in Southwest City, Missouri. See Gunn, *Oliver Cowdery*, 219-21; Dear, *Whitmer Family*, 48.

Kant, Immanuel (1724-1804) was born on 22 April 1724 in Königsberg, East Prussia (modern Russia), son of Johann Georg Cant and Anna Regina Reuter. Appointed chair of logic and metaphysics at University of Königsberg in 1770. Published *Kritik der reinen Vernunft (Critique of Pure Reason)*, 1781; *Kritik der praktischen Vernunft (Critique of Practical Reason)*, 1788; *Kritik der Urteilskraft (Critique of Judgment)*, 1790. Died on 12 February 1804 in Königsberg. See Kuehn, *Kant*.

Kinkade, William (1783-1832) was born on 22 September 1783 in Pennsylvania, son of Samuel Kinkade and Elizabeth Wilson. Baptized in September 1802, ordained a minister about 1809. Served two sessions in Illinois State Senate in early 1820s. Married Anna Gregory in 1823. Published *A Sermon on Election*, 1824; *The Bible Doctrine of God, Jesus Christ, the Holy Spirit, Atonement, Faith, and Election*, 1829. Died on 20 September 1832. See Purviance, *Biography*, 205-11.

Lee, Thomas LaFlesh (1828-1890) was born on 12 January 1828 in Winchester, Indiana, son of Alfred Lee and Elizabeth LaFlesh. Married Harriet Wolkitt in July 1849 and had thirteen children. Operated first tannery and shoe factory in Tooele, Utah Territory. Polygamously married Primrose Shields in March 1857 and had eleven children. Set apart for mission to the states in November 1871, returned in April the next year. Probably visited McLellin in November or December 1871. Arrested for unlawful cohabitation in August 1886. Died on 22 October 1890 in Milton, Utah Territory. See Esshom, *Pioneers,* 1001-1002.

Locke, John (1632-1704) was born on 29 August 1632 in Wrington, Somerset, England, son of John Locke and Agnes Keene. Elected to Royal Society in 1668. Published *A Letter concerning Toleration* and *Two Treatises of Government* in 1689; *An Essay concerning Human Understanding,* 1690; *Some Thoughts concerning Education,* 1693; *The Reasonableness of Christianity,* 1695. Died on 28 October 1704 in Oates, Essex, England. See Thomson, *Locke.*

Luther, Martin (1483-1546) was born on 10 November 1843 in Eisleben, Germany, son of Hans Luther and Margarethe Ziegler, and baptized into Roman Catholic Church the day after his birth. Ordained a priest in April 1507. Visited Rome in 1510, shocked by worldliness of papal court. Received doctorate in theology in 1512. Circulated ninety-five theses in 1517 denouncing sale of indulgences. Published *An den christlichen Adel deutscher Nation* (*To the Christian Nobility of the German Nation*) in 1520, asserting a priesthood of all believers. Excommunicated in January 1521. Published German translation of New Testament, 1522; *De servo arbitrio (The Will in Bondage),* 1525. Married Katharina von Bora, a former Cistercian nun, June 1525, and had six children. Died on 18 February 1546 in Eisleben. See Schwarz, *True Faith*; Lilje, *Martin Luther.*

Mahomet [*or* Muhammad] (ca. 570-632) was born in Mecca (modern Saudi Arabia), son of Abdullah, who died before Muhammad's birth, and Amina, who died when he was six years old. Had vision of archangel Gabriel about 610, bidding him to preach. Began preaching about 613. Married the widow Khadija about 595, had four daughters who grew to maturity and sons who died in infancy–Khadija died about 619. Married the widow Sawda and fled with about seventy followers in 622 to Yathrib, renamed Medina. Polygamously married (1) Aisha, reportedly nine years old, (2) Hafsa, (3) Hind, (4) cousin Jahsh, (5) Umm Salama, (6)

Juwayriyya, (7) Ramla or Umm Habiba, (8) Safiyya, and (9) Maymuna. Had son Ibrahim by Coptic concubine Mariyah about 630, but Ibrahim died in infancy. Received revelations which were compiled posthumously in the Qur'an or Koran. Died in Medina in 632. See Peters, *Muhammad.*

Marks, William (1792-1872) was born on 15 November 1792, in Rutland, Vermont, son of Cornell Marks and Sarah Goodrich. Married Rosannah Robinson in May 1813 and had eleven children; his wife died in 1863. Baptized and ordained a priest before April 1835. Edited *The Latter Day Saints' Messenger and Advocate* in 1837, appointed to Kirtland high council in September. In 1838 became president of Kirtland Stake, the next year president of Nauvoo Stake. Initiated into Masonry, April 1842, endowed the next month, and appointed to Council of Fifty in March 1844. Sympathized with Sidney Rigdon's claims after Joseph Smith's death, rejected as Nauvoo Stake president in October 1844. Appointed counselor to James J. Strang in March 1846, assumed role 1847-50. Joined with Charles B. Thompson to found the New Organization in 1852, withdrew the next year. Received into the Reorganization in 1859, appointed counselor to Joseph Smith III in 1863. Married Julia Durfee in September 1866. Died on 22 May 1872 in Plano, Illinois. See Cook, *Revelations*, 230-31; Knisley, *Biographical Dictionary*.

McLellin, Charles William (1834-1880) was born on 14 April 1834 in Liberty, Missouri, son of William McLellin and Emeline Miller. Died on 11 November 1880. See Porter, "Odyssey," 310, 355.

McLellin, Emeline Miller (1809-1907) was born on 4 September 1809 in Pomfret, Vermont, daughter of Martin Miller and Rebecca Jacobs. Married William E. McLellin in April 1832 and had six children. Baptized into Reorganized Church in July 1888. Died on 1 November 1907 in Denison, Texas. See Porter, "Odyssey," 302-03, 358; Black, *RLDS Members*, 4:371-72.

McLellin, Marcus Nelson (1848-1881) was born on 9 February 1848 in Kirtland, Ohio, son of William McLellin and Emeline Miller. Died on 5 February 1881. See Porter, "Odyssey," 344, 355.

Narcissus (d. 215) was bishop of Jerusalem in late second century. Due to advanced age, shared bishopric of Jerusalem with Alexander beginning about 211.

Neil [Neill], William (1778-1860) was born near McKeesport, Pennsylvania, son of William Neill and Jane Snodgrass. Graduated from College of New Jersey (now Princeton University) in 1803. Married Elizabeth Van Dyke in October 1805 and had two children, but wife died in 1809. Became minister of Presbyterian church in Cooperstown, New York, in 1805. Married Frances King in February 1811 and had three children; his wife died in 1832. Served as moderator of Presbyterian General Assembly in 1815, minister of Presbyterian church in Philadelphia in 1816, editor of *The Presbyterian Magazine,* 1821-22, president of Dickinson College, 1824-29. Married Sarah Elmer in April 1835 and had two children. Published *Lectures on Biblical History,* 1846; *A Practical Exposition of the Epistle to the Ephesians,* 1850; *The Divine Origin and Authority of the Christian Religion,* 1854; autobiographical *Discourse Reviewing a Ministry of Fifty Years,* 1857. Died on 8 August 1860 in Philadelphia. See Faris, "William Neill"; Herringshaw, *Encyclopedia,* 687.

Noble, Joseph Bates (1810-1900) was born on 14 January 1810 in Egremont, Massachusetts, son of Ezekiel Noble and Theodocia Bates. Baptized into Church of Christ in fall of 1832. Participated in paramilitary campaign, Zion's Camp, in 1834. Married Mary Adeline Beman, September 1834, and had nine children. Ordained Seventy in February 1835. In April 1841 performed plural marriage of Joseph Smith and Louisa Beaman, Smith dictating ceremony and Noble repeating it. From 1843 polygamously married (1) Sarah B. Alley, (2) Mary Ann Washburn, (3) Susan Hammond, (4) Millicent London, (5) Julia Rosetta Thurston, (6) Loretta Sylvia Meacham, (7) Jane Wallace, (8) Hannah Keer, (9) Catherine Wallace, and (10) Sarah Wallace. Received temple endowment in January 1845. Immigrated to Utah, set apart for mission to states in October 1871, returned in March 1872. Probably visited McLellin in November or December 1871. Died on 17 August 1900 in Wardboro, Idaho. See Boyack, *Nobleman.*

Origen (Origin) (ca. 185-254), son of Leonides, was probably born in Alexandria. Became principal theologian of early Greek church, appointed head of Alexandrian catechetical school about 203. Began ascetic life of fasting and praying, castrating himself in obedience to Matthew 19:12. Ordained a priest about 230. Constructed monumental *Hexapla* with parallel columns of Old Testament in Hebrew, Hebrew transliteration, and Greek translations of Aquila, Symmachus, Theodotion, and the Septuagint. Wrote *Peri Archon (On First Principles)* reconciling Greek philosophy with Christian theology. Wrote *Contra Celsum* against second-century pagan critic Celsus. Imprisoned and tortured during Decian persecution, 250-51. Died after being released, probably in Tyre. See Trigg, *Origen.*

Orton, Roger (1799-1851) was born on 20 January 1799 in Tyringham, Massachusetts, son of Roger Orton and Esther Avery. Married Clarissa Mary Bicknell in 1822 and had six children. Baptized into Church of Christ and ordained an elder in 1832. Participated in paramilitary expedition, Zion's Camp, in 1834. Ordained a Seventy and appointed to Kirtland high council in 1835, credited with having seen an angel during dedication of Kirtland Temple in January 1836. Excommunicated in November 1837, although re-baptized soon after. Sustained as one of seven presidents of Seventy in March 1845, dropped from office in October 1845 for not responding to appointment. Died on 24 November 1851, near South Augusta, Iowa. See Quinn, *Origins*, 566.

Page, Hiram (1800-1852) was born in Vermont. Married Catherine Whitmer in November 1825 and had nine children. Became one of eight witnesses of Book of Mormon in 1829. In 1830 baptized into Church of Christ and, through seer stone or "peepstone," received revelations accepted by Oliver Cowdery, the Whitmers, and others even though in contradiction to Joseph Smith. At church conference in September, Page recanted. Helped found town of Far West, Missouri, 1836. Left church in 1838. Died on 12 August 1852 near Excelsior Springs, Missouri. See Stewart, "Hiram Page"; Westergren, *Historian to Dissident*, 62-63.

Pamphilus, St. (d. 309) was born in Berytus (modern Lebanon). Reopened school of Caesarea, founded by Origen. Ordained a priest by Bishop Agapius about 290. Arrested in 307 and held in prison for two years. Wrote *Apology for Origen* during imprisonment. Decapitated at Caesarea, Palestine, during persecution of Maximinus Daia. See Crouzel, "Pamphilus."

Partridge, Edward (1793-1840) was born on 27 August 1793 at Pittsfield, Massachusetts, son of William Partridge and Jemima Bidwell. Married Lydia Clisbee in August 1819 and had seven children. Joined Campbellites in 1828. Baptized into Church of Christ by Joseph Smith in December 1830, ordained an elder soon after. Called as bishop over Missouri in February 1831, ordained a high priest in June; in October 1839 appointed bishop of a ward in Nauvoo, Illinois. Died on 27 May 1840 in Nauvoo. See Wixom, *Edward Partridge*; Black, *Who's Who*, 213-16.

Pelagius (ca. 354-ca. 425) was probably born in Britain. Wrote *On Nature* about 414, was excommunicated by Pope Innocent I in 417, and wrote a response the same year, *Libellus fidei.* Excommunicated again by Pope Zosimus in 418. Taught human freedom against Manichaean fatalism. See Rees, *Pelagius*; Smith, "Pelagianism."

Peterson, Ziba (ca. 1808-1849) was born in Burke County, North Carolina. Baptized into Church of Christ in April 1830; in June received written elder's license with added designation of "apostle of Jesus Christ." Called "into the wilderness among the Lamanites" (D&C 32) in October 1830. Married Rebecca Hooper in August 1831 and had eight children. Left church in May 1833 and was excommunicated in June 1833. Became sheriff of Dry Diggins, later Placerville, California, in 1848. Died in Placerville. See Cook, *Revelations*, 45; Black, *Who's Who*, 221-23; Quinn, *Origins*, 569.

Phelps, William Wines (1792-1872) was born on 17 February 1792 in Hanover, New Jersey, son of Enon Phelps and Mehitabel Goldsmith. Married Sally Waterman in April 1815 and had ten children. Baptized into Church of Christ and ordained an elder in June 1831. Appointed church printer the next month; edited *The Latter Day Saints' Messenger and Advocate*, 1832-33. Appointed to Missouri church presidency in 1834. Wrote lyrics for twenty-nine songs in 1835 LDS hymnal. Rejected as church counselor in February 1838, excommunicated by high council the next month, excommunicated by church conference in March 1839. Re-baptized in 1840. From 1847 polygamously married (1) Laura Stowell, (2) Elizabeth Dunn, (3) Mary Jones, (4) Sarah Betsy Gleason, and (5) Harriet Schrider. Ordained a high priest in Nauvoo, Illinois, and served on city council in 1844. Participated in church leadership prayer circle, 1856-58. Died on 6 March 1872 in Salt Lake City, Utah Territory. See Bowen, "Phelps"; Van Wagoner and Walker, *Book of Mormons*, 204-209.

Pious [Pius] IX, Pope (1792-1878) was born Giovanni Maria Mastai Ferretti on 13 May 1792 in Senigallia, Italy. Ordained a priest in April 1819 after receiving special dispensation due to epilepsy. Appointed archbishop of Spoleto in May 1827, bishop of Imola in February 1832, pope in June 1846, taking name of Pius IX. Promulgated doctrine of immaculate conception of Blessed Virgin Mary in 1854. Convoked First Vatican Council in 1869, confirming papal primacy and infallibility. Died on 7 February 1878 in Rome, making him longest reigning pope in history. See Hasler, *How the Pope.*

Pratt, Orson (1811-1881) was born on 19 September 1811 in Hartford, New York, son of Jared Pratt and Charity Dickinson. Baptized into Church of Christ in September 1830 and ordained an elder in December, then a high priest in February 1832. Participated in paramilitary campaign, Zion's Camp, in 1834. Served on Kirtland high council, 1834-35. Appointed to Quorum of Twelve in April 1835. Married Sarah Marinda Bates in July 1836 and had twelve children. Published *A[n] Interesting Account of Several Remarkable Visions* in 1840. Served on Nauvoo city council, 1841-45. Excommunicated in August 1842 for believing wife's accusation against Joseph Smith. Re-baptized and reinstated as apostle, January 1843. From 1844 polygamously married (1) Charlotte Bishop, (2) Adelia Ann Bishop, (3) Mary Ann Merrill, (4) Sarah Louisa Chandler, (5) Marian Ross, (6) Sarah Louise Lewis, (7) Juliaet Ann Phelps, (8) Eliza Crooks, and (9) Margaret Graham. Appointed to Council of Fifty, March 1844. Edited *New York Messenger,* 1845. Received endowment, December 1845; evicted from Nauvoo temple next month over conflict with brother Parley, but next day returned to fellowship. Entered Salt Lake Valley with Erastus Snow in July 1847. Edited *The Latter-Day Saints' Millennial Star,* 1848-50. Published *Divine Authenticity of the Book of Mormon,* 1850; *Great First Cause or the Self-Moving Forces of the Universe,* 1851. Delivered address to publicly announce polygamy, August 1852. Edited pro-polygamy magazine, *The Seer,* 1853-54. Served in Utah territorial legislature, 1855. Published debate with the Rev. John P. Newman, *Great Discussion! Does the Bible Sanction Polygamy!* in 1874. Visited William E. McLellin with Joseph F. Smith in September 1878. Divided Book of Mormon into shorter chapters with verses and geographical identifications, 1879. Died on 3 October 1881 in Salt Lake City, Utah Territory. See England, *Orson Pratt*; Bergera, *Conflict*; Quinn, *Origins*, 569-71.

Pratt, Parley Parker (1807-1857) was born on 12 April 1807 in Burlington, New York, son of Jared Pratt and Charity Dickinson. Married Thankful Halsey in September 1827 and had one child, but wife died in 1837. Baptized into Sidney Rigdon's Campbellite (Reformed Baptist Society) movement in late 1820s. Baptized into Church of Christ and ordained an elder in September 1830. Called "into the wilderness among the Lamanites" (D&C 32) in October. Ordained a high priest, June 1831. Participated in paramilitary expedition, Zion's Camp, in 1834. Served on Kirtland high council, 1834-35. Called to original Quorum of Twelve, February 1835, and published *The Millennium: A Poem* the same year. Married Mary Ann Frost in May 1837 and had four children. Published *A Voice of Warning* in 1837. Imprisoned with Joseph Smith in Liberty Jail, Clay County, Missouri, 1838-39. Edited *Latter Day Saints Millennial Star,* 1840-42. From 1843 polygamously married (1) Elizabeth Brotherton, (2) Mary Wood, (3) Hannahette Snively, (4) Belinda B. Marden, (5) Sarah Houston, (6) Phoebe Sopher, (7) Martha Monks, (8) Ann Agatha Walker, (9) Keziah Downes, and (10) Eleanor J. McComb McLean. Edited newspaper, *The Prophet*, in New York City, 1844-45. Published *Key to the Science of Theology,* 1855. Assassinated on 13 May 1857, at Van Buren, Arkansas, by Hector McLean, legal husband of Pratt's last wife. See Proctor and Proctor, *Parley P. Pratt*; Van Wagoner and Walker, *Book of Mormons*, 217-23; Quinn, *Origins*, 571-73.

Pratt, Sarah Marinda Bates (1817-1888) was born on 5 February 1817 in Henderson, New York, daughter of Cyrus Bates and Lydia Harrington. Baptized in June 1835 by Orson Pratt; married him in July 1836 and had twelve children. Rejected Joseph Smith's marriage proposal in early 1840s. Re-baptized, January 1843, at same time as husband, though never excommunicated. Voted into endowment quorum, December 1844; evicted from Nauvoo temple, January 1845, but received second anointing next day. Separated (but not divorced) from husband in 1860s. Excommunicated for apostasy, October 1874. Died on 25 December 1888 in Salt Lake City, Utah Territory. See Van Wagoner and Van Wagoner, "Sarah M. Pratt"; Compton, *Sacred Loneliness*, 634.

Publius (d. 150s) was bishop of Athens, late second century. Probably died during persecution under Antoninus Pius.

Quadratus (d. 140s) was the earliest Christian apologist and is sometimes counted among the Apostolic Fathers. Wrote apology for Christian religion in mid-120s, addressed to emperor Hadrian. See, *Apostolic Fathers*, 257-59; Holmes, *Apostolic Fathers*, 3, 293.

Quadratus (d. 170s) was bishop of Athens in the late second century. Died probably during persecution under Antoninus Pius.

Rich, Leonard (1800-1868) was born in Connecticut or New York. Married a woman named Keziah about 1823 and had at least eight children. Participated in paramilitary maneuver, Zion's Camp, in 1834. Ordained a president of Seventy in February 1835, released in April 1837. Died in Kirtland, Ohio. See Westergren, *Historian to Dissident*, 159-60; Quinn, *Origins*, 574-75.

Rigdon, Sidney S. (1793-1876) was born on 19 February 1793 in Saint Clair Township, Pennsylvania, son of William Rigdon and Nancy Gallaher. Became Baptist preacher in 1819. Married Phebe Brooks in June the next year and had eleven children. Became pastor of First Baptist Church in Pittsburgh in 1821, pastor of Grand River Association church in Mentor, Ohio, in 1826. Broke with Alexander Campbell and Walter Scott in 1830 to set up a communal society. Baptized into Church of Christ in November 1830 and was soon ordained an elder; became scribe for Joseph Smith's revision of Bible in December. Ordained a high priest in June 1831. Ordained second counselor to Smith in March 1832. Disfellowshipped and dropped from office in July for preaching against Smith's alleged avarice, but re-ordained later that month. Became Smith's first counselor in March 1833. Prepared and delivered seven "Lectures on Faith," 1834-35, published in Doctrine and Covenants to 1920. Edited *The Latter Day Saints' Messenger and Advocate* in 1837. Delivered so-called "Salt Sermon" in June 1838 threatening violence against dissenters and non-Mormons. Imprisoned with Smith in Liberty Jail in Clay County, Missouri, 1838-39. Served on Nauvoo city council in 1841. Joined Masonic lodge in 1842. Disfellowshipped in August 1843, but later reinstated. Appointed to Council of Fifty in March 1844, became Joseph Smith's running mate on Jeffersonian Democracy ticket for presidency of United States, but was disfellowshipped and finally excommunicated in September. Published *The Latter Day Saint Messenger and Advocate* (later *Messenger and Advocate of the Church of Christ*), 1844-46. Organized own Church of Christ, April 1845, in Pittsburgh. Appointed Stephen Post as spokesman, 1856; led Church of Jesus Christ of the Children of Zion from 1863 to death on 14 July 1876 in Friendship, New York. See Van Wagoner, *Sidney Rigdon*; Fletcher, "Sidney Rigdon"; Quinn, *Origins*, 576-78.

Robinson, Ebenezer (1816-1891) was born on 25 May 1816 in Floyd, New York, son of Nathan Robinson and Mary Brown. Baptized into Church of the Latter Day Saints in October 1835. Married Angelina Eliza Works two months later and had one child. Wife died in 1880. Ordained an elder in 1836. Edited *Times and Seasons* in Nauvoo, 1839-42. Supported Sidney Rigdon in late 1844 and called as Rigdon's counselor in April 1845. Printed weekly newspaper, *The Conococheague Herald*, at Greencastle, Pennsylvania, 1849. Married Martha A. Cunningham in February 1885. Edited *The Return,* 1889-91. Died on 11 March 1891 in Davis City, Iowa. See Shields, *Bibliography*, 30-31.

Robinson, George W. (1814-1890s) was born on 14 May 1814 in Pawlet, Vermont. Married Athalia Rigdon in April 1837. Appointed church recorder and First Presidency clerk, April 1838. Served as regimental colonel of Danites that year and was imprisoned in November. Became first postmaster of Nauvoo, 1840, and was released as church recorder in October. In 1842 lost faith due to Joseph Smith's marriage proposal to Nancy Rigdon. Supported Sidney Rigdon's Church of Christ in April 1845 and was named a counselor. Separated from Rigdon in early 1850s. Died in Friendship, New York. See Knisley, *Biographical Dictionary*; Van Wagoner, *Sidney Rigdon*.

Rogers, Israel Lewis (1818-1899) was born on 4 April 1818 in Stephentown, New York, son of David Rogers and Betsy Allen. Raised in Baptist church. Married Mahala Salisbury in February 1839 and had six children; his wife died in 1892. Baptized into LDS Church in 1840. Joined William Smith's church about 1850 and was ordained a counselor but soon left. Ordained a high priest and bishop of Reorganized Church in April 1860. Procured printing press for *True Latter Day Saints' Herald* in 1862, served on publication committee. Resigned as bishop in 1882, served as branch president. Married Rachel Trout in October 1893. Died on 8 November 1899 in Sandwich, Illinois. See Black, *RLDS Members*, 5:176-78; Knisley, *Biographical Dictionary*.

Septimus [Septimius] Severus (145-211) was born Lucius Septimius Severus near Lepcis Magna in Libya, son of P. Septimius Geta and Fulvia Pia. Married Paccia Marciana about 175, though she died about 185. Married Julia Domna in 187 and had two sons. Became emperor of Rome in 193. Fought Caledonians in Scotland in 208. Died in February 211 at York, England. See Birley, *Septimius Severus*.

Sheen, Isaac Joseph (1810-1874) was born on 22 December 1810 in Littlethorpe, Leicestershire, England, son of William and Jane Sheen. Baptized into LDS Church in August 1840, ordained an elder in May 1841. Married Drucilla Babbitt in May 1841. Edited *Melchisedek and*

Aaronic Herald, 1849-50, favoring William Smith's organization. Baptized into Reorganized Church in October 1861. Began editing *The True Latter Day Saints' Herald* in 1863 and wrote numerous pamphlets through the early 1870s: *The Kingdom of God*, *Millennial State*, *The Narrow Way*, *The Plan of Salvation*, *Universalism Examined*, and *Zion in America*. Died on 3 April 1874 in Plano, Illinois. See Black, *LDS Members*, 38:926; Black, *RLDS Members*, 5:354-55.

Smith, Don Carlos (1816-1841) was born on 25 March 1816 in Norwich, Vermont, son of Joseph Smith Sr. and Lucy Mack. Baptized into Church of Christ in June 1830. Married Agnes M. Coolbrith in July 1835 and had three children. Ordained a high priest and appointed president of Kirtland high priests quorum, January 1836. Edited *Times and Seasons* in Nauvoo, 1839-41; appointed president of Nauvoo high priests quorum, January 1841. Elected brigadier-general of Nauvoo Legion, February 1841; Nauvoo city councilman, February 1841. Died on 7 August 1841 in Nauvoo, Illinois. See Cook, *Revelations*, 274-75; Black, *Who's Who*, 269-71.

Smith, Emma Hale (1804-1879) was born on 10 July 1804 in Harmony Township, Pennsylvania, daughter of Isaac Hale and Elizabeth Lewis. Married Joseph Smith in January 1827, had nine children and adopted two others. Baptized into Church of Christ in June 1830 and confirmed two months later. Compiled first LDS hymn book, 1835. Became first president of Female Relief Society, March 1842. Received endowment, May 1843. After Joseph Smith's death, married Lewis C. Bidamon in December 1847. Joined Methodist church in 1848. Became member of Reorganized Church, 1860. Died on 30 April 1879 in Nauvoo, Illinois. See Newell and Avery, *Mormon Enigma*; Madsen, "Emma Hale Smith."

Smith, Hyrum (1800-1844) was born on 9 February 1800 in Tunbridge, Vermont, son of Joseph Smith Sr. and Lucy Mack. Joined Masons (Mount Moriah Lodge, New York) sometime before 1826. Married Jerusha Barden in November 1826 and had six children, though wife died in 1837. Baptized in June 1829 before church was organized. Became one of eight witnesses of Book of Mormon later that month. Became charter member of Church of Christ on 6 April 1830, ordained a priest in June and elder later that year, ordained a high priest in 1831. Participated in paramilitary maneuver, Zion's Camp, in 1834. Sustained as assistant president of the church, December 1834; assistant counselor to First Presidency, September 1837; second counselor in First Presidency, November 1837. Married Mary Fielding in December 1837 and had two children. Imprisoned with Joseph Smith in Liberty Jail in Clay County, Missouri, 1838-39. Ordained as presiding patriarch and associate president of church in January 1841. Served on Nauvoo city council and as brevet-major general of Nauvoo Legion, 1841-44; senior warden and worshipful master of Nauvoo Masonic lodge, 1842-44. From 1843 polygamously married (1) Mercy Rachel Fielding, (2) a woman surnamed Perry, and (3) a Mrs. Derbot. Appointed to Council of Fifty in March 1844; murdered by armed vigilantes on 27 June 1844, in Carthage, Illinois. See Corbett, *Hyrum Smith*; Van Orden, "Hyrum Smith"; Quinn, *Origins*, 583-85.

Smith, Joseph, Jr. (1805-1844) was born on 23 December 1805 in Sharon, Vermont, son of Joseph Smith Sr. and Lucy Mack. Married Emma Hale in January 1827, had nine children and adopted two others. Baptized by Oliver Cowdery in May 1829. Using a seer stone, dictated text of Book of Mormon in 1829, published it in March 1830. Designated first elder of church at organization on 6 April 1830. Dictated biblical revisions, 1830-1833, using King James Version as base text. In 1832 wrote earliest account of first vision, was sustained as president of high priesthood. From 1833 polygamously married at least thirty women. Received revelations which were compiled in Book of Commandments, 1833, revised and expanded in Doctrine and Covenants, 1835. Commander of Mormon militia, Zion's Camp, in 1834. Using seer stone, dictated Book of Abraham beginning in 1835 (published in 1842), using Egyptian funerary texts as source. Dedicated Kirtland Temple, January 1836. Edited *The Latter Day Saints' Messenger and Advocate,* 1837; *Elders' Journal,* 1837-38. In 1838 initiated as a Danite, changed church name to Church of Jesus Christ of Latter-day Saints, was imprisoned at Liberty Jail in Clay County, Missouri. Served as church treasurer, 1839-41; Nauvoo city councilman, 1841-42; lieutenant general of the Nauvoo Legion, 1841-44; Nauvoo mayor and chief justice of municipal court, 1842-44. Joined Nauvoo Masonic lodge, 1842. Organized Council of Fifty, March 1844; anointed "prophet, priest, and king over Israel on earth" in April. Ran as Jeffersonian Democracy candidate for president of United States in 1844. Ordered city marshal to destroy *Nauvoo Expositor,* June 1844. Murdered by armed vigilantes on 27 June 1844, in Carthage, Illinois. See Hill, *Joseph Smith*; Compton, *Sacred Loneliness*; Quinn, *Origins*, 587-91; Bushman and Jesse, "Joseph Smith."

Smith, Joseph, III (1832-1914) was born on 6 November 1832 in Kirtland, Ohio, son of Joseph Smith Jr. and Emma Hale. Ordained by father to be his successor in June 1844. Married Emmeline Griswold in October 1856 and had five children, but his wife died in 1869. Appointed president of Reorganized Church in April 1860. Published *Reply to Orson Pratt* in 1869. Married Bertha Madison in November 1869 and had nine children; his second wife died in 1896. Published *Reply of Pres. Joseph Smith to L. O. Littlefield in Refutation of the Doctrine of Plural Marriage* in 1885. Married Ada Rachel Clark in January 1898 and had three children. Published four-volume *History of the Church of Jesus Christ of Latter Day Saints,* 1902-03; *Plural Marriage in America,* 1903. Died on 10 December 1914 in Independence, Missouri. See Launius, *Joseph Smith III.*

Smith, Joseph F. (1838-1918) was born on 13 November 1838 in Far West, Missouri, son of Hyrum Smith and Mary Fielding. Ordained a Seventy in March 1858. Married cousin Levira Annett Clark Smith in April 1859. Ordained a high priest in October 1859. From 1866 polygamously married (1) Julina Lambson, (2) Sarah Ellen Richards, (3) Edna Lambson, (4) Alice Ann Kimball, and (5) Mary Taylor Schwartz. Ordained an apostle and counselor to First Presidency in July 1866, became member of Quorum of Twelve in October 1867. With Orson Pratt, visited William E. McLellin in September 1878. Sustained as president of church in October 1901. Died on 19 November 18 in Salt Lake City, Utah. See Gibbons, *Joseph F. Smith.*

Smith, Samuel Harrison (1808-1844) was born on 13 March 1808 in Tunbridge, Vermont, son of Joseph Smith Sr. and Lucy Mack. Baptized in May 1829 before church was organized. Became one of eight witnesses of Book of Mormon in 1829. Became a charter member of Church of Christ and was re-baptized on 6 April 1830. Received written license of an elder in June 1830, with added designation as "apostle of Jesus Christ." Ordained a high priest in June 1831. Served on Kirtland high council in February 1834. Married Mary Bailey in August 1834 and had four children, but wife died in 1841. Participated in battle of Crooked River, October 1838. In 1841, called by revelation (D&C 124) to be counselor to Nauvoo ward bishop Vinson Knight, became member of Nauvoo Legion, and married Levira A. Clark, with whom he had three children. Called as bishop of a Nauvoo ward, August 1842, but refused position. Received endowment in December 1843. Died on 30 July 1844 in Nauvoo, Illinois. See Jarman, "Samuel Smith"; Smith, "Samuel Harrison Smith."

Smith, Sylvester Marshall (1806-1880) was born on 28 March 1806 in Tyringham, Massachusetts, son of Chileab Smith and Nancy Marshall. Married Elizabeth Frank in 1827 and had eight children. Baptized into Church of Christ and ordained an elder sometime before June 1831; ordained a high priest in October. Participated in paramilitary campaign, Zion's Camp, in 1834, then tried for "traducing" the character of Joseph Smith during the march. Appointed to Kirtland high council, February 1835; released, January 1836. Ordained a Seventy in February 1835, and as president of First Quorum of Seventy the next month. Became charter member of Kirtland Safety Society, January 1837. Honorably released as president of Seventy, April 1837, due to previous high priest ordination. Became disaffected, was excommunicated in December 1837, and worked as an agent for William Smith's publication in 1849. Died on 22 February 1880 in Council Bluffs, Iowa. See Westergren, *Historian to Dissident*, 158-59; Black, *Who's Who*, 298-99; Quinn, *Origins*, 593-94.

Stewart, Dugald (1753-1828) was born on 22 November 1753 in Edinburgh, Scotland, son of Matthew Stewart. Advocate "common sense" school of philosophy. Married Helen Bannatyne in 1783 and had one son, but wife died in 1787. Appointed chair of mathematics and then of moral philosophy, University of Edinburgh, 1785. Married Miss Cranstoun in 1790 and had two children. Wrote three-volume *Elements of the Philosophy of the Human Mind,* 1792; *Outlines of Moral Philosophy,* 1793; *Philosophical Essays,* 1810; *The Philosophy of the Active and Moral Powers of Man,* 1828. Died on 11 June 1828. See Madden, "Stewart"; Hamilton, *Dugald Stewart.*

Strang, James Jesse (1813-1856) was born on 21 March 1813 in Scipio, New York, son of Clement Strang and Abigail James. Married Mary Perce in November1836. Baptized into LDS Church in February 1844. Found ancient plates, published as *The Book of the Law of the Lord* in 1856. Denounced Mormon polygamy in *Voree Herald* in 1847. From 1848 polygamously married (1) Elvira Field, (2) Betsy McNutt, (3) Sarah Wright, and (4) Phoebe Wright. Was shot in mid-June 1856, dying on 9 July 1856 in Voree, Wisconsin. See Van Noord, *Michigan King.*

Swift, Jonathan (1667-1745) was born on 30 November 1667 in Dublin, Ireland, son of English parents Abigaile and, posthumously, Jonathan Swift. Educated at Trinity College in 1680s and received an M.A. from Oxford in 1692. Ordained priest in Church of Ireland (Anglican) in 1695. Received D.D. from Dublin University in 1702. Published *A Tale of* *a Tub* and *The Battle of the Books* in 1704, *Gulliver's Travels* (anonymously) in 1726. Declared insane in 1742 and died on 19 October 1745. See Glendinning, *Jonathan Swift*.

Theodoret (ca. 393-ca. 466), born in Antioch, became bishop of Cyrrhus in 423. Wrote *Historia religosa (Religious History)*, 444-49, with biographies of Syrian monks. Supported Nestorius and two-nature Christology. Condemned by Dioscorus of Alexandria and deposed in 449 by Robber Synod of Ephesus, exiled to monastery at Apamea. Forced at council of Chalcedon in 451 to denounce Nestorius to regain his see. See Urbainczyk, *Theodoret*.

Trajan (ca. 56-117) was born Marius Ulpius Traianus on 18 September 56 (or thereabout) in Italica, Spain, son of Marius Ulpius Traianus and Marcia. Assigned to Roman legion in Syria about 75. Married Pompeia Plotina about 78. Adopted by Nerva and made co-emperor in 97, sole emperor in 98. Dedicated Trajan's Column in 113. Died in August 117 at Selinus. See Bennett, *Trajan*.

Traughber, John Logan (1854-1908) was born on 23 November 1854 in Missouri, son of John L. Traughber Sr. and Ellen Keziah Ross, and was a school teacher and farmer. Joined Reorganized Church. Married Mattie Elmira Felkins in January 1888 in Taney County, Missouri, and had nine children. Received William E. McLellin notebooks in 1880s, offered to sell them in 1901 to Salt Lake City minister Theodore Schroeder, then sold most in 1908, including copy of 1833 Book of Commandments, to LDS Church for fifty dollars. Retained three notebooks and other miscellany. Died on 8 December 1908 in Doucette, Texas.

Webster, Noah (1758-1843) was born on 16 October 1758 in West Hartford, Connecticut, son of Noah Webster and Mercy Steele. Graduated from Yale College in 1778. Published spelling books, 1783-1829, which helped standardize American spelling. Married Rebecca Greenleaf in October 1789 and had eight children. Published *A Compendious Dictionary of the English Language*, 1806; *An American Dictionary of the English Language*, 1828, with 70,000 entries; and a modern-English edition of the Bible in 1833 with gender-neutral language. Died on 28 May 1843 in New Haven, Connecticut. See Unger, *Noah Webster*.

Wesley, John (1703-1791) was born on 17 June 1703 at Epworth, Lincolnshire, England, son of Samuel Wesley and Susanna Annesley.

Ordained a priest in September 1728, led an Oxford study group the next year that was known for its methodical approach to scripture. Served mission to American colony of Georgia, 1735-37. Converted at religious meeting, May 1738, his heart being "strangely warmed," and formed Methodist Societies the next year. Accepted principle and practice of lay preaching in 1740. Published *Sermons on Several Occasions,* 1746; *Primitive Physick,* a medical self-help manual, 1747. Married the widow Mary "Molly" Vazeille in February 1851, though not happy and later separated. Published *Explanatory Notes on the New Testament,* 1754; *A Calm Address to Our American Colonies,* defending England's right to tax colonists, 1775. Died on 2 March 1791 in London. See Stone, *John Wesley*; Collins, *Real Christian.*

Whitmer, David D. (1805-1888) was born on 7 January 1805, at Harrisburg, Pennsylvania, son of Peter Whitmer Sr. and Mary Elsa Musselman. Became one of three witnesses of Book of Mormon in 1829. Baptized, confirmed, and ordained an elder in June 1829 before church was organized. Designated an apostle in 1829 by revelation. Became charter member of Church of Christ and re-ordained elder on 6 April 1830; received written elder's license in June with added designation of "apostle of Jesus Christ." Married Julia Ann Jolley in January 1831 and had two children. Appointed president of Missouri church, Clay County high council, and successor to Joseph Smith in July 1834. Assisted Oliver Cowdery and Martin Harris in choosing and ordaining twelve apostles in 1835. Rejected as president of Missouri church in February 1838, excommunicated in April for failure to observe Word of Wisdom, neglecting meetings, writing unfavorable letters, and signing name to official documents after being dismissed from office. Became president of a new Church of Christ in Kirtland, 1847-48, then another Church of Christ about 1875. Stated in June 1885 that "he did see them [gold plates] and the angel and heard him speak. But that it was indiscribable[,] that it was through the power of God ... [like] Paul hearing and seeing Christ but his associates did not. Because it is only seen in the Spirit." Published *An Address to All Believers in Christ* in 1887: "If you believe my testimony to the Book of Mormon; if you believe that God spake to us three witnesses by his own voice, then I tell you that in June, 1838, God spake to me again by his own voice from the heavens, and told me to 'separate myself from among the Latter Day Saints.'" Died on 25 January 1888, in Richmond, Missouri. See Anderson, *Lucy's Book*, 883; Quinn, *Origins*, 600; Vogel, "Witnesses' Testimonies."

Whitmer, David J. (1833-1895) was born on 27 November 1833, son of David Whitmer and Julia Ann Jolley. Married Sylvia R. Stockwell. Died on 14 June 1895. See Dear, *Whitmer Family*, 41.

Whitmer, David P. (1829-1883) was born on 4 August 1829, son of Jacob Whitmer and Elizabeth Ann Schott. Married cousin Vashti Whitmer (Peter Whitmer Jr.'s daughter) in April 1859 and had two children. Died on 21 February 1883. See Dear, *Whitmer Family*, 11; Anderson, *Lucy's Book*, 884.

Whitmer, Elizabeth Schott (1803-1876) was born on 28 January 1803 in Pennsylvania. Married Jacob Whitmer in September 1825 and had nine children. See Dear, *Whitmer Family*, 10.

Whitmer, Jacob C. (1800-1856) was born on 27 January 1800 in Harrisburg, Pennsylvania, son of Peter Whitmer Sr. and Mary Elsa Musselman. Married Elizabeth Schott in September 1825 and had nine children. Became one of eight witnesses of Book of Mormon in 1829. Baptized into Church of Christ by Oliver Cowdery on 11 April 1830. Served on Far West high council. Left church in 1838, supported David Whitmer's Church of Christ, 1847-48. Died on 21 April 1856 in Richmond, Missouri. See Anderson, *Lucy's Book*, 884; Dear, *Whitmer Family*, 10.

Whitmer (Whitmore), John (1802-1878) was born on 27 August 1802, in Fayette Township, New York, son of Peter Whitmer Sr. and Mary Elsa Musselman. Became one of eight witnesses of Book of Mormon in 1829, baptized in June before Church of Christ was organized. Re-baptized a year later and received elder's license with added designation of "apostle of Jesus Christ." Appointed church historian and ordained a high priest in 1831. Married Sarah Maria Jackson in February 1833 and had five children. In 1834 served on high council in Missouri, then as counselor in Missouri presidency from July on. Edited *Latter Day Saints' Messenger and Advocate*, 1835-36. Rejected as counselor in Missouri presidency, February 1838; excommunicated for apostasy in March; supported David Whitmer's Church of Christ, 1847-48, 1876. Died on 11 July 1878 at Far West, Missouri. See Westergren, *Historian to Dissident*, vii-xi; Anderson, *Lucy's Book*, 884.

Whitmore [Whitmer], Peter, Jr. (1809-1836) was born on 27 September 1809 in Fayette Township, New York, son of Peter Whitmer Sr. and Mary

Elsa Musselman. Became one of eight witnesses of Book of Mormon in 1829. In 1830 became charter member of Church of Christ on 6 April, ordained an elder by June, called "into the wilderness among the Lamanites" (D&C 32) in October. Ordained a high priest a year later. Married Vashti Higley in October 1832 and had three children. Appointed member of the Clay County high council, 1836. Died on 22 September 1836 near Liberty, Missouri. See Anderson, *Lucy's Book*, 884; Westergren, *Historian to Dissident*, 15.

Whitmer, Vashti P. (1837-1903) was born on 20 May 1837, daughter of Peter Whitmer Jr. and Vashti Higley. Married cousin David P. Whitmer (Jacob Whitmer's son) in April 1859 and had two children. Died on 23 December 1903. See Dear, *Whitmer Family*, 11, 47.

Whitney, Newell Kimball (1795-1850) was born on 5 February 1795 in Marlborough, Vermont, son on Samuel Whitney and Susannah Kimball. Joined the Masonic order at the Meridian Orb Lodge, Ohio, in 1817. Married Elizabeth Ann Smith in October 1822 and had twelve children. Was a Unitarian until 1829, then baptized into the Disciples of Christ or Campbellite church. Baptized a member of the Church of Christ in November 1830 and ordained an elder soon thereafter. Ordained a high priest in 1831. Called to be the first bishop in Kirtland in December 1831. Appointed a bishop of one of the wards in Nauvoo in October 1839. Received his endowment in May 1842. Served as treasurer of the Nauvoo Masonic lodge from 1842 to about 1845. Received second anointing in October 1843. Appointed to the council of fifty in March 1844. Sustained as First Bishop in the Church in October 1844. From 1845 polygamously married (1) Emmeline B. Woodward and (2) Anne Houston. Sustained as presiding bishop of the church in April 1847. Called as a local bishop in Salt Lake City in 1849. Died on 23 September 1850 in Salt Lake City, Utah Territory. See Quinn, *Origins*, 601-602; Black, *Who's Who*, 339-41.

Wight, Lyman (1796-1858) was born on 9 May 1796 at Fairfield Township, New York, son of Levi Wight and Sarah Corbin. Enlisted in militia and fought in Battle of Sackettt's Harbor in War of 1812. Married Harriet Benton in January 1823 and had nine children. Baptized into Church of Christ, November 1830; ordained an elder a week later, a high priest in June 1831. Participated in paramilitary expedition, Zion's Camp, in 1834. Served as Danite colonel in Missouri, 1838, and stake presidency to 1841. Imprisoned with Joseph Smith at Liberty Jail in Clay County, Missouri, 1838-39. Ordained an apostle, April 1841. Served on Nauvoo city council, 1841-43; joined Masonic order, Nauvoo lodge, 1842; appointed to Council of Fifty, May 1844, but was dropped in February 1845. Commissioned by apostles in August 1844 to find a location for church in Texas. From 1845 polygamously married (1) Mary Hawley, (2) Mary Ann Otis, and (3) Jane Margaret Ballantyne. Sustained as an apostle in William Smith's church, October 1848, and disfellowshipped by LDS Pottawattamie high council the same month; excommunicated in December. Appointed second counselor to William Smith in November 1849 and relocated twelve followers to Texas colony in May 1850. In Texas, served as chief justice of Gillespie County, 1850-51, and began temple ordinances in Zodiac, February 1851. Died on 31 March 1858 in Dexter, Texas. See Wight, *Wild Ram*; Quinn, *Origins*, 602-604.

Williams, Frederick Granger (1787-1842) was born on 28 October 1787 in Suffield, Connecticut, son of William Wheeler Williams and Ruth Granger. Married Rebecca Swain in December 1815 and had four children. A Baptist, then Disciple of Christ (Campbellites), was baptized into Church of Christ and ordained an elder in November 1830. Ordained a high priest in October 1831. Called as counselor to Joseph Smith, March 1832, and as second counselor in First Presidency, March 1833. Participated in paramilitary campaign, Zion's Camp, in 1834. Edited *Northern Times*, 1835-36. Rejected as counselor and dropped from the First Presidency, November 1837. Apparently excommunicated, December 1837, and re-baptized, August 1838; excommunicated again, March 1839, then restored and re-baptized, April 1840. Moved from church headquarters and was excommunicated a third time in 1841 or 1842. Died on 10 October 1842, in Quincy, Illinois. See Thomas, "Frederick G. Williams"; Williams, "Frederick Granger Williams"; Quinn, *Origins*, 604-605.

Young, Brigham (1801-1877) was born on 1 June 1801 in Whitingham, Vermont, son of John Young and Abigail Howe. Married Miriam Works in October 1824 and had two children, though she died in 1832. Joined Methodist church in 1824. Baptized into Church of Christ and ordained an elder in April 1832. Married Mary Ann Angell in February 1834 and had six children. Participated in paramilitary excursion, Zion's Camp, in 1834. Ordained one of original twelve apostles in February 1835. Became charter member and stockholder in Kirtland Safety Society, January 1837. Sustained as president of the Quorum of Twelve in April 1840. Served as commander in chief of Nauvoo Legion, 1841-46; Nauvoo city councilman, 1841-45. Joined Masonic lodge, April 1842. From 1842 polygamously married at least twenty-six women. Appointed to Council of Fifty in March 1844, claimed church leadership in August, and dedicated Nauvoo temple in October. Left Nauvoo for western exodus, February 1846, arriving in Great Salt Lake Valley, July 1847. Sustained as president of church, December 1847; ordained "king, priest, and ruler over Israel on earth," December 1848. Served as governor of independent state of Deseret, 1848-52; Utah territorial governor and superintendent of Indian affairs, 1851-58. Laid cornerstone for Salt Lake Temple, April 1853. Introduced Deseret Alphabet, 1859. Relinquished governorship, April 1858; continued as head of "ghost government," 1862-70. Served on Salt Lake City council, 1872-77. Dedicated St. George Temple, April 1877. Died on 29 August 1877 in Salt Lake City, Utah Territory. See Arrington, *Brigham Young*; Quinn, *Origins*, 607-11.

D.

FROM THE ILLINOIS PATRIOT, 1831

On 10 September 1831, William E. McLellin preached in a courthouse in Jacksonville, Illinois, accompanied by his mission companion, Hyrum Smith. The *Illinois Patriot* summarized the content of the sermon. Unfortunately the *Patriot* is no longer extant for the date in question,[1] but because the article was reprinted in other newspapers such as the *New Hampshire Gazette*[2] it is possible to present the transcript which follows on pages 569-70. Even though the newspaper neglected to identify the preacher by name, McLellin's diary and a letter to his family confirm that it was him.[3] The article is consistent with all other sources for the period in reporting that the story of Mormonism began with the appearance of an unnamed angel to Joseph Smith, translation of the gold plates by means of a seer stone, and announcement of the millennial headquarters of Christ at Independence, Missouri.

---

1. The article presumably first appeared on 17 September 1831.

2. "Miscellany," *New Hampshire Gazette,* 25 Oct. 1831, p. 4, Readex Early American Newspaper Series for Portsmouth, New Hampshire, 1756-1833, American Antiquarian Society, Worcester, Massachusetts, copy in the William E. McLellin Collection, Accn 1827, Marriott Library, University of Utah. Our appreciation to H. Michael Marquardt for sharing this source with us, also for making the connection to McLellin, documented in note 3.

3. See Jan Shipps and John W. Welch, eds., *The Journals of William E. McLellin, 1831-1836* (Provo and Urbana: BYU Studies and University of Illinois Press, 1994), 39, 81.

NEW-HAMPSHIRE GAZETTE.

[$2 per annum.] PUBLISHED BY GIDEON BECK, PUBLISHER OF THE LAWS OF THIS STATE AND OF THE UNITED STATES. [half in advance.]

VOL. LXXVI. *PORTSMOUTH, TUESDAY, OCTOBER 25, 1831.* NO. 50.

MISCELLANY.

Mormonism.—The following article from the Illinois Patriot, will give some idea of the absurdities of this new faith.

The Mormonites.—A Preacher of this sect visited us last Saturday. We heard a part of his lecture, which occupied more than two hours. From his account, this sect came into existence a little more than a year since in the following manner:—A young man about 23 years of age somewhere in Ontario county, N. Y. was visited by an *angel!* (here the preacher looked around him apparently to see it the credulity of the people in this enlightened age, could be thus imposed on) who informed him three times in one night that by visiting a certain place in that town he would have revealed to him something of importance. The young man was disturbed, but did not obey the summons until the following day, when the angel again visited him. At the place appointed he found in the earth a box which contained a set of thin plates resembling gold, with Arabic characters inscribed on them. The plates were minutely described as being connected with rings in the shape of the letter D, which facilitated the opening and shutting of the book. The preacher said he found in the same place two stones with which he was enabled by placing them over his eyes and putting his head in a dark corner to decypher the hieroglyphics on the plates!—This we were told was performed to admiration, and now, as the result, we have a book which the speaker informed us was the Mormon Bible—a book second to no other—without which the holy bible, he seemed to think, would be of little use.

It appears from his statement, that three of the offspring of Joseph, by his youngest son Ephraim, whose names were Laman, Nephi and Lehigh, as near as we could understand, were the persons from whom sprang Mormon.—Laman and Nephi rather declined from walking in the right way, but Lehigh was firm in the faith. Mormon, who was a prophet, led them eastward until they came to the sea, as we suppose, where they built a ship and came to this western world. To prove this, the preacher referred us to Genesis, 49th chapter and 22d verse, and said the branches running over the wall was neither more nor less than the progeny of Joseph, leaving their own and coming to this country! He went into a detail of the reasons which induced him to join himself to this people—that on account of so many sects being in the world, and the discrepances in their opinions, he became sceptical—that hearing of these people in July last, he joined himself to them, believing them to constitute the true Church—and that he came this way to meet a convocation of elders in Jackson county, Missouri, which is to be their New Jerusalem, but was disappointed in not seeing them there. He insisted on the bible being joined with his book, by quoting the 16th and 17th verses of the 37th chapter of Ezekiel, and comparing the bible and Mormon's book to the two sticks there spoken of. We thought this part of his subject too ludicrous to be refuted by any man in his right mind. We cannot now enter into the merits of his discourse, nor should we have given this hastily written sketch, had we not been requested to say something on the subject. Some of these men may be sincere; but does this prove they are in the right? The worshippers of Juggernaut are sincere, or they would not sacrifice their lives by throwing themselves under the wheel of its life destroying car. As far as we are acquainted with the bible we now have, we are satisfied that the Mormonites are a deluded set of men, whose doctrines are not only dangerous—but, notwithstanding all their professions, they are calling down the curse of God on their own heads.

An article from the *Illinois Patriot*, reprinted in the *New Hampshire Gazette*, 25 October 1831, p. 4. The masthead is from page 1; the long column is given here as two for the sake of space.

MISCELLANY.

Mormonism.—The following article from the Illinois Patriot, will give some idea of the absurdities of this new faith.

The Mormonites.—A Preacher of this sect visited us last Saturday. We heard a part of his lecture, which occupied more than two hours. From his account, this sect came into existence a little more than a year since in the following manner:—A young man about 23 years of age somewhere in Ontario county, N.Y. was visited by an *angel!* (here the preacher looked around him apparently to see if the credulity of the people in this enlightened age, could be thus imposed on) who informed him three times in one night that by visiting a certain place in that town he would have revealed to him something of importance. The young man was disturbed, but did not obey the summons until the following day, when the angel again visited him. At the place appointed he found in the earth a box which contained a set of thin plates resembling gold, with Arabic characters inscribed on them. The plates were minutely described as being connected with rings in the shape of the letter D, which facilitated the opening and shutting of the book. The preacher said he found in the same place two stones with which he was enabled by placing them over his eyes and putting his head in a dark corner to decypher the hieroglyphics on the plates!—This we were told was performed to admiration, and now, as the result, we have a book which the speaker informed us was the Mormon Bible—a book second to no other—without which the holy bible, he seemed to think, would be of little use.

It appears from his statement, that three of the offspring of Joseph, by his youngest son Ephraim, whose names were Laman, Nephi and Lehigh, as near as we could understand, were the persons from whom sprang Mormon.—Laman and Nephi rather declined from walking in the right way, but Lehigh was firm in the faith. Mormon, who was a prophet, led them eastward until they came to the sea, as we suppose, where they built a ship and came to this western world. To prove this, the preacher referred us to Genesis, 49th chapter and 22d verse, and said the branches running over the wall was neither more nor less than the progeny of Joseph, leaving their own and coming to this country! He went into a detail of the reasons which induced him to join himself to this people—that on account of so many sects being in the world, and the discrepances in their opinions, he became sceptical—that hearing of these people in July last, he joined himself to them, believing them to constitute the true Church—and that he came this way to meet a convocation of elders in Jackson county, Missouri, which is to be their New Jerusalem, but was disappointed in not seeing them there. He insisted on the bible being joined with his book, by quoting the 16th and 17th verses of the 37th chapter of Ezekiel, and comparing the bible and Mormon's book to the two sticks there spoken of. We thought this part of his subject too ludicrous to be refuted by any man in his right mind. We cannot now enter into the merits of his discourse, nor should we have given this hastily written sketch, had we not been requested to say something on the subject. Some of these men may be sincere; but does this prove they are in the right? The worshippers of Juggernaut are sincere, or they would not sacrifice their lives by throwing themselves under the wheel of its life destroying car. As far as we are acquainted with the bible we now have, we are satisfied that the Mormonites are a deluded set of men, whose doctrines are not only dangerous–but, notwithstanding all their professions, they are calling down the curse of God on their own heads

E.

BIBLIOGRAPHY

Ahlstrom, Sidney E. *A Religious History of the American People.* 2 vols. New York: Doubleday, 1975.

Allen, James B., and Glen M. Leonard. *The Story of the Latter-day Saints.* 2d ed. rev. Salt Lake City: Deseret Book, 1992.

Allen, James B., Ronald W. Walker, and David J. Whittaker. *Studies in Mormon History, 1830-1997: An Indexed Bibliography.* Urbana and Provo: University of Illinois Press and BYU Smith Institute for LDS History, 2000.

Anderson, Karl Ricks. *Joseph Smith's Kirtland: Eyewitness Accounts.* Salt Lake City: Deseret Book, 1989.

Anderson, Lavina Fielding, ed. *Lucy's Book: A Critical Edition of Lucy Mack Smith's Family Memoir.* Salt Lake City: Signature Books, 2001.

Anderson, Mary Audentia Smith, ed. *The Memoirs of President Joseph Smith III (1832-1914).* Independence, MO: Price Publishing, 2001.

Anderson, Richard L. "Oliver Cowdery, Esq.: His Non-Church Decade." In *To the Glory of God: Mormon Essays on Great Issues,* eds. Truman G. Madsen and Charles D. Tate Jr. Salt Lake City: Deseret Book, 1972.

________. "What Changes Have Been Made in the Name of the Church?" *Ensign,* Jan. 1979, 13-14.

________. *Investigating the Book of Mormon Witnesses.* Salt Lake City: Deseret Book, 1981.

________. "The Mature Joseph Smith and Treasure Searching." *BYU Studies* 24 (Fall 1984-86): 489-560.

________. "Cowdery, Oliver." In *Encyclopedia of Mormonism,* ed. Daniel H. Ludlow.

Andrews, Bob L. "McClellan Family Sketch." *Smith County Historical and Genealogical Society Newsletter,* vol. 1, issue 2.

Andrus, Hyrum L., and Helen Mae Andrus, comps. *They Knew the Prophet.* Salt Lake City: Bookcraft, 1974; rpt. Deseret Book, 1999.

Arnold, Marvin M. *Nicaea and the Nicene Council of A.D. 325*. Washington, Mich.: Arno Publications, 1987.

Arrington, Leonard J. *Brigham Young: American Moses*. New York: Alfred A. Knopf, 1985.

Ashment, Edward H. "The Facsimiles of the Book of Abraham: A Reappraisal." *Sunstone*, Dec. 1979, 33-48.

Attwater, Donald, comp. *A New Dictionary of Saints*. Collegeville, Minn.: Liturgical Press, 1993.

Backman, Milton V., Jr. *The Heavens Resound: A History of the Latter-day Saints in Ohio, 1830-1838*. Salt Lake City: Deseret Book, 1983.

________. *Eyewitness Accounts of the Restoration*. Salt Lake City: Deseret Book, 1986.

Barlow, Philip L. "Decoding Mormonism." *Christian Century*, 17 Jan. 1996, 52-55.

Barnes, Jonathan. *The Cambridge Companion to Aristotle*. Cambridge, Eng.: Cambridge University Press, 1995.

Barron, Howard H. *Orson Hyde: Missionary, Apostle, Colonizer*. Bountiful, Utah: Horizon Publishers, 1977.

Bennett, Julian. *Trajan Optimus Princeps: A Life and Times*. Bloomington: Indiana University Press, 1997.

Benson, Ezra Taft. "Flooding the Earth with the Book of Mormon." *Ensign*, Nov. 1988.

Bergera, Gary James. "Seniority in the Twelve: The 1875 Realignment of Orson Pratt." *Journal of Mormon History* 18 (Spring 1992): 19-58.

________. *Conflict in the Quorum: Orson Pratt, Brigham Young, Joseph Smith*. Salt Lake City: Signature Books, 2002.

Berrett, LaMar C. "An Impressive Letter from the Pen of Joseph Smith." *BYU Studies* 11 (Summer 1971): 517-23.

Best, Karl F. "Changes in the Revelations, 1833 to 1835." *Dialogue: A Journal of Mormon Thought* 25 (Spring 1992): 87-112.

Bigler, David L., ed. *A Winter with the Mormons: The 1851 Letters of Jotham Goodell*. Salt Lake City: Tanner Trust Fund and J. Willard Marriott Library, 2001.

Birley, Anthony Richard. *Hadrian: The Restless Emperor*. London: Routledge, 1997.

________. *Septimius Severus: The African Emperor.* Rev. ed. New Haven, Conn.: Yale University Press, 1988.

Bitton, Davis. Review of *The Refiner's Fire* by John L. Brooke. *BYU Studies* 34 (1994): 182-92.

Black, Susan Easton, comp. *Membership of the Church of Jesus Christ of Latter-day Saints, 1830-1848.* 50 vols. Provo, Utah: BYU Religious Studies Center, 1984-1988.

________. "Name of the Church." In *Encyclopedia of Mormonism,* ed. Daniel H. Ludlow.

________, comp. *Early Members of the Reorganized Church of Jesus Christ of Latter Day Saints.* 6 vols. Provo, Utah: BYU Religious Studies Center, 1993.

________. *Who's Who in the Doctrine and Covenants.* Salt Lake City: Bookcraft, 1997.

Bledsoe, Albert Taylor. "Foreknowledge and Free Will." *Southern Review* 15 (1874): 91-109.

________. Review of Victor Cousin's *Course of the History of Modern Philosophy. Southern Review* 20 (1876): 196-210.

________. "Augustinism: Original Sin." *Southern Review* 22 (1877): 5-61.

________. "Of the Application of the Maxim that Every Effect Must Have a Cause." *Southern Review* 23 (1878): 26-33.

________. "The Relation of the Will to the Feelings." *Southern Review* 23 (1878): 339-51.

Bowen, Francis, ed. *The Metaphysics of Sir William Hamilton.* Boston: John Allyn, 1873.

Bowen, Norman R., ed. *A Gentile Account of Life in Utah's Dixie, 1872-73: Elizabeth Kane's St. George Journal.* Salt Lake City: Tanner Trust Fund and J. Willard Marriott Library, 1995.

Bowen, Walter Dean. "The Versatile W. W. Phelps—Mormon Writer, Educator, and Pioneer." M.S. thesis, Brigham Young University, 1958.

Boyack, Hazel Noble. *A Nobleman in Israel.* Cheyenne, Wyo.: Pioneer Printing, 1962.

Brooke, John L. *The Refiner's Fire: The Making of Mormon Cosmology, 1644-1844.* New York: Cambridge University Press, 1994.

Brown, Peter. *Augustine of Hippo: A Biography.* Berkeley: University of California Press, 2000.

Brown, S. Kent. "Apostle." In *Encyclopedia of Mormonism,* ed. Daniel H. Ludlow.

Brox, Norbert. *A Concise History of the Early Church.* New York: Continuum, 1995.

Buck, Charles. *A Theological Dictionary containing Definitions of All Religious Terms.* Philadelphia: J. J. Woodward, 1832.

Burnett, M. Dallas. "General Conference." In *Encyclopedia of Mormonism,* ed. Daniel H. Ludlow.

Bushman, Richard L. "Mormon Persecutions in Missouri, 1833." *Brigham Young University Studies* 3 (Autumn 1960): 11-20.

________. *Joseph Smith and the Beginnings of Mormonism.* Urbana: University of Illinois Press, 1984.

________. "The Mysteries of Mormonism." *Journal of the Early Republic* 15 (1995): 501-08.

Bushman, Richard L., and Dean C. Jessee. "Smith, Joseph: The Prophet." In *Encyclopedia of Mormonism,* ed. Daniel H. Ludlow.

Cannon, Brian Q., et al., "Priesthood Restoration Documents." *Brigham Young University Studies* 35 (Winter 1996): 163-207.

Cannon, Donald Q. "Licensing in the Early Church." *Brigham Young University Studies* 22 (Winter 1982): 96-105.

________ and Lyndon W. Cook, eds. *Far West Record: Minutes of the Church of Jesus Christ of Latter-day Saints, 1830-1844.* Salt Lake City: Deseret Book, 1983.

Cannon, George Q. *Life of Joseph Smith the Prophet.* Salt Lake City: Deseret Book, 1986.

Chase, Harold W., et al., eds. *Dictionary of American History.* Rev. ed. New York: Charles Scribner's Sons, 1976.

Christoph, Florence A., ed. *The Van Voorhees Family in America.* North Haledon, N.J.: Van Voorhees Association, 2000.

Clark, James R. *The Story of the Pearl of Great Price.* Salt Lake City: Bookcraft, 1955.

Collier, Fred C., and William S. Harwell, eds. *Kirtland Council Minute Book.* Salt Lake City: Collier's Publishing, 1996.

Collins, Kenneth J. *A Real Christian: The Life of John Wesley.* Nashville, Tenn.: Abingdon Press, 1999.

Compton, Todd. *In Sacred Loneliness: The Plural Wives of Joseph Smith.* Salt Lake City: Signature Books, 1997.

Condie, Spencer J. "Missionary, Missionary Life." In *Encyclopedia of Mormonism*, ed. Daniel H. Ludlow.

Coogan, Michael David, ed. *The New Oxford Annotated Apocrypha*. 3d ed. New York: Oxford University Press, 2001.

Cook, Lyndon W. *The Revelations of the Prophet Joseph Smith: A Historical and Biographical Commentary of the Doctrine and Covenants*. Salt Lake City: Deseret Book, 1985.

________. *William Law: Biographical Essay, Nauvoo Diary, Correspondence, Interview*. Orem, Utah: Grandin Book, 1994.

Corbett, Pearson H. *Hyrum Smith, Patriarch*. Salt Lake City: Deseret Book, 1963.

Corrill, John. *A Brief History of the Church of Christ of Latter Day Saints*. St. Louis, Mo.: By the author, 1839.

Cowan, Richard O. "Branch, Branch President." In *Encyclopedia of Mormonism*, ed. Daniel H. Ludlow.

Craig, Edward, ed. *Routledge Encyclopedia of Philosophy*. London: Routledge, 1998.

Cronon, William. "A Place for Stories: Nature, History, and Narrative." *Journal of American History* 78 (Mar. 1992): 1347-76.

Crouzel, Henri. "Pamphilus." In *New Catholic Encyclopedia*, ed. William J. McDonald. D.C.: Catholic University of America, 1967.

Davis, Inez Smith. *The Story of the Church*. 6th ed. Independence, Mo.: Herald Publishing House, 1959.

Dear, Mary Cleora, comp. *Two Hundred Thirty-Eight Years of the Whitmer Family, 1737-1976*. Richmond, Mo.: Beck Printing, 1976.

Draper, Maurice L. "The Sociology of Dissent and the Reorganized Church." In *Let Contention Cease*, eds. Launius and Spillman.

Dudley, Dean A. "Bank Born of Revelation: The Kirtland Safety Society Anti-Banking Company." *Journal of Economic History* 30 (Winter 1970): 848-53.

Duffy, John-Charles. "The New Missionary Discussions and the Future of Correlation." *Sunstone*, Sept. 2005, 32-34.

________. "Clyde Forsberg's Equal Rites and the Exoticizing of Mormonism." *Dialogue: A Journal of Mormon Thought* 39 (Spring 2006), 4-34.

Duncan, Jon M. "Multiple Discourses in Early Mormon Religion." M.A. thesis, Brigham Young University, 1998.

Dyer, Alvin R. *The Refiner's Fire: The Significance of Events Transpiring in Missouri.* 3d ed. rev. Salt Lake City: Deseret Book, 1972.

Edwards, F. Henry. *The Edwards Commentary on the Doctrine and Covenants.* Independence, Mo.: Herald Publishing House, 1986.

Ehat, Andrew F. "Joseph Smith's Introduction of Temple Ordinances and the 1844 Mormon Succession Question." M.A. thesis, Brigham Young University, 1982.

Ehrman, Bart D. *The New Testament: A Historical Introduction to the Early Christian Writings.* New York: Oxford University Press, 1997.

Elliott, J. K. *The Apocryphal New Testament: A Collection of Apocryphal Christian Literature in an English Translation.* Oxford: Clarendon Press, 1993.

England, Breck. *The Life and Thought of Orson Pratt.* Salt Lake City: University of Utah Press, 1985.

England, Eugene. "Healing and Making Peace in the World and the Church." *Sunstone,* Dec. 1991, 38.

Ensign. "June Videoconference: Accomplishing the Mission of the Church," Sept. 1987.

Esplin, Ronald K. "The Emergence of Brigham Young and the Twelve to Mormon Leadership, 1830-1841." Ph.D. diss., Brigham Young University, 1981.

________. "Joseph, Brigham, and the Twelve: A Succession of Continuity." *Brigham Young University Studies* 21 (Summer 1981): 301-41.

Esshom, Frank. *Pioneers and Prominent Men of Utah.* 2 vols. Salt Lake City: Utah Pioneers Publishing, 1913.

Etheridge, J. W. *The Life of the Rev. Adam Clarke, LL.D.* New York: Carlton and Porter, 1858.

Faris, Paul P. "Neill, William." In *Dictionary of American Biography,* ed. Dumas Malone. New York: Charles Scribner's Sons, 1934.

Faulring, Scott H., ed. *An American Prophet's Record: The Diaries of Journals of Joseph Smith.* 2d ed. Salt Lake City: Signature Books and Smith Research Associates, 1989.

Faust, James E. "Keeping Covenants and Honoring the Priesthood." *Ensign,* Nov. 1993.

Fielding, Robert Kent. "The Mormon Economy in Kirtland, Ohio." *Utah Historical Quarterly* 27 (Oct. 1959): 331-56.

Firmage, Edwin Brown, and Richard Collin Mangrum. *Zion in the Courts: A Legal History of the Church of Jesus Christ of Latter-day Saints, 1830-1900*. Urbana: University of Illinois Press, 2001.

Flake, Lawrence R. *Prophets and Apostles of the Last Dispensation*. Provo, Utah: BYU Religious Studies Center, 2001.

Fletcher, Galen L. "Sidney Rigdon: First Counselor to Joseph Smith (1833-1844)." In *Counselors to the Prophets*, comp. Michael K. Winder.

Gates, Paul W. "Half-Breed Tract." In *Dictionary of American History*, eds. Chase et al.

Gibbons, Francis M. *Joseph F. Smith: Patriarch and Preacher, Prophet of God*. Salt Lake City: Deseret Book, 1984.

Glazier, Michael, and Monika K. Hellwig. *The Modern Catholic Encyclopedia*. Collegeville, Minn.: Liturgical Press, 1994.

Glendinning, Victoria. *Jonathan Swift: A Portrait*. New York: Henry Holt, 1999.

Godfrey, Kenneth W., Audrey M. Godfrey, and Jill Mulvay Derr, eds. *Women's Voices: An Untold History of the Latter-day Saints, 1830-1900*. Salt Lake City: Deseret Book, 1982.

Goodrich, Charles A. *Outlines of Ecclesiastical History*. N.p.: 1829.

Goodspeed, Edgar J. *The Apostolic Fathers: An American Translation*. New York: Harper and Brothers, 1950.

Grandstaff, Mark R. "Having More Learning than Sense: William E. McLellin and the Book of Commandments Revisited." *Dialogue: A Journal of Mormon Thought* 26 (Winter 1993): 23-48.

Grant, Bruce. *Concise Encyclopedia of the American Indian*. Rev. ed. New York: Wings Books, 1989.

Grant, Michael. *Constantine the Great: The Man and His Times*. New York: Scribner's, 1994.

Grant, Robert M. *Eusebius as Church Historian*. Oxford: Clarendon Press, 1980.

________. *Irenaeus of Lyons*. London: Routledge, 1997.

Greenhow, John. "To the Church of Jesus Christ." *Zion's Reveille*, 4 Feb. 1847, 16.

Groat, Joel B. "Apostle William McLellin and the Integrity Issue." *Heart and Mind: Newsletter of Gospel Truths Ministries*, Summer 1993, 1-2.

Gunn, Stanley R. *Oliver Cowdery: Second Elder and Scribe.* Salt Lake City: Bookcraft, 1962.

Hales, Brian C. *Modern Polygamy and Mormon Fundamentalism: The Generations after the Manifesto.* Salt Lake City: Greg Kofford Books, 2005.

Hall, David D., ed. *The Antinomian Controversy, 1636-1638: A Documentary History.* Rev. ed. Durham, N.C.: Duke University Press, 1990.

Hamblin, William J. Review of *The Refiner's Fire* by John L. Brooke. *BYU Studies* 34 (1994): 167-81.

Hamblin, William J., Daniel C. Peterson, and George L. Mitton. "Mormon in the Fiery Furnace: Or Loftes Tryk Goes to Cambridge." *FARMS Review of Books* 6/2 (1994): 3-58.

Hamilton, William, ed. *The Collected Works of Dugald Stewart.* 11 vols. Edinburgh: T. Constable, 1854-60.

Harper, Steven C. "Drawing Lessons from a Life: William E. McLellin, 1831-1832," In *Lives of the Saints: Writing Mormon Biography and Autobiography*, ed. Jill Mulvay Derr.

Hartley, William G. *My Best for the Kingdom: History and Autobiography of John Lowe Butler, a Mormon Frontiersman.* Salt Lake City: Aspen Books, 1993.

________. "The McLellin Journals and Early Mormon History." In *Journals of McLellin,* eds. Shipps and Welch.

Hasler, August. *How the Pope Became Infallible: Pius IX and the Politics of Persuasion.* Trans. Peter Heinegg. Garden City, N.Y.: Doubleday, 1981.

Hatch, Nathan. *The Democratization of American Christianity.* New Haven: Yale University Press, 1989.

Hays, Willard Murrell. "Polemics and Philosophy: A Biography of Albert Taylor Bledsoe." Ph.D. diss., University of Tennessee, 1971.

Heinerman, Joseph. *Temple Manifestations.* Manti, Utah: Mountain Valley Publishers, 1974.

Herringshaw, Thomas William. *Herringshaw's Encyclopedia of American Biography of the Nineteenth Century.* Chicago: American Publishers' Association, 1898.

Hill, Donna. *Joseph Smith: The First Mormon.* Garden City, N.Y.: Doubleday, 1977; rpt. Signature Books, 1999.

Hill, Marvin S. "Cultural Crisis in the Mormon Kingdom: A Reconsideration of the Causes of Kirtland Dissent." *Church History* 49 (Fall 1980): 286-97.

________. *Quest for Refuge: The Mormon Flight from American Pluralism.* Salt Lake City: Signature Books, 1989.

Hill, Marvin S., C. Keith Rooker, and Larry T. Wimmer. "The Kirtland Economy Revisited: A Market Critique of Sectarian Economics." *Brigham Young University Studies* 17 (Summer 1977): 391-475.

Holmes, Michael W., ed. *The Apostolic Fathers.* 2nd ed. Grand Rapids, Mich.: Baker Book House, 1989.

Holzapfel, Richard Neitzel, and T. Jeffery Cottle. *Old Mormon Kirtland and Missouri: Historic Photographs and Guide.* Santa Ana, Calif.: Fieldbrook Productions, 1991.

Howard, Richard P. "William E. McLellin–Restless Son of Tennessee–Come Home." *Saints Herald,* July 1974, 42.

________. *The Church through the Years.* 2 vols. Independence, Mo.: Herald Publishing House, 1992-93.

________. "William E. McLellin: 'Mormonism's Stormy Petrel." In *Differing Visions,* eds. Launius and Thatcher.

________. *Restoration Scriptures: A Study of Their Textual Development.* 2d ed. rev. & enl. Independence, Mo.: Herald Publishing House, 1995.

Howe, E. D. *Mormonism Unvailed.* Painsville. Ohio: By the author, 1834.

Humble, Bill J. *Light from Above: The Life of Alexander Campbell.* Nashville, Tenn.: Gospel Advocate, 1988.

Hyde, Myrtle Stevens. *Orson Hyde: The Olive Branch of Israel.* Salt Lake City: Agreka Books, 2000.

Jahn, Johann. *Jahn's Biblical Archaeology.* Trans. Thomas C. Upham. New York: Mark H. Newman, 1849.

James, Rhett Stephens. "Harris, Martin." In *Encyclopedia of Mormonism,* ed. Daniel H. Ludlow.

________. "Lucy Harris: Toward a Compassionate Reinterpretation." *Nauvoo Journal* 9 (Spring 1997): 49-57.

Jarman, Dean. "The Life and Contributions of Samuel Harrison Smith." M.S. thesis, Brigham Young University, 1961.

Jennings, Warren A. "Factors in the Destruction of the Mormon Press in Missouri, 1833." *Utah Historical Quarterly* 35 (Winter 1967): 57-76.

________. "The Expulsion of the Mormons from Jackson County, Missouri." *Missouri Historical Review* 64 (Oct. 1969): 41-63.

Jenson, Andrew. "The Twelve Apostles." *Historical Record*, Mar. 1886, 39.

________. *Latter-day Saint Biographical Encyclopedia*. 4 vols. Salt Lake City: Andrew Jenson History Company, 1901-36.

Jessee, Dean C., ed. "Joseph Knight's Recollection of Early Mormon History." *Brigham Young University Studies* 17 (Autumn 1976): 29-39.

________, ed. *The Papers of Joseph Smith*. 2 vols. Salt Lake City: Deseret Book, 1989-92.

________, ed. *Personal Writings of Joseph Smith*. Rev. ed. Salt Lake City and Provo: Deseret Book and BYU Press, 2002.

Johnson, Benjamin F. *My Life's Review*. Independence, Mo.: Zion's Printing and Publishing, 1947.

Jones, William. *The History of the Christian Church from the Birth of Christ*. New York: S. H. Cone, 1824.

Jorgensen, Lynne Watkins. "The Mantle of the Prophet Joseph Passes to Brother Brigham: A Collective Spiritual Witness." *BYU Studies* 36 (Winter 1997): 125-204.

Kelly, J. N. D. *Golden Mouth: The Story of John Chrysostom, Ascetic, Preacher, Bishop*. London: Duckworth, 1995.

________. *Jerome: His Life, Writings, and Controversies*. Peabody, Mass.: Hendrickson, 1998.

Kenney, Scott G., ed. *Wilford Woodruff's Journal, 1833-1898*. 9 vols. Midvale, Utah: Signature Books, 1983-85.

Kerr, Howard, and Charles L. Crow, eds. *The Occult in America: New Historical Perspectives*. Urbana: University of Illinois Press, 1983.

Kimball, Stanley B., ed., *On the Potter's Wheel: The Diaries of Heber C. Kimball*. Signature Books and Smith Research Associates, 1987.

Kitto, John. *A Cyclopaedia of Biblical Literature*. 2 vols. New York: Mark H. Newman, 1845.

Knight, Newell. "Newel Knight's Journal." In *Scraps of Biography:*

Tenth Book of the Faith-Promoting Series. Salt Lake City: Juvenile Instructor Office, 1883.

Knisley, Alvin. *Biographical Dictionary of the Latter Day Saints Ministry*. Independence, Mo.: Alvin Knisley, 1948.

Kuehn, Manfred. *Kant: A Biography*. Cambridge, Eng.: Cambridge University Press, 2001.

Lang, Amy Schranger. *Prophetic Woman: Anne Hutchinson and the Problem of Dissent in the Literature of New England*. Berkeley: University of California Press, 1987.

Larson, Charles M. *By His Own Hand upon Papyrus: A New Look at the Joseph Smith Papyri*. Rev. ed. Grand Rapids, Mich.: Institute for Religious Research, 1992.

Lattin, Don. "Musings of the Main Mormon." *San Francisco Chronicle*, 13 Apr. 1997.

Launius, Roger D. *The Kirtland Temple: A Historical Narrative*. Independence, Mo.: Herald Publishing House, 1986.

________. *Joseph Smith III: Pragmatic Prophet*. Urbana: University of Illinois Press, 1988.

________. "An Ambivalent Rejection: Baptism for the Dead and the Reorganized Church Experience." *Dialogue: A Journal of Mormon Thought* 23 (Summer 1990): 61-84.

Launius, Roger D., and W. B. Spillman. *Let Contention Cease: The Dynamics of Dissent in the Reorganized Church of Jesus Christ of Latter Day Saints*. Independence, Mo.: Graceland College and Park Press, 1991.

Launius, Roger D., and Linda Thatcher, eds. *Differing Visions: Dissenters in Mormon History*. Urbana: University of Illinois Press, 1994.

LDS Church News. "McLellin Became Enemy of Church," Oct. 27, 1985.

________. "Writings Shed Light on Church History," Oct. 24, 1992.

LeBaron, E. Dale. *Benjamin Franklin Johnson: Friend to the Prophets*. Provo, Utah: Grandin Book, 1997.

Legg, Phillip R. *Oliver Cowdery: The Elusive Second Elder of the Restoration*. Independence, Mo.: Herald Publishing House, 1989.

Leopold, David. "Cousin, Victor." In *Routledge Encyclopedia of Philosophy*, ed. Edward Craig.

LeSueur, Stephen C. *The 1838 Mormon War in Missouri*. Columbia: University of Missouri Press, 1987.

Lilje, Hanns. *Martin Luther: 1483/1983*. Trans. Patricia Crampton. Bonn, Ger.: Inter Nationes, 1983.

Lindsey, Robert. *A Gathering of Saints: A True Story of Money, Murder, and Deceit*. New York: Simon and Schuster, 1988.

Littlefield, Lyman O. *Reminiscences of Latter-day Saints, Giving an Account of Much Individual Suffering Endured for Religious Conscience*. Logan: Utah Journal, 1888.

Livesey, Richard. *An Exposure of the Mormons*. Preston, Eng.: J. Livesey, 1838.

Ludlow, Daniel H., ed. *Encyclopedia of Mormonism: The History, Scripture, Doctrine, and Procedure of the Church of Jesus Christ of Latter-day Saints*. New York: Macmillan Publishing, 1992.

Lundwall, Nels B., comp. *Temples of the Most High*. Salt Lake City: Bookcraft, 1968.

Mackenzie, Robert. *John Brown of Haddington*. London: Banner of Truth Trust, 1964.

Madden, E. H. "Stewart, Dugald." In *Routledge Encyclopedia of Philosophy*, ed. Edward Craig.

Madison, Robert B. "Baptism for the Dead: One RLDS Perspective." *Restoration: Journal of Latter Day Saint History* 7 (Apr. 1988): 18-23.

Madsen, Carol Cornwall. "Smith, Emma Hale." In *Encyclopedia of Mormonism*, ed. Daniel H. Ludlow.

Magness, J. Lee. *Sense and Absence: Structure and Suspension in the Ending of Mark's Gospel*. Atlanta: Scholars Press, 1986.

Marquardt, H. Michael. *The Joseph Smith Revelations: Text & Commentary*. Salt Lake City: Signature Books, 1999.

Marty, Martin E. *Pilgrims in Their Own Land: Five Hundred Years of Religion in America*. Boston: Little, Brown, 1984.

Maxwell, Neal A. "Remember How Merciful the Lord Hath Been." *Ensign*, May 2004.

McBrien, Richard P., ed. *The Harper Collins Encyclopedia of Catholicism*. San Francisco: Harper San Francisco, 1995.

McConkie, Joseph Fielding, and Craig J. Ostler. *Revelations of the Restoration: A Commentary on the Doctrine and Covenants and Other Modern Revelations*. Salt Lake City: Deseret Book, 2000.

McCune, George M., ed. *Personalities in the Doctrine and Covenants and Joseph Smith History*. Salt Lake City: Hawkes Publishing, 1991.

McGuckin, John Anthony. *St. Gregory of Nazianzus: An Intellectual Biography*. Crestwood, N.Y.: St. Vladimir's Seminary Press, 2001.

McKiernan, F. Mark, Alma R. Blair, and Paul M. Edwards, eds. *The Restoration Movement: Essays in Mormon History*. Lawrence: Coronado Press, 1973.

McKiernan, F. Mark, and Roger D. Launius, eds. *An Early Latter Day Saint History: The Book of John Whitmer, Kept by Commandment*. Independence, Mo.: Herald Publishing House, 1980.

McKinsey, C. Dennis. *The Encyclopedia of Biblical Errancy*. Amherst, N.Y.: Prometheus Books, 1995.

Metzger, Bruce M. *A Textual Commentary on the Greek New Testament*. London: United Bible Societies, 1971.

"Miscellany." *New Hampshire Gazette*, 25 Oct. 1831, p. 4.

Morgan, Dale L. "A Bibliography of the Churches of the Dispersion." *Western Humanities Review* 7 (Summer 1953): 255-66.

Mosheim, Johann Lorenz. *Institutes of Ecclesiastical History, Ancient and Modern*. New Haven: A. H. Malby, 1832.

Mounce, H. O. "Hamilton, William." In *Routledge Encyclopedia of Philosophy*, ed. Edward Craig.

Naifeh, Steven, and Gregory White Smith. *The Mormon Murders: A True Story of Greed, Forgery, Deceit, and Death*. New York: Weidenfeld and Nicolson, 1988.

Nelson, William O. "Quorum of the Twelve Apostles." In *Encyclopedia of Mormonism,* ed. Daniel H. Ludlow.

Newell, Linda King, and Valeen Tippetts Avery. *Mormon Enigma: Emma Hale Smith*. 2d ed. Urbana: University of Illinois Press, 1994.

Nibley, Hugh. *Abraham in Egypt*. Salt Lake City: Deseret Book, 1981.

Nichols, Stephen J. *Jonathan Edwards: A Guided Tour of His Life and Thought*. Phillipsburg, N.J.: P & R Publications, 2001.

N[icholson], J[ohn]. "My First Experience on the Frontier: How I Became a Party to a Lawsuit." *Juvenile Instructor,* 15 May 1883, 158-59.

Niebuhr, Reinhold. *The Nature and Destiny of Man*. New York: C. Scribner's Sons, 1941-43.

Oaks, Dallin H. "Criticism." *Ensign*, Feb. 1987.

_______. "Alternate Voices." *Ensign*, May 1989.

Osborn, Eric. *Irenaeus of Lyons*. Cambridge, Eng.: Cambridge University Press, 2001.

Pace, Glenn L. "Follow the Prophet." *Ensign*, May 1989.

Packer, Boyd K. "The Mantle Is Far, Far Greater than the Intellect." *Brigham Young University Studies* 21 (Summer 1981): 259-78.

_______. "Scriptures." *Ensign*, Nov. 1982.

_______. *Let Not Your Heart Be Troubled*. Salt Lake City: Bookcraft, 1991.

Packer, Lynn. "Lost and Found." *Utah Holiday,* Nov. 1992, 33-39.

Palmer, Grant H. *An Insider's View of Mormon Origins*. Salt Lake City: Signature Books, 2002.

Parkin, Max H. "The Nature and Cause of Internal and External Conflict of the Mormons in Ohio between 1830 and 1838." M.A. thesis, Brigham Young University, 1966.

_______. "A History of the Latter-day Saints in Clay County, Missouri, from 1833 to 1837." Ph.D. diss., Brigham Young University, 1976.

Parry, Jay A., and Larry E. Morris. *The Mormon Book of Lists*. Salt Lake City: Bookcraft, 1987.

Partridge, Scott H. "The Failure of the Kirtland Safety Society." *Brigham Young University Studies* 12 (Summer 1972): 437-54.

Pelikan, Jaroslav. *The Reformation of the Bible: The Bible of the Reformation*. New Haven, Conn.: Yale University Press, 1996.

Perkins, Keith W. "Whitmer, David." In *Encyclopedia of Mormonism,* ed. Daniel H. Ludlow.

Peters, Francis E. *Muhammad and the Origins of Islam*. Albany: State University of New York Press, 1994.

Peterson, Daniel C. "Editor's Introduction: Questions to Legal Answers." *Review of Books on the Book of Mormon* 4 (1992): vii-lxxvi.

Peterson, H. Donl. *The Pearl of Great Price: A History and Commentary*. Salt Lake City: Deseret Book, 1987.

_______. "Sacred Writings from the Tombs of Egypt." In *The Pearl of Great Price: Revelations from God*, ed. H. Donl Peterson and Charles D. Tate, Jr. Provo, Utah: BYU Religious Studies Center, 1989.

Robinson, Stephen E. Review of *Early Mormonism and the Magic World View* by D. Michael Quinn. *BYU Studies* 27 (Fall 1987): 88-95.

________. *Believing Christ: The Parable of the Bicycle and Other Good News*. Salt Lake City: Deseret Book, 1992.

Romig, Ronald E. "Locating McLellin's Grave." *Missouri Mormon Frontier Foundation,* Fall 1994, 5.

________. "David Whitmer: Faithful Dissenter, Witness Apart." In *Differing Visions,* eds. Launius and Thatcher.

Romig, Ronald E., and John H. Seibert. "First Impressions: The Independence, Missouri, Printing Operation, 1832-33." *John Whitmer Historical Journal* 10 (1990): 51-66.

Russell, William D. "The RLDS Church and Biblical Criticism: The Early Response." *John Whitmer Journal* 7 (1987): 62-68.

________. "The LDS Church and Community of Christ: Clearer Differences, Closer Friends." *Dialogue: A Journal of Mormon Thought* (Winter 2003): 177-90.

Sampson, D. Paul, and Larry T. Wimmer. "The Kirtland Safety Society: The Stock Ledger Book and the Bank Failure." *Brigham Young University Studies* 12 (Summer 1972): 427-36.

Scherer, Mark A. "'Called by a New Name': Mission, Identity, and the Reorganized Church." *Journal of Mormon History* 27 (Fall 2001).

Schwarz, Hans. *True Faith in the True God: An Introduction to Luther's Life and Thought.* Trans. Mark William Worthing. Minneapolis: Augsburg, 1996.

Secor, Philip B. *Richard Hooker: Prophet of Anglicanism.* Tunbridge Wells, Eng.: Burns and Oates, 1999.

Shields, Steven L. *The Latter Day Saint Churches: An Annotated Bibliography*. New York: Garland Publishing, 1987.

________. *Divergent Paths of the Restoration: A History of the Latter Day Saint Movement.* 4th ed. rev. and enl. Los Angeles: Restoration Research, 1990.

________. "An Overview of Dissent in the Reorganization." In *Let Contention Cease,* eds. Launius and Spillman.

Shipps, Jan. *Mormonism: The Story of a New Religious Tradition*. Urbana: University of Illinois Press, 1985.

________. "Another Side of Early Mormonism." In *Journals of McLellin,* eds. Shipps and Welch.

________. *Sojourner in the Promised Land.* Urbana: University of Illinois Press, 2000.

Shipps, Jan, and John W. Welch, eds. *The Journals of William E. McLellin, 1831-1836.* Provo and Urbana: BYU Studies and University of Illinois Press, 1994.

Sillitoe, Linda, and Allen D. Roberts. *Salamander: The Story of the Mormon Forgery Murders.* 2d ed. Salt Lake City: Signature Books, 1989.

Simon, Jules. *Victor Cousin.* London: George Routledge and Sons, 1888.

Smith, George D., ed. *An Intimate Chronicle: The Journals of William Clayton.* Salt Lake City: Signature Books and Smith Research Associates, 1991.

Smith, Heman C. *The Truth Defended; or, A Reply to Elder D. H. Bays' Doctrines and Dogmas of Mormonism.* Lamoni, Iowa: Reorganized Church of Jesus Christ of Latter Day Saints, 1901.

Smith, Joseph, III. "The Last Testimony of Sister Emma." *Saints' Herald,* 1 Oct. 1879.

Smith, Joseph, III, and Heman C. Smith. *History of the Church of Jesus Christ of Latter Day Saints.* 4 vols. Lamoni, Iowa: Reorganized Church of Jesus Christ of Latter Day Saints, 1897-1903.

Smith, Lucy Mack. *Biographical Sketches of Joseph Smith the Prophet and His Progenitors for Many Generations,* ed. Orson Pratt. Liverpool, Eng.: S. W. Richards, 1853.

Smith, Melvin T. "Samuel Harrison Smith." Unpublished paper, delivered at the 2002 Sunstone Symposium, J. Willard Marriott Library, Salt Lake City.

Smith, Thomas. "Pelagianism." In *The Harper Collins Encyclopedia of Catholicism,* ed. Richard P. McBrien. San Francisco: Harper San Francisco, 1995.

Smith, William. *William Smith on Mormonism.* Lamoni, Iowa: Herald Steam Book and Job Office, 1883.

Snow, Erastus. "Ancient Prophecy, Relating to the Time of the Restitution of All Things, To Be Fulfilled." *Journal of Discourses* 16 (1874): 200-08.

Staker, Susan, ed. *Waiting for World's End: The Diaries of Wilford Woodruff.* Salt Lake City: Signature Books, 1993.

Stewart, Bruce G. "Hiram Page: An Historical and Sociological

Analysis of an Early Mormon Prototype." M.A. thesis, Brigham Young University, 1987.

Stewart, Kenneth M. "Half-Breeds." In *Dictionary of American History*, eds. Chase et al.

Stone, Ronald H. *John Wesley's Life and Ethics*. Nashville, Tenn.: Abingdon Press, 2001.

Strickland, W. P., ed. *Autobiography of Peter Cartwright, the Backwoods Preacher*. New York: Carlton & Porter, 1857.

Stuy, Brian H., ed. *Collected Discourses Delivered by President Wilford Woodruff, His Two Counselors, the Twelve Apostles, and Others*. 5 vols. Burbank, Calif.: B. H. S. Publishing, 1987-92.

Styles, John. *Memoirs and Remains of the Late Rev. Charles Buck*. Philadelphia: Anthony Finley, 1817.

Suderman, Jeffrey M. *Orthodoxy and Enlightenment: George Campbell in the Eighteenth Century*. Montreal: McGill and Queen's University Press, 2001.

Sunstone. "Comments on Temple Changes Elicit Church Discipline," June 1990, 59-61.

________. "Church Issues Statement on 'Symposia,'" Oct. 1991, 58-59.

________. "Six Intellectuals Disciplined for Apostasy," Nov. 1993, 65-73.

Talbot, Wilburn D. *The Acts of the Modern Apostles*. Salt Lake City: Randall Book, 1985.

Tanner, Jerald, and Sandra Tanner, eds. *Clayton's Secret Writings Uncovered: Extracts from the Diaries of Joseph Smith's Secretary William Clayton*. Salt Lake City: Modern Microfilm, [1982].

Tanner, N. Eldon. "Judge Not, That Ye Be Not Judged." *Ensign*, July 1972.

Thomas, John C. "Frederick G. Williams: Second Counselor to Joseph Smith (1833-1837)." In *Counselors to the Prophets*, comp. Michael K. Winder.

Thomasson, Gordon C. "Lamanites." In *Encyclopedia of Mormonism*, ed. Daniel H. Ludlow.

Thompson, John E. "The Far West Dissenters and the Gamblers at Vicksburg: An Examination of the Documentary Evidence and Historical Context of Sidney Rigdon's Salt Sermon." *Restoration* 5 (Jan. 1986): 21-27.

Thomson, Garrett. *On Locke*. Belmont, Calif.: Wadsworth and Thomson Learning, 2001.

Tinney, Thomas Milton. *Fanny Alger, the First Plural Wife of the Prophet Joseph Smith Jr.: A Preliminary Genealogical Report*. Salt Lake City: Tinney GenSearch Consultants, 1986.

Todd, Jay M. *The Saga of the Book of Abraham*. Salt Lake City: Deseret Book, 1969.

Trigg, Joseph Wilson. *Origen*. London: Routledge, 1998.

Turley, Richard E., Jr. *Victims: The LDS Church and the Mark Hofmann Case*. Urbana: University of Illinois Press, 1992.

________. "The Provenance of William E. McLellin's Journals." In *Journals of McLellin,* eds. Shipps and Welch.

Tyler, S. Lyman. *Modern Results of the Lamanite Dispersion: The Indians of the Americas*. Provo, Utah: BYU Division of Continuing Education, 1965.

Tyree, Alan D. "The Nature of New Revelation." *Saints' Herald,* Feb. 1984.

Ulrich, Laurel Thatcher. Foreword. In *Journals of McLellin,* eds. Shipps and Welch.

Unger, Harlow G. *Noah Webster: The Life and Times of an American Patriot*. New York: John Wiley and Sons, 1998.

Urbainczyk, Theresa. *Theodoret of Cyrrhus: The Bishop and the Holy Man*. Ann Arbor: University of Michigan Press, 2002.

Vaganay, Leon. *An Introduction to New Testament Textual Criticism*. 2d ed. rev., eds. Christian-Bernard Amphoux and Jenny Heimerdinger. Cambridge, Eng.: Cambridge University Press, 1991.

Van Biena, David. "Kingdom Come." *Time,* 4 Aug. 1997.

Van Noord, Roger. *Assassination of a Michigan King: The Life of James Jesse Strang*. Ann Arbor: University of Michigan Press, 1997.

Van Orden, Bruce A. "Hyrum Smith: Second Counselor to Joseph Smith (1837-1841)." In *Counselors to the Prophets,* comp. Michael K. Winder.

Van Wagoner, Richard S. *Mormon Polygamy: A History*. 3d ed. Salt Lake City: Signature Books, 1992.

________. *Sidney Rigdon: A Portrait of Religious Excess*. Salt Lake City: Signature Books, 1994.

________. "The Making of a Mormon Myth: The 1844 Transfiguration of Brigham Young." *Dialogue: A Journal of Mormon Thought* 28 (Winter 1995): 1-24.

Van Wagoner, Richard S., and Mary C. Van Wagoner. "Sarah M. Pratt: The Shaping of an Apostate." In *Mormon Mavericks: Essays on Dissenters*, eds. John Sillito and Susan Staker. Salt Lake City: Signature Books, 2002.

Van Wagoner, Richard S., and Steven C. Walker. *A Book of Mormons*. Salt Lake City: Signature Books, 1982.

Vogel, Dan. *Religious Seekers and the Advent of Mormonism*. Salt Lake City: Signature Books, 1988.

________, comp. and ed. *Early Mormon Documents*. 5 vols. Salt Lake City: Signature Books, 1996-2002.

________. "The Validity of the Witnesses' Testimonies." In *American Apocrypha*, eds. Dan Vogel and Brent Lee Metcalfe.

Vogel, Dan, and Brent Lee Metcalfe, eds. *American Apocrypha: Essays on the Book of Mormon*. Salt Lake City: Signature Books, 2002.

Walker, Ronald W. "Joseph Smith: The Palmyra Seer." *BYU Studies* 24 (Fall 1984-86): 461-72.

Waterman, Bryan, and Brian Kagel. *The Lord's University: Freedom and Authority at BYU*. Salt Lake City: Signature Books, 1998.

Watson, Elden Jay, ed. *Manuscript History of Brigham Young, 1801-1844*. Salt Lake City: Smith Secretarial Service, 1968.

Weinfeld, Moshe. *Deuteronomy 1-11: A New Translation with Introduction and Commentary*. Anchor Bible Series. New York: Doubleday, 1991.

Welch, John W. "The Acts of the Apostle William E. McLellin." In *Journals of McLellin*, eds. Shipps and Welch.

________. "The Miraculous Translation of the Book of Mormon." In *Opening the Heavens*, eds. Welch and Carlson.

Welch, John W., and Erik B. Carlson, eds. *Opening the Heavens: Accounts of Divine Manifestations, 1820-1844*. Provo and Salt Lake City: Brigham Young University Press and Deseret Book, 2005.

Welch, John W., and Trevor Packer. "The Newly Found Manuscript of Doctrine and Covenants Section 65." *Brigham Young University Studies* 33 (Summer 1993): 331-36.

Westergren, Bruce N., ed. *From Historian to Dissident: The Book of John Whitmer*. Salt Lake City: Signature Books, 1995.

Whitmer, David. *An Address to All Believers in Christ by a Witness to the Divine Authenticity of the Book of Mormon.* Richmond, Mo.: By the author, 1887.

________. *An Address to Believers in the Book of Mormon.* Richmond, Mo.: By the author, 1887.

Whittaker, David J. "Substituted Names in the Published Revelations of Joseph Smith." *Brigham Young University Studies* 23 (Winter 1983): 103-12.

Wight, Jeremy Benton. *The Wild Ram of the Mountain: The Story of Lyman Wight.* [Bedford, Wyo.]: Star Valley Llama, 1996.

Williams, Frederick G. "Frederick Granger Williams of the First Presidency of the Church." *Brigham Young University Studies* 12 (Spring 1972): 243-61.

Williams, Nancy C. *After One Hundred Years.* Independence, Mo.: Zion's Printing and Publishing, 1951.

Williams, Selma R. *Divine Rebel: The Life of Anne Marbury Hutchinson.* New York: Holt, Reinhart, and Winston, 1981.

Wilson, William A. Review of *Early Mormonism and the Magic World View* by D. Michael Quinn. *BYU Studies* 27 (Fall 1987): 96-104.

Wimmer, Larry T. "Kirtland Economy." In *Encyclopedia of Mormonism,* ed. Daniel H. Ludlow.

Winder, Michael K., comp. *Counselors to the Prophets.* Roy, Utah: Eborn Books, 2001.

Wixom, Hartt. *Edward Partridge: The First Bishop of the Church of Jesus Christ of Latter-day Saints.* Springville, Utah: Cedar Fort, 1998.

Wood, Gordon S. "Evangelical America and Early Mormonism." *New York History* 61 (Winter 1980): 359-86.

Woodford, Robert J. "The Historical Development of the Doctrine and Covenants." Ph.D. diss., Brigham Young University, 1974.

________. "A Survey of Textual Changes in the Doctrine and Covenants." In *The Seventh Annual Sidney B. Sperry Symposium: The Doctrine and Covenants.* Provo, Utah: BYU Religious Instruction, 1979.

________. "The Story of the Doctrine and Covenants." *Ensign,* Dec. 1984, 32-39.

________. "Book of Commandments." In *Encyclopedia of Mormonism,* ed. Daniel H. Ludlow.

________. "Doctrine and Covenants Editions." In *Encyclopedia of Mormonism,* ed. Daniel H. Ludlow.

Woodruff, Wilford. "History of William McLellin." *Deseret News*, May 12, 1858.

Woodward, Kenneth L. "A Mormon Moment." *Newsweek*, Sept. 10, 2001, 48.

Woodworth, Steven E. "Bledsoe, Albert Taylor." In *American National Biography*, eds. John A. Garraty and Mark C. Carnes. New York: Oxford University Press, 1999.

Wyl, W. [Wilhelm, Ritter von Wymetal]. *Mormon Portraits; or, The Truth about the Mormon Leaders from 1830 to 1886*. Salt Lake City: Tribune Printing and Publishing, 1886.

INDEX